Selected chapters from

DYNAMIC BUSINESS LAW

SECOND EDITION

NANCY K. KUBASEK
Bowling Green State University

M. NEIL BROWNE
Bowling Green State University

DANIEL J. HERRON
Miami University

ANDREA GIAMPETRO-MEYER
Loyola College

LINDA L. BARKACS
University of San Diego

LUCIEN J. DHOOGE
Georgia Tech University

CARRIE WILLIAMSON
DLA Piper US LLP
East Palo Alto, California

 Learning Solutions

Boston   Burr Ridge, IL   Dubuque, IA   New York   San Francisco
St. Louis   Bangkok   Bogotá   Caracas   Lisbon   London   Madrid
Mexico City   Milan   New Delhi   Seoul   Singapore   Sydney   Taipei   Toronto

Selected chapters from
DYNAMIC BUSINESS LAW, Second Edition
Franklin University

1 2 3 4 5 6 7 8 9 0   QDB QDB 13 12 11

ISBN-13: 978-0-07-757004-0
ISBN-10: 0-07-757004-9
part of
ISBN-13: 978-0-07-757264-8
ISBN-10: 0-07-757264-5

Learning Solutions Representative: Ann Hayes
Production Editor: Nichole Birkenholz
Printer/Binder: Quad/Graphics

About the Authors

 **Nancy K. Kubasek** received her J.D. from the University of Toledo College of Law in 1981 and her B.A. from Bowling Green State University in 1978. She joined the BGSU faculty in 1982, became an associate professor in 1988, and became a full professor in 1993.

During her tenure at Bowling Green State University, she has primarily taught courses in business law, legal environment of business, environmental law, health care law, and moral principles. She has published over 75 articles, primarily in law reviews and business journals. Most of her substantive articles focus on environmental questions. She has helped get students involved in legal research, and a number of her articles have been coauthored with students. She has also published a number of pedagogical articles in teaching journals, focusing primarily on the teaching of critical thinking and ethics.

She wrote the first environmental law text for undergraduate students, *Environmental Law,* and coauthored *The Legal Environment of Business: A Critical Thinking Approach.* She has written supplemental materials, such as study guides, test banks, and instructors' manuals.

Active in many professional organizations, she has served as president of the Academy of Legal Studies in Business, the national organization for professors of legal studies in colleges of business. She has also served as president of the Tri-State Academy of Legal Studies in Business, her regional professional association.

In her leisure time, she and her husband, Neil Browne, fish for halibut and salmon in Alaska, as well as largemouth bass in Florida. In addition, they are regular participants in polka, waltz, zydeco, and Cajun dance festivals in Europe and the United States. For almost 30 years, they have been successful tournament blackjack players. Both are avid exercisers—lifting weights, doing yoga, and running almost every day.

 **M. Neil Browne** is a senior lecturer and research associate and a Distinguished Teacher professor emeritus at Bowling Green State University. He received his B.A. in history and economics at the University of Houston, his Ph.D. in economics at the University of Texas, and his J.D. from the University of Toledo. He has been a professor at Bowling Green for more than four decades.

Professor Browne teaches courses in economics and law, legal research, jurisprudence, ethical reasoning, critical thinking, and economics at both the undergraduate and graduate levels. He has received recognition as the Silver Medalist National Professor of the Year, the Ohio Professor of the Year, and Distinguished Teacher and Master Teacher at Bowling Green State University, as well as numerous research awards from his university and from professional organizations. His consulting activities with corporate, governmental, and educational institutions focus on improving the quality of critical thinking in those organizations. In addition, he serves as a Rule 26 expert with respect to the quality of the reasoning used by expert witnesses called by the party opponent in legal actions.

Professor Browne has published 25 books and over 140 professional articles in law journals, as well as in economics, sociology, and higher-education journals. His current research interests focus on the relationship between orthodox economic thinking and legal policy. In addition, he is in the midst of writing books about the power of questionable assumptions in economics, the usefulness of asking questions as a learning strategy, and the deficiencies of legal reasoning.

Daniel J. Herron is a professor of business legal studies at Miami University in Oxford, Ohio. He received his law degree from Case Western Reserve University School of Law in 1978 and is a member of the Ohio and federal bars. He has taught at Miami University, his alma mater, since 1992, having previously taught at the University of Wyoming, Western Carolina University, the University of North Carolina–Wilmington, and Bowling Green State University. He has been a member of the Academy of Legal Studies in Business for nearly 25 years and has served as its executive secretary since 1991. His research interests focus on law and ethics, employment law, and legal history.

He has been married for over 30 years to his wife, Deborah, and they have two children, Elisabeth and Christopher, a daughter-in-law, Amanda, and one grandchild, Jack. Herron and his wife reside in Oxford, Ohio, with their two beagles, Max and Missy.

Andrea Giampetro-Meyer is chair of the Law & Social Responsibility Department in the Sellinger School of Business & Management at Loyola College in Maryland. She received her B.S. in business administration from Bowling Green State University and her J.D. from the Marshall-Wythe School of Law at the College of William & Mary.

Professor Giampetro's research focuses primarily on legal responses to race and gender discrimination in employment. Her teaching interests are wide-ranging. She teaches at all levels of higher education, from courses designed especially for first-year college students to courses designed for high-level business executives. Professor Giampetro's preferred courses are the undergraduate legal environment of business course and the graduate ethics and corporate social responsibility course.

Professor Giampetro has earned both national and local awards for teaching, including the Charles M. Hewitt Teaching Award from the Academy of Legal Studies in Business and the Henry W. Rodgers III Distinguished Teacher of the Year Award from Loyola College. She has experience helping new teachers understand how to work toward teaching excellence. At Loyola College, she serves as a faculty mentor, especially to teachers struggling with how to encourage students to engage in high-level discussion in class. Professor Giampetro has also written several instructors' manuals for textbooks. In these manuals, she strives to provide practical information that gives teachers ideas about how to engage students in meaningful ways.

Professor Giampetro has also received the Holmes-Cardozo Award from the Academy of Legal Studies in Business in recognition of excellence in legal scholarship. She has published numerous articles, and they have appeared in leading journals. In keeping with Loyola College's Jesuit mission, her favorite articles pursue themes related to social justice, especially as it relates to eliminating discrimination and oppression.

Linda L. Barkacs received her J.D. from the University of San Diego in 1993. She also has a B.A. in political science from San Diego State University and an A.A. in accounting from Irvine Valley College.

Upon graduating from law school and passing the California bar exam, Professor Barkacs became an associate at a downtown San Diego law firm. During her time with that firm, she was involved in a number of high-profile trials, including a sexual harassment case against the City of Oceanside that resulted in a $1.2 million verdict. In 1997, Professor Barkacs and her husband Craig (also a professor at USD) started their own law firm specializing in business and civil litigation (in both federal and state courts), employment law cases, and appeals. They were also involved in numerous mediations and arbitrations.

Professor Barkacs began teaching at USD in 1997 and went full-time in Spring 2002. As an educator, she has designed and taught numerous courses on law, ethics, and negotiation. She teaches in USD's undergraduate and graduate programs, including the Master of Science in Executive Leadership (a Ken Blanchard program), the Master of Science in Global Leadership, and the Master of Science in Supply Chain Management. Professor Barkacs often teaches in USD's study-abroad classes and has traveled extensively throughout Europe, Asia, and South America.

Professor Barkacs has received numerous awards for her teaching at USD, including the 2008 USD Outstanding Undergraduate Business Educator; 2008 and 2007 Professor of the Year, USD Senior Class (universitywide); 2007 Creative and Innovative Teaching Award, Academy of Education Leadership (national); and 2009 and 2010 nominee for U.S. Professor of the Year (Carnegie Foundation).

She and her husband are principals in The Barkacs Group (www.tbgexecutivetraining.com), a consulting firm that provides negotiation, ethics, and team training for the private sector. Professor Barkacs has published numerous journal articles in the areas of law, ethics, and negotiation. She and her husband are coauthoring a book on negotiation. She has been the president, vice president, conference chair, and treasurer of the Pacific Southwest Academy of Legal Studies in Business (www.pswalsb.net).

Professor Barkacs currently spends her time teaching, publishing, consulting for The Barkacs Group, and doing volunteer work for various civic causes. She enjoys walking, weight lifting, and spending her free time with her husband and their three cats, Phoenix, Violet, and Vanessa.

Lucien J. Dhooge is the faculty director of the Global Executive MBA Program and is the Sue and John Staton Professor of Law at Georgia Tech University. He teaches international trade and commercial law, real estate law, and the legal and ethical environment of business.

After completing an undergraduate degree in history at the University of Colorado, Professor Dhooge attended the University of Denver College of Law, where he received his J.D. in 1983. He received his LL.M. in 1995 from the Georgetown University Law Center, where he specialized in international and comparative law. Before coming to the University of the Pacific, Professor Dhooge spent 11 years in the practice of law in Washington, D.C., and Denver.

Professor Dhooge is the author of three books and more than 40 law review articles and has presented research papers and courses throughout the United States as well as in Europe and Asia. Professor Dhooge is the recipient of numerous research awards given by the Academy of Legal Studies in Business, including six Ralph C. Hoeber Awards granted annually for excellence in research. He was designated the outstanding junior business law faculty member in the United States by the academy in 2002 and received the Kay Duffy Award for outstanding service in 2005. In 2003, the University of the Pacific designated him as an Eberhardt Teacher-Scholar. He was designated as an International Scholar by the Soros Foundation in 2006. Professor Dhooge currently serves on the executive committee of the Academy of Legal Studies in Business and is a past editor-in-chief of the *American Business Law Journal* and the *Journal of Legal Studies Education.*

A native of Chicago but raised in Denver, Professor Dhooge enjoys spending time with his family and following the fortunes of the Chicago Cubs and the Colorado Rockies professional baseball teams.

Carrie Williamson is an associate in the intellectual property litigation group at DLA Piper US LLP. She has participated in three patent infringement trials. She earned her J.D. from Boalt Hall, University of California at Berkeley, and her B.A. from Bowling Green State University.

She has coauthored *Practical Business Ethics: A Guide for a Busy Manager,* and six legal journal articles. Her research interests include critical thinking, ethics, the use of expert testimony, women's legal issues, and patent litigation issues.

Preface

We wrote this book because our primary sense of who we are as professionals is that we are teachers. We play various roles in our careers, but we are especially dedicated to our students. We want them to listen, read, create, and evaluate more effectively as a result of their experience in a business law class.

We tried to construct a book that is both comprehensive and readable. But the features integrated into the chapters provide its distinctive worth. Each feature stands by itself as an aid to the kind of learning we hope to encourage. Yet the features are also a cohesive unit, contributing both to the liberal education of the students who use this book and to their skills as decision makers in a market economy.

Specifically, we provide what competing texts deliver, a comprehensive examination of all the relevant questions, concepts, and legal rules of business law. Our text must address the power and authority of constitutions, statutes, case law, and treaties as sources of law. Together the various elements of what we call "the law" make up the foundation and structure of the market exchange process.

Decisions to trade and produce require trust—trust that consumers, firms, workers, financial institutions, and asset owners will do as they promise and that violations of such promises will be unacceptable in the marketplace. Without guarantees that promises will be kept, market exchanges would grind to a halt. Business law provides these guarantees and the boundaries within which certain promises can be made and enforced.

Market decisions are made in a context—a persistently changing context. The law, in turn, is dynamic in response. New technologies and business practices bring new disputes over rights and responsibilities in a business setting. Future business leaders need knowledge of existing business law, as well as a set of skills permitting them to adjust efficiently and effectively to new legal issues that arise over the course of their careers.

We are excited about the contents of our features and want to explain the function of each of them in preparing our students for leadership in business.

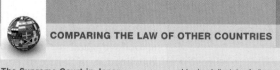

COMPARING THE LAW OF OTHER COUNTRIES

The Supreme Court in Japan

The supreme court of Japan, located in Tokyo, consists of 15 justices, including one chief justice. Because the justices ascend from lower courts, they are usually at least 60 years old. The full bench of the supreme court does not hear every appealed case. Rather, a petit (small) bench of five justices first hears each case to determine whether to transfer the case to a hearing before the full bench. The petit court transfers a case to the full bench if it believes that the appellant can prove that the law or decision in question is unconstitutional. Because proving the unconstitutionality of a law is extremely difficult, the full bench generally hears fewer than 10 cases annually.

A. COMPARING THE LAW OF OTHER COUNTRIES BOXES

This first feature highlights the emerging, interconnected market. Each chapter contains multiple Comparing the Law of Other Countries boxes. Because so many market decisions are made in an international context, learners need to familiarize themselves with the likelihood that a particular legal principle essential to doing business in one country may not be appropriate in other countries. The Comparing the Law of Other Countries boxes provide heightened awareness of this likelihood by illustrating how unique the law in a certain country often is. After reading dozens of these "stories of difference," readers will certainly better understand the need to discover relevant law in all jurisdictions where their market decisions have legal implications.

We believe that students learn innumerable valuable lessons about U.S. business law by contrasting the concepts of our business law system with those of our primary trading partners. We typically use Canada, Japan, China, Russia, Mexico, and the European Union for our comparisons because modern business managers will more likely be interacting with the law in those particular jurisdictions.

B. E-COMMERCE BOXES

A central feature of modern business decisions is new technology, specifically the rapid spread of electronic commerce. This development has created new challenges and opportunities that were unforeseeable until very recently.

Our initial approach was to construct an e-commerce chapter that stood by itself. But the more we thought about that approach and listened to our reviewers, we decided to place E-Commerce boxes in most of

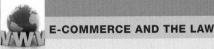

E-COMMERCE AND THE LAW

The Sliding-Scale Standard for Internet Transactions

Does a business that has Internet contact with a plaintiff in a different state satisfy the minimum-contacts standard? Anyone who engages in transactions over the Internet should be concerned about this question.

A federal district court established the following "sliding-scale" standard in the 1997 case *Zippo Mfg. Co. v. Zippo Dot Com, Inc.*:

[T]he likelihood that personal jurisdiction can be constitutionally exercised is directly proportionate to the nature and quality of commercial activity that an entity conducts over the Internet. This sliding scale is consistent with well developed personal jurisdiction principles.

At one end of the spectrum are situations in which a defendant clearly does business over the Internet. If the defendant enters into contracts with residents of a foreign jurisdiction that involve the knowing and repeated transmission of computer files over the Internet, personal jurisdiction is proper.

At the opposite end are situations in which a defendant has simply posted information on an Internet Web site that is accessible to users in foreign jurisdictions. A passive Web site that does little more than make information available to those who are interested in it is not grounds for the exercise of personal jurisdiction.

The middle ground is occupied by interactive Web sites at which a user can exchange information with the host computer. In such cases, the exercise of jurisdiction is determined by examining the level of interactivity and commercial nature of the exchange of information that occurs on the Web site.

*952 F. Supp. 1119, 1124 (W.D. Pa. 1997).

our chapters, as well as to integrate the e-commerce material throughout relevant chapters. By this infusion approach, we think we can best convince students of the pervasive influence of this new, complicating aspect of business decisions.

C. CONNECTING TO THE CORE

The business curriculum, as experienced by students, can easily be seen as a collection of silos, with each silo, or academic department, walled off from the others with its own special language and issues. But successful business decisions start with the recognition that decision makers should take advantage of the interrelatedness of the various subject areas.

not authorized to accept service on behalf of the company, and the court could not find any address for the company in Costa Rico. Rio Properties then filed a motion for alternative service of process with the court for permission to serve RII via its e-mail address, and the motion was granted by the district court. The court of appeals upheld the validity of the district court's order, noting that the Constitution does not require any specific means of service, only a means of service "reasonably calculated to provide notice and an opportunity to respond."[1] Because the method seemed to be the method of service most likely to reach RII, the court found that it clearly met the standard.

If the defendant is a corporation, courts generally serve either the president of the corporation or an agent that the corporation has appointed to receive service. Most states require that corporations appoint an agent for service when they incorporate. Corporations are subject to *in personam* jurisdiction in three locations: the state of their incorporation, the location of their main offices, and the geographic areas in which they conduct business.

Courts have *in personam* jurisdiction only over persons within a specific geographic region. In the past, a state court could not acquire *in personam*

To read more about how the choice of where to incorporate relates to jurisdiction, please see the **Connecting to the Core** activity on the text Web site at www.mhhe.com/kubasek2e.

[1] *Rio Properties, Inc. v. Rio International Interlink*, 284 F.3d 1007 (2002).

The purpose of the Connecting to the Core feature is to drive home the point that concepts from finance, accounting, marketing, management, and economics are closely linked to concepts and dilemmas in business law. The study of business law is best seen as a foundational component of the larger study of business administration. This feature for the second edition has been placed on the Web site assigned to *Dynamic Business Law*.

D. CRITICAL THINKING

After each case in the book, we have provided critical thinking questions to highlight the need to think critically about the reasoning used by the court. In addition, we include in every chapter a Point/Counterpoint problem that encourages the reader to evaluate the conflicting reasoning surrounding a key issue in the chapter.

But we do much more than just ask a lot of critical thinking questions at particular locations throughout the chapters. We encourage the use of a step-by-step critical thinking approach that has been developed and used in classrooms in many countries. We do

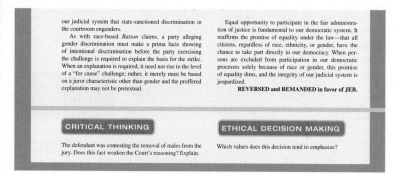

our judicial system that state-sanctioned discrimination in the courtroom engenders.

As with race-based *Batson* claims, a party alleging gender discrimination must make a prima facie showing of intentional discrimination before the party exercising the challenge is required to explain the basis for the strike. When an explanation is required, it need not rise to the level of a "for cause" challenge; rather, it merely must be based on a juror characteristic other than gender and the proffered explanation may not be pretextual.

Equal opportunity to participate in the fair administration of justice is fundamental to our democratic system. It reaffirms the promise of equality under the law—that all citizens, regardless of race, ethnicity, or gender, have the chance to take part directly in our democracy. When persons are excluded from participation in our democratic processes solely because of race or gender, this promise of equality dims, and the integrity of our judicial system is jeopardized.

REVERSED and REMANDED in favor of JEB.

CRITICAL THINKING

The defendant was contesting the removal of males from the jury. Does this fact weaken the Court's reasoning? Explain.

ETHICAL DECISION MAKING

Which values does this decision tend to emphasize?

not just repeatedly urge students to "think critically." Instead, we describe for them what is meant by that phrase in the context of business law. We include this step-by-step approach in Appendix 1A at the end of Chapter 1. Instructors who want to emphasize critical thinking can use that appendix as a structured approach for learning how to evaluate legal reasoning.

E. ETHICAL REASONING

Our book emphasizes consideration of all stakeholder interests in every market decision. Business ethics should never be an afterthought or something firms consider because they think they must.

Instead, business ethics is what provides the social legitimacy for markets, what distinguishes markets from the life of the jungle. While market decisions are calculating and purposeful, they must at the same time reflect awareness that the good and the right provide social borders that elevate those decisions above simple greed and egoism.

Ethical discussion focuses on the basic observation that we are socially and globally interdependent as entrepreneurs, asset owners, workers, businesspeople, and consumers. Our inescapable contact with one another requires that our aspirations be defined, at least in part, by their impact on others.

Our text has several ethical reasoning possibilities in each chapter. But for the reader to make use of this emphasis requires a practical step-by-step approach. In other words, our students need more than just a discussion about values or ethics. They need to have some sense that the discussion is headed somewhere. They want to know, "How will my behavior be any more ethical after I have read the chapter and participated in the class discussions?" Our text answers their question.

Chapter 2 provides a clear explanation of our approach—an approach that students can use on a regular basis. The language and organization of our model of ethical reasoning leans implicitly on standard ethical theories. But it meets the challenge of a fast-paced business world. It pushes stakeholders to the forefront of market decisions, where they belong, and does so in a manner that is both powerful and doable without becoming tedious.

Business ethics are the guidelines we use to shape the world we want to create. As such, they provide guidance for the kind of business behavior we want to reinforce. After each case excerpt, we pause to think about the ethics of business law by asking a question derived from the practical approach to business ethics developed in Chapter 2. Because we want students to see stakeholder interests as having numerous ethical dimensions, we have included frequent references to the ethical questions arising in modern business enterprises.

The second edition has been substantially revised to update the case law and case problems at the end of each chapter. Also, we have greatly expanded the exhibits in the book to make the material more accessible to visual learners. In addition, we have highlighted the legal principles and learning objectives in each chapter to make the text more user-friendly.

Acknowledgments

This final element of the Preface contains a palpable tone of gratitude and humility. Any project the scope of *Dynamic Business Law* is a collective activity; the authors are but the visible component of a remarkably large joint effort. We want to thank several contributors by name, but there are doubtlessly many other students, colleagues, and friends who made essential contributions to these pages.

Our largest gratitude goes to the dozens of business law colleagues who saved us from many embarrassing errors, while tolerating our stubborn reluctance to adhere to certain of their suggestions. Many thanks go to our manuscript reviewers and focus group participants:

Wayne Anderson
Missouri State University

Jennifer Barger Johnson
University of Central Oklahoma

Curtis J. Bell
Western Michigan University

Dr. Jon D. Bible
Texas State University–San Marcos

Robert W. Bing
William Patterson University

Joyce Birdoff
Nassau Community College

Eli Bortman
Babson College

Daniel R. Cahoy
Pennsylvania State University

Anita Cava
University of Miami–Coral Gables

Michael Chikeleze, JD
Cincinnati State College

Wade Chumney
Georgia Institute of Technology

Mark Conrad
Fordham University

Angelo J. Corpora
Palomar College

Richard E. Custin
University of San Diego

Dr. Raven Davenport
Houston Community College System

Howard Davidoff
Brooklyn College

Peter Dawson
Collin County Community College–Plano

Mary Elena Ellison
Florida Atlantic University

Joseph L. Flack. Jr.
Washentaw Community College

Darrell G. Ford
University of Central Oklahoma

Joan Gabel
Florida State University

Gary S. Gaffney
Florida Atlantic University

Christopher Giles
Virginia Tech

Robert Gonzalez
American River College

Dale Arrison Grossman
Cornell University

Francine Guice
Indiana Purdue University–Fort Wayne

William Harwood
Dutchess Community College

Norman Hawker
Western Michigan University

Lynda F. Hodge
Guilford Technical Community College

Karen A. Holmes
Hudson Valley Community College

Russell Holmes
Des Moines Area Community College

Catherine Jones-Rikkers
Grand Valley State University

Steve Kaber
Baldwin-Wallace College

Brian Keliher
Grossmont College

Cheryl Kirschner
Babson College

Gordon Klein
University of California–Los Angeles

Patricia Laidler
Massasoit Community College

Elizabeth W. Lane
Columbia College

Laurie A. Lucas
Oklahoma State University

James Mac Donald
Weber State University

Bruce Mather
State University of New York–New Paltz

Catherine McKee
Mt. San Antonio College

James L. Molloy
University of Wisconsin–Whitewater

Ann Morales Olazábal
University of Miami

Sandra Mullings
Bernard M. Baruch College

George A. Nation III
Lehigh University

Jan Novak
Chabot College

Gary Patterson
University of California–Riverside

Mark Patzkowski
Northwestern Oklahoma

George A. Redmond
Franklin University

Linda Reid
University of Wisconsin–Whitewater

Bruce Rich
California State University–San Marcos

Keith Roberts
University of Redlands

Thomas Rossi
Broome Community College

Don Sanders
Texas State University–San Marcos

Dr. Martin Segal
University of Miami

Lou Ann Simpson
Drake University

George Swan
North Carolina A & T University

John Swenson
University of Missouri–Columbia

Robert Scott Taylor
Moberly Area Community College

Cheryl Thomas
Fayetteville Technical Community College

Carol A. Vance
University of South Florida–Tampa

Russell A. Waldon
College of the Canyons

Norman Young
California State Poly University–Pomona

Thomas Young
Lone Star College Tomball

Mary-Kathryn Zachary
University of West Georgia

Bruce Zucker
California State University–Northridge

In addition, the second edition of the book could not have been written without the competent and dedicated research assistance we received from Lauren Biksacky, Kendall Johnson, and Jill Hagerman.

Finally, a book is but a raw, unsold manuscript until the talent team at a publishing house starts to refine it. Our manuscript benefited immeasurably from the guidance of the multiple levels of skill provided to us by McGraw-Hill/Irwin. We respect and honor our Sponsoring Editor, John Weimeister; our Development Editor, Megan Richter; the book's Marketing Manager, Sarah Schuessler; and its Project Manager, Bruce Gin.

Brief Contents

Appendixes

Contents

Part Six
AGENCY

Part Seven
BUSINESS ORGANIZATIONS

Part Eight
EMPLOYMENT AND LABOR RELATIONS

Part Ten
PROPERTY

CHAPTER 48
The Nature of Property, Personal Property, and Bailments   1059

CHAPTER 49
Real Property   1078

List of Cases

Chapter 51: INSURANCE LAW

Chapter 52: WILLS AND TRUSTS

An Introduction to Dynamic Business Law

LEARNING OBJECTIVES

After reading this chapter, you will be able to answer the following questions:

1   What is business law?

2   How does business law relate to business education?

3   What are the purposes of law?

4   What are alternative ways to classify the law?

5   What are the sources of the law?

6   What are the various schools of jurisprudence?

This book is for future business managers, especially those who wish to be leaders. The preparation for that career requires, in part, an awareness of the legal issues arising in business. Businesses need to finance capital growth, purchase inputs, and hire and develop employees. They must sell to consumers, please owners, and comply with government rules. All these activities are full of potential legal conflicts. Appendix 1A explains the role of critical thinking in resolving these conflicts.

Business law consists of the enforceable rules of conduct that govern commercial relationships. For example, a firm is required by law to obey the antitrust laws when it considers merging with another firm. In other words, buyers and sellers interact in market exchanges within the rules that specify the boundaries of legal business behavior. Constitutions, legislatures, regulatory bodies, and courts spell out what market participants may and may not legally do.

Business activities must follow legal guidelines. All contracts, employment decisions, and payments to a supplier are constrained and protected by business law. Each of the six functional areas of business—management, production and transportation, marketing, research and development, accounting and finance, and human resource management—sits on a foundation of business law, as Exhibit 1-1 illustrates.

Law and Its Purposes

As individuals, few of us can impose rules on others, but a majority of citizens in a democracy can agree to permit certain authorities to make and enforce rules of behavior in their community. These rules are the *law,* and they are enforceable in the courts the community maintains. Exhibit 1-2 lists just a few of the many purposes fulfilled by the law.

Each is important, but taken together they remind us why we are proud to say we are a society of laws. The respect we give the law as a source of authority is in part our recognition that in its absence, we would rely solely on the goodwill and dependability of one another. Most of us greatly prefer the law.

Classification of the Law

There are many ways of dividing laws into different groups. Some include national versus international law, federal versus state law, and public versus private law. **Private law** regulates disputes between private individuals or groups. If a store owner is delinquent in paying rent to the landlord, the resulting dispute is governed by private law. **Public law** controls disputes between private individuals or groups and their government. If a store dumps waste behind its building in violation of local, state, or federal environmental regulations, public law will resolve the dispute.

Another distinction we make is between civil and criminal law. (See Exhibit 1-3.) **Civil law** delineates the rights and responsibilities implied in relationships between persons and between persons and their government. It also identifies the remedies available when someone's rights are violated. For example, in 1993 the restaurant chain Jack-In-the-Box was ordered to pay civil damages after a two-year-old child died of food poisoning and several other people became ill from eating meat tainted with *E. coli* bacteria.

Criminal law, in contrast, regulates incidents in which someone commits an act against the public as a whole, such as by conducting insider trading on the stock exchange. Insider trading occurs when an individual uses insider, or secret, company information to increase her or his own finances or those of family or friends. Several years ago an IBM secretary allegedly told her husband, who in turn told several other people, that the company was

LO1

What is business law?

LO2

How does business law relate to business education?

LO3

What are the purposes of law?

LO4

What are alternative ways to classify the law?

Exhibit 1-1

Business Law and the Six Functional Areas of Business

FUNCTIONAL AREA OF BUSINESS	RELEVANT AREAS OF BUSINESS LAW
Corporate management	International and comparative law
	White-collar crime
	Contracts
	Corporate law
	Antitrust law
	Administrative law
	Agency law
	Insurance law
	Employment law
Production and transportation	Tort law
	Contracts
	Environmental law
	Consumer law
Marketing	Tort law
	Contracts
	Antitrust law
	Consumer law
	Intellectual property
Research and development	Product liability
	Intellectual property
	Property law
	Consumer law
Accounting and finance	Liability of accountants
	Contracts
	Negotiable instruments and banking
	Bankruptcy
	White-collar crime
Human resource management	Agency law
	Contracts
	Employment and labor law
	Employment discrimination

Exhibit 1-2

Purposes of the Law

- Providing order such that one can depend on a promise or an expectation of obligations.
- Serving as an alternative to fighting.
- Facilitating a sense that change is possible, but only after a rational consideration of options.
- Encouraging social justice.
- Guaranteeing personal freedoms.
- Serving as a moral guide by indicating minimal expectations of citizens and organizations.

Exhibit 1-3

Civil versus Criminal Law

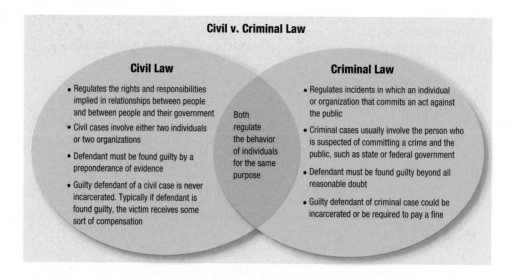

Civil v. Criminal Law

Civil Law
- Regulates the rights and responsibilities implied in relationships between people and between people and their government
- Civil cases involve either two individuals or two organizations
- Defendant must be found guilty by a preponderance of evidence
- Guilty defendant of a civil case is never incarcerated. Typically if defendant is found guilty, the victim receives some sort of compensation

Both regulate the behavior of individuals for the same purpose

Criminal Law
- Regulates incidents in which an individual or organization that commits an act against the public
- Criminal cases usually involve the person who is suspected of committing a crime and the public, such as state or federal government
- Defendant must be found guilty beyond all reasonable doubt
- Guilty defendant of criminal case could be incarcerated or be required to pay a fine

going to take over operations of Lotus Development. The leaked information spread among a number of individuals, 25 of whom bought stock that increased greatly in value following IBM's public announcement of the takeover. The Securities and Exchange Commission filed charges against them for creating an unfair trading environment for the public. Criminal law cases are prosecuted not by individuals but by the state, federal, or local government.

While some new laws have been adopted to regulate the kinds of activities businesses can now conduct online, **cyberlaw** is based primarily on existing laws. Laws governing contracts, for instance, are essentially the same in all situations, yet adaptations are necessary because contracts can now be made and signed online through retailers such as Amazon and eBay. Activities by companies such as Napster and YouTube have raised the question of whether and when the copying of certain intellectual property, such as music and video, constitutes theft.

Sources of Business Law

How is law created, and where do we look to find the laws? The sources of law are discussed below and summarized in Exhibit 1-4.

L05

What are the sources
of the law?

CONSTITUTIONS

The United States Constitution and the constitution of each state establish the fundamental principles and rules by which the United States and the individual states are governed. The term **constitutional law** refers to the general limits and powers of these governments as stated in their written constitutions. The U.S. Constitution is the supreme law of the land, the foundation for all laws in the United States. It is the primary authority to study when trying to identify the relationship between business organizations and government.

STATUTES

The assortment of *statutes,* or rules and regulations put forth by legislatures, is what we call **statutory law.** These legislative acts are written into the United States Code when they are passed by Congress or into the appropriate state codes when they are enacted by state legislatures. The codes are a collection of all the laws in one convenient location.

Exhibit 1-4
Sources of Law

Constitutional law	A collection of fundamental rules and regulations concerning the power and limits of governments as well as the relationships between the levels of government. Constitutional laws are usually stated in the form of a written constitution, and each level of government has its set of constitutional law, with the highest level (federal) being the foundation for the lower levels.
Statutory law	A collection of rules and regulations put forth by legislating bodies; considered the primary law under the constitution. Under state government, these laws or statutes are typically grouped by subject matter and referred to as codes. Under the federal government, these laws are organized by subject-matter titles, under the United States Code. Under local government, these laws are usually within the city and county ordinances.
Administrative law	A collection of rules and regulations put forth by agencies of executive bodies of government. Each level of government has dozens of administrative agencies that are responsible for particular areas of government function, and administrative law consists of the decisions made by these agencies.
Common law	A collection of judicial interpretations put forth by judicial bodies; also referred to as *case law.* This source is considered law unless later statutory law revokes the interpretation. When deciding a case, courts will use current law as well as past decisions in similar cases to reach a decision, or, in other words, they obey the principle of stare decisis.
Treaty	A legally binding agreement, similar to a contract, between two or more nations or international organizations.
Executive order	An order by the head of the executive governing body, such as the president or state governor, that either implements a new law or interprets existing law.

Business managers must also be familiar with the local city and county ordinances that govern matters not covered by federal or state codes. These ordinances address important business considerations such as local taxes, environmental standards, zoning, and building codes. If you wish to open a Krispy Kreme franchise in Santa Fe, New Mexico, you must follow local guidelines regarding where you may build your store, the materials you may use, and the state minimum wage you must pay employees making donuts. The regulations will be different if you wish to open your franchise in Toledo, Ohio, or Seattle, Washington.

While they are not a source of law in the same sense as constitutions and statutory law, **model** or **uniform laws** serve as a basis for some statutory law at the state level. Business activity is made more difficult when laws vary from state to state. To prevent such problems, a group of legal scholars and lawyers formed the National Conference of Commissioners on Uniform State Laws (NCC). The NCC regularly urges states to enact model laws to provide greater uniformity. The response is entirely in the hands of the state legislatures. They can ignore a suggestion or adopt part or all of the proposed model law.

The proposals of the NCC, while not laws themselves, have been adopted on more than 200 occasions by state legislatures. The NCC is an especially important influence on business law. Paired with the publications of the American Law Institute, it became the source of the *Uniform Commercial Code (UCC)*. The UCC is a body of law so significant for business activities that it will be the focus of intensive study in several chapters of this text. The UCC laws include sales laws and other regulations affecting commerce, such as bank deposits and collections, title documents, and warranties. For example, these laws govern the different types of warranties that companies such as Microsoft, Sony, and Honda provide with their products.

CASES

Constitutions, legislatures, and administrative agencies encourage certain behaviors and prevent others. But laws are seldom self-explanatory and often require interpretation. **Case law,** also called **common law,** is the collection of legal interpretations made by judges. These interpretations are law unless revoked later by new statutory law.

Case law is especially significant for businesses that operate in multiple legal jurisdictions. Courts in two different business locations may interpret similarly worded statutes differently.

Courts issue judicial decisions that often include interpretations of statutes and administrative regulations, as well as the reasoning they used to arrive at a decision. Such reasoning depends heavily on **precedent,** past decisions in similar cases that guide later decisions, thereby providing greater stability and predictability to the law.

Business managers must pay attention to changes in the law and cases in which new precedents are set and take them into account when making business decisions. After a woman was severely burned by very hot coffee, McDonald's was found negligent for failing to provide a warning label on its hot-beverage cups. Now many retailers provide warning labels on their beverage cups because of the precedent set by this case.

When courts rely on precedent, they are obeying the principle of **stare decisis** ("standing by their decision"), in which rulings made in higher courts become binding precedent for lower courts. When an issue is brought before a state court, the court will determine whether the state supreme court has made a decision on a similar issue, which creates a binding precedent or pattern of law the lower court must follow. If there is no binding decision, both state courts need to look for other rulings on similar cases.

They are not bound by each other's decisions and might decide differently on the same issue. Decisions in lower courts can be appealed to the state appeals court, however, and the appeals court's decision can be appealed to the state supreme court. If the state supreme court rules on the case, its decision is binding for the state in that and future cases but does not affect earlier decisions made by state courts.

Perhaps the most well-known case associated with stare decisis is *Roe v. Wade.*[1] This landmark case, decided in 1973, made a decision on the issue of abortion. The U.S. Supreme Court decided that until a fetus is "viable," a woman may terminate her pregnancy for any reason. The Court went on to define *viable* as the ability of the fetus "to live outside the mother's womb, albeit with artificial aid." The Court added that such a capability could occur around 24 weeks, although usually around 7 months. The decision in *Roe v. Wade* has been upheld in cases since. The precedent still stands today, despite attempts to overturn it. In 1992, *Planned Parenthood of Southeastern Pennsylvania v. Casey*[2] used the decision to determine that a woman has a constitutional right to have an abortion, although the standard for restricting abortions was lowered.

Another case that has been used in accordance with stare decisis as a binding precedent is *Brown v. Board of Education,*[3] which abolished discriminatory policies for individuals of different racial backgrounds. In *Regents of the University of California v. Bakke,*[4] the plaintiff, a white male, had applied to the University of California at Davis medical school two years in a row and been denied admittance. He alleged the admissions process was discriminatory because 16 of 100 slots were reserved for members of minority races. The U.S. Supreme Court found the school's admissions policy was not lawful, referencing *Brown* and stating that the basic principle behind it and similar cases was that individuals could not be excluded on the basis of race or ethnicity. The Court wrote, "Preferring members of any one group for no reason other than race or ethnic origin is discrimination for its own sake."

Another U.S. Supreme Court case that relied in part on *Brown v. Board of Education* was *Wygant v. Jackson Board of Education.*[5] The Board of Education and teachers' union in Jackson, Michigan, had agreed that if teachers were laid off, those with more seniority would be retained and the minority teachers' percentage of the layoffs would not be higher than their percentage of all teachers employed by the school district at the time of the layoffs. When layoffs did occur, nonminority teachers were laid off and minority teachers with less seniority were retained. The nonminority teachers sued. When the case was brought before the Supreme Court, the Court ruled that the layoff policy was not lawful because "[c]arried to the logical extreme, the idea that black students are better off with black teachers could lead to the very system the Court rejected in *Brown v. Board of Education.*" Again in accordance with *Brown,* the Court ruled that singling people out on the basis of race was not lawful.

However, the case *Plessy v. Ferguson*[6] is an interesting circumstance in regard to stare decisis. In this case, the court decided that separate accommodations for blacks and whites was acceptable as long as such separation was "separate but equal." This case essentially made the legal acknowledgment of a difference between blacks and whites, and different treatment, acceptable. Interestingly, in 1954, *Brown v. Board of Education* did not follow the precedent established by *Plessy v. Ferguson.* In fact, the ruling established in *Plessy* was overturned. The Supreme Court determined that segregation of blacks and whites

[1] 410 U.S. 113 (1973).
[2] 505 U.S. 833 (1992).
[3] 347 U.S. 483 (1954).
[4] 438 U.S. 265 (1978).
[5] 476 U.S. 267 (1986).
[6] 163 U.S. 537 (1896).

violated the equal protection clause of the Fourteenth Amendment of the Constitution. Thus, the court overturned the precedent and created a new one, one that has been used in decisions made by courts ever since.

Just as state statutes have been strongly influenced by the suggestions of the NCC, common law evolves with the assistance of a mechanism called **Restatements of the Law.** These are summaries of the common law rules in a particular area of the law that have been enacted by most states. The American Law Institute prepares these Restatements for contracts, agency, property, torts, and many other areas of law that affect business decisions. While the Restatements are not themselves a source of business law, judges frequently use them to guide their interpretations in a particular case.

In addition to the Restatements, many influences are at work in the minds of judges when they interpret constitutions, statutes, and regulations. Their own values and social backgrounds function as lights and shadows, moving the judges toward particular legal decisions.

Courts in one jurisdiction need not obey precedents in other jurisdictions, but they may be influenced by them. At least two current Supreme Court justices are using law in other countries as a basis for rethinking certain laws in the United States. The logic of this reliance on precedent is based on respect for those who have already wrestled with the issue and provided us guidance with their earlier decision.

ADMINISTRATIVE LAW

Constitutions and statutes never cover all the detailed rules that affect relationships between government and business. The federal, state, and local governments have dozens of administrative agencies whose task is to perform a particular government function. For example, the Environmental Protection Agency (EPA) has broad responsibilities to enforce federal statutes in the area of environmental protection. The Occupational Safety and Health Administration (OSHA) oversees health and workplace safety and makes sure working conditions are not hazardous. In 1994, OSHA settled a complaint that United Parcel Service (UPS) was not providing adequate safety measures and equipment for workers who handled hazardous waste by making sure UPS adapted its practices to follow federal safety guidelines.

Administrative law is the collection of rules and decisions made by all these agencies. Just glance at Exhibit 1-5 to get a sense of the scope of a few of the major federal administrative agencies.

TREATIES

A **treaty** is a binding agreement between two states or international organizations. It may be an international agreement, a covenant, an exchange of letters, a convention, or protocols. In the United States, a treaty is generally negotiated by the executive branch. To be binding, it must then be approved by two-thirds of the Senate.

A treaty is similar to a contract in two important ways. Both treaties and contracts are attempts by parties to determine rights and obligations among themselves, and when a party fails to obey a treaty or a contract, international law imposes liability on it.

EXECUTIVE ORDERS

The president and state governors can issue directives requiring that officials in the executive branch perform their functions in a particular manner. The Code of Federal Regulations (CFR) contains all the executive orders created by the president. (It is online at

Exhibit 1-5

Major Federal
Administrative Agencies

INDEPENDENT AGENCIES	EXECUTIVE AGENCIES
• Commodity Futures Trading Commission (CFTC) http://www.cftc.gov/ • Consumer Product Safety Commission (CPSC) http://www.cpsc.gov/ • Equal Employment Opportunity Commission (EEOC)http://www.eeoc.gov/ • Federal Trade Commission (FTC) http://www.ftc.gov/ • Federal Communications Commission (FCC) http://www.fcc.gov/ • National Labor Relations Board (NLRB) http://www.nlrb.gov/ • National Transportation Safety Board (NTSB) http://www.ntsb.gov/ • Nuclear Regulatory Commission (NRC) http://www.nrc.gov/ • Securities and Exchange Commission (SEC) http://www.sec.gov/	• Federal Deposit Insurance Corporation (FDIC) http://www.fdic.gov/ • Occupational Safety and Health Administration (OSHA) http://www.osha.gov/ • General Services Administration (GSA) http://www.gsa.gov/ • National Aeronautics and Space Administration (NASA) http://www.nasa.gov/ • Small Business Administration (SBA) http://www.sba.gov • U.S. Agency for International Development (USAID) http://www.usaid.gov/ • National Science Foundation (NSF) http://www.nsf.gov/ • Veterans Administration (VA) http://www.va.gov/ • Office of Personnel Management (OPM) http://www.opm.gov/

www.gpoaccess.gov/cfr/index.html.) Presidents claim the power to issue such orders on the basis of their Article II, Section 1, constitutional power to "take care that the laws be faithfully executed." President George W. Bush issued 284 executive orders during the eight years of his presidency.

An especially controversial executive order is Order 9066, issued by President Franklin Roosevelt during World War II, which sent Japanese-Americans on the West Coast, as well as thousands of Italian-American and German-American families, to internment camps for the duration of the war.

Exhibit 1-6 summarizes the various locations where you can find particular laws.

SCHOOLS OF JURISPRUDENCE

When legislators or courts make law, they do so guided by certain habits of mind and specific beliefs about human nature. Beliefs are deeply rooted within a person's emotions and habits, and thus they are sure to guide one's opinions and decisions. Such beliefs may be commonly held and thus create various larger schools of thought. Once one determines what schools of thought influence certain types of decisions and opinions, one is sure to better understand such decisions. This section briefly describes several of the more common guides to legal interpretation.

Natural Law.   The term natural law describes certain ethical laws and principles believed to be morally right and "above" the laws devised by humans. Under natural law individuals have not only basic human rights but also the freedom to disobey a law enacted

LO6

What are the various schools of jurisprudence?

Exhibit 1-6   Where to Locate the Law

TYPE OF LAW	Source by Level of Government		
	FEDERAL	STATE	LOCAL
Statutes	United States Code (USC) United States Code Annotated (USCA) United States Statutes at Large	State code	Municipal ordinances
Administrative law	Code of Federal Regulations (CFR) *Federal Register*	State administrative code	Municipality administrative regulations
Common law	United States Reports (U.S.) United States Supreme Court Reporter (S. Ct.) Federal Reporter (F. F.2d) Federal Supplement (F.Supp.)	Regional reporters State reporters	Check the clerk's office at the local courthouse
Executive order	Title 3 of Code of Federal Regulations Codification of Presidential Proclamations and Executive Orders	See state government Web site	n/a
Treaty	See http://www.asil.org/treaty1.cfm	n/a	n/a

by people if their conscience goes against it and they believe it is wrong. Dow Chemical wants its suppliers to conform to U.S. environmental and labor laws, not just the local laws in the supplier's country, where regulations may not be as stringent. This policy reflects the beliefs that people have a right to be treated fairly in their jobs and a right as human beings to have a clean environment.

Legal Positivism.   The concept of legal positivism sees our proper role as obedience to duly authorized law. That law is quite distinct from morality, and moral questions about the law should not interfere with our inclination to obey it. A judge with leanings in the direction of legal positivism might write that she is deciding to enforce the law in question but that her decision does not necessarily mean she sees the law as the morally correct rule.

Identification with the Vulnerable.   Closely linked to pursuing legal change through natural law is pursuing change through identification with the vulnerable, on the grounds that some higher law or body of moral principles connects all of us in the human community. Some members of our society are able to take care of themselves in terms of most life situations. Others, especially the ill, children, the aged, the disabled, and the poor, require assistance to meet their fundamental needs of life, health, and education.

This guide to legal change is tied closely to the pursuit of fairness, a "level playing field," in our society. We might look at a particular employment contract and feel outrage that "it is just not fair." That outrage can be a stimulus for legal change. Minimum-wage laws reflect the belief that workers should receive a minimum hourly wage and that employers should not be allowed to pay them less.

Historical School: Tradition.   One of the guidelines most often used for shaping the law is tradition, or custom. Stare decisis is rooted in this *historical school.* When we follow tradition, instead of reinventing the wheel we link our behavior to the behavior of those who faced similar problems in earlier periods. We assume past practice was the product of careful thought.

Legal Realism.   Legal realism is based on the idea that, when ruling on a case, judges need to consider more than just the law; they also weigh factors such as social and economic conditions, since legal guidelines were designed by humans and exist in an ever-changing environment. Judges who follow this school of thought are more likely to depart from past court decisions to account for the fact that our society is constantly shifting and evolving. They believe the law can never be enforced with complete consistency and argue that because judges are human, they will bring different methods of reasoning to very similar cases.

One law enacted to reflect social changes is the Family and Medical Leave Act. This act mandates that businesses employing more than 50 people provide their workers with up to 12 weeks' unpaid leave every year to take care of family-related affairs, including caring for oneself or ill parents and adopting or having a child. The law also protects pregnant women who take time off work, as their employers must provide them with the same pay and the same or an equivalent job when they return to work. More mothers are working outside the home, and more women are returning to work soon after they have a child. The act protects them against some types of discrimination that might occur after they return.

Cost-Benefit Analysis.   Suppose we could attach a monetary figure to the benefits of a particular law or legal decision. We would next need to examine all its costs and place a monetary value on it. If we possessed these figures, we could use cost-benefit analysis as a guide to legal change, choosing the alternatives that maximized benefits and minimized costs.

This approach is tied closely to the pursuit of efficiency. If the law to be applied yields more benefits than costs, then we have saved resources that we can, in turn, use to obtain more goods and services. Our economy is thus more efficient because it produces more with less.

Polluted land is an economic loss as it cannot be used for farming or recreation. Polluted water can be toxic for fish and cannot be used for drinking. Polluted air can cause health problems and result in higher health care costs. While complying with EPA pollution controls may cost companies more initially, the price of environmental cleanup and lost productivity in the economy as a whole may be even greater.

Global and Comparative Law

Advances in technology and transportation make trade with other countries far easier today than in the past. Boeing Co. can make hundreds of components for the same airliner all over the world and then assemble them in the United States. An antique store can operate in Poughkeepsie but sell to customers in Moscow or Taipei through a Web site.

This ease in trade means business managers must be familiar with laws that regulate business practices between nations. The United States has entered into trade agreements, such as the North American Free Trade Agreement (NAFTA) with Canada and Mexico and the General Agreement on Tariffs and Trade (GATT) with about 150 other countries, that help establish the conditions of global trade.

Future managers should also understand comparative law, which studies and compares the laws in different countries. The European Union (EU) regulates taxes on Internet sales and the amount of pollution firms can release differently than does the U.S. government. Companies doing business in the EU must take these standards into account. The Chinese government does not want its citizens to have access to certain information and Web sites. To do business there, Google had to conform to Chinese standards by restricting the content of searches performed on Google.cn. Some felt that by thus restricting access to information, Google had violated its own mission statement to "do no evil."

Business law tells managers the basic rules of the business game. Play any game without having first studied the rules, and you will probably fail. But unlike an ordinary game, business has a rule book that is changing dynamically. So modern business managers must have an ongoing fascination with the law to function effectively.

Key Terms

administrative law 8	cost-benefit analysis 11	legal realism 11	public law 2
business law 2	criminal law 2	model (uniform)	Restatements
case law 6	cyberlaw 4	laws 6	of the Law 8
civil law 2	identification with the	natural law 9	stare decisis 6
common law 6	vulnerable 10	precedent 6	statutory law 5
constitutional law 5	legal positivism 10	private law 2	treaty 8

Looking for more review material?

The Online Learning Center at **www.mhhe.com/kubasek2e** contains this chapter's "Assignment on the Internet" and also a list of URLs for more information, entitled "On the Internet." Find both of them in the Student Center portion of the OLC, along with quizzes and other helpful materials.

Success in business requires the development of **critical-thinking skills**—the ability to understand the structure of what someone is saying and then apply a set of criteria to evaluate its worth. In other words, businesspeople need to be able to sort sense from nonsense by developing critical attitudes and abilities. There is no better context in which to develop these skills than the study of the laws that affect business.

Legal reasoning is like other kinds of reasoning in some ways. The stimulus that gets us thinking is an *issue,* stated as a question that requires us to *do* something, to think about answers.

We may be interested in such issues as the following:

- When are union organizers permitted under the National Labor Relations Act to trespass on an employer's property?
- Do tobacco manufacturers have liability for the deaths of smokers?
- Must a business fulfill a contract with an unlicensed contractor in a state requiring that all contractors be licensed?

These questions have several potential answers, but which best accomplishes a particular business objective? Which is consistent with the law? Here is where critical thinking is essential to business success. Some answers can get the decision maker into trouble; others will advance the intended purpose. Each answer is called a *conclusion.*

Business firms are both consumers of and contributors to legal conclusions. As they learn about and react to decisions or conclusions made by courts, businesspeople can respond in two ways:

1. Understand the conclusions in the case, and use this understanding as a guide for future business decisions.
2. Make judgments about the quality of the conclusions.

This book encourages you to do both. Critical thinking is active; it challenges each of us to form judgments about the quality of the link between a set of reasons and the conclusion derived from them. In particular, we will be focusing on the link between a court's reasons and its conclusions.

The following structure for critical thinking is a thoroughly tested method used by successful market decision makers. Every time you read a case, try to follow it.

1. Find the *facts.*
   Here we are looking for the most basic building blocks in a legal decision or argument. They provide the environment or context in which the legal issue is to be resolved. Certain events occurred; certain actions were or were not taken; particular persons behaved or failed to behave in specific ways. We always want to know, What happened in this case?
2. Look for the *issue.*
   The issue is the question that caused the lawyers and their clients to enter the legal system.
3. Identify the judge's *reasons and conclusion.*
   We want a world rich with opinions so that we can have a broad field of choice. But we should agree with only those legal opinions that have convincing reasons supporting the

conclusion. Asking "Why?" is our respectful way of saying, "I want to believe you, but you have an obligation to help me by sharing the reasons for your conclusion."

4. Locate in the decision the *rules of law* that govern the judge's reasoning.

Judges cannot offer just any reasoning that they please. They must always look back over their shoulders at the laws and previous court decisions that together provide an anchor for current and future decisions. What makes legal reasoning so complex is that statutes and legal findings are never *crystal* clear. They may seem very clear, but judges and businesspeople have room for interpretive flexibility in their reasoning.

5. Apply *critical thinking* to the reasoning.

A judge's reasoning, once we have laid it out by following the steps discussed here, is a message we may either accept or reject. *Critical thinking in the legal context* consists of examining the legal opinion in search of potential problems in the reasoning.

One of the most exciting things about our legal system is its potential for change. Here is a small sample of some especially useful critical-thinking tools for business managers when thinking about business law:

- Look for potential ambiguity in the reasoning. *Ambiguity* is a lack of clarity in a word or phrase. Many words have multiple meanings; until we know the intended one, we cannot tell whether we agree or disagree with the reasoning.
- Ask whether the analogies used in the decision are strong. When judges follow precedents, they are saying the facts in the precedent and those in the case at hand are so similar that it makes sense to apply the same rule of law in both. Are there key differences in the facts that raise questions about the quality of that analogy?
- Check the quality of the judge's reasoning. Is the judge's supporting evidence both abundant enough and reliable enough that we should agree with the reasoning?
- Think about the extent to which missing information prevents you from being totally confident about the judge's reasoning. Is there information you would need to have before making up your mind?
- Consider the possibility of rival causes. When the judge claims one action caused another, think about whether some alternative cause may have been responsible.

Working through these steps accomplishes several things. First, walking through this process familiarizes you at a deeper level with what the judge is saying. You have to wrestle with the judge's logic and use of evidence to complete the critical-thinking activity. Second, the critical thinking provides a sense that the law evolves as we put together the strengths and weaknesses of previous thinking by judges and legal scholars. Most importantly, critical thinking enables us to practice interacting with the law, always with an eye to considering ways to improve our legal system.

This chapter has enabled you to understand several important things. First, you should now be acquainted with what business law is and how business law and business education are intertwined. Second, you should understand the purposes of law, be acquainted with different kinds of law, and have a basic understanding of how different courts and agencies cooperate with one another. You should also now know about the interplay between case law and stare decisis, or binding precedent. You should also be able to pinpoint where various kinds of laws come from.

More importantly, however, you should realize that all of our courts and legal documents are thought to be just and that justice is an idea based on other ideas. Different schools of thought arise from deep-rooted, commonly held beliefs, and these schools guide decisions about what is fair and just and why. Finally, you should be able to critically evaluate a judge's or court's opinion. Only by doing so can you sort through the logic of the decision and pinpoint all the factors that went into the decision, including not only precedent and case law but the perspective flowing from schools of legal thought, rooted in personal beliefs and opinions.

Key Terms

critical-thinking skills   13

2 Business Ethics

LEARNING OBJECTIVES

After reading this chapter, you will be able to answer the following questions:

1 What are business ethics and the social responsibility of business?

2 How are business law and business ethics related?

3 How can we use the WPH framework for ethical business decisions?

CASE OPENER
Chinese Factories and Toxic Toothpaste

The Chinese export industry is highly competitive, with each manufacturer continuously seeking to cut costs, even if by only one-half of 1 percent. In May 2007, the international community expressed its dismay at the manufacturers' latest cost-cutting technique: replacing glycerin with diethylene glycol. Glycerin is a harmless thickening agent. Diethylene glycol is a poisonous thickening agent used to make antifreeze. The end product exported from China was poisonous toothpaste, none of which was labeled to indicate that the products contained diethylene glycol.

When the poisonous chemical was found in Chinese toothpaste, the FDA issued a warning, telling consumers to discard all Chinese toothpaste as a precaution. The Chinese government responded by telling consumers that the FDA warning was unscientific and unjustified. In 2000, a Chinese study had found that toothpaste containing diethylene glycol was harmless if the chemical concentration was below 15.6 percent. The contaminated toothpaste found in America contained diethylene glycol in concentrations of 3 to 5 percent. The FDA warned that diethylene glycol was unsafe in any concentration, particularly for children, as well as individuals with liver and kidney illnesses.

In July 2007, due to growing international concern about the safety of Chinese toothpaste, the Chinese government banned all manufacturers from using diethylene glycol in toothpaste. Investigators believed that the toothpaste originated from two small manufacturers in the Danyang coastal region, although the manufacturers denied fault. The contaminated toothpaste was found in at least seven countries, including the United States. As of the writing of this book, there had been no confirmed illnesses or deaths due to use of the contaminated toothpaste.

1. If you were one of the small Chinese manufacturers of toothpaste, would you be willing to substitute diethylene glycol for glycerin?

2. If you were manufacturing toothpaste and decided to substitute diethylene glycol for glycerin, would you consider it your ethical obligation to list diethylene glycol as an ingredient in your toothpaste?

The Wrap-Up at the end of the chapter will answer these questions.

What a business manager in the situation described in the opening scenario should do is not altogether clear. Ethical conversation is less about finding the one and only right thing to do than it is about finding the better thing to do. Whatever you choose to do, some stakeholders will be hurt and others will benefit.

This chapter provides some assistance for thinking systematically about issues of right and wrong in business conduct. Initially, we need to sort through the meaning of key terms like *business ethics* and *social responsibility*. Then, because it is helpful to have a useful approach to ethical decision making, we provide a practical method by which future business managers can think more carefully about the ethical dilemmas they will face during their careers.

Business Ethics and Social Responsibility

Ethics is the study and practice of decisions about what is good, or right. Ethics guides us when we are wondering what we should be doing in a particular situation. **Business ethics** is the application of ethics to the special problems and opportunities experienced by businesspeople. For example, as a business manager, you might someday decide what is best for a company, such as one of those Chinese toothpaste manufacturers described in the Case Opener. Is the company doing the right thing when it attempts to reduce the costs of production by substituting diethylene glycol for glycerin?

Such questions present businesses with ethical choices, each of which has advantages and disadvantages. An **ethical dilemma** is a problem about what a firm should do for which no clear, right decision is available. Reasonable people can expect to disagree about optimal solutions to ethical dilemmas.

For example, imagine yourself in the position of a business manager at Wells Fargo Bank. You know that providing bank accounts for customers has costs attached to it. You want to cover those costs by charging the customers the cost of their checking accounts. By doing so, you can preserve the bank's revenue for shareholders and employees of Wells Fargo. So far, the decision seems simple. But an ethical dilemma soon appears.

You learn from recent government reports that 12 million families cannot afford to have bank accounts when they are charged a fee to maintain one. You want to do the right thing in this situation. But what would that be? The study of business ethics can help you resolve this dilemma by suggesting approaches you can use that will show respect for others while maintaining a healthy business enterprise.

Making these decisions would be much easier if managers could focus only on the impact of decisions on the firm. If, for example, a firm had as its only objective the

L01

What are business ethics and the social responsibility of business?

To see how ethics relates to accounting, please see the **Connecting to the Core** activity on the text Web site at www.mhhe.com/kubasek2e.

maximization of profits, the "right thing" to do would be the option that had the largest positive impact on the firm's profits.

But businesses operate in a community. Communities have expectations for behavior of individuals, groups, and businesses. Different communities have different expectations of businesses. Trying to identify what those expectations are and deciding whether to fulfill them complicate business ethics. The community often expects firms to do much more for it than just provide a useful good or service at a reasonable price. For example, a community may expect firms to resist paying bribes, even when the payment of such fees is an ordinary cost of doing business in certain global settings. The **social responsibility of business** consists of the expectations that the community imposes on firms doing business inside its borders. These expectations must be honored to a certain extent, even when a firm wishes to ignore them, because firms are always subject to the implicit threat that legislation will impose social obligations on them. So, if the community expects businesses to obey certain standards of fairness even when the standards interfere with profit maximization, firms that choose to ignore that expectation do so at their peril. See Exhibit 2-1 for a brief look at General Electric's approach to social responsibility.

Consider also the 2008 financial meltdown that resulted when Wall Street investors traded packages of faulty mortgages. Fannie Mae, a government-sponsored company, was in the business of buying, selling, and guaranteeing high-risk mortgages in an effort to make mortgages more affordable for the American people. When borrowers defaulted on their mortgages, Fannie Mae was obligated to pay the balance. Financial advisers warned the company that it was assuming too much risk (guaranteeing more than $270 billion in loans to risky borrowers between 2005 and 2008), but the company continued to buy high-risk mortgages in an effort to keep up with the current market trends. As Wall Street began trading more and more high-risk mortgages, and more borrowers began defaulting on those mortgages, Fannie Mae faced a crisis. In September 2008, the federal government spent $200 billion to rescue Fannie Mae and its counterpart Freddie Mac from their risky investment decisions. Fannie Mae had not only failed in its profit-oriented goals but also failed in its attempts to make mortgages more affordable for Americans, engaging instead in irresponsible behaviors that cost taxpayers billions of dollars.

Exhibit 2-1

Good Citizenship and Profits

Given the number of corporate accounting scandals that have been revealed in the past few years, many corporations are making a point of assuring their investors that their corporate goals are not focused solely on profit. As investors lost millions of dollars during the collapse of companies such as WorldCom and Enron, some corporations have been placing increased emphasis on promoting themselves not only as profitable but as conscientious and ethical.

For example, the following three statements that compose GE's Citizenship Framework seek to assure current and potential investors that the company is dedicated to both stock performance and company integrity.

GE's Citizenship Framework

1. Strong economic performance and stakeholder impact.
2. Rigorous compliance with fundamental accounting and legal requirements.
3. Going beyond compliance by supporting ethical actions.

In linking *performance* and *integrity,* the company endeavors to pair high profits and compliance with government ethics regulations, promoting itself as a company that is worthy of investment and will be honest with shareholders. Whereas in years past companies may have focused solely on their profitability in an attempt to gain new investors, today many business managers realize that corporate honesty has become just as important to those who are seeking to buy stock.

Business Law and Business Ethics

LO2

How are business law
and business ethics
related?

Before business managers consider the social responsibilities of firms in their communities, they need to gather all the relevant facts.

The Chinese manufacturers' decision to substitute diethylene glycol for glycerin depends on a huge array of facts: alternative costs of production, competition among manufacturers, the legal and regulatory framework in each relevant country, and the social responsibilities of the manufacturers, just to name a few. But experienced managers know that assembling the facts is just the beginning of a thoughtful business decision. Next, it makes sense to ask, *Is it legal to go forward with this decision?*

The legality of the decision is the minimal standard that must be met. But the existence of that minimum standard is essential for the development of business ethics. To make this point, let's take a look at the growing practice of bribery in the absence of such legal standards. In some countries businesses must pay bribes to receive legitimate supplies. Though the businessperson may be morally opposed to paying the bribes, the supplies are necessary to stay in business and there may be no other means of obtaining them.

Thus, multinational companies face an ethical dilemma: They must decide whether to pay bribes or find alternative sources of supplies. For instance, when McDonald's opened its doors in Moscow, it made arrangements to receive its supplies from foreign providers. These arrangements ensured that the franchise did not have to engage in questionable business practices.

Regardless of the ethical and legal implications, there are still multinational corporations that choose to use bribes as a means of doing business in foreign markets. For example, in December 2008, multinational giant Siemens AG was ordered to pay the largest Foreign Corrupt Practices Act (FCPA) fine in history after admitting to acts of bribery worldwide. The company had been using off-the-book slush funds, middlemen posing as agents or company consultants, and even money-filled briefcases to bribe government officials and secure contracts overseas. An FBI agent involved in the Siemens investigation went so far as to say that executives for Siemens used bribery as "standard operating procedure" and "a business strategy." As a result, $1.6 billion later, Siemens AG is now forced to restructure itself to do business ethically and legally.

Future business professionals ought to consider not just the moral and monetary costs of engaging in unethical business practices but also the cost of lost business. A tarnished reputation could mean losing contracts, sales, and partnerships in the future.

Look at Case 2-1 as an exercise in comparing what is legal with what is ethical. Business law affects ethics because it provides a floor for managerial ethics. At a minimum, ethics requires a presumption in favor of obedience to law. As you review the Kipps case, consider the relationship between law and ethics.

CASE 2-1   REXFORD KIPPS ET AL. v. JAMES CAILLER ET AL.
U.S. COURT OF APPEALS, FIFTH CIRCUIT 197 F.3D 765 (1999)

Several universities actively recruited Kyle Kipps, a talented football player in southern Louisiana, in 1996 and 1997. Kyle's father, Rexford Kipps, was an assistant football coach at the University of Southwestern Louisiana (USL) *for eleven years. In March 1996, Nelson Stokley, USL's head football coach, told Rexford Kipps that Kyle was to attend either USL or a college or university outside of Louisiana. When Kyle notified Stokley that he had orally* committed to play at Louisiana State University (LSU) on a football scholarship, Stokley told Rexford Kipps to forbid his son to play football for LSU. Rexford Kipps argued that he could not and would not force his son to refuse to play for LSU. Consequently, Stokley terminated Kipps's employment with LSU. Both Nelson Schexnayder, Jr., USL Director of Athletics, and Ray Authement, President of USL, approved Kipps's termination. The President of the Board of Trustees, James Caillier, also approved Kipps's termination.

Rexford Kipps brought constitutional and state law claims against defendants Caillier, Schexnayder, Authement, and Stokley. These defendants filed for summary judgment, arguing that the at-will employment status of Kipps precluded any wrongful termination action. Furthermore, they claimed that they were entitled to qualified immunity and Kipps's termination was justified because Kyle's choice would affect USL's ability to recruit athletes. The district court granted Stokley, Schexnayder, and Authement's motion for summary judgment on qualified immunity grounds. Kipps appealed to the U.S. Court of Appeals, 5th District.

JUDGE PARKER: Public officials acting within the scope of their official duties are shielded from civil liability by the qualified immunity doctrine. Government officials are entitled to qualified immunity "insofar as their conduct does not violate clearly established statutory or constitutional rights of which a reasonable person would have known."

In order to establish that the defendants are not entitled to qualified immunity, plaintiffs must satisfy a three-part test. First, "[a] court evaluating a claim of qualified immunity must first determine whether the plaintiff has alleged the deprivation of a constitutional right at all."

Second, the court must "determine whether that right was clearly established at the time of the alleged violation." Finally, the court "must determine whether the record shows that the violation occurred, or at least gives rise to a genuine issue of material fact as to whether the defendant actually engaged in the conduct that violated the clearly-established right." If it is determined that the official's conduct was unconstitutional, then the court must decide whether the conduct was nonetheless "objectively reasonable."

Assuming arguendo that defendants violated Kipps's clearly established constitutional liberty interest in familial association, the resolution of this issue turns on whether the defendants' actions were "objectively reasonable." Because we find that defendants' actions were objectively reasonable, we affirm the district court's dismissal of Kipps's 1983 claim on the basis of qualified immunity.

Even if defendants violated Kipps's clearly established constitutional right, they are still entitled to qualified immunity if their actions were objectively reasonable. . . . The record indicates that Kipps was fired because his son chose to play football for a Louisiana school other than USL. Notwithstanding the defendants' subjective motivation and belief as to the lawfulness of their conduct, we find the defendants' motivation for terminating Kipps was objectively reasonable. Defendants' motivation, according to the record in this case, was to mitigate the damage that Kyle's attendance at LSU as opposed to USL would have on alumni relations and recruiting efforts.

The summary judgment record of this appeal contains no facts upon which we could find that defendants' actions were objectively unreasonable.

AFFIRMED.

CRITICAL THINKING

What reasons did the judge offer to support his decision that Kipps's termination was legal? Which facts in the case are most important in your mind when evaluating the reasoning?

Identify various meanings of the phrase "objectively reasonable." Which meaning do you think the court is using? Is it clear? How does this affect the validity of the argument given by Judge Parker?

ETHICAL DECISION MAKING

The Kipps case provides a snapshot of the complexity of the link between ethics and the law. Do you believe that some view of what it means to do the right thing is responsible for the legal decision in this case?

Exhibit 2-2
Ethical Business
Practices

General Motors'
Code of Business Conduct

The foundation for all conduct by GM and its employees is one of our core values: Integrity. Integrity is essential to achieving our vision of becoming the world leader in transportation products and services, earning the enthusiasm of our customers, working together as a team, innovating, and continuously improving. We call this Winning With Integrity.

These Guidelines are designed to help GM and its employees understand and meet fundamental obligations that are vital to our success. Some of those obligations are legal duties. They are established by the laws, regulations, and court rulings applicable to our business. Other obligations result from policies GM establishes to make sure our actions align with our core values and cultural priorities. Compliance with both types of obligation—our legal duties and our internal policies—is vital to our goal of winning with integrity.

Employees who violate these guidelines may be subject to disciplinary action which, in the judgment of management, is appropriate to the nature of the violation and which may include termination of employment. Employees may also be subject to civil and criminal penalties if the law has been violated.

As the Kipps case demonstrates, business managers must sometimes decide whether to hire and fire particular employees. Their decisions will be guided by legal rules that have both ethical foundations and implications for needed legal reform.

In addition, the definition of business ethics refers to *standards* of business conduct. *It does not result in a set of correct decisions.* Business ethics can improve business decisions by serving as a reminder not to choose the first business option that comes to mind or the one that enriches us in the short run. But business ethics can never produce a list of correct business decisions that all ethical businesses will make.

Well-managed firms try to provide ethical leadership by establishing codes of ethics for the firm. For example, Exhibit 2-2 addresses the attempt by General Motors, a major automobile maker, to make a statement about the importance of business ethics to its firm. Notice, however, that this corporate code can never do more than provide guidance. The complications associated with managerial decisions do not permit any ethical guide to provide definitive lists of right and wrong decisions.

At the same time that business ethics guides decisions within firms, ethics helps guide the law. Law and business ethics serve as an interactive system—informing and assessing each other. For example, our ethical inclination to encourage trust, dependability, and efficiency in market exchanges shapes many of our business laws. See Exhibit 2-3, for instance. The principles of contract law facilitate market exchanges and trade because the parties to an exchange can count on the enforceability of agreements. Legal rules that govern the exchange have been shaped in large part by our sense of commercial ethics.

Of course, different ethical understandings prevail in different countries. Thus, ethical conceptions shape business law and business relationships uniquely in each country. Increasingly, business leaders require sensitivity to the differences in legal guidelines in the various countries in which they operate. These differences are based on somewhat different understandings of ethical behavior among businesspeople in diverse countries.

Business Gifts and Favors in China

In China, the practice of using *guanxi* has become an integral part of doing business for firms already located in the country and for those interested in entering the Chinese market. *Guanxi*, which refers to a sort of relationship building, is an intricate system of interpersonal networks woven together by social ties. The concept of *guanxi* is important to individuals involved in business because having good *guanxi* means having connections that can assist you in getting things that may normally be out of reach to you or your business. The rules and regulations in China can be burdensome, but the right *guanxi*, or connections, can make many processes much easier. The *guanxi* system is built on reciprocity, and if someone does a favor for you, you'll be expected to return that favor in the future. A favor could technically be any number of things, from access to partnerships, contacts, and government officials to special consideration or useful information.

The process of creating and maintaining *guanxi* may seem somewhat taboo to westerners because businesses in the United States often have strict rules about accepting gifts, doing favors

and offering preferential treatment or consideration to clients. However, Dan Mintz, a Brooklyn native with no college degree, who is now the CEO of one of the largest advertising agencies in China, claims *guanxi* is a necessity when doing business in China. After moving to Beijing with no contacts and little experience, Mintz established his own business (Dynamic Marking Group) with two Chinese partners, Peter Xiao and Wu Bing. Both Xiao and Bing had extensive *guanxi*, networks that extended into high levels of Chinese government and banking. The trio spent their time targeting potential clients, delivering gifts, and hosting dinners as means to strengthen their *guanxi* and improve their business opportunities. Through their hard work and strong *guanxi* Mintz, Xiao, and Bing were eventually able to secure deals with some of the biggest brands in the world: Budweiser, Kraft, Audi, Volkswagen, and Nike.

Source: Flora F. Gu, Kineta Hung, and David K. Tse, "When Does Guanxi Matter? Issues of Capitalization and Its Dark Sides," *Journal of Marketing* 72 (July 2008), pp. 12–28; www.fastcompany.com/magazine/104/open_mintz.html?page=0%2C0; and www.chinasuccessstories.com/2008/02/07/dmg-chinese-advertising/.

Exhibit 2-3

Enron, WorldCom, and Shifts in Business Regulation

During the past several years, ethics violations have been uncovered in the accounting practices of a number of large companies. Enron and WorldCom were two of the perpetrators in these scandals. Both companies failed to report or record billions of dollars in profit losses, which resulted in stockholders' believing that the companies were in a much better financial state than actually was the case.

Enron's tangled web involved the company's creating multiple subsidiaries and related companies. These businesses were often treated as companies independent of Enron and not shown on the accounting books. Enron used the subsidiaries to conceal debts and losses in a very complex fraud scheme. When the company went bankrupt, employees who had based their retirement plans around Enron stock lost almost everything. Additionally, Enron auditor Arthur Andersen was found guilty of shredding documents about Enron's audits.

In June 2002, shortly after the Enron bankruptcy was announced, WorldCom revealed that it also had engaged in unethical accounting practices. WorldCom's violations included counting profits twice and concealing billions of dollars in expenses when making reports to the SEC. The company thereby made itself appear profitable when it was actually losing money. In total, WorldCom had more than $7 billion in misreported debt.

These two cases, among others, left investors understandably concerned about the truthfulness of individuals who were in charge of operating large corporations. Those in charge of these companies had been awarded million-dollar bonuses while completely disregarding stockholders and employees, who lost millions of dollars when the companies collapsed.

The revelations of Enron and WorldCom suggested quite blatantly that the business world could not be allowed to regulate itself ethically. Their downfall in part led to many federal regulations designed to promote truthfulness and ethical practices among business managers. In this new business environment, there is a much greater degree of government oversight to ensure that companies maintain high standards of ethical behavior. Companies are required to make their accounting records far more transparent, to satisfy not only the federal government but their understandably wary investors.

As we mentioned above, business ethics does not yield one "correct" decision. So how are business managers to chart their way through the ethical decision-making process? One source of assistance consists of the general theories and schools of thought about ethics. Each ethical system provides a method for resolving ethical dilemmas by examining duties, consequences, virtues, justice, and so on. A detailed look at each of these ethical systems can be found in Appendix 2A.

In the interest of providing future business managers with a practical approach to business ethics *that they can use,* we suggest a three-step approach: the **WPH process of ethical decision making.** This approach offers future business managers some **ethical guidelines,** or practical steps, that provide a dependable stimulus to ethical reasoning in a business context. Appendix 2A provides the theoretical basis for the WPH approach used in this book.

The WPH Framework for Business Ethics

A useful set of ethical guidelines requires recognition that managerial decisions must meet the following primary criteria:

L03

How can we use the WPH framework for ethical business decisions?

- The decisions affect particular groups of stakeholders in the operations of the firm. The pertinent question is thus, *Whom* would this decision affect?
- The decisions are made in pursuit of a particular *purpose.* Business decisions are instruments toward an ethical end.
- The decisions must meet the standards of action-oriented business behavior. Managers need a doable set of guidelines for *how* to make ethical decisions.

The remainder of this chapter explains and illustrates this framework. See Exhibit 2-4 for a summary of the key WPH elements.

1. **W—WHO (Stakeholders):**
   Consumers
   Owners or investors
   Management
   Employees
   Community
   Future generations
2. **P—PURPOSE (Values):**
   Freedom
   Security
   Justice
   Efficiency
3. **H—HOW (Guidelines):**
   Public disclosure
   Universalization
   Golden Rule

Exhibit 2-4

The WPH Process of Ethical Decision Making

WHO ARE THE RELEVANT STAKEHOLDERS?

The **stakeholders** of a firm are the many groups of people affected by the firm's decisions. Any given managerial decision affects, in varying degrees, the following stakeholders:

1. Owners or shareholders.
2. Employees.
3. Customers.
4. Management.
5. The general community where the firm operates.
6. Future generations.

Exhibit 2-5 gives a portrait of General Mills' commitments to its primary stakeholders and demonstrates that General Mills is aware of the people involved in its various decisions.

When you consider the relevant stakeholders, try to go beyond the obvious. In the Case Nugget, Maria's encounter with her company's vice president clearly highlights certain common interests of management and its employees. However, a useful exercise for all of us is to force ourselves to think more broadly about additional stakeholders who may be affected just as much in the long run. Then we will be less likely to make decisions that have unintended negative ethical impacts.

Maria's ethical dilemma is complex. Many of the issues in the dilemma pertain to her career and the welfare of her firm. But consider the many stakeholders whose interests

Exhibit 2-5

Commitments to General Mills' Stakeholders

We share a common purpose and a common responsibility with our stakeholders. We want them to know that they can depend on us—and that they can trust us. We know too that we must depend on them. We want every stakeholder of General Mills to feel they are part of something special.

Our Consumers

Our consumers trust General Mills to deliver quality and value when they are shopping for the most important people in their lives—their families.

Our Customers

Our customers trust General Mills to deliver quality and value for their customers—the consumers of our products—and they look to us to help them grow.

Our Partners

We treat our suppliers, vendors, and other partners with respect—conducting ourselves with integrity in every aspect of every relationship.

Our Team

We are diverse, talented, committed individuals of integrity—constantly learning and growing and contributing to our communities.

Our Shareholders

Our shareholders trust General Mills to deliver superior performance and superior total investment returns.

Our Communities

We are committed to making a positive difference in people's lives by making a positive difference in our communities.

www.generalmills.com/corporate/commitment/stakeholders.aspx (accessed October 30, 2008).

HYPOTHETICAL CASE NUGGET

The Many Stakeholders in a Business Decision

Maria Lopez

Maria recently became the purchasing manager of a small lawn-mower manufacturing firm. She is excited about the opportunity to demonstrate her abilities in this new responsibility. She is very aware that several others in the firm are watching her closely because they do not believe she deserves the purchasing manager position.

Her new job at the firm requires that she interact with several senior managers and leaders. One vice president in particular, Brian O'Malley, is someone she admires because he has earned the respect of the CEO on the basis of his success at making profits for the firm. Again and again, he just seems to know how to discover and take advantage of competitive opportunities that end up paying off royally for the firm.

Maria's first responsibility is to buy the motors for the assembly line. The motors constitute 30 percent of the total construction cost of the lawn mowers. Consequently, even a small error on Maria's part would have huge implications for the firm's profitability. The bids from the motor suppliers are required to be secret in order to maximize competition among the suppliers. The bids are due at 5 p.m. today.

At 3 p.m., Maria accidentally sees Brian returning the submitted bids to the locked safe where they are to be stored, according to company policy, until all bids have been submitted at 5 p.m. Then at 4:45 p.m., she notices a postal delivery of a bid from Stein's Motor Company. Her head buzzes as it hits her that Stein's president is one of Brian O'Malley's cousins.

She has no idea what to do. However, she knows she has to decide quickly.

were not introduced into the conversation. When we overlook important, relevant stakeholders, we are ignoring a significant component of ethical reasoning.

Consider the negative impact that results when a firm fails to show adequate respect for a major stakeholder. On December 3, 1984, a horrible catastrophe occurred at a chemical plant in Bhopal, India. The plant was a subsidiary of Union Carbide. Damage to some equipment resulted in the emission of a deadly gas, methyl isocyanate, into the atmosphere. The emission of the gas caused injuries to more than 200,000 workers and other people in the neighborhood of the chemical plant. Several thousand people died.

Many factors, including worker error, faulty management decisions, equipment failures, and poor safety standards combined to cause the accident. Union Carbide was accused of not demanding the same rigorous safety standards in India as it had in the United States. Citizens of both India and the United States demanded that the corporation be held responsible for its evident neglect of safety. Union Carbide argued that it could not operate the plant if it were required to obey rigid Indian safety standards and that the economic benefits of the plant to India outweighed the risks of not following these standards. After years of litigation in both U.S. and Indian courts, Union Carbide was eventually ordered to monetarily compensate the victims of the accident. Among other factors, Union Carbide's failure to respect the interests of a major stakeholder resulted in a disaster for the firm and for the community.

After we consider stakeholders, the next step in the WPH framework is to consider the purpose of business decisions. In the next section, we look first at the parties involved, and then we explore the purposes that bring these various parties together in a common effort.

WHAT ARE THE ULTIMATE *PURPOSES* OF THE DECISION?

When we think about the ultimate reason or purpose for why we make decisions in a business firm, we turn to the basic unit of business ethics—values. **Values** are positive abstractions that capture our sense of what is good or desirable. They are *ideas* that underlie conversations about business ethics. We derive our ethics from the interplay of values. Values represent our understanding of the purposes we will fulfill by making particular decisions.

For example, we value honesty. We want to live in communities where the trust that we associate with honesty prevails in our negotiations with one another. Business depends on the maintenance of a high degree of trust. No contract can protect us completely against every possible contingency. So we need some element of trust in one another when we buy and sell.

When that trust is lacking, businesses fall apart. Between January and October 2008, more than 400 people were arrested for mortgage-fraud-related crimes. One of the people arrested was Wayne Puff, who started the business New Jersey Affordable Homes. Over the course of a decade, Puff solicited more than $123 million from investors, who did not know that Puff was running a Ponzi scheme. Puff was using money from later investors to pay "returns" to earlier investors, thereby fooling people into believing his business was profitable. All the while, Puff and his associates were committing mortgage fraud to maintain the appearance of their business scheme.

If we think about the definition of values for a moment, we realize two things immediately. First, there are a huge number of values that pull and push our decisions. For example, Puff may have thought of honesty as an important value, but perhaps his desire for personal success weighed more heavily on his decision making than the need for honesty did. Second, to state that a value is important in a particular situation is to start a conversation about what is meant by that particular value. For example, some people may consider success a measure of one's character, whereas one may presume from Puff's actions that his definition of success was largely based on financial achievement.

To help make WPH useful to you as a manager, Exhibit 2-6 outlines an efficient way to apply this second step in the WPH framework. The exhibit identifies four of the most important values influencing business ethics and presents alternative meanings for each.

Exhibit 2-6

Primary Values and Business Ethics

VALUE	ALTERNATIVE MEANINGS
Freedom	1. To act without restriction from rules imposed by others.
	2. To possess the capacity or resources to act as one wishes.
	3. To escape the cares and demands of this world entirely.
Security	1. To possess a large-enough supply of goods and services to meet basic needs.
	2. To be safe from those wising to interfere with your property rights.
	3. To achieve the psychological condition of self-confidence to such an extent that risks are welcome.
Justice	1. To receive the products of your labor.
	2. To treat all humans identically, regardless of race, class, gender, age, and sexual preference.
	3. To provide resources in proportion to need.
	4. To possess anything that someone else is willing to grant you.
Efficiency	1. To maximize the amount of wealth in society.
	2. To get the most from a particular output.
	3. To minimize costs.

Exhibit 2-6 should not only help clarify the importance of values in your own mind but also enable you to question others who claim to be acting in an ethical fashion.

For instance, a manager might be deciding whether to fire an employee whose performance is less than impressive. In making this decision, the manager explores alternative visions of key values such as justice and efficiency and then makes choices about which action to take. Values and their alternative meanings are often the foundation for different ethical decisions.

To avoid ambiguity, many companies summarize their values in brief statements. Nortel Networks' statement of core values, shown in Exhibit 2-7, identifies for Nortel's stakeholders which positive abstractions guide its business decisions.

HOW DO WE MAKE ETHICAL DECISIONS?

Making ethical decisions has always been one of our most confusing *and* important human challenges. In the process of meeting this challenge, we have discovered a few general, ethical guidelines to assist us. An *ethical guideline* provides one path to ethical conduct. Notice that all three ethical guidelines below reflect a central principle of business ethics: consideration for stakeholders.

The Golden Rule.   The idea that we should interact with other people in a manner consistent with the way we would like them to interact with us has deep historical roots. Both Confucius and Aristotle suggested versions of that identical guideline. One scholar has identified six ways the Golden Rule can be interpreted:

1. Do to others as you want them to gratify you.
2. Be considerate of others' feelings as you want them to be considerate of yours.
3. Treat others as persons of rational dignity like you.

Exhibit 2-7
Core Values: A Guide to Ethical Business Practice

NORTEL NETWORKS' CORE VALUES

1. We create superior value for our customers.
2. We work to provide shareholder value.
3. Our people are our strength.
4. We share one vision. We are one team.
5. We have only one standard—excellence.
6. We embrace change and reward innovation.
7. We fulfill our commitments and act with integrity.

New ways of organizing people and work within the corporation are giving each of us more decision-making responsibility. Given the complexity and constantly changing nature of our work and our world, no book of hard-and-fast rules—however long and detailed—could ever adequately cover all the dilemmas people face. In this context, every Nortel Networks' employee is asked to take leadership in ethical decision making.

In most situations, our personal values and honesty will guide us to the right decision. But in our capacity as employees and representatives of Nortel Networks, we must also always consider how our actions affect the integrity and credibility of the corporation as a whole. Our business ethics must reflect the standard of conduct outlined in this document—a standard grounded in the corporation's values and governing Nortel Networks' relationships with all stakeholders.

4. Extend brotherly or sisterly love to others, as you would want them to do to you.

5. Treat others according to moral insight, as you would have others treat you.

6. Do to others as God wants you to do to them.

Regardless of the version of the Golden Rule we use, this guideline urges us to be aware that other people—their rights and needs—matter.

Let's return to the ethical problem outlined at the beginning of this chapter. Using the Golden Rule as your ethical guideline, how would you behave? Would you hide the information about the chemicals used to make your toothpaste, or would you disclose the information? Put yourself in the consumer's position. As a consumer, would you want to know that your toothpaste contained a potentially toxic chemical? Are there other stakeholders in the organization whose interests should be the focus of your application of the Golden Rule? The focus on others that is the foundation of the Golden Rule is also clearly reflected in a second ethical guideline: the public disclosure test.

Public Disclosure Test.   Applying what you have learned to the ethical dilemma faced by the Chinese toothpaste manufacturers, suppose you decide to ignore the complaints about the use of diethylene glycol instead of glycerin. Now suppose that your decision to ignore the complaints is printed in the newspaper. How would the public react? How would you feel about the public's having full knowledge of what you intend to do?

We tend to care about what others think about us as ethical agents. Stop for a moment and think of corporations that failed to apply the public disclosure test and generated negative reactions as a result. For example, in July 2006, a company named Trafigura attempted to dump waste from one of its ships at a port in Holland. The ship initially reported that it was dumping "regular slops," or wastewater from the ship's hold, and agreed to pay $15,000.

As the port's workers began to empty the waste, they noticed that the waste had an unusual consistency and smell. Upon testing, the workers discovered that the waste was toxic and would cost $300,000 to treat and dispose of properly. Trafigura refused to pay, insisting that the waste was not toxic.

Trafigura had its waste reloaded onto the ship and left without paying to dispose of any of the waste. The ship then headed toward Africa, where Trafigura had reportedly found a company capable of disposing the waste. The disposal company, called Tommy, was allegedly a shell corporation created by Trafigura specifically for this job. Tommy charged Trafigura a mere $20,000 to dispose of the toxic waste. The waste was pumped from the ship into trucks that drove into Abidjan, an extremely poor part of the Ivory Coast, where the waste was dumped in 18 different residential areas during the night. The waste was not treated in any way.

Over the course of the following days, people throughout Abidjan suffered from headaches, nausea, open sores on their skin, and even death. At least 10 people died from exposure to the toxic waste, and tens of thousands of people were injured. When the international community heard that tons of toxic waste had been dumped in impoverished residential areas, the outcry was noticeable.

Trafigura disclaimed all blame, saying first that the waste was not toxic and second that the company at fault was Tommy, the company that physically dumped the waste in Abidjan. As a result of the companies' actions, criminal charges were filed against some of the key players. In October 2008, the Nigerian man who hired the trucks that dumped the waste was sentenced to 20 years in prison, and an Ivorian port official was sentenced to 5 years in prison. Seven other port and government officials were acquitted at trial.

In February 2007, Trafigura agreed to pay $200 million to the Ivory Coast government, although the company stated that the settlement was not an admission of guilt. Trafigura claimed that the money would help pay for medical care for the tens of thousands of injured people and also help with the cleanup of the waste. Trafigura would likely have behaved differently had it considered the public disclosure test before paying to dump toxic waste in Abidjan. The company may have realized that the international community would be outraged by Trafigura's disregard for the well-being of tens of thousands of people, and the company may even have considered that its decision would cost far more money than it would save. Presumably, Trafigura would have chosen a different waste disposal option, one that would have saved its reputation, its money, and the lives of others.

Another way to think of the public disclosure test is to view it as a ray of sunlight that makes our actions visible, rather than obscured. As Exhibit 2-8 suggests, the issue of transparency of behavior is often seen as a method of improving ethical behavior. The public disclosure test is sometimes called the "television test," for it requires us to imagine that our actions are being broadcast on national television. The premise behind the public disclosure test is that ethics is hard work, labor that we might resist if we did not have frequent reminders that we live in a community. As a member of a community, our self-concept is tied, at least in part, to how that community perceives us.

Universalization Test.   A third general guideline shares with the other two a focus on the "other"—the stakeholders whom our actions affect. Before we act, the universalization test asks us to consider what the world would be like were our decision copied by everyone else. Applying the universalization test causes us to wonder aloud: "Is what I am about to do the kind of action that, *were others to follow my example,* makes the world a better place for me and those I love?"

THE SARBANES-OXLEY ACT

The Corporate and Criminal Fraud Accountability Act, also known as the Sarbanes-Oxley Act, was signed by President Bush in 2002 in the wake of several corporate accounting scandals. The act is intended to promote high ethical standards among business managers and employees through a series of stringent requirements and controls that regulate several different facets of corporate operation.

Among other things, the act created the Public Company Accounting Oversight Board. This board is responsible for ensuring that auditors and public accounting firms compile accurate and truthful financial reports for the companies they audit. The act also requires that companies devise a system that allows employees to report suspicions of unethical behavior within the company. The act also protects these whistle-blowers from being fired or from retaliation by their employer for reporting a possible problem within the company.

Additionally, the chief executive officer (CEO) or chief financial officer (CFO) must personally vouch that the company's financial statements are correct, meet all SEC requirements for disclosure, and represent company finances accurately. The act provides for very harsh penalties in the case of violations. If the CEO or CFO knows that the company's financial reports are incorrect but claims they are truthful, or if he or she destroys or changes financial documents, the imposed fine can run into the millions of dollars.

Exhibit 2-8
A Mandate for Ethical Behavior

E-COMMERCE AND THE LAW

Computer Use and Ethics

The use of computers to store and transfer important business information has resulted in a new set of ethical concerns. How private is the computer screen? Are companies allowed to collect information about their customers? Who owns the information customers give to e-businesses? E-commerce law is gradually adjusting to such questions. But as the beginning of this chapter pointed out, knowing the law is just the first step in discovering ethical business decisions.

One case that considered questions related to e-commerce and privacy involved Toysmart.com and its privacy policy. In 2000, the Federal Trade Commission (FTC) filed a complaint against Toysmart.com, charging the online retailer with selling customer lists despite earlier privacy statements that its customers' personal data would never be shared with a third party. The customer lists were included as assets to be sold as part of the company's bankruptcy proceedings. The FTC issued a settlement with Toysmart.com allowing the lists to be sold as long as (1) the sale occurred before July 2001, (2) the lists would be sold to a family-oriented company, and (3) the buyer would agree to abide by the original Toysmart.com privacy policy. After the FTC imposed these restrictions, the end result was that customers' personal information was not sold.

The Toysmart.com case makes it clear that, for both ethical and legal reasons, companies that adopt a privacy policy need to think that policy through before announcing it to customers.

In summary, business managers can apply the WPH approach to most ethical dilemmas. The WPH framework provides a practical process suited to the frequently complex ethical dilemmas that business managers must address quickly in today's society.

CASE OPENER WRAP-UP

Chinese Toothpaste Manufacturers

Chinese toothpaste manufacturers, as well as other firms, affect the lives of many stakeholders in many countries. The manufacturers' owners, workers, and customers are perhaps the most obvious stakeholders in decisions the manufacturers make about their production, labeling, and distribution policies. It is clear that the manufacturers' decisions have potentially deadly consequences for customers who use the contaminated toothpaste, but the manufacturers' decisions may also affect the business climate among other manufacturers, which may be tempted to engage in similarly questionable business practices to cut costs. All of the manufacturers' decisions have ethical implications.

What those decisions are can be guided by an appreciation of the conflicting values that lie under the surface when we make decisions that affect others. The WPH system of ethical decision making stimulates the Chinese toothpaste manufacturers and similar companies to ask questions about their behavior that highlight their possible effects on the community.

All of us would probably agree that the manufacturers have a responsibility to try to be sustainable business enterprises. Toward that end, profits are essential. But production practices that cut costs may not be an effective way to make long-run profits because the multiple stakeholders disagree about the benefits of such practices. While the Chinese government initially defended the manufacturers by reporting that diethylene glycol was not dangerous in low concentrations, the international outrage resulting from the discovery of the contaminated toothpaste caused even the Chinese government to ban the manufacturers from using diethylene glycol in toothpaste. By failing to disclose their use of diethylene glycol, the manufacturers lost credibility among international consumers, substantially damaging their ability to be competitive and successful business firms.

Key Terms

business ethics   17

ethical dilemma   17

ethical guidelines   23

ethics   17

social responsibility
of business   18

stakeholders   24

values   25

WPH process of ethical
decision making   23

Summary of Key Topics

**Business Ethics and
Social Responsibility**

Business ethics is the application of ethics to the special problems and opportunities experienced by businesspeople.

The *social responsibility of business* consists of the expectations that the community imposes on firms doing business with its citizens.

**Business Law and
Business Ethics**

Business ethics builds on business law. The law both affects and is affected by evolving ethical patterns. But business law provides only a floor for business ethics, telling business leaders the minimally acceptable course of action.

**The WPH Framework
for Business Ethics**

Who are the relevant stakeholders? This question determines which interests (consumers, employees, managers, owners) are being pushed and prodded. *What are the ultimate purposes of the decision?* This question determines which values (freedom, efficiency, security, and justice) are being upheld by the decision.

How do we make ethical decisions? This question leads us to apply general ethical guidelines:

- *Golden Rule:* Do unto others as you would have them do unto you.
- *Public disclosure test:* If the public knew about this decision, how would you decide?
- *Universalization test:* What would the world be like were our decision copied by everyone else.

Point / Counterpoint

Sarbanes-Oxley Act of 2002

Are the Costs Associated with the Sarbanes-Oxley Act Reason for Reform?	
NO	YES
Corporate and accounting scandals, such as Enron, were the reason the Sarbanes-Oxley Act of 2002 was drafted. The act promotes honesty and accountability in financial reporting, thus bringing increased security to investors. For example, corporations must now ensure the segregation of all duties related to accounting procedures.	Corporations need incentives to remain or go public. The Sarbanes-Oxley Act of 2002 is not an incentive. Although there may have been ample motivation for the development of an act that addresses accounting scandals, the costs associated with Sarbanes-Oxley are much too high. Simply purchasing and learning to use the materials needed for compliance with the act would cost approximately $3.5 million.

Although critics assert that the financial burden associated with the act is reason for reform, the compliance costs about which they speak are beginning to fall as individuals become familiar with the new systems. In addition, the Dow Jones Industrial Average is rising as a result of increased investor confidence. This confidence is the direct result of the requirement that corporations disclose information and allow for investigations by the Public Company Accounting Oversight Board.

Since the passing of the Sarbanes-Oxley Act, there have not been any known major accounting scandals. Without public disclosure, corporations would have little incentive to engage in rigorous evaluation of their own accounting practices. By forcing corporations to disclose information, they are being held to higher ethical standards than they were previously.

Those who argue that the act should not be reformed often focus on the idea that every corporation is now being held to the same standards. However, as a result of the substantial economic costs associated with implementation of the guidelines, smaller businesses that would like to go public are forced to remain private to avoid the costs. Among small businesses that are already public, many are not able to gather the resources necessary to comply with the act.

In addition to the costs associated with the act, corporations are now monitored by commissions that are appointed rather than elected. These commissions lack the accountability that is necessary to make decisions about how to regulate, tax, and punish companies and individuals that may violate the provisions of the act. Thus, the act as it is currently written does not provide an equal opportunity to all corporations and businesses.

Questions & Problems

1. How do business ethics and business law interact with each other? Is one highly ethical and the other less ethical?

2. If business ethics does not offer guidance about what is always the right thing to do, is one behavior as good as the next?

3. How does the WPH approach to ethics approach an ethical problem?

4. Jarold Daniel Friedman worked as a temporary computer contractor for a pharmaceutical warehouse. The warehouse offered him a permanent position, but the warehouse required that he get a mumps vaccine, grown in chicken embryos, as a condition of his permanent employment. Friedman, a vegan, believed that the vaccination would violate his religious beliefs and declined to be vaccinated. As a result, the warehouse withdrew its offer of employment. Friedman claimed that the warehouse discriminated against him on the basis of religion. Do you agree with Friedman? Do employers have a duty to respect the beliefs of their employees? If so, what happens when that duty conflicts with employers' duty to provide a safe and healthy work environment? [*Friedman v. Southern California Permanente Medical Group*, 102 Cal. App. 4th 39 (2002).]

5. Jennifer Erickson sued her employer, Bartell Drug Company, contending that its decision not to cover prescription contraceptives under its employee prescription drug plan constituted sex discrimination. Bartell argued that its decision was not sex discrimination because contraceptives were preventive, were voluntary, and did not treat an illness. With whom do you agree? Why? What values did you use to reach your conclusion? [*Erickson v. Bartell Drug Co.*, 141 F. Supp. 2d 1266 (2001).]

6. Entertainment Network, Inc. (ENI), a business that provided news, entertainment, and information via the Internet, sued government officials who prohibited the company from filming the execution of Oklahoma City bomber Timothy McVeigh and selling the footage of the execution online. The government officials argued that a Justice Department regulation prohibiting audio and visual recording devices at federal executions applied in the case at hand. ENI, however, argued that the regulation violated the company's First Amendment right to free speech. How do you think the court should have ruled in this case? Do you think ENI might have altered its decision to broadcast the execution if it had applied the Golden Rule? [*Entm't Network, Inc. v. Lappin*, 134 F. Supp. 2d 1002 (2001).]

7. Ernest Price went to a doctor in 1997, seeking Oxycontin to treat pain related to sickle cell anemia. Between November 1999 and October 2000, Price sought Oxycontin prescriptions from at least ten different doctors at ten different clinics in two cities, filling the prescriptions at seven pharmacies in three cities. The doctors were notified of Price's medication-seeking behavior, and the doctors discontinued Price's treatment. Price then filed suit, claiming his doctors, pharmacies, and the pharmaceutical companies that manufactured Oxycontin had breached their duty by failing to adequately warn Price of the addictive nature of Oxycontin. How do you think the court responded to Price's claims? Think about all the stakeholders involved in such a case; how would those parties be affected by a ruling in favor of Price? In favor of the doctors and pharmaceutical companies? [*Ernest Price v. The Purdue Pharma Co.,* 920 So. 2d 479; 2006 Miss. LEXIS 67 (2006).]

8. Javier Galindo, the husband of Richard Clark's housekeeper, was sitting in his car, parked in the driveway of Clark's house, waiting to pick up his wife. While he was waiting, a leaning 80-foot tree located on an adjacent property fell on Galindo's car and killed him. Galindo's wife sued Clark, alleging that Clark was liable for failing to notify Galindo about the danger posed by the leaning tree. Do you think that Clark had a legal responsibility to tell Galindo about the tree? Do you think Clark had an ethical responsibility to tell Galindo about the tree? Why might the answer to these questions be different? [*Galindo v. Town of Clarkstown,* 2 N.Y.3d 633 (2004).]

9. Doctors diagnosed Leo Guilbeault with lung cancer. He had been smoking the same brand, Camel cigarettes, since 1951. Guilbeault filed a complaint against the manufacturer of Camel cigarettes, R. J. Reynolds Tobacco Co. According to Guilbeault, Reynolds failed to adequately warn consumers about the dangers of smoking. Prior to 1970, Camel cigarettes were sold without a warning label. After the Labeling Act of 1966, Reynolds began to put warning labels on packages of cigarettes. Guilbeault believes that Reynolds knew about the adverse health consequences of smoking before 1970 and, therefore, that Reynolds had a duty to warn consumers of these consequences. Do you agree with his argument? Should Reynolds have warned consumers earlier? [*Guilbeault v. R. J. Reynolds Tobacco Co.,* 44 Fed. R. Serv. 3d 124 (1999).]

10. Brazos Higher Education Service Corporation, Inc., was a nonprofit student loan company. Brazos allowed one of its employees to store customers' personal financial information on a laptop with an unencrypted hard drive. The laptop was subsequently stolen from the employee's home during a robbery. Brazos had no way of knowing which customers' information was contained on the laptop's hard drive or whether the information would be accessed by a third party. As a precaution, Brazos notified all of its customers that their information may have been accessed by a third party and offered each customer six months of identity-theft monitoring. One customer, Guin, brought suit against Brazos for negligence, claiming that Brazos had failed to adequately protect his financial information, thereby causing Guin harm. Guin's information was never accessed by a third party, and Guin never suffered identity theft. How might other businesses be affected if Guin's lawsuit succeeded? Do you think Brazos was wrong to store its customers' financial information on an unencrypted laptop hard drive? [*Stacy Lawton Guin v. Brazos Higher Education Service Corporation, Inc.,* 2006 U.S. Dist. LEXIS 4846 (2006).]

Looking for more review material?

The Online Learning Center at **www.mhhe.com/kubasek2e** contains this chapter's "Assignment on the Internet" and also a list of URLs for more information, entitled "On the Internet." Find both of them in the Student Center portion of the OLC, along with quizzes and other helpful materials.

Ethical Relativism and Situational Ethics

An ethical school of thought that may seem appealing on the surface is ethical relativism. **Ethical relativism** is a theory of ethics that denies the existence of objective moral standards. Rather, according to ethical relativism, individuals must evaluate actions on the basis of what they feel is best for themselves. Ethical relativism holds that when two individuals disagree over a question about morality, both individuals are correct because no objective standard exists to evaluate their actions. Instead, morality is relative, and thus no one can criticize another's behavior as immoral. Many people find ethical relativism attractive because it promotes tolerance.

Ethical relativism may appear attractive at first glance, but very few people are willing to accept the logical conclusions of this theory. For example, ethical relativism requires that we see murder as a moral action as long as the murderer believes that the action is best for himself or herself. Once a person accepts the appropriateness of criticizing behavior in some situations, the person has rejected ethical relativism and must develop a more complex ethical theory.

Situational ethics is a theory that at first appears similar to ethical relativism but is actually substantially different. Like ethical relativism, **situational ethics** requires that we evaluate the morality of an action by imagining ourselves in the position of the person facing the ethical dilemma. But unlike ethical relativism, situational ethics allows us to judge other people's actions. In other words, situational ethics holds that once we put ourselves in another person's shoes, we can evaluate whether that person's action was ethical.

While situational ethics provides a useful rule of thumb to use when thinking about the ethical decision-making process, it does not offer specific-enough criteria to be useful in many real-world situations. Once we imagine ourselves in the position of a person facing an ethical dilemma, situational ethics does not tell us *how* to evaluate that person's actions. An alternative school of ethical thought, however, provides a much more judgmental approach to ethical dilemmas.

Absolutism

Absolutism, or *ethical fundamentalism,* requires that individuals defer to a set of rules to guide them in the ethical decision-making process. Unlike ethical relativism and situational ethics, absolutism holds that whether an action is moral does not depend on the perspective of the person facing the ethical dilemma. Rather, whether an action is moral depends on whether the action conforms to the given set of ethical rules.

Of course, people disagree about which set of rules to follow. Why should we accept and act on any one absolutist set of rules? Absolutism cannot tell us, for example, why we ought to follow the doctrines set forth in the Koran and not Hindu doctrines.

Moreover, the unquestionable nature of the rules in most absolutist repositories seems overly inflexible when applied to different situations. For instance, "Thou shalt not kill" seems to be an absolute rule, but, in practice, killing in self-defense seems to be an acceptable exception to this rule.

Consequentialism

In contrast to absolutism, consequentialism does not provide a rigid set of rules to follow regardless of the situation. Rather, as the word *consequentialism* suggests, this ethical approach "depends on the consequences." Consequentialism is a general approach to ethical dilemmas that requires that we inquire about the consequences to relevant people of our making a particular decision.

Utilitarianism is one form of consequentialism that business managers may find useful. Like many consequentialist theories of ethics, utilitarianism urges managers to take those actions that provide the greatest pleasure after having subtracted the pain or harm associated with the action in question.

Utilitarianism has two main branches: act utilitarianism and rule utilitarianism. Act utilitarianism tells business managers to examine all the potential actions in each situation and choose the action that yields the greatest amount of pleasure over pain for all involved. For example, according to act utilitarianism, a business manager who deceives an employee may be acting morally if the act of deception maximizes pleasure over pain for everyone involved.

Rule utilitarians, on the other hand, see great potential for the abuse of act utilitarianism. Instead of advocating the maximization of pleasure over pain in each individual situation, rule utilitarianism holds that general rules that *on balance* produce the greatest amount of pleasure for all involved should be established and followed in each situation. Thus, even if the business manager's decision to deceive an employee maximizes pleasure over pain in a given situation, the act probably would not be consistent with rule utilitarianism because deception does not generally produce the greatest satisfaction.

Rule utilitarianism underlies many laws in the United States. For example, labor laws prohibit employers from hiring children to do manufacturing work, even though in some situations the transaction would maximize pleasure over pain.

One form of utilitarianism commonly applied by firms and government is cost-benefit analysis. When a business makes decisions based on cost-benefit analysis, it is comparing the pleasure and pain of its optional choices, as that pleasure and pain are measured in monetary terms.

As we have shown, consequentialism is not altogether helpful because of the extreme difficulty in making the required calculations about consequences. Another issue raises an important additional objection to consequentialist thinking: Where does the important social value of justice fit into consequentialist reasoning? Many business decisions could be beneficial in their consequences for a majority of the population, but is it fair to require that a few be harmed so that the majority can be improved? Consequentialism does not provide definite answers to these questions, but an alternative ethical theory does.

Deontology

Deontology is an alternative theoretical approach to consequentialism. When you see references to *Kantian ethics,* the analysis that follows the reference will be a discussion of the most famous of the deontological approaches to business ethics. Unlike a person espousing consequentialism, a person using a deontological approach will not see the relevance of making a list of harms and benefits that result from a particular decision. Instead, deontology consists of acting on the basis of the recognition that certain actions are right or wrong, regardless of their consequences. For example, a business leader might consider it wrong to terminate a person whose spouse has terminal cancer because a firm has an obligation to support its employees when they are vulnerable, *period.*

But how are business managers to decide whether an action is right or wrong? The German deontological philosopher Immanuel Kant proposed the categorical imperative to determine whether an action is right. According to the categorical imperative, an action is moral only if it would be consistent for everyone in society to act in the same way. Thus, for example, applying the categorical imperative would lead you to conclude that you should not cheat on a drug test, because if everyone acted in the same way, the drug test would be meaningless.

From the deontological viewpoint, the duties or obligations that we owe one another as humans are much more ethically significant than are measurements of the impacts of business decisions. For example, a person using a deontological theory of ethics may see any business behavior that violates our duty of trust as being wrong. To sell a car that one knows will probably not be usable after four years is, from this perspective, unethical. No set of positive consequences that might flow from the production decision can overcome the certainty of the deontological recognition that the sale is wrong.

The duties that we owe others imply that human beings have fundamental rights based on the dignity of each individual. This principle of rights asserts that whether a business decision is ethical depends on how the decision affects the rights of all involved. This principle is foundational to Western culture: the Declaration of Independence, for example, asserts that everyone has the right to "life, liberty, and the pursuit of happiness."

But just as consequentialism is incredibly complicated, deontology is difficult to apply because people disagree about what duties we owe to one another and which duties are more important than others when they conflict. For example, imagine the dilemma of a scientist working for a tobacco firm who discovers that cigarettes are carcinogenic. She owes a duty of trust to her employer, but she also has a conflicting duty to the community to do no harm. Where would a business manager find a list of relevant duties under the deontological framework, and why should we accept and act on any particular list?

In addition, as with absolutism, the absolute nature of many deontological lists of duties and rights seems overly rigid when applied to a wide variety of contexts. For instance, saying that we owe a duty to respect human life sounds absolute. In application, however, we might be forced to harm one life to preserve other life. An alternative theory of ethics, called *virtue ethics,* avoids this rigidity problem by providing us with abstract goals to pursue continually.

Virtue Ethics

Virtue ethics is an ethical system in which the development of virtues, or positive character traits such as courage, justice, and truthfulness, is the basis for morality. A morally excellent (and thus good) person develops virtues and distinguishes them from vices, or negative character traits, such as cowardice and vanity. This development of virtues occurs through practice. Virtues are the habits of mind that move us toward excellence, the good life, or human flourishing.

As a guide to business ethics, virtue ethics requires that managers act in such a way that they will increase their contributions to the good life. Virtue ethics tells them to follow the character traits that, upon introspective reflection, they see as consistent with virtue. Identifying the relevant virtues and vices requires reasoning about the kind of human behavior that moves us toward the good, successful, or happy life.

A difficulty with the application of virtue ethics is the lack of agreement about the meaning of "the good life." Without that agreement, we are not able to agree about what types of behavior are consistent with our achievement of that goal. Even so, virtue ethics is useful in reminding us that ethics is grounded in a sense of what it means to be virtuous— we need some moral beacon to call us toward a more morally excellent condition. An alternative theory of business ethics, the ethics of care, offers a clear conception of what is virtuous.

Ethics of Care

The ethics of care holds that the right course of action is the option most consistent with the building and maintaining of human relationships. Those who adhere to an ethic of care argue that traditional moral hierarchies ignore an important element of life: relationships. Care for the nurturing of our many relationships serves as a reminder of the importance of responsibility to others.

According to someone who adheres to an ethic of care, when one person cares for another person, the first person is acting morally. When other ethical theories emphasize different moral dimensions as a basis for resolving ethical dilemmas, they rarely consider the harm they might do to relationships; thus, from the perspective of the ethics of care, alternative theories of business ethics often encourage unethical behavior.

Ethics-of-care theorists argue that when one individual, the *caregiver,* meets the needs of one other person, the *cared-for* party, the caregiver is actually helping to meet the needs of all the individuals who fall within the cared-for party's *web of care.* Thus, by specifically helping one other individual, the caregiver is assisting numerous people.

The strength of this theoretical approach is that it focuses on the basis of ethics in general: the significance of the interests of other people. The urging to care for relationships speaks to the fundamental basis of why we are concerned about ethics in the first place. Most of us do not need any encouragement to think about how a decision will affect us personally. But ethical reasoning requires that we weigh the impact of decisions on the larger community.

Let's examine how these ethical theories are applied in real-world firms. Exhibit 2A-1 is an abridged version of the Johnson & Johnson Credo, or statement of shared corporate values. General Robert Wood Johnson, who guided Johnson & Johnson from a small, family-owned business to a worldwide enterprise, believed the corporation had social responsibilities beyond the manufacturing and marketing of products. In 1943, he wrote and published the Johnson & Johnson Credo, a document outlining those responsibilities. Does the credo depend more on ethical relativism, situational ethics, absolutism, consequentialism, deontology, virtue ethics, or the ethics of care for its ethical vision?

Exhibit 2A-1

Johnson & Johnson's
Credo

The Credo

We believe our first responsibility is to the doctors, nurses and patients, to mothers and fathers and all others who use our products and services. In meeting their needs everything we do must be of high quality. We must constantly strive to reduce our costs in order to maintain reasonable prices. Customers' orders must be serviced promptly and accurately. Our suppliers and distributors must have an opportunity to make a fair profit.

We are responsible to our employees, the men and women who work with us throughout the world. Everyone must be considered as an individual. We must respect their dignity and recognize their merit. They must have a sense of security in their jobs. Compensation must be fair and adequate, and working conditions clean, orderly and safe. We must be mindful of ways to help our employees fulfill their family responsibilities. Employees must feel free to make suggestions and complaints. There must be equal opportunity for employment, development and advancement for those qualified. We must provide competent management, and their actions must be just and ethical.

We are responsible to the communities in which we live and work and to the world community as well. We must be good citizens—support good works and charities and bear our fair share of taxes. We must encourage civic improvements and better health and education. We must maintain in good order the property we are privileged to use, protecting the environment and natural resources.

Our final responsibility is to our stockholders. Business must make a sound profit. We must experiment with new ideas. Research must be carried on, innovative programs developed and mistakes paid for. New equipment must be purchased, new facilities provided and new products launched. Reserves must be created to provide for adverse times. When we operate according to these principles, the stockholders should realize a fair return.

Used with permission of Johnson & Johnson.

Exhibit 2A-2 summarizes the ethical theories discussed in this appendix.

Exhibit 2A-2

At a Glance

Theories of Business Ethics	
ETHICAL APPROACH	**DESCRIPTION**
Ethical relativism	Asserts that morality is relative.
Situational ethics	Requires that when we evaluate whether an action is ethical, we imagine ourselves in the position of the person facing the ethical dilemma.
Consequentialism	Considers the consequences (i.e., harms and benefits) of making a particular decision.
Deontology	Recognizes certain actions as right or wrong regardless of the consequences.
Virtue ethics	Encourages individuals to develop virtues (e.g., courage and truthfulness) that guide behavior.
Ethics of care	Holds that ethical behavior is determined by actions that care for and maintain human relationships.

Key Terms

absolutism   34

act utilitarianism   35

categorical
   imperative   36

consequentialism   35

cost-benefit
   analysis   35

deontology   36

ethical relativism   34

ethics of care   37

principle of rights   36

rule utilitarianism   35

situational ethics   34

utilitarianism   35

virtue ethics   36

LEARNING OBJECTIVES

After reading this chapter, you will be able to answer the following questions:

1   What are the different types of jurisdiction a court must have before it can render a binding decision in a case?

2   What is venue?

3   How is our dual court system structured?

4   What are the threshold requirements that must be met before a court will hear a case?

5   What are the steps in civil litigation?

CASE OPENER
Questionable Jurisdiction over Caterpillar

James Lewis, a resident of Kentucky, sustained an injury while operating a Caterpillar bulldozer. He filed suit against Caterpillar, a company incorporated in Delaware but with its principal place of business in Illinois. Lewis also filed suit against the supplier of the bulldozer, Whayne Supply Company, whose principal place of business was Kentucky. Lewis filed his case in a Kentucky state court, alleging defective manufacture, negligence, failure to warn, and breach of warranty. Lewis and Whayne Supply Company agreed to settle out of court. Caterpillar then filed a motion to exercise its right of removal (its right to move the case from the state to the federal court system), arguing that the federal court had jurisdiction over the case because Caterpillar and Lewis were from different states. Lewis disagreed with Caterpillar's contention, claiming that because he had not completed his settlement with Whayne, the case still included a defendant (Whayne) from Lewis's state, Kentucky. Thus, Lewis argued, federal courts did not have jurisdiction over the case.

The court agreed with Caterpillar's argument and moved the case to a federal district court. Shortly thereafter, Lewis and Whayne finalized their settlement agreement, and the district court dismissed Whayne from the lawsuit. The federal district court granted

Caterpillar a favorable judgment. Lewis, however, appealed the district court's decision, renewing his argument that the district court did not have jurisdiction over the case. The court of appeals agreed with Lewis, holding that because Whayne was a defendant in the case at the time that Caterpillar moved the case from state to federal court, the diversity of citizenship necessary to give the federal court jurisdiction over the case was absent. Thus, a state court should have resolved the dispute. Consequently, the appellate court vacated the district court's decision. Caterpillar then appealed to the U.S. Supreme Court.

1. What factors determine whether the state or federal court system hears a case?
2. If you were a businessperson with Caterpillar, why might you prefer a federal court to hear the dispute with Lewis instead of a state court?

The Wrap-Up at the end of the chapter will answer these questions.

As the opening scenario illustrates, when a dispute arises, parties in this country do not simply "go to court." They often must choose between federal and state court systems. This chapter examines these systems, as well as the trial procedures that apply in civil cases.

Jurisdiction

The word **jurisdiction** comes from the Latin terms *juris,* meaning "law," and *diction,* meaning "to speak." A useful way to understand jurisdiction is to think of it as referring to courts' power to hear cases and render decisions that bind the parties before them. A court must have several types of jurisdiction to decide any particular case.

ORIGINAL VERSUS APPELLATE JURISDICTION

Trial courts, or **courts of original jurisdiction,** have the power to hear and decide cases when they first enter the legal system. In these courts, the parties present evidence and call witnesses to testify. Most state court systems refer to trial courts as *courts of common pleas* or *county courts.* The federal system calls them *district courts.*

Courts of appellate jurisdiction, or **appellate courts,** have the power to review previous judicial decisions to determine whether trial courts erred in their decisions. Appellate courts do not hold trials. Rather, appellate judges review transcripts of trial court proceedings and occasionally consider additional oral and written arguments from each party.

Appellate courts handle primarily questions of law, not questions of fact. A *question of law* is an issue concerning the interpretation or application of a law. In contrast, a *question of fact* is a question about an event or characteristic in a case. For example, whether a student yelled racial slurs on a college campus is a question of fact. On the other hand, whether the First Amendment protects the student's right to utter racial slurs is a question of law.

Only judges can decide questions of law. Questions of fact are determined in the trial court. In a *bench trial* (a trial with no jury), the judge decides questions of fact; in a *jury trial,* the jury decides questions of fact. Appellate courts can, however, overrule trial courts' decisions on questions of fact, but only when the trial court's finding was clearly erroneous or when no trial evidence supports the trial court's finding.

L01

What are the different types of jurisdiction a court must have before it can render a binding decision in a case?

Legal Principle: **The court in which a case is first heard is called the** *court of original jurisdiction,* **and the court to which a decision made by that court is appealed is called the** *court of appellate jurisdiction.*

JURISDICTION OVER PERSONS AND PROPERTY

In personam **jurisdiction** (literally, "jurisdiction over the person") is a court's power to render a decision affecting the rights of the specific persons before the court. Generally, a court's power to exercise *in personam* jurisdiction extends only over a specific geographic region. In the state court system, a court's *in personam* jurisdiction usually extends to the state's borders. In the federal system, on the other hand, each court's jurisdiction extends across its geographic district.

A court acquires *in personam* jurisdiction over a person (the **plaintiff**) when she files a lawsuit with the court. The court acquires jurisdiction over the person the plaintiff is suing (the **defendant**) when it gives him a copy of the complaint and a summons. The **complaint** specifies the factual and legal basis for the lawsuit and the relief the plaintiff seeks. The **summons** is a court order that notifies the defendant of the lawsuit and explains how and when to respond to the complaint.

Service of process is the procedure by which courts present these documents to defendants. Traditionally, courts use **personal service:** An officer of the court hands the summons and complaint to the defendant. Recently, however, courts have employed other methods of service, including *residential service,* in which a court representative leaves the summons and complaint with a responsible adult at the defendant's home, and *service by certified* or *ordinary mail.*

There has even been one case in which a court of appeals upheld service of process by e-mail to be appropriate. The facts of the case, however, created an unusual situation in which no other means of service was really possible. Rio Properties, Inc., operators of the Rio All Suites Resort Casino in Las Vegas, Nevada, decided to put some of its gaming activities on the Internet and discovered that a Costa Rican company, Rio International Interlink (RII), was operating an online, international sports book that allegedly infringed on Rio Properties' registered trademark. When the court attempted to serve RII at its U.S. address, the court found that it was only an address for an international courier that was not authorized to accept service on behalf of the company, and the court could not find any address for the company in Costa Rico. Rio Properties then filed a motion for alternative service of process with the court for permission to serve RII via its e-mail address, and the motion was granted by the district court. The court of appeals upheld the validity of the district court's order, noting that the Constitution does not require any specific means of service, only a means of service "reasonably calculated to provide notice and an opportunity to respond."[1] Because the method seemed to be the method of service most likely to reach RII, the court found that it clearly met the standard.

If the defendant is a corporation, courts generally serve either the president of the corporation or an agent that the corporation has appointed to receive service. Most states require that corporations appoint an agent for service when they incorporate. Corporations are subject to *in personam* jurisdiction in three locations: the state of their incorporation, the location of their main offices, and the geographic areas in which they conduct business.

Courts have *in personam* jurisdiction only over persons within a specific geographic region. In the past, a state court could not acquire *in personam*

To read more about how the choice of where to incorporate relates to jurisdiction, please see the **Connecting to the Core** activity on the text Web site at www.mhhe.com/kubasek2e.

[1] *Rio Properties, Inc. v. Rio International Interlink,* 284 F.3d 1007 (2002).

A Question of Minimum Contacts

Jones v. Williams

Jones lived in California, and for four years received weekly psychotherapy and dream counseling over the telephone from Williams, a licensed therapist living in New Mexico. Williams made several trips to California at Jones's request to provide additional treatment. For one year, Jones also received shamanic counseling over the phone from Williams's wife, Ritzman. Jones ceased treatment and sued Williams and Ritzman for medical malpractice in California. The defendants moved to have the complaint dismissed for lack of personal jurisdiction.

In examining the facts of the case, the court found that the defendants had sufficient contacts for establishing specific jurisdiction with respect to a medical malpractice case arising out of their treatment of Jones. The court said that sufficient contacts existed for *in personam* jurisdiction in a specific case when (1) the nonresident defendant purposefully availed himself of the privilege of conducting activities in the forum state by some affirmative act or conduct; (2) the plaintiff's claim arises out of or results from the defendant's forum-related activities; and (3) the exercise of jurisdiction is reasonable. In this case, the defendants engaged in counseling in the state, both in person and via the telephone; the lawsuit arose out of the counseling that occurred in that state; and the defendants should have recognized that in light of their providing services in that state they would be subject to suit there for activities arising from providing that service.

jurisdiction over out-of-state defendants unless it served the defendants within the court's home state. Thus, defendants who injured plaintiffs could evade legal action by leaving the state and remaining outside its borders. To alleviate this problem, most states have enacted **long-arm statutes,** which enable the court to serve defendants outside the state as long as the defendant has sufficient minimum contacts within the state and it seems fair to assert long-arm jurisdiction over him or her. The U.S. Supreme Court established this "minimum-contacts" standard in the 1945 case *International Shoe Co. v. State of Washington.*[2]

Each state has its own minimum-contact requirements, but most state statutes hold that acts like committing a tort or doing business in the state are sufficient to allow the state to serve a defendant. In the opening scenario, the company sold products in Kentucky, and its products caused an injury in that state. These two facts were sufficient minimum contacts to allow the Kentucky court to serve Caterpillar, even though it was an out-of-state company. Compare the facts of the Caterpillar case to those in the Case Nugget, where the court found that the contacts were sufficient to give the court jurisdiction over the out-of-state resident, even when the primary contact in the state was over the telephone.

In contrast to the situations in the Case Nugget and in the opening scenario, the Florida appellate court did not find minimum contacts with that state to enable a foreign corporation to sue Columbia University, located in New York City, for a tort that allegedly occurred in New York. The court found that the fact that Columbia had alumni associations in Florida, owned some interactive classrooms in that state, and offered some online classes to residents did not constitute sufficient minimum contacts for a lawsuit in which none of the tortuous acts were alleged to have occurred in the state.[3]

If a defendant has property in a state, a plaintiff may file suit against the defendant's property instead of the owner. For example, suppose a Utah resident had not paid property taxes on a piece of land she owned in Idaho. Idaho courts have *in rem* jurisdiction (Latin for "jurisdiction over the thing") over the property. Thus, an Idaho state court has the power to seize the property and sell it to pay the property taxes in an *in rem* proceeding.

Courts can also gain **quasi *in rem* jurisdiction,** or *attachment jurisdiction,* over a defendant's property *unrelated* to the plaintiff's claim. For example, suppose Charlie, a Massachusetts resident, ran a red light while he was vacationing in California and collided with

---

[2] 326 U.S. 310.

[3] *Trustees of Columbia University v. Ocean World, SA,* 2009 WL 1212229, Ct. App. Fla.

The Sliding-Scale Standard for Internet Transactions

Does a business that has Internet contact with a plaintiff in a different state satisfy the minimum-contacts standard? Anyone who engages in transactions over the Internet should be concerned about this question.

A federal district court established the following "sliding-scale" standard in the 1997 case *Zippo Mfg. Co. v. Zippo Dot Com, Inc.:*

[T]he likelihood that personal jurisdiction can be constitutionally exercised is directly proportionate to the nature and quality of commercial activity that an entity conducts over the Internet. This sliding scale is consistent with well developed personal jurisdiction principles.

At one end of the spectrum are situations in which a defendant clearly does business over the Internet. If the defendant enters into contracts with residents of a foreign jurisdiction that involve the knowing and repeated transmission of computer files over the Internet, personal jurisdiction is proper.

At the opposite end are situations in which a defendant has simply posted information on an Internet Web site that is accessible to users in foreign jurisdictions. A passive Web site that does little more than make information available to those who are interested in it is not grounds for the exercise of personal jurisdiction.

The middle ground is occupied by interactive Web sites at which a user can exchange information with the host computer. In such cases, the exercise of jurisdiction is determined by examining the level of interactivity and commercial nature of the exchange of information that occurs on the Web site.

*952 F. Supp. 1119, 1124 (W.D. Pa. 1997).

Jessica's car. Suppose further that Jessica suffered extensive injuries from the accident and successfully sued Charlie for $200,000 in a California state court. The California court can exercise quasi *in rem* jurisdiction over Charlie's California vacation home by seizing it, selling it, and transferring $200,000 to Jessica to satisfy her judgment against Charlie. If Charlie's vacation home is worth more than $200,000, however, the court must return the excess proceeds to Charlie.

SUBJECT-MATTER JURISDICTION

Subject-matter jurisdiction is a court's power to hear certain kinds of cases. Most industrialized countries have a single court system, with courts that have the power to hear both national law cases and local law cases. In contrast, the United States has both a state and a federal court system. Subject-matter jurisdiction determines which court system may hear a particular case. Cases may fall under state jurisdiction, exclusive federal jurisdiction, or concurrent jurisdiction. Exhibit 3-1 illustrates the subject-matter-jurisdiction divisions.

Exclusive Federal Jurisdiction.   The federal court system has exclusive jurisdiction over very few cases: admiralty cases, bankruptcy cases, federal criminal prosecutions, lawsuits in which one state sues another state, claims against the United States, and cases involving federal copyrights, patents, or trademarks. Additionally, federal courts have exclusive jurisdiction over claims arising under federal statutes that specify exclusive federal jurisdiction.

State Jurisdiction.   The state court system has a broad range of jurisdiction; state courts have the power to hear all cases not within the exclusive jurisdiction of the federal court system. State courts also have exclusive jurisdiction over certain cases, such as cases concerning adoption and divorce. Most cases, therefore, fall under state court jurisdiction.

The Caterpillar case fell under state court jurisdiction because its subject matter—product liability and negligence—did not place the case under the exclusive jurisdiction of the federal court system.

Concurrent Federal Jurisdiction.   Concurrent federal jurisdiction means that both state and federal courts have jurisdiction over a case. Concurrent jurisdiction covers

Exhibit 3-1
Subject-Matter-
Jurisdiction Divisions

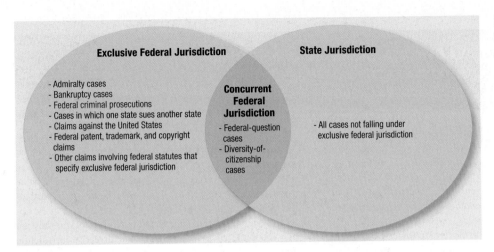

two types of cases: federal-question and diversity-of-citizenship cases. *Federal-question* cases require an interpretation of the United States Constitution, a federal statute, or a federal treaty. For example, suppose a plaintiff alleges that a Florida campaign financing law violates his First Amendment free speech rights. Because this case raises a federal question, it falls under concurrent jurisdiction, and both state and federal courts have the power to hear it.

A *diversity-of-citizenship* case must satisfy two conditions: (1) The plaintiff(s) does (do) not reside in the same state as the defendant(s), and (2) the controversy concerns an amount in excess of $75,000. Courts use the location of a party's residence to determine whether diversity of citizenship exists. Most federal court cases are based on diversity of citizenship.

A business may reside in two states: the state of its incorporation and the state of its principal place of business. Thus, in the opening scenario, Caterpillar was a resident of Delaware, the state where it incorporated, and of Illinois, the state of its primary place of business.

Diversity must be complete, however, for a case to fall under concurrent jurisdiction. In the Caterpillar case, Lewis argued that diversity was not complete because both he and the supply company, the second defendant he originally sued, were residents of Kentucky. The appellate court agreed with his argument and overturned the district court's decision because the district court lacked subject-matter jurisdiction.

Legal Principle: **Concurrent jurisdiction exists whenever there is a federal question or diversity of citizenship and at least $75,000 at issue.**

When a case falls under concurrent jurisdiction, the plaintiff initially chooses which court will hear the case by filing in whichever court system the plaintiff wishes the case to be heard in. If a plaintiff files the case in a state court, however, the defendant has a *right of removal.* This right entitles the defendant to transfer the case to the federal court system. Thus, either party to a case involving concurrent jurisdiction has the ability to ensure that the case will be heard in the federal court system: The plaintiff can file the case in federal court initially, or the defendant can transfer the case to federal court by exercising her right of removal if the case is initially filed in state court. In the opening scenario, Caterpillar exercised its right of removal, and the state trial court moved the case to a federal district court.

The issue of subject-matter jurisdiction often arises when the parties to a lawsuit disagree about whether to try the case in state or federal court, as Case 3-1 illustrates.

WACHOVIA BANK, N. A. v. SCHMIDT
UNITED STATES SUPREME COURT
126 S. CT. 941 (2006)

Petitioner Wachovia Bank, National Association (Wachovia), is a national banking association with its designated main office in North Carolina and branch offices in many states, including South Carolina. Plaintiff-respondent Schmidt and other South Carolina citizens sued Wachovia in a South Carolina state court for fraudulently inducing them to participate in an illegitimate tax shelter. Shortly thereafter, Wachovia filed a petition in Federal District Court, seeking to compel arbitration of the dispute. As the sole basis for federal-court jurisdiction, Wachovia claimed there was diversity of citizenship between the parties.

The District Court denied Wachovia's petition on the merits. On appeal, the Fourth Circuit determined that the District Court lacked subject-matter jurisdiction over the action, vacated the judgment, and instructed the District Court to dismiss the case. The appeals court observed that for diversity purposes, Wachovia is a citizen of "the States in which they are respectively located." Therefore the appellate court found Wachovia to be "located" in, and therefore a "citizen" of, every State in which it maintains a branch office. Thus, Wachovia's South Carolina branch operations rendered it a citizen of that State. Given the South Carolina citizenship of the opposing parties, the court concluded that the matter could not be adjudicated in federal court.

Wachovia appealed to the United States Supreme Court.

JUSTICE GINSBURG: This case concerns the citizenship, for purposes of federal-court diversity jurisdiction, of national banks, i.e., corporate entities chartered not by any State, but by the Comptroller of the Currency of the U.S. Treasury. Congress empowered federal district courts to adjudicate civil actions between citizens of different States where the amount in controversy exceeds $75,000.

A business organized as a corporation, for diversity jurisdiction purposes, is deemed to be a citizen of any State by which it has been incorporated and, since 1958, also of the State where it has its principal place of business. State banks, usually chartered as corporate bodies by a particular State, ordinarily fit comfortably within this prescription. Federally chartered national banks do not, for they are not incorporated by "any State." For diversity jurisdiction purposes, therefore, Congress has discretely provided that national banks "shall . . . be deemed citizens of the States in which they are respectively located."

The question presented turns on the meaning, in § 1348's context, of the word "located." Does it signal, as the petitioning national bank and the United States, as *amicus curiae,* urge, that the bank's citizenship is determined by the place designated in the bank's articles of association as the location of its main office? Or does it mean, in addition, as respondents urge and the Court of Appeals held, that a national bank is a citizen of every State in which it maintains a branch?

Recognizing that "located" is not a word of enduring rigidity, but one that gains its precise meaning from context, we hold that a national bank, for § 1348 purposes, is a citizen of the State in which its main office, as set forth in its articles of association, is located. Were we to hold, as the Court of Appeals did, that a national bank is additionally a citizen of every State in which it has established a branch, the access of a federally chartered bank to a federal forum would be drastically curtailed in comparison to the access afforded state banks and other state-incorporated entities. Congress, we are satisfied, created no such anomaly.

REVERSED in favor of Wachovia.

CRITICAL THINKING

What guideline does Justice Ginsburg provide for determining which alternative interpretation of a word is the most appropriate in a certain context? In other words, what did she suggest as a guideline for sorting out solutions to ambiguity?

ETHICAL DECISION MAKING

What is the ethical problem suggested by this case?

Why does it matter who has jurisdiction in a case like this one?

While the question of which court system will hear a case is a matter that we think of as arising once a dispute has occurred, sometimes companies' decisions about where to locate are influenced by their knowledge about the court system in a state they are considering. And some organizations actually encourage companies to take a state's court system into account. As you already know, companies take into account the laws of the states where they are considering locating and doing business. Another factor some businesses consider is whether a state's courts seem hospitable to businesses. The American Tort Reform Association (ATRA), a national organization based in Washington, D.C., attempts to eliminate some of the "legal guesswork" for businesses by creating a list of the nation's top "Judicial Hellholes" each year. ATRA identifies its top hellholes as places where the law is applied in an "inequitable manner, generally against defendants in civil lawsuits."[4] One state in particular, West Virginia, continues to top the ATRA charts and has been named the number-one Judicial Hellhole in the United States for both 2007 and 2008. ATRA mentions that one of West Virginia's major legal shortcomings is that it happens to be only one of two states in the country that does not "guarantee the right to appeal a civil verdict."[5]

Also crippling West Virginia's ability to offer a favorable business environment is its reputation as being a lawsuit- and plaintiff-friendly state. For example, a judge in West Virginia recently ordered the DuPont company to pay $196 million in punative damages and $55 million for site cleanup and to commit $130 million to medical monitoring and testing after several West Virginia citizens filed suit against the company, claiming one of its plants contaminated their city and posed serious health risks, even though at the time of the verdict none of the residents were ill or showed health effects. High-profile and high-award cases like the DuPont case, coupled with an arguably flawed judicial system, could be enough to deter businesses from locating in West Virginia in the future. The DuPont case demonstrates that, as with any business decision, the costs and benefits of doing business in a particular state and legal climate need to be evaluated before moving forward.

Venue

Once a case is in the proper court system, **venue** determines which trial court in the system will hear the case. Venue is a matter of geographic location determined by each state's statutes. Usually, the trial court where the defendant resides is the appropriate venue. If a case involves property, the trial court where the property is located is also an appropriate venue. Finally, if the focus of the case is a particular incident, the trial court where the dispute occurred is an appropriate venue. The plaintiff initially chooses from among the appropriate venues when she files the case.

If the location of the court where the plaintiff filed the case is an inconvenience to the defendant or if the defendant believes it will be difficult to select an unbiased jury in that venue, he may request that the judge move the case by filing a motion for a change of venue. The judge has the discretion to grant or deny the motion.

For example, one particular reason a defendant might choose to request a change of venue is negative pretrial publicity. In May 2008, Sholom Rubashkin, the manager of the nation's largest kosher slaughterhouse, was arrested in an immigration raid, and he now faces roughly 100 charges ranging from document fraud and identity theft to child-labor and minimum-wage violations. The scale of the raid, which led to the arrest of approximately 400 of Rubashkin's employees, and the severity of Rubashkin's charges attracted national media attention. Fearing that he would not be able to receive a fair trial or an

LO2

What is venue?

---

[4] www.atra.org/reports/hellholes/.

[5] Ibid.

unbiased jury,[6] Rubashkin filed a request to have his trial moved from Iowa to either Minneapolis or Chicago. A federal district court judge disagreed with Rubashkin, and denied his initial request for a new venue. However, the judge did acknowledge that publicity may increase even more as the trial draws near and mentioned that she may allow Rubashkin to renew his argument for a new venue at that time.

Legal Principle: **Venue is appropriate in the county where the defendant resides or where the incident took place over which the lawsuit arose.**

The Structure of the Court System

L03

How is our dual court system structured?

The U.S. legal system has two parallel court structures: a federal system and a state system. Once a plaintiff files a case in one of the systems, the case remains in that system throughout the appeals process. The only exception to this rule occurs when a party to a lawsuit appeals the decision of a state supreme court to the U.S. Supreme Court.

THE FEDERAL COURT SYSTEM

The federal court system derives its power from Article III, Section 2, of the U.S. Constitution and consists of three main levels: trial courts, intermediate appellate courts, and the court of last resort. Exhibit 3-2 illustrates this system.

Federal Trial Courts.   In the federal court system, the trial courts, or courts of original jurisdiction, are U.S. district courts. The United States has 94 districts; each district has at least one trial court of general jurisdiction. Courts of general jurisdiction have the power to hear a wide range of cases and can grant almost any type of remedy. Almost every case in the federal system begins in one of these courts.

A small number of cases, however, do not begin in trial courts of general jurisdiction. For cases concerning certain subject matter, Congress has established special trial courts of limited jurisdiction. The types of cases for which Congress has established these special trial courts include bankruptcy cases, claims against the U.S. government, international trade and customs cases, and disputes over certain tax deficiencies.

Exhibit 3-2   The Federal Court System

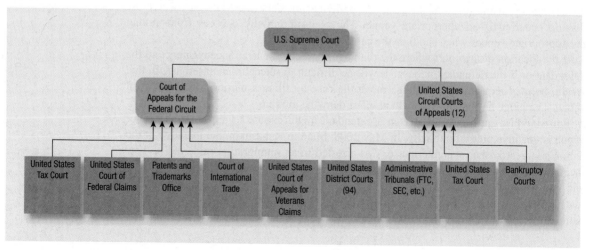

[6] www.nytimes.com/2008/10/31/us/31immig.html?hp; and seattletimes.nwsource.com/html/businesstechnology/2008881497_apkosherslaughterhousetrial.html.

In an extremely limited number of cases, the U.S. Supreme Court functions as a trial court of limited jurisdiction. These cases include controversies between states and lawsuits against foreign ambassadors.

Intermediate Courts of Appeal.   The U.S. circuit courts of appeal make up the second level of courts in the federal system. The United States has 12 circuits, including a circuit for the District of Columbia. Each circuit court hears appeals from district courts in its geographic area. Additionally, a federal circuit court of appeals hears appeals from government administrative agencies. Exhibit 3-3 illustrates the geographic circuit divisions.

The Court of Last Resort.   The U.S. Supreme Court is the final appellate court in the federal system. Nine justices, who have lifetime appointments, make up the high court. Exhibit 3-4 shows the nine justices on the U.S. Supreme Court in 2010.

The U.S. Supreme Court hears appeals of cases from the court of last resort in a state system. The Court will not, however, hear cases considering questions of pure state law. The Court also functions as a trial court in rare occasions. The structure and functioning of the U.S. Supreme Court system differ from those of similar courts in other countries, as the Comparing the Law of Other Countries box illustrates.

STATE COURT SYSTEMS

No uniform state court structure exists because each state has devised its own court system. Most states, however, have a structure similar to the federal court system's structure.

Exhibit 3-3   The Circuits of the Federal Court System

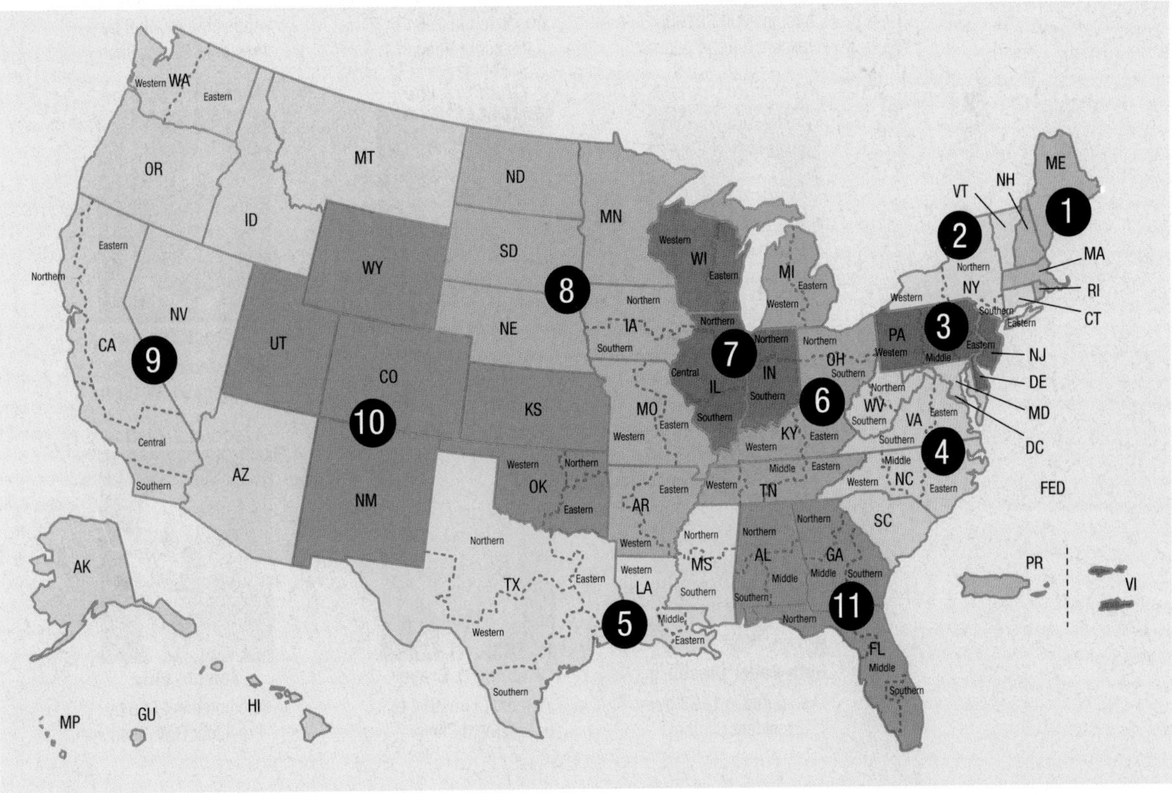

The Supreme Court in Japan

The supreme court of Japan, located in Tokyo, consists of 15 justices, including one chief justice. Because the justices ascend from lower courts, they are usually at least 60 years old. The full bench of the supreme court does not hear every appealed case. Rather, a petit (small) bench of five justices first hears each case to determine whether to transfer the case to a hearing before the full bench. The petit court transfers a case to the full bench if it believes that the appellant can prove that the law or decision in question is unconstitutional. Because proving the unconstitutionality of a law is extremely difficult, the full bench generally hears fewer than 10 cases annually.

State Trial Courts. In state court systems, most cases begin in a trial court of general jurisdiction. As in the federal system, state trial courts of general jurisdiction have the power to hear all cases over which the state court system has jurisdiction except those cases for which the state has established special trial courts of limited jurisdiction. Most states have a trial court of general jurisdiction in each county. The names of these courts

Exhibit 3-4

U.S. Supreme Court
Justices, 2010

Associate Justice	Associate Justice	Associate Justice
Elena Kagan Appointed in 2010 by President Barack Obama	**Antonin Scalia** Appointed in 1984 by President Reagan	**Anthony M. Kennedy** Appointed in 1988 by President G.H.W. Bush
Associate Justice	Chief Justice	Associate Justice
Sonia Sotomayor Appointed in 2009 by President Barack Obama	**John G. Roberts** Appointed in 2005 by President G.W. Bush	**Clarence Thomas** Appointed in 1991 by President G.H.W. Bush
Associate Justice	Associate Justice	Associate Justice
Ruth Bader Ginsburg Appointed in 1993 by President Clinton	**Stephen G. Breyer** Appointed in 1994 by President Clinton	**Samuel Alito** Appointed in 2006 by President G.W. Bush

vary by state, but most states refer to them as *courts of common pleas* or *county courts.* In some states, these courts have specialized divisions: domestic relations, probate, and so on.

Most states also have trial courts of limited jurisdiction. Usually, these courts can grant only certain remedies. For example, small claims courts, a common type of court of limited jurisdiction in most states, may not grant damage awards larger than a specified amount. Other courts of limited jurisdiction have the power to hear only certain types of cases. For example, probate courts hear only cases about asset and obligation transfers after an individual's death.

Intermediate Courts of Appeal.   Intermediate courts of appeal, analogous to federal circuit courts of appeal, exist in approximately half the states. These courts usually have broad jurisdiction, hearing appeals from courts of general and limited jurisdictions, as well as from state administrative agencies. The names of these courts also vary by state, but most states call them *courts of appeal* or *superior courts.*

Courts of Last Resort.   Appeals from the state intermediate courts of appeal lead cases to the state court of last resort. Most states call this court the *supreme court,* although some states refer to it as the *court of appeals.* Because approximately half the states lack intermediate courts of appeal, appeals from trial courts in these states go directly to the state court of last resort.

Threshold Requirements

Before a case makes it to court, it must meet three *threshold requirements.* These requirements ensure that courts hear only cases that genuinely require adjudication. The three requirements are standing, case or controversy, and ripeness.

STANDING

A person who has the legal right to bring an action in court has **standing** (or *standing to sue*). For a person to have standing, the outcome of a case must personally affect him or her. For example, if you hire a landscaper to mow your lawn every week and she fails to show up every other week, you have standing to sue your landscaper. But if your friend hired the landscaper to mow his lawn, you lack the standing to sue on your friend's behalf because you do not have a personal stake in the outcome of the case. The American legal system requires that a plaintiff have a personal stake in the outcome of the case because, the theory goes, the plaintiff's personal stake stimulates her to present the best possible case.

Standing requirements are subject to frequent litigation when citizen groups sue to enforce environmental laws. For example, the standing of the plaintiff, Friends of the Earth (FOE), was a central issue in the 2000 U.S. Supreme Court case *FOE v. Laidlaw Environmental Services.*[7] In the case, FOE filed a lawsuit against Laidlaw, alleging that it had violated the Clean Water Act by discharging excessive amounts of pollutants into a river.

Writing for the majority, Justice Ginsburg cited three factors plaintiffs need for standing: (1) The plaintiff must have an injury in fact that is concrete and actual or imminent; (2) the injury must be fairly traceable to the challenged action of the defendant; and (3) it must be likely that the injury will be redressed by a favorable decision.[8] In applying those criteria to the Laidlaw case, the Supreme Court found that FOE members' testimony

L04

What are the threshold requirements that must be met before a court will hear a case?

[7] 120 S. Ct. 923 (2000).
[8] Ibid.

that they were afraid to fish and swim in a river they previously enjoyed satisfied the first two criteria. The Court held that although the FOE members would not directly receive money from a penalty against Laidlaw, they would benefit because the penalties would deter Laidlaw and other companies from polluting the river in the future.[9] The Court ruled in FOE's favor and assessed Laidlaw a $405,800 penalty payable to the U.S. Treasury.

CASE OR CONTROVERSY

The **case or controversy** (or *justiciable controversy*) requirement ensures that courts do not render advisory opinions. Three criteria are necessary for a case or controversy to exist. First, the relationship between the plaintiff and the defendant must be adverse. Second, actual or threatened actions of at least one of the parties must give rise to an actual legal dispute. Third, courts must have the ability to render a decision that will resolve the dispute. In other words, courts can give final judgments that solve existing problems; they cannot provide rulings about hypothetical situations.

RIPENESS

The case or controversy requirement is closely linked to the **ripeness** requirement. A case is *ripe* if a judge's decision is capable of affecting the parties immediately. Usually the issue of ripeness arises when one party claims that the case is moot—in other words, there is no point in the court's hearing the case because no judgment can affect the situation between the parties.

In the Laidlaw case cited previously, Laidlaw also argued that the case was moot because by the time the case went to trial, the company had complied with the requirements of its discharge permits. Thus, Laidlaw argued, the only remedy left to the courts—a penalty Laidlaw must pay to the government—would not affect the plaintiffs. The Supreme Court disagreed, ruling that the fact that a defendant voluntarily ceases a practice once litigation has commenced does not deprive a federal court of its power to determine the legality of the practice, because such a ruling would leave the defendant free to return to his old unlawful practices. Thus, the Court found the case was not moot because imposing a penalty on the defendant would have an important deterrent effect.[10]

Legal Principle: **Before a case can be heard, it must meet the three threshold requirements of standing, case or controversy, and ripeness.**

Steps in Civil Litigation

L05

What are the steps in civil litigation?

The U.S. litigation system is an adversary system: a neutral fact finder—a judge or jury—hears evidence and arguments that opposing sides present and then decides the case on the basis of the facts and law. Strict rules govern the types of evidence fact finders may consider. Theoretically, fact finders make informed and impartial rulings because each party has an incentive to find all relevant evidence and make the strongest possible arguments on behalf of her or his position.

Critics of the adversary system, however, point out several drawbacks: the time and expense each lawsuit requires, the damage a suit may cause to the litigating parties' relationship, and the unfair advantage to those with wealth and experience using the court system.

---

[9] Ibid.
[10] Ibid.

THE PRETRIAL STAGE

The *rules of civil procedure* govern civil case proceedings. The Federal Rules of Civil Procedure apply in all federal courts. Each state has its own set of rules, but most states' rules are very similar to the Federal Rules of Civil Procedure. In addition, each court usually has its own set of local court rules.

Informal Negotiations.   The initial attempt to resolve a business dispute is usually informal: a discussion or negotiation among the parties to try to find a solution. If the parties are unable to resolve their dispute, one party often seeks an attorney's advice. Together, the attorney and client may be able to resolve the dispute informally with the other party.

Pleadings.   The first formal stage of a lawsuit is the *pleading stage.* The plaintiff's attorney initiates a lawsuit by filing a *complaint* in the appropriate court. The complaint states the names of the parties to the action, the basis for the court's subject-matter jurisdiction, the facts on which the plaintiff bases his claim, and the relief the plaintiff seeks. The pleadings prevent surprises at trial; they allow attorneys to prepare arguments to counter the other side's claims. Exhibit 3-5 shows a typical complaint.

Service of Process.   To obtain *in personam* jurisdiction over a defendant and to satisfy due process, a court must notify the defendant of the pending lawsuit. Service of process occurs when the defendant is given a copy of the complaint and summons by a process server or by certified or ordinary mail.

The complaint explains the basis of the lawsuit to the defendant. The summons tells the defendant that if he or she does not respond to the lawsuit within a certain period of time, the plaintiff will receive a default judgment. A **default judgment** is a judgment in favor of the plaintiff that occurs when the defendant fails to answer the complaint and the plaintiff's complaint alleges facts that would support such a judgment.

Defendant's Response.   The defendant responds to the complaint with an **answer.** In this document, the defendant denies, affirms, or claims no knowledge of the accuracy of the plaintiff's allegations.

A defendant uses an *affirmative defense* when her or his answer admits that the facts contained in the complaint are accurate but also includes additional facts that justify the defendant's actions and provide a legally sound reason to deny relief to the plaintiff. For example, if a woman sued a man for battery because he punched her in the face, he might claim that he hit her only because she aimed a gun at him and threatened to shoot. His claim that he was acting in self-defense is an affirmative defense.

If the defendant plans to raise an affirmative defense, he must raise it in his answer to give the plaintiff adequate notice. If he fails to raise an affirmative defense in the answer, the judge will likely not allow him to raise it during the trial.

Upon receiving the complaint, if the defendant believes that even though all the plaintiff's factual allegations are true, the law does not entitle the plaintiff to a favorable judgment, the defendant may file a **motion to dismiss,** or *demurrer.* (A **motion** is a request by a party for the court to do something; in this instance, the request is to dismiss the case.)

Exhibit 3-5

Typical Complaint

THE COURT OF COMMON PLEAS OF CLARK COUNTY, NEVADA

Bob Lyons and Sue Lyons, Plaintiffs

v.

Christine Collins, Defendant

COMPLAINT FOR NEGLIGENCE

Case No.

Now come the plaintiffs, Bob Lyons and Sue Lyons, and, for their complaint, allege as follows:

1. Plaintiffs, Bob Lyons and Sue Lyons, both of 825 Havercamp Street, are citizens of Clark County, in the state of Nevada, and defendant, Christine Collins, 947 Rainbow Ave., is a citizen of Clark County in the state of Nevada.

2. On May 1, 2001, the Defendant built a wooden hanging bridge across a stream that runs through the plaintiffs' property at 825 Havercamp Street.

3. Defendant negligently used ropes in the construction of the bridge that were not thick enough to sustain human traffic on the bridge.

4. At approximately 4:00 p.m., on May 20, 2001, the plaintiffs were attempting to carry a box of landscaping stones across the bridge when the ropes broke, and the bridge collapsed, causing plaintiffs to fall seven feet into the stream.

5. As a result of the fall, plaintiff, Bob Lyons, suffered a broken arm, a broken leg, and a skull fracture, incurring $160,000 in medical expenses.

6. As a result of the fall, plaintiff, Sue Lyons, suffered two broken cervical vertebrae, and a skull fracture, incurring $300,000 in medical expenses.

7. As a result of the fall, the landscaping stones, which had cost $1,200, were destroyed.

8. As a result of the foregoing injuries, plaintiff, Bob Lyons, was required to miss eight weeks of work, resulting in a loss of $2,400 in wages.

9. As a result of the foregoing injuries, plaintiff, Sue Lyons, was required to miss twelve weeks of work, resulting in a loss of $3,600 in wages.

   WHEREFORE, Plaintiffs demand judgment in the amount of $467,200, plus costs of this action.

   Harlon Elliot

   Attorney for Plaintiff

   824 Sahara Ave.

   Las Vegas, Nevada 89117

   JURY DEMAND

   Plaintiff demands a trial by jury in this matter.

In deciding whether to grant a motion to dismiss, a judge accepts the facts as stated by the plaintiff and rules on the legal issues in the case. Judges generally grant a motion to dismiss only when it appears beyond a doubt that the plaintiff cannot prove any set of facts to justify granting the judgment she seeks.

If the defendant believes he has a claim against the plaintiff, he includes this **counterclaim** with the answer. As Exhibit 3-6 shows, the form of a counterclaim is identical to the form of a complaint. The defendant states the facts supporting his claim and asks for relief.

If the defendant files a counterclaim, the plaintiff generally files a reply. A **reply** is an answer to a counterclaim. In the reply, the plaintiff admits, denies, or claims a lack of

Exhibit 3-6
Defendant's Answer and Counterclaim

THE COURT OF COMMON PLEAS OF CLARK COUNTY, NEVADA

Bob Lyons and Sue Lyons, Plaintiffs v. Christine Collins, Defendant ANSWER AND COUNTER-CLAIM FOR BREACH OF CONTRACT Case No.

Now comes the defendant, Christine Collins, and answers the complaint of plaintiff herein as follows:

First Defense

1. Admits the allegations in paragraphs 1 and 2.
2. Denies the allegation in paragraph 3.
3. Is without knowledge as to the truth or falsity of the allegations contained in paragraphs 4, 5, 6, 7, 8, and 9.

Second Defense

4. If the court believes the allegations contained in paragraph 3, which the defendant expressly denies, plaintiffs should still be denied recovery because they were informed prior to the construction of the bridge that there should be no more than one person on the bridge at one time and that no individual weighing more than 200 pounds should be allowed to walk on the bridge.

Counterclaim

5. On April 15, the parties agreed that Defendant would build a wooden hanging bridge across a stream that runs through the defendants' property at 825 Havercamp Street, in exchange for which plaintiffs would pay defendant $2,000 upon completion of construction.
6. On May 1, 2001, the Defendant built the agreed upon ornament, wooden, hanging bridge across a stream that runs through the defendants' property at 825 Havercamp Street, but Plaintiffs failed to pay the agreed upon price for the bridge.
7. By their failure to pay, plaintiffs breached their contract and are liable to defendant for the contract price of $2,000.

WHEREFORE, defendant prays for a judgment dismissing the plaintiffs' complaint, and granting the defendant a judgment against plaintiff in the amount of $2,000 plus costs of this action.

Melissa Davenport

Attorney for Defendant

777 Decatur Ave.

Las Vegas, Nevada 89117

knowledge as to the accuracy of the facts of the defendant's counterclaim. If the plaintiff plans to use an affirmative defense, she must raise it in the reply.

Pretrial Motions.   The early pleadings establish the legal and factual issues of the case. After the pleadings, the plaintiff or defendant may file a motion to conclude the case early, eliminate some claims, or gain some advantage. A party may move, or request, that the court do almost anything pertaining to the case. For example, if the plaintiff files a suit about the right to a piece of property, she may move that the court prohibit the current possessor of the land from selling it. Courts may grant or deny such motions at their discretion.

When a party files a motion with the court, the court sends a copy to the opposing attorney, who may respond to the motion, usually by requesting that the judge deny the motion. In many cases, the judge rules on the motion immediately. In other cases, the judge holds a hearing at which the attorneys for both sides argue how the judge should decide the motion.

Two primary pretrial motions are a motion for judgment on the pleadings and a motion for summary judgment. Once the parties file the pleadings, either party can file a **motion for judgment on the pleadings.** The motion is a request for the court to consider that all the facts in the pleadings are true and to apply the law to those facts. The court grants the motion if, after this process, it finds that the only reasonable decision is in favor of the moving party.

Either party can file a **motion for summary judgment** after the discovery process (described below). The motion asserts that no factual disputes exist and that if the judge applied the law to the undisputed facts, her only reasonable decision would be in favor of the moving party. The difference between this motion and a motion for judgment on the pleadings is that in a motion for summary judgment, the moving party may use affidavits (sworn statements from the parties or witnesses), relevant documents, and depositions or interrogatories (a party's sworn answers to written questions) to support his motion. The judge grants the motion if, after examining the evidence, she finds no factual disputes. If, however, she finds any factual issues about which the parties disagree, she denies the motion and sends the case to trial.

Discovery.   After filing the initial pleadings and motions, the parties gather information from each other through **discovery.** The discovery process enables the parties to learn about facts surrounding the case so that they are not surprised in the courtroom. Three common discovery tools are interrogatories, requests to produce documents, and depositions.

Interrogatories are written questions that one party sends to the other to answer under oath. Frequently, a *request to admit certain facts* accompanies interrogatories. Attorneys work with their clients to answer interrogatories and requested admissions of facts.

A **request to produce documents** (or other items) forces the opposing party to produce (turn over) certain information unless it is privileged or irrelevant to the case. Parties may request documents such as photographs, contracts, written estimates, medical records, tax forms, and other government documents. In tort cases, the defendant frequently asks the plaintiff to submit a mental- or physical-examination report.

Finally, the parties may obtain testimony from a witness before trial through a deposition. At a **deposition,** attorneys examine a witness under oath. A court reporter (stenographer) records every word the witnesses and attorneys speak. Both parties receive a copy of the testimony in document form. Depositions provide information and may also set up inconsistencies between a witness's testimony at the deposition and his testimony at trial. If a party discovers an inconsistency in the testimony of one of the other party's witnesses, she can bring the inconsistency to the fact finder's attention to diminish the witness's credibility. The parties may also use depositions when a witness is elderly, moving, or ill such that he may be unavailable at the time of the trial.

If a party does not comply with requests for discovery, the court may admit the facts the other party sought to discover. Attorneys who feel that certain material is outside the scope of the case often argue that the material is irrelevant to the case. If the court disagrees, however, the party must supply the requested information. Although these discovery tools are important in the United States, not all countries have a discovery process.

In discovery, as in other areas, technology is having an impact. It is estimated that 90 percent of all documents and communications are created and maintained in electronic formats. In December 2006, the Federal Rules of Civil Procedure were amended to reflect changes in technology. Parties are now required to "make provisions for disclosure or discovery of electronically stored information"[11] at the start of the litigation

---

[11] Rule 16(B), Federal Rules of Civil Procedure.

process, and they must develop a discovery plan during their pretrial conferences. Once it appears that litigation is imminent, litigants have an obligation not to delete or destroy electronic files that may be discoverable. However, "absent exceptional circumstances, a court may not impose sanctions . . . on a party for failing to provide electronically stored information lost as a result of the routine, good-faith operation of an electronic information system."[12]

Parties who might become embroiled in litigation, however, probably should not count on using the good-faith exception because the consequences of destroying electronic data can be significant. For example, in the sex discrimination case of *Zubulake v. UBS Warburg LLC*,[13] the judge found that the company's employees had intentionally deleted e-mail messages, lost a number of backup tapes, and failed to produce files as requested. As a sanction, she issued an *adverse-inference* instruction to the jury, basically telling them that they could assume that any documents not produced would have been harmful to the company's case. The jury ultimately awarded the woman $29.3 million in damages.

Morgan Stanley had to pay an even bigger price for its failure to meet its obligations for electronic discovery of relevant e-mail messages and documents. In *Coleman Holdings Inc. v. Morgan Stanley & Co.*,[14] the firm produced more than 1,300 pages of e-mail messages but failed to reveal in a timely fashion the existence of 1,423 backup tapes. In that case, the court also issued an adverse-inference instruction, stating that Morgan Stanley would have to bear the burden of proving that it lacked knowledge of the fraud. The jury found in favor of the plaintiff and awarded damages in the amount of $1.6 billion. Morgan Stanley also had to pay the U.S. Securities and Exchange Commission $15 million in fines for failure to comply with discovery requirements in a related commission investigation.

What organizations can learn from these cases is that as soon as they reasonably anticipate that litigation will occur, they must suspend their routine policy for retaining and destroying documents and put in place a "litigation hold" to make sure that documents that might be relevant to the lawsuit are preserved. Some plaintiffs' lawyers are now sending *litigation-hold demand* letters to potential defendants, making it almost impossible for a firm to claim that relevant documents were innocently deleted.

Pretrial Conference.   A pretrial conference precedes the trial. A **pretrial conference** is an informal meeting of the judge with the attorneys representing the parties. During this conference, the parties try to narrow the legal and factual issues and possibly work out a settlement. If the parties cannot reach a settlement, the attorneys and the judge discuss the administrative details of the trial: its length, witnesses, and any pretrial stipulations of fact or law to which the parties agree.

THE TRIAL

If a plaintiff seeks at least $20 in monetary damages, the Seventh Amendment to the U.S. Constitution entitles the parties to a jury trial. The plaintiff must, however, demand a jury trial in his or her complaint. Following the English tradition, most civil trials have 12 jurors; however, in many jurisdictions the number of required jurors has been reduced by the legislature. In some jurisdictions, fewer than 12 jurors may be allowed if both parties consent. If the plaintiff seeks an equitable remedy (an injunction or other court

---

[12] Rule 37(F), Federal Rules of Civil Procedure.
[13] 231 F.R.D. 159, 2005 U.S. Dist. LEXIS 1525 (S.D.N.Y., Feb. 2, 2005).
[14] 2005 WL 679071 (Fla. Cir. Ct., Mar. 1, 2005).

order) or if the parties have waived their right to a jury, a judge serves as the fact finder in the case.

Trials have six stages: jury selection, opening statements, examination of witnesses, closing arguments, conference on jury instructions, and posttrial motions. The following sections describe these stages.

Jury Selection.   The jury selection process begins when the clerk of the courts randomly selects a number of potential jurors from the citizens within the court's jurisdiction. Once the potential jurors have reported for jury duty, the **voir dire,** or jury selection, process begins. The voir dire process selects the jurors who will decide the case, as well as two or three "alternate jurors" who will watch the trial and be available to replace any juror who, for some legitimate reason, must leave jury duty before the trial ends.

During voir dire, the judge and/or attorneys question potential jurors to determine whether they are able to render an unbiased opinion in the case. If a potential juror's response to a question indicates that she or he may be biased, either attorney may challenge, or ask the court to remove, that potential juror "for cause." For example, a lawyer could challenge for cause a potential juror who was a college roommate of the defendant. In most states, each party has a certain number of **peremptory challenges.** These peremptory challenges allow a party to challenge a certain number of potential jurors without giving a reason.

Peremptory challenges, however, may lead to abuse. For example, in the past, attorneys have used peremptory challenges to eliminate a certain class, ethnic group, or gender from the jury. In the 1986 case *Batson v. Kentucky,*[15] the U.S. Supreme Court ruled that race-based peremptory challenges in criminal cases violate the equal protection clause of the Fourteenth Amendment to the U.S. Constitution. (Chapter 5 discusses the amendments to the Constitution in more detail.) The Supreme Court later extended the ban on race-based challenges to civil cases. In Case 3-2, the U.S. Supreme Court addressed the issue of whether the equal protection clause covers gender-based challenges.

[15] 476 U.S. 79 (1986).

CASE **3-2**   **J.E.B. v. ALABAMA, EX. REL. T.B.**
UNITED STATES SUPREME COURT
114 S. CT. 1419 (1994)

The State of Alabama filed a complaint for paternity and child support against J.E.B. on behalf of T.B., the unwed mother of a minor child. The court called a panel of twelve males and twenty-four females as potential jurors. Only ten males remained after three individuals were removed for cause. The state used its peremptory challenges to remove nine male jurors, and J.E.B. removed the tenth, resulting in an all female jury. The trial court rejected J.E.B.'s objection to the gender-based challenges, and the jury found J.E.B. to be the father. J.E.B. appealed, and the court of appeals affirmed the trial court's ruling that the Equal Protection Clause does not prohibit gender-based challenges. The

Alabama Supreme Court declined to hear the appeal, and J.E.B. appealed to the U.S. Supreme Court.

JUSTICE BLACKMUN: Discrimination in jury selection, whether based on race or on gender, causes harm to the litigants, the community, and the individual jurors who are wrongfully excluded from participation in the judicial process. The litigants are harmed by the risk that the prejudice which motivated the discriminatory selection of the jury will infect the entire proceedings. The community is harmed by the State's participation in the perpetuation of invidious group stereotypes and the inevitable loss of confidence in our judicial system that state-sanctioned discrimination in the courtroom engenders.

As with race-based *Batson* claims, a party alleging gender discrimination must make a prima facie showing of intentional discrimination before the party exercising the challenge is required to explain the basis for the strike. When an explanation is required, it need not rise to the level of a "for cause" challenge; rather, it merely must be based on a juror characteristic other than gender and the proffered explanation may not be pretextual.

Equal opportunity to participate in the fair administration of justice is fundamental to our democratic system. It reaffirms the promise of equality under the law—that all citizens, regardless of race, ethnicity, or gender, have the chance to take part directly in our democracy. When persons are excluded from participation in our democratic processes solely because of race or gender, this promise of equality dims, and the integrity of our judicial system is jeopardized.

REVERSED and REMANDED in favor of JEB.

CRITICAL THINKING

The defendant was contesting the removal of males from the jury. Does this fact weaken the Court's reasoning? Explain.

ETHICAL DECISION MAKING

Which values does this decision tend to emphasize?

The voir dire process has become more sophisticated over time. In cases involving significant amounts of money, rather than relying on their instinct or experience during jury selection, attorneys use professional jury selection services to identify demographic data to help select ideal jurors.

Jury selection firms also provide additional services, including mock trials and shadow juries. Jury selection firms set up **mock trials** by recruiting individuals who match the demographics of the real jury to listen to attorneys' arguments and witnesses' testimony. These mock trials give attorneys a sense of how their approach to the case will appear to the actual jurors. If the mock jury is not receptive to a particular argument or witness's testimony, the attorneys can modify their approach before trial.

Parties also often hire jury selection firms to provide shadow juries. Like a mock trial, a **shadow jury** uses individuals whose demographics match the demographics of a trial's real jurors. A shadow jury, however, sits inside the courtroom to watch the actual trial. At the end of each day of the trial, the shadow jury deliberates, giving the attorneys an idea of how the real jurors are reacting to the case. If the shadow jury finds the opposing side to be winning, the attorneys can modify their strategy.

Many attorneys believe that these services increase their clients' chances of winning cases. Critics argue, however, that jury selection services give an unfair advantage to one side when only one party can afford these services.

Opening Statements. Once the attorneys have impaneled, or selected, a jury, the case begins with opening statements. Each party's attorney explains to the judge and jury which facts he or she intends to prove, the legal conclusions to which these facts lead, and how the fact finder should decide the case based on those facts.

The Examination of Witnesses and Presentation of Evidence. Following opening statements, the plaintiff and defendant, in turn, present their cases-in-chief by examining witnesses and presenting evidence. The plaintiff has the burden of proving the case, meaning that if neither side presents a convincing case, the fact finder must rule in favor of the defendant. Thus, the plaintiff presents her case first.

The procedure for each witness is the same. First, the plaintiff's attorney questions the witness in *direct examination.* The plaintiff's attorney asks the witness questions to elicit facts that support the plaintiff's case-in-chief. Questions must relate to matters about which the witness has direct knowledge. Attorneys cannot elicit "hearsay" from the witnesses. *Hearsay* is testimony about what a witness heard another person say. Hearsay is impermissible because the opposing attorney cannot question the person who made the original statement to determine the statement's veracity.

The federal rules of evidence also prohibit attorneys from asking leading questions. Leading questions are questions that imply a specific answer. For example, an attorney cannot ask a witness, "Did the defendant come to your office and ask you to purchase stock from him?" Instead, attorneys must ask questions such as, "When did you first encounter the defendant?"

After direct examination, opposing counsel may *cross-examine* the witness. Opposing counsel, however, may ask only questions related to the witness's direct examination. On cross-examination, attorneys can ask leading questions. Attorneys try to show inconsistencies in the witness's testimony, cast doubt on the claims of the plaintiff's case, and elicit information to support the defendant's case.

After cross-examination, the plaintiff's attorney may conduct a *redirect examination,* a series of questions to repair damage done by the cross-examination. At the judge's discretion, opposing counsel has an opportunity to *re-cross* the witness to question his testimony on redirect examination. The parties follow this procedure for each of the plaintiff's witnesses.

Immediately following the plaintiff's presentation of her case, the defendant may move for a **directed verdict.** This motion is a request for the court to direct a verdict for the defendant because even if the jury accepted all the evidence and testimony presented by the plaintiff as true, the jury would still have no legal basis for a decision in favor of the plaintiff. The federal court system refers to a motion for a directed verdict as a *motion for a judgment as a matter of law.* Courts rarely grant motions for a directed verdict because plaintiffs almost always present at least *some* evidence to support each element of the cause of action.

If the court denies the defendant's motion for a directed verdict, the defendant then presents his case. The parties question the defendant's witnesses in the same manner as they questioned the plaintiff's witnesses, except that the defendant's attorney conducts direct and redirect examination and the plaintiff's attorney conducts cross-examination and re-cross-examination.

Closing Arguments.   After the defendant's case, the attorneys present closing arguments. In the *closing argument,* each attorney summarizes evidence from the trial in a manner consistent with his or her client's case. The plaintiff's attorney presents her closing argument first, followed by the defendant's attorney, and the plaintiff has the option to present a rebuttal of the defendant's closing argument.

Jury Instructions.   In a jury trial, the judge "charges the jury" by instructing the jurors how the law applies to the facts of the case. Both sides' attorneys submit statements to the judge explaining how they believe he should charge the jury. The judge's instructions are usually a combination of both sides' suggestions.

Different types of cases require different standards of proof. In most civil cases, the plaintiff must prove her case by a *preponderance of the evidence;* in other words, she must show that her claim is more likely to be true than the defendant's claim. In some civil cases, particularly cases involving fraud or oral contracts, the plaintiff must prove her case by *clear and convincing evidence,* a higher standard of proof. Criminal cases have an even higher burden of proof: The prosecution must prove its case *beyond a reasonable doubt.*

Trials in Japan

Civil procedure in Japan differs significantly from American civil procedure. The Japanese legal system has no juries and no distinct pretrial stage. Instead, a trial is a series of discrete meetings between the parties and the judge. At the first meeting, the parties identify the most critical and contested issues. They choose one and recess to gather evidence and marshal arguments on the issue.

At the next meeting, the judge rules on the chosen issue. If the judge decides against the plaintiff, the case is over. If the plaintiff wins, the process continues with the next issue. The process continues until the plaintiff loses an issue or until the judge decides all issues in the plaintiff's favor, resulting in a verdict for the plaintiff.

In addition, the discovery process in the Japanese court system is not as simple as it is in the United States. To obtain evidence, parties must convince the judge to order others to testify or produce documents. The judge can fine or jail parties who refuse to comply with such orders. Additionally, if a party does not comply with the judge's requests for discovery, the judge may admit the facts the other party sought to discover.

After the judge charges the jury, the jurors retire to the jury room to deliberate. Once they reach a decision, they return to the courtroom, where the judge reads their verdict and discharges them from their duty.

Trial procedures in the United States are quite different from trial procedures in other countries, as the Comparing the Law of Other Countries box illustrates.

Posttrial Motions.   Once the trial ends, the party who received the favorable verdict files a *motion for a judgment in accordance with the verdict.* Until the judge enters the judgment, the court has not issued a legally binding decision for the case.

The party who loses at trial has a number of available options. One option is to file a *motion for a judgment notwithstanding the verdict,* or *judgment non obstante verdicto,* asking the judge to issue a judgment contrary to the jury's verdict. To grant the motion, the judge must find that, when viewing the evidence in the light most favorable to the nonmoving party, a reasonable jury could not have found in favor of that party. In other words, as a matter of law, the judge must determine that the trial did not produce sufficient evidence to support the jury's verdict. This motion is similar to a motion for a directed verdict, except the parties cannot make this motion until *after* the jury issues a verdict. The federal court system refers to this motion as a *motion for judgment as a matter of law.*

The losing party can also file a *motion for a new trial.* Judges grant motions for a new trial only if they believe the jury's decision was clearly erroneous but they are not sure that the other side should necessarily have won the case. A judge often grants a motion for a new trial when the parties discover new evidence, when the judge made an erroneous ruling, or when misconduct during the trial may have prevented the jury from reaching a fair decision.

APPELLATE PROCEDURE

Either party may appeal the judge's decision on posttrial motions or on her or his final judgment. Sometimes, both parties appeal the same decision. For example, if a jury awarded the plaintiff $10,000 in damages, the plaintiff and the defendant may both appeal the amount of the judgment. Appellate courts, however, reverse only about 1 out of every 10 trial court decisions on appeal.

To be eligible for appeal, the losing party must argue that a prejudicial error of law occurred during the trial. A **prejudicial error of law** is a mistake so significant that it likely affected the outcome of the case. For example, a prejudicial error could occur if the judge improperly admitted hearsay evidence that allowed the plaintiff to prove an element of her case.

To appeal a case, the attorney for the appealing party (the appellant) files a notice of appeal with the clerk of the trial court within a prescribed time. The clerk then forwards the record of appeal to the appeals court. The record of appeal typically contains a number of items: the pleadings, a trial transcript, copies of the trial exhibits, copies of the judge's rulings on the parties' motions, the attorneys' arguments, jury instructions, the jury's verdict, posttrial motions, and the judgment order.

The appellant then files a **brief,** or written argument, with the court. Appellants file briefs to explain why the judgment in the lower court was erroneous and why the appeals court should reverse it. The attorney for the party who won in the lower court (the appellee) files an answering brief. The appellant may then file a reply brief in response to the appellee's brief. Generally, however, appellants do not file reply briefs.

The appeals court then usually allows the attorneys to present oral arguments before the court. The court considers these arguments, reviews the record of the case, and renders a decision.

An appellate court may render four basic decisions. The court can accept the lower court's judgment by *affirming* the decision of the lower court. Alternatively, if the appellate court concludes that the lower court's decision was correct but the remedy was inappropriate, it *modifies* the remedy. If the appellate court decides that the lower court was incorrect in its decision, it *reverses* the lower court's decision. Finally, if the appeals court thinks the lower court committed an error but does not know how that error affected the outcome of the case, it *remands* the case to the lower court for a new trial.

An appellate court usually has a bench with at least three judges. Appellate courts do not have juries; rather, the judges decide the case by majority vote. One of the judges who votes with the majority records the court's decision and its reasons in the *majority opinion.* These decisions have precedential value—that is, judges use these prior appellate court decisions to make decisions in future cases. Also, these decisions establish new guidelines in the law that all citizens must follow. If a judge agrees with the majority's decision, but for different reasons, she may write a *concurring opinion,* stating the reasons she used to reach the majority's conclusion. Finally, judges disagreeing with the majority may write a *dissenting opinion,* giving their reasons for reaching a contrary conclusion. Attorneys arguing that a court should change the law frequently cite dissenting opinions from previous cases in their briefs. Likewise, appellate judges who change the law often cite dissenting opinions from past cases.

For most cases, only one appeal is available. In states with both an intermediate and a final court of appeals, a losing party may appeal from the intermediate appellate court to the state supreme court. In a limited number of cases, the losing party can appeal the decision of a state supreme court or a federal circuit court of appeals to the U.S. Supreme Court.

Appeal to the U.S. Supreme Court.   Every year thousands of individuals file appeals with the U.S. Supreme Court. The Court, however, hears, on average, only 80 to 90 cases each year. To file an appeal to the U.S. Supreme Court, a party files a petition asking the Court to issue a **writ of certiorari,** an order to the lower court to send to the Supreme Court the record of the case. The Court issues very few writs.

The justices review petitions and issue a writ only when at least four justices vote to hear the case (the *rule of four*). The court is most likely to issue a writ in four instances: (1) The case presents a substantial federal question that the Supreme Court has not yet addressed; (2) multiple circuit courts of appeal have decided the issue of the case in different ways; (3) a state court of last resort has ruled that a federal law is invalid or has upheld a state law that may violate federal law; or (4) a federal court has ruled that an act of Congress is unconstitutional. If the Supreme Court does not issue a writ of certiorari, the lower court's decision stands.

CASE OPENER WRAP-UP

Caterpillar

The timing of events was crucial to the outcome of the Caterpillar case. At the time Lewis filed the case in the state court system, one of the defendants and the plaintiff were from the same state, so the state court system had jurisdiction. Once the supply company reached an agreement with Lewis, the other defendant, Caterpillar, filed a motion to exercise its right of removal because diversity of citizenship existed in the absence of the Kentucky defendant. But the agreement was not final at the time of the motion because the agreement was subject to the insurer's approval. Thus, the appellate court ruled that because the supply company was still a party to the agreement, the federal court system could not exercise jurisdiction over the case.

The U.S. Supreme Court, however, overruled the appellate court. The Supreme Court ruled that the state court should not have granted Caterpillar's initial motion to remove the case because at the time of removal, the insurer had not accepted the settlement agreement, the supply company remained a party in the case, and, therefore, the diversity of citizenship was not complete. The Supreme Court held further, however, that the district court's error in hearing the case was not fatal because the settlement agreement was approved and the case satisfied the jurisdictional requirements by the time the federal court issued its decision. The Court ruled that to require the district court to send the case back to the state system would be an undue waste of judicial resources.

Why might Caterpillar have wanted to move the case to the federal court system? First, the case involved product liability claims. Data suggest that average damage awards in product liability cases tend to be higher in state courts than in federal courts. Second, Caterpillar may have feared local prejudice. While all judges must strive for neutrality, out-of-state defendants may fear that state judges are slightly biased in favor of in-state parties.

Key Terms

Summary of Key Topics

Jurisdiction	*In personam jurisdiction* is the power of a court to render a decision affecting a person's legal rights. *Subject-matter jurisdiction* is the power of a court to render a decision in a particular type of case. The three forms of subject-matter jurisdiction are state, exclusive federal, and concurrent.
Venue	*Venue* is the geographic location of the trial.
The Structure of the Court System	The U.S. has two parallel court structures: the state and federal systems. The federal structure has *district courts* (trial courts), *circuit courts of appeal,* and the *U.S. Supreme Court.* The state court structure varies by state, but generally includes courts of common pleas (trial courts), state courts of appeal, and a state supreme court.
Threshold Requirements	*Standing:* For a person to have the legal right to file a case, the outcome of the case must personally affect that person.

Case or controversy: There must be an issue before the court that a judicial decision is capable of resolving. Parties cannot ask the judge for an "advisory opinion."

Ripeness: The case cannot be moot; it must be ready for a decision to be made. |
| **Steps in Civil Litigation** | The stages of a civil trial include the pretrial, trial, posttrial, and appellate stages.

Pretrial includes consultation with attorneys, pleadings, the discovery process, and the pretrial conference.

The *trial* begins with jury selection, followed by opening statements, the plaintiff's case, the defendant's case, closing arguments, jury instructions, jury deliberations, the jury's verdict, and the judgment.

After the trial, parties may file *posttrial motions.*

The parties may then file *appeals* to the appropriate appellate court and, in some cases, to the U.S. Supreme Court. |

Point / Counterpoint

Is the Adversarial System the Most Effective Approach to Justice?	
YES	**NO**
Proponents of the adversarial system argue that justice is best served when each individual's rights and freedoms are protected. The adversarial system requires that the fact finder remain a neutral and objective party, free from bias. The parties are responsible for developing their own individual theories of the case. By allowing individuals to decide what information they wish to present as a part of their case, the system allows them to take a more active role in the legal process.

In addition to promoting individual rights, the adversarial system also helps prevent the abuse of power by the finder of fact. Proponents argue that excluding the finder of fact from question asking and evidence collection | Critics of the adversarial system argue that the quest for truth should be central to the administration of justice. By pitting parties against one another in the courtroom, the adversarial system becomes more interested in solving controversies than discovering the truth. Since the parties are allowed to decide what evidence they do and do not wish to present to the fact finder, it is likely that a decision will be rendered on the basis of incomplete and biased information.

In addition to overemphasizing controversy, the adversarial system creates a wealth disparity between parties. For example, if Suzie the secretary decides to sue her employer, Giant Corporate Entity, the sheer size and |

prevents them from reaching a premature decision or abusing their power.

In response to critics who argue that the adversarial system is more about resolving a dispute than finding the truth, proponents argue that by pitting the two sides against one another, the truth will emerge. The parties involved in the litigation have a stronger motivation to uncover and disclose the facts relevant to the case than does any neutral party (such as the judge in the inquisitorial system). Individual rights and zealous advocacy will best lead to the administration of justice.

financial strength of her opponent puts her at an immediate disadvantage. While Suzie may be able to afford an attorney, it is likely that her employer will be able to afford a team of attorneys, paralegals, and support staff. The adversarial system quickly goes from a "system designed to protect individual rights" to a system that primarily protects the rights of the wealthy few who can afford better attorneys and fund a lengthy litigation.

Rather than having the adversarial system, the country would be better served by an inquisitorial system. In the inquisitorial system, the finder of fact, not the parties, is responsible for gathering evidence and investigating. The finder of fact has the opportunity to gather as much information as necessary before rendering an opinion. In the inquisitorial system, the truth, not the controversy, guides the way.

Questions & Problems

1. Explain the two types of jurisdiction that a court must have to hear a case and render a binding decision over the parties.

2. Explain the differences between trial courts and appellate courts.

3. Identify and define the alternative tools of discovery.

4. Explain the three threshold requirements a plaintiff must meet before he or she can file a lawsuit.

5. Missouri was International Shoe Corporation's principal place of business, but the company employed between 11 and 13 salespersons in the state of Washington who exhibited samples and solicited orders for shoes from prospective buyers in Washington. The state of Washington assessed the company for contributions to a state unemployment fund. The state served the assessment on one of International Shoe Corporation's sales representatives in Washington and sent a copy by registered mail to the company's Missouri headquarters. International Shoe's representative challenged the assessment on numerous grounds, arguing that the state had not properly served the corporation. Is the corporation's defense valid? Why or why not? [*International Shoe Co. v. Washington,* 326 U.S. 310 (1945).]

6. The Robinsons, residents of New York, bought a new Audi car from Seaway Volkswagen Corp., a retailer incorporated in New York and with its principal place of business there. World-Wide Volkswagen, a company incorporated in New York and doing business in New York, New Jersey, and Connecticut, distributed the car to Seaway. Neither Seaway nor World-Wide did business in Oklahoma, and neither company shipped cars there. The Robinsons were driving through Oklahoma when another vehicle struck their Audi in the rear. The gas tank of the Audi exploded, injuring several members of the family. The Robinsons brought a product liability suit against the manufacturer, distributor, and retailer of the car in an Oklahoma state court. Seaway and World-Wide argued that the Oklahoma state court did not have *in personam* jurisdiction over them. After the state's trial court and supreme court held that the state did have *in personam* jurisdiction over Seaway and World-Wide, the companies appealed to the U.S. Supreme Court. How do you think the Court decided in this case? Why? [*World-Wide Volkswagen Corp. v. Woodson,* 444 U.S. 286 (1980).]

7. The plaintiff, a Texas resident, and the defendants, Colorado residents, were cat breeders who met at a cat show in Colorado. Subsequently, the plaintiff sent two cats to the defendants in Colorado for breeding and sent a third cat to them to be sold. A dispute over the return of the two breeding cats arose, and the plaintiff filed suit against the defendants in Texas. The defendants alleged that

the Texas court lacked personal jurisdiction over them because they did not have minimum contacts within the state of Texas.

The Texas statute provides that the Texas court could exercise jurisdiction over an out-of-state defendant only if (1) the defendant has purposefully established minimum contacts with the forum state and (2) the exercise of jurisdiction comports with traditional notions of fair play and substantial justice. The defendants were not residents of Texas and had no business in Texas. The only contact the defendants had with Texas was a single trip they made to Texas to pick up two other cats, not related to the litigation, that they were going to take to a cat show. During that same visit, the defendants took a cat unrelated to the lawsuit to see a Texas veterinarian, and the plaintiff's husband assisted the defendants with a Web page for their business. The trial court found that sufficient minimum contacts had been established. The defendants appealed. How do you believe the appellate court would rule in this case, and why? [*Hagan v. Field,* Court of Appeals of Texas, Fifth District, Dallas, 2006 Tex. App. LEXIS 393.]

8. Le Cabaret 481, Inc., an adult entertainment corporation, wanted to open a strip club in the city of Kingston. Kingston, however, passed an ordinance prohibiting adult businesses from operating within 300 feet of any church, school, nursery, public park, or residential property. Le Cabaret 481 filed a suit against the city, arguing that the ordinance left no feasible locations in the city for an adult business and thus violated the company's First Amendment right to free expression. The city, on the other hand, argued that Le Cabaret 481 did not present a ripe case to the court because the company had not applied for a building permit for its adult business. The company argued that it could not find a location for which it could apply for a permit. Do you think Le Cabaret 481 satisfied the ripeness requirement for its suit against the city? Why or why not? [*Le Cabaret 481, Inc. v. Municipality of Kingston,* 2005 U.S. Dist. LEXIS 706 (2005).]

9. Thirteen record labels filed a copyright violation suit against Hummer Winblad Venture Partners (Hummer), an owner of Napster, a peer-to-peer file-sharing network for online distribution of music. Hummer filed a counterclaim alleging antitrust violations against the record labels because they conspired to exclude independent music distributors like Napster from the online music distribution market. The record labels argued that Hummer lacked standing to make its counterclaims because Hummer, not Napster, made the counterclaims and Hummer never competed directly with the record labels. Hummer, on the other hand, argued that it had standing because it financed Napster, a participant in the online music distribution market. How do you think the court ruled in this case? Why? [*In re Napster Copyright Litig. v. Hummer Winblad Venture Partners,* 354 F. Supp. 2d 1113 (2005).]

10. The plaintiffs, parents of underage children, sued the Advanced Brands and Importing Co., an importer of alcoholic beverages, seeking an injunction prohibiting advertisers from advertising its beers and damages in the form of compensation for the money spent by their children on illegal purchases of beer. The parents argued that the advertising campaign of the defendant causes underage children, like theirs, to illegally purchase the defendant's beer. The trial court dismissed the claim, in part, based on lack of standing, and the parents appealed. Do you think the appellate court found that they had standing? Why or why not? [*Alston v. Advanced Brands and Importing Co.,* 494 F.3d 562 (6th Cir. 2007).]

Looking for more review material?

The Online Learning Center at **www.mhhe.com/kubasek2e** contains this chapter's "Assignment on the Internet" and also a list of URLs for more information, entitled "On the Internet." Find both of them in the Student Center portion of the OLC, along with quizzes and other helpful materials.

Introduction to Contracts

LEARNING OBJECTIVES

After reading this chapter, you will be able to answer the following questions:

1   What is a contract?

2   What are the sources of contract law?

3   How can we classify contracts?

4   What are the rules that guide the interpretation of contracts?

CASE OPENER
A Questionable Contract

Mary Kay Morrow began working for Hallmark in 1982. At the beginning of 2002, Hallmark adopted the "Hallmark Dispute Resolution Program," which required, among other things, that claims against the company be resolved in binding arbitration rather than litigation. Hallmark assumed that employees who remained at Hallmark after the policy became effective were bound by the new company policy. Additionally, Hallmark reserved the right to modify the program at any time and excluded claims it brought from the arbitration requirement.

Fifteen months after the policy became effective, Hallmark terminated Morrow's employment. Morrow filed a claim against Hallmark, claiming that she had not been fired for just cause but, rather, had been terminated because of age discrimination and retaliation resulting from her earlier complaints about company policies. In response to the suit, which was filed in the circuit court of Jackson County, Hallmark filed a motion to stay the litigation and compel arbitration in accordance with its Dispute Resolution Program. The court granted Hallmark's motion.

After several additional failed attempts to get the circuit court to hear the case, Morrow proceeded with the only route she had left—arbitration. The arbitrator dismissed Morrow's claims for lack of timeliness and ruled that the program constituted a valid contract and was not unconscionable. In yet another effort to have the case heard, Morrow went back to the trial court with a motion to vacate the arbitrator's ruling. The motion was denied. Morrow appealed the case to the Missouri Court of Appeals on the grounds that the Dispute Resolution Program did not constitute an enforceable contract.

1. By what standard would the courts determine whether a contract existed?
2. Did each party to the supposed contract make a valid promise that would support the existence of the contract?

The Wrap-Up at the end of the chapter will answer these questions.

The Definition of a Contract

L01

What is a contract?

This part of the text focuses on contracts, but what is a contract? The Restatement (Second) of Contracts defines a **contract** as "a promise or set of promises for the breach of which the law gives a remedy or the performance of which the law in some way recognizes a duty."[1] Another way to think of a contract is as a set of legally enforceable promises. Contracts play a fundamental role in business; after all, almost all business relationships are created by contracts.

One of the most important business relationships, the relationship that exists between employers and employees, is often created through contracts. Typically, during the hiring process, an employer will establish an employment contract, which lists the terms and obligations a new employee must agree to before starting work. One particular type of employment contract is a **covenant not to compete.** Covenants not to compete restrict what an employee may do after leaving a company, and they often dictate where, when, and with whom an employee may work. Employers justify the use of covenants not to compete by saying they are necessary to protect their trade secrets, talent, and proprietary information.

Noncompete contracts are especially common in industries such as technology and sales, where possession of cutting-edge information or client lists can greatly affect the competition between companies. For example, in 2008, IBM and Apple found themselves in a court battle over employee Mark Papermaster. Apple had hired Papermaster away from his high-level position at IBM and wished to put him in charge of Apple's iPhone and iPod division. In turn, IBM argued that Papermaster's move to Apple violated his covenant not to compete, which stated that he would not work for a competitor during the year after he left IBM. Former employer IBM also argued that because Papermaster had been a top executive at IBM, he was in possession of confidential and proprietary information that could be valuable to Apple. The court agreed with IBM and thus issued an injunction barring Papermaster from starting work at Apple until after a trial had taken place. Apple and IBM opted to reach an agreement out of court, and Papermaster was cleared to start work at his new position in April 2009.[2] Covenants not to compete are discussed in greater detail in Chapter 16 of this text.

ELEMENTS OF A CONTRACT

We can flesh out the definition of a contract by examining the four elements that are necessary for it to exist. These elements are the agreement, the consideration, contractual capacity, and a legal object. The **agreement** consists of an **offer** by one party, called the

---

[1] Restatement (Second) of Contracts, sec. 1.

[2] See www.networkworld.com/community/node/37835 and http://library.findlaw.com/2003/Feb/5/132530.html.

offeror, to enter into a contract and an **acceptance** of the terms of the offer by the other party, called the *offeree* (see Exhibit 13-1). This first element is discussed in detail in Chapter 14.

The second element of the contract is the **consideration,** the bargained-for exchange or what each party gets in exchange for his or her promise under the contract. We discuss consideration in Chapter 15.

The third element is **contractual capacity.** Capacity is the legal ability to enter into a binding agreement. Most adults over the age of majority have capacity; those under the age of majority, people suffering from mental illness, and intoxicated persons do not. Chapter 16 explains further cases that limit or prohibit capacity.

Exhibit 13-1   The Formation of a Contract

This exhibit illustrates the first element of the contract, the agreement. For a contract to exist, the parties also must have legal capacity to enter into a contract, exchange valid consideration, and be entering into a contract with a legal purpose. The contract is formed as soon as the second party makes his or her promise.

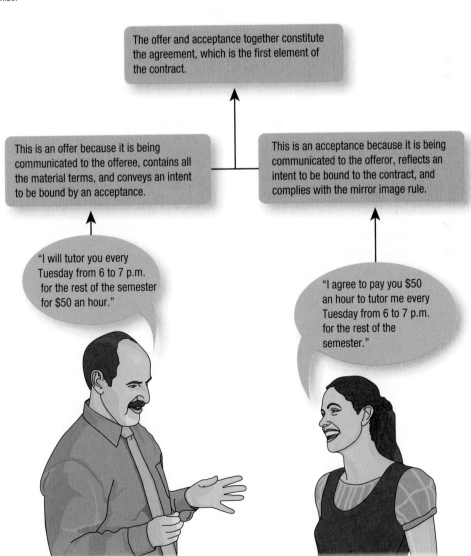

Contract Formation and E-Commerce

Contract law operates on the Internet, with adjustments for special issues that range from jurisdiction to payment. Which state's or country's laws apply if the parties to an e-contract end up in a dispute? What happens if an online company engages in fraud by using a customer's credit card information in ways the customer never intended?

Contract formation via the Internet is especially important. Issues regarding contract formation range from timing to contract terms. For instance, given the speed with which e-mails go back and forth between parties, it is sometimes difficult to know when the parties have created a contract. Once a contract is formed, additional questions arise: What specific terms does the contract include? Can a company post standard terms on a Web site rather than in a document or on a ticket?

Fortunately, legislators have drafted and implemented key pieces of legislation that clarify issues related to contract formation and e-commerce. Two examples of e-commerce legislation are the Electronic Signatures in Global and National Commerce (ESIGN) Act and the Uniform Electronic Transactions Act (UETA).

Congress passed ESIGN to facilitate the use of electronic records and signatures in e-commerce. The federal law affirms e-contracts as legally valid. This law makes it clear that documents produced electronically are as valid as documents produced on paper. Congress did not write or pass UETA. Instead, the National Conference of Commissioners on Uniform State Laws proposed this piece of legislation, which almost every state has adopted. UETA's intent was similar to Congress's intent regarding ESIGN. In addition to affirming electronic contracts as legally valid, UETA attempts to make state laws consistent regarding topics such as the validity of signatures created online.

Chapter 16 also discusses the fourth element of a binding legal contract, legal object. This means that to be enforceable, the contract cannot be either illegal or against public policy.

Legal Principle: **A legally binding contract requires four elements: agreement, consideration, capacity, and legal object.**

DEFENSES TO THE ENFORCEMENT OF A CONTRACT

Sometimes a contract appears to be legally binding because all four elements of a contract are present, but one of the parties may have a defense to its enforcement. Such defenses fall into two categories. The first is a lack of genuine assent (Chapter 17). A contract is supposed to be entered into freely by both parties, but sometimes the *offeror* (the party proposing the contract) secures acceptance of the agreement through improper means such as fraud, duress, undue influence, or misrepresentation. In these situations, there is no genuine assent to the contract, and the *offeree* (the person who agreed to or accepted the contract) may be able to raise that lack of genuine assent as a defense to enforcement of the agreement.

The second defense, discussed in Chapter 18, is that the contract lacks the *proper form*, which typically means it lacks a writing. As Chapter 18 will explain, the contract itself does not have to be in writing, but a writing meeting certain criteria that confirms the existence of the contract must exist.

Exhibit 13-2 summarizes the requirements of an enforceable contract.

Legal Principle: **Two defenses to the enforcement of a contract are lack of genuine assent and lack of proper form.**

THE OBJECTIVE THEORY OF CONTRACTS

Contract law is based on an *objective theory of contracts*, which means we base the existence of a contract on the parties' outward manifestations of intent and we base its interpretation on how a reasonable person would interpret it. Thus, the subjective intent of the parties is not usually relevant; what matters is how they represented their intent through their actions and words.

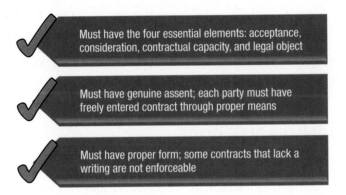

Exhibit 13-2
Requirements of an
Enforceable Contract

The subjective intent may be relevant, however, under a limited number of circumstances. As Chapter 17 explains in its discussion of mistake, if a mutual misunderstanding between the parties exists, and if as a result they did not really come to a meeting of the minds, there is no contract. The courts may then look at how each party subjectively interpreted the situation to determine whether the parties really reached an agreement.

Legal Principle: In determining whether parties intended to enter into a contract, the courts look at their objective words and behavior and do not try to figure out what they might have been secretly intending.

Sources of Contract Law

The two most important sources of contract law are case law and the Uniform Commercial code (UCC). A third source of law, which has become more important with increasing globalization, is the Convention on Contracts for International Sales of Goods (CISG). In this part of the book we focus primarily on the law of contracts as established by the common law. (Part Three, "Domestic and International Sales Law," focuses more on the law as set out by the UCC and CISG.)

LO2

What are the sources of contract law?

COMMON LAW

Today's law of contracts actually originated in judicial decisions in England, later modified by early courts in the United States. Since then, contract law has been further modified by U.S. legislatures and court rulings. The law of contracts is primarily common law. Therefore, to find out what the law is, we could go to the Reporters and read the decisions, but it is easier to go to the Restatement (Second) of the Law of Contracts. Prominent legal scholars, recruited by the American Law Institute, organized the principles of the common law of contracts into the original *Restatement of the Law, Contracts*. The compilation has been revised and published as *Restatement of the Law Second, Contracts*.

The Restatement (Second) is not actually the law itself, although judges frequently cite it because it is an authoritative statement of what the law is. As the common law of contracts evolved, not all states interpreted all aspects of it in the same way, so while we can make generalizations about the law of contracts, you will always want to know exactly what the law at issue is in your own state. In the Restatement (Second), the drafters often explain what the law about a particular matter is in the majority of states and then provide alternative approaches other states have adopted.

China

Countries outside the United States have slightly different laws for different types of contracts. China, for example, has seven chapters of general provisions for contracts but also has chapters with special provisions for 15 different types of contracts governing sales, leases, loans, donations, construction projects, storage, and transportation.

UNIFORM COMMERCIAL CODE

Having different laws governing contracts in different states did not make interstate commerce flow smoothly. To remedy some of the difficulties created by a patchwork of different laws governing commercial transactions, the National Conference of Commissioners on Uniform State Laws and the American Law Institute drafted a set of commercial laws that could be applicable to all states. This effort was called the **Uniform Commercial Code (UCC).** The UCC became law in each state that adopted it in whole or in part as an element of its state code. Thus, if a firm enters into a contract governed by the Uniform Commercial Code in Ohio, it will be operating under the Ohio Uniform Commercial Code.

Legal Principle: **All contracts are governed by either the common law or the Uniform Commercial Code (UCC). If the contract is for the sale of a good, it falls under Article 2 of the UCC; if it is for anything else, it falls under the common law.**

The part of the Uniform Commercial Code relevant to contracts is Article 2, which governs contracts for the sale (exchange for a price) of goods (tangible, movable objects). In this part of the book we will sometimes point out important differences between the UCC and the common law, but we discuss contracts governed by the UCC primarily in Part Three. Also relevant to contract law is UCC Article 2A, which governs contracts for the lease of goods. For instance, if Rashad leases a car from a dealership, the lease contract is governed by Article 2A. If Rashad purchases the car, the purchase contract is governed by Article 2 of the UCC.

Classification of Contracts

LO3

How can we classify contracts?

Contracts are classified in a number of different ways. Different classifications are useful for different purposes. This section describes the primary ways by which we classify contracts.

BILATERAL VERSUS UNILATERAL CONTRACTS

All contracts are either unilateral or bilateral. Knowing whether a contract is unilateral or bilateral is important because that classification determines when the offeree is legally bound to perform. Exhibit 13-3 highlights the difference between unilateral and bilateral contracts.

If the offeror wants a promise from the offeree to form a binding contract, the contract is a **bilateral contract,** commonly defined as a promise in exchange for a promise. As soon as the promises are exchanged, a contract is formed and the parties' legal obligations arise. When Shannon promises to pay Gary $1,000 in exchange for his promise to paint her car on July 1, they have a bilateral contract. If either party fails to perform, the other may sue for breach. In the opening scenario, Hallmark wanted its employees to promise to submit any claims against it to arbitration rather than litigation. At issue in this case is, among other things, the question of whether Hallmark promised anything in return.

Exhibit 13-3

Bilateral vs. Unilateral Contracts

A PROMISE + A PROMISE = A *BILATERAL* CONTRACT

A PROMISE + A REQUESTED ACTION = A *UNILATERAL* CONTRACT

Another example of a bilateral contract can be found in the bidding process used by eBay. When an auction on eBay's Web site has closed, a bilateral contract exists between the seller and the individual who made the highest bid. The seller has promised to send the item (which needs to be comparable to the item described in the listing) to the bidder. The bidder has promised to make payment to the seller in the full amount of his or her bid. Should either party fail to perform, the other party make seek legal remedy according to the terms and conditions set forth by eBay's seller-bidder agreements.

In a **unilateral contract,** the offeror wants the offeree to *do* something, not to promise to do something. Perhaps the most common kind of unilateral offer is a reward. If Jim loses his dog, he may post a sign saying, "$50 reward for the safe return of my Poodle, Frenchie." When Michiko calls Jim and says, "Don't worry, I'll find your dog," she is not making a contract because the unilateral offer calls for an action, not a promise.

Just as the offeree is under no obligation to actually perform the act called for by the offeror, the offeror may revoke the offer at any time before performance. Initially this situation created problems because a person could be halfway through the performance and the offeror could revoke the offer. Because of the unfairness of such a scenario, today the courts hold that once an offeree begins performance, the offeror must hold the offer open for a reasonable time to allow the offeree to complete it.

Sometimes the key issue in a case is whether the offer is for a unilateral or bilateral contract. Case 13-1 demonstrates why it's important to distinguish between a unilateral and a bilateral contract.

CASE 13-1   D.L. PEOPLES GROUP, INC. v. HAWLEY
COURT OF APPEAL OF FLORIDA, FIRST DISTRICT
804 SO. 2D 561, FLA. APP. 1 DIST. (2002)

Hawley responded to an ad in a Missouri newspaper designed to recruit Admissions Representatives to recruit Missouri residents to attend Appellant's college in Florida. The Appellant's representative interviewed Hawley in Missouri and recommended that Hawley be hired as a recruiter to recruit students from Missouri. An Admissions Representative Agreement (agreement) was mailed to Hawley, who signed it on November 16, 1996, in Missouri. The agreement was subsequently mailed to Appellant's President, for the "final say," and he executed the agreement on December 2, 1996, in his office in Kissimmee, Florida. Hawley was then trained exclusively in Missouri. Hawley was shot and killed in Missouri while attempting to make one of his first calls.

The agreement provided that Appellant was to pay Hawley a commission if Hawley successfully recruited students for Appellant's school, to provide Hawley with an opportunity to participate in Appellant's health and life insurance plans, and to provide appropriate payroll taxes for social security, unemployment and workers' compensation. Hawley agreed, among other things, to devote exclusive time

and effort to Appellant's business, to operate in the territory assigned by Appellant, to maintain a certain level of liability and property damage insurance, to maintain certain licenses and levels of expertise in applicable areas, and to attend and complete Appellant's training program.

The heirs of Hawley argued that they should be entitled to workers' compensation from the state of Florida for his death. The trial court, however, denied their claim because the Florida statute provided that workers' compensation would be paid only when the contract of employment was formed in Florida, and Hawley's employment contract was a unilateral contract that could be formed solely by employee's performance in Missouri. Thus, because the contract was not formed in Florida, he was not covered by workers' compensation. Hawley's heirs appealed on grounds that the contract was in fact a bilateral contract formed in Florida when executed by the Appellant's President.

JUDGE BROWNING: . . . These mutual responsibilities constitute a bilateral contract. To form a bilateral contract, there must be mutuality of obligation. . . . Thus, the agreement is a bilateral contract, and Chapter 440 must be examined to determine the resulting consequences.

Section 440.09(1)(d), Florida Statutes (1999), provides in pertinent part, that:

[I]f an accident happens while the employee is employed elsewhere than in this state, which would entitle the employee or his or her dependents to compensation if it had happened in this state, the employee or his or her dependents are entitled to compensation *if the contract of employment was made in this state,* or the employment was principally localized in this state.

Thus, based on the plain language of the statute, if a contract is formed in Florida, the accident is compensable under Florida workers' compensation law. . . . The employment contract between Appellant and Hawley was executed in Florida. A contract is created where the last act necessary to make a binding agreement takes place. . . . Where one contracting party signs the contract, and the other party accepts and signs the contract, a binding contract results. . . . It is undisputed that Hawley signed the agreement then sent it to Appellant in Kissimmee, Florida, where it was signed and executed by Appellant's President. Because the last act necessary to complete the agreement, i.e., Appellant's President's signature, was performed in Florida, the contract was made in Florida. Accordingly, Florida workers' compensation law applies. The JCC erred by finding the agreement was a unilateral contract and Florida workers' compensation law inapplicable. . . .

REVERSED.

CRITICAL THINKING

Give an example of a realistically possible piece of missing information that could change the acceptability of Judge Browning's reasoning. What effect would this new information have?

In what way is the case especially subject to the proper definition of pertinent terms? What words or phrases are particularly crucial? Are alternate definitions possible, and if so, how could they affect your willingness to accept the validity of the conclusion?

ETHICAL DECISION MAKING

Who are the stakeholders primarily affected by this ruling? What ethical theory might justify the consequences imposed on the relevant parties? How?

What do you think a public disclosure test of this ruling would yield? How might the outcome vary between regions or countries? Why?

EXPRESS VERSUS IMPLIED CONTRACTS

We can classify contracts as express or implied depending on how they are created. The terms of **express contracts** are all clearly set forth in either written or spoken words. In the opening scenario, Hallmark contended that the Dispute Resolution Program constituted an express contract because it had laid out the terms for the contract in a writing received by its employees. **Implied contracts,** in contrast, arise not from words but from the conduct of the parties. If you have a dental emergency and the dentist pulls your severely infected tooth without prior negotiation about payment, or even any mention of payment, you have an implied contract for payment for her services. However, if you go to the dentist's office, ask how much it will cost to whiten your teeth, and sign a written agreement that stipulates exactly what the process will entail and how much you will pay, you have an express contract.

Apple's iTunes store provides another example of express contracts. Apple has several express contracts with music labels and television stations to sell music and television shows online. As a result of each sale, Apple retains a percentage of the profit and submits the remainder to the music label or television station. Should Apple, or the label, not receive the appropriate percentage of the sale, a breach-of-contract suit could be filed.

As a general rule, three conditions must be met for the courts to find an implied, or *implied-in-fact,* contract. First, the plaintiff provided some property or service to the defendant. Second, the plaintiff expected to be paid for such property or service, and a reasonable person in the position of the defendant would have expected to pay for it. Third, the defendant had an opportunity to reject the property or service but did not. In Case 13-2, the court had to decide whether the facts gave rise to an implied-in-fact contract.

CASE 13-2 PACHE v. AVIATION VOLUNTEER FIRE CO.
SUPREME COURT OF NEW YORK, APPELLATE DIVISION, THIRD DEPARTMENT 20 A.D.3D 731, 800 N.Y.S.2D 228 (2005)

Mr. Pache was the fire chief of the Aviation Volunteer Fire Company, which serves several neighborhoods in the Bronx. Mr. Pache suffered a fatal heart attack at the scene of a fire. His widow applied for Workers' Compensation, and was ultimately granted benefits by the Workers' Compensation Board. The decision was based on a finding that there was an implied contract between Aviation and the City of New York giving rise to the City's liability pursuant to the Volunteer Fireman's Benefit Law. The City appealed.

MERCURE, J.: . . . The City initially contended that claimant was not a covered employee within the meaning of Volunteer Firefighters' Benefit Law because the City had no written contract with Aviation. In relevant part, Volunteer Firefighters' Benefit Law § 30(2) provides:

> If at the time of injury the volunteer fire[fighter] was a member of [an incorporated] fire company . . . and located in a city, . . . protected under a contract by the fire department or fire company of which the volunteer fire[fighter] was a member, any benefit under this chapter shall be a city . . . charge.

Having conceded at oral argument that an implied contract against the City is a legal possibility, the City argues that it was error to find an implied contract in this case because there was no evidence that the Commissioner of the Fire Department of the City of New York (hereinafter FDNY) ever approved such a contract and there was insufficient proof of the elements of formation of an implied contract. We find both contentions to be unavailing.

In general, "it is well settled that a contract may be implied in fact where inferences may be drawn from the facts and circumstances of the case and the intention of the parties as indicated by their conduct." . . . However, there cannot be a valid implied contract with a municipality when the

Legislature has assigned the authority to enter into contracts to a specific municipal officer or body or has prescribed the manner in which the contract must be approved, and there is no proof that the statutory requirements have been satisfied.

Here, the City relies on several provisions of the City Charter for the proposition that the Commissioner of the FDNY has the exclusive authority to enter into contracts on behalf of the FDNY (New York City Charter §§ 16-389, 17-394, 19-487). To the extent that this argument—explicitly asserted for the first time before this Court—is properly before us, it is unpersuasive because these provisions, individually and in conjunction, do not include an express assignment of exclusive contracting authority to the Commissioner.

The City further contends that there was insufficient evidence to support the Board's finding of an implied-in-fact contract because there was no evidence of assent by the City to the alleged contract. While acknowledging the absence of direct evidence on the issue of assent, we conclude that the Board's finding of an implied contract between the City and Aviation should not be disturbed. The Board was presented with evidence that Aviation had been in existence since 1923, and that it worked "hand in hand" with the local FDNY company to fight fires. There was evidence that the local fire company occasionally called Aviation to request its assistance. A representative of the City provided evidence that the City was aware of Aviation, and knew that it fought fires in conjunction with the FDNY. If Aviation arrived at the scene of a fire before the local FDNY company, Aviation would be in charge of a fire scene until the FDNY company arrived and would thereafter continue working under its supervision. There was no evidence that City officials or the local fire company ever objected to or rejected the services of Aviation. Moreover, although the City was directed to produce an employee from the

[continued]

local FDNY company with knowledge of the relationship between the local fire company and Aviation as well as other facts relevant to the implied contract issue, it failed to do so. . . . Inasmuch as the Board was entitled to draw reasonable and adverse inferences from the City's failure to produce a knowledgeable employee, we are satisfied that substantial evidence supports the Board's determination that an implied-in-fact contract existed between the City and Aviation.

AFFIRMED in favor of Plaintiff.

CRITICAL THINKING

Do you agree that enough evidence has been considered in establishing an implied-in-fact contract? If so, what makes the evidence strong; and if not, what further evidence do you feel is necessary to make a confident claim?

Can you find an appreciable body of evidence in this case in support of an opposite contention? What is it?

ETHICAL DECISION MAKING

Justify the decision reached by the court by using different guidelines for ethical decision making. Which guideline fits most strongly with the case data? Why?

What values might the court be attempting to uphold with this ruling? What values are necessarily sacrificed to these interests? Can you justify this preference, and if so how?

QUASI-CONTRACTS

Quasi-contracts are sometimes called *implied-in-law contracts,* but they are not actually contracts. Rather, in order to prevent one party from being unjustly enriched at the expense of another, the courts impose contractual obligations on one of the parties *as if* that party had entered into a contract.

Assume Diego hears a noise in his driveway. He looks out and sees a group of workers apparently getting ready to resurface it. The doorbell rings, but he does not answer it. He goes down to his basement office and stays there until the workers have gone and he has a resurfaced driveway. When he receives a bill from the paving company, Diego refuses to pay on the grounds that he did not ask to have the driveway paved. In such a case, where the defendant knew the company was getting ready to bestow on him a benefit to which he was not entitled, the court will probably impose a quasi-contract, requiring that Diego pay the paving company the fair market value of the resurfacing. Imposing such a duty prevents him from being unjustly enriched at the expense of the paving company.

There are limits to the doctrine, however; specifically, the enrichment must be unjust. Sometimes a benefit may be conferred on you simply because of a mistake by the other party, and the courts will not make people pay for others' mistakes. Had Diego been out of town when his driveway was repaved, he would have just gotten lucky. The courts are not going to make him pay for the pavers' mistake when he could have done nothing to prevent the benefit from being bestowed on him.

A defendant, however, does not need to acknowledge the subcontractor's role, as was the case in Case 13-3, for a quasi-contract to exist.

Legal Principle: **Recovery in quasi-contract may be obtained when (1) a benefit is conferred by the plaintiff upon the defendant; (2) the defendant has knowledge of the benefit that is being bestowed upon her; and (3) the defendant retains the benefit under circumstances where it would be unjust to do so without payment.**

CASE **13-3**

REISENFELD & CO. v. THE NETWORK GROUP, INC.; BUILDERS SQUARE, INC.; KMART CORP.
U.S. COURT OF APPEALS FOR THE SIXTH CIRCUIT
277 F.3D 856 U.S. APP. (2002)

Network Group ("Network") was contracted by BSI to assist in selling or subleasing closed Kmart stores in Ohio. A few years later, Network entered into a commission agreement with Reisenfeld, a real estate broker for Dick's Clothing and Sporting Goods ("Dicks"). Dicks then subleased two stores from BSI. According to executed assignment and assumption agreements signed in November of 1994, BSI was to pay a commission to Network. Network was then responsible, pursuant to the commission agreement with Reisenfeld, to pay a commission of $1 per square foot to Reisenfeld. There was no direct agreement made between BSI and Reisenfeld.

During this time, Network's sole shareholder was defrauding BSI. This shareholder was convicted of several criminal charges stemming from his fraudulent acts. Network was ordered by the district court to disgorge any commissions received from BSI, and BSI was relieved of any duty to pay additional commissions to Network. As such, Reisenfeld never received his commission related to the Dicks sublease.

Reisenfeld sued in state court for the $160,320 in commissions he had not been paid. In addition to suing Network, Reisenfeld also named BSI as a defendant. The suit alleged, among other things, that based on a theory of quasi-contracts, BSI was jointly and severally liable for the commission.

JUDGE BOOGS: . . . A contract implied-in-law, or "quasi-contract," is not a true contract, but instead a liability imposed by courts in order to prevent unjust enrichment. . . . Under Ohio law, there are three elements for a quasi-contract claim. There must be: (1) a benefit conferred by the plaintiff upon the defendant; (2) knowledge by the defendant of the benefit; and (3) retention of the benefit by the defendant under circumstances where it would be unjust to do so without payment. . . .

There is no disagreement as to the first two requirements. It is clear that Reisenfeld's work as broker benefited BSI and that BSI was aware of the work Reisenfeld was doing. The disagreement rests on the third requirement—whether it would be unjust for BSI to retain the benefit it received without paying Reisenfeld for it. . . . Unreported Ohio Court of Appeals cases support the proposition that, in the contractor/ subcontractor context, when the subcontractor is not paid by the contractor and the owner has not paid the contractor for the aspect of the job at issue, the subcontractor can look to the owner for payment under a theory of unjust enrichment. . . . Further, another Ohio case, in dicta, supports the proposition that nonpayment by the owner would make payment on an unjust enrichment theory appropriate. . . .

[H]ere, BSI has not paid Network on this contract, and the losses suffered by BSI at Network's hands were "soft" losses of additional profits Network might have made, rather than quantifiable losses (due, for example, to theft) that might be held to constitute payment. . . . Therefore, though not controlling of this matter, the Ohio contractor/subcontractor cases involving property owners who have not paid the contractors provide persuasive support for the proposition that Reisenfeld may hold BSI accountable on a theory of quasi-contract for the benefits it provided to BSI, and for which it was not compensated by Network. . . .

Of course, liability under quasi-contract does not necessarily imply liability for the amount of money promised Reisenfeld under its contract with Network. Instead, the proper measure of liability is the reasonable value of the services Reisenfeld provided to BSI. We must therefore vacate the district court's order and remand the case for a determination of value.

REMANDED for consideration of damages.

CRITICAL THINKING

What words or phrases important to the reasoning of this decision might be ambiguous? What alternate definitions are possible? How does this ruling appear to be defining the words or phrases? Would another choice affect the acceptability of the conclusion?

Provide an example of one piece of new evidence that might lead Judge Boggs to a different conclusion, and explain how this information changes the consideration.

ETHICAL DECISION MAKING

Does this ruling establish a positive precedent in terms of the potential effect on future participants in disputes of this sort?

Does this decision appear to follow the Golden Rule guideline? Why or why not? How is this question particularly relative to the person making the judgment, and what sorts of interpersonal differences might lead to a variety of responses?

VALID, VOID, VOIDABLE, AND UNENFORCEABLE CONTRACTS

What everyone hopes to enter into, of course, is a **valid** contract, one that contains all the legal elements set forth in the beginning of this chapter. As a general rule, a valid contract is one that will be enforced. However, sometimes a contract may be valid yet **unenforceable** when a law prohibits the courts from enforcing it. The statute of frauds (Chapter 18) requires that certain contracts must be evidenced by a writing before they can be enforced. Similarly, the statute of limitations mandates that an action for breach of contract must be brought within a set period of time, thereby limiting enforceability.

A **void** contract is in effect not a contract at all. Either its object is illegal or it has some defect so serious that it is not a contract. If you entered into a contract with an assassin to kill your business law professor, that contract would be void because it is obviously illegal to carry out its terms.

A contract is **voidable** if one or both parties has the ability to either withdraw from the contract or enforce it. If the parties discover the contract is voidable after one or both have partially performed, and one party chooses to have the contract terminated, both parties must return anything they had already exchanged under the agreement so that they will be restored to the condition they were in at the time they entered into it.

Certain types of errors in the formation of a contract can make it voidable. Typically, the person who can void the contract is the person the court is attempting to protect, or the party the court believes might be taken advantage of by the other. For example, contracts by minors are usually voidable by the minor (Chapter 16). Contracts entered into as a result of fraud, duress, or undue influence, as described in Chapter 17, may be voided by the innocent party. In the opening scenario, Morrow attempted to prove that the Dispute Resolution Program was a voidable contract because it did not include mutual promises, could be changed at any time without approval, and lacked genuine assent from the employees.

EXECUTED VERSUS EXECUTORY CONTRACTS

Once all the terms of the contract have been fully performed, the contract has been **executed.** As long as some of the terms have not yet been performed, the contract is **executory.** If Randolph hires Carmine to paint his garage on Saturday for $800, with $200 paid as a down payment and the balance due on completion of the job, the contract becomes executory as soon as they reach agreement. When Randolph makes the down payment and Carmine's work is half complete, it is still executory. Once the painting has been finished and the final payment made, the contract is an executed contract. In the opening scenario, Hallmark assumed that any employee who remained at the company had executed the contract.

FORMAL VERSUS INFORMAL CONTRACTS

Contracts can be formal or informal. **Formal contracts** have a special form or must be created in a specific manner. The Restatement (Second) of Contracts identifies the following four types of formal contracts: (1) contracts under seal, (2) recognizances, (3) letters of credit, and (4) negotiable instruments.

When people hear the term *formal contract,* what often comes to mind is a *contract under seal,* named in the days when contracts were sealed with a piece of soft wax into which an impression was made. Today, sealed contracts may still be sealed with wax or

A Special Kind of Contract in Iraq

While most foreign states recognize the marriage contract, a different kind of marriage contract, sanctioned by Shiite clerics, is legal in Iraq. Called *muta'a* ("contract for a pleasure marriage"), it can last anywhere from an hour to 10 years and is renewable. Under the contract, the male typically receives sexual intimacy, in exchange for which the woman receives money. For a one-hour contract, she can generally expect the equivalent of $100; for a longer-term arrangement, $200 a month is typical, although she might receive more. The couple agrees to not have children, and if the woman does get pregnant, she can have an abortion but then must pay a fine to a cleric. The male can usually void the contract before the term ends, but the female can do so only if such a provision is negotiated when the contract is formed. *Muta'as* originally developed as a way for widows and divorced women to earn a living and for couples whose parents would not allow a permanent marriage to be together. Many women's rights advocates, however, see these contracts as exploiting women and are opposed to their increased popularity after the fall of Saddam Hussein in 2003. But as the war in Iraq continues to produce greater numbers of widows, increasing numbers of them are turning to this method of putting food on the table for themselves and their children.

Source: Rick Jervic, "'Pleasure Marriages' Regain Popularity in Iraq," *USA Today,* May 5, 2005, p. 8A; Bobby Caina Calvin, "In Shiite Iraq, Temporary Marriage May Be Rising," *McClatchy News,* www.mcclatchydc.com/103/story/21584.html (accessed June 9, 2009).

some other soft substance, but they are more likely to be simply identified with the word *seal* or the letters *L.S.* (an abbreviation for *locus sigilli,* which means "the place for the seal") at the end. Preprinted contract forms with a printed seal can be purchased today, and parties using them are presumed, without evidence to the contrary, to be adopting the seal for the contract.

U.S. states today do not require that contracts be under seal. However, 10 states still allow a contract without consideration to be enforced if it is under seal.

A **recognizance** arises when a person acknowledges in court that he or she will perform some specified act or pay a price upon failure to do so. A bond used as bail in a criminal case is a recognizance. The person agrees to return to court for trial or forfeit the bond.

A **letter of credit** is an agreement by the issuer to pay another party a sum of money on receipt of an invoice and other documents. The Uniform Commercial Code governs letters of credit.

Negotiable instruments (discussed in detail in Chapters 26 and 27) are unconditional written promises to pay the holder a specific sum of money on demand or at a certain time. The most common negotiable instruments are checks, notes, drafts, and certificates of deposit. They are governed primarily by the UCC.

Any contract that is not a formal contract is an **informal contract,** also called a **simple contract.** Informal contracts may in fact be quite complex, but they are called "simple" because no formalities are required in making them. Even though informal, or simple, contracts may appear less official, they are just as important and legally binding as their more formal counterparts. One particular case, *Baum v. Helget Gas Products, Inc.,* proved that something as basic as handwritten notes can be considered an enforceable employment contract in a court of law.

In *Baum v. Helget Gas Products, Inc.,*[3] Robert Baum alleged that a series of handwritten notes, which were compiled during his interview with Helget Gas Products, constituted a three-year employment contract with the company. The notes Baum took during the interview process outlined three years' worth of salary, bonuses, benefits, and vacation time as

[3] 440 F.3d 1019; 2006 U.S. App. (accessed on Lexis Nexis, April 4, 2009).

Exhibit 13-4   Classification of Contracts

BILATERAL	or	UNILATERAL
Consists of a promise in exchange for a promise		Requires a performance by the offeree to form a contract

EXPRESS	or	IMPLIED
The terms of the contract are clearly formed either in written or spoken words		Arises from the conduct of the parties rather than their words

EXECUTED	or	EXECUTORY
A contract whose terms have been fully performed		A contract in which not all the duties have been performed

FORMAL	or	INFORMAL
Contracts created in a specific manner: contracts under seal, recognizances, letters of credit, and negotiable instruments		Simple contracts that require no formalities in making them; payment can be demanded by the payee at any time (e.g., checks)

VALID	or	VOID	or	UNENFORCEABLE	or	VOIDABLE
A contract that has all the legal elements of a contract and thus can be enforced		Not a contract because either its object is illegal or it has a serious defect		A valid contract that can't be enforced because some law prohibits it		A contract in which one or both parties has the ability to either withdraw from or enforce the contract

discussed in the meetings. After being hired by the company, Baum also added "contract with Helget Gas Products St. Louis Mo. Market" to the top of the notes and had a Helget executive sign the document. Helget countered by saying that Baum, a salesman for the company, knew that he must meet certain performance goals each month or risk being fired. Thus, Helget's decision to fire Baum, based on his poor performance only a year after being hired, was legitimate. Helget further said that the itemizations produced by Baum in his notes were simply specifications of what Baum would receive if he remained employed by the company for the duration of three years and were not the components of an employment contract.

Initially, the district court agreed with Helget Gas Products and ruled against Baum on his breach-of-contract claim. However, Baum appealed, and the U.S Court of Appeals for the Eighth Circuit reversed the district court's judgment on the breach-of-contract claim. For business students, *Baum v. Helget Gas Products, Inc.,* demonstrates the importance of being aware of what you are agreeing to when you sign a document, regardless of how informal, or simple, it may seem.

For a summary of contract classification, see Exhibit 13-4.

A Question of Interpretation

Davco Holding Co. v. Wendy's International
2008 U.S. Dist. LEXIS 27108

Plaintiff Davco Holding Co., a franchisee of Wendy's, sued the company for breach of the franchise agreement for refusing to allow Davco to sell Pepsi from an unapproved supplier. The franchise agreement permits franchisees desiring to purchase products from an unapproved supplier to submit a written request to Wendy's for approval to do so. In response to Davco's written request to obtain beverage syrup from unapproved Pepsi, Wendy's informed Davco that CCF was the only approved supplier for fountain beverages and, further, that Pepsi syrup was not even an equivalent to Coke syrup because the drinks were made from two different secret formulas. The plaintiff alleged that Wendy's failed to adequately consider its request to solicit bids from Pepsi or to investigate Pepsi as a potential supplier and that this failure resulted in a breach by Wendy's of the franchise agreement.

The paragraph discussing the request for using an unapproved supplier contained the following language:

> Franchisor shall have the right to require that Franchisor be permitted to inspect the supplier's facilities, and that samples from the supplier be delivered, either to Franchisor or to an independent laboratory designated by Franchisor for testing. . . . Franchisor reserves the right to reinspect the facilities and products of any such approved supplier and to revoke its approval upon the supplier's failure to continue to meet any of Franchisor's then-current criteria. Nothing in the foregoing shall be construed to require Franchisor to approve any particular supplier, nor to require Franchisor to make available to prospective suppliers, standards and specifications for formulas that Franchisor, in its sole discretion, deems confidential.

The plaintiff claimed that Wendy's breached the agreement because it didn't inspect the facilities of Pepsi, request samples, or make its criteria available to Pepsi.

In interpreting the contract, the court said that where the terms of an existing contract are clear and unambiguous, the court "cannot create a new contract by finding an intent not expressed in the clear and unambiguous language of the written contract," and that a written agreement that appears complete and unambiguous on its face will not be given a construction other than that which the plain language of the contract provides.

As the court pointed out in dismissing the plaintiff's claims, the clause gives Wendy's the right to inspect a potential supplier, but giving someone a right to do something is not imposing a duty to do so. Thus, Wendy's failure to inspect cannot be a breach. Likewise, the terms of the clause clearly state that approval of another supplier lies within the sole discretion of Wendy's and that Wendy's does not have to share its criteria with the potential supplier.

Interpretation of Contracts

Perhaps the best-known rule of interpretation is the **plain-meaning rule,** which states that if a writing, or a term in question, appears to be plain and unambiguous on its face, we must determine its meaning from just "the four corners" of the document, without resorting to outside evidence, and give the words their ordinary meaning.

Although parties try to draft contracts as clearly as possible, sometimes they disagree about exactly what their obligations are under the agreement. Over time, the courts have developed some general guidelines to aid them in interpreting contracts and ascertaining the intentions of the parties:

- A judge should interpret a contract so as to give effect to the parties' intentions at the time they entered into the contract and to ensure the agreement makes sense as a whole. If possible, the court should ascertain the parties' intentions from the writing.

- If multiple interpretations are possible, the court should adopt the interpretation that makes the contract lawful, operative, definite, reasonable, and capable of being carried out.

LO4

What are the rules that guide the interpretation of contracts?

- If the contract contains ambiguity, the judge should interpret it against the interests of the drafter. After all, the drafter is the one who could have prevented the ambiguity in the first place.

- If there is a conflict between preprinted and handwritten terms, the handwritten ones prevail. If numerals and numbers written out in words conflict, the written words prevail. If there is a conflict between general terms and specific ones, the specific terms apply.

- The court should interpret technical words in a contract as they are usually understood by persons in the profession or business to which they relate, unless clearly used in a different sense.

The Case Nugget on page 317 illustrates how some of these principles can be important in determining the outcome of a case.

CASE OPENER WRAP-UP

A Questionable Contract

The main issue in the Hallmark case was whether a valid contract existed. Hallmark argued that by staying with the company beyond the effective date of the program, employees were agreeing to the terms of the contract. To Hallmark, the bargained-for exchange was continued employment in exchange for a promise to submit to arbitration in lieu of litigation. The circuit court sent the case to arbitration, where the arbitrator found that the program constituted a valid contract.

The appellate court, however, using the objective standard for determining whether a contract existed, found that there was not a valid contract. For a valid, bilateral contract to exist, both sides would have to be making a valid promise. Hallmark was not binding itself to anything. The program did not require Hallmark to submit its claims to arbitration or in any way bind the company to keep any other promise mentioned in the Dispute Resolution Program (DRP). Further, Hallmark had reserved the right to "modify or discontinue the DRP at any time."

In response to the claim that continued employment was given to the employees in exchange for their promise to submit all disputes to arbitration, the court found that no such promise had been made by Hallmark. The employees to be bound by the program were at-will employees. As such, employment could be terminated at any time by Hallmark. Thus, the employees were receiving no rights in regard to employment that they did not already have. Because no mutually binding promises were exchanged, the appellate court ruled that the trial court had erred in accepting the arbitrator's award. In other words, because there was no consideration from Hallmark, there was no binding contract to submit disputes to arbitration. The case was remanded for further proceedings on Morrow's discrimination and retaliation claims.[4]

[4] *Mary Kaye Morrow v. Hallmark Cards*, 273 S.W.3d 15, 2008 Mo. App. LEXIS 908.

Key Terms

acceptance 305	executed 314	letter of credit 315	Uniform Commercial
agreement 304	executory 314	negotiable instruments 315	Code (UCC) 308
bilateral contract 308	express contracts 310	offer 304	unilateral contract 309
consideration 305	formal contracts 314	plain-meaning rule 317	valid 314
contract 304	implied contracts 310	quasi-contracts 312	void 314
contractual capacity 305	informal contract 315	recognizance 315	voidable 314
covenant not	lack of genuine	simple contract 315	
to compete 304	assent 306	unenforceable 314	

Summary of Key Topics

The Definition of a Contract

Contracts at their simplest level are legally enforceable agreements. A *valid contract* is generally one that has the following elements:

- *Agreement,* which is made up of the offer and the acceptance.
- *Consideration,* which is the bargained-for exchange.
- *Legal object,* which means that the subject matter does not violate the law or public policy.
- *Parties with contractual capacity,* which means they are at least the age of majority and do not suffer from any defect that renders them unable to understand the nature of the contract or their obligations under it.

Sources of Contract Law

The two most important sources of contract law are state common law and the Uniform Commercial Code. The Uniform Commercial Code, in Article 2, governs contracts for the sale of goods. All other contracts are also governed by the UCC.

Classification of Contracts

Contracts may be classified in a number of ways. Every contract is either unilateral or bilateral; express or implied; valid, voidable, void, or enforceable; executed or executory; and formal or informal.

- A *unilateral contract* requires a performance in order to form a contract.
- A *bilateral contract* consists of a promise in exchange for a promise.
- An *express contract* has all the terms clearly set forth in either written or spoken words.
- An *implied contract* arises from the conduct of the parties rather than their words.
- A *valid contract* is one that contains *all* the legal elements of a contract (agreement, consideration, contractual capacity, and legal object).
- A contract is *void* when either its object is illegal or it has some defect so serious that it is not actually a contract.
- A contract is *unenforceable* when some law prohibits the court from enforcing an otherwise valid contract.
- A contract is *voidable* if one or both of the parties has the ability to withdraw from the contract or to enforce it.
- *Executed contracts* are those whose terms have been fully performed.
- A contract is considered *executory* when some of the duties have not yet been performed.

Interpretation of Contracts

Courts have established rules to help interpret contracts so that they can ascertain and enforce the intent of the agreement.

The *plain-meaning rule* requires that if a writing, or a term in question, appears to be plain and ambiguous, its meaning must be determined from the instrument itself, with the words given their ordinary meaning.

Point / Counterpoint

Should the Distinction between Sealed and Unsealed Contracts Be Abolished?

NO	YES
The distinction between sealed and unsealed contracts was drawn for several reasons, many of which are still relevant. As such, the distinction should remain intact despite the many attempts to have it abolished.	Advocates of abolishing the distinction between sealed and unsealed contracts argue that the distinction has become unnecessary and outdated. Sealed contracts can be dated back to medieval England when a substantial portion of the population was illiterate and many people were unable to sign their own names. As a result, each party to a sealed contract was responsible for impressing on the physical document a wax seal or some other mark bearing his or her individual sign of identification. The seals, in place of signatures, became proof of the parties' identities as well as the authenticity of the document.
Sealed contracts, at common law, did not require consideration. In many instances today, consideration is not a necessary part of the agreement. These instances include releases, modifications and discharges, promises to keep offers open, promises based on past consideration, and promises to make gifts. In these instances, one party is offering to give something without consideration. For example, an individual wishing to make a charitable donation could enter into a binding agreement to make the donation without receiving any consideration in return. By sealing the contract, the charitable organization receiving the donation would be protected against lawsuits arising from a lack of consideration. In this instance, the distinction between a sealed and unsealed contract would be the difference between a judgment in favor of the charitable organization despite the lack of consideration and an outright dismissal.	The practice of actually affixing a seal to a document is no longer necessary. Today, the parties to a sealed contract need only write the words "under seal," "sealed," or "l.s" (locus sigilli) for the document to be given the privileged status of a sealed document.
Additionally, sealed contracts are often accompanied by an increased statute of limitations. In instances when there are potentially long-term ramifications tied to the signing of a contract, a sealed contract would provide a much longer period in which the parties could sue than would be the case if the contract were left unsealed.	In response to those who argue that sealed contracts are necessary to bind contracts that do not contain consideration, abolishment advocates argue that there are other, and perhaps more meaningful, methods of accomplishing this. Instead of sealing a contract, one could (1) require that the promise without consideration be explicitly referenced and agreed to in the text itself; or (2) require that witnesses be present at the signing of the contract (as is the practice with regard to wills); or (3) simply rewrite the contract to provide for consideration.
Given the protections offered by sealed contracts, abolishing them would be irresponsible. Moreover, the elimination of the sealed-unsealed distinction would necessarily result in the creation of another method of enforcement. Why should we abolish a technique that provides protection to the parties involved in the making of a contract only to turn around and create a similar distinction under a different name?	The practice of sealing contracts is outdated and irrelevant. Parties to contracts lacking consideration could be more protected from lawsuits by using different methods of enforcement. The sealed contract should be abolished in all states (as has already been done in several states).

Questions & Problems

1. What are the elements of a valid contract?

2. What is the difference between an offer for a unilateral contract and an offer for a bilateral contract? Why might that difference be important to understand?

3. Explain how a valid contract differs from one that is void or voidable.

4. What is the objective theory of contracts?

5. What must a party prove to recover under the theory of quasi-contract?

6. What is the difference between a formal and an informal contract?

7. What is the plain-meaning rule?

8. AES was formed in 1996, hiring eight employees. At a meeting of these employees in 1997, they expressed concern that the company might not survive as it was using outdated equipment. At that meeting, a company executive asked the employees to remain with the firm and stated that the company was likely to merge with another firm, and if it did, the original eight employees would receive 5% of the value of the sale or merger as a reward for staying. In 2001, the firm was bought by another firm, and the seven employees who had stayed sought to collect their 5%. The company refused to pay on grounds there was no contract. Did the company and employees have a bilateral or a unilateral contract? Explain. [*Vanegas v. American Energy Services*, 302 S.W.3d 299 (2009 WL 4877734, Sup. Ct., Texas, 2009).]

9. Michael Merkle was fired from T-Mobile USA, Inc., after he had allegedly been seen drunk at a company conference. Merkle, who had worked for T-Mobile for 11 years, denied being drunk at the event. During a meeting between Merkle and the senior human resource manager, Merkle was simultaneously informed of the allegations against him and fired. When Merkle began employment at T-Mobile, he was given the company handbook, which sets forth T-Mobile's policy of internally investigating all claims of suspected or alleged employee misconduct. Merkle claimed that no internal investigation had been conducted. T-Mobile did not deny the existence of the investigation portion of the handbook or the lack of investigation in this case. The company did, however, contend that there were sufficient disclaimers throughout the handbook which stated that no portion of the handbook constituted a contract. Merkle further asserted that as a result of T-Mobile's investigations of other employees (one employee had actually been drunk) as well as the company's track record for providing warnings, a precedent had been set to provide a warning or investigation before termination. Merkle filed suit against T-Mobile for breach of an implied contract of employment. Do you think that T-Mobile's handbook and prior disciplinary actions constitute an implied contract of employment? Why or why not? [*Michael Merkle v. T-Mobile USA, Inc.,* 2008 U.S. Dist. LEXIS 63614.]

10. Anthony Maglica and Claire Halasz lived together, held themselves out as a married couple, and acted as companions toward each other. Claire changed her last name to "Maglica," even though the couple never married. Together, they worked in a business owned solely by Anthony, although Claire participated in a substantial part of the work and the two were paid equal salaries. The company, Mag Instrument, was incorporated in 1974, and all shares went to Anthony. After the company began manufacturing flashlights, the company grew rapidly, exceeding hundreds of millions of dollars in net worth. In 1992, Claire and Anthony separated, and subsequently Claire filed suit against Anthony for breach of contract and claimed damages under a theory of quasi-contract. No contract existed between Anthony and Claire. Does Claire have any remedy under a theory of quasi-contract? If so, what must she prove? [*Maglica v. Maglica,* 1998 Cal. App. LEXIS 750.]

Looking for more review material?

The Online Learning Center at **www.mhhe.com/kubasek2e** contains this chapter's "Assignment on the Internet" and also a list of URLs for more information, entitled "On the Internet." Find both of them in the Student Center portion of the OLC, along with quizzes and other helpful materials.

Agreement

PART 2

Contracts

LEARNING OBJECTIVES

After reading this chapter, you will be able to answer the following questions:

1   What are the elements of a valid offer?

2   How may an offer terminate?

3   What are the elements of an acceptance?

CASE OPENER
The Problematic Promotion

A Pepsi promotion encouraged consumers to collect "Pepsi points" and redeem them for merchandise. If they did not have quite enough points for the prize they wanted, they could buy additional points for 10 cents each; however, at least 15 original Pepsi points had to accompany each order.

In an early commercial for the promotion, which can be viewed on the Web at www. youtube.com/watch?v=U_n5SNrMaL8, three young boys are sitting in front of a high school, one reading his Pepsi Stuff catalog while the others drink Pepsi. All look up in awe at an object rushing overhead as the military march in the background builds to a crescendo. A Harrier Jet swings into view and lands by the side of the school building, next to a bicycle rack. Several students run for cover, and the velocity of the wind strips one hapless faculty member down to his underwear. The voice-over announces: "Now, the more Pepsi you drink, the more great stuff you're gonna get."

A teenager opens the cockpit of the fighter and can be seen, without a helmet, holding a Pepsi. He exclaims, "Sure beats the bus," and chortles. The military drumroll sounds a final time as the following words appear: "Harrier Fighter 7,000,000 Pepsi Points." A few seconds later, the following appears in more stylized script: "Drink Pepsi—Get Stuff."

A 21-year-old student named John Leonard decided to accept what he believed was Pepsi's offer of the Harrier fighter jet for 7 million Pepsi points. He quickly realized it

The plaintiff in the opening scenario hoped to obtain a jet like this one.

would be easier to raise the money to buy points than to collect 7 million points. In early March 1996, he filled out an order form requesting the jet and submitted it to Pepsi, along with 15 Pepsi points and a check for $700,000.

In response, Pepsi sent him a letter saying, "The item that you have requested is not part of the Pepsi Stuff collection. It is not included in the catalogue or on the order form, and only catalogue merchandise can be redeemed under this program." Leonard sued for breach of contract.

1. Did Pepsi offer to sell the Harrier jet for 7 million points?
2. Did Leonard's submission of the order form constitute an acceptance of an offer?

The Wrap-Up at the end of the chapter will answer these questions.

Elements of the Offer

LO1

What are the elements of a valid offer?

The first element of a contract is the agreement, which is made up of an offer and an acceptance, as shown in Exhibit 14-1. Formation of the agreement begins when the party initiating the contract, called the *offeror,* makes an offer to another party, called the *offeree.* The elements of an offer are (1) serious intent by the offeror to be bound to an agreement, (2) reasonably definite terms, and (3) communication to the offeree. Remember, this chapter focuses on the elements of a contract under the common law. Some of these elements have been modified under the UCC for contracts for the sale of goods, and we discuss these changes in Chapter 21.

INTENT

The first element of the offer is **intent.** The offeror must show intent to be bound by the offeree's acceptance. As explained in Chapter 13, we interpret contracts using an objective standard, meaning the courts are concerned only with the party's outward manifestations

Exhibit 14-1

The Formation of an Agreement

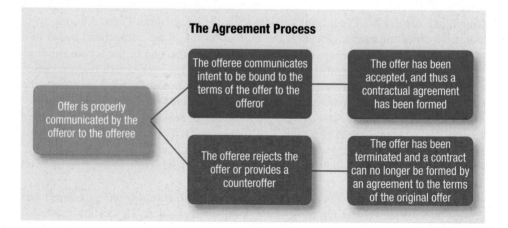

The Agreement Process

Offer is properly communicated by the offeror to the offeree

The offeree communicates intent to be bound to the terms of the offer to the offeror → The offer has been accepted, and thus a contractual agreement has been formed

The offeree rejects the offer or provides a counteroffer → The offer has been terminated and a contract can no longer be formed by an agreement to the terms of the original offer

of intent, not internal thought processes. The courts interpret the parties' words and actions the way a reasonable person would interpret them.

Thus, if Jude is clearly joking or speaking in anger, a reasonable person would not think Jude seriously intended to make an offer and the courts will not treat his words as an offer. If someone tries to accept Jude's offer, the courts will find a contract has not been made.

Sometimes an offeror may try to avoid being bound to a contract by later claiming she was only joking when she made the offer, but the courts are not interested in her hidden intent. As Case 14-1 demonstrates, if you joke too well, you may find yourself in an unwanted contract.

CASE 14-1   LUCY v. ZEHMER
SUPREME COURT OF APPEALS OF VIRGINIA
196 VA. 493, 84 S.E.2D 516 (1954)

Plaintiffs W. O. and J. C. Lucy had wanted to purchase Ferguson Farm from the Zehmers for at least eight years. One night, Lucy stopped by the establishment the Zehmers operated and said that he bet Zehmer wouldn't accept $50,000 for the place. Zehmer replied that he would, but he bet that Lucy wouldn't pay $50,000 for it. Over the course of the evening, the parties drank whiskey and engaged in casual conversation, with the talk repeatedly returning to the sale of Ferguson Farm. Eventually Lucy got Zehmer to draw up a contract for the sale of the farm for $50,000.

When Lucy later attempted to enforce the agreement, Zehmer refused to complete the sale, arguing that he had been drunk, and that the agreement to sell the property had been made in jest. Lucy sued to enforce the agreement. The trial court found for the defendants and the plaintiffs appealed.

JUSTICE BUCHANAN: If it be assumed, contrary to what we think the evidence shows, that Zehmer was jesting about selling his farm to Lucy and that the transaction was intended by him to be a joke, nevertheless the evidence shows that Lucy did not so understand it but considered it to be a serious business transaction and the contract to be binding on the Zehmers as well as on himself. The very next day he arranged with his brother to put up half the money and take a half interest in the land. The day after that he employed an attorney to examine the title. The next night, Tuesday, he was back at Zehmer's place and there Zehmer told him for the first time, Lucy said, that he wasn't going to sell, and he told Zehmer, "You know you sold that place fair and square." After receiving the report from his attorney that the title was good, he wrote to Zehmer that he was ready to close the deal.

Not only did Lucy actually believe, but the evidence shows he was warranted in believing, that the contract represented a serious business transaction and a good faith sale and purchase of the farm.

In the field of contracts, as generally elsewhere, "We must look to the outward expression of a person as manifesting his intention rather than to his secret and unexpressed intention. 'The law imputes to a person an intention corresponding to the reasonable meaning of his words and acts.'"

At no time prior to the execution of the contract had Zehmer indicated to Lucy by word or act that he was not in earnest about selling the farm. They had argued about it and discussed its terms, as Zehmer admitted, for a long time. Lucy testified that if there was any jesting it was about paying $50,000 that night. The contract and the evidence show that he was not expected to pay the money that night. Zehmer said that after the writing was signed he laid it down on the counter in front of Lucy. Lucy said Zehmer handed it to him. In any event there had been what appeared to be a good faith offer and a good faith acceptance, followed by the execution and apparent delivery of a written contract. Both said that Lucy put the writing in his pocket and then offered Zehmer $5 to seal the bargain. Not until then, even under the defendants' evidence, was anything said or done to indicate that the matter was a joke. Both of the Zehmers testified that when Zehmer asked his wife to sign he whispered that it was a joke so Lucy wouldn't hear and that it was not intended that he should hear.

The mental assent of the parties is not requisite for the formation of a contract. If the words or other acts of one of the parties have but one reasonable meaning, his undisclosed intention is immaterial except when an unreasonable meaning which he attaches to his manifestations is known to the other party.

The law, therefore, judges of an agreement between two persons exclusively from those expressions of their intentions which are communicated between them.

An agreement or mutual assent is of course essential to a valid contract but the law imputes to a person an intention corresponding to the reasonable meaning of his words and acts. If his words and acts, judged by a reasonable standard, manifest an intention to agree, it is immaterial what may be the real but unexpressed state of his mind.

So a person cannot set up that he was merely jesting when his conduct and words would warrant a reasonable person in believing that he intended a real agreement. . . .

Whether the writing signed by the defendants and now sought to be enforced by the complainants was the result of a serious offer by Lucy and a serious acceptance by the defendants, or was a serious offer by Lucy and

an acceptance in secret jest by the defendants, in either event it constituted a binding contract of sale between the parties.

Defendants contend further, however, that even though a contract was made, equity should decline to enforce it under the circumstances. These circumstances have been set forth in detail above. They disclose some drinking by the two parties but not to an extent that they were unable to understand fully what they were doing. There was no fraud, no misrepresentation, no sharp practice and no dealing between unequal parties. The farm had been bought for $11,000 and was assessed for taxation at $6,300. The purchase price was $50,000. Zehmer admitted that it was a good price. There is in fact present in this case none of the grounds usually urged against specific performance.

REVERSED and REMANDED in favor of Plaintiff.

CRITICAL THINKING

How can someone be held to have made a contract when the necessary acceptance was "in secret jest"? In other words, why must a joke be visibly a joke to a reasonable observer for there to be no acceptance?

ETHICAL DECISION MAKING

What stakeholders are being protected by this ruling? What value is playing the largest role in shaping this ruling?

Legal Principle: **In determining intent to enter into a contract, the court looks at the person's objective manifestation of intent and does not try to interpret what the person may have been secretly thinking.**

Preliminary Negotiations. An invitation to negotiate or an expression of possible interest in an exchange is not an offer because it does not express any willingness to be bound by an acceptance. For example, if Rachael asked Bill whether he would sell his car for $5,000, she is not making an offer; she is just inquiring about his potential willingness to sell. Likewise, when a firm or government entity requests bids for a construction project, the request is just an invitation for contractors to make offers. The bids, however, would be offers.

While it may seem easy to distinguish an offer from an invitation to negotiate, whether an offer in fact existed is a question of fact and sometimes ends up being litigated. When you are either making an offer or attempting to begin negotiations about a possible contract, you should use very precise language that clearly expresses your intent.

Advertisements. Another illustration of an offer to make an offer is the advertisement. If a custom furniture maker places an advertisement in the paper that reads, "Old-fashioned, hand-crafted cedar rocking chairs only $250 the first week in May," the store is merely inviting potential customers to come to the store and offer $250 for a rocker. Because no reasonable person would expect the store to be able to sell a rocking chair to

CASE NUGGET

When Is an Ad an Offer?

Lefkowitz v. Great Minneapolis Surplus Store, Inc.
251 Minn. 188, 86 N.W.2d 689 (1957)

Great Minneapolis Surplus Store published a newspaper announcement stating: "Saturday 9 AM Sharp, 3 Brand New Fur Coats, Worth up to $1,000.00, First Come First Served $1 Each." Morris Lefkowitz arrived at the store, dollar in hand, but was informed that under the defendant's "house rules," the offer was open to ladies but not gentlemen. The court ruled that because the plaintiff had fulfilled all the terms of the advertisement, and the advertisement was specific and left nothing open for negotiation, a contract had been formed.

From this case came the often-quoted exception to the rule that advertisements do not create any power of acceptance in potential offerees: an advertisement that is "clear, definite, and explicit, and leaves nothing open for negotiation." In that circumstance, "it constitutes an offer, acceptance of which will complete the contract." Unlike the illustration of the offer for an offer in the text, where the store obviously could not give every person who came to the store a rocking chair, in the Lefkowitz case, it was very clear that there were three new fur coats and the first three people who showed up with $1 would receive them. There was nothing indefinite or unclear about how to accept the offer.

every person who might see the ad, the court will interpret the intent of the store as being to invite readers to make an offer.

Under limited circumstances, however, an ad can be treated as an offer. If it appears from the wording that the store did, in fact, intend to make an offer, that is, the ad specifies a limited quantity and provides a specific means by which the offer can be accepted, the courts will treat the ad as an offer, as demonstrated by the Case Nugget.

John Leonard, the plaintiff in the case described in the opening scenario, tried to rely on the *Lefkowitz* decision to argue that the Pepsi commercial was an offer because it was "clear, definite, explicit, and left nothing to negotiation." After all, the commercial clearly stated that 7 million points earned a Harrier jet, and the catalog provided an additional means of buying the points for cash.

The court, however, found that the commercial could not be regarded as sufficiently definite because it specifically reserved the details of the offer to a separate writing, the catalog. Also, the commercial itself made no mention of the steps a potential offeree would be required to take to accept the alleged offer of a Harrier jet.

The court further found that the only offer in this scenario was the plaintiff's letter of March 27, 1996, along with the order form and appropriate number of Pepsi points. Since Pepsi rejected this offer with its letter, there is no contract.

Sometimes, however, unlike in the opening scenario, the advertiser's intent does appear to be to enter into a contract, even thought that is not what the advertiser subjectively had in mind. A good example of such a situation occurred when Cathy McGowan called in to a U.K. radio station to enter a contest and win the advertised prize: a brand new car. The radio DJ told McGowan that to win the new car, a Renault Clio, she would have to identify a scrambled version of a song. McGowan did correctly identify the song and was told that she could come down to the radio station to collect her prize. It was not until she arrived at the radio station that McGowan became aware that she was going to receive not an actual new car but, instead, a toy version of the Renault Clio.

An upset McGowan took her case to court and argued that the radio station broadcasters gave no indication to their listeners that the contest prize was actually a toy version of the car. A Derby crown court judge agreed with McGowan and ruled that the radio station had a legal contract to provide the contest winner with a new car. The judge further said that after reviewing the broadcast, he saw nothing that suggested the radio DJ was joking or intended to award contest winners with toy cars. Cathy McGowan was thus awarded £8,000, the cost of a new Renault Clio. The case, although from the United Kingdom, still has important implications for U.S. business students. In many respects U.K. contract laws are very similar to those of the United States, and had this case occurred on U.S. soil, a similar outcome would have been reached.[1]

To prevent possible "bait-and-switch" advertising that would appear as offers, some states have consumer protection laws requiring advertisers to state in their ads either that quantities of the item are limited to the first X number of people or that rain checks will be available if the item sells out.

Auctions.   Another situation in which what seems to be an offer may not be is the auction. When Janine places a good with an auctioneer for sale by auction, is she making an offer, or is Kevin, who bids on it? It depends on what kind of auction is taking place.

If nothing is stated to the contrary in the terms of the auction, an auction is presumed to be *with reserve,* which means that the seller is merely expressing intent to receive offers. The auctioneer may withdraw the item from auction at any time before the hammer falls, signaling the acceptance of the bid. The bidder may also revoke the bid before that point.

In an auction *without reserve,* the seller is treated as making an offer to accept the highest bid and therefore must accept it. Not surprisingly, very few auctions are without reserve.

Legal Principle: **If an auction is without reserve, the auctioneer must accept the lowest bid; if it is with reserve, the auctioneer may refuse to sell the item if he or she is not satisfied with the size of the highest bid.**

DEFINITE AND CERTAIN TERMS

Under the common law, the terms of the offer must be definite and certain. In other words, all the material terms must be included.[2] The material terms allow a court to determine damages in the event that one of the parties breaches the contract. They include the subject matter, price, quantity, quality, and parties.

Sometimes an offer contains not the material term itself but a method for determining it. For example, Hampton's Construction Company is building a new garage for Jones, and the parties want to make it possible for Jones to pay one-third of the price of the garage in advance, one-third upon completion, and one-third in 12 monthly payments, with interest, beginning a month after completion. Rather than stipulating an interest rate to be charged on the monthly payments, the contract might specify an external standard according to which the interest rate would be set through the course of the 12-month payment period.

The question of whether the terms of an alleged offer were adequate for the formation of a valid contract often arises when one party believes a contract has been formed and the other believes the terms were not definite enough. That issue is the focus of Case 14-2.

COMMUNICATION TO THE OFFEREE

The third element of the offer is communication. The offer must be communicated to the offeree or the offeree's agent. Only the offeree (or his agent acting on his behalf) can accept the offer. If Bill overhears Sam offer to sell his car to Helen for $5,000, Bill cannot walk over and form a contract with Sam by accepting the offer to Helen. If he says to Sam, "I'll give you $5,000 for your car," he is not accepting the offer but, rather, is making a new offer.

---

[1] www.dailymail.co.uk/news/article-40153/8-000-Clio-winner-handed-toy.html.

[2] See UCC § 2-204 or Chapter 21 of this text for the modification of this element for sales of goods contracts.

ANDRUS v. STATE, DEPARTMENT OF TRANSPORTATION, AND CITY OF OLYMPIA
WASHINGTON STATE APPELLATE COURT
117 P.3D 1152 (WASH. APP. 2005)

Scott Andrus applied for a position as a building inspector with the city of Olympia. He received a call from Tom Hill, an engineering supervisor with the city. Hill stated, "You're our number one choice, and I'm offering you the job." Andrus responded "Great" and "Yes." Hill did not discuss the specifics of the job, so Andrus asked Hill to fax him those details. The city never sent such a fax or a written job offer and request for acceptance.

On the same day that Andrus received the call from Hill, the city checked Andrus's employment references, including his current employer (the Washington Department of Transportation), which proved unsatisfactory. Hill called Andrus the next day, informing him that the city had withdrawn the job offer because of further reference checks.

Andrus sued the city and the DOT, claiming wrongful discharge and arguing that the phone call from Hill offering the position was an employment contract. He also alleged

the DOT was liable for defamation for providing a bad employment reference to the city. The superior court granted the city's request to dismiss his claims without a trial, and he appealed only the breach of contract claim against the city.

JUSTICE QUINN-BRINTNALL: An enforceable contract requires, among other things, an offer with *reasonably certain* terms. Restatement (Second) of Contracts §33 (1979) ("The fact that one or more terms of a proposed bargain are left open or uncertain may show that a manifestation of intention is not intended to be understood as an offer or as an acceptance"). Hill's "job offer" contained no starting date, salary, or benefit information. Moreover, it was to be followed by a written offer and request for acceptance. Under these facts, the July 13 phone conversation did not form an employment contract.

AFFIRMED in favor of the city.

CRITICAL THINKING

How could the original phone call from Hill be considered an employment contract? What would have to be included in the conversation? What could be left out? How different do you think the call would have needed to be to qualify as an employment contract between the plaintiff and the city? Why?

ETHICAL DECISION MAKING

How well does this decision hold up under examinations of ethicality, such as the public disclosure test and the universalization test? Do you think Justice Quinn-Brintall took such examinations into account in reaching this decision? Why or why not?

Legal Principle: To have a valid offer under the common law, you need (1) the intent to be bound by an acceptance, (2) definite and certain terms, and (3) communication to the offeree.

Termination of the Offer

Offers, once made, do not last forever. At some point in time they terminate. When an offer is terminated, the offeree can no longer accept it to form a binding contract. Termination of an offer can occur in one of five ways: revocation by the offeror, rejection or counteroffer by the offeree, death or incapacity of the offeror, destruction or subsequent illegality of

L02

How may an offer terminate?

the subject matter of the offer, or lapse of time or failure of other conditions stated in the offer. Each method is discussed below and summarized in Exhibit 14-2.

REVOCATION BY THE OFFEROR

To see how the six components of communication relate to the making of an agreement, please see the **Connecting to the Core** activity on the text Web site at www.mhhe.com/kubasek2e.

The offeror is said to be the "master of his or her offer" and, as such, can revoke it at any time, even if the offer states it will be open for a specified period of time. If Jim sends Carol a letter offering to mow her yard every week during the summer for the price of $20 per week as long as she responds to his offer within the next month, he can still change his mind and tell her at any time before she responds that he is no longer interested in working for her, thereby revoking his offer.

As a general rule, a **revocation** is effective when the offeree receives it. If it is really important to the offeror that the offeree know the offer has been revoked, the offeror should deliver the revocation personally.

Exceptions to the Revocability of the Offer. An offeree who wishes to ensure that an offer will in fact be held open for a set period of time may do so by entering into an option contract with the offeror. In an **option contract** the offeree gives the offeror a piece of consideration in exchange for holding the offer open for the specified period of time.

There is no requirement as to the value of the consideration. If it is money, the parties may agree that if the offer is eventually accepted and a contract is formed, the consideration will become part of the offeree's payment under the contract. This situation frequently arises in real estate contracts. Jose may be considering opening a restaurant and would like to have the option of purchasing a lot owned by Simone, so he gives her $1,000 for a 30-day option to purchase, with the provision that she will deduct the $1,000 from the purchase price if Jose purchases the property. If he does not, Simone will keep the $1,000.

Detrimental reliance on the offer may also form the basis for the court's not allowing the offeror to revoke an offer. If the offeree had reasonably relied on the offeror's promise to hold the offer open and had taken action in reliance on the offer, the courts may use the doctrine of promissory estoppel to estop, or prevent, the offeror from revoking his offer.

Detrimental reliance also comes into play to prevent a party who made a unilateral offer from revoking the offer once the offeree has begun performance of the action necessary to accept the unilateral offer. While the contract cannot be considered formed until the action requested has been completed, most courts recognize that to allow the offeror to revoke her offer after the offeree has expended significant amounts of time or money in

Exhibit 14-2

Ways an Offer Can Be Terminated

Revocation	The offeror can revoke the offer at any time unless the offeree entered into an option contract with the offeror.
Rejection	The offeree can reject the offer.
Counteroffer	If the offeree offers a counteroffer, the original offer is terminated.
Death or incapacity	If the offeror becomes incapacitated or dies, the offer immediately terminates.
Illegality	If the subject matter of the offer becomes illegal, the offer immediately terminates.
Lapse of time	The offer will expire after a reasonable amount of time, which depends on the subject matter of the offer, unless a specific time condition is given.

reliance on the offer would be to allow an unjustifiable injustice to occur. Therefore, once significant partial performance in reliance has begun, most courts require that the offeror give the offeree a reasonable amount of time to complete performance.

REJECTION OR COUNTEROFFER BY THE OFFEREE

The second means by which an offer can be terminated is **rejection** by the offeree. Regardless of how long the offer was stated to be open, once the offeree rejects it, it is terminated. In our earlier illustration, if Carol calls Jim and says she is not interested in his working for her this summer or any summer because of the poor quality of his work but then she calls him back an hour later to say she has changed her mind and would like to hire him in accordance with his proposed terms, it is too late. There is no offer for her to accept because her rejection terminated it.

In the same illustration, if Carol tells Jim she would indeed like him to cut her grass every week this summer but will pay him only $15 each week, she has made a **counteroffer,** defined by the Restatement as "an offer made by an offeree to his offeror relating to the same matter as the original offer and proposing a substituted bargain differing from that proposed by the original offer."[3] A counteroffer terminates the original offer, and so Carol's counteroffer terminates Jim's original offer. Thus, if you receive an offer that you might want to accept but you are wondering whether you can get better terms, you should inquire about how set the offeror is on the terms proposed before you make a counteroffer. For example, Carol might have simply asked Jim whether he would consider doing the job at any other price.

DEATH OR INCAPACITY OF THE OFFEROR

An offer terminates immediately if the offeror dies or loses the legal capacity to enter into the contract, even if the offeree does not know of the terminating event. If the parties had already entered into an option contract to hold the offer open for a set period of time, however, the administrator of the offeror's estate or the guardian of the offeror must hold the offer open until it expires in accordance with the option contract.

DESTRUCTION OR SUBSEQUENT ILLEGALITY OF THE SUBJECT MATTER

If the subject matter of the offer is destroyed or becomes illegal, the offer immediately terminates. For example, if Jamie offers Mercedes a job managing the riverboat casino he plans to open on January 1 but, before Mercedes accepts the offer, the state decides to no longer allow riverboat casinos to operate, the offer of employment terminates.

LAPSE OF TIME OR FAILURE OF ANOTHER CONDITION SPECIFIED IN THE OFFER

We've noted that the offeror has the power to revoke the offer at any time, even if the offer states that it will be held open for a set period. But if the offer states that it will be held open for only a certain time, it terminates when that time expires. In the absence of such a time condition, the offer will expire after the lapse of a reasonable amount of time. What constitutes a reasonable amount of time varies, depending on the subject matter of the offer. An offer by a retailer to purchase seasonal goods from a wholesaler would lapse sooner than an offer to purchase goods that could be easily sold all year long. The Case Nugget illustrates

---

[3] Restatement (Second) of Contracts, sec. 39 (1981).

The Importance of Conditions in Offers

Adone v. Paletto
2005 NY Slip Op 50196U; 6 Misc.
3d 1026A; 800 N.Y.S.2d 341

On July 26, 2004, the defendants' counsel made an "Offer to Compromise" and settle the action in the amount of $500,000, plus costs accrued to that date, which represented the entire available coverage under the defendants' insurance policy. Part of the offer stated:

> If within ten days thereafter the claimant serves a written notice that he accepts the offer, either party may file the summons, complaint, and offer, with proof of acceptance, and thereupon the clerk shall enter judgment accordingly. If the offer is not accepted and the claimant fails to obtain a more favorable judgment, he shall not recover costs from

the time of the offer, but shall pay costs from that time. An offer of judgment shall not be made known to the jury.

On August 9, 2004, the parties appeared before the court for a settlement conference in which the plaintiffs' counsel made a demand of $700,000 to settle the case. This demand was clearly not an acceptance of the offer to compromise; instead, it was a counteroffer that rejected that $500,000 offer.

The plaintiffs' $700,000 demand was not acceptable to the defendants, and the case was not settled. On September 24, 2004, the plaintiffs' counsel sent a letter to the defendants accepting the $500,000 judgment offered two months earlier, which was to include interest from the date of the summary judgment and costs. On September 28, the defendants rejected the acceptance in writing because it was not within 10 days of the offer.

The plaintiffs' motion for a judgment to enforce the offer to compromise was denied because the acceptance was not within the 10-day time frame.

the consequences of not paying attention to the time or other limiting conditions specified in an offer, and a summary of the ways a contract can be terminated can be found in Exhibit 14-2.

The Acceptance

LO3

What are the elements of an acceptance?

Once an offer has been made, the offeree has the power to accept that offer and form a contract. Under the common law, the basic requirements for a valid **acceptance** parallel those for a valid offer. There should be a manifestation of intent to be bound by the acceptance to the contract, agreement to the definite and certain terms of the offer, and communication to the offeror.

MANIFESTATION OF INTENT TO BE BOUND TO THE CONTRACT

In general, there are two ways an offeree can manifest intent to enter into the contract: by performance or by a return promise. The offeree must either do or say something to form the contract.

Recall, from Chapter 12, the distinction between a bilateral and a unilateral contract. If the offer is for a unilateral contract, the offeree can accept only by providing the requested performance. If Bill offered to pay $500 to anyone who returned his lost dog to him, Mary could accept the offer only by returning the dog. Bill did not want her promise, and if she called and promised to return the dog to him, that promise would have no legal effect because the only way to accept a unilateral offer is by performance.

Remember from the previous section that the offeror has the right to revoke the offer at any time before it has been accepted. This rule is slightly modified with respect to unilateral offers so that if one party has begun performance, the offeror must give the offeree a reasonable time to complete it.

In a bilateral contract, what the offeror wants is not performance but, rather, a return promise. Sometimes, however, it is not clear what the offeror wants. Then the offeree has the option of either performing or making a return promise.

Contracts in Japan

The Japanese tend to view contracts as ongoing relationships in which parties work with each other to smooth out any problems that arise in performance of the contract. Often suspicious of long, detailed contracts, they have a distinct preference for short, flexible agreements that leave a number of terms to be decided later.

Silence as a Form of Acceptance. Silence, as a general rule, cannot be used to form a contract. Lisa and Marie both work at a local diner where the manager is very flexible about their hours and lets them trade shifts. Marie leaves Lisa a voice-mail message saying, "I can't work my three night shifts this week. If you can cover them for me, I'll pay you an extra $40 on top of the money you'll receive from the boss for working my shifts. If I don't hear from you by 7 p.m. tomorrow, I'll assume we have a deal. Thanks so much!" If Lisa does not call back, no contract has been formed because silence under these circumstances will not constitute acceptance.

There are, however, a few situations in which silence *can* mean acceptance. In the most common, the parties, by their previous course of dealing with each other, have established a pattern of behavior whereby it is reasonable to assume silence communicates acceptance. If a wholesaler and a retailer have a long-standing relationship in which the retailer will reject a shipment that does not meet his needs, when a shipment is not sent back it is reasonable for the wholesaler to assume that the retailer means to accept it.

Silence can also be acceptance when the offeree receives the benefits of the offered services with reasonable opportunity to reject them and knowledge that some form of compensation is expected yet remains silent. In this case, an implied-in-fact contract is created. Because many unscrupulous businesspersons once took advantage of this rule and sent unordered merchandise to people, stating the goods could be returned or be kept on payment of a set price, most states have passed laws providing that unsolicited merchandise does not have to be returned and the recipient may keep it as a gift, with no contract being formed.

A third situation occurs when the parties agree that silence will be an acceptance. For example, a person may join a book club whose contract provides that a new book will be sent every month if the member does not send notification rejecting the month's selection.

ACCEPTANCE OF DEFINITE AND CERTAIN TERMS: THE MIRROR-IMAGE RULE

When a bilateral contract is being formed under the common law, the mirror-image rule applies to the acceptance. The **mirror-image rule** says that the terms of the acceptance must mirror the terms of the offer. If they do not, no contract is formed. Instead, the attempted acceptance is a counteroffer.[4]

COMMUNICATION TO THE OFFEROR

An offeror has the power to control the means by which the acceptance is communicated, so if the offeror specifies that only a certain means of communication will be accepted, then only an acceptance by that means forms a valid contract. Suppose Jennifer offers to paint Rashad's car for $500 but says he must accept the offer by telephone before midnight

---

[4] See UCC § 2-207 and Chapter 21 for an explanation of how the UCC modifies the mirror-image rule for contracts for the sale of goods.

on Thursday. If Rashad sends Jennifer an e-mail Thursday morning accepting her offer, there is no contract. Even though e-mail might be a valid means of accepting a contract offer if no means is specified, when the offer is limited to a specific means of communicating the acceptance, only that means results in a valid contract. Thus, Rashad's attempted acceptance was simply a new offer.

If no means of communicating the acceptance is specified, any reasonable means is generally acceptable. Telephone, mail, fax, and e-mail are all valid means of accepting an offer, as is accepting it in person. When drafting an offer, if a person wishes acceptance to be only by a particular means, the offer must make it clear that only certain means are allowed. As Case 14-3 illustrates, courts will carefully interpret provisions specifying the means of acceptance.

CASE 14-3   OSPREY L.L.C. v. KELLY-MOORE PAINT CO.
SUPREME COURT OF OKLAHOMA
984 P.2D 194, 1999 OKLA. LEXIS 64

The plaintiff leased commercial premises to the defendant. The lease required that defendant provide notice of its intent to renew the lease at least six months prior to the lease's expiration, and notice was to be given in writing and delivered personally or through registered first class mail. Defendant attempted to extend the lease by faxing a renewal letter on the last day of the six-month notification period. Although fax and telephone records confirmed the fax was transmitted, the plaintiff denied receiving it.

The plaintiff refused to renew the lease and demanded the defendant vacate the premises at the end of the current lease term. The defendant refused to vacate the premises, so the plaintiff filed an action for forcible entry and detainer.

The trial court found the faxed notice effectively renewed the lease, and the appeals court reversed. The supreme court granted certiorari.

JUDGE KAUGER: . . . The precise issue of whether a faxed or facsimile delivery of a written notice to renew a commercial lease is sufficient to exercise timely the renewal option of the lease is one of first impression in Oklahoma. Neither party has cited to a case from another jurisdiction which has decided this question, or to any case which has specifically defined "personal delivery" as including facsimile delivery.

Osprey argues that: 1) the lease specifically prescribed limited means of acceptance of the option, and it required that the notice of renewal be delivered either personally or sent by United States mail, registered or certified; 2) Kelly-Moore failed to follow the contractual requirements of the lease when it delivered its notice by fax; and 3) because the terms for extending the lease specified in the contract

were not met, the notice was invalid and the lease expired on August 31, 1997. Kelly-Moore counters that: 1) the lease by the use of the word "shall" mandates that the notice be written, but the use of the word "may" is permissive; and 2) although the notice provision of the lease permits delivery personally or by United States mail, it does not exclude other modes of delivery or transmission which would include delivery by facsimile. Kelly-Moore also asserts that the lease specified that time was of the essence and that faxing the notice was the functional equivalent of personal delivery because it provided virtually instantaneous communication.

Although the question tendered is novel in Oklahoma, the sufficiency of the notice given when exercising an option contract or an option to renew or extend a lease has been considered by several jurisdictions. A few have found that delivery of notice by means other than hand delivery or by certified or registered mail was insufficient if the terms of the contract specifically referred to the method of delivery. However, the majority have reached the opposite conclusion. These courts generally recognize that, despite the contention that there must be strict compliance with the notice terms of a lease option agreement, use of an alternative method does not render the notice defective if the substituted method performed the same function or served the same purpose as the authorized method.

Language in a contract is given its plain and ordinary meaning, unless some technical term is used in a manner meant to convey a specific technical concept. . . . The lease does not appear to be ambiguous. "Shall" is ordinarily construed as mandatory and "may" is ordinarily construed as permissive. The contract clearly requires that notice "shall" be in writing. The provision for delivery, either personally or by certified or registered mail, uses the permissive "may" and it does not bar other modes of transmission which are just as effective.

The purpose of providing notice by personal delivery or registered mail is to insure the delivery of the notice, and to settle any dispute which might arise between the parties concerning whether the notice was received. A substituted method of notice which performs the same function and serves the same purpose as an authorized method of notice is not defective. Here, the contract provided that time was of the essence. Although Osprey denies that it ever received the fax, the fax activity report and telephone company records confirm that the fax was transmitted successfully, and that

it was sent to Osprey's correct facsimile number on the last day of the deadline to extend the lease. The fax provided immediate written communication similar to personal delivery and, like a telegram, would be timely if it were properly transmitted before the expiration of the deadline to renew. Kelly-Moore's use of the fax served the same function and the same purpose as the two methods suggested by the lease and it was transmitted before the expiration of the deadline to renew. Under these facts, we hold that the faxed or facsimile delivery of the written notice to renew the commercial lease was sufficient to exercise timely the renewal option of the lease.

REVERSED in favor of Defendant.

CRITICAL THINKING

Could the information provided in this case lead to a different conclusion than that reached by the court? Would some elements need to be considered differently? How would their interpretation need to be changed?

Might a different court have viewed this dispute differently? Come up with a short list of personal characteristics that might lead the deciding body to rule in this way and a contrasting list of characteristics that might have led the court to an opposite conclusion.

ETHICAL DECISION MAKING

Consider Osprey's denial of receiving the fax in question from Kelly-Moore. If this denial does amount to a false claim, what is the motivation for it? What is its ultimate purpose?

How might different ethical perspectives lead to contradictory opinions regarding this behavior? Does it necessarily amount to a blameworthy action? Why or why not?

The Mailbox Rule. Because not all acceptances are made in person, the courts needed a rule to determine the point at which an acceptance made through the mail became effective. They settled on the **mailbox rule,** which provides that an acceptance is valid when the offeree places it in the mailbox, whereas a revocation is effective only when the offeree receives it. The mailbox rule is not applicable when there is instantaneous communication, such as over the phone, in person, or by telex.

Since the mailbox rule does not apply to instantaneous communications, when are faxes, text messages, and e-mail effective? Are these instantaneous forms of communication? Text messages seem the easiest to answer yes to. There is still some disagreement among jurisdictions as to whether faxes and e-mail should be effective on dispatch or receipt. The majority rule with respect to faxes appears to be that faxes are instantaneous transmissions and therefore effective on receipt, but some jurisdictions have applied the mailbox rule to them. There seems to be greater split among the jurisdictions over how to treat e-mail transmissions. The Uniform Electronic Transactions Act seems to create an electronic version of the mailbox rule, providing that an e-mail is sent when properly addressed to an information processing system designated by the recipient, in a form capable of being processed by that system, and enters an information processing system out of the control of the sender. It is considered received when it enters the information processing system designated by the recipient.

Authorized Means of Acceptance. The means by which the offeree can communicate acceptance to the offeror may either be expressly stated in the offer, which is called an *express authorization,* or be implied from the facts and circumstances surrounding the communication of the offer to the offeree. If the offer specifies that acceptance must be communicated by a specific mode, that mode is the only means for accepting the offer, and once the acceptance is dispatched, the contract has been formed. If any other attempted means of acceptance is used, there is no valid contract. For example, if the offer says acceptance must be by certified mail, then as soon as the acceptance is taken to the post office, there is a valid contract. If the offeree instead faxes an acceptance, there is no contract.

According to the Restatement, if no mode of communication is specified in the offer, any reasonable means of acceptance is valid. To determine the reasonableness of the means, courts look at such factors as the means by which the offer was communicated and the surrounding circumstances.

Effect of an Unauthorized Means of Acceptance. As noted above, when an offer specifies that acceptance must be communicated by a particular mode, no other form of acceptance is valid. However, if the offer merely authorizes certain modes of acceptance but does not condition acceptance on the use of those modes, use of an unauthorized means of acceptance is acceptable but the contract is not formed until the acceptance is received by the offeror. For example, if Beth sends an offer to Joe via a fax, saying in the offer that acceptance may be via fax or e-mail, and Joe accepts her offer by overnight mail, his acceptance is valid but it is effective only on receipt.

If the offeree makes a mistake and sends the acceptance to the wrong address, there is no acceptance on dispatch. However, if a correction is made and the letter eventually reaches the offeror, the acceptance is valid on receipt, assuming the offer was still open.

The Effect of an Acceptance after a Rejection. We've seen that if an acceptance is received after a rejection, the acceptance is not valid because the rejection terminated the offer. However, sometimes a rejection is dispatched, but before it is received, the acceptance is communicated to the offeror. In that case, a valid contract has been formed because the rejection is not effective until it is received. Suppose Brenda e-mails an offer to Harry, and he puts a rejection in the mail; then, before it is received, Harry calls Brenda and tells her he accepts. A valid contract has been formed, and the rejection will have no effect when Brenda receives it. However, if Harry telephoned after Brenda had received the rejection, there could be no contract.

CASE OPENER WRAP-UP

Harrier Jet

Much to the plaintiff's dismay, the court in the Pepsi case found that the commercial could not be regarded as sufficiently definite to be an offer, because it specifically reserved the details of the offer to a separate writing, the catalog.[5] Also, the commercial itself made no mention of the steps a potential offeree would be required to take to accept the alleged offer of a Harrier jet. As in most cases where a consumer attempts to place an order for an advertised item, the court regarded the plaintiff's purported acceptance as an offer. And it was an offer that Pepsi obviously rejected. And while the court did not specifically mention this factor, common sense should have indicated to the plaintiff and his family that Pepsi did not really intend to give a harrier jet as one of the promotional prizes.

Key Terms

acceptance   332
communication   328
counteroffer   331

definite and certain terms   328
intent   324
mailbox rule   335

material terms   335
mirror-image rule   333
option contract   330

rejection   331
revocation   330
termination   329

Summary of Key Topics

Elements of the Offer	A valid offer requires (1) the manifestation of the offeror's intent to be bound, (2) definite and certain terms, and (3) communication to an offeree.
Termination of the Offer	An offer can be terminated by revocation by the offeror; rejection or counteroffer by the offeree; death or incapacity of the offeror; destruction or subsequent illegality of the subject matter of the offer; or lapse of time or failure of other conditions stated in the offer.
The Acceptance	An acceptance is valid when a manifestation of intent to be bound to the terms of the offer is communicated to the offeror by the offeree.

[5] *Leonard v. Pepsico*, 210 F.3d 88, 2000 U.S. App. LEXIS 6855.

Point / Counterpoint

Should Internet Click-Wrap and Browse-Wrap Agreements Be Treated as Legally Binding Contacts?

YES	NO

YES

Nearly all computer users have, at some point, encountered form contracts while browsing the Internet. Whether they pertain to downloading software, signing up for a free e-mail service, or making an online purchase, many online forms are designed to protect the host company or retail store's interests. To protect these companies and ensure continued online commerce, these contracts *must* be viewed as legally binding.

The two types of Internet contracts are click-wrap and browse-wrap contracts. A click-wrap contract requires that users read all terms and conditions before clicking an "I Agree" button. Such contracts give users the ability to *choose* whether to accept the conditions and proceed or decline and withdraw. This process includes an offer by the offeror (the terms and conditions as listed) and acceptance by the offeree (clicking the "I Agree" button). The contract includes a clear manifestation of the offeree's intent to be bound when he or she clicks the accept button.

In the second type of Internet contract, the browse-wrap agreement, the user is not required by the site to click any button but is seen under the law as having accepted the terms by viewing the Web site. In such instances, the site provides its terms and conditions via a hyperlink at the top of a Web page. By posting the link, the Web site has provided users with notice that there are terms and conditions associated with the site and that users who continue making use of the site should be bound by those terms. By viewing the site (the performance), the user is bound to the terms (the offer).

Given the large quantity of transactions occurring over the Internet, browse-wrap and click-wrap agreements offer an efficient means for governance. In an effort to protect companies and ensure compliance by consumers, these agreements *must* be treated as legally binding contracts.

NO

Nearly all computer users have agreed to and proceeded beyond click-wrap agreements. Many of these computers users have used Web sites that have browse-wrap agreements embedded within their pages. But the mere existence of these agreements does not mean that they are valid contracts under existing contract laws; they should not.

In both click-wrap and browse-wrap agreements, the terms are decided prior to the user even installing the software or visiting the site. The user is not given an opportunity to negotiate the terms; in essence, there is no meeting of the minds. If the user wishes to use the Web site, software, or e-mail system, he/she must accept the prewritten terms.

Click-wrap agreements have become so prevalent throughout recent years that Internet users often ignore the text of the agreement and simply click the "I Agree" box. Without reading and understanding the terms of the agreement, lawyers, consumers, and companies are left to wonder whether the user lacked genuine assent.

Browse-wrap agreements, unlike click-wrap agreements, are not even located on the general Web page. In order to view the terms and conditions of use, the user must find the hyperlink on a page, click on it, read the terms, and then decide whether or not to continue reading the Web page. The site owners cannot be certain that users will find, read, or understand the terms and conditions of use before they browse the site. Without knowledge, Internet users should not be bound to the terms and conditions.

Finally, when paper contracts are signed, one can be certain whom the relevant parties are. With electronic contracts, that certainty quickly dissipates. Even though a click-wrap agreement is offered and accepted, without proper verification, one cannot be certain who was using the computer at the time the contract was formed. If, for example, a friend uses your computer while visiting your dorm room and enters into a click-wrap agreement, which you later violate unknowingly, who is accountable? Can you prove you were not the one who agreed to the terms? Identifying the parties associated with electronic contracts would be more difficult than identifying those associated with paper contracts.

Questions & Problems

1. What is the mirror-image rule?

2. What is the mailbox rule?

3. In response to an excessive supply of 1954 Ford models, Capital City Ford heavily advertised in newspapers and on the radio the following message:

TWO FOR ONE . . . For two weeks BUY A NEW '54 FORD NOW TRADE EVEN FOR A '55 FORD. Don't Wait—Buy a 1954 Ford now, when the 1955 models come out we'll trade even for your '54. You pay only sales tax and license fee. Your '55 Ford will be the same model, same body style, accessory group, etc. A sure thing for you—a gamble for us, but we'll take it. Hurry, though, this offer good only for the remainder of September. The 1954 car must be returned with only normal wear and tear. Physical damage, such as dented fenders, torn upholstery, etc. must be charged to owner or repaired at owner's expense. No convertibles or Skyliners on this basis.

In response to the advertisement, Leland Johnson purchased a 1954 Ford and later requested that Capital City Ford accept his 1954 as an even trade for the new 1955 model. However, Capital City Ford refused, claiming that the advertisement was merely an invitation to bargain. In response, Johnson sued for specific performance of the contract, claiming that the advertisement was an offer and that his purchasing of the 1954 model operated as an acceptance. Which argument do you find most persuasive? Why? What did the court hold? [*Johnson v. Capital City Ford Co.,* 85 So. 2d 75, 79 (La. Ct. App. 1955).]

4. Michael and Laurie Montgomery negotiated with Norma English with regard to the potential sale of the Montgomerys' home. English submitted a bid for $272,000, but she included a request to purchase some of the Montgomerys' personal property and expressed that an "as-is" provision was not applicable to the sale. When the Montgomerys received the offer, they deleted the personal property provision, deleted provisions related to latent defects and a building inspection, and added a specific as-is rider. English's agent then delivered the counteroffer to English, who initialed many, but not all, of the Montgomerys' modifications, such as the deletion of the personal property provision. The Montgomerys refused to proceed with the sale, so English filed suit for specific performance of the contract. Under the mirror-image rule, did a contract exist between the Montgomerys and English? Why or why not? [*Montgomery v. English,* 2005 Fla. App. LEXIS 4704.]

5. Wilbert Heikkila, wanting to sell eight of his parcels of land, signed an agreement with Kangas Realty. Thereafter, David McLaughlin met with a Kangas representative, who created a handwritten offer to purchase three of the parcels. McLaughlin signed the offer and provided the Kangas agent with three earnest-money checks for each parcel. The agent then created three separate purchase agreements, which McLaughlin did not sign, but his wife did sign and initial all three agreements. Two days later, Heikkila met with the Kangas agent, changing the price on all three parcels by writing on the purchase agreements. Heikkila also altered the closing dates for the parcels and reserved mineral rights for each parcel. The McLaughlins did not make any additional marks or signings on the purchase agreements. However, the Kangas agent returned the checks to the McLaughlins, indicating that Heikkila had withdrawn his offer to sell the parcels. The court held that this transaction was subject to the statute of frauds, which requires that a contract for the sale of land be in writing. Were there an offer and an acceptance, thereby creating an enforceable contract? Why or why not? [*McLaughlin v. Heikkila,* 2005 Minn. App. LEXIS 591.]

6. The Pennsylvania Department of Transportation (PennDOT) issued a Request for Bid Proposal for Vending Machine Services for rest areas on highways in the state. ATI submitted the lowest bid for the sites. PennDOT selected ATI for a contract for 35 vending sites. Enclosed with the notice of award sent to ATI was a service purchase contract to be executed by ATI, by PennDOT, by the commonwealth comptroller, and by PennDOT's attorney. Also, "if required," signature lines for the Office of General Counsel and the Attorney General's Office were provided. The award notice indicated that the contract would become effective "after all approvals have been received from the administrative and fiscal personnel in Harrisburg" and further stated that

no activities may be performed until the contract is fully executed. ATI returned an executed contract to PennDOT. PennDOT's director of the Bureau of Maintenance and Operations and a representative from its legal department executed the agreement. The comptroller and Office of General Counsel subsequently signed the contract; however, the Attorney General's Office refused to execute the agreement. The Attorney General's Office subsequently filed criminal charges, related to sales tax issues, against ATI's president. As a result, the Attorney General's Office notified PennDOT it would not approve the contract.

PennDOT never returned an executed contract to ATI or provided a notice-to-proceed to ATI. Instead, PennDOT notified ATI it would not enter into the contract because it determined ATI is not a responsible contractor. ATI filed a complaint alleging PennDOT breached a valid contract. After the hearing, the board determined that PennDOT never delivered an acceptance of the offer to ATI and, as a result, a contract was never formed. ATI appealed, arguing that the board erred in finding a contract did not exist because PennDOT's representatives, who signed the contract, intended to bind PennDOT to the terms of the contract. How did the court rule on appeal? Did the documents contain a proper acceptance? [*Makoroff v. DOT,* 938 A.2d 470 (Pa. Commw. Ct. 2007).]

7. Plaintiff Business Systems Engineering, Inc., was one of several subcontractors that agreed to provide technical consultants for defendant IBM's work on a transit project. In a "plan of utilization" provided by IBM to the transit authority, IBM had listed Business Systems as one of its intended subcontractors, with $3.6 million listed on that document under the heading "contract amount." The terms of the arrangement between IBM and its subcontractors for the job were that when IBM needed technical consultants for a part of the project, the subs would submit bids and when the subcontractor's bid was accepted, the subcontractor would receive a specific statement of work detailing the scope of the specific project, the time frame, the conditions under which the task would be deemed complete, and the hourly wage, followed by a work authorization. The transit authority retained the authority to reject any individual consultant who was selected by the subcontractor, and the contract between the subcontractors and IBM incorporated by reference the contract between IBM and the transit authority. Work was not to begin until a final work authorization was issued. At the

end of the project, 38 work authorizations had been issued to the plaintiff by the defendant for a total of $2.2 million, rather than the $3.6 million that had been projected in the original estimate IBM had provided to the transit authority. IBM had paid the plaintiff the $2.2 million for the work done on the work authorizations, but the plaintiff argued that it should have been entitled to the full $3.6 million contained in the estimate that was incorporated by reference in the contracts between IBM and the subcontractors. The plaintiff argued that it had a contract with IBM for the full $3.6 million. The district court granted summary judgment for the defendant. What do you think the plaintiff's argument was on appeal? What do think the outcome of the appeal was and why? [*Business Systems Engineering, Inc. v. International Business Machines Corp.,* 547 F.3d 883, 2008 U.S. App LEXIS 23682.]

8. Plaintiff VanHierden injured his thumb and finger at work and had it surgically repaired. He later developed a persistent pain at the base of his thumb. He went to see the defendant about having a sympathectomy to alleviate his pain. The defendant told the plaintiff, "We're going to get rid of your pain and get you back to work." The plaintiff then signed a written consent form to have the surgery, which included the following:

The procedure listed under paragraph 1 has been fully explained to me by Dr. Swelstad and I completely understand the nature and consequences of the procedure(s). I have further had explained to me and discussed available alternatives and possible outcomes, and understand the risk of complications, serious injury or even death that may result from both known and unknown causes. I have been informed that there are other risks that are adherent to the performance of any surgical procedure. I am aware that the practice of medicine and surgery is not an exact science and I acknowledge that no guarantees have been made to me concerning the results of the operation or procedure(s).

The defendant performed the sympathectomy, but it did not alleviate the plaintiff's pain; nor was he able to return to work, so he sued the defendant for breach of a contract to cure the pain. The district court granted summary judgment for the defendant, finding that no contract had been formed as a matter of law. On appeal, do you believe the court found a valid agreement between the parties? Why or why not? [*Ronald VanHierden v. Jack Swelstad, MD,* 2010 WI App. 16, 2009 Wis. App. LEXIS 1013.]

9. R-Vision manufactures recreational vehicles (RVs). Representatives of Associated Home met R-Vision's regional sales manager, Darrell Higgins, and the product manager, Timothy Cunningham, at a convention where they discussed the possibility of using Associated Home as a dealer of R-Vision's RVs in Albuquerque, New Mexico. At the time of the convention, Rocky Mountain RV was R-Vision's dealer in Albuquerque. Higgins contacted Rocky Mountain and told it that if Rocky Mountain did not make better efforts to represent R-Vision's product, then R-Vision would find another dealer in Albuquerque. Higgins closed out the conversation by informing Rocky Mountain that R-Vision would "pursue somebody else." R-Vision faxed Associated Home an application to become R-Vision's dealer in Albuquerque. Associated Home faxed in return a completed dealer application form. Higgins then called Associated Home to explain that Associated Home needed to submit orders for RVs as part of the dealer application. In response to that telephone call, Associated Home submitted orders for four RV units. Higgins then contacted Rocky Mountain to tell it that R-Vision had "another dealer in your area that wants the product, that has ordered product and is going to represent the product." Rocky Mountain's owner called Higgins, and Higgins told him that Rocky Mountain would no longer be R-Vision's dealer in Albuquerque. At that point, Rocky Mountain's owner informed Higgins that, under New Mexico law, R-Vision had to give Rocky Mountain 90 days' written notice of its action and that Rocky Mountain could still be the dealer by placing orders before the expiration of the 90-day period. Thereafter, Rocky Mountain ordered more RVs.

   By this point, Higgins had already told Associated Home that it would be the dealer. Higgins told Associated Home about the 90-day issue with Rocky Mountain but also told Associated Home that they would work it out and that Associated Home would be the dealer. Associated Home did not receive any RVs from R-Vision. Associated Home filed a complaint charging that R-Vision breached a contract with it by not delivering four RVs. Associated Home argues that the order forms confirm the contract. Did the forms meet the requirements of a valid contract? [*Associated Home and RV Sales, Inc. v. R-Vision, Inc.,* 2006 U.S. Dist. LEXIS 95631 (D.N.M. 2006).]

10. Sarah and Eddie Hogan wanted to sell 2.5 acres of land through their real estate agent, Darita Richardson. On December 10, 2001, Warren Kent offered to purchase the land for $52,500. An "Agreement to Buy or Sell" was created, which Kent signed right away. One term of the agreement was that the offer would expire on December 11, 2001, at 3 p.m., and it stated additionally, "Time is of the essence and all deadlines are final except where modifications, changes, or extensions are made in writing and signed by all parties." Although Richardson scheduled a meeting on December 11, 2001, at 2 p.m. with the Hogans, the Hogans failed to appear. However, the parties agreed to a two-day extension, lasting until December 13, 2001, at 3 p.m., and the extension was binding and irrevocable according to the "Addendum to Agreement to Purchase or Sell." The Hogans signed both documents at 9 a.m. on December 13, 2001. At about 11 a.m., Kent also signed the addendum. However, neither Kent's agent nor Richardson contacted the Hogans before 3 p.m. about Kent's acceptance. After 3 p.m., Richardson realized that the Hogans had not placed the date and time next to their signatures. When she met with the Hogans, the Hogans placed the date and the time as 4:48 p.m., informing Richardson that they, the Hogans, had changed their minds about the sale. Kent sued for specific performance of the contract. What effect, if any, did the failure to communicate the acceptance of the offer before 3 p.m. have in terms of whether a contract was formed? What was the appellate court's reasoning? [*Kent v. Hogan,* 2004 La. App. LEXIS 2539.]

Looking for more review material?

The Online Learning Center at **www.mhhe.com/kubasek2e** contains this chapter's "Assignment on the Internet" and also a list of URLs for more information, entitled "On the Internet." Find both of them in the Student Center portion of the OLC, along with quizzes and other helpful materials.

15 Consideration

LEARNING OBJECTIVES

After reading this chapter, you will be able to answer the following questions:

1   What is consideration?

2   What are the rules regarding consideration?

3   What is promissory estoppel, and when can it be used?

4   What is an illusory promise?

5   How are the UCC rules regarding consideration different from the common law rules regarding consideration?

6   What is the difference between a liquidated debt and an unliquidated debt?

7   What is an accord and satisfaction?

CASE OPENER

Upper Deck—Contract Liability or Gift?

In 1988 the Upper Deck Company was a company with an idea for a better baseball card: one that had a hologram on it. By the 1990s the firm was a major corporation worth at least a quarter of a billion dollars.

In 1988, however, its outlook hadn't been so bright. Upper Deck lacked the funds for a $100,000 deposit it needed to buy some special paper by August 1. Without that deposit its contract with the Major League Baseball Players Association would have been jeopardized.

Upper Deck's corporate attorney, Anthony Passante, Jr., loaned the company the money. That evening, the directors of the company accepted the loan and, in gratitude, agreed to give Passante 3 percent of the firm's stock. Passante never sought to collect the stock, and later the company reneged on its promise. Passante sued for breach of oral contract.[1]

[1] *Passante v. McWilliam,* 53 Cal. App. 4th 1240 (1997).

1. If you were on the jury, how would you decide the case? Was the offer of 3 percent of the firm's stock legal consideration for the loan? Or was it a mere gift?
2. Does Upper Deck have a moral obligation to give Passante the stock? If so, is this obligation legally enforceable?

The Wrap-Up at the end of the chapter will answer these questions.

What Is Consideration?

LO1

What is consideration?

Consideration is required in every contract. It is what a person will receive in return for performing a contract obligation. Suppose Dan agrees to purchase Marty's car for $1,000. Dan's payment of $1,000 is the consideration Marty will receive for the car. Title to and possession of the car are the consideration Dan will receive in exchange. Consideration can be anything, as long as it is the product of a bargained-for exchange. In a business context it is often (but not always) money. Exhibit 15-1 provides other examples of consideration.

Rules of Consideration

LO2

What are the rules regarding consideration?

The key to understanding consideration is understanding the rules that govern it and their exceptions. We explore them below.

LACK OF CONSIDERATION

A court will enforce one party's promise only if the other party promised some consideration in exchange. For example, in a bilateral contract (a promise for a promise), the consideration for each promise is a return promise. Suppose Nicole promises to pay Mike $2,000 tomorrow for his car. Mike promises to sell Nicole his car tomorrow for $2,000. There is an oral contract between them. Nicole's promise is her consideration to Mike. Mike's promise is his consideration to Nicole. There has been a mutual exchange of something of value.

An example of a bilateral contract, or a promise for a promise, occurred when the U.S. government seized control of insurance giant American International Group (AIG). The government agreed to lend AIG up to $85 billion in exchange for nearly 80 percent of AIG's stock. The consideration AIG received was the promise of up to $85 billion in

Exhibit 15-1
Examples of Consideration

TYPE OF CONSIDERATION	EXAMPLE
A benefit to the promisor	A promise to stay in a job until a particular project is complete (this is a benefit to the employer)
A detriment to the promisee	A promise to your football coach to refrain from riding your motorcycle during football season even though you love riding it
A promise to do something	A promise to cook dinner for your roommate for the next six months
A promise to refrain from doing something	A promise to stop drinking alcohol during exam week

U.S. government loans. The consideration the government received was a promise of almost 80 percent of AIG's stock.[2]

In a unilateral contract (a promise for an act), one party's consideration is the promise and the other party's consideration is the act. Suppose your professor made the following statement in class: "If any student shows up at my house on Saturday and does the gardening, I will pay that student $100." You show up and do the gardening. The professor's consideration to you is the promise of the payment of $100 on completion of the gardening, and your consideration to the professor is the act of completing the gardening. Once again, there has been a mutual exchange of something of value.

See Exhibit 15-2 for an explanation of bilateral and unilateral contracts.

Legal Principle: **For a promise to be enforced by the courts, there must be consideration.**

L03

What is promissory estoppel, and when can it be used?

One exception to the rule requiring consideration is **promissory estoppel.** Promissory estoppel occurs when three conditions are met:

- One party makes a promise knowing the other party will rely on it.
- The other party does rely on the promise.
- The only way to avoid injustice is to enforce the promise.

How does promissory estoppel work? Suppose upon graduation from college, Amanda receives a job offer across the country. She gives up her apartment, cancels all her other job interviews, and moves all her possessions. Upon arriving, she rents a new apartment and shows up for work. Amanda is then told there is no job! May she sue the employer? The answer in most states is yes, under the theory of promissory estoppel. Amanda may be able to recover her *reliance damages* (money she spent in "reliance" on the job offer). Promissory estoppel is not awarded regularly, but in the right case it can provide a remedy where no other remedy exists.

In a recent case, the Ninth Circuit Court of Appeals held that Yahoo's promise to remove a nude photo from its Web site was subject to a claim of promissory estoppel. In that case, the plaintiff learned that her ex-boyfriend, pretending to be her, had posted nude photos of her on Yahoo. He also included all her contact information and an invitation for men to contact her for sexual purposes.[3] The plaintiff contacted Yahoo (in accordance with its established policies) and requested that the photo be removed. Yahoo agreed but, despite repeated requests, did not remove the photo for six months. The court held that Yahoo's promise to depost the profile meant that Yahoo had a duty to the plaintiff. As such, the plaintiff's claim of promissory estoppel could be maintained. If the plaintiff is able to prove that she reasonably relied on Yahoo's promise to her detriment, she may well prevail on her claim.

Exhibit 15-2

Type of Consideration Based on Type of Contract

TYPE OF CONTRACT	PROMISOR	PROMISEE
Bilateral	A promise	A promise
Unilateral	A promise	An act

[2] "U.S. Seizes Control of AIG with $85 Billion Emergency Loan," *Washington Post*, September 17, 2008, www.washingtonpost.com/wp-dyn/content/article/2008/09/16/AR2008091602174 (accessed May 25, 2009).

[3] "Do Interactive Websites Have a Legal Duty to Remove Malicious Content?" http://writ.news.findlaw.com/scripts/printer_friendly.pl?page=/ramasastry/20090519.html (accessed May 25, 2009) [discussing *Barnes v. Yahoo, Inc.*, 2009 U.S. App. LEXIS 10940 (9th Cir. 2009)].

Promissory Estoppel

Double AA Builders, Ltd. v. Grand State Construction L.L.C.
114 P.3d 835 (Ariz. Ct. App. 2005)

In anticipation of submitting a bid for the construction of a Home Depot Store in Mesa, Arizona, Double AA solicited bids from subcontractors for various portions of the work. Grand State faxed a written but unsigned bid to Double AA in the amount of $115,000 for installation of the exterior insulation finish system (EIFS) on the project. The proposal stated: "Our price is good for 30 days." Double AA relied on several subcontractor bids, including Grand State's, in preparing its overall price for the project.

On December 21, 2001, Home Depot advised Double AA it was the successful bidder for the project. On January 11, 2002, within the 30-day "price is good" period, Double AA sent a subcontract for the EIFS work to Grand State to be signed and returned. Grand State advised Double AA it would not sign the subcontract or perform on the project. Double AA subsequently entered into a subcontract with a replacement subcontractor to install the EIFS

at a cost of $131,449, which exceeded Grand State's quoted price by $16,449. Double AA demanded that Grand State pay the difference between its bid and Double AA's ultimate cost to perform the same work. After Grand State refused, Double AA filed suit based on promissory estoppel.

When a general contractor prepares an overall bid for a competitively bid construction project, it receives bids and quotes from subcontractors for portions of the work. The general contractor uses the bids in preparing its overall price for the project. A subcontractor's refusal to honor its bid can be financially disastrous for the general contractor, because the general contractor will typically be bound by the bid price it submitted to the project owner.

Promissory estoppel may be used to require that the subcontractor perform according to the terms of its bid to the contractor if the contractor receives the contract award, because the contractor has detrimentally relied on the subcontractor's bid and must perform for a price based on that reliance. Double AA prevailed. Nonperformance by the subcontractor resulted in damages equal to the difference between what the contractor had to pay and what it would have paid had the subcontractor performed.

A second exception to the rule requiring consideration is a *contract under seal*. In the past, contracts were sealed with a piece of soft wax into which an impression was made. Today, sealed contracts are typically identified with the word *seal* or the letters *L.S.* (an abbreviation for *locus sigilli,* which means "the place for the seal") at the end. Consumers may also purchase contract forms with a preprinted seal. The parties using them are presumed, without evidence to the contrary, to be adopting the seal for the contract. States in the U.S. no longer require that contracts be under seal. However, 10 states still allow a contract without consideration to be enforced if it is under seal.

Legal Principle: Promissory estoppel and contracts under seal are exceptions to the common law rule requiring consideration.

In Case 15-1, the court must decide whether continued employment is consideration for signing a noncompete agreement.

CASE 15-1

ANTHONY A. LABRIOLA v. POLLARD GROUP, INC.
SUPREME COURT OF WASHINGTON
100 P.3D 791 (SUP. CT. WASH. 2004)

In 1997, Employer hired Employee to work as a commercial print salesperson, and the parties entered into an employment agreement. Under the agreement, Employer could terminate Employee without cause. Employee's

compensation consisted of a base salary and commission from sales. The agreement also contained a clause prohibiting Employee from competing with Employer in the custom printing business for a period of three years after employment ended. The agreement had no geographical limitations.

Nearly five years later, in April 2002, Employer requested and Employee executed a "Noncompetition and Confidentiality Agreement" (noncompete agreement). The noncompete agreement required Employee to refrain from accepting employment with a competitor for a period of three years within 75 miles of Employer's business in Tacoma, Washington. Employee remained an "at will" employee and received no additional benefits. Employer incurred no additional obligations from the noncompete agreement. The noncompete agreement also contained clauses for confidentiality, severability, and an award of attorneys' fees and costs.

A few months later, in July 2002, Employer announced a new commission sales compensation schedule. The old schedule's threshold had paid commission when an employee generated sales of at least $25,000 for the month, while the new schedule required sales to exceed $60,000. Employee determined the new schedule would reduce his income by about 25 percent and sought employment for a similar position elsewhere. On November 12, 2002, Employer discovered Employee's intention to seek employment with a competitor and terminated him. Employer also sent a letter to the competitor interested in hiring Employee, stating its intent to enforce Employee's noncompete agreement. The competitor did not hire Employee. Employee remains unemployed despite actively seeking a position similar to the one he held with Employer.

The Employee sued the Employer. The trial court ruled against the employee and the employee appealed to the state supreme court.

JUDGE IRELAND: . . . Issue 1. Is there consideration for the formation of a contract when an employee, already employed by the employer, executes a noncompete agreement but receives no new benefit and the employer incurs no further obligations?

Employee claims that the noncompete agreement fails for lack of consideration; in other words, a contract was not formed. Employer contends that the noncompete agreement is enforceable because future and continued employment and/or job training served as the Employer's consideration in exchange for Employee's execution of the noncompete agreement. . . . The general rule in Washington is that consideration exists if the employee enters into a noncompete agreement when he or she is first hired. . . . A noncompete agreement entered into after employment will be enforced if it is supported by independent consideration. . . . Independent, additional consideration is required for the valid formation of a modification or subsequent agreement. There is no consideration when "one party is to perform some additional obligation while the other party is simply to perform that which he promised in the original contract." [Citations omitted]. Independent consideration may include increased wages, a promotion, a bonus, a fixed term of employment, or perhaps access to protected information. . . . Independent consideration involves new promises or obligations previously not required of the parties. . . .

In the present case, Employer contends that continued employment served as consideration for the 2002 noncompete agreement . . . [but] Employee's noncompete agreement made no promises as to future employment and wages. Further, during deposition, Robin Pollard, Employer's president, conceded that "no extra benefits or consideration or promises [were] made to [Employee] if he signed the noncompete."

Consideration is a bargained-for exchange of promises. A comparison of the status of the employer before and after the noncompete agreement confirms that the 2002 noncompete agreement was entered into without consideration. Employer did not incur additional duties or obligations from the noncompete agreement. Prior to execution of the 2002 noncompete agreement, Employee was an "at will" Employee. After Employee executed the noncompete agreement, he still remained an "at will" employee terminable at Employer's pleasure. We hold that continued employment in this case did not serve as consideration by Employer in exchange for Employee's promise not to compete.

We hold that the 2002 noncompete agreement lacked independent consideration and is not enforceable against the Employee.

REVERSED in favor of Employee.

CRITICAL THINKING

What is the reasoning used by the court to support its decision? Are there any ambiguous words or phrases in that reasoning that you would want defined before you decided whether to agree with the court's ruling?

ETHICAL DECISION MAKING

Return to the WPH framework. Who are the stakeholders in this case? Is the decision of the employer consistent with how someone would act when using the Golden Rule as a guide?

ADEQUACY OF CONSIDERATION

The court does not weigh whether you made a good bargain. Suppose Donna purchases a flat-screen TV from Celia, a friend in her business law class. Donna pays $500 for the TV but later realizes it is worth less than $100! May Donna sue Celia? Typically, the answer is no. It is Donna's responsibility to do her research and determine what price she should pay. The court will not set aside the sale because she made a bad deal. Conversely, if the court believes fraud or undue influence occurred, the court may look at adequacy of consideration. (For example, suppose a person divests himself of all his assets for pennies on the dollar and then declares bankruptcy—the court would likely review the consideration paid to determine whether there was fraud by the debtor against the creditors.)

Legal Principle: **The court seldom considers adequacy of consideration.**

Is a promise to refrain from something you are legally entitled to do appropriate consideration for a contract? See Case 15-2.

CASE 15-2

HAMER v. SIDWAY
COURT OF APPEALS OF NEW YORK
124 N.Y. 538 (1891)

Plaintiff sought to enforce against the defendant estate a promise made by his now-deceased uncle to pay plaintiff a sum of money if plaintiff refrained from the use of alcohol and tobacco for a period of years. Plaintiff so refrained and sought recovery of the sum promised.

J. PARKER: In 1869, William Story, 2d, promised his nephew that if he refrained from drinking liquor, using tobacco, swearing, and playing cards or billiards for money until he was 21 years of age, then he would pay him the sum of $5,000. William Story, the nephew, agreed and fully performed.

The defendant (the deceased uncle's estate) now contends that the contract was without consideration to support it, and, therefore, invalid. He asserts that the nephew, by refraining from the use of liquor and tobacco, was not harmed but benefited; that that which he did was best for him to do independently of his uncle's promise, and insists that it follows that unless the nephew was benefited, the contract was without consideration. This contention, if well founded, would seem to leave open for controversy in many cases whether that which the promisee did or omitted to do was, in fact, of such benefit to him as to leave no consideration to support the enforcement of the promisor's agreement.

Such a rule could not be tolerated, and is without foundation in the law. Consideration means not so much that one party is profiting as that the other abandons some legal right in the present or limits his legal freedom of action in the future. Now, applying this rule to the facts before us, the promisee used tobacco, occasionally drank liquor, and he had a legal right to do so. He abandoned that right for a period of years based upon the promise of his uncle that for such forbearance he would give him $5,000. We need not speculate on the effort which may have been required to give up the use of those stimulants. It is sufficient that he restricted his lawful freedom of action within certain prescribed limits upon the faith of his uncle's agreement. Now, having fully performed the conditions imposed, it makes no difference whether such performance was actually a benefit to the promisor, and the court will not inquire into it. Even if it were a proper subject of inquiry, we see nothing in this record that would permit a determination that the uncle was not benefited in a legal sense. It is deemed established for the purposes of this appeal, that on January 31, 1875, defendant's testator was indebted to William E. Story, 2d, in the sum of $5,000. All concur.

The order reversing the trial court judgment in favor of plaintiff is reversed on the grounds that plaintiff's promise to abandon his legal right to use tobacco and alcohol was sufficient consideration to enforce the contract.

In Case 15-3, the court had to consider whether $1 plus "love and affection" was adequate consideration for the transfer of property.

CASE 15-3

THELMA AGNES SMITH v. DAVID PHILLIP RILEY
COURT OF APPEALS OF TENNESSEE, EASTERN SECTION, AT KNOXVILLE
2002 TENN. APP. LEXIS 65 (2002)

The plaintiff, Thelma Agnes Smith, lived with the defendant out of wedlock for several years. When the relationship ended, she sued the defendant, seeking to enforce two written agreements with him regarding the sale and assignment of property to her. The trial court enforced the agreements and divided the parties' property. The defendant appealed, arguing the agreements lacked consideration and were void as against public policy.

JUDGE CHARLES D. SUSANO: . . . Thelma Agnes Smith and David Phillip Riley, both of whom then resided in Florida, separated from their respective spouses in 1997 and began a romantic relationship. In early 1998, the two moved to Tennessee and began cohabitating. . . . Smith and Riley opened a joint checking account in March, 1998. Over time, Smith deposited into that account $9,500—the proceeds from an insurance settlement and monies received when her divorce later became final; she also deposited her monthly social security check of $337 into the same account. Smith continued to deposit her social security check in the joint account until December, 1998, when she opened her own checking account. Riley also contributed to the joint account. He placed a settlement of $84,000 from

the Veteran's Administration into the account. In addition, he deposited his monthly pension check of $2,036 into the same account. . . .

On July 31, 1998, Riley entered into a lease with Jerry Strickland and Wanda Strickland with respect to a residence owned by them; the lease was accompanied by an option to purchase. Almost four months later, on November 20, 1998, Smith and Riley returned to their attorney's office, at which time the attorney prepared a bill of sale and an assignment. In the bill of sale, Riley transferred [to Smith] a one-half undivided interest in seven items of personal property. . . . Riley also assigned to Smith a one-half undivided interest in the lease and option to purchase with the Stricklands, which interest included a right of survivorship in the one-half interest retained by Riley as well. The property Riley sold and assigned to Smith in the two agreements was stated in each to be "for and in consideration of the sum of One Dollar ($1.00) and other and good and valuable consideration, the sufficiency of which is hereby acknowledged. . . ."

When Smith and Riley separated in April, 1999, Smith filed suit against Riley in the trial court, seeking the dissolution of their "domestic partnership." Smith alleged that she and Riley had been living together for several years without the benefit of marriage and had acquired both real and personal property, some of which Riley had assigned to her. As a result, she asked the court to award her 50 percent of the "partnership" assets, leaving the other 50 percent to Riley. . . . [The trial court ruled in favor of Smith and Riley appealed.]

Riley first argues that the trial court erred in finding that the bill of sale and assignment are supported by valid consideration. Specifically, Riley relies on Smith's statements at trial that she considered their pending engagement and the funds she deposited into their joint account to be consideration for their agreements.

It is a well-settled principle of contract law that in order for a contract to be binding, it must, among other things, be supported by sufficient consideration. [Citations omitted.] In expounding on the adequacy of consideration, the Tennessee Supreme Court has stated that it is not necessary that the benefit conferred or the detriment suffered by the promisee shall be equal to the responsibility assumed. Any consideration, however small, will support a promise. In the absence of fraud, the courts will not undertake to regulate the amount of the consideration. The parties are left to contract for themselves, taking for granted that the consideration is one valuable in the eyes of the law. . . .

Quoting the United States Supreme Court, the Tennessee Supreme Court went on to state that "[a] stipulation in consideration of $1 is just as effectual and valuable a consideration as a larger sum stipulated for or paid." [Citations omitted.] Indeed, the consideration of love and affection has been deemed sufficient to support a conveyance. . . .

Both the bill of sale and the assignment recite that they are undertaken "for and in consideration of the sum of One Dollar ($1.00) and other and good and valuable consideration, the sufficiency of which is hereby acknowledged. . . ." Facially, the documents are therefore supported by sufficient consideration, as clearly recognized by the Supreme Court. . . . Moreover, Smith's "society and consortium"— a concept comparable to the love and affection . . . is further evidence of sufficient consideration to support these conveyances.

Riley calls our attention to Smith's statement at trial that she considered the funds she deposited into their joint account to be consideration for the conveyances. If this were the only consideration involved in this case, Riley's argument regarding past consideration supporting a present transaction might have some merit. However, the recitals of nominal consideration that are present in both agreements, as well as the consideration of Smith's love and affection, are adequate consideration and will support the conveyances represented by the assignment and bill of sale. . . .

Judgment affirmed in favor of Plaintiff.

CRITICAL THINKING

What is the reasoning of the appellant in terms of why the consideration was not adequate to cause the contracts to be enforceable? What key rule of law did this reasoning overlook?

ETHICAL DECISION MAKING

What values are being advanced by the logic of the relevant rule of law in this case? In other words, what values prevent the rule of law from being that "consideration must be in an amount similar in value to the item or services being transferred in order for the contract to be enforceable"?

ILLUSORY PROMISE

What is an illusory promise? Suppose Shawn offers to sell Molly his skis for $300. Molly responds, "I'll look at them in the morning, and if I like them, I'll pay you." At this point, Molly has not committed to doing anything. The law considers this an **illusory promise**— it is not a promise at all.

LO4

What is an illusory promise?

Legal Principle: **An illusory promise is not consideration.**

PAST CONSIDERATION

For a court to enforce a promise, both sides must offer consideration. Imagine you graduate from college and get a great job. After five years, your boss says to you, "Because you have done such a great job the last five years, I am going to give you 5 percent of the

Deeds in England

England has the same requirement for consideration as the United States and even shares the exception of promissory estoppel. However, England has an additional exception: specialty contracts or deeds. In England, a *deed* creates a binding obligation between parties without consideration when certain formalities are honored.

These formalities include a written document signed by the person making it, a witness to the maker's signature, and delivery of the document to the other party with a statement or an accompanying act indicating the maker's intention to be bound by the deed. Deeds are used in England to create enforceable promises of gifts to charity. This exception to the requirement for consideration also exists in Canadian law.

---

company stock." Six months later, you still have not received the stock. May you sue your boss to enforce the promise? The answer is no. For a promise to be enforceable, there must be bargaining and an exchange. Because your work has already been performed, you have given nothing in exchange, and the court will not enforce the promise. A promise cannot be based on consideration provided before the promise was made. You are at the mercy of your boss's goodwill.

    Legal Principle: **Past consideration is no consideration at all.**

    As you have probably guessed by now, there is an exception to this rule. Under the Restatement (Second) of Contracts (a persuasive, though not binding, authority), promises based on past consideration may be enforceable "to the extent necessary to avoid injustice." In some cases, if past consideration was given with expectation of future payment, the court may enforce the promise.

PREEXISTING DUTY

There are two parts to the **preexisting duty** rule. *Performance of a duty you are obligated to do under the law is not good consideration.* Part of a police officer's sworn public duty is catching suspected criminals. If someone offers a reward for the capture of a suspect, the police officer may not collect it, as he or she was already obligated to apprehend the suspect. Moreover, *performance of an existing contractual duty is not good consideration.* Gene decides to have a pool built in his backyard. Under the existing contract, the pool is to be completed by June 1, just in time for summer. The pool contractor then explains that due to a shortage of workers, the completion date cannot be met; however, if Gene were to pay an extra $5,000, additional workers could be hired and the pool completed on time. Gene tells the contractor he will pay the $5,000. On June 1, the pool is completed and the contractor asks for the additional payment. Is Gene legally obligated to pay? The answer is no. The pool contractor had a preexisting contractual duty to complete the pool by June 1. Gene is under no obligation to pay the additional money.

    Legal Principle: **A promise to do something that you are already obligated to do is not valid consideration.**

Exceptions to the Preexisting Duty Rule.   There are exceptions to the preexisting duty rule: unforeseen circumstances, additional work, and UCC Article 2 (sale of goods).

    If *unforeseen circumstances* cause a party to make a promise regarding an unfinished project, that promise is valid consideration. Suppose the pool contractor has been building pools in Gene's neighborhood for the last 20 years and has never had any problem with rocks—until now. While bulldozing the hole for the pool in Gene's backyard, the pool contractor hits solid rock. It will cost an additional $5,000 to clear the rock with jackhammers, possibly even dynamite. The contractor says unless Gene agrees to pay the additional money, he will not be able to finish the pool. Gene agrees to pay. When the pool is completed, the contractor asks for the additional $5,000. Will a court enforce Gene's promise? The answer is yes. Even though the contractor is completing only what he was obligated to do under the contract, neither party knew of the solid rock. The contractor has given additional consideration (removal of the rock) and Gene will be held to his promise to pay the additional money.

If a party to a contract agrees to do *additional work* (more than the contract requires), the promise to do it is valid consideration. If the contractor asks Gene for an additional $10,000 but agrees to add a waterfall and a deck to the pool, the promise to do the additional work is consideration. If Gene agrees to pay the $10,000, that is his consideration. Both parties are now bound.

UCC Exceptions.   The rules and exceptions we've discussed fall under the common law of contracts, which the Uniform Commercial Code (UCC) has changed in significant ways. Under UCC 2-209:[4]

1. An agreement modifying a contract within this Article needs no consideration to be binding.
2. A signed agreement which excludes modification or rescission except by a signed writing cannot be otherwise modified or rescinded, but except as between merchants such a requirement on a form supplied by the merchant must be separately signed by the other party.

Gary is a manufacturer of blow dryers. He sends a purchase order for 10,000 white on/ off switches to a switch manufacturer. Later, Gary telephones the switch manufacturer and changes his order to 5,000 white switches and 5,000 red switches. Under the UCC, no additional consideration is required for the modification of the agreement to be binding. Moreover, unless stated otherwise, such an agreement need not be in writing.

Legal Principle: Under Article 2 (sale of goods), an agreement modifying a contract needs no consideration to be binding.

L05

How are the UCC rules regarding consideration different from the common law rules regarding consideration?

Uniform Commercial Code: Requirement and Output Contracts

A requirement contract is an agreement whereby the buyer agrees to purchase all his or her goods from one seller. No quantity is stated in the contract. Under common law, such a contract would be void because the buyer has made no commitment and therefore there is no consideration. An output contract is an agreement whereby the seller guarantees to sell everything he or she produces to one buyer. Once again, no quantity is stated, and under common law, consideration is lacking. Because such contracts are valued by merchants, however, under the UCC both are valid, with the limitation that the output or requirement must be made in "good faith." The consideration, then, is that the parties act in good faith. Neither may take advantage of the other by requiring or producing more than was expected when the deal was signed.

Legal Principle: Under UCC Section 2-306, requirement and output contracts are permitted for the sale of goods.

L06

What is the difference between a liquidated debt and an unliquidated debt?

Partial Payment of a Debt

Partial payment of a debt may or may not be valid consideration, depending on whether the debt is liquidated or unliquidated. In a liquidated debt, there is no dispute that money is owed or how much. Natalie calls her credit card company and explains she is a poor

---

[4] www.law.cornell.edu/ucc/2/article2.htm#s2-209.

CASE NUGGET

Requirement Contracts

Mast Long Term Care v. Forest Hills Rest Home et al.
156 N.C. App. 556 (N.C. Ct. App. 2003)

Mast Long Term Care and Forest Hills Rest Home entered into an agreement whereby the rest home was to buy from Mast all the drugs needed for its patients that were not commonly stocked at the rest home. The rest home argued that the agreement was not a valid contract since it contained vague purchasing terms, obligating it to buy only those drugs not commonly stocked.

At the hearing, Forest Hills Rest Home argued that the agreement lacked consideration. It also did not state any price terms.

The court ruled that North Carolina law permitted requirement contracts and that the sale of drugs was governed by the North Carolina Uniform Commercial Code (UCC). Under the UCC, the failure to omit certain material terms such as definite amounts did not invalidate the contract, as courts were permitted to read into a contract good-faith requirements. Moreover, consideration need not consist of a promise to pay money for goods or services. Instead, it can take the shape of mutual promises to perform some act or to forbear from taking some action.

In this case, the consideration consisted of the plaintiff's promise to supply the defendant with certain pharmaceuticals and the defendant's counterpromise to stock the plaintiff's products at its pharmacy and sell them to its patients. Accordingly, the agreement does not fail for either lack of consideration or lack of specificity.

L07

What is an accord and satisfaction?

student and cannot afford to pay the entire $3,000 she owes. The credit card company agrees to accept $2,000 as payment in full. The following month, Natalie receives her new credit card statement showing she owes the remaining $1,000. May the credit card company collect the additional $1,000? Yes! A creditor's promise to accept less than owed, when the debtor is already obligated to pay the full amount, is not binding.

The exception to the rule regarding liquidated debt occurs when the debtor offers different performance. Suppose Natalie offered the credit card company her car in full settlement of the $3,000 debt. If the credit card company accepts, regardless of the value of the car, the debt is paid in full and the credit card company may not sue Natalie for any additional money.

In an **unliquidated debt,** the parties either disagree about whether money is owed or dispute the amount. They can settle for less than the full amount if they enter into an **accord and satisfaction,** which must meet three requirements to be enforceable:

1. The debt is unliquidated (the amount or existence of the debt is in dispute).
2. The creditor agrees to accept as full payment less than it claims is owed.
3. The debtor pays the amount they have agreed on.

Under these circumstances, the debt is fully discharged. The *accord* is the new agreement to pay less than the creditor claims is owed. The *satisfaction* is the debtor's payment of the reduced amount. It pays to keep your word: If the debtor fails to pay the new amount, the creditor may sue for the full amount of the original debt. Exhibit 15-3 clarifies the accord-and-satisfaction process.

Legal Principle: **When a debt is unliquidated, the parties may enter into an accord and satisfaction.**

Debtors sometimes attempt to create an accord and satisfaction by sending the creditor a check with "paid in full" written on it. Under the common law, in many states this did create an accord and satisfaction, and if the creditor cashed the check, he or she was bound to accept the lesser amount as payment in full. The UCC has reduced the scope of this rule, however. Under UCC Section 3-311, effective in 30 states, the rule has two major exceptions.

Exhibit 15-3 Accord and Satisfaction

DEBT DISPUTED?	STATUS OF DEBT	PAYMENT?	CREATE AN ACCORD?	CREATE A SATISFACTION?
Yes—*amount* of debt in dispute	Unliquidated	Debtor offers to pay less money than creditor believes is owed as full payment, and creditor agrees.	Yes	Yes. Once debtor pays the money agreed to, the debt is satisfied and the creditor may not collect any additional money.
Yes—*existence* of debt in dispute	Unliquidated	Debtor offers to pay a sum of money as full payment when debtor does not believe anything is owed, and creditor agrees.	Yes	Yes. Once the debtor pays the money agreed to, the debt is satisfied and the creditor may not collect any additional money.
No dispute over amount of debt or existence of debt	Liquidated	Debtor offers to pay less money than is owed as full payment, and creditor agrees.	No	No. Even if the debtor pays the money agreed to, the creditor may still sue for the balance it believes is owed.
No dispute over amount of debt or existence of debt	Liquidated	Debtor offers a *different* payment (e.g., her car) as full payment.	Yes	Yes. Once the debtor makes a *different* payment, the debt is satisfied and the creditor may not collect anything else.

First, business organizations can receive thousands of checks each day. To protect themselves, they may notify their debtors that any offer to settle a claim for less than the amount owed must be sent to a particular address and/or person. If you check the terms printed on your credit card statement, you will likely find language directing you to send such payments to a different address and person than regular payments are sent to. This safeguard protects businesses from inadvertently creating accord-and-satisfaction agreements. Below is a typical clause you might find on any credit statement regarding conditional payments:

> *Conditional Payments:* Any payment check or other form of payment that you send us for less than the full balance that is marked "paid in full" or contains a similar notation, or that you otherwise tender in full satisfaction of a disputed amount, must be sent to [address omitted]. We reserve all rights regarding these payments (e.g., if it is determined that there is no valid dispute or if any such check is received at any other address, we may accept the check and you will still owe any remaining balance).[5]

In the second exception, if a business does inadvertently cash a "paid-in-full" check, it has 90 days to offer the debtor repayment in the same amount. For example, if John owed his credit card company $3,000 and sent a $2,000 check marked "paid in full" to the correct address and person, the credit card company has 90 days to offer to repay John the $2,000. Once the business has made that offer, no accord and satisfaction exists.

To see how an accord and satisfaction relates to income taxation, please see the **Connecting to the Core** activity on the text Web site at www.mhhe.com/kubasek2e.

[5] From Chase Visa statement.

CASE NUGGET

Accord and Satisfaction

Thomas v. CitiMortgage, Inc.
2005 U.S. Dist. LEXIS 14641 (Dist. Ct. Ill. 2005)

In November 1979, Thomas assumed an existing mortgage, which CitiMortgage now holds, that required him to make a payment on the first of each month. Beginning in April 1996, his payments became sporadic. On December 16, 1996, Thomas sent a letter to CitiMortgage. He wrote:

> My primary concern is the effect on my credit rating and the fact that I have an application to refinace [*sic*] the mortgage which cannot be finalized, at great cost to me, unless this matter is resolved and my credit cleared up. I have enclosed a check in the amount of the monthly payment on condition that it be applied to tha [*sic*] May payment and that it will allow you to remove the negative material relative to my credit rating.

CitiMortgage cashed the check enclosed with the December 16 letter and credited it to Thomas's account. At CitiMortgage as of 1996, mail was sorted in a central mail room. The persons processing checks lacked the authority either to accept conditions on payments or to change credit reports. In his breach-of-contract claim, Thomas asserted that he and CitiMortgage had entered an agreement whereby he would make a payment on his mortgage in exchange for CitiMortgage's agreement to "remove the negative material" from his credit rating. He further claimed that CitiMortgage accepted the contract when it cashed the check he enclosed with his December 16 letter. Whether Thomas's claim was considered an accord and satisfaction or a simple contract, he could not prevail unless he established that consideration supported the agreement.

Consideration can consist of a promise, an act, or a forbearance. The preexisting duty rule provides, however, that when a party does what it is already legally obligated to do, there is no consideration because there has been no detriment. Thomas claimed that the payment he made with his December 16 letter constituted consideration for the agreement. As of that date, however, he was already two months in arrears on his mortgage payment. Thus, he was already legally obligated—under the terms of the mortgage—to make the payment he enclosed with the letter. Accordingly, that payment could not be consideration for an additional agreement to "remove the negative material" from his credit rating.

CASE OPENER WRAP-UP

Upper Deck

As you know from the Case Opener, Passante sued Upper Deck for breach of oral contract. At trial, the jury awarded him close to $33 million—the value of 3 percent of Upper Deck's stock at the time of the trial in 1993. Upper Deck appealed.

As a matter of law, any claim by Passante for breach of contract is necessarily based on the rule that consideration must result from a bargained-for exchange. In this case, the appellate court held that if the stock promised was truly bargained for, then Passante had an obligation to give Upper Deck the opportunity to have separate counsel represent it in the course of that bargaining. The legal profession has certain rules regarding business transactions with clients. Bargaining between the parties might have resulted in Passante's settling for just a reasonable finder's fee.

All Passante's services in arranging the $100,000 loan for Upper Deck had already been rendered (even though the board had not formally accepted the loan) before the idea of giving him stock came up. There was no evidence he had any expectation of receiving stock in return. If there is no expectation of payment by either party when services are rendered, the promise is a mere promise to make a gift and not enforceable. The promise of 3 percent of the stock represented a moral obligation but was legally unenforceable.

Key Terms

accord and
   satisfaction   352
consideration   343

illusory promise   349
liquidated debt   351
output contract   351

preexisting duty   350
promissory
   estoppel   341

requirement contract   351
unliquidated debt   352

Summary of Key Topics

What Is Consideration?	*Consideration* is something of value given in exchange for something else of value; it must be the product of a mutually bargained-for exchange.
Rules of Consideration	The key to understanding consideration is understanding the various rules: • For a promise to be enforced by the courts, there must be consideration. • *Exception: Promissory estoppel* occurs when one party makes a promise knowing the other party will rely on it, the other party does rely on it, and the only way to avoid injustice is to enforce the promise even though it is not supported by consideration. • The court seldom considers adequacy of consideration. • An *illusory promise* is not consideration. • Past consideration is no consideration at all. • A promise to do something you are already obligated to do is not valid consideration. (This is the *preexisting duty rule.*)
Uniform Commercial Code: Requirement and Output Contracts	In a *requirement contract* the buyer agrees to purchase all his or her goods from one seller. No quantity is stated in the contract. An *output contract* is an agreement whereby the seller guarantees to sell everything he or she produces to one buyer. Once again, no quantity is stated. The consideration, then, in both a requirement contract and an output contract, is that the parties act in *good faith* in what they either require or produce.
Partial Payment of a Debt	In a *liquidated debt,* there is no dispute that money is owed or the amount. In an *unliquidated debt,* the parties dispute either the fact that money is owed or the amount. To be enforceable, an *accord and satisfaction* must meet three requirements: (1) The debt is unliquidated (the amount or existence of the debt is in dispute); (2) the creditor agrees to accept as full payment less than the creditor claims is owed; and (3) the debtor pays the amount they agree on.

Point / Counterpoint

Should the Courts Require Consideration to Create a Binding Contract?	
YES	**NO**
The rules of consideration have been established for many years and precedent should be followed.	All promises should be enforced, eliminating the need to distinguish between binding and nonbinding promises.

Requiring consideration gives the court a way to distinguish between binding and nonbinding promises, or between a promise made as a gift and a promise made as part of a contract.

We have enough exceptions to the rule requiring consideration to make enforcement fair. If a promise was made and there was expectation of economic benefit, some courts will permit enforcement under the moral-obligation exception.

If we suddenly did not require consideration to create binding contracts, the courts would fill with civil cases of people trying to enforce all kind of promises.

If a person makes a promise, its timing should not make a difference. If Barbara's grandmother promises her $50,000 for "all you have done for me these last five years," why should Barbara be denied the money because it was based on acts she did in the past? The right thing, ethically and morally, is to enforce this promise whether or not Barbara acted with expectation of payment. Under current law, some states can use the moral-obligation exception to reward those who expect something when they do good and punish those who do the right thing with no expectation of reward.

Questions & Problems

1. List the four types of consideration described in the text.

2. What is required to prove promissory estoppel when consideration is missing?

3. Can $1 be adequate consideration? Why or why not?

4. List and describe the three exceptions to the preexisting duty rule.

5. List the three elements of accord and satisfaction.

6. When Holloman applied for a job at Circuit City, she signed a "Dispute Resolution Agreement" (DRA) that stated: "This agreement requires you and Circuit City to arbitrate certain legal disputes related to your application for employment with Circuit City." The job application then added, "Circuit City will consider your application only if this agreement is signed." Finally, the DRA contained this statement: "I understand that my employment, compensation and terms and conditions of employment can be altered or terminated, with or without cause, and with or without notice, at any time, at the option of either Circuit City or myself." Holloman was hired but later quit and sued Circuit City, claiming she had been discriminated against and constructively discharged. Holloman argued that the arbitration agreement was illusory and not supported by consideration because of Circuit City's unilateral ability to terminate or modify the agreement. How should the court rule? Explain your reasoning. [*Holloman v. Circuit City Stores,* 162 Md. App. 332 (Md. Ct. App. 2005).]

7. Martin was employed as a retail associate by UPS for over two years. He had no written employment agreement. On December 5, 2004, Martin's boss called him at his home and told him that he was terminating Martin's employment. The parties disagreed, however, as to the content of the rest of the conversation. Martin testified that his boss had said that Martin was fired because the other employees felt intimidated by him and that Martin would be given a severance package of two weeks' pay if he would not litigate. Martin's mother corroborated this version of the conversation. In contrast, Martin's boss stated that he told Martin that he was fired because of his continued personal use of company computers and because of the multiple downloads on company computers. The boss claims he indicated that he would give Martin his last week's pay and his November bonus and that he would consider giving him two weeks of severance pay in a few weeks. Martin never received severance pay from the company. The company now argues that the offer of severance pay was not supported by consideration and that Martin was not prejudiced by his boss's rescission of his offer to pay severance. How should the court decide? Why? [*Richard A. Martin v. Ost Mark, Inc.,* 2006 Ohio App. LEXIS 3938 (Ohio Ct. of Appeals, 2006).]

8. On February 1, 2004, Zhang entered into a contract to buy former realtor Frank Sorichetti's Las Vegas home for $532,500. The contract listed a March

closing date and a few household furnishings as part of the sale. On February 3, Sorichetti told Zhang that he was terminating the sale "to stay in the house a little longer" and that Nevada law allows the rescission of real property purchase agreements within three days of contracting. Sorichetti stated that he would sell the home, however, if Zhang paid more money. Zhang agreed. Another contract was drafted, reciting a new sales price, $578,000. This contract added to the included household furnishings drapes that were not listed in the February 1 agreement, and it set an April, rather than March, closing date. The primary issue before the court was whether a real property purchase agreement is enforceable when it is executed by the buyer only because the seller would not perform under an earlier purchase agreement for a lesser price. Should the court enforce the second contract? Why or why not? [*Zhang v. The Eighth Judicial District Court of the State of Nevada,* 103 P.3d 20 (Sup. Ct. Nev. 2004).]

9. This appeal arises out of the trial court's division of property in a divorce case. Vincent Simmons appeals from the trial court's order awarding to his wife, Dorothy Simmons, a one-half interest in land that he had inherited from his parents. Vincent contends that the land is nonmarital property and, consequently, should have remained his separate property. Vincent and Dorothy Simmons were married in 1976. Vincent's mother executed a trust in order to convey the land in Florida to her children, Vincent and his sister, upon her death.

Louise Simmons died on April 1, 1999, but the land remained in trust for several years after her death. After Louise died, Dorothy became concerned that she would not receive an interest in the Florida land if Vincent died before the trust was distributed, so she hired an attorney in Monticello, David Chambers, to prepare a document to protect her interest. In the document, Vincent states, in part, "It is my intention, through this affidavit, to convey to my said wife marital interest in said real property. If I should die prior to the above-stated Trust being dissolved, then my said wife shall receive my share of said real property as her own property." In 2003, Dorothy filed for divorce. Vincent argued that there was a total absence of consideration to support a contract in this case. Dorothy argued that her ongoing marriage to Vincent constituted adequate consideration to support the contract. Who is correct? Why? [*Vincent Simmons v. Dorothy Simmons,* 98 Ark. App. 12 (Ark. Ct. App. 2007).]

10. Five employees of American Electric Power (AEP) Service Corp. invented a new product. "In consideration of the sum of One Dollar (1.00), and of other good and valuable consideration paid to the undersigned Assignor," each employee signed an agreement giving AEP exclusive patent rights to the invention. Some of the employees sued, alleging that there was no contract because AEP never paid the one dollar. How do you think the court ruled? Explain your reasoning. [*Bennett et al. v. American Electric Power Service Corporation,* 2001 Ohio App. LEXIS 4357 (Ohio Ct. App. 2001).]

Looking for more review material?

The Online Learning Center at **www.mhhe.com/kubasek2e** contains this chapter's "Assignment on the Internet" and also a list of URLs for more information, entitled "On the Internet." Find both of them in the Student Center portion of the OLC, along with quizzes and other helpful materials.

16 Capacity and Legality

LEARNING OBJECTIVES

After reading this chapter, you will be able to answer the following questions:

1 What is the legal effect of a lack of capacity on a person's ability to enter into a contract?

2 Under what circumstances would a party have limited capacity to enter into a contract?

3 What is the legal effect of entering into a contract for an illegal purpose?

CASE OPENER
A Wasted Education

Ten months before he attained the age of majority, John Adamowski paid for and received a course in elementary aviation from Curtiss-Wright Flying Service. Five months later, he purchased and received a limited commercial pilot's course from the same company. Two months later, he entered into a contract with Curtiss-Wright for an advanced course of instruction to become a transport pilot, but he withdrew from the course within a month and paid nothing.

Six months after reaching the age of majority, Adamowski received a bill from Curtiss-Wright for the balance due on his course. He visited Curtiss-Wright's attorney and denied liability but said nothing about disaffirmance (exercising his legal right to end the contract). He took no further action until a few days shy of a year from the date on which he had attained the age of majority. At that time, he filed suit against Curtiss-Wright, seeking to disaffirm his contracts for the aviation courses and recover the money he had paid for them on grounds that he had entered into the contracts as a minor and thus had the right to disaffirm them and receive his money back. Curtiss-Wright argued that the courses were necessaries and, as such, Adamowski was not entitled to disaffirm the contracts for them.[1]

---

[1] *John P. Adamowski v. The Curtiss-Wright Flying Service, Inc.,* 300 Mass. 281, 15 N.E.2d 467, 1938 Mass. LEXIS 942.

1. Were the contracts for necessaries and, as such, not subject to being disaffirmed?
2. Even if the plaintiff had the right to disaffirm the contracts, was almost a year too long to wait to disaffirm them?

The Wrap-Up at the end of the chapter will answer these questions.

Capacity

LO1

What is the legal effect of a lack of capacity on a person's ability to enter into a contract?

Capacity is the third element of a legally binding contract. A person who has legal capacity has the mental ability to understand his or her rights and obligations under a contract and therefore presumably to comply with the terms. *Incapacity,* or *incompetence* as it is sometimes called, is the possession of a mental or physical defect that prevents a natural person from being able to enter into a legally binding contract. Depending on the nature and extent of the defect, a person may have either no capacity, the complete inability to enter into contracts, or limited capacity, the ability to form only voidable contracts.

Historically, people with limited or no capacity included married women, minors, and insane persons. Other categories were added by statutes, such as people for whom guardians had been appointed, including habitual drunkards, narcotic addicts, spendthrifts, the elderly, and convicts. Today, married women have been removed from the category of those lacking contractual capacity, although in a few states their capacity to enter into certain kinds of contracts is still limited. In this section of the chapter, we explain the current law limiting the capacity of some categories of persons to enter into legally binding agreements.

LO2

Under what circumstances would a party have limited capacity to enter into a contract?

MINORS

One of the oldest limitations on capacity is the fact that minors may enter into only voidable contracts. Today, in all but three states, a *minor* is someone under the age of 18.[2] In most states, however, a person is given full legal capacity to enter into contracts when he or she becomes emancipated before reaching the age of majority. *Emancipation* occurs when a minor's parents or legal guardians give up their right to exercise legal control over the minor, typically when the minor moves out of the parents' house and begins supporting himself or herself. Often the minor will petition the court for a declaration of emancipation. In most cases, when a minor marries, she or he is considered emancipated.

Legal Principle: As a general rule, any contract entered into by a minor is voidable by the minor until he or she reaches the age of majority or a reasonable time thereafter.

Disaffirmance of the Contract. Because their contracts are voidable, minors have the right, until a reasonable time after reaching the age of majority, to disaffirm or void their contracts. Note that it is only the minor who has the right to disaffirm, never the adult with whom the minor entered into the agreement. No formalities are required to disaffirm the contract; the minor need only show an intention to rescind it, either by words or actions. However, the minor must void the entire contract; he or she cannot choose to disaffirm only a portion of it.

---

[2] In Alabama, Nebraska, and Wyoming, full capacity to contract does not arise until the person reaches the age of 19, which is the age of majority in those states. In Mississippi, the age of majority is still 21.

The Age of Majority in Great Britain

People in the United States take the idea of an "age of majority" for granted; the only question is whether it should be 18, 19, or 21. Yet in Great Britain there is no magical age at which a young person suddenly acquires the legal capacity to enter into a contract. British courts will not enforce contracts with immature minors. However, they make the decision of whether a person is too immature to enter into a contract on a case-by-case basis. If the courts consider a person under 18 to be able to look out for his or her own interests, the contract will be enforced. If not, it will be void. A key factor is often the fairness of the agreement. If the agreement is one-sided and favors the adult, the young person is usually considered to lack the maturity to enter into it.

The minor's obligations on disaffirmance vary from state to state. Traditionally, most states simply required the minor to notify the competent party and return any consideration received, regardless of its condition. If the consideration had been damaged or destroyed, the other party had no recourse against the minor. For instance, if William, a minor, purchased a flat-screen TV from Sound Systems, Inc., under a six-month contract and dropped the TV a week after he took it home, he could return it in its broken condition and tell the store owner he wished to rescind the contract. He would be entitled to the return of his down payment and would owe no further obligations to the store.

The traditional rule makes sense if we view minors as innocents in need of protection from competent adults who would otherwise take advantage of them. However, it is not going to encourage competent parties to enter into contracts with minors, and some argue that it allows a knowledgeable and unethical minor to take advantage of a competent party. Thus, a number of states have modified the duty of the minor on disaffirmance, holding that the minor has a duty of restitution, requiring that she or he place the competent party back in the position that party was in at the time the contract was made. In these states, William would have a duty of restoration that would require him to compensate the store owner for the difference between the value of the TV when he got it and its value when he returned it. Case 16-1 illustrates the application of the majority rule for return of consideration on disaffirmance.

CASE 16-1 SWALBERG v. HANNEGAN
UTAH COURT OF APPEALS
883 P.2D 931 (UTAH APP. 1994)

The parties entered into a contract for the sale and purchase of the automobile. The minor's age was not discussed and there was no allegation he misrepresented it. The minor made a down payment and promised to pay the balance three months later. Thereafter, he disaffirmed the contract on the basis of his minority. The seller filed the complaint asking for enforcement of the contract or to be put back into his precontract state. The seller argued the minor did not properly restore the automobile under Utah Code Ann. § 15-2-2 (1986) because it was returned in a condition worth substantially less than the purchase price. The trial court awarded the seller a sum representing the balance owed minus the value of the automobile when it was returned. The plaintiff appealed.

JUDGE BENCH: The dispositive issue on appeal is whether a minor who disaffirms a contract is required to restore the full value of the property received under the contract. Defendant argues that Utah law does not require a disaffirming minor to restore the other party to his or her precontractual status. Utah Code Ann. § 15-2-2 (1986) provides:

[continued]

A minor is bound not only for the reasonable value of necessities but also for his contracts, unless he disaffirms them before or within a reasonable time after he obtains his majority and restores to the other party all money or property received by him by virtue of said contracts and remaining within his control at any time after attaining his majority.

. . . This statute requires only that the property remaining within the minor's control be returned to the other party. The trial court held, however, that defendant was required to return the property in its original condition or be liable for the difference in value. This holding is clearly contrary to the provisions of this unamended nineteenth century statute, as interpreted by controlling Utah case law.

In Blake v. Harding . . . , a minor sold a pony, harness, and buggy to an adult at an agreed value of $150, for which the adult delivered 3,000 shares of stock in a mining company. The minor later disaffirmed the contract and returned the stock to the adult. The minor sued to recover $150 since the adult had sold the pony, harness, and buggy. The jury was instructed that "if you believe that the contract in evidence was fair and reasonable, and was free from any fraud or bad faith on the part of the [adult], and if you further find that the mining stock traded to the [minor] by the [adult] is now worthless, the [minor] is not entitled to recover in this action." A jury returned a verdict in favor of the adult. The Utah Supreme Court reversed the verdict and held that the jury instruction was in "direct conflict with our statute." The Supreme Court stated that this jury instruction would require the minor to place the adult in his precontractual status, which would "disregard and misapply the purpose of

the law. The law is intended for the benefit and protection of the minor; and hence an adult, in dealing with a minor, assumes all the risk of loss." Id.

Further, in Harvey v. Hadfield, . . . (1962), a minor contracted with an adult to buy a house-trailer. The minor paid $1,000 as a down payment without selecting a trailer. The minor later disaffirmed the contract, requesting the return of his money. When the adult refused to return the money, the minor brought an action against the adult. . . . The supreme court stated that section 15-2-2 "cannot be tortured to support the adult's contention that the disaffirming minor must compensate the adult for damages the adult may have incurred" so long as the property is returned to the adult.

In view of these Utah cases interpreting the language of section 15-2-2, the trial court erred in requiring defendant to restore plaintiff to his precontractual status. . . .

Section 15-2-2 requires that a disaffirming minor must only return the property remaining within his or her control. The Utah Supreme Court has interpreted this statute to allow a minor to effectively disaffirm the underlying contract without restoring the full value of the property received under the contract. Although we do not necessarily believe in the wisdom of this approach, we are not in a position to hold contrary to controlling case law under the doctrine of stare decisis. If a contracting and disaffirming minor is to be held responsible for waste of property received under a contract, it is for the legislature to so provide. Alternatively, the Supreme Court might . . . overrule existing case law.

REVERSED in favor of defendant.

CRITICAL THINKING

How does the explicitly stated reliance on legal precedent affect the acceptability of the reasoning of this ruling? Is the conclusion reached the result of fair consideration of all available evidence? What issues are raised by this question regarding the workings of the U.S. legal system at large? How do you think these problems would best be resolved?

ETHICAL DECISION MAKING

Does this decision maintain an awareness of the interests of all relevant stakeholders? Are these interests properly weighted? Does any party receive unequal or unjustified treatment? Why or why not? Can you discern a larger purpose from the ruling of the court in this case? Does Judge Bench appear to be acting out of any value preferences?

The disaffirmance must occur before or within a reasonable time of the minor's reaching the age of majority. What constitutes a reasonable time is determined on a case-by-case basis. For example, in the opening scenario, the court found that it was not unreasonable for the defendant to disaffirm his contract almost a year after attaining the age of majority. In deciding to allow the disaffirmance, the court explained that the contracts were wholly executed and there was no evidence that an earlier disaffirmance would have benefited the defendant or saved it from any harm. The court further noted that the plaintiff had made no use of his education in aviation, which had been of no apparent benefit to him. Under such circumstances, the court felt that a year was a reasonable time period within which to disaffirm a contract.

As indicated in the paragraph above, the laws created to protect minors from being victimized by competent adults do not necessarily protect competent adults from being taken advantage of by knowledgeable and unethical minors. Thus, individuals operating or working in businesses that are subject to laws requiring that their customers be the age of majority or older must familiarize themselves with the laws pertaining to minors, because often the responsibility of making sure that a business is dealing with people who are of legal age falls on the employees and the owner. However, since some minors use false identification or misrepresent themselves as adults, it is difficult for business owners and employees to recognize which customers are truly of age.

For example, as CEO of Girls Gone Wild (GGW), Joe Francis runs a business that requires he be familiar with the laws surrounding minors. In fact, Francis has said that GGW has very specific procedures in place to prevent filming underage girls and even teaches its camera crew ways to ensure that the girls the crew is selecting to appear in GGW spring break videos are of age. During the selection procedure, the GGW camera crew is required to check the IDs of girls wanting to be filmed, obtain signed written release forms in which the girls give their consent to be filmed, and videotape the girls' IDs as well as the actual process of signing the release forms. Regardless of his company's strict policies, Francis found himself in the middle of a heated legal battle in 2003 when seven girls claimed that they were underage when the GGW camera crew filmed them on vacation in Panama City, Florida. Francis fought back, saying that the girls misrepresented themselves, knowingly sought out the GGW crew and wanted to exploit the company in order to obtain a monetary settlement. After four years of court proceedings and intense media coverage, Francis reached an undisclosed settlement with the women, who reportedly wanted a total of $70 million.[3]

Exceptions to the Minor's Right to Disaffirm the Contract.

The minor's right to disaffirm is designed to protect the minor from competent parties who might otherwise take advantage of him or her. But primarily for public policy reasons, in most states, courts or state legislatures have determined that the minor should *not* have the right to disaffirm contracts for life insurance, health insurance, psychological counseling, the performance of duties related to stock and bond transfers and bank accounts, education loan contracts, child support contracts, marriage contracts, and enlistment in the armed services.

Most of these exceptions apply in most, but not all, states. Another issue on which the states disagree is what should happen when a minor misrepresents his or her age. While the majority rule is that a minor's misrepresentation of age does not affect the minor's right to disaffirm the contract, some states hold that when a minor who appears to be of the age of majority misrepresents his or her age and a competent party relies on that misrepresentation in good faith, the minor gives up the right to disaffirm the agreement and can be treated as an adult. One justification for this rule is that any minor who is going to misrepresent his or her age does not need the protection that disaffirmance is designed to provide.

Other states have compromised, either by requiring that the minor restore the competent party to that party's precontract position before allowing the

To see how marketing research relates to the legal system's protection of minors, please see the **Connecting to the Core** activity on the text Web site at www.mhhe.com/kubasek2e.

---

[3] www.meetjoefrancis.com/legalstory/; www.associatedcontent.com/article/280397/two_florida_women_sue_girls_gone_wild.html?cat=17; and www.usatoday.com/life/people/2007-06-13-joe-francis_N.htm.

disaffirmance or by allowing the minor to disaffirm but then giving the competent party the right to sue the minor in tort and recover damages for fraud.

Liability of Minors for Necessaries.   A necessary is a basic necessity of life, generally including food, clothing, shelter, and basic medical services. Technically, minors can disaffirm contracts for necessaries, but they will still be held liable for the reasonable value of the necessary. The purpose of this limitation on the minor's right to disaffirm is to ensure that sellers will not be reluctant to provide minors the basic necessities of life when their parents will not provide them.

Food, clothing, shelter, and basic medical services are clearly necessaries, but it is sometimes difficult to determine whether something is in fact a necessary. Some courts define a necessary as what a minor needs to maintain his or her standard of living and financial and social status, but this can lead to a problem when an item considered a necessary for a child of upper-income parents is a luxury to a child of lower-income parents. Whether an item is considered a necessary also depends on whether the minor's parents are willing to provide it.

One of the issues raised in the opening scenario was whether the aviation classes constituted a necessary. The court found that, given the defendant's social class, it would be difficult to find them so, although perhaps some forms of education might constitute a necessary under certain circumstances.

Ratification.   Once a person reaches the age of majority, he or she may ratify, or legally affirm, contracts made as a minor. Once ratified, the contract is no longer voidable. Ratification may be either express or implied (see Exhibit 16-1).

An *express ratification* occurs when, after reaching the age of majority, the person states orally or in writing that he or she intends to be bound by the contract entered into as a minor. For example, when she is 17, Marcy enters into an agreement to purchase an automobile from Sam for 10 monthly payments of $1,000. After making the fifth payment, Marcy turns 18 and decides to move out of state. She e-mails Sam and tells him not to worry because even though she is moving, she still intends to make her monthly payments to purchase the car. Marcy has expressly ratified the contract.

An *implied ratification* occurs when the former minor takes some action after reaching the age of majority consistent with intent to ratify the contract. Going back to the previous example, if the day after she turns 18 Marcy enters into an agreement with Joe to sell him the car in six months, that action is obviously consistent with intent to finish purchasing the car, so she has impliedly ratified the contract with Sam. Most courts find that continuing to act in accordance with the contract, such as continuing to make regular payments

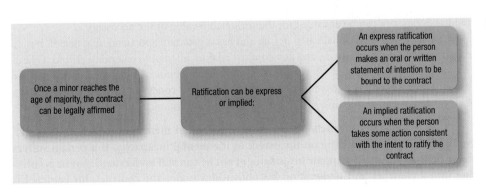

Exhibit 16-1

Ratifying a Contract

after reaching the age of majority, constitutes ratification. So, if (without the agreement with Joe) Marcy continued using the car and making payments on it for several months after reaching the age of majority, the courts would probably find that she had ratified the contract.

Parents' Liability for their Children's Contracts, Necessaries, and Torts.   As a general rule, parents are not liable for contracts entered into by their minor children. Thus, merchants are often reluctant to enter into contracts with minors unless some competent person is willing to cosign and become legally bound to perform if the minor no longer wishes to live up to the terms of the contract. Parents do, however, have a legal duty to provide their children with the basic necessities of life, such as food, clothing, and shelter. Thus, they may be held liable in some states for the reasonable value of necessaries for which their children enter into contracts.

In most states, minors, not their parents, are liable for a minor's personal torts. In many states, however, parents may be liable when a child causes harm if it can be proved that the parent failed to properly supervise the child, thereby subjecting others to an unreasonable risk of harm.

MENTALLY INCAPACITATED PERSONS

Persons suffering from a mental illness or deficiency may have full, limited, or no legal capacity to enter into a binding contract, depending on the nature and extent of their deficiency. If a person suffers from mental problems yet still understands the nature of the contract and the obligations it imposes, that person may enter into a binding, legal agreement. Suppose Gina suffers from the delusion that she is a rock star. When an encyclopedia salesperson comes to her door, she buys a set from him because she believes it is important to be knowledgeable to set a good example for her fans. As long as she understands that she is binding herself through a contract to make monthly payments for two years, Gina is bound to the contract. If, after making a year of payments, she no longer suffers from her delusions and wishes to disaffirm the contract, she will not be able to do so because her delusions had not affected her understanding of what she was legally agreeing to do when she entered into the contract.

However, a person has only limited capacity to enter into a contract if she suffers from a mental illness or deficiency that prevents her from understanding the nature and obligations of the transaction. If, in the above scenario, Gina's delusions persuaded her that she was giving the salesperson her autograph when she signed the contract, the contract is voidable. She may disaffirm it at any time until a reasonable time after she no longer suffers from the mental deficiency. Once the deficiency has been removed, Gina may also choose to ratify the contract.

As with contracts of minors, a contract for necessaries by a person suffering from a mental deficiency can be enforced for the reasonable value of the necessary.

If a person has been adjudicated insane and has a guardian appointed, that person has no capacity to enter into contracts and any contract he does attempt to enter into is void. Guardians may also be appointed for persons who have been adjudicated habitual drunkards and for those whose judgment has been impaired because of a condition such as Alzheimer disease. The guardian has the sole legal capacity to enter into contracts on such a person's behalf.

Legal Principle: **Contracts of a person with limited mental capacity can be valid, voidable, or void, depending on the extent of the mental incapacity. If a person suffers from delusions that may impair his judgment but he can still understand that he is entering into a contract and understand his obligations under the contract, his contract is**

valid; if his delusions prevent him from understanding that he is entering into a contract or the nature and extent of his obligations under the contract, his contract is voidable; and if he has been adjudicated insane, his contract is void.

INTOXICATED PERSONS

For purposes of determining capacity, intoxicated persons include those under the influence of alcohol or drugs. Most states follow the Restatement of Contracts, Section 16, which provides that contracts of an intoxicated person are voidable if the other party had reason

The degree of intoxication is crucial when determining the capacity to agree to a legal contract.

to know that intoxication rendered the person unable to understand the nature and consequences of the transaction or unable to act in a reasonable manner in relation to the transaction. If the intoxication merely causes someone to exercise poor judgment, the person's capacity is not affected unless the other party unfairly capitalizes on this impaired judgment. Exhibit 16-2 presents the key points regarding contracts made by intoxicated persons.

Recall the case of *Lucy v. Zehmer,* discussed in Chapter 14. Another argument Zehmer tried to make in that case was that he was "high as a Georgia pine" when he signed the agreement and that the transaction was "just a bunch of two doggoned drunks bluffing to see who could talk the biggest and say the most."[4] Lucy, however, testified that while he felt the drinks, he was not intoxicated and that, from the way Zehmer handled the transaction, he did not think Zehmer was either. Zehmer's discussion of the terms of the agreement made it clear that he did in fact understand the nature of the transaction and thus could not claim a lack of capacity due to intoxication.

Similarly, if one party had no way of knowing that the other was intoxicated and if the agreement is a fair one, most courts will uphold it. Suppose Lisa e-mails Rob and offers to buy his antique car for $8,000. Rob has been drinking all day and immediately responds with a yes. Lisa has no way of knowing Rob is intoxicated, so they would have a valid contract in most states.

Exhibit 16-2
Intoxicated Individuals

Generally, contracts made by intoxicated persons are voidable. However, there are exceptions:

1. If the intoxication just causes the person to exercise poor judgment, the contract is not voidable unless the other party unfairly capitalized on the impaired judgment.

2. When the intoxicated person becomes sober, the contract can be ratified or disaffirmed; however, the courts will fairly liberally interpret behavior that seems like ratifying the contract once the intoxicated person becomes sober.

[4] *Lucy v. Zehmer,* 84 S.E.2d 516 (1954).

Once sober, the previously intoxicated person has the ability to either ratify or disaffirm the contract. Because public policy does not favor intoxication, the courts tend to not be sympathetic to intoxicated parties and will fairly liberally interpret behavior that seems like ratification as ratifying the contract. If Jim became intoxicated at a bar one evening and Randi took advantage by getting him to sign a contract to sell her his 2010 SUV for $8,000, any act Jim takes consistent with ratification after becoming sober will result in a binding contract. If Randi appears at his house the next morning with the cash, shows him the contract drafted on a napkin he signed, and asks for the keys and the title, by giving her the keys and saying, "I knew I shouldn't have drunk that much," Jim has entered into a binding contract.

If the contract is disaffirmed on the basis of intoxication, each party must return the other to the condition he or she was in at the time they entered into the contract. And, just as with contracts of minors and mentally incapacitated persons, the courts will enforce an intoxicated person's contract for necessaries for their reasonable value.

Exhibit 16-3 summarizes the general rules on incapacity and contracts.

Exhibit 16-3
The Three *I*'s of Incapacity: General Rules

TYPE OF INCAPACITY	CONSIDERATIONS	IF THE ANSWER IS YES, THE GENERAL RULE IS:
*In*fancy	Is the person under the age of majority (a minor)?	The contract is voidable.
*In*sanity	Is the person suffering from mental deficiencies that prevent him from understanding his legal obligations under the contract he is entering into?	The contract is voidable.
	Does the person's mental deficiency simply impair her judgment about the desirability of the contract but not prohibit her from understanding her obligations under it?	The contract is valid.
	Is the person adjudicated insane?	The contract is void.
*In*toxication	Is the sober party aware that the intoxicated person is so impaired that he is unable to understand his legal obligations under the contract he is entering into?	The contract is voidable.
	Is the intoxication such that it impairs only the intoxicated person's judgment but not her understanding of her contractual obligations?	The contract is valid.
	Has the intoxicated person been adjudicated a habitual drunkard?	The contract is void.

Legality

To be enforceable, contracts must have legal subject matter and must be able to be performed legally. They cannot violate either state or federal law. A contract overturned for illegal subject matter or for being illegal to perform is generally declared void. A contract need not be in violation of a statute to be illegal; agreements against generally accepted public policy are also illegal and unenforceable.

Contracts that are made for an illegal purpose or that cannot be carried out by legal means are made void for two main reasons: First, making them void clearly indicates that such agreements are not socially acceptable, and, second, doing so prevents the legal system's being used to promote agreements that are harmful to society.

CONTRACTS THAT VIOLATE STATE OR FEDERAL STATUTES

There are any number of ways in which contracts can violate a state or federal statute. Some of the more common ones are discussed below and summarized in Exhibit 16-4.

Agreements to Commit a Crime or Tort.   Again, contracts cannot be for illegal purposes or require illegal acts for performance. Any agreement to commit a crime or tort is illegal and unenforceable. However, should a legal contract be formed and its subject later become illegal under a new statute, the contract is considered to be discharged by law. Suppose Jim agrees to paint Hiroki's house and, in exchange, Hiroki agrees to be a poker dealer at Jim's casino, starting in two weeks. Before Hiroki can begin work, however, the state amends its gaming statute, making all games of chance other than slot machines illegal. Because it is now illegal for Jim's casino to offer poker, it would be illegal for Hiroki to perform the contract. Because a change in the law has made the subject matter of the contract illegal, both parties are discharged from their obligations under the contract.

Licensing Statutes.   All 50 states have statutes requiring that people in certain professions obtain a license before practicing their craft. For example, doctors of all varieties, plumbers, cosmetologists, lawyers, electricians, teachers, and stockbrokers are all required to obtain a license before practicing. While this list is far from exhaustive, it demonstrates how widespread the licensing requirement can be. For most of these licensed professions, licenses are typically issued only after extensive schooling, training, and/or demonstrating some degree of competence. These requirements reflect the value society places on proper performance of duties in the licensed professions.

Licensing statutes have three main purposes in addition to indicating this value. The first is to give the government some control over which people, and how many people,

L03

What is the legal effect of entering into a contract for an illegal purpose?

Agreements to commit a crime or tort are illegal in all states.

Agreements made for the purpose of protecting the public's health, safety, or welfare by a party unlicensed to do so are typically illegal in all states.

Agreements regarding usurious loans may be illegal in some states.

Agreements regarding gambling are illegal in most states.

Agreements that violate Sabbath or Sunday laws are illegal in some states.

Exhibit 16-4

Contracts That Violate State or Federal Statutes

can perform certain jobs. Second, by charging for licenses, the government can obtain revenue.

The third purpose of licensing statutes, the protection of the public's health, safety, and welfare, is related to the public interest. By imposing legal standards on a profession, the government can try to prevent harm to public health, safety, and welfare due to substandard work. For instance, it is not in the public's best interest to allow an unqualified person to perform the delicate and complicated process of medical surgery. To limit the number of people who might be harmed during surgery, the government requires that prospective surgeons, even after extensive schooling, obtain a license.

Given these different reasons for licensing various professionals, different outcomes can result when someone enters into an agreement with a person who is unlawfully unlicensed, depending on the purpose of the licensing statute. The state in which the unlicensed person is practicing is relevant, because many licensing statutes occur at the state level and thus vary from state to state. In some states the rule is "no license, no contract." These states will not enforce any agreement with an unlawfully unlicensed professional.

However, in other states the courts typically consider the purpose of licensing. If it is to provide government control over the profession or generate revenue, most states allow enforcement of the contract. Although the unlicensed professional is acting in violation of the law and is usually required to pay a fine for working without a license, there are no grave reasons the contract should not be carried out.

If the licensing statute is intended to protect the public's health, safety, and welfare, however, the agreement is typically deemed illegal and unenforceable. For example, the public would not be made safer if the government allowed unlicensed people to perform surgery. Therefore, a person cannot enter into a contract for professional service with an unlicensed professional when the law requires a license out of intent to protect the public.

Legal Principle: If the licensing statute is intended simply to generate revenue, then the contract of an unlicensed person is valid; if the purpose of the licensing statute is to protect the public's health, safety, and welfare, however, the agreement of an unlicensed person is typically deemed illegal and unenforceable.

Usury.   Almost as widespread as licensing statutes, statutes prohibiting usury are found on the books of nearly every state. Usury occurs when a party gives a loan at an interest rate exceeding the legal maximum. The legal maximum interest rate varies from state to state, but it is easy to determine the rate of any given state.

While usury statutes act as a ceiling on rates, there are a few legal exceptions whereby loans may exceed the predetermined maximum. To facilitate business transactions and keep the economy healthy, for example, most states with usury statutes allow corporations willing to pay more to lend and borrow at rates exceeding the maximum. The rationale behind the corporation exception is that if a business needs money to expand and is willing to pay the higher interest rate, the corporation should be afforded the opportunity to borrow. The converse is that if a corporation is willing to borrow at a high interest rate, parties should be allowed to lend at that rate for corporations only. The intent is to facilitate business transactions in order to keep the economy in a healthy state.

Many states also allow parties to make small loans at rates above the maximum to parties that cannot obtain a needed loan at the statutory maximum. The belief is that if people need money and the statutory maximum is not inducing others to lend, certain parties will make the necessary loans at a higher rate as long as the loan is "small." This exception allows cash advance institutions to operate.

If no exception allows a usurious loan, the legal outcome varies by state. A few states declare all usurious loans void, which means the lender is not entitled to recover either interest or principal from the borrower. A larger number of states allow lenders to recover the principal but no interest. States most favorable toward lenders allow recovery of the principal as well as interest up to, but not exceeding, the statutory maximum.

Gambling.   All states regulate gambling. As used in this chapter, the term *gambling* refers to agreements in which parties pay consideration (money placed during bets) for the chance, or opportunity, to obtain an amount of money or property. Industry officials, however, prefer to use the term *gaming*.

While gambling is illegal in most states, some allow casino gambling, notably Nevada, New Jersey, and Louisiana. Some allow certain other types of gambling, either intentionally or through legal loopholes. For example, given California's definition of gambling, betting on draw poker is legal. Some states make other exceptions, such as for horse tracks, casinos on Native American reservations, or state-run lotteries, which, although most people do not consider them to be such, are a form of gambling.

Sabbath Laws.   A large number of states still have *Sabbath, Sunday,* or *blue* laws on the books. Sabbath laws limit the types of business activities in which parties can legally engage on Sundays. In Colonial times, these laws prohibited store operations and all work on the "Lord's day" (Sunday). Today these laws vary by state. Most prohibit the sale of all alcohol, or specific types, either all day or at particular times on Sundays. Some Sabbath laws also make it illegal to enter into any contract on a Sunday. However, an executed, or fully performed, contract created on a Sunday cannot be rescinded.

There are exceptions to Sabbath laws. Most states allow the performance of charity work on Sundays. In addition, the laws typically do not apply to contracts for obtaining "necessities," including prescription medication, food, and anything else related to health or survival.

Regardless of how widespread Sabbath laws are, the vast majority of states do not enforce some or all of their Sabbath laws. In fact, some have been held to violate the First Amendment. If they are on the books, however, they can be applied, and some states do apply them. Prudent businesspersons should always find out whether Sabbath laws exist in their state and whether authorities enforce them.

AGREEMENTS IN CONTRADICTION TO PUBLIC POLICY

Some types of agreements are not illegal per se, as they are not in violation of any statute or legal code, but are nevertheless unenforceable because courts have deemed them to be against public policy. Public policy involves both the government's concern for its citizens and the beliefs people hold regarding the proper subject of business transactions. The focus is what is "in society's best interest."

Contracts in Restraint of Trade.   It is a widely held belief in economics, and in U.S. culture in general, that competition drives down prices, which is good for consumers. Thus, agreements that restrain trade, called *anticompetitive agreements,* are viewed as being harmful to consumers and against public policy. They also frequently violate antitrust laws. See Chapter 47 for an in-depth discussion of antitrust law.

When courts determine a restraint on trade is reasonable, however, and the restraint is part of a subordinate, or ancillary, clause in the contract, the restraint is typically allowed. Such restraints are known as covenants not to compete, or *restrictive covenants.* There are two types.

The first enforceable type of restrictive covenant is one made in conjunction with the sale of an ongoing business. The public policy argument in favor of supporting restrictions regarding the sale of a business involves the fairness of the sale, as illustrated by the following hypothetical: Suppose you purchase a jewelry store from Ann, a well-respected member of the community, whose business has been around for many years. The people in the community know the store, and they trust Ann to provide fair exchanges. As a well-informed businessperson, you know about Ann's good reputation and it made the purchase more appealing.

Now suppose a month later Ann opens another jewelry store a block away. Ann's loyal customers are likely to go to her new store because they still trust her. In the meantime, Ann's good name is no longer associated with your store, and your business suffers accordingly. You entered into the sales agreement thinking you would benefit from Ann's good name, but in the end you overpaid for a business that lacks that benefit, because Ann took her name with her when she went into competition with your store. In the interest of fairness, courts are willing to impose restrictions preventing Ann, or others in her position, from going into immediate competition with you, or others in your position. Public policy requires fairness in business transactions, which does not occur when people profit from the sale of a business and then start a new business that destroys the one they just sold.

Remember, if the covenant not to compete is an integral part of the main agreement, not subordinate, the agreement is typically considered unenforceable and void, because it goes against public policy by creating unreasonable restraints on trade. When the covenant is subordinate, however, the specific noncompetition clause can be removed and the agreement can go forward as planned. In Case 16-2, the court had to determine the reasonableness of a covenant not to compete that was included in a separation agreement.

CASE 16-2   WILLIAM CAVANAUGH v. MARGARET McKENNA
SUPERIOR COURT OF MASSACHUSETTS, AT MIDDLESEX
22 MASS. L. REP. 694; 2007 MASS. SUPER. LEXIS 298

Defendant entered into a separation agreement with the plaintiff at the time of their divorce. The agreement provided in part that defendant would not accept full-time employment or open her own funeral business in Wilmington so long as the plaintiff maintained his funeral business. The trial court found that plaintiff had breached the agreement by competing with defendant by working for, and later owning, Nichols Funeral Home. On appeal, the defendant argued that the covenant not to compete was unenforceable as a restraint of trade that violated public policy.

JUSTICE SMITH: A covenant to not compete must be reasonable in time and scope, serve to protect a party's legitimate business interest, be supported by consideration,

and be consonant with the public interest. . . . While most covenants not to compete arise either in the context of an employment relationship or the sale of a business, there are situations which do not "fit neatly into existing standards for reviewing such covenants" which require analogy. *Boulanger v. Dunkin' Donuts, Inc.,* . . . (2004) (finding covenant in franchise agreement akin to that of covenant in sale of business). With the sale of a business, "courts look less critically at covenants not to compete because they do not implicate an individual's right to employment to the same degree as in the employment context." . . . Courts will consider whether the parties were represented by counsel in making the agreement and entered the agreement without compulsion. . . .

The reasonableness of a covenant not to compete must be determined by the facts of each case. . . . Factors considered in determining the reasonableness of a restriction as to time include: 1) the nature of the business; 2) the type of employment involved; 3) the situation of the parties; 4) the legitimate business interests; and 5) a party's right to work and earn a livelihood. . . . Legitimate business interests include trade secrets, confidential business information, and good will. *Id.*, 779–80.

Here, the covenant not to compete contained within the separation agreement is most analogous to the sale of a business. While McKenna worked at Cavanaugh Funeral Home before her divorce, she was not considered to be an employee. Her relinquishment of the right to operate a competing funeral home is akin to her sale of an asset. As such, the covenant not to compete should be construed more liberally. Also important in this consideration is the fact that McKenna was represented by counsel when she agreed to the noncompete provision, and there is no allegation that she was in any way coerced.

The Court finds that her covenant not to compete in the funeral business in the town of Wilmington for as long as Cavanaugh operates his funeral home there is reasonable in time and space. The restriction only applies to the town of Wilmington. Nothing prevents McKenna from entering the funeral business in another town (in fact, she worked for a funeral business in the town of Newton previously). In addition, it is important to note that there are only two funeral homes in Wilmington, Cavanaugh's and Nichols Funeral Home, and the defendant's utilization of the personal relationships forged while working at the plaintiff's funeral home would, in effect, misappropriate the good will of the plaintiff's business.

As part of the separation agreement, Cavanaugh gave up his right to the marital home and assumed the mortgage, and, in the modification, agreed to make weekly support payments, obtaining protection for the good will of his business in return. Allowing McKenna to compete in the same town while soliciting his clientele can be expected to eviscerate the good will of his business, the protection of which he received in return for his contractual undertakings.

In these circumstances, the Court finds that her covenant not to compete is enforceable. . . . Accordingly, the Court grants summary judgment to the plaintiff on Count I, leaving the issue of damages for trial.

AFFIRMED in favor of Plaintiffs.

CRITICAL THINKING

Provide an example of a piece of evidence that the defendant could have provided to indicate the unreasonableness of the scope of the covenant in this case. How does your example weigh in comparison to the evidence provided to the contrary? Do you think it would or should be sufficient to change the conclusion of the court? Defend your answer.

ETHICAL DECISION MAKING

What values are in conflict in this case? Which are supported by the ruling, and which are not? How well can the ethical stance taken by the court in this area be defended, and what ethical guidelines might be used in the effort to do so?

Legal Principle: Covenants not to compete in conjunction with the sale of a business are generally enforceable if they are for a reasonable length of time and involve a reasonable location.

The second category of permissible restraints on trade is covenants not to compete in employment contracts. The employee is agreeing, in the event of her leaving, not to compete with her boss (by starting her own company or working for competitors) for a designated period of time within a designated geographic area. These covenants are not unusual. In fact, many middle or upper-level managers enter into them.

Covenants not to compete in employment contracts are legal in most states, but they must protect a legitimate business interest. They must also apply to a period of time and geographic area that are reasonable for that purpose and not unlawfully impinge on the employee's rights. Not surprisingly, the enforceability of covenants not to compete in employment contracts varies from state to state. California does not allow any covenants not to compete. Texas requires that the employee gain or be given a specific benefit beyond employment before its courts will enforce even a reasonable covenant not to compete.

Employers and employees may therefore attempt to file suit or have their cases heard in the location that can provide them with the most favorable legal environment given their situation. Thus, business owners who create covenants not to compete may prefer to file suit in a location that is more tolerant of covenants not to compete, and employees may wish to have their cases heard in a location, such as California, that generally prohibits the enforceability of covenants not to compete.

For example, when executive Kai-Fu Lee left his job with Microsoft to join rival Google, Microsoft filed suit in the state of Washington, alleging that Lee's decision was in violation of his noncompete contract. Google fought back by filing suit against Microsoft in California, the state where Google is based, saying that under California laws Lee's noncompete contract was unenforceable. Both companies fought one another in court to have the case heard in the state where one or the other had the best chance of winning. In the end, a district court judge ruled that the case would first be tried in Washington, and if Google wanted to pursue the case further in California, it could do so after the trial. Early decisions made by the judge in Washington state court seemed to fall in Microsoft's favor, and Lee was initially barred from doing certain tasks for Google until after the trial. However, before the trial could end, the two companies reached a private settlement agreement.[5]

Unconscionable Contracts or Clauses.   When courts are asked to review contracts, fairness is not usually high on their list of things to look for. Instead, they typically assume that the contracting parties are intelligent, responsible adults who enter into contracts because they want to. Nevertheless, some agreements are so one-sided that the courts will not make the innocent party be harmed by fulfilling his or her contractual duties. These heavily one-sided agreements are known as **unconscionable** agreements. The term *unconscionable* refers to the fact that the agreement in question is so unfair that it is void of conscience.

The common law would not enforce contracts the courts deemed unconscionable. Now rules against unconscionable contracts exist in both the Restatement (Second) of Contracts and the Uniform Commercial Code. UCC Section 2-302 states:

> (1) If the court as a matter of law finds the contract or any clause of the contract to have been unconscionable at the time it was made, the court may refuse to enforce the contract, or it may enforce the remainder of the contract without the clause, or it may so limit the application of any unconscionable clause as to avoid any unconscionable result; (2) When it is claimed or appears to the court that the contract or any clause thereof may be unconscionable, the parties shall be afforded a reasonable opportunity to present evidence as to its commercial setting, purpose, and effect to aid the court in making the determination.

[5] http://news.cnet.com/Kai-Fu-Lees-California-case-put-on-hold/2100-1022_3-5918672.html; www.forbes.com/2005/12/23/gates-microsoft-google-cx_cn_1223autofacescan02.html; and http://news.cnet.com/Microsoft-sues-over-Google-hire/2100-1014_3-5795051.html.

Every state except California and Louisiana has incorporated this section into its UCC. Section 208 of the Restatement also incorporates the above section.

There are two main types of unconscionable agreements, procedural and substantive. **Procedural unconscionability** describes conditions that impair one party's understanding of a contract, as well as the integration of terms into a contract. These conditions can be anything from tiny, hard-to-read print on the back of an agreement to excessive use of legalese (unnecessarily technical legal language) or even a person's inability to fully read a contract and ask questions before being required to sign.

Procedural unconscionability usually arises in an **adhesion contract,** an agreement presented on a take-it-or-leave-it basis or as the only chance the presented party (the *adhering party*) will have to enter into it. While adhesion contracts are legal, they do raise red flags for courts, which will try to determine how voluntary the agreement really was.

Substantive unconscionability occurs when an agreement is overly harsh or lopsided. Courts would find the following, for example, to be substantively unconscionable: large differences between cost and price in a sales agreement; agreements in which one party gains vastly more than the other; agreements in which one party is prevented from having equal benefit or has little to no legal recourse; and portions of an agreement unrelated to either party's business risk.

Exculpatory Clauses.   An **exculpatory clause** releases one of the contracting parties from all liability, regardless of who is at fault or what injury is suffered. Because tort law attempts to return the wronged party to a state he or she was in before the wrong occurred, anything preventing this corrective mechanism is against public policy. It does not benefit society to allow some parties to get away with not having to pay for wrongs they commit simply because they state they will not be liable in various contracts. In fact, the patently unfair nature of an exculpatory clause is closely tied to the idea of unconscionable contracts.

Exculpatory clauses frequently show up in rental agreements for commercial or residential property. It does not serve the public's interest to allow landlords, especially of residential property, to disavow in advance all liabilities for injuries due to carelessness, negligence, or other wrongdoing. If they were allowed to do so, nothing would require them to fix problems in their rental units, including potentially lethal problems like faulty wiring or the presence of lead-based paint.

A basic test to determine whether an exculpatory clause is enforceable is to see whether the enforcing party engages in a business directly related to the public interest, as does a bank, transportation provider, or public utility. Courts believe it is against the public interest to allow businesses engaging in work in the public's interest *not* to be held accountable to the public they are serving.

Businesses serving the public interest can also possess unfair bargaining power in negotiating a contract; they could simply demand that all customers accept the exculpatory clause, thereby escaping all liability. Worse, there would then be no financial motive for them to conduct operations carefully, and the potential for increased accidents would be great. Obviously, it is not in the public's interest to have unsafe businesses not be accountable to the public. Thus, these businesses cannot enforce exculpatory clauses.

Case 16-3 details a court's determination that an illegal exculpatory clause existed.

Eric Lucier and Karen A. Haley, a young married couple, were first-time home buyers. They contracted with the Williams's to purchase a single-family residence. Lucier and Haley engaged the services of Cambridge Associates, Ltd. (CAL), to perform a home inspection. Al Vasys had formed CAL and was its president. Lucier dealt directly with Vasys, and Vasys performed the inspection and issued the home inspection report on behalf of CAL.

The home inspection agreement contains a provision limiting CAL's liability to "$500, or 50% of fees actually paid to CAL by Client, whichever sum is smaller." This provision, like several others in the form agreement prepared by CAL, was followed by a line for the clients' initials. Lucier initialed this provision. The fee for the home inspection contract was $385, which Lucier paid to CAL.

Lucier claims when he began to read the agreement, in Vasys' presence, he felt some of the language was unfair and confusing. According to Lucier, Vasys stated he would not change any provisions, that it was a standard contract based upon home inspections done in New Jersey, and Lucier would have to sign the agreement "as is" or not at all. Vasys does not dispute this but relies upon Lucier's signing the agreement and initialing the limitation of liability clause. Likewise, Lucier does not deny signing the contract or initialing that clause.

Lucier and Haley obtained title to the property from the Williams's. Shortly after, they noticed leaks in the house. They engaged the services of a roofing contractor and found the roof was defective. Lucier and Haley argue Vasys should have observed and reported the problem to them. The cost of repair was about $8,000 to $10,000.

Lucier and Haley brought suit against the Williams's, CAL, and Vasys, seeking damages to compensate them for the loss occasioned by the alleged defect. CAL and Vasys moved for partial summary judgment seeking a declaration that the limit of their liability in the action, if any, was one-half the contract price, or $192.50. The motion for partial summary judgment was granted. Lucier and Haley then filed this appeal, seeking review of the partial summary judgment order.

JUDGE LISA: There is no hard and fast definition of unconscionability. As the Supreme Court explained in *Kugler v. Romain,* unconscionability is "an amorphous concept obviously designed to establish a broad business ethic." The standard of conduct that the term implies is a lack of "good faith, honesty in fact and observance of fair dealing."

In determining whether to enforce the terms of a contract, we look not only to its adhesive nature, but also to "the subject matter of the contract, the parties' relative bargaining positions, the degree of economic compulsion motivating the 'adhering' party, and the public interests affected by the contract." Where the provision limits a party's liability, we pay particular attention to any inequality in the bargaining power and status of the parties, as well as the substance of the contract.

We also focus our inquiry on whether the limitation is a reasonable allocation of risk between the parties or whether it runs afoul of the public policy disfavoring clauses which effectively immunize parties from liability for their own negligent actions. To be enforceable, the amount of the cap on a party's liability must be sufficient to provide a realistic incentive to act diligently.

Applying these principles to the home inspection contract before us, we find the limitation of liability provision unconscionable. We do not hesitate to hold it unenforceable for the following reasons: (1) the contract, prepared by the home inspector, is one of adhesion; (2) the parties, one a consumer and the other a professional expert, have grossly unequal bargaining status; and (3) the substance of the provision eviscerates the contract and its fundamental purpose because the potential damage level is so nominal that it has the practical effect of avoiding almost all responsibility for the professional's negligence. Additionally, the provision is contrary to our state's public policy of effectuating the purpose of a home inspection contract to render reliable evaluation of a home's fitness for purchase and holding professionals to certain industry standards.

This is a classic contract of adhesion. There were no negotiations leading up to its preparation. The contract was presented to Lucier on a standardized preprinted form, prepared by CAL, on a take-it-or-leave-it basis, without any opportunity for him to negotiate or modify any of its terms.

The bargaining position between the parties was grossly disparate. Vasys has been in the home inspection business for twenty years. He has inspected thousands of homes. He has an engineering degree. He has served as an expert witness in construction matters. He holds various designations in the building and construction field. He advertises his company and holds it and himself out as possessing expertise in the home inspection field. Lucier and Haley, on the other hand, are unknowledgeable and unsophisticated in matters of home construction. They are consumers. They placed their trust in this expert. They had every reason to expect he would act with diligence and competence in inspecting the home they desired to purchase and discover and report major defects. The disparity in the positions of these parties is clear and substantial.

The foisting of a contract of this type in this setting on an inexperienced consumer clearly demonstrates a lack of fair dealing by the professional. The cost of homes in New Jersey is substantial.

The limitation of liability clause here is also against public policy. First, it allows the home inspector to circumvent the state's public policy of holding professional service providers to certain industry standards. Second, it contravenes the stated public policy of New Jersey regarding home inspectors.

With professional services, exculpation clauses are particularly disfavored. The very nature of a professional service is one in which the person receiving the service relies upon the expertise, training, knowledge and stature of the professional. Exculpation provisions are antithetical to such a relationship.

In summary, the limitation of liability provision in this contract is unconscionable and violates the public policy of our State. The contract is one of adhesion, the bargaining power of the parties is unequal, the impact of the liability clause is negligible to the home inspector while potentially severe to the home buyer, and the provision conflicts with the purpose of home inspection contracts and our Legislature's requirement of accountability by home inspectors for their errors and omissions.

REVERSED and REMANDED.

CRITICAL THINKING

In this decision, does Judge Lisa make any assumptions regarding the facts of the case without proper evidence to support them as a reasoning step? For instance, what evidence supports her characterization of Lucier? Is it possible he is significantly different from the way he has been presented? How might such differences affect the acceptability of the conclusion? Can you locate any other assumptions in this ruling? How do they affect the reasoning?

ETHICAL DECISION MAKING

Examine the actions of each party leading up to this dispute. Who behaved in a blameworthy fashion, and who in a praiseworthy fashion? What facts from the case and what ethical theories or guidelines support your claim?

Now consider each party's stance in the legal dispute. Does either one appear more or less ethical, relative to that party's earlier actions? Why or why not?

While businesses closely linked to the public interest cannot enforce exculpatory clauses, not all such clauses are unlawful. To prevail, the party seeking enforcement must be a private business or individual *not* important to the public interest. These private businesses or individuals provide nonessential services and thus do not have the same bargaining power as the previously discussed groups, such as banks, utilities, or airlines. Given their lack of huge bargaining power, courts assume such businesses and individuals will enter a contract voluntarily and on relatively equal terms.

Private businesses that *can* enforce exculpatory clauses thus include skiing facilities such as resorts or rental places, private gyms or health clubs, any business offering sky diving or bungee jumping, and amusement parks, to name a few. Because their services and those of others in this category are not related to the public interest and are not activities in which people *must* engage, these parties are allowed to deny liability if the other party agrees to the exculpatory clause. Just because these parties *might* be able to enforce an exculpatory clause, however, does not mean the clause is always automatically enforceable.

EFFECT OF ILLEGAL AGREEMENTS

When an agreement is deemed illegal, courts will usually label it void. The reason is the legal principle of *in pari delicto,* which means both parties are equally responsible for the illegal agreement. In that case, it does not make sense for the courts to attempt to salvage the agreement or reward either party. Therefore, neither party can enforce the agreement, and neither is entitled to recovery.

But what if both parties are *not* at fault? What if one is significantly more culpable? Then it sometimes makes sense to allow one party to an illegal agreement to recover various damages.

The first exception to the general rule occurs when a member of a protected class is party to an agreement that contradicts a statute intended to protect the specific class. That party is allowed to sue for performance. The reasoning is that a statute intended to protect a specific class should not be allowed to harm those in the class.

For example, a work agreement between Diego and his employer may specify that Diego gets paid for the number of hours he works as a truck driver. Yet certain statutes limit the number of hours truck drivers may drive in a given time period. If Diego accidentally drives more than the allowable hours, he has technically violated a statute. However, this violation does not allow his employer to refuse to pay him for the extra hours. Rather, Diego may sue his employer to enforce the work agreement.

The second exception to the voiding of illegal agreements occurs when *justifiable ignorance of facts* leaves one party unaware of a provision of the agreement that would make it illegal. While ignorance of the law does not excuse illegal behavior, not knowing that the other party intended to fulfill the agreement through illegal means does function as an excuse.

When one party is relatively innocent, the court may give back any consideration that party gave or may require exchange for partial performance such that both parties can be returned to the positions they were in before they entered into the agreement. If one party is completely innocent of any illegality and has completed his or her portion of the contract, then—depending on the reason the contract is considered illegal and which state's laws are in question—the court might enforce the entire agreement.

A third exception to the general rule occurs when one of the parties withdraws from an illegal agreement. The key to any recovery is that the party must have withdrawn before any illegality occurred. The party may then recover value for whatever partial or full performance has been completed. However, a party involved in the illegal activity in any way cannot recover at all.

Severable Contracts. Severable contracts, also known as *divisible contracts,* contain multiple parts that can each be performed separately and for which separate consideration is offered. In essence, a severable contract is like

What happened to you?!?!

The court severed my illegal provision. Man, it hurts.

stus.com

Determining the Legality of an Arbitration Clause

Buckeye Check Cashing, Inc. v. Cardegna et al.
United States Supreme Court
126 S. Ct. 1204, 163 L. Ed. 2d 1038 (2006)

The respondents, Cardegna et al., entered into a number of deferred-payment transactions with Buckeye Check Cashing. Each agreement they signed contained a provision requiring binding arbitration to resolve disputes arising out of the agreement. The respondents filed a class action suit against Buckeye in Florida state court, alleging that Buckeye charged usurious interest rates and that the agreement violated various Florida laws, rendering it illegal on its face. The trial court denied Buckeye's motion to compel arbitration, holding that a court rather than an arbitrator should resolve a claim that a contract is illegal and void *ab initio*. A state appellate court reversed, but its decision was in turn reversed by the Florida Supreme Court, which reasoned that enforcing an arbitration agreement in a contract challenged as unlawful would violate state public policy and contract law. The case was appealed to the U.S. Supreme Court to determine whether the courts or an arbitrator should determine the legality of a potentially illegal contract containing a binding arbitration clause.

The Court answered this question by relying on three established propositions. First, as a matter of substantive federal arbitration law, an arbitration provision is severable from the remainder of the contract. Second, unless the challenge is to the arbitration clause itself, the issue of the contract's validity is considered by the arbitrator in the first instance. Third, this arbitration law applies in state as well as federal courts. Applying these propositions to the case, the high court concluded that when an agreement as a whole, but not specifically its arbitration provisions, is challenged, the arbitration provisions are enforceable apart from the remainder of the contract. The challenge to the legality of the contract itself should therefore be considered by an arbitrator, not a court.

---

numerous contracts in one. An **indivisible contract,** on the other hand, requires complete performance by both parties, even if it appears to contain multiple parts.

With respect to illegality, severable contracts have a huge advantage: If they have both legal and illegal portions, the court can void only the illegal sections and enforce the rest as long as they represent the main purpose of the original agreement. Indivisible contracts must be enforced or rejected in their entirety. If declaring parts of a contract void substantially alters it, the court is not likely to enforce the remaining portions. Courts ultimately want to facilitate business transactions and enforce the legal wishes of parties, and severable contracts enable them to do so.

Legal Principle: If the court can sever the illegal part of a contract from the legal part, it will generally do so and enforce only the legal part; if the contract is indivisible, then it generally will be unenforceable.

CASE OPENER WRAP-UP

A Wasted Education

On appeal, the judge agreed with the trial court judge that education in aviation was not a necessary.

The court further found that the plaintiff's delay in disaffirming the contracts for nearly a year after reaching the age of majority did not, as a matter of law, constitute a ratification of them. The court reasoned that the contracts were wholly executed and there was no evidence that an earlier disaffirmance would have benefited the defendant or saved it from harm. In addition, the plaintiff had not made use of his education in aviation during that time, or at any other time, so the plaintiff received no benefit from the delay.

Key Terms

adhesion contract   373

capacity   359

covenants not
    to compete   369

exculpatory clause   373

gambling   369

indivisible contract   377

in pari delicto   376

procedural
    unconscionability   373

Sabbath laws   369

severable
    contracts   376

substantive
    unconscionability   373

unconscionable   372

usury   368

Summary of Key Topics

Capacity

Natural persons over the age of majority are presumed to have the full legal capacity to enter into binding legal contracts.

A person has only limited capacity to enter into a legally binding contract, and therefore can enter into only voidable contracts, if the person is either:

- A minor.
- Suffering from a mental deficiency that prevents the person from understanding the nature and obligations of contracts.
- Intoxicated.

A person has no capacity to enter into a contract if the person either:

- Has been adjudicated insane.
- Has been adjudicated a habitual drunkard.
- Has had a legal guardian appointed to enter into contracts on his or her behalf.

Necessaries: Even if a party has the ability to disaffirm a contract, if the contract is for a necessary—something like food, clothing, or shelter—the party cannot completely disaffirm the contract; she will be held liable for the reasonable value of the necessary.

Legality

Contracts that do not have a legal object are not valid.

Contracts that lack a legal object because they violate a statute or violate public policy are not valid.

When a contract is partly legal and partly illegal, if the illegal part can be severed, then the legal part will still be enforced, but if the contract is indivisible, it will be void and not enforced.

Point / Counterpoint

Should the Age at Which Minors Have Full Capacity to Enter into Binding Contracts Be Lowered to 16?	
YES	**NO**
Given the rights and responsibilities currently granted to 16-year-olds, lowering the age at which minors can enter into legally binding contracts seems logical.	Under the law, teenagers are not viewed as adults until they have reached the age of majority. In nearly every state, the age of majority is at least 18. The age at which

One of the most widely argued reasons given against lowering the age requirement pertains to a teenager's ability to fully understand a contract and comprehend the consequences associated with it. In response, proponents argue that society has already given children responsibilities and rights that are associated with long-term consequences; 16-year-olds are viewed, in the eyes of the law, as being able to consent to a sexual relationship. Along with this right comes the responsibility of understanding the potential for pregnancy and/or disease (which are *extremely* long-term consequences).

Perhaps as a result of their ability to consent to sexual relationships, 16-year-olds are often able to marry if the female is pregnant. Marriage is, by definition, a contract. These teenagers are already able, albeit in a limited fashion, to enter into binding contracts.

Furthermore, at the age of 16, a teenager can request a work permit and begin employment. As a result of this employment, the teenager is able to earn an income and make purchases. By maintaining the current age at which teenagers are seen as having the legal capacity to enter into a contract, society is, in effect, limiting the teenager's ability to make transactions he or she would otherwise be able to make. This limitation not only restricts teenagers' freedoms but also reduces commerce in this country. Society *should* lower the age requirement to 16.

teenagers can enter into binding contracts should *not* be lower than the age of majority.

At the age of 16, teenagers are still in the process of completing high school. They have not taken courses in financial management and have not been adequately introduced to contracts through life experiences. As such, these youths lack the ability to fully understand or comprehend the nature of or consequences associated with entering into contracts.

Additionally, at the age of 16, nearly all teenagers are still residing within the home of a parent and/or guardian. Parents are held liable for many actions and decisions of their children. To cite but one potential example, if a child under the age of majority entered into a cell phone contract and was eventually unable to pay the related bills, it is possible that under parental liability law the parents will be held responsible for the funds owed. In short, society could prevent this undue burden from being placed on parents by keeping the age at which youths have the capacity to enter into contracts equal to, or greater than, the age of majority. Parents should have the ability to decide whether or not they wish to sign a contract on their child's behalf if it is potentially they who will ultimately be held responsible.

Questions & Problems

1. How does the concept of the age of majority differ in Great Britain from that in the United States?

2. Explain the obligations of a minor who chooses to disaffirm a contract.

3. Go back to the discussion of contracts that cannot be disaffirmed by minors, and explain the policy reasons that support each of the exceptions. Can you make an argument for any additional kinds of contracts that should not be subject to disaffirmance by minors?

4. If all you know about a man is that his neighbors think he is crazy, you do not know whether the contract he entered into was valid, voidable, or void. Why not?

5. What factors determine whether a covenant not to compete is legal or illegal?

6. What is the relationship between contracts in restraint of trade and unconscionable contracts?

7. Roger Bannister was the director of technical and product development for Bemis. Bannister entered into a covenant not to compete with Bemis, which prohibited Bannister from working for a Bemis competitor for 18 months after the termination of his employment. The covenant not to compete included a provision which stated that Bemis was to pay Bannister his monthly salary if he was unable to find work due solely to the covenant not to compete, providing that he provide the relevant paperwork.

    Bemis terminated Bannister's employment. Bannister's counsel sent a letter to Bemis requesting payment of his monthly salary under the covenant not to compete because he was unemployed due solely to the covenant not to compete. In this letter, Bannister included a letter he had received from Mondi, which informed him that Mondi would hire him if not for the covenant not to compete. Bannister sent a job contacts log to Bemis that detailed his job search and again requested that Bemis start paying his monthly salary under the covenant not to compete. Bemis responded by allowing Bannister out of the covenant not to compete, with the exception that he could not work for Mondi because of a separate agreement Bemis had with Mondi. Bannister responded by letter, stating that the Bemis correspondence was the first notice of his release to pursue employment with any competitor other than Mondi and that he considered the release a partial release because of the Mondi exception. Bemis then confirmed in a letter that Bannister could accept "employment with any company other than [Mondi]" and reiterated its position that there were no damages due under the covenant not to compete "based on the fact that Mr. Bannister has been released to seek employment with any company other than [Mondi]."

Bannister accepted a position with Bancroft Bag, Inc., a Bemis competitor. He brought a claim against Bemis for its failure to pay his monthly salary for the nine-month period during which he was out of work under the covenant not to compete. The district court found in Bannister's favor. Bemis appealed. How did the appellate court rule, and why? [*Bannister v. Bemis Co., Inc.*, 556 F.3d 882 (2009).]

8. Paul Stewart and Ellen Chalk bought a wireless LAN PC card, manufactured by Sony, to connect wirelessly to the Internet through service provided by T-Mobile. Stewart and Chalk also signed a one-year service agreement with T-Mobile. The service agreement mandated arbitration and prohibited class action lawsuits. For approximately three weeks after the purchase of the card, Stewart and Chalk were able to insert it into their IBM ThinkPad laptop and connect to the Internet without any difficulty. They then did not attempt to use the card again for a few months, at which time they were unable to insert the card into their ThinkPad. They contacted T-Mobile technical support several times and received refurbished cards on three separate occasions. None of the refurbished cards fit into the ThinkPad. After Stewart and Chalk were unable to insert the third card, staff from T-Mobile technical support informed them that they would have to pursue the issue at the T-Mobile store where they purchased the original card. At the store, a Sony representative attempted to insert the card, but he failed as well. He then promised to contact them

about how to solve the problem. They never heard back from him, despite multiple e-mail inquiries.

Ultimately, Stewart and Chalk filed a class action lawsuit against T-Mobile and Sony. The complaint alleged that Sony and T-Mobile knew or should have known that the card "was not compatible and/or did not fit into the IBM ThinkPad laptop" computers and that Sony and T-Mobile allowed customers to purchase cards and enter into long-term service contracts from which consumers would receive no benefit without a compatible card. Sony and T-Mobile filed a motion to compel arbitration. Stewart and Chalk opposed the motion, contending that the arbitration clause was unconscionable and therefore unenforceable. The district court ruled in favor of Sony and T-Mobile. Stewart and Chalk appealed. Is the arbitration agreement unconscionable? If you were an attorney for Stewart and Chalk, would you argue that the arbitration clause was procedurally unconscionable, substantively unconscionable, or both? Why? [*Chalk v. T-Mobile, USA, Inc.*, 560 F.3d 1087 (2009).]

9. Seigneur joined NFI, a health and fitness facility, to lose weight and become fit. She was in poor physical condition and had back problems that she discussed with NFI before signing a contract with the facility. The contract she ultimately signed contained a clause that said NFI was not responsible for injuries sustained during exercise. Seigneur claimed that she tore a muscle in her shoulder while doing a series of tests to evaluate her physical condition. The tear required surgery to be repaired, and her surgeon stated that he believed the injury was caused by her using an upper-torso weight machine during her fitness evaluation. She sued NFI for negligence. NFI filed a motion for summary judgment on the basis of the exculpatory clause. The trial court granted NFI's motion, and Seigneur appealed. Do you believe the appellate court upheld the motion for summary judgment? Why or why not? [*Seigneur v. National Fitness Institute, Inc.*, 752 A.2d 631 (Ct. App. Md. 2000).]

10. On July 16, 1997, Chicago Steel entered into a contract with ADT in which ADT agreed to design, sell, install, and/or maintain a fire alarm system and provide fire alarm monitoring and reporting services for Chicago Steel's plant at 6630 W. Wrightwood Avenue in Chicago. Under the terms

of the contract, ADT was to maintain the fire alarm system and inspect it four times a year. Chicago Steel was to pay ADT $3,472 annually.

The contract stated that ADT was not an insurer and would be exempt from liability for damage to property, whether based on breach of contract, negligence, or strict liability. The contract also contained a limitation-of-damages clause limiting any liability on ADT's part to the greater of 10 percent of the annual service charge or $1,000. The contract, however, gave Chicago Steel the option of paying for an allocation of additional liability to ADT. The record reflects that Chicago Steel did not exercise that option.

On January 2, 1999, after the alarm system's installation, a fire occurred at the Wrightwood plant, causing substantial damage to property located there. The plaintiffs sued ADT, alleging that the failure of the alarm system and/or ADT's failure to maintain and monitor the system caused a delay in notification to the Chicago fire department and resulted in substantial property damage. Their complaint included four counts: (1) strict product liability, (2) breach of contract, (3) negligence, and (4) gross negligence.

ADT filed a motion to dismiss the plaintiffs' complaint, based in part on the exculpatory clause contained in its fire alarm installation and maintenance contract with Chicago Steel, which released ADT from future negligence, breach of contract, and strict-liability claims. The trial court granted the motion. On appeal, do you think the exculpatory clause was enforced by the appellate court? Why or why not? [*Chicago Steel Rule and Die Fabricators Company and Travelers Indemnity Company of Illinois v. ADT Security Systems, Inc., ADT Security Services, Inc.,* 327 Ill. App. 3d 642, 763 N.E.2d 839 (2002).]

Looking for more review material?

The Online Learning Center at **www.mhhe.com/kubasek2e** contains this chapter's "Assignment on the Internet" and also a list of URLs for more information, entitled "On the Internet." Find both of them in the Student Center portion of the OLC, along with quizzes and other helpful materials.

CHAPTER

17 Legal Assent

LEARNING OBJECTIVES

After reading this chapter, you will be able to answer the following questions:

1 Why is legal assent important?

2 What are the elements of mistake?

3 What are the elements of misrepresentation?

4 What are the elements of undue influence?

5 What are the elements of duress?

6 What are the elements of unconscionability?

CASE OPENER

A Disagreement over an Agreement

In spring 1989, Michael Jordan and the Chicago Bulls were in Indianapolis, Indiana, to play against the Indiana Pacers. At the same time, Karla Knafel was singing with a band at a hotel in Indianapolis. After Knafel's performance, a National Basketball Association referee approached her and introduced her to Jordan via telephone. Knafel and Jordan began a long-distance telephone relationship that continued for several months.

In December 1989, Knafel traveled to Chicago to meet with Jordan, where the couple had unprotected sex for the first time. In November 1990, the couple had unprotected sex again while in Phoenix, Arizona. Shortly after this second meeting, Knafel learned that she was pregnant. Knafel was "convinced that she was carrying Jordan's baby" despite having had sex with other male partners. Later, during spring 1991, Knafel informed Jordan "she was pregnant with his child."

As a result of several conversations about the baby, Knafel alleged that the two had agreed that Jordan would pay her $5 million when he retired from professional basketball. In return, Knafel promised she would not file a paternity suit against him and would keep their relationship a secret.

In July 1991, the baby was born. Jordan paid some hospital bills and medical costs, and he paid Knafel $250,000 for "her mental pain and anguish arising from her relationship with him." Knafel continued to keep the relationship and paternity a secret.

After Jordan retired from professional basketball, a lawsuit arose between the parties in 2000. Jordan sought declaratory judgment and an injunction against Knafel, who had been approaching him for the $5 million. Knafel filed a counterclaim for Jordan's alleged breach of contract. The trial court dismissed all claims, but the appellate court remanded Knafel's claim for breach of contract. Although Jordan had originally denied the existence of the agreement, on remand he did not contest the existence of the alleged settlement agreement. Instead, Jordan argued that the alleged agreement was not enforceable because it either was fraudulently induced or was based on a mutual mistake of fact. In support of his argument, Jordan produced the affidavit of Dr. Storm, who, after DNA testing, concluded that Jordan was not the child's father.

In response to Jordan's argument, Knafel claimed that the paternity of the child was irrelevant to the enforceability of the alleged agreement. An obstetrician had told Knafel that the baby was conceived on November 19 or 20, 1990 (while she was in Phoenix with Jordan). As a result of this information, Knafel believed that the baby was Jordan's. Additionally, Knafel asserted that the paternity was irrelevant because Jordan entered into the agreement knowing that she had been having sex with other men.

The trial court ruled in favor of Jordan, finding that "as a result of Knafel's fraudulent misrepresentation to Jordan that he was the child's father or, alternatively, as a result of a mutual mistake of fact, the alleged settlement contract is voidable and is therefore unenforceable against Jordan." Knafel appealed.

1. Imagine you are the judge in this case. Do you think that both parties were able to legally assent to the agreement?
2. Under which ethical system, if any, should Knafel be able to recover the $5 million for breach of contract?

The Wrap-Up at the end of the chapter will answer these questions.

The Importance of Legal Assent

L01

Why is legal assent important?

When two people talk in the hope that an exchange will take place between them, all kinds of things can go wrong. Yet global business needs dependability. Imagine what transactions would be like if "Yes" meant "Maybe!" Deals would be closed only to be reopened again and again. The costs of all purchases would soar. Businesses would be forced to charge extra to pay for all the extra time they had to spend to finally get to the point where "Yes" really meant "Yes."

To make business transactions smoother and more dependable, courts have developed rules about when an assent to do something is a **legal assent,** that is, a promise the courts will require the parties to obey.

The courts see some forms of assent as more genuine or real than others. It is important for businesspeople to know the differences among the various kinds of assent. Why do the differences matter? Jamal may think he has sold his tutoring services to Harrison. However, without legal assent the contract may be **voidable,** a circumstance that can cost a business large profits when the transaction is significant. A voidable contract can be **rescinded,** or canceled, permitting the person who canceled the contract to require the return of everything she gave the other party. She must herself return whatever she has received. An enormous waste of time and an unnecessary cost of doing business may be the result.

The major theme of this chapter is that *best-practice firms aim for legal assent in their contracts.* This chapter shows you how to achieve legal assent. It explains the major obstacles to legal assent: mistake, misrepresentation, undue influence, duress, and unconscionability. By knowing about these potential problems, you will be in a good position to avoid them.

Mistake

L02

What are the elements of mistake?

When people agree to buy or sell, they do so with a particular understanding about the nature of the good or service they are about to exchange. However, one or both parties may think they consented to exchange a particular thing only to find out later that no meeting of the minds had occurred. People may misunderstand either some fact about the deal or the value of what is being exchanged. We focus on misunderstandings about facts, because they are the only issues that raise the potential of rescission (the rescinding of a contract) in U.S. courts. Mistaken beliefs about the subjective value of an item do not affect the validity of the contract.

In contract law a **mistake of fact** is an erroneous belief about the facts of the contract *at the time the contract is concluded.* Legal assent is absent when a mistake of fact occurs. Later in this chapter, when we discuss misrepresentation, our focus will be on incorrect beliefs about the facts of the contract caused by the other party's untrue statements. Mistakes in contract law do *not* result from these untrue statements.

Mistakes can be **unilateral,** the result of an error by *one* party about a material fact, that is, a fact that is important in the context of the particular contract. Or mistakes can be **mutual,** shared by both parties to the agreement. As we see next, this distinction is important in determining which contracts are voidable.

The insurance companies are fighting about "mutual mistake." I thought they were talking about the accident, but it's actually about the wording of the insurance documents.

stus.com

The European View about Mistakes about Value

European courts take a different approach to mistakes about the *value of performance* of the contract. In general, they agree with the reluctance of U.S. courts to interfere with a contract just because the value of the item in question has changed since the agreement. The parties are assumed to have accepted the risk that the value might change after they made the contract. However, European courts permit rescission of the contract for a mistake of value when the mistake involves more than 50 percent of the value at the time of the contract.

UNILATERAL MISTAKE

Because courts are hesitant to interfere when one of the parties has a correct understanding of the material facts of the agreement, a unilateral mistake does not generally void a contract. For instance, a widow seeking to rescind her and her husband's election to have his retirement benefits paid out over *his* life was not permitted to receive survivor's pension benefits. The court held that representatives of the retirement system had provided sufficient information to the plaintiff and her husband before they elected that particular form of payout.[1]

On rare occasions, however, rescission *is* permitted for unilateral mistakes. Because our economic well-being depends so heavily on reliable contracts, we want to be fully aware of the circumstances under which unilateral mistakes permit rescission. Any of the following conditions would permit a court to invalidate a contract on grounds of unilateral mistake:

1. One party made a mistake about a material fact, and the other party knew or had reason to know about the mistake.
2. The mistake was caused by a clerical error that was accidental and did not result from gross negligence.
3. The mistake was so serious that the contract is unconscionable, that is, so unreasonable that it is outrageous.

These situations are rare, but it is important to be aware of them because any rescission can be costly in terms of time and lost opportunities.

MUTUAL MISTAKE

When both parties are mistaken about a current or past material fact, either can choose to rescind the contract. Rescission is fair because any agreement was an illusion: Ambiguity prevented a true meeting of the minds.

The famous story of the ship *Peerless*[2] has taught generations of students the importance of being very clear in defining material facts in any contract. The parties in the case had agreed that the vessel *Peerless* would deliver the cotton they were exchanging. Unfortunately for them, there were two ships named *Peerless*. So when the deal was made, one party had one *Peerless* in mind while the other meant the second. The times the ships sailed were materially different, so the court rescinded the contract. *Warning:* Anticipate ambiguity in material facts, and clarify them in advance to save yourself headaches later.

---

[1] *Ricks v. Missouri Local Government Employees Retirement System,* 1999 WL 663217 (Mo. App. WD).

[2] *Raffles v. Wichelhaus,* 159 Eng. Rep. 375 (1864).

A Questionable "Mistake"

Mary W. Scott (Respondent-Appellant) v. Mid-Carolina Homes, Inc. (Appellant-Respondent)
Court of Appeals of South Carolina
293 S.C. 191 (1987)

Mary Scott signed a contract to purchase a repossessed 1984 mobile home from Mid-Carolina Homes, Inc., for $5,644 to be paid in full before delivery. Scott gave the salesperson a check for $2,913.71, and agreed to pay the balance before the end of the month. Within the next week, the salesman called Scott and told her that according to the standards of the South Carolina Manufactured Housing Board he could not sell her the home because it had a bent frame. Scott offered to buy it as is and sign a waiver, but the salesman said that would not be legal. A few weeks later, Mid-Carolina sold the mobile home to another couple for $9,220.

Scott sued and was awarded $3,600 actual damages, $6,400 punitive damages for breach of contract accompanied by a fraudulent act, and $3,000 actual damages for violation of a state consumer protection law. The appeals court upheld the award.

On appeal, Mid-Carolina argued that it was entitled to rescind the contract because the salesperson was acting under a mistake of fact when he gave Scott the sales price. In upholding the award, the state supreme court explained that a contract may be rescinded for unilateral mistake only when the mistake has been induced by fraud, deceit, misrepresentation, concealment, or imposition of the party opposed to the rescission, without negligence on the part of the party claiming rescission, or when the mistake is accompanied by very strong and extraordinary circumstances that would make it a great wrong to enforce the agreement. Mid-Carolina had not demonstrated the presence of any of these. The salesperson was in the superior bargaining position to know the price, and the buyer's reliance on a salesperson's representation of the price was reasonable.

For a mutual mistake to interfere with legal consent, all the following must be present:

1. A basic assumption about the subject matter of the contract.
2. A material effect on the agreement.
3. An adverse effect on a party who did not agree to bear the risk of mistake at the time of the agreement.

Courts will not void contracts for reason of mutual mistake if even one of these conditions is missing. (See Exhibit 17-1.) Let's see why they matter.

To rise to the level of a basic assumption, a mistake must be about the existence, quality, or quantity of the items to be exchanged. To be material, condition 2, the mistake must affect the essence of the agreement. A fact is material when it provides a basis for a person's agreeing to enter into the contract. Neither party can void the contract simply by falsely claiming that the item to be exchanged is not the one he intended.

The third condition protects those who bargain with someone who agreed, at the time of the agreement, to bear the risk of mistake but then later wishes to avoid that risk when the contract does not work out as well as he or she had planned. This situation might arise, for instance, if the adversely affected party had agreed in the contract to accept items "as is" but later felt they were not worth the price paid. In the opening scenario,

Exhibit 17-1

Enforceability of a Mutual Mistake

Before a contract can be voided for a mutual mistake, you must answer each of the following questions with a yes:

1. Is the mistake about a basic assumption that affects the subject matter of the contract?
2. Does the mistake have a material effect on the agreement?
3. Would enforcement of the contract have an adverse effect on the party who did not agree to bear the risk of mistake at the time of the agreement?

had Jordan agreed to pay Knafel the $5 million regardless of the outcome of any future paternity tests, the outcome of the case would have been very different. Instead, Jordan had allegedly agreed to pay Knafel the money on the basis of misinformation that the child was definitely his. Upon learning that the child was not his, Jordan wanted to have the contract rescinded on the basis, partly, of the mutual mistake made between himself and Knafel. Case 17-1 demonstrates the elements of mutual mistake in the sale of a business.

CASE 17-1   RONALD JACKSON AND WILLA JACKSON, APPELLANT v. ROBERT R. BLANCHARD, HELEN M. BLANCHARD, MAYNARD L. SHELLHAMMER, AND PHILIP SCHLEMMER, APPELLEE
COURT OF APPEALS OF INDIANA, FOURTH DISTRICT
601 N.E.2D 411 (1992)

The Blanchards owned the Corner Cupboard Restaurant until 1985, when they sold it on contract. Schlemmer and Shellhammer became the new assignees under the contract and took over operations of the Corner Cupboard.

In late 1988, Schlemmer and Shellhammer sold the Corner Cupboard to the Jacksons. Before finalizing the sale, Ronald Jackson and Schlemmer discussed the septic system and a certain well located on the restaurant property. Schlemmer said he had been told there was a workable well on the property, but neither he nor the previous owners had ever used it; they had always purchased their water from the filling station across the street. Schlemmer also told Jackson the septic system had backed up on occasion, but he thought this problem had been fixed.

At the closing, the Jacksons met the Blanchards, who were there to give them a warranty deed to the restaurant. Before executing the deed, Blanchard confirmed to Jackson there was a working well on the property that neither he nor any of the previous owners had used.

Soon after the sale, Jackson attempted to supply the restaurant with water from the well and realized it was plugged; his only recourse was to drill a new well. Then he discovered two other landowners were hooked into the septic discharge line, which was illegally dumping into a lake and subjecting him to penalties up to $25,000 per day. Finally, Jackson found numerous underground petroleum storage tanks had been buried on the property.

The Jacksons sued, seeking, among other claims, rescission of the assignment contract from Schlemmer and Shellhammer based on mutual mistake of fact. Defendants filed a motion for summary judgment, which was granted. The Jacksons appealed.

JUDGE MILLER: Mutual assent is a prerequisite to the creation of a contract. However, "where both parties share a common assumption about a vital fact upon which they based their bargain, and that assumption is false, the transaction may be voided if because of the mistake a quite different exchange of values occurs from the exchange of values contemplated by the parties." It is not enough that both parties are mistaken about any fact; rather, the mistaken fact complained of must be one that is "of the essence of the agreement. . . ."

The Jacksons argue that the existence of a working well was a material fact going to the heart of the agreement. Our review of the designated materials shows that this is not the case. It was only several months after purchasing the restaurant and purchasing their water from the filling station that the Jacksons attempted to supply the restaurant with well water. Thus, the Jacksons knew at the time they purchased the restaurant that the well was unusable without a new pump and piping, and that until such work, they would have to purchase their water from another source. We cannot conclude that an operable well was an essential factor in the Jacksons' decision to purchase the restaurant. . . . The fact that the well was actually unable to provide water, while contrary to the assumptions of both parties, was not a mistake of material fact.

The Jacksons next argue that because they and Schlemmer and Shellhammer were unaware of the existence of the underground storage tanks, this constituted grounds for rescinding the contract. . . . While the discovery of the underground storage tanks might have been an unfortunate surprise . . . [i]t does not affect the suitability of the premises for the purpose of operating a restaurant—the very thing bought by the Jacksons. . . . We cannot say that ignorance of the existence of the underground storage tanks constituted a mutual mistake.

Finally, the Jacksons contend that there was no meeting of the minds because neither party was aware of the problems with the septic system. . . . We conclude that what the Jacksons bargained for was a functioning restaurant, not necessarily one that would avoid all infringements of the law. Thus, in order to qualify as a material mistake, the Jacksons must prove that any subsequently discovered conditions regarding the septic system rendered it, and the restaurant, inoperable.

The Jacksons do not dispute that the restaurant's septic system is functional; their sole complaint is that the current method of discharge may subject them to civil penalties. From this alone, we could determine that the subsequently discovered problems were not material. As we stated earlier, it is only those mistakes which are material or essential to the parties' agreement that properly fall within the definition of mutual mistake.

AFFIRMED.

CRITICAL THINKING

What is fundamentally at issue in this dispute? That is, what basic question do the two sides disagree on? What evidence does each use to defend its position?

ETHICAL DECISION MAKING

On the basis of the provided information, sketch the ethical considerations taken into account by each side before the lawsuit. Does your projection paint either as approaching matters from the ethical high ground?

Misrepresentation

L03

What are the elements of misrepresentation?

Misrepresentations are similar to mistakes in that at least one of the parties is in error about a fact material to the agreement. But a **misrepresentation** is an untruthful assertion by one of the parties about that material fact; it prevents the parties from having the mental agreement necessary for a legal contract. They only *appeared* to agree, so their contract lacked legal assent.

The courts insist on a meeting of the minds for a valid contract. Thus, they might rescind a contract even though the person making the false assertion was entirely innocent of any intentional deception.

The topic of misrepresentation should be particularly important to future business professionals, especially those interested in marketing or advertising careers, as it may one day be your job to develop promotional materials for a company's products. Marketing and advertising professionals must exercise special care when developing product labels, packaging, and advertisements because consumers often depend on the information provided by a company when deciding whether to purchase a product. Thus, if the marketing materials created by a company are seen as being inaccurate or appear to misrepresent what a product truly is or what benefits the product offers, consumers may attempt to take legal action.

For example, in 1991 a Michigan man, Richard Overton, filed suit against Anheuser-Busch, claiming that the company's commercials made untrue statements and misrepresentations that caused him to continually buy and consume the company's beer. More specifically, Overton alleged that Anheuser-Busch was liable for creating advertisements that falsely suggested drinking its beer would result in fantasies coming to life (tropical settings, beautiful women, and happiness). Overton sought to recover $10,000 in damages from Anheuser-Busch for causing him physical and mental injury as well as emotional distress and financial loss. A circuit court granted summary judgment in favor of the defendant. Richard Overton appealed, and the Michigan Court of Appeals affirmed the lower court's ruling.[3] While the company won the case, it still had the expense of defending its actions. It is always better to try to avoid being sued in the first place.

[3] 205 Mich. App. 259; 517 N.W.2d 308 (case summary accessed on Lexis Nexis May 25, 2009).

INNOCENT MISREPRESENTATION

An **innocent misrepresentation** results from a false statement about a fact material to an agreement that the person making it believed to be true. The person had no knowledge of the claim's falsity. We say he or she lacked **scienter** (from the Latin root of the word meaning "knowledge").

Innocent misrepresentations permit the misled party to rescind the contract. However, because the other party had no intent to mislead, the aggrieved party cannot sue for damages. The reasoning in these cases resembles the arguments in a mutual mistake case, as you might expect.

NEGLIGENT MISREPRESENTATION

In some contract negotiations, one party makes a statement of material fact that he thinks is true. If he could have known the truth by using reasonable care to discover or reveal it, his statement is a **negligent misrepresentation.**

Even though he had no intent to deceive, in contract law the party is treated as if he did. If this standard seems unfair to you, remember that the courts find negligent misrepresentation only when the party making the false statement should have known the truth using the skills and competence required of a person in his position or profession. The impact of negligent misrepresentation is identical to that of fraudulent misrepresentation, discussed next.

FRAUDULENT MISREPRESENTATION

Any fraud on the part of a party to a contract provides a basis for rescission. The parties cannot be said to have assented when one of the parties was tricked into the "agreement" by a fraudulent misrepresentation. Thus, the agreement was not voluntary and can be rescinded on the ground that there was no meeting of the minds.

Even in countries trying to encourage joint ventures and global commercial activity, such as the People's Republic of China, fraudulent claims can end the country's hospitality to agreements with outsiders.[4] In China, accusations of outsiders' fraudulent misrepresentation have resulted in heavy fines and even refusals to allow the fraudulent party to enter into any more agreements with Chinese firms. In most, if not all, cultures, little judicial sympathy exists for those who consciously mislead others in commercial activities.

A **fraudulent misrepresentation** is a consciously false representation of a material fact intended to mislead the other party. It is also referred to as **intentional misrepresentation.** Here scienter is clear: the party making the misrepresentation either knows or believes that the factual claim is false or knows there is no basis for it.

To understand the requirements for a finding of fraudulent misrepresentation, start with the two elements from the definition:

1. *A false statement about a past or existing fact that is material to the contract.*
2. *Intent to deceive,* which can be inferred from the particular circumstances.

Then add a third necessary element:

3. *Justifiable reliance on the false statement by the innocent party to the agreement:* Justifiable reliance is generally present unless the injured party knew, or should have known by the extravagance of the claim, that the false statement was indeed false.

---

[4] Charles D. Paglee, "Contracts and Agreements in the People's Republic of China," www.qis.net/chinalaw/explan1.htm, updated March 6, 1998.

For example, a homeowner could not justifiably rely on a claim by a gardener that if she will pay him to apply a special fertilizer to her trees once a week, the trees would never die.

Finally, if damages are sought, the defrauded party must have been injured by the misrepresentation.

In the opening scenario, Jordan claimed that he had been the victim of a fraudulent misrepresentation made by Knafel. To meet the three requirements, Jordan argued that Knafel told him that he was definitely the child's father despite her knowledge that she had been having sexual relationships with other men during the same time period. According to Jordan, Knafel had reason to believe that her representation could be false and still made it with certainty in an effort to deceive him. Finally, it was based on the assertion that he was the father that Jordan allegedly agreed to pay Knafel $5 million. Hence, according to Jordan, he had proved that the statement qualified as a fraudulent misrepresentation. Does Knafel's representation that Jordan was the child's father amount to a fraudulent misrepresentation?

Each of the three aforementioned elements can become a source of debate in any attempt to rescind a contract on grounds of fraudulent misrepresentation. Thus, it is your responsibility as a person who will be involved with dozens of contracts in your business activities to know these elements. A rescinded contract is a time-consuming and expensive business opportunity that has gone wrong. And don't forget that you can collect damages only from parties you can locate.

Before we go into greater detail about the elements of fraudulent misrepresentation, please consider Case 17-2. Follow the court's reasoning as it works through the elements of the attempt to rescind a contract.

CASE 17-2   GARY W. CRUSE AND VENITA R. CRUSE v. COLDWELL BANKER/GRABEN REAL ESTATE, INC.
SUPREME COURT OF ALABAMA
667 SO. 2D 714 (1995)

Mr. and Mrs. Cruse sued Mr. and Mrs. Harris, Coldwell Banker, and Graben Real Estate, Inc., alleging defective workmanship in the construction of a house they had bought from the Harrises and fraudulent misrepresentation and/or suppressed material facts about the condition of the house.

When the Cruses began looking for a home, they contacted Graben Real Estate, and a Graben agent took them to see the Harrises' house. Randy Harris, a building contractor, had built the house for sale, and he and his wife were occupying it at that time. Graben listed the house as "new" in its advertisements, and the agent told the Cruses it was new. She also told them it was comparable to, or even better than, other houses in the neighborhood, that it was a good buy, and that if they purchased it they could look forward to years of convenient, trouble-free living.

The Cruses signed a contract on November 11, 1992, to purchase the house from the Harrises. When they told the agent they wanted to hire an independent contractor to assess its condition, she told them it was not really necessary to do so because Randy Harris was a contractor and the house was well-built.

The Cruses signed an "Acceptance Inspection Contract," which stated that they had inspected the property or waived the right to do so, accepted it in "as-is" condition, and based their decision to purchase on their own inspection and not on any representations by the broker.

Plaintiffs took possession of the residence in mid-December 1992 and soon began noticing many defects in the structure and electrical wiring. They contacted Graben Real Estate, which sent an agent to remedy the problems.

The defects continued and multiplied, so the Cruses sued. At the trial, defendants moved for summary judgment, which was granted. Plaintiffs appealed.

JUSTICE BUTTS: To establish fraudulent misrepresentations, the Cruses are required to show that Graben Real Estate made a false representation concerning a material fact and that they relied upon that representation, to their detriment. The Cruses contend that Graben Real Estate represented to them that the house was new; that, in reliance on that representation, they decided not to hire a contractor to inspect the house and discover its defects; and that reliance resulted in damage to them.

The unequivocal term "new," when applied to real estate, is not merely descriptive. It is a definite legal term that carries with it the implied warranty of habitability and prevents the realtor from invoking the protection of the doctrine of caveat emptor. Graben Real Estate marketed the house as "new," both in print and in direct response to the Cruses' queries. In so doing, Graben Real Estate made statements that went beyond the patter of sales talk and became representations of material fact. Moreover, Gary Cruse testified . . . that he relied upon this representation in failing to hire a contractor to inspect the house before he bought it.

Graben Real Estate argues that even if it did misrepresent the newness of the house, the Cruses could not have justifiably believed the misrepresentation and relied upon it to the point that they would not closely inspect the house before buying it. Graben Real Estate relies heavily on the fact that the Cruses knew that the house was being occupied by the Harrises at the time of the sale, and concludes that this alone should have proved to the Cruses that the house was not actually new. . . . We do not agree that the mere knowledge of the Harrises' prior occupancy so wholly contradicted the printed and spoken representations of Graben Real Estate that the Cruses could not, as a matter of law, have justifiably relied upon them.

Graben Real Estate also argues that, regardless of whether the house was new or was used, the Cruses cannot recover because they signed an "as-is" agreement at the time of the sale, thereby, Graben Real Estate says, accepting the condition of the house without a prior inspection. Graben Real Estate relies on Hope v. Brannan, wherein this Court held that buyers of a 58-year-old house who signed a statement accepting the house "as-is," without independently inspecting it for defects, could not maintain an action for fraud arising from the seller's statements concerning the condition of the house.

Graben Real Estate's reliance on Hope is misplaced; in Hope, the house was not new, nor was it represented to be new. A buyer's failure to inspect the premises of a 58-year-old house before signing an "as-is" agreement is hardly the equivalent of the Cruses' failure to inspect the premises of a house that their realtor had represented to be new.

The evidence establishes that Graben Real Estate misrepresented a material fact and creates a jury question as to whether the Cruses could have justifiably relied upon this misrepresentation in deciding not to closely inspect the house before buying it. The fact that the Cruses knew the house was occupied by a third party before they bought it, along with the fact that they signed an "as-is" agreement, separate from the purchase contract, for a house they claim to have regarded as new, are elements for the jury to consider.

REVERSED and REMANDED.

CRITICAL THINKING

Several key points in the reasoning of this decision rely on personal testimony. On the basis of your life experience and any knowledge you may have accumulated through your educational career, how reliable do you think witness testimony is as a form of evidence in legal disputes? What are some of the ways that this testimonial evidence might be flawed? What are its particular strengths? In this case, do you think the testimonies are valid? Why or why not?

ETHICAL DECISION MAKING

What general values might the court be interested in protecting in this ruling? How are they similar to values upheld by other cases in this chapter? How are they different? What opposing values are less important in these rulings?

The elements of fraudulent misrepresentation become more complicated in the context of actual disagreements. Let's revisit them for more insight.

False Assertion of Fact.   For fraudulent misrepresentation to be the basis for a contract rescission, the statement of fact need not be an actual assertion. It can also be an act of concealment or nondisclosure. **Concealment** is the *active* hiding of the truth about a material fact, for example, removing 20,000 miles from the odometer on your car before selling it. **Nondisclosure** is a failure to provide pertinent information about the projected contract. The courts have until recently been hesitant to use nondisclosure as a basis for rescinding a contract because it is a passive form of misleading conduct. Under ordinary situations associated with a legal bargain, it is not the obligation of one party to bring up any and all facts he or she might possess. Each individual is, to a large extent, treated as a responsible decision maker.

However, courts will now find nondisclosure as having the same legal effect as an actual false assertion under certain conditions:

1. *A relationship of trust exists between the parties to the contract.* In this situation the relationship provides a reasonable basis for one person's expectation that the other would never act to defraud him or her.
2. *There is failure to correct assertions of fact that are no longer true.* Caroline's failure to inform Vito of the recent outbreak of rust on her "rust-free" car that Vito agreed to purchase next month is nondisclosure.
3. *A statute requires the disclosure,* such as mandatory disclosures under residential real estate sales laws.
4. *The nondisclosure involves a dangerous defect,* such as bad brakes in a car that is being sold.

Nondisclosure is especially likely to provide the basis for rescission when one party has information about a basic assumption of the deal that is unavailable to the other party. Sellers thus have a special duty to disclose because they know more about the structural makeup of the item being purchased.

Intent to Deceive.   *Scienter* is present when the party making the fraudulent assertion believed it was false or had no regard for whether it was true or false. *Intent to deceive* occurs when the party making the false statement claims to have or implies having personal knowledge of its accuracy. Any resulting assent is not legal because the injured party was not allowed to join the mind of the deceiving party. The party with scienter or intent to deceive wanted the contract to be fulfilled on the basis of a falsehood.

Justifiable Reliance on the False Assertion.   What responsibilities does the injured party have in a case of false assertion? As we've said, the injured party has no justifiable claim of fraud after relying on assertions whose falsity should have been obvious. Anyone who pays for a house in reliance on the claim that it was "built before the founding of our country" cannot later rescind the contract on grounds of fraudulent misrepresentation.

Nor can parties successfully claim they justifiably relied on a false assertion when its falsity would have been clear to anyone who inspected the item. However, the duty to inspect is declining in modern contract law, and courts are giving increasing responsibility to the person who made the erroneous assertion.

As you might infer from the foregoing discussion, the process of determining whether intentional misrepresentation has occurred can be an extremely difficult task. This process

COMPARING THE LAW OF OTHER COUNTRIES

Consumer Contracts Law in Japan

In 1997, after studying the application of civil law in the country, the Japanese Social Policy Council, an advisory body to the prime minister, recognized that the consumer environment was growing more diversified and that a significant gap existed between consumers and businesses in their access to information and knowledge and their negotiating power. Because it cannot honestly be said that consumers and businesses are equal, as contracting parties are presumed to be under the country's Civil Code, the council developed a special Consumer Contracts Law. This legislation is considered to place consumers and businesses on a more equal footing in transactions.

Under the Consumer Contracts Law, a consumer may cancel the contract whenever a business (1) fails to provide information about the contents of the contract, (2) fails to provide information necessary for the consumer to decide to enter into the contract, or (3) makes misrepresentations. In many such cases, the consumer would not have been entitled to relief under the Civil Code because of its strict requirements for the application of fraud.

can become even more complex when the defendant believes that the other party was never misled in the first place. Such was the case when several individuals involved in the movie *Borat* filed suit against Sacha Baron Cohen and Twentieth Century Fox for fraudulent and negligent misrepresentation as well as other various claims. The plaintiffs in the case were lawyers who represented the locals of the Romanian village of Glod, where the opening scenes of the movie were filmed. In their suit, the villagers alleged that Cohen and Twentieth Century Fox convinced them that they were taking part in a documentary film about poverty in Romania, not a blockbuster movie set in Kazakhstan. Further, the lawsuit asserted that Cohen and Twentieth Century Fox "used their superior educational background, stature, influence and economic position" to exploit the villagers and that the company also encouraged villagers to sign documents that they did not understand and that had not been fully explained.

Twentieth Century Fox defended its film and claimed that the villagers of Glod knew they were participating in a movie and not a documentary. The company further defended its position by stating that the villagers were paid more than the average going wage for movie extras. Eventually, the lawsuit was thrown out by a U.S district court judge who stated that the allegations against Sacha Baron Cohen and Twentieth Century Fox needed to be more specific. The lawyers of the Glod villagers said that they intended to file a new suit in the future.[5]

Before we conclude this section about misrepresentation, consider what would have happened if Karla Knafel, in the opening scenario, had told Jordan there was a strong probability that the child was his. Would Jordan have been able to claim that their contract lacked assent because of Knafel's misrepresentation?

Legal Principle: **The effect of both a negligent misrepresentation and a fraudulent misrepresentation is that the victim can either rescind the contract or keep the contract and sue for damages, whereas if the mistake is innocent, the victim can seek only rescission.**

To see how certain aspects of marketing relate to misrepresentation, please see the **Connecting to the Core** activity on the text Web site at www.mhhe.com/kubasek2e.

Undue Influence

When legal assent is present, the courts assume both parties have made their own choices based on complete freedom to accept or reject the terms of the bargain. However, many factors can work to make our choices anything but free. **Undue influence** refers to those

L04

What are the elements of undue influence?

[5] http://news.bbc.co.uk/2/hi/europe/7686885.stm; and http://74.125.113.132/search?q=cache:jQ0M5aR16wUJ:www.courthousenews.com/onpoint/borat_NY.pdf+Twentieth+century+fox+v+michael+witti+and+ed+fagan&cd=1&hl=en&ct=clnk&gl=us.

A Case of Undue Influence

Evan Rothberg v. Walt Disney Pictures
1999 U.S. App. 1472

Robert Jahn was a senior executive at Walt Disney Pictures until he died of complications from AIDS. Within days before his death, a Disney official visited him at the hospital and convinced him to sign a release that waived his rights to approximately $2 million in employee benefits, including life insurance, stock options, bonuses, and deferred compensation. After his death, his estate sued to recover the benefits waived in the release. Disney received a motion for summary judgment, and the plaintiff appealed. In reversing the

motion for summary judgment, the court ruled that the question of whether the release had been procured by undue influence was a question for a jury. The court pointed out that undue influence requires (1) undue susceptibility on the part of the weaker party and (2) application of excessive pressure by the stronger party. In this case, the first fact was self-evident. The defendant was in the hospital and was fearful that Disney would expose information that would destroy his reputation. Regarding the second element, however, the court noted that in most undue-influence cases, and this case was no exception, direct evidence is rarely obtainable and thus the jury must decide the issue on the basis of inferences drawn from all the facts and circumstances. Thus, the court said that summary judgment was improper.

special relationships in which one person takes advantage of a dominant position in a relationship to unfairly persuade the other and interfere with that person's ability to make his or her own decision. When people bargain with their attorney, doctor, guardian, relative, or anyone else in a relationship that includes a high degree of trust, they are susceptible to being persuaded by unusual pressures unique to that relationship. Consequently, the assent that results may not be legal consent. The courts may see the undue influence of the relationship as interfering with the free choice required for an enforceable contract. Whatever contracts result from undue influence are voidable.

Are all contracts in which undue influence might arise likely to be rescinded? Not necessarily. The courts look to the mental condition of the person relying on the guidance of the dominant person. Courts look to the extent to which the dominant person used the persuasive powers of his or her dominance to secure assent.

Factors that enter into the finding of undue influence are the following:

1. Was the dominant party rushing the other party to consent?
2. Did the dominant party gain undue enrichment from the agreement?
3. Was the nondominant party isolated from other advisers at the time of the agreement?
4. Is the contract unreasonable because it overwhelmingly benefits the dominant party?

The more of these factors present, the more likely a court is to rescind the contract on grounds of undue influence. The following Case Nugget provides an illustration of undue influence.

Legal Principle: The essential element of undue influence is the existence of a dominant-subservient relationship, so if you are going to enter into a contract with someone with whom you have such a relationship, to ensure that the agreement will be enforced in the future, make sure that the person in the subservient position has independent advice before entering into the contract.

Duress

L05

What are the elements of duress?

Duress is a much more visible and active interference with free will than is undue influence. **Duress** occurs when one party is forced into the agreement by the wrongful act of another.

Duress in Australia

Australia recognizes a special category called *duress of goods,* which occurs whenever one party makes an illegitimate threat to hold goods unless another party makes payment or enters into an agreement. Note that this is different from a situation in which someone legitimately holds goods when money is owed on them or the goods have been used as security for a loan.

Australia also recognizes economic duress, which is the unacceptable use of economic power to leave someone with no practical alternative but to submit to the accompanying demand.

To prove economic duress, a plaintiff must establish that (1) pressure was used to procure his or her assent to an agreement or to the payment of money, (2) the pressure was illegitimate in the circumstance, (3) the pressure in fact contributed to the person's assenting to the transaction, and (4) the person's assent to the transaction was reasonable in the circumstances.

Just as with economic duress in the United States, it is often unclear when pressure is illegitimate. A threat to do something unlawful is almost always undue pressure. A threat to use the civil legal process is usually considered lawful, unless the contemplated legal action would clearly be an abuse of process. "Driving a hard bargain" or refusing to do any more business with someone in the future is generally not regarded as economic duress.

The wrongful act may come in various forms. Any of the following would trigger a successful request for rescission on grounds of duress:

- One party threatens physical harm or extortion to gain consent to a contract.
- One party threatens to file a criminal lawsuit unless consent is given to the terms of the contract. (Threats to bring civil cases against a party to a lawsuit do not constitute duress unless the suit is frivolous.)
- One party threatens the other's economic interests (this is known as *economic duress*). For instance, a person refuses to perform according to a contract unless the other person either signs another contract with the one making the threat or pays that person a higher price than specified in the original agreement.

The injured party makes the case for duress by demonstrating that the threat left no reasonable alternatives and that the free will necessary for legal consent was removed by the specifics of the threat.

Legal Principle: **When one party is forced to enter into a contract by the wrongful threat of another, the contract is voidable by the innocent party due to duress.**

Unconscionability

A final way to question the appropriateness of consent arises when one of the parties has so much more bargaining power than the other that he or she dictates the terms of the agreement. Such an agreement can be rescinded on grounds of **unconscionability** (as discussed in Chapter 4). The disproportionate amount of power possessed by one party to the contract has made a mockery of the idea of free will, a necessity for legal consent. The resulting contract is called an **adhesion contract.**

Although unconscionability has traditionally been limited to the sale of goods under the Uniform Commercial Code, many courts have not followed that tradition. When they see contracts written by one party and presented to the other with the threat to "take it or leave it," they sometimes extend the idea of unconscionability beyond the sale of goods.

Follow the judge's reasoning in Case 17-3 to review the type of reasoning that makes up a claim for unconscionability.

LO6

What are the elements of unconscionability?

ORVILLE ARNOLD AND MAXINE ARNOLD, PLAINTIFFS v. UNITED COMPANIES LENDING CORPORATION, A CORPORATION, AND MICHAEL T. SEARLS, AN INDIVIDUAL, DEFENDANTS
SUPREME COURT OF APPEALS OF WEST VIRGINIA
1998 WL 8651015

On September 17, 1996, Michael Searls came to the residence of Orville and Maxine Arnold, an elderly couple, and offered to arrange a loan for them, acting as a loan broker. He procured a loan for them. From the loan proceeds, a mortgage broker fee of $940.00 was paid to Searls and/or Accent Financial Services, with which Searls was affiliated.

At the loan closing, United Lending had the benefit of legal counsel, while the Arnolds apparently did not. During the course of the transaction, the Arnolds were presented with more than twenty-five documents to sign. Among these were a promissory note, reflecting a principal sum of $19,300.00 and a yearly interest rate of 12.990%; a Deed of Trust, giving United Lending a security interest in the Arnolds' real estate; and a two-page form labeled "Acknowledgment and Agreement to Mediate or Arbitrate," which stated that all legal controversies arising from the loan would be resolved through nonappealable, confidential arbitration, and that all damages would be direct damages, with no punitive damages available. However, this agreement not to arbitrate did not limit the lender's right to pursue legal actions in a court of law relating to collection of the loan.

On July 10, 1997, the Arnolds filed suit against United Lending and Searls, seeking a declaratory judgment adjudging the arbitration agreement to be void and unenforceable. On August 11, 1997, United Lending moved to dismiss the entire action on the basis of the compulsory arbitration agreement. The circuit court certified three questions to the state supreme court.

JUSTICE McCUSKEY: We reformulate the question as follows: Whether an arbitration agreement entered into as part of a consumer loan transaction containing a substantial waiver of the consumer's rights, including access to the courts, while preserving for all practical purposes the lender's right to a judicial forum, is void as a matter of law.

The drafters of the Uniform Consumer Credit Code explained that the [basic test] of unconscionability is whether . . . the conduct involved is, or the contract or clauses involved are, so one-sided as to be unconscionable under the circumstances existing at the time the conduct occurs or is threatened or at the time of the making of the contract. . . . [T]his Court stated:

["W]here a party alleges that the arbitration provision was unconscionable, or was thrust upon him because he was unwary and taken advantage of, or that the contract was one of adhesion, the question of whether an arbitration provision was bargained for and valid is a matter of law for the court to determine by reference to the entire contract. . . ."

A determination of unconscionability must focus on the relative positions of the parties, the adequacy of the bargaining position, the meaningful alternatives available to the plaintiff, and "the existence of unfair terms in the contract."

Applying the rule . . . leads us to the inescapable conclusion that the arbitration agreement between the Arnolds and United Lending is "void for unconscionability" as a matter of law. . . . The relative positions of the parties, a national corporate lender on one side and elderly, unsophisticated consumers on the other, were "grossly unequal." In addition, there is no evidence that the loan broker made any other loan option available to the Arnolds. In fact, the record does not indicate that the Arnolds were seeking a loan, but rather were solicited by defendant Searls. Thus, the element of "a comparable, meaningful alternative" to the loan from United Lending is lacking. Because the Arnolds had no meaningful alternative to obtaining the loan from United Lending, and also did not have the benefit of legal counsel during the transaction, their bargaining position was clearly inadequate when compared to that of United Lending.

Given the nature of this arbitration agreement, combined with the great disparity in bargaining power, one can safely infer that the terms were not bargained for and that allowing such a one-sided agreement to stand would unfairly defeat the Arnolds' legitimate expectations.

Finally, the terms of the agreement are "unreasonably favorable" to United Lending. United Lending's acts or omissions could seriously damage the Arnolds, yet the Arnolds' only recourse would be to submit the matter to binding arbitration. At the same time, United Lending's access to the courts is wholly preserved in every conceivable situation where United Lending would want to secure judicial relief against the Arnolds. The wholesale waiver of the Arnolds' rights together with the complete preservation of United Lending's rights "is inherently inequitable and unconscionable because in a way it nullifies all the other provisions of the contract."

Judgment in favor of Plaintiffs.

[continued]

CRITICAL THINKING

This case highlights the importance of language in the legal system. Phrases quoted from the law are subject to significant judicial discretion, which allows rulings like this to be possible. Using the contextual clues found in the information given, choose two descriptions in quotes and write your idea of how the judge must be defining the relevant phrase. Then come up with some other ways these phrases could have been defined. Would the use of your alternatives significantly affect the reasonableness of the conclusion?

ETHICAL DECISION MAKING

Does this case lend itself very well to considerations of ethicality? What sort of theoretical approach do you see the court taking with this ruling?

On the basis of other decisions you have encountered in this book, what do you think is probably the most common ethical framework U.S. courts use in guiding their rulings? How well does this case fit with larger trends? Support your answer.

 CASE OPENER WRAP-UP

A Disagreement over an Agreement

The trial court agreed with Michael Jordan's argument regarding a mutual mistake or fraudulent misrepresentation in the contract. Knafel appealed, and the court affirmed the lower court's decision. The court held that Knafel's representation to Jordan that he was the father met the requirements of being (1) a material fact, (2) made for the purpose of inducing Jordan to act, (3) that either was known by Knafel to be false or was not actually believed by her on reasonable grounds to be true, but Jordan reasonably believed it to be true, and (4) that was relied on by Jordan to his own detriment. Thus, the appellate court found that Knafel's representation that Jordan *was* the father constituted fraud. The agreement can be rescinded because Jordan would not have entered into the agreement but for the fraudulent representation made by Knafel. Even if Knafel did not act fraudulently, at the time the agreement was created both parties believed that the child was Jordan's. After conducting paternity tests and learning that the baby was *not* Jordan's, the agreement could still be rescinded based on a mutual mistake of fact.

Key Terms

adhesion contract   395
concealment   392
duress   394
fraudulent
    misrepresentation   389
innocent
    misrepresentation   389

intentional
    misrepresentation   389
legal assent   383
misrepresentation   388
mistake
    of fact   384
mutual   384

negligent
    misrepresentation   389
nondisclosure   392
rescinded   383
scienter   389
unconscionability   395
undue influence   393

unilateral   384
voidable   383

Summary of Key Topics

The Importance of Legal Assent

If assent is not genuine, or legal, a contract may be voidable.

Mistake

Mistakes are erroneous beliefs about the material facts of a contract at the time the agreement is made. They may be either unilateral or mutual. Only under certain rare conditions are unilateral mistakes a basis for rescinding a contract. However, if both parties to a contract are mistaken about a material fact, either can opt to rescind it. The agreement was not based on a meeting of the minds, a basic criterion for a legal assent.

Misrepresentation

Misrepresentation is an intentional untruthful assertion by one of the parties about a material fact. An innocent misrepresentation occurs when the party making the false assertion believes it to be true. The misled party may then rescind the contract. When a misrepresentation is fraudulent, any assent is gained by deceit and the courts permit rescission. In addition to requiring a false assertion and intent to deceive, fraudulent misrepresentation also requires the innocent party's justifiable reliance on the assertion.

Undue Influence

Undue influence is the persuasive efforts of a dominant party who uses a special relationship with another party to interfere with the other's free choice of the terms of a contract. Any relationship in which one party has an unusual degree of trust in the other can trigger concern about undue influence.

Duress

Duress occurs when one party threatens the other with a wrongful act unless assent is given. Such assent is not legal assent because coercion interferes with the party's free will. For the courts to rescind the agreement, the injured party must demonstrate that the duress left no reasonable alternatives to agreeing to the contract.

Unconscionability

Unconscionability may be a basis for avoiding a contract if one party has so much relative bargaining power that he or she in effect dictates the terms. The resulting agreement is an adhesion contract.

Point / Counterpoint

Are Payday Loans, and the Accompanying Interests Rates, Unconscionable?	
NO	**YES**
The companies that supply payday loans offer short-term solutions to difficult financial situations. For consumers who find themselves strapped and in dire need of cash, payday loans provide a means to repair a broken-down car, pay the rent, or pay other accumulating bills. Although the interest rates are high, these loans do not violate any laws and the consumers' loan agreements are not unconscionable.	The consumers who take out payday loans are often desperate and lack other methods of obtaining a loan. For these consumers, getting a loan from a bank is impossible due to their poor credit ratings or lack of necessary collateral. The companies that offer these consumers payday loans are preying on a vulnerable population by exploiting their lack of bargaining power. Payday loans are unconscionable.
When consumers approach a payday lender for a loan, they are greeted by a plethora of signs indicating relevant interest rates. Before signing the loan documents, the consumer is given numerous documents containing the interest rates. Additionally, many states require that the	Regardless of the amount of advertising a lender may provide, consumers who find themselves in need of payday loans lack the necessary bargaining power to make these loans conscionable. For a loan to be unconscionable, one of the parties has to have so much more bargaining

lender verbally state the interest rates to consumers. These consumers have numerous opportunities to walk away from the lender if they are unwilling to accept the high interest rates.

In response to those who argue that these loans are unconscionable, supporters argue that consumers still have the free will to choose whether or not to enter into the loan agreement. These loans do not involve any coercion or enticing.

Furthermore, the high interest rates tied to payday loans are the reason these lenders are able to make small (often between $100 and $500) loans to otherwise risky consumers. Without the ability to raise interest rates, these companies would not be able to offset their own risk in providing the loans. Therefore, these loans are *not unconscionable.*

power than the other that he or she dictates the terms of the agreement; in payday loans it is the lender that has the power to dictate the terms. Desperate consumers often feel that they are left with no choice but accepting the terms offered by the payday lenders.

Additionally, payday loans exploit the financial hardships experienced by consumers and often result in increased hardship. A typical bank loan is usually capped at an APR of 35 percent; payday loans average an APR of 530 percent. The consumers' ability to pay back the loans is often limited by the individuals' impoverished situation, and, as a result, these loans will often roll over, making it impossible for consumers to recover. As a result of the consumers' limited bargaining power, payday loans trap disadvantaged populations in high–interest rate loans they cannot afford. Thus, payday loans are *inherently unconscionable.*

Questions & Problems

1. Explain the difference between a unilateral mistake and a mutual mistake.

2. Explain when a unilateral mistake can lead to a contract's being voidable.

3. Distinguish innocent misrepresentation from fraudulent misrepresentation.

4. Explain how nondisclosure can be treated as misrepresentation.

5. Explain the primary differences between duress and undue influence.

6. The personal representatives of the plaintiff's estate hired an appraiser to appraise personal property in preparation for an estate sale. The appraiser told the representatives that she was no judge of fine art and that they would have to hire an additional appraiser if she found any fine art. She did not report finding any fine art, and relying on her silence, the representatives priced and sold two oil paintings at $60. The defendant came to the estate sale and bought the paintings. Although he had bought and sold some art before, he was not an educated purchaser and had made no more than $55 on any art that he had previously sold; he had bought many paintings that ended up being forgeries. He assumed that the paintings were not originals, given their price and the fact that professionals were managing the sale, but he liked the subject matter of one and the frame

of the other. Once home with the paintings, he compared their signatures to those in a book of artists' signatures and thought they looked like those of Martin Johnson Head. As he had done with other art, he sent photos of the paintings to Christie's in New York, which confirmed the signatures and offered to auction the paintings for him. The auction netted the defendant $911,000. After finding out what had happened, the estate sued the defendant buyer, alleging that the contract should have been rescinded on grounds of mutual mistake and unconscionability. The trial court granted summary judgment in favor of the defendant, and the plaintiff appealed. How do you think the appellate court ruled, and why? [*Estate of Martha Nelson v. Carl Rice and Anne Rice,* 12 P.3d 238, 2000 LEXIS APP 159 (2000).]

7. Audrey Vokes was a 51-year-old widow who wanted to become an "accomplished dancer." She was invited to attend a "dance party" at J. P. Davenports' School of Dancing, an Arthur Murray franchise. She subsequently signed up for dance classes, at which she received elaborate praise. Her instructor initially sold her eight half-hour dance lessons for $14.50 each, to be used one each month. Eventually, after being continually told that she had excellent potential and that she was developing into a beautiful dancer—when, in fact, she

was not developing her dance ability and had no aptitude for dance—she ended up purchasing a total of 2,302 hours' worth of dance lessons for a total of $31,090.45. When it finally became clear to Vokes that she was not developing her dance skills, in part because she had trouble even hearing the musical beat, she sued Arthur Murray. What would be the basis of her argument? Her case was initially dismissed by the trial court. What do you think the result of her appeal was? [*Okes v. Arthur Murray,* 212 So. 2d 906 (1968).]

8. Arnold Olson and his now-deceased spouse deeded their property to their six children in perpetuity until they die. During a subsequent conversation with his son and daughter-in-law, in the presence of two other children, Olson granted his son part of that property, which included the home and several buildings, as long as they did not sell it while he was alive, because he wanted to live in a trailer on the property. He then executed a second deed conveying the property but failed to include the life estate in this second deed.

   The father lived in his trailer on the property for four years. Then the son told him he would have to move because they were selling the property. Olson and his other children sued to have the contract reformed on the grounds of mistake. The trial court agreed and reformed the contract to include the provision for the father's life estate. Why do you think the appellate court either affirmed or reversed the lower court's decision? [*Olson v. Olson,* 1998 WL 170111.]

9. The Winklers were interested in purchasing a home in the Valleyview Farms housing development. They contacted the developer, Galehouse, and selected a lot that cost $57,000. They asked the developer to show them plans for houses for which the construction costs would range from $180,000 to $190,000, indicating this was the price they would be willing to spend for construction only and wasn't to include the lot price. The developer gave them several books and plans to look at.

   After the Winklers had several conversations with Galehouse, the developer drafted plans for a 2,261-square-foot house and gave the Winklers a quote of $198,000 for construction. The lot price was not included. After several months of adding options and upgrades to the plan, the cost rose to $242,000, excluding the lot. The parties then engaged in a couple of weeks of negotiations regarding the price of the construction and lot. Eventually they reached a compromise price of $291,000 ($243,000 for the construction and $48,000 for the lot).

   Galehouse prepared a written contract to reflect the parties' agreement, but the developer forgot to include the lot price. The Winklers paid Galehouse $48,000, the lot price, as a deposit on the contract. When the construction was completed, and the Winklers were finalizing their loan from the bank, the parties discovered the drafting error. Galehouse sued to have the contract reformed to reflect the agreed-on price. Should the contract be reformed? Why or why not? [*Galehouse v. Winkler,* 1998 WL 312527.]

10. Plaintiff Stirlen was the chief financial officer for Supercuts. On numerous occasions he informed Lipson, to whom he reported directly, and other corporate officers of various operating problems he felt contributed to the general decline in Supercuts' retail profits and of "accounting irregularities" he feared might be in violation of state and federal statutes and regulations. After Stirlen brought his concerns to the company's auditor, Lipson allegedly reprimanded him, accused him of being a "troublemaker," and told him that if he did not reverse his position on the issues taken to the auditor he would no longer be considered a "member of the team." Stirlen was terminated the following month and subsequently filed suit for wrongful discharge. Supercuts' general counsel moved to compel arbitration under the compulsory arbitration provision of the employment contract between the parties.

    The contract provided that all claims arising from an individual's employment, including civil rights actions and tort claims, must be submitted to arbitration within one year of the date on which the dispute arose or the employee waived his right to pursue the claim. Damages that could be awarded through arbitration were limited to "a money award not to exceed the amount of actual damages for breach of contract, less any proper offset for mitigation of such damages, and the parties shall not be entitled to any other remedy at law or in equity, including but not limited to other money damages, punitive damages, specific performance, and/or injunctive relief." In the event that an employee did submit a dispute to arbitration, the employee's employment would immediately cease, as would any claims he had to unpaid benefits, without any penalty to the company, pending the outcome of the arbitration.

The agreement did not totally prevent the use of the courts, however. It provided that the following need not be submitted to arbitration: "Any action initiated by the Company seeking specific performance or injunctive or other equitable relief in connection with any breach . . . of this Agreement."

The trial court found this agreement was unconscionable. How do you believe the appellate court ruled on this case? Why? [*Stirlen v. Supercuts, Inc., et al.*, 51 Cal. App. 1519 (1997).]

Looking for more review material?

The Online Learning Center at **www.mhhe.com/kubasek2e** contains this chapter's "Assignment on the Internet" and also a list of URLs for more information, entitled "On the Internet." Find both of them in the Student Center portion of the OLC, along with quizzes and other helpful materials.

Agency Formation and Duties

LEARNING OBJECTIVES

After reading this chapter, you will be able to answer the following questions:

1   What is agency law?

2   How is an agency relationship created?

3   What are the different types of agency?

4   What are the different types of agency relationships?

5   What are the duties of the agent?

6   What are the rights and remedies of the agent and principal?

CASE OPENER
FedEx and Independent Contractors

In July 2006, the International Brotherhood of Teamsters, Local Union 25, filed two petitions and held an election for a collective bargaining representative at two FedEx locations. However, FedEx refused to bargain with the union. FedEx did not contest the vote count of the election; instead, FedEx refused to collectively bargain because it believed that its single-route drivers were not "employees" but, rather, "independent contractors," and the rules of collective bargaining in this situation apply only to employees. However, the National Labor Relations Board concluded that FedEx committed an unfair labor practice by refusing to bargain with the union certified as the collective bargaining representative of the drivers. FedEx sought judicial review of the decision of the board, and the board cross-applied for enforcement of its order requiring that the company bargain.

1. Do you agree with the National Labor Relations Board's ruling that FedEx engaged in an unfair labor practice? Why?

2. What duties and rights would the FedEx drivers have if they were considered employees? How would their duties and rights differ if the drivers were considered independent contractors of the company?

The Wrap-Up at the end of the chapter will answer these questions.

One of the most important relationships in the business world is the agency relationship, in which the employee may be an agent of the employer and have the ability to bind that employer legally. The use of agents and independent contractors allows corporations to enter into contracts and conduct business in multiple locations simultaneously. This chapter explores the nature and creation of the agency relationship, as well as the legal obligations of the parties in such a relationship.

Introduction to Agency Law

LO1

What is agency law?

Agency is generally defined as a relationship between a principal and an agent. In the **agency relationship,** the agent is authorized to act for and on behalf of the principal, who hires the agent to represent him or her. The Restatement of Agency defines **agency** as "the fiduciary relationship that results from the manifestation of consent by one person to another that the other shall act in his behalf and subject to his control, and consent by the other so to act."[1] (A *fiduciary* is a person who has a duty to act primarily for another person's benefit. A lawyer, for example, is a fiduciary for his or her client. We discuss fiduciaries in greater depth later in this chapter.)

Agency law is primarily state law. Thus, it can vary somewhat from state to state. At least 27 states have enacted statutes governing the behavior of sports agents. Twenty-three of those states impose civil penalties or damages on the agent for violations of the athlete agent statutes. Twenty-four states (including California and Florida) have established criminal penalties for sports agents who violate the state statute. In contrast, only five states have criminalized violations of the statute by the athletes themselves. In addition to state laws protecting athletes and agents, players associations' model contracts describe the nature of the services agents can perform on behalf of their principals and the duties the parties owe to one another. For example, the Major League Baseball Players Association's (MLBPA's) Regulations Governing Player Agents expressly state that agents act in a fiduciary capacity vis-à-vis their athlete clients.

Agency law is especially important for U.S. firms doing business globally. While foreign countries offer fresh markets and eager consumers, U.S. companies often run into legal difficulties due to language barriers or lack of knowledge about local laws. To avoid such problems, many companies hire agents familiar with local laws, customs, and customers to help them function smoothly in foreign markets.

Creation of the Agency Relationship

LO2

How is an agency relationship created?

Agency relationships are consensual relationships formed by informal oral agreements or formal written contracts. There are two criteria for the creation of agency relationships. First, like contracts, they can be created only for a lawful purpose; thus, a principal could

---

[1] Restatement (Second) of Agency, sec. 1(1). A valuable reference that summarizes agency law, the Restatement is well respected in the legal profession and frequently cited by judges as well as attorneys and scholars in making legal arguments.

not hire an agent to kill someone on his or her behalf.[2] Second, almost anyone can act as an agent; however, an individual who does not have contractual capacity, such as a minor, cannot hire an agent to make contracts on his or her behalf.

As long as these two criteria are met, agency relationships can be created on the basis of any of the following four forms of authority:

1. By expressed agency or agency by agreement.
2. By implied authority.
3. By apparent agency, or agency by estoppel.
4. By ratification.

The following pages discuss all four forms. Agency agreements usually do not need to be in writing, with two important exceptions. First, the agreement must be in writing whenever an agent will enter into a contract that the statute of frauds requires to be in writing. Janet wants Phil to act as her agent and grants him the power to enter into contracts. The statute of frauds, or, more specifically, the equal dignities rule, mandates that the type of contracts Phil is allowed to enter into must be in writing. Therefore, Phil's agreement with Janet must also be in writing. Second, the agreement must be in writing whenever an agent is given power of attorney (discussed below).

A *gratuitous agent* is one who acts without consideration; that is, such an agent is not paid for his or her services. Gratuitous agents function much like regular agents, with a few exceptions noted later in this chapter.

Legal Principle: **Agency relationships cannot be created to conduct illegal activities.**

Types of Agency

EXPRESSED AGENCY (AGENCY BY AGREEMENT)

When parties form an agency relationship by making a written or oral agreement, the agency is known as an **expressed agency,** or agency by agreement. Expressed agency is the most common type of agency and gives the agent the authority to contract on behalf of the principal. While a contract is not necessary to form the agency, if there is one it must meet all the elements of a contract discussed in Chapter 13. If the principal agrees to hire no other agent for a period of time or until a particular job is done, the principal and agent have entered into an exclusive agency contract.

LO3

What are the different types of agency?

A *power of attorney* establishes an agency by agreement that gives an agent authority to sign legal documents on behalf of the principal. A general power of attorney grants broad authority, while a specific power of attorney gives authority only for the specific areas or purposes listed in the agreement.

Powers of attorney are often given for business and health care purposes. Hence, an agent can make decisions about a principal's medical care if the principal cannot. Given that a principal must have the ability to enter into contracts to create an agency relationship, a principal may not enact a power of attorney after becoming incompetent. Therefore, a principal may preemptively enact a *durable power of attorney,* a written document expressing his or her wishes for an agent's authority not to be affected by the principal's subsequent incapacity. Alternatively, a durable power of attorney might become active only after a principal becomes incapacitated in any matter. (See Exhibit 33-1 for a comparison of a power of attorney and a durable power of attorney.) The Case Nugget examines the boundaries of the durable power of attorney.

---

[2] Restatement (Second) of Agency, sec.19.

Durable Power of Attorney

**Penny Garrison et al. v. The Superior Court
of Los Angeles et al.
132 Cal. App. 4th 253 (2005)**

On Ella Needham's request, her daughter, Penny Garrison, was designated Needham's agent through a durable power of attorney. Needham was later admitted to a residential care facility. As part of the admissions process, Garrison, acting under the durable power of attorney, executed two arbitration agreements. After Needham's death, Garrison and Needham's other daughters sought to sue the facility for a number of concerns the family had regarding the care their mother had received. The facility sought to enforce the two arbitration agreements. However, the family contended that the agreements were unenforceable because Garrison could not legally enter into them.

The durable power of attorney had given Garrison power to (1) make all health care decisions for Needham according to what she believed was in Needham's best interest and (2) make decisions relating to Needham's personal care, including but not limited to determining where she lived. Therefore, Garrison was legally in charge of picking the residential care facility, and she had the power to enter into agreements regarding Needham's care.

Nowhere in the enumerated legal powers did the durable power of attorney state that Garrison could not enter into arbitration clauses. Moreover, the arbitration clauses were optional to the original contract, and they allowed a 30-day period during which Garrison could cancel them. Because the durable power of attorney was legal and enforceable, Garrison could not cancel the agreements into which she entered.

The Restatement says, "[A]n agency relation exists only if there has been a manifestation by the principal to the agent that the agent may act on his account, and consent by the agent so to act."[3] Therefore, in addition to the above criteria, the principal must agree to have the person act as an agent, and the agent must agree to act for the principal. As noted below, the parties can reach this agreement in several ways.

AGENCY BY IMPLIED AUTHORITY

In some cases, an agency relationship is not created by an express agreement but is instead implied by the conduct of the parties. For example, if a homeowner asked a real estate broker to help sell her home, her words imply that an agency relationship has been formed. The circumstances determine the extent of an agent's ability to conduct business on behalf of the principal. However, implied authority cannot conflict with any express authority.

Exhibit 33-1
Comparison of Powers of Attorney

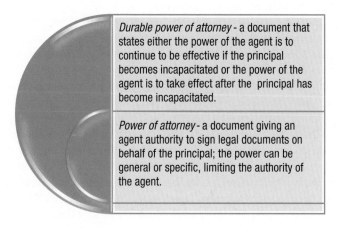

Durable power of attorney - a document that states either the power of the agent is to continue to be effective if the principal becomes incapacitated or the power of the agent is to take effect after the principal has become incapacitated.

Power of attorney - a document giving an agent authority to sign legal documents on behalf of the principal; the power can be general or specific, limiting the authority of the agent.

[3] Restatement (Second) of Agency, sec. 15.

Formation of Power of Attorney under Civil Law in France

In the United States and other common law jurisdictions, a power of attorney authorizes the agent only to "conduct a series of transactions" under instruction from the principal. This limitation makes the power of attorney in common law distinctly different from that provided by civil law, which authorizes the agent to do "everything and anything which the principal himself could do." Under French Civil Code, the common law definition would actually be classified as portraying a special agent.

France recognizes the danger in granting unlimited power to the agent. Therefore, in 1988, the French amended their Civil Code to say that power of attorney will refer only to acts of management and not those of disposition (transfer of property). Thus, before signing a contract, the principal must carefully specify every type of disposition transaction in which the agent may engage.

Despite the danger associated with the broad definition in current civil law, Germany maintains that a power of attorney authorizes the agent to do "everything and anything."

Legal Principal: Agency by implied authority cannot conflict with any express authority.

APPARENT AGENCY (AGENCY BY ESTOPPEL)

Suppose a principal falsely leads a third party to believe another individual serves as his or her agent. Does an agency relationship exist? Yes, because by his or her conduct, the principal has created **apparent agency** or **agency by estoppel.** According to the principal's conduct, the agent has apparent authority to act; thus, the principal is estopped, or prevented, from denying that the individual is an agent.[4] An apparent agency can be created only on the acts of the principal—never on the basis of what the purported agent says or does. When a third party relies on the principal's conduct and makes an agreement with an apparent agent, the principal must uphold any agreements made by the agent. If the principal attempts to deny that an agency relationship existed, the third party must dem-

onstrate that he or she reasonably believed, on the basis of the principal's conduct, that an agency relationship existed. The court will consider the principal's conduct in determining whether an agency relationship existed.

Suppose a salesman enters the office of a third party claiming he represents a company that wants to do business. If he is really not an agent for the company and provides no evidence of a link with it, the company will not be held responsible under apparent agency because the third party had no interaction

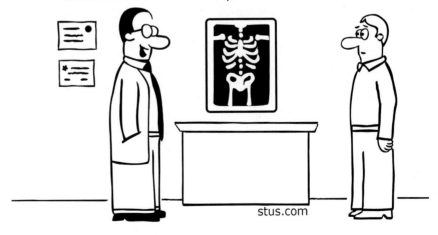

Yes, I'm a radiologist. And yes I work at the hospital. And yes I'm the only choice the hospital offers. But why would you think I work for the hospital?

stus.com

---

[4] Restatement (Second) of Agency, sec. 8B.

with it. The third party had no reason to believe an agency relationship existed, other than the agent's words. However, if the president of the company suggests to the third party that the salesman *is* a representative of the company, the president's conduct suggests that the salesman is an agent. Thus, the company would have to uphold any agreement the third party made with the apparent agent. In Case 33-1, pay close attention to how the court focuses on the principal's actions in this agency issue.

CASE 33-1   THOMAS & LINDA GENOVESE v. THERESA BERGERON
COURT OF APPEALS OF SOUTH CAROLINA
327 S.C. 567 (1997)

From October 1988 to December 1993, Theresa Bergeron paid $1,300 a month according to a yearly lease to rent a residence on Hilton Head Island from Thomas and Linda Genovese. Throughout the period, Doris Warner managed the property. In December 1993, Bergeron told Warner she had been offered employment in New York and wanted to either terminate the lease or sublease the property. Warner told Bergeron the landlords did not want her to sublease the property and were considering selling it. She said Bergeron should put her wish to terminate the lease in writing along with the fact she was vacating the premises.

In January 1994, when Bergeron was moving out, Warner inspected the property and told Bergeron she had to pay $1,360 for damages to it. Because Bergeron's security deposit covered only $1,000 of the damages, Bergeron wrote a check to the Genoveses for $360.

The Genoveses brought a suit against Bergeron to recover unpaid rent and property damages. Bergeron argued Warner had the apparent authority to release her from the lease. The trial court ruled in favor of the Genoveses, and Bergeron appealed.

JUDGE GOOLSBY: Apparent authority to do a particular act "is created as to a third person by written or spoken words or any other conduct of the principal which, reasonably interpreted, causes the third person to believe the principal consents to have the act done on his behalf by the person purporting to act for him." Muller v. Myrtle Beach Golf and Yacht Club, 303 S.C. 137, 142, 399 S.E. 2d 430, 433 (Ct. App. 1990) (citing RESTATEMENT (SECOND) OF AGENCY § 27 (1958)). The principal must either intend to cause the third person to believe the agent is authorized to act for him, or he should realize his conduct is likely to create such belief.

It is undisputed Warner was the landlords' agent. At issue, then, is the extent of Warner's agency. Genovese testified he gave Warner broad authority to manage the property. For instance, as the rental property manager for the landlords

throughout the five-year period during which the tenant occupied the property, Warner managed the lease, received rent payments, and ordered necessary repairs to the property. Warner also prepared the rental agreements between the landlords and the tenant for their signing and negotiated the terms with the tenants. The landlords always dealt with the tenant through Warner and there were no contacts between the landlords and the tenant except through Warner.

When the tenant requested in writing whether she could terminate the lease or be allowed to sublet the property, Warner told the tenant the landlords were thinking about selling the property, and the landlords did not want the tenant to sublease it, so the tenant could vacate the property. The landlords did not communicate their opposition to this arrangement between the tenant and Warner until they filed this lawsuit.

Viewing the evidence in the light most favorable to the tenant, as we are required to do [because the case was decided on summary judgment], we find there is some evidence in the record for a jury to conclude, under the doctrine of apparent authority, the conduct of the landlords in clothing Warner with so much authority to manage the property would allow a reasonably prudent person in the tenant's position to believe Warner had the authority to release the tenant from her obligations under the lease. See Rickborn v. Liberty Life Ins. Co., 321 S.C. 291, 468 S.E. 2d 292 (1996) (under the doctrine of apparent authority, a principal is bound by the acts of its agent when it has placed the agent in such a position persons of ordinary prudence, reasonably knowledgeable with business usages and customs, are led to believe the agent has certain authority and they in turn deal with the agent based on that assumption); Fernander v. Thigpen, 278 S.C. 140, 293 S.E. 2d 424 (1982) (agency may be implied or inferred and may be shown directly or circumstantially by the conduct of the purported agent exhibiting a pretense of authority with the knowledge of the alleged principal).

AFFIRMED.

CRITICAL THINKING

Is any important information missing from this decision that might further clarify the nature of the relationships between the concerned parties? Could it change the acceptability of the judge's reasoning?

ETHICAL DECISION MAKING

Does this ruling appear to follow a coherent ethical guideline? If so, what form does it take? Who are the stakeholders in this situation? Are they awarded proper consideration under the selected ethical guideline?

AGENCY BY RATIFICATION

Francisco is driving home and sees a car with a "For Sale" sign in the window. He stops to look at it because his friend Miles wants to buy a used car. Impressed by the car's price and quality, Francisco tells the owner his friend wants to buy it. The owner claims another individual is coming to probably buy the car in an hour. To ensure that Miles gets the car, Francisco signs a contract to purchase it but notes on the contract that he is an agent of Miles. Because Francisco is not his agent, Miles is not required to uphold the contract.

However, if Miles does agree to purchase the car, he has accepted Francisco as his agent for the contract. Miles is now bound by the contract, and Francisco cannot be held liable for misrepresenting himself. This type of agency relationship is *agency by ratification*. As the example suggests, it has two requirements:

1. An individual must misrepresent himself or herself as an agent for another party.
2. The principal must accept or ratify the unauthorized act.

For ratification to be effective, two additional requirements must be met:

3. The principal must have complete knowledge of all material facts regarding the contract.
4. The principal must ratify the entirety of the agent's act. (The principal cannot accept certain parts of the agent's act and reject others.)

Agency Relationships

Agency laws are relevant to three types of business relationships: the principal-agent relationship, the employer-employee relationship, and the employer–independent contractor relationship (see Exhibit 33-2). We discuss all three in the following sections.

PRINCIPAL-AGENT RELATIONSHIP

The *principal-agent relationship* typically exists when an employer hires an employee to enter into contracts on its behalf. This is the most basic type of agency relationship. Suppose a salesclerk at Abercrombie sells Amanda a shirt. The clerk is acting on behalf of Abercrombie's owner; consequently, any sales she makes are binding on it. Think of all the advertisements you've seen in which a professional athlete speaks on behalf of a product. The athlete usually hires an agent to find and make agreements on his or her behalf to promote products.

LO4

What are the different types of agency relationships?

Exhibit 33-2
Types of Agency
Relationships and
Their Significance

RELATIONSHIP	HOW TO IDENTIFY	SIGNIFICANT FOR WHAT ISSUES?
Principal-agent	Parties have *agreed* that agent will have power to bind principal in contract.	Contract law
Employer-employee	Employer has right to *control* conduct of employees.	Tort law, tax law, wage law, discrimination law, copyright law
Employer–independent contractor	Employer has *no control* over details of conduct of independent contractor.	Tort law, tax law, wage law, discrimination law, copyright law

EMPLOYER-EMPLOYEE RELATIONSHIP

Whenever an employer hires an employee to perform some sort of physical service, the parties have created an *employer-employee relationship* in which the employee is subject to the employer's control.[5] Generally, all employees are considered agents of the employer, even those not legally authorized to enter into contracts binding their employer or to interact with third parties. However, not all agents are employees.

Legal Principle: **Employees are agents of an employer.**

EMPLOYER–INDEPENDENT CONTRACTOR RELATIONSHIP

The Restatement of Agency defines an *independent contractor* as "a person who contracts with another to do something for him but who is not controlled by the other nor subject to the other's right to control with respect to his physical conduct in the performance of the undertaking."[6] Building contractors, doctors, stockbrokers, and lawyers are types of independent contractors. They are also agents, but not employees. However, not all independent contractors are agents. They cannot enter into contracts on behalf of the principal unless the principal authorizes them to do so.

Legal Principle: **Independent contractors cannot enter into contracts on behalf of the principal unless the contractor possesses authority from the principal.**

Employee or Independent Contractor?   The question of whether a worker is an employee or an independent contractor has important implications because the employer-employee relationship is subject to the workers' compensation, workplace safety, employment discrimination, and unemployment statutes, while the employer–independent contractor relationship is not. Employers are also generally liable in tort for the actions of their employees, while they are generally not liable for the actions of independent contractors (see Chapter 34).

When courts are deciding whether a worker is an employee or an independent contractor, perhaps the most important consideration is employer control.[7] If the employer has the

---

[5] Restatement (Second) of Agency, sec. 2.

[6] Restatement (Second) of Agency, sec. 2.

[7] Restatement (Second) of Agency, sec. 2(3).

Formation of Agency in Italian Law

The Italian legal system has created an agency relationship that gives the agent unique powers. Although not formally recognized by the Italian Civil Code, this relationship is common in business practices and has been upheld in a number of court cases.

The agency relationship begins much like agency in the United States: The principal and agent enter into a contract under which the agent agrees to the principal's stipulations. This contract, however, also requires that the agent maintain the principal's property.

Under Italian law, the agent then becomes legal owner of the property and can transfer or contract it without the principal's consent. Such autonomous powers are not granted to agents in the United States, who must maintain communication with and receive permission from principals unless otherwise specified.

The extended freedom of the agent under the Italian Civil Code results in considerably lengthy and detailed contracts between agents and principals. Both parties are looking to protect their own interests.

right to substantially control the worker's day-to-day operations, the worker is generally considered an employee. Employers will sometimes have some control over the operations of a contractor; however, this control does not always mean that the contractor is an employee. In the Case Opener, the main issue for the court to determine was whether the FedEx drivers were employees or contractors. To do so, the court relied on the standard agency principle of determining how much control the employer exerted over the agent drivers. (See Exhibit 33-3 for more criteria that distinguish employees and independent contractors.)

The IRS also must decide who is an employee and who is an independent contractor to ensure that the employer is not simply trying to lower its tax burden. The IRS has outlined 20 different criteria for its auditors to consider in determining whether someone is an independent contractor. In 1997, under advisement of the court, the IRS changed its criteria to focus on one element: how much control the employer exerts over the agent. The IRS needs to determine when people are employees and when they are independent contractors because of different tax liabilities employers face. When the IRS determines an independent contractor is really an employee, the employer becomes liable for all applicable taxes, such as Social Security and unemployment taxes.

Exhibit 33-3   Independent Contractor or Employee?

CRITERIA	EMPLOYEE	INDEPENDENT CONTRACTOR
Does the worker engage in a distinct occupation or an independently established business?	No	Yes
Is the work done under the employer's supervision, or does a specialist without supervision complete the work?	Employer supervision	Specialist without supervision
Does the employer supply the tools?	Yes	No
What skill is required for the occupation?	No specialized skill	Great degree of skill
What is the length of time for which the worker is employed?	Long time	Varies
Is the worker a regular part of the business of the employer?	Yes	No
How is the worker paid?	Regular payments according to time	When the job is completed

Case 33-2 provides an illustration of the court's consideration of the criteria that establish whether a worker is an employee or an independent contractor.

CASE 33-2

CYNTHIA WALKER v. JOHN A. LAHOSKI ET AL.
COURT OF APPEALS OF OHIO, NINTH APPELLATE DISTRICT, SUMMIT COUNTY 1999 OHIO APP. LEXIS 3435 (1999)

In 1995, Cynthia Walker contracted with Genny's Home Health Care to find her employment as a home health-care worker. When Ben Lahoski contacted Genny's to obtain twenty-four-hour home health care for his wife Ann, Walker and another worker were assigned to her. Each would stay at the Lahoski's for either forty-eight or seventy-two hours, at which time the two would switch. In September 1995, while Walker was mopping the floor in the Lahoski home, the mop handle knocked a cast iron clock off the wall. Walker was hit on the head by the clock and suffered a sprain of the neck and contusions on her face, scalp, and neck. Walker filed a claim with the Ohio Bureau of Workers' Compensation, naming Ben and Ann Lahoski as her employers. The Ohio Bureau refused Walker's claim by arguing the Lahoskis were not Walker's employers.

Walker filed a claim in court against the Lahoskis for denying her workers' compensation. The trial court granted summary judgment to the Lahoskis. Walker appealed.

JUDGE BAIRD: To prevail in her workers' compensation claim, Ms. Walker would have to establish she was an employee of Ben and Ann Lahoski at the time her injury occurred. The trial court's denial of her claim is based on its finding she was not their employee, but an independent contractor.

Appellees in this matter argue Walker was an independent contractor. In support of their position they point out there was no contract between Walker and the Lahoskis, the Lahoskis did not pay Walker but paid the agency, and Walker's contract with the agency specifically stated she was an independent contractor.

Courts have distinguished an employee from an independent contractor by resolving two key questions. The first is whether the "employer" controls the "manner or means" by which the work is done or if the "employer" is interested only in the results to be achieved. In the first case, the worker would be an employee while in the second case the worker would be an independent contractor.

The second question is how the worker is paid. If the worker is paid on an hourly basis, this tends to indicate the worker was an employee, while payment by the job tends to indicate the worker was an independent contractor. Thus, the overriding consideration for the fact-finder in these cases is who has the right to control the manner or means of the work performed.

In the instant case, Walker signed a contract in which she acknowledged she was an independent contractor relative to Genny's and she would be an independent contractor relative to the customer, absent agreement by the customer she could be considered the customer's employee. However, such a contract provision is not necessarily controlling. The trial court must look to the substance of the relationship, not merely to a label attached to the relationship.

Appellees also assert when Walker and her coworker Peggy J. Seifert began to work for Ben Lahoski, Mr. Lahoski only briefly gave the women a tour of the house, then left it to them to perform their work as they saw fit. However, Cynthia Walker has testified otherwise, asserting Ben Lahoski was actively involved in directing her work for Mrs. Lahoski. In considering whether summary judgment was appropriate in this case, we must resolve the conflict in testimony in favor of the nonmoving party, Ms. Walker. Furthermore, the factual determination to be made in this case is who had the right to exercise control over the manner or means of the work performed.

[T]he "right to control" is agreeably the key factor in making the determination of whether an individual is an independent contractor or an employee. . . .

In the instant case, appellees merely assert "it is clear that Ben Lahoski did not reserve the right to control the manner or means of Appellant's work[.]" In point of fact, it is not clear Mr. Lahoski did not exercise such control. The statements of the two workers conflict on this point. Furthermore, even if Ben Lahoski did not exercise right to control, there is sufficient evidence to indicate he had the right to exercise that control.

The record below contains disputed facts and several indicia of employee status, such as hourly payment, control of hours worked, and control over the manner or means the work was performed. Appellees failed to meet their burden to show there was no genuine issue of material fact and reasonable minds could only decide favorably for the appellees. Thus, the trial court erred in granting summary judgment in favor of the defendants.

REVERSED.

CRITICAL THINKING

Clearly, all relevant information regarding the agreement is critical to the judge's conclusion. What missing information might be reason for the judge to form a different conclusion?

ETHICAL DECISION MAKING

The court felt that the law governing agency in this particular fact pattern was unclear enough that the lower court should not grant a summary judgment. But Walker and Seifert worked for the Lahoskis. Are there values that employers in a position like that of the Lahoskis should act on in their relationship with those who work for them? Should these values push employers beyond what they are required to do by law?

The classification as an employee or independent contractor is also important in determining who owns the output of a work project. According to the Copyright Act of 1976,[8] when an employee completes work at the request of the employer, the product is considered a "work for hire" and the employer owns the copyright. Conversely, an independent contractor normally maintains ownership of copyrights for his or her work product. Only by an agreement of both parties that a specific work is a work for hire may an employer gain copyright ownership of the work of an independent contractor.

Duties of the Agent and the Principal

An agency relationship is a fiduciary relationship of trust, confidence, and good faith. Thus, its formation creates certain duties that the principal and agent owe each other (see Exhibit 33-4). We discuss them in the following sections.

L05

What are the duties of the agent?

PRINCIPAL'S DUTIES TO THE AGENT

The principal owes certain duties to the agent. If these duties are not fulfilled, the principal has violated the agent's rights and the agent can sue for contract or tort remedies. The agent can also refuse to act on behalf of the principal until the failure is remedied.

Legal Principle: **The principal owes specific duties to the agent. Failure to fulfill these rights provides the basis for a tort or contract action against he principal.**

Duty of Compensation. The principal has a duty to compensate the agent for services provided, unless the parties have agreed the agent will act gratuitously. The agency contract will usually specify the type and amount of compensation as well as the time at which it will be paid. If there is no agreement on the amount, the courts suggest compensation should be calculated according to the customary fee in the situation.[9] The Case Nugget examines which individuals are responsible under the duty to compensate.

---

[8] 17 U.S.C. § § 101-810.

[9] Restatement (Second) of Agency, sec. 443.

CASE NUGGET

Duty to Compensate

Ralph T. Leonard et al. v. Jerry D. McMorris et al.
320 F.3d 1116 (2003)

NationsWay was one of the largest privately held trucking companies in the United States, with 3,200 employees operating in 43 different states. In 1999, NationsWay filed for Chapter 11 bankruptcy and terminated most of its employees. Ralph Leonard, and a number of the other employees who were terminated, sued Jerry McMorris and other NationsWay executives, arguing they were personally liable for unpaid wages under their duty to compensate arising from the employer-employee relationship.

The defendants argued they could not be held personally liable for agreements made between the employees and the corporation.

As the case began, NationsWay was continuing its bankruptcy filings, under which the former employees were to receive approximately $3 million in unpaid wages. However, the plaintiffs wanted additional amounts covering accrued vacation pay, sick-leave pay, holiday pay, and other nonwage compensation, as well as a 50 percent penalty and attorney fees.

In deciding the case, the court addressed "[w]hether officers of a corporation are individually liable for the wages of the corporation's former employees under the Colorado Wage Claim Act." The court concluded, "[U]nder Colorado's Wage Claim Act, the officers and agents of a corporation are *not* jointly and severally liable for payment of employee wages and other compensation the corporation owes to its employees under the employment contract and the Colorado Wage Claim Act." Although there is a duty to compensate for the corporation, the executives who were the defendants were not individually liable to the former employees for the unpaid wages.

Duty of Reimbursement and Indemnification. The principal has a duty of reimbursement and indemnification to the agent. If an agent makes authorized expenditures in the course of working on behalf of the principal, the principal has a duty to reimburse the agent for that amount of money.[10] Thus, if an agent takes a trip on behalf of the principal, the principal must have authorized this trip if the agent is to be reimbursed.

Exhibit 33-4 Duties of Principal and Agent

PRINCIPAL DUTIES	
Compensation	The principal has a duty to compensate the agent for services provided unless the parties have agreed that the agent will act gratuitously.
Reimbursement and indemnification	The principal has a duty to reimburse or indemnify the agent for any authorized expenditures or any losses the agent incurs in the course of working on behalf of the principal.
Cooperation	The principal must assist the agent in the performance of his or her duties and cannot interfere with the reasonable conduct of the agent.
Safe working conditions	The principal has a duty to ensure safe working conditions and to warn the agent if the principal is aware of any potential danger.

AGENT DUTIES	
Loyalty	The agent has a responsibility to act in the best interest of the principal; this duty is important because the agency relationship is founded on trust.
Notification	The agent must notify the principal of any relevant information in a timely manner.
Obedience	The agent must follow the lawful instruction and direction of the principal.
Accounting	The agent must keep an accurate account of the transactions made on behalf of the principal and provide the accounting information to the principal on request.
Performance	The agent must perform the duties as specified in the agency agreement with reasonable skill, care, and professionalism.

[10] Restatement (Second) of Agency, sec. 438.

Similarly, the principal has the duty to indemnify or reimburse the agent for any losses the agent incurs while working within the scope of authority on the principal's behalf.[11] Suppose an agent makes an agreement with a third party on behalf of the principal and the principal fails to uphold the agreement. The third party could sue the agent for damages, but the principal has a duty to indemnify the agent for the losses the third party regains.

Duty of Cooperation.   The principal also owes a *duty of cooperation* to the agent and must therefore assist the agent in the performance of his or her duties. Furthermore, the principal can do nothing to interfere with the agent's reasonable conduct. If Suzi hires someone to sell her car for her, she must be willing to let the agent show the car to interested buyers.

Duty to Provide Safe Working Conditions.   The principal has a *duty to provide safe working conditions* for the agent, including equipment and premises. A principal aware of unsafe working conditions has a duty to warn the agent and make necessary repairs. Federal and state statutes, such as the Occupational Safety and Health Act (OSHA), set specific standards for the working environment. Employers that violate these standards may be subject to fines.

AGENT'S DUTIES TO THE PRINCIPAL

Because the agent makes agreements on behalf of the principal in a fiduciary relationship of trust and confidence, he or she can also harm the principal. Suppose an agent makes numerous contracts the principal could not possibly carry out all at once. The third parties may sue the principal for not carrying out the agreements. If the agent breaches his or her duties, the principal can sue the agent and may be entitled to a variety of contract and tort remedies beyond those stated in the contract.

Legal Principle: **When an agent fails to fulfill his duties to the principal, that failure provides the basis for a contract or tort action against the agent.**

Duty of Loyalty.   Courts suggest that the **duty of loyalty** is the most important duty an agent owes to a principal. Because of their fiduciary relationship, the agent has a responsibility to act in the interest of the principal,[12] including avoiding conflicts of interest and protecting the principal's confidentiality.

An agent cannot represent both the principal and a third party in an agreement, because there could be a conflict of interest. The agent also has a duty to notify the principal of any offers from third parties. Suppose Tony has hired a real estate agent to make land purchases for him. A third party notifies the real estate agent that some of her property will soon be going up for sale and wants to know whether Tony would be interested in buying it. The real estate agent cannot decide to buy that property for himself or herself until (1) the real estate agent has communicated the offer to Tony and (2) Tony has considered and rejected the offer.

The duty of loyalty also requires that the agent keep confidential any information about the principal, during the course of agency as well as after the agency relationship has been terminated. The agent cannot disclose or misuse any information received during or after the agency relationship with the principal.

---

[11] Restatement (Second) of Agency, secs. 438 and 439.

[12] Restatement (Second) of Agency, sec. 401.

E-COMMERCE AND THE LAW

Electronic Agents and Contract Formation

Some scholars believe that it is only a matter of time until individuals and companies send nonhuman agents to the Internet to transact business on their behalf. Some have suggested that robots will one day be able to "trawl the Internet" and make decisions on behalf of their owners. The possibility that agency relationships could be created without human involvement raises some interesting legal questions. For example, can there be a "meeting of the minds" if a computer program participates in a negotiating process? Can a robot exceed its authority?

Duty of Notification. The agent has to communicate not only offers from third parties but also, under the duty of notification, any information he or she thinks could be important to the principal.[13] If a third party has made an agreement with a principal through an agent and fails to meet the agreement, the agent must notify the principal in a timely manner. The law typically assumes that the principal is aware of all information revealed to the agent, regardless of whether the agent shares it with the principal. Case 33-3 pays special attention to the duties of the agent to the principal and explains what happens when an agent violates the specific duty of loyalty.

[13] Restatement (Second) of Agency, sec. 381.

CASE 33-3   INTERNATIONAL AIRPORT CENTERS v. JACOB CITRIN
COURT OF APPEALS FOR THE SEVENTH DISTRICT
440 F.3D 418 (2006)

The defendant, Mr. Citrin, was employed by the plaintiffs' real estate business, IAC. In the course of their business relationship, IAC lent Citrin a laptop to use to record work data. Eventually Mr. Citrin quit his job at IAC and started his own business, which was in breach of his employment contract. Before returning the laptop to IAC, he deleted all of the business data in the computer. Ordinarily, pressing the "delete" key on a computer merely removes the index entry and such "deleted" files are easily recoverable. But Mr. Citrin loaded into the laptop a secure-erasure program to prevent the recovery of the files. Subsequently, IAC sued him for violating the Computer Fraud and Abuse Act and his duty of loyalty that agency law imposes on an employee. The district court dismissed the suit and IAC appealed.

JUDGE POSNER: [Mr. Citrin's] authorization to access the laptop terminated when, having already engaged in misconduct and decided to quit IAC in violation of his employment contract, he resolved to destroy files that incriminated himself and other files that were also the property of his employer, in violation of the duty of loyalty that agency law imposes on an employee.

Muddying the picture some, the Computer Fraud and Abuse Act distinguishes between "without authorization" and "exceeding authorized access," 18 U.S.C. § § 1030(a) (1), (2), (4), and, while making both punishable, defines the latter as "accessing a computer with authorization and . . . using such access to obtain or alter information in the computer that the accesser is not entitled so to obtain or alter." § 1030(e)(6). That might seem the more apt description of what Citrin did.

The difference between "without authorization" and "exceeding authorized access" is paper thin, but not quite invisible. In *EF Cultural Travel BV v. Explorica, Inc.,* for example, the former employee of a travel agent, in violation of his confidentiality agreement with his former employer, used confidential information that he had obtained as an employee to create a program that enabled his new travel company to obtain information from his former employer's website that he could not have obtained as efficiently without the use of that confidential information. The website was open to the public, so he was authorized to use it, but he exceeded his authorization by using confidential information to obtain better access than other members of the public.

Our case is different. Citrin's breach of his duty of loyalty terminated his agency relationship (more precisely, terminated any rights he might have claimed as IAC's agent—he could not by unilaterally terminating any duties he owed his principal gain an advantage) and with it his authority to access the laptop, because the only basis of his authority had been that relationship. "Violating the duty of loyalty, or failing to disclose adverse interests, voids the agency relationship." *(State v. DiGiulio.)* "Unless otherwise agreed, the authority of the agent terminates if, without knowledge of the principal, he acquires adverse interests or if he is otherwise guilty of a serious breach of loyalty to the principal."

Citrin points out that his employment contract authorized him to "return *or destroy*" data in the laptop when he ceased being employed by IAC. But it is unlikely, to say the least, that the provision was intended to authorize him to destroy data that he knew the company had no duplicates of and would have wanted to have—if only to nail Citrin for misconduct. The purpose of the provision may have been to avoid overloading the company with returned data of no further value, which the employee should simply have deleted. More likely the purpose was simply to remind Citrin that he was not to disseminate confidential data after he left the company's employ—the provision authorizing him to return or destroy data in the laptop was limited to "Confidential" information. There may be a dispute over whether the incriminating files that Citrin destroyed contained "confidential" data, but that issue cannot be resolved on this appeal.

REVERSED and REMANDED.

CRITICAL THINKING

Why do you think the original trial court ruled in the opposite manner? Why might you conclude that the agent in the case (Citrin) did not violate his duties to the principal (IAC)?

ETHICAL DECISION MAKING

Recall the WPH framework for ethics. A classmate argues that Citrin made the correct decision in deleting the data because he himself was a stakeholder and deleting the data bettered his own position. Do you agree? Who are the relevant stakeholders negatively affected by Citrin's decision to destroy the business data on the computer?

Duty of Performance. The *duty of performance* the agent owes the principal is twofold. First, the agent must perform the duties as specified in the agency agreement. Suppose an insurance agent contacts Bethany about purchasing a car insurance policy. Bethany agrees to purchase it, but for some reason the agent never obtains the policy for her. Bethany discovers the insurance agent's mistake when she gets into a car accident. The insurance agent did not meet the duty of performance; thus Bethany could bring a claim against the agent.

Second, the agent must perform the specified duties with the same skill, care, and professionalism as a reasonable person in the same situation would provide. An attorney who advertises he is a specialist in certain types of law will be held to the reasonable standard of care in that specialty.[14] A gratuitous agent cannot be found liable for a breach of contract for failure to perform because no contract exists between the principal and the agent. However, if a gratuitous agent begins to act as an agent and the principal affirms the relationship, a duty to perform arises insofar as the agent has begun a specific task for the principal.

---

[14] Restatement (Second) of Agency, sec. 379.

Duty of Obedience.   Under the *duty of obedience,* the agent must follow the lawful instruction and direction of the principal.[15] An agent who makes an unauthorized agreement has failed to meet the duty of obedience. However, if the principal gives unlawful or unethical instructions, the agent is not required to behave in accordance with them. Let us say a principal tells an agent to sell a basketball autographed by Michael Jordan and the agent knows that the principal forged the signature. The agent is not required to obey this instruction.

Duty of Accounting.   Under the *duty of accounting,* the agent must keep an accurate account of the transactions of money and property made on behalf of the principal.[16] If the principal asks to see this accounting, the agent has a duty to provide it. The agent must also keep separate accounts for the principal's funds and the agent's funds and not allow them to mix.

Rights and Remedies
PRINCIPAL'S RIGHTS AND REMEDIES AGAINST THE AGENT

L06

What are the rights and remedies of the agent and principal?

Because the agency relationship generally *is* a contractual relationship, a principal has available contract remedies, discussed in depth in Chapter 20, for breach of fiduciary duties. In addition, a principal may utilize tort remedies for an agent's misrepresentations, negligence, or other business failings causing damage to the principal. When an agent breaches his or her fiduciary duties, the principal has the right to terminate the agency relationship. Of numerous remedies available to the principal, the three main ones are constructive trust, avoidance, and indemnification.

> **Legal Principle: When an agent breaches his or her duties to the principal, the principal can terminate the agency relationship and seek remedies.**

Constructive Trust.   Agency relationships exist primarily for the benefit of the principal. Therefore, principals are the legal owners of anything an agent may come to possess through the employment or agency relationship. Accordingly, an agent who through deceit or other means retains such profits or goods has breached his or her fiduciary duties. Joy, an agent of Sarah's selling real estate, sells a piece of property for $2,000 more than Sarah anticipated. Joy keeps the extra $2,000 and reports the sale at the price Sarah anticipated. By law the profits belong to Sarah, and Joy has breached her fiduciary duties by keeping the money.

An agent also may not use the agency relationship to obtain goods or property for himself or herself when the principal desired to obtain the same goods or property; the principal always has right of first refusal. If Joy were to buy a piece of land for herself that she knew Sarah wanted to purchase, she again would have breached her fiduciary duties to Sarah.

When an agent illegally benefits from the agency relationship, the principal may enact a **constructive trust** on the profits, goods, or property in question. A constructive trust is an equitable trust imposed on someone who wrongfully obtains or holds legal right to property he or she should not possess. The court then rules that the agent is merely holding the property or goods in trust for the principal, granting the principal legal right or possession.

[15] Restatement (Second) of Agency, secs. 383 and 385.
[16] Restatement (Second) of Agency, sec. 382.

Duties of the Agent in Australia

Agents in Australia and the United States share many of the same duties to the principal, including following the principal's instructions, exercising reasonable care and skill, and not inappropriately divulging or concealing confidential information.

Agents in Australia do have a unique duty, however. They are obligated to "act personally" on behalf of the principal. Suppose an agent is hired to sell apartments owned by the principal. If the agent hires an individual to sell the apartments for him, he cannot receive commission from the sale.

The basis for such a law is quite logical. The agent was hired to exercise personal skills, such as availability, in the absence of the principal. When no personal skill is demonstrated, the agent shall not be granted any compensation or reward. Specifying that duties must be performed personally may seem like an obvious and unnecessary stipulation, but this specificity is important in protecting the interests of the principal.

Avoidance. When an agent breaches an agency contract or his fiduciary duties, the principal may use her right of *avoidance* to nullify at her discretion any contract the agent negotiated.

Indemnification. A third party who believes that an agent is acting with actual or apparent authority may sue the principal for any breach of contract. However, if the breach was caused by the agent's negligence, the principal has a right to *indemnification;* that is, when sued by a third party, a principal may sue his agent to recover the amount assessed to the third party. As Ricardo's agent, Mercedes enters into a contract with Christina knowing that Ricardo cannot possibly fulfill it. Christina sues Ricardo for breach of contract and recovers damages. Ricardo, under indemnification, is entitled to sue Mercedes to recover what he had to pay.

A principal can also recover if an agent fails to follow the principal's instructions. Ricardo tells Mercedes not to take any more orders for the widgets he produces. While Ricardo is out of town, Mercedes takes Christina's order for 1,000 widgets. When Christina sues Ricardo for breach of contract, he can recover damages from Mercedes because she did not follow his instructions. Courts have had difficulty determining when a principal gives limiting instructions and when she merely gives advice. Going against advice does not impose liability on an agent, but violating limiting instructions does. To avoid a potential lawsuit from a third party, the principal should notify the third party whenever a relationship with an agent ceases or limiting instructions are given.

AGENT'S RIGHTS AND REMEDIES AGAINST THE PRINCIPAL

While agency relationships are intended to benefit the principal, the agent is not without rights and remedies. Whenever a duty is imposed on the principal, a corresponding right exists for the agent. Agents have available tort and contract remedies, in addition to the right to demand an accounting.

Tort and Contract Remedies. Tort and contract remedies available when a principal violates an agency agreement are the standard tort and contract remedies discussed in Chapters 8 and 20, respectively.

Demand for an Accounting. An agent who feels she is not being properly compensated, especially when working on commission, may *demand an accounting* and may withhold further performance of her duties until the principal supplies appropriate accounting data. Hal is a used-car salesman working for Not a Lemon Car Dealers.

When he receives his pay, he believes he has been shorted the appropriate amount he made on commission. Hal can request that Not a Lemon obtain an auditor to perform an audit and determine whether he was in fact paid the proper amount for his sales.

Specific Performance.   When a contract exists and a principal agrees to certain conditions but fails to perform, under contract remedies the agent may seek court assistance in forcing the principal to perform the contract as stipulated. However, when the agency relationship is not contractual or the contract is for personal services, an agent does not have this right. The agent may recover for services rendered and/or future damages but may not force the principal to fulfill the specific contractual agreements or even to continue to employ the agent.

CASE OPENER WRAP-UP

FedEx and Independent Contractors

Ultimately, the court ruled in favor of FedEx and found that the board's decision was unenforceable because the drivers in question were independent contractors rather than employees. To determine whether the FedEx drivers should be classified as employees or independent contractors, the court applied traditional agency law principles. They discovered that FedEx "may not prescribe hours of work, whether or when the drivers take breaks, what routes they follow, or other details of performance"; drivers "are not subject to reprimands or other discipline"; and the owners of the FedEx stores (called *contractors*) are responsible for all the costs associated with operating and maintaining their vehicles Therefore, FedEx does not exercise the degree of control necessary for the relationship to be considered employer-employee. Rather, in this situation, the route drivers are independent contractors who have "significant entrepreneurial opportunity for gain or loss" because they can operate multiple routes, hire additional drivers and helpers, sell routes without permission, and negotiate their price to deliver the packages. Therefore, the rights and duties of employees as agents discussed throughout the chapter do not apply to FedEx drivers.

This case illustrates the importance of understanding agency relations and whether a person is an employee or independent contractor. Although FedEx was successful in the case, this case suggests that it is essential for businesses to have knowledge of the kinds of agency relationships involved in their transactions. In the future, your knowledge about agency relationships could save you or your company large amounts of time and money spent on litigation.

Key Terms

Summary of Key Topics

Introduction to Agency Law	*Agency:* The relationship between a principal and an agent.
	Agent: One authorized to act for and on behalf of a principal.
	Principal: One who hires an agent to represent him or her.
	Fiduciary: One with a duty to act primarily for another person's benefit.
Creation of the Agency Relationship	Agency relationships can be created only for a lawful purpose, and almost anyone can serve as an agent. Agency relationships are consensual relationships formed by informal oral agreements or formal written contracts.
Types of Agency	*Expressed agency:* Agency formed by making a written or oral agreement.
	Power of attorney: Document giving an agent authority to sign legal documents on behalf of the principal.
	Durable power of attorney: Power of attorney intended to continue to be effective or to take effect after the principal has become incapacitated.
	Agency by implied authority: Agency formed by implication through the conduct of the parties.
	Agency by estoppel: Agency formed when a principal leads a third party to believe that another individual serves as his or her agent but the principal had made no agreement with the so-called agent.
	Agency by ratification: Agency that exists when an individual misrepresents himself or herself as an agent for another party and the principal accepts or ratifies the unauthorized act.
Agency Relationships	An *agency relationship* is a fiduciary relationship (a relationship of trust) in which an agent acts on behalf of the principal.
	A *principal-agent relationship* exists when an employer hires an employee to enter into contracts on behalf of the employer.
	An *employer-employee relationship* exists when an employer hires an employee to perform some sort of physical service.
	An *employer–independent contractor relationship* exists when an employer hires persons, other than employees, to conduct certain tasks.
Duties of the Agent and the Principal	*The duties of the principal:*
	• Duty of compensation
	• Duty of reimbursement and indemnification
	• Duty of cooperation
	• Duty of safe working conditions
	The duties of the agent:
	• Duty of loyalty
	• Duty of performance
	• Duty of notification
	• Duty of obedience
	• Duty of accounting

Rights and Remedies

The rights and remedies of the principal:

- Constructive trust
- Avoidance
- Indemnification

The rights and remedies of the agent:

- Tort and contract remedies
- Demand for an accounting
- Specific performance

Point / Counterpoint

Should an Agent Fulfill the Duty of Loyalty If a Product Is Faulty but No Laws Have Been Broken?	
YES	**NO**
According to the duty of loyalty, the relationship between the agent and the principal is a fiduciary relationship and the agent is obligated to act in the best interest of his or her principal under all legal circumstances. The agent can act on behalf of only one party in an agreement and so cannot be obligated to advise the consumer while acting on behalf of his or her principal. A conflict of interest would then arise, because the best interests of the consumer are not necessarily those of the principal. Also, it is the responsibility of the consumer, not the agent, to become fully informed about the risks and potential problems with a product *before* purchasing. Consumers can quickly access product reviews on the Internet, study frequently asked questions on company Web sites, and perform simple Internet searches for potential problems before purchasing. The responsibility of the agent is to his or her principal, no one else. Consumers are responsible for their own choices.	The agent should not remain loyal to the principal when she or he knows the product is faulty, even if no laws are being broken. A moral rule is a moral rule and exists to protect people from businesses that are willing to bend laws to increase profits. If we allow people to obey or disobey such rules as they saw fit, then they are not a guide to moral behavior but just a way for people to justify what they were going to do anyway. Agents do not need to reveal to consumers that they think a competitor's product is better; in fact, they need not reveal their opinion at all. However, an employee who knows that a new computer he is selling will break a month after the warranty expires should feel obligated to inform the consumer. This transparency is not a matter of revealing trade secrets or secret recipes. Agents should simply provide sufficient information to allow a careful decision to be made in a healthy, competitive business atmosphere. "Protecting" the employer under the guise of a duty of loyalty does not excuse an agent from fulfilling his or her moral obligations to honestly and fully inform consumers.

Questions & Problems

1. What are the similarities and differences between the types of agency relationships?

2. How is apparent agency, or agency by estoppel, different from expressed agency?

3. What are a principal's duties to an agent and an agent's duties to a principal?

4. William Roberts operated a McDonald's restaurant under a franchise agreement with McDonald's Corporation. Roberts hired 23-year-old David Mabin, who was just released from jail for robbery, drug use, and theft, as an hourly worker. Soon Roberts promoted Mabin to assistant manager on the night shift at the restaurant. A 15-year-old girl began

working at the McDonald's, and she quickly became involved with Mabin, who provided her with free food, alcohol, and drugs (including ecstasy) and kissed her openly in the workplace. Just before the girl's 16th birthday, Mabin took her to a motel where they spent the night and engaged in sexual intercourse. The girl and her family later brought suit against McDonald's Corporation on the basis that McDonald's Corporation was the principal to Roberts through apparent agency. McDonald's Corporation was supposed to be a business with a wholesome reputation and safe workplace, but instead the minor was taken advantage of by her assistant manager. The girl argued for apparent agency with McDonald's as the principal because she claimed that as far as she was concerned, she worked for McDonald's Corporation, not just the franchise. She had a McDonald's logo on her uniform, her paycheck, and restaurant products. However, the application she filled out for employment stated, "I understand that my employer is an independent Owner/Operator of a McDonald's franchise and that I am not employed by McDonald's Corporation or any of its subsidiaries. The independent Owner/Operator of this restaurant is solely responsible for all terms, conditions and any other issues concerning my employment." Was there an apparent agency relationship between McDonald's Corporation and the franchise? Why or why not? [*D.L.S. et al. v. David Mabin et al.*, 130 Wn. App. 94; 121 P.3d 1210 (2005).]

5. R. Edwin Powell was CEO and president of CAIRE, Inc., in addition to being a minority shareholder in Holdings, owning 11.9 percent of the company. In 1996, a group of investors decided to acquire Holdings and CAIRE. They formed MVE Investors, LLC. MVE purchased the shares of three retiring Holdings shareholders as part of a recapitalization of the company. MVE paid the retiring shareholders $125.456 per share and became its primary owner. Powell did not sell his stock at this time and remained CAIRE's CEO and president. In response to CAIRE's financial setbacks, David O'Halloran, Holdings' CEO and president, met with Powell on January 23, 1997, to fire Powell. While the two men agreed on a number of provisions in Powell's severance package, they disagreed on the terms for the disposition of Powell's stock. Powell testified that O'Halloran agreed, on behalf of Holdings, to buy Powell's stock at the same

price the retiring shareholders had been paid at the recapitalization. O'Halloran maintained he did not promise Powell that Holdings would buy Powell's stock. But O'Halloran conceded that at the meeting he gave Powell a detailed chart showing the number of shares Powell owned and how much money Powell would receive if those shares were sold or redeemed at the same price the retiring shareholders had received. O'Halloran also admitted he wrote a letter terminating Powell's employment if he chose not to resign. In the letter, O'Halloran expressed Holdings' intent to buy Powell's stock in the same manner as it had bought the retiring shareholders' stock. Holdings fired O'Halloran from his position as CEO and president. Powell brought action against Holdings, claiming, among other things, that Holdings had contracted to buy back his shares and then breached that contract. The district court found that Holdings had contracted to buy Powell's stock and breached the contract. The district court awarded Powell the amount Powell would have received had he sold his nonpledged stock for $125.456 per share. Holdings appealed, claiming that O'Halloran did not have authority to agree on its behalf to buy Powell's stock, the district court's finding that O'Halloran and Powell entered into a contract was contrary to the evidence, and any agreement was not the parties' final expression, is void for lack of consideration, and is against public policy. As an agent of Holdings, did O'Halloran enter into a contract on Holdings' behalf? Why? [*Powell v. MVE Holdings, Inc.*, 626 N.W.2d 451 (2001).]

6. Ward Manufacturing, Inc., decided to construct a casting facility on its property located in Blossburg, Pennsylvania. Ward entered into a written contract with Welliver-McGuire, Inc. Under the terms of the contract, Welliver agreed to indemnify Ward for any and all claims for bodily injury and property damage arising out of the performance of the work identified in the contract. Welliver assumed control, possession, and responsibility over the construction site throughout the project. Ward did, however, maintain an on-site representative to act as liaison and monitor the status of the project. Ward also had a safety representative on-site periodically to inspect the work site. Jonathon Olin worked as a carpenter for Welliver. Olin, while engaged in surveying activities on the Ward construction site, fell into an unbarricaded excavation pit allegedly

covered with water and mud. As a result of the fall, Olin purportedly suffered severe injuries. Since the date of the accident, Olin had received total disability workers' compensation benefits from Welliver. Olin brought suit against Ward for negligence. Ward argued that Olin, through Welliver, was an independent contractor and that Ward therefore was not liable to Olin for damages. Furthermore, Ward argued that Welliver, and not Ward, was in charge of the site. Ward then moved for summary judgment. Was Ward successful in its motion for summary judgment? Why? [*Olin v. George E. Logue, Inc.,* 119 F. Supp. 2d 464 (2000).]

7. Ford Motor Company is the defendant in several product liability suits pending in the circuit court of Greene County. In each case, Ford raised a defense of improper venue and moved to transfer the case to a county where venue was proper. Venue in Missouri is determined by statute, which requires that actions be filed where the cause of action occurred or where the corporation has an office or agent conducting regular business. The cause of action was not in Greene County, and Ford does not have an office in Greene County. However, Ford Motor Credit Company, Ford's wholly-owned subsidiary, does maintain an office in Greene County. Ford Credit has its own offices and directors. It also has its own articles of incorporation and is organized under the laws of Delaware. Its principal place of business is Dearborn, Michigan. Ford Credit is in the business of purchasing retail contracts and leases of automobiles entered into by the dealer and its retail and commercial customers. Ford Credit also participates in commercial lending, including providing automobile wholesale inventory financing and capital, revolving credit, and mortgage loans to Ford and non-Ford dealers. A consumer is not required to finance a Ford Motor Company vehicle through Ford Credit. A consumer may choose to finance a vehicle through a bank or another credit service that may offer similar products and services. The manufacturer is not a party at any time to the retail installment contract or to lease agreements. Interest and principal payments from consumers and dealers are received by Ford Credit and not held in trust for Ford Motor Company. Ford Motor Company and Ford Credit are not parties to any agreement restricting or conditioning Ford Credit's ability to finance a customer's purchase of a vehicle or a dealer's inventory purchases. Is Ford Credit an agent of Ford Motor Company? Why? [*State ex rel. Ford Motor Co. v. Bacon,* 63 S.W.3d 641 (2002).]

8. John Ray Lawrence, an employee of H.W. Campbell Construction Company, was killed when his head was crushed in the "pinch point" area of a crane. Coastal Marine Services of Texas, Inc., owned the crane, and Campbell employees were using it on Coastal's property when the accident occurred. Campbell took custody of the crane and began continued occupation of Coastal's property. Campbell was an independent contractor of Coastal, and no written contract existed between the two companies. Coastal employees were not directing or supervising Campbell's work on the project, nor were they on the job site when the accident occurred. Lawrence's surviving family and estate sued Campbell and Coastal, alleging, among other things, negligence. During the trial Coastal asserted that the Lawrences had presented no evidence that Coastal retained the right to control Campbell's work, a prerequisite for finding Coastal liable under a premises liability theory. The trial court agreed and submitted an instruction precluding a finding of negligence based on the manner in which Coastal controlled the premises. The jury found no negligence on Coastal's part. At trial, in response to a series of hypothetical questions, Campbell employees testified that they would have complied with any instructions from Coastal about the movement of the crane if Coastal had given such instructions. On the basis of the Campbell employees' testimony, the court of appeals reversed the trial court's judgment, concluding that the testimony created a fact issue about Coastal's right to control the crane. Coastal appealed. What duties did Coastal owe Campbell as an independent contractor? How did the court rule on appeal? [*Coastal Marine Serv., Inc. v. Lawrence,* 988 S.W.2d 223 (1999).]

9. In 2000, Loretta Henry was pregnant and experiencing pain in her abdomen. After visiting a clinic, she was referred to Flagstaff Medical Hospital. Once there, she was examined and treated by Dr. Kraig Knoll, a physician with a physician's group providing a service for the hospital. Knoll advised her to have her gallbladder removed, and he performed the surgery. Although Henry read and signed two

consent forms, she was never told that Knoll was not an employee of the hospital and was instead an independent contractor. Subsequently, Henry sued the hospital for negligence when after her child was born, both mother and child sustained injuries. She claimed there was an apparent agency relationship. The hospital argued that Henry could not establish an agency relationship between Flagstaff Hospital and Knoll. What duties did Flagstaff Hospital owe Knoll as an independent contractor? Did the court find enough evidence to establish an agency relationship? [*Loretta Henry/Charles Arnold v. Flagstaff Medical*, 212 Ariz. 365; 132 P.3d 304; 2006 Ariz. App. LEXIS 53; 476 Ariz. Adv. Rep. 11.

10. Nu-Look Design, Inc., operated as a residential home improvement company. During calendar years 1996, 1997, and 1998, Ronald A. Stark not only was Nu-Look's sole shareholder and president but also managed the company. He solicited business, performed necessary bookkeeping, otherwise handled finances, and hired and supervised workers. Rather than pay Stark a salary or wages, Nu-Look distributed its net income during 1996, 1997, and 1998 to him "as Mr. Stark's needs arose." Nu-Look reported on its tax returns in 1996, 1997, and 1998 net incomes of $10,866.14, $14,216.37, and $7,103.60, respectively. Stark, in turn, reported the very same amounts as nonpassive income on his 1996, 1997, and 1998 tax returns. On June 8, 2001, the IRS issued to Nu-Look a "Notice of Determination Concerning Worker Classification." The notice advised that the IRS had classified an individual at Nu-Look as an employee for purposes of federal employment taxes and that such taxes "could" be assessed for calendar years 1996, 1997, and 1998. Nu-Look challenged this determination by filing a petition for redetermination in the United States Tax Court, disputing the propriety of the determination that Stark was an employee, and also sought relief from that determination. The tax court found that Stark performed more than minor services for Nu-Look and had received remuneration for those services. As a result, the court held that Stark was an employee of Nu-Look and that Nu-Look was not entitled to relief. Nu-Look appealed. Does Stark meet the requirements for an employee? Should Nu-Look be liable for a tax assessed under the assumption that Stark is an employee? [*Nu-Look Design, Inc. v. Commission of Internal Revenue*, 356 F.3d 290 (2004).]

Looking for more review material?

The Online Learning Center at **www.mhhe.com/kubasek2e** contains this chapter's "Assignment on the Internet" and also a list of URLs for more information, entitled "On the Internet." You can find both of them in the Student Center portion of the OLC, along with quizzes and other helpful materials.

34 Liability to Third Parties and Termination

LEARNING OBJECTIVES

After reading this chapter, you will be able to answer the following questions:

1   Under what circumstances might a principal be held liable to a third party on a contract negotiated by an agent?

2   Under what circumstances might a principal be held liable for the tortious behavior of its agent or independent contractor?

3   How can an agency relationship be terminated?

CASE OPENER

Liability and the "Wardrobe Malfunction" of Super Bowl XXXVIII

On February 1, 2004, CBS presented a live broadcast of the National Football League's Super Bowl XXXVIII, which included a halftime show produced by MTV Networks. The show featured musical artists Janet Jackson and Justin Timberlake as performers. Justin Timberlake's performance of his popular song "Rock Your Body" ended with Timberlake singing, "Gonna have you naked by the end of this song," and simultaneously tearing away part of Jackson's bustier, exposing her breast on national television for nine-sixteenths of one second. Jackson's exposed breast caused a sensation and resulted in a large number of viewer complaints to the Federal Communications Commission.

On September 22, 2004, the FCC issued a Notice of Apparent Liability, finding that CBS had violated federal law and FCC rules restricting the broadcast of indecent material. After its review, the commission determined that CBS was apparently liable for a forfeiture penalty of $550,000. The FCC claimed that CBS should be held vicariously liable through the doctrine of *respondeat superior* for the actions of its agents, Jackson and Timberlake. CBS contends that it is not vicariously liable through *respondeat superior* because the musical performers were independent contractors, not employees.

1. If you were an executive for CBS, what would you have done differently to avoid litigation?
2. As an employee of the FCC, who would you hold liable—the principal, the agents/independent contractors, or both?

The Wrap-Up at the end of the chapter will answer these questions.

In the preceding chapter, we discussed how an agency relationship and its resulting authority could be created. We also introduced (1) expressed agency, or agency by agreement; (2) implied agency; and (3) agency by estoppel. Each of these avenues for creating agency includes a corresponding form of agent authority.

Contractual Liability of the Principal and Agent

When making decisions about an agency relationship's liability to third parties, courts must first identify the type of authority an agent has (see Chapter 33) and then determine the classification of the principal. Finally, the court must decide whether the principal authorized the actions of the agent. A special type of express agent authority is known as a **power of attorney.** The power of attorney is a specific form of express authority, usually in writing, granting an agent specific powers. There are two basic types of power of attorney: special and general. A **special power of attorney** grants the agent express authority over specifically outlined acts. In contrast, a **general power of attorney** allows the agent to conduct all business for the principal. While powers of attorney tend to terminate on the principal's death or incapacitation, a **durable power of attorney** specifies that the agent's authority is intended to continue beyond the principal's incapacitation.

Even with explicit instructions given through express authority, sometimes conflicts arise between principal-agent relationships in power of attorney. Case 34-1 examines how a court determines the extent of power of attorney. What links this chapter with the preceding chapter is the necessity of being careful about the allocation of legal responsibility in an agency relationship.

LO1

Under what circumstances might a principal be held liable to a third party on a contract negotiated by an agent?

CASE **34-1**   **SHARON D. JONES v. RENEE S. BRANDT**
SUPREME COURT OF VIRGINIA
274 VA. 131; 645 S.E.2D 312 (2007)

W. Leigh Ansell, an attorney practicing in Virginia Beach, had represented Warren Dean Davis, Sr., for many years. At Mr. Davis' request, Ansell prepared a durable power of attorney appointing Ansell attorney-in-fact to act for Davis. The power of attorney contains very broad powers, including the power to make gifts, but lacks a specific grant of power to make a change of beneficiaries of the principal's certificates of deposit. Mr. Davis acknowledged the

document on April 8, 2004. Renee S. Brandt, a widow, lived with Davis from 2002 until his death on September 30, 2004. Davis was in failing health during his last year. In accordance with Davis' directions, Ansell prepared a will that Davis executed within a few days of signing the power of attorney. The will appointed Brandt trustee and executrix but gave her no interest in Davis' estate except the right to occupy and use the home in which they had lived, along with all personal property therein, rent-free, "so long as she lives in the premises." Davis, who personally handled his own estate planning, told Ansell that he intended to take care of Ms. Brandt outside of the will.

On August 4, 2004, Mr. Davis orally directed Mr. Ansell to designate Brandt as the beneficiary "payable on death" of a certificate of deposit in the amount of $250,000. The certificate of deposit previously had named no beneficiary other than Mr. Davis, its owner. Mr. Davis died months later. The will's other chief beneficiaries were Davis' daughters, Sharon Jones and Jody Clark. The two daughters brought suit against Ms. Brandt, asserting that there was no express language in the power of attorney granting Ansell the authority "to change the beneficiary of the certificate of deposit." The Circuit Court found that as an attorney-in-fact, Mr. Ansell had the authority, by the durable power of attorney under which he acted, to change the beneficiary of a particular certificate of deposit (CD) belonging to the principal. The plaintiffs appealed.

JUDGE KOONTZ: Brandt concedes that the power of attorney did not expressly grant Ansell the authority to change the beneficiary of Davis' certificate of deposit at Wachovia Bank, but points to the following provisions of the power of attorney as granting such power by necessary implication:

3. To sign, endorse or assign any note, check or other instrument of any nature whatsoever, negotiable or nonnegotiable, for deposit, discount, collection or otherwise;

4. To open accounts, make deposits, write checks upon or otherwise withdraw some or all funds or account balances now or hereafter outstanding to my credit or to the credit of my attorney, whether or not the check or other instrument is drawn to the order of my attorney;

. . .

10. To instruct any entity or person having custody or control of any assets of mine, or any assets in which I may have an interest, in any agency, fiduciary or other capacity, and I authorize that person or entity to rely upon such instructions;

. . .

13. To make, sign, acknowledge and deliver any contract, deed or other document relating to real estate or personal property or both and to perform any contract binding either me or my attorney;

. . .

24. It is my intention that the grant herein of power to my attorney-in-fact be as broad as possible and the list above of specifically enumerated powers shall not be construed or interpreted to narrow the granted powers but rather they are meant to indicate my intention to grant as broad a grant of power as possible, and this Power of Attorney should be broadly construed to accomplish this intention.

25. Without limiting the above powers, generally to perform any other acts of any nature whatsoever, that ought to be done or in the opinion of my attorney ought to be done, in any circumstances as fully and effectively as I could do as part of my normal, everyday business affairs if acting personally.

Initially, we note that this is not a case of an attorney-in-fact, under a durable power of attorney, engaging in self-dealing with regard to his principal's personal property. Indeed, there is no suggestion of fraudulent conduct by the principal's agent. Nor is this a case involving the authority of an attorney-in-fact, under a durable power of attorney, to make a gift of his principal's personal property. The beneficiary designation of the certificate of deposit in question did not become a final disposition of Davis' certificate until his death on September 30, 2004, and conveyed no present interest in the certificate, but only at best an expectancy. Consequently, neither *Estate of Casey v. Commissioner,* 948 F.2d 895 (4th Cir. 1991), upon which the appellants principally rely, nor the provisions of Code § 11-9.5 resolve the issue presented in this case.

There is no dispute that in directing Ansell's actions to designate Brandt as the beneficiary POD on this certificate of deposit, Davis acted to accomplish, at least in part, his previously expressed intent to "take care of [Brandt] outside of [his] will." Undoubtedly, Davis and Ansell considered the provisions of the power of attorney sufficient to authorize Ansell to act in accord with Davis' direction to Ansell with regard to designating Brandt as the beneficiary of Davis' certificate of deposit. Nevertheless, the appellants assert that without express language in the power of attorney granting Ansell the authority "to change the beneficiary of the certificate of deposit," Ansell's act in doing so was a nullity. We disagree.

In Virginia, powers of attorney have been strictly construed for over a century. The authority granted by such an instrument is never considered to be greater than that warranted by its language, or indispensable to the effective operation of the authority granted. The authority given is not extended beyond the terms in which it is expressed.

This general rule of construction essentially provides that expansive language, such as that contained in paragraphs 24 and 25 of the power of attorney in this case, should be interpreted as intending only to confer those incidental powers necessary to accomplish objects as to which express authority has been given to the attorney-in-fact. The policy that supports this rule of construction is that the power to dispose of the principal's property is so susceptible of abuse that the power should not be implied. That abuse of the agent's power is particularly dangerous in a case involving a durable power of attorney, which by its nature remains in effect after the principal has become incapable of monitoring the agent's conduct. We do not retreat from the rationale of these guidelines of construction.

However, in this case we are not concerned with the power to make a gift or to transfer the principal's property but, rather, the power to contract on behalf of the principal. Among the 35 numbered paragraphs included in Davis' power of attorney, paragraph 3 authorized Ansell "[t]o sign, endorse or assign any note, check or other instrument of any nature whatsoever, negotiable or nonnegotiable, for deposit, discount, collection or otherwise." A certificate of deposit is an instrument for deposit. Additionally, paragraph 13 authorized Ansell "[t]o make, sign, acknowledge and deliver any contract . . . or other document relating to . . . personal property." A certificate of deposit including the designation of the beneficiary POD thereon is a contract between the depositor and the bank relating to personal property.

It is highly doubtful that every power of attorney, even as in this case one carefully drawn by a skilled draftsman, will always expressly confer the authority necessary to address every specific circumstance in which the principal nevertheless intends to give authority to the attorney-in-fact.

Undoubtedly, standard provisions granting broad general power to the agent are intended by the principal to become applicable so as to avoid any potential unintended limitation in the authority expressly granted. Such is the case here as evidenced by the language in paragraph 25, stating that "[w]ithout limiting the above powers, generally to perform any other acts of any nature whatsoever, . . . in any circumstances as fully and effectively as I could do as part of my normal, everyday business affairs if acting personally." Surely, the change of a beneficiary designation on a certificate of deposit is an act within "the normal, everyday business affairs" of the owner of a certificate of deposit at a bank.

The very nature of the task of interpreting language in a document is a fact specific one. Here, we are called upon to determine the intent of the principal with regard to the beneficiary designation of the principal's certificate of deposit. We are of opinion that Davis, the principal, sufficiently expressed the intent to authorize Ansell, the attorney-in-fact, to make a change in the beneficiary designation under the provisions of paragraphs 3, 13, and 25 of the power of attorney when those provisions are considered in concert. For these reasons, we hold that the circuit court did not err in finding that Ansell was authorized to designate Brandt as the beneficiary POD of Davis' certificate of deposit at Wachovia Bank.

AFFIRMED.

CRITICAL THINKING

A classmate argues that the power-of-attorney document did not express that Ansell should have the authority to change certificates of deposit; therefore, the decision should have been reversed. What reasoning did the court use to come to the conclusion that the power of attorney did include certificates of deposit? If you were a judge, would you have found that Ansell was authorized to make Brandt the beneficiary of the certificate of deposit?

ETHICAL DECISION MAKING

Recall the ethical theory of absolutism. The classmate from the previous question argues that the court erred in its decision because absolutism suggests that we should always follow the written rules of contracts when we enter into them. In this case, the power of attorney was an explicit contract between a principal and an agent. How would you persuade your classmate to reconsider absolutism in this case?

CLASSIFICATION OF THE PRINCIPAL

We classify principals from the perspective of the third party's knowledge about them. The law of agency places special weight on this viewpoint of the agency relationship.

When the third party is aware that the agent is making an agreement on behalf of a principal and also knows who the principal is, the principal is a **disclosed principal.** If the third party is aware of the principal's existence but not his or her identity, we classify the principal as a **partially disclosed principal** or an **unidentified principal**. Finally, if the third party does not know that an agent is acting on behalf of a principal, we have an **undisclosed principal**. Classification of the principal is important because it helps determine the principal's liability.[1] If a principal is partially disclosed, the agent and the principal are both considered parties to the contract and each may be liable separately from the other.

AUTHORIZED ACTS

An agent who acts within the scope of her authority on behalf of a disclosed or partially disclosed principal is not liable for the acts of the principal.[2] The principal is liable only if the agent has authority to act on the principal's behalf. With a disclosed principal, the agent is not liable because she is not a party to the transaction. If the principal is *partially* disclosed, the agent herself can be held liable for contractual nonperformance because the courts generally treat the agent as a party to the contract.[3] Whether disclosed or partially disclosed, apart from any liability the agent might have, the principal is liable for the agreements made with the third party.

When the agent acts within her authority on behalf of an undisclosed principal, the law will likely hold her liable for the agreement. In the eyes of the third party, the agent is the only person who could be liable. Yet, if the agent is liable to the third party, then the undisclosed principal is liable to the agent. However, in certain situations the agent is the only party liable for the contract. These situations are:

1. The contract expressly excludes the principal from the contract. If the principal was not a party to the contract, he or she has no liability to the agent.
2. The agent enters into a contract that is a negotiable instrument. The Uniform Commercial Code (UCC) governs negotiable instruments and states that other parties, that is, principals, cannot be liable for them if their name is not on the instrument or if the agent's signature does not indicate that it was made in a representative capacity.[4]
3. The third party enters into a contract with the agent such that the agent's performance is required and the third party may reject the performance of the principal. For example, if the agent is a photographer and he enters into a contract for his principal without disclosing this fact, the third party may reject the principal's attempt to fulfill the contract by taking the third party's picture.
4. The principal or agent knows a third party would not enter into a contract with the principal if the principal's identity were disclosed but the agent does so anyway. The agent will be the only party liable should the third party rescind the contract.

When the third party comes to know of the undisclosed principal's identity, a judgment for the third party against the agent releases the principal from liability.[5] A judgment against a previously undisclosed principal likewise frees the agent from liability.[6]

Exhibit 34-1 summarizes contractual liability to third parties for authorized acts of the agent.

---

[1] Restatement (Second) of Agency, sec. 4.

[2] Restatement (Second) of Agency, sec. 320.

[3] Restatement (Second) of Agency, sec. 321.

[4] UCC § 3-402(b)(2).

[5] Restatement (Second) of Agency, sec. 210.

[6] Restatement (Second) of Agency, sec. 337.

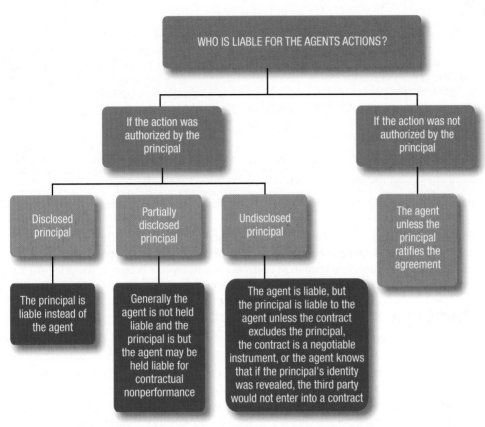

Exhibit 34-1
Contractual Liability
to Third Parties for
Authorized Agent Acts

UNAUTHORIZED ACTS

If an agent has no authority to act on behalf of a principal but still enters into a contract with a third party, the principal, regardless of the classification, is not bound to the contract unless the principal ratifies the agreement.

When the agent exceeds his authority to act on behalf of the principal, the agent will likely be personally liable to the third party. Yet, when the third party is aware that the agent does not represent the principal, the law does not hold the agent liable for the agreement. In almost all other cases in which the agent claims to have authority to contract on behalf of the principal, the law holds the agent liable to the third party. If an agent enters into a contract knowingly misrepresenting his alleged authority, the agent is liable to the third party in a tort action.

Agents who go beyond their authority when the principal is disclosed or partially disclosed are liable for a breach of implied warranty. They cannot be liable for breach of contract because they were never an intended party to the contract, even when exceeding their authority. The agent can breach the implied warranty intentionally, through a knowing misrepresentation, or unintentionally, through a good-faith mistake such as simply misjudging his or her authority. In either case, the agent is liable if the third party relied on the agent's alleged status.

Legal Principle: **As a general rule, when an agent commits an unauthorized act, the principal is neither bound to the contract nor liable.**

Tort Liability and the Agency Relationship

An agent who commits a tort that injures a third party is personally liable for his or her actions, regardless of both the classification and the liability of the principal.[7] The principal

LO2

Under what circumstances might a principal be held liable for the tortious behavior of its agent or independent contractor?

[7] Restatement (Second) of Agency, sec. 343.

Respondeat Superior in Iraq

Unlike the United States' broad employment of the *respondeat superior* doctrine, the Iraqi Civil Code generally rejects the idea of *respondeat superior*. Iraq's Civil Code is partially influenced by classical Islamic law, in which there is no separate concept of tort and which suggests that those who cause harm should repair it. Thus, classical Islamic legal systems tend to follow a rule of strict and "specific" liability for torts. This notion of specific liability rejects the idea of vicarious liability of superiors and custodians and constrains liability to the actual wrongdoer. However, Iraqi law does contain

some limited exceptions in which *respondeat superior* principles are permitted. These include the liability of owners of animals for damage caused by the animals, the liability of a parent of a minor who causes injury, the liability of owners of buildings that collapse, and the liability of government municipalities and commercial entities for injuries caused by their employees during the course of their service.

Sources: Dan E. Stiggal, "A Closer Look at Iraqi Property and Tort Law," *La. L. Rev.* 68 (2008), p. 765; and Dan E. Stiggal, "Refugees and Legal Reform in Iraq: The Iraqi Civil Code, International Standards for the Treatment of Displaced Persons, and the Art of Attainable Solutions," *Rutgers L. Rec.* 34 (2009), p. 1.

may also be held liable for the agent's authorized or unauthorized acts. Furthermore, tortious liability of the principal can be established directly or indirectly. Finally, if an agent is an employee and the principal/employer controls the employee's behavior, the principal can be found liable. The next section introduces these methods of establishing tortious liability.

PRINCIPAL'S TORTIOUS CONDUCT

The law holds a principal directly responsible for his or her own tortious conduct on two conditions. First, a principal who directs the agent to commit a tort is authorizing the agent's unlawful behavior and thus is liable for any damages caused by the tort.[8] Similarly, the principal who ratifies an agent's tortious act knowing that the agent acted illegally is liable, even if she does not condone the agent's conduct.[9]

Second, if the principal fails to provide proper instruments or tools or gives inadequate instructions to the agent concerning the necessity to employ competent agents, the law holds the principal liable to a third party for negligent hiring of an agent. If an agent commits a tort against a customer, the customer often argues that the principal is liable because she should have taken more care in hiring the agent.

Respondeat Superior. The doctrine of *respondeat superior* (a Latin phrase meaning "let the superior speak") applies in the context of the principal/employer–agent/employee relationship. The principal/employer holds **vicarious liability,** which is liability assigned without fault, for any harm the agent/employee causes while working for the principal. In other words, the principal/employer is liable not because he was personally at fault but because he negligently hired an agent. The rationale is that if the employer is benefiting by the work of the employee, the employer should also be responsible for the harms the employee caused.

Thus, a third party injured through the negligence of an employee can sue either the employee or the employer.[10] To establish employer liability, the third party must show that the wrongful act occurred within the scope of the employment. The courts consider the following in determining this element:[11]

1. Did the employer authorize the employee's act?
2. Did the act occur within the time and space limits of employment?

---

[8] Restatement (Second) of Agency, sec. 212.

[9] Restatement (Second) of Agency, sec. 218.

[10] Restatement (Second) of Agency, secs. 216 and 219.

[11] Restatement (Second) of Agency, sec. 229.

3. Was the act performed, at least in part, on behalf of the employer?

4. To what extent were the employer's interests advanced by the act?

5. To what extent were the private interests of the employee involved?

6   Did the employer provide the means (tools) by which the act occurred?

7. Did the employee use force not expected by the employer?

8. Did the employer know that the act would include the commission of a serious crime?

If a delivery driver negligently injures a third party while making deliveries on behalf of the employer, both the employee and the employer will be held liable. Suppose the driver is using the company vehicle when he stops at a drive-through to get coffee. Could the employer be liable to a third party for an accident caused by the driver? If an agent makes a substantial departure from the course of the employer's business, the employer is not liable.

Courts often refer to an employee's substantial departure as a "frolic of his own." However, if the deviation from the employer's business is *not* substantial, the employer can be held liable. In Case 34-2, the court considers the scope of the employment relationship.

Legal Principle: As a general rule, a principal is vicariously liable for the actions of his or her agent.

CASE 34-2   IGLESIA CRISTIANA LA CASA DEL SENOR, INC., ETC. v. L.M.
COURT OF APPEAL OF FLORIDA, THIRD DISTRICT
783 SO. 2D 353 (2001)

L.M. sued Ali Pacheco, the former pastor of Iglesia Cristiana La Casa Del Senor, Inc. (the Church), as well as the Church, alleging Pacheco had sexually assaulted her in July 1991 when she was a minor. The allegation of sexual assault formed the basis of L.M.'s claims against the Church based on respondeat superior. When the criminal act occurred, L.M. was sixteen years old.

Before the criminal act took place, Pacheco visited L.M.'s residence twice when L.M. had been left home alone. On another occasion, Pacheco visited L.M. at her school. L.M. told her mother about Pacheco's visit, but did not advise anyone from the Church.

According to L.M., on July 8, 1991, Pacheco called her at work and invited her to lunch to discuss her parents' marital problems. L.M. accepted, and Pacheco picked her up from work. L.M. noticed a sandwich and soft drink in the car. Pacheco drove to a Marriott Hotel. L.M. testified Pacheco led her to a room he had rented, and told her not to worry because she would finally be cured. He then proceeded to sexually assault her. Pacheco testified L.M. consented to having sex.

According to him, their meeting was prearranged. They had discussed the matter and had in fact been to the Marriot Hotel the previous day intending to have sexual relations but had decided against it. Pacheco testified he knew what he was doing was wrong but explained it was a great temptation in his life.

The jury returned a verdict in L.M.'s favor, finding the Church liable for Pacheco's criminal act on the grounds of respondeat superior. The Church appealed.

PER CURIAM: Under the doctrine of respondeat superior, an employer cannot be held liable for the tortious or criminal acts of an employee, unless the acts were committed during the course of the employment and to further a purpose or interest, however excessive or misguided, of the employer. An employee's conduct is within the scope of his employment, where (1) the conduct is of the kind he was employed to perform, (2) the conduct occurs substantially within the time and space limits authorized or required by the work to be performed, and (3) the conduct is activated at least in part by a purpose to serve the master. An exception may exist

[continued]

where the tort-feasor was assisted in accomplishing the tort by virtue of the employer/employee relationship.

In this case, the sexual assault did not occur on Church property, and the record does not support a finding Pacheco's criminal act against L.M. constituted the kind of conduct he was employed to perform, or he was in any way motivated by his desire to serve the Church. On the contrary, the record establishes Pacheco's purpose in arranging the meeting that day was to satisfy his personal interests, not to further the Church's objectives. Regardless of the stated reason for the meeting between Pacheco and L.M., it is undisputed no counseling occurred on the day of the crime. While Pacheco may have had access to L.M. because of his position as the Church pastor, whom L.M. and her family had become

friends with over time, he was not engaging in authorized acts or serving the interests of the Church during the time he tried to seduce her or on the day he raped her. The sexual assault was an independent, self-serving act by Pacheco; an act he knew was wrong to commit and the Church would surely have tried to prevent had it known of his plans.

We agree with the Church that Pacheco's sexual assault of L.M. did not occur within the scope of his employment. Accordingly, we find, as a matter of law, the Church cannot be held vicariously liable for Pacheco's criminal act.

Therefore, we reverse the trial court's final judgment and remand with instructions to enter judgment in favor of Appellant.

REVERSED and REMANDED.

CRITICAL THINKING

Assume L.M.'s account of the crime is true. Examine the exception to the "scope of employment" criteria mentioned by the judge. How could the plaintiff make an argument, using that exception, that Pacheco's conduct was within the scope of his employment?

ETHICAL DECISION MAKING

The judge in this case outlines a doctrine for determining the liability of an employer for the actions of employees. What value preference is highlighted by that doctrine?

If the third party is able to establish employee negligence such that the employer is liable, the employer has the right to recover from the employee any damages he paid the third party as a result of the employee's negligence. The right to recover damages is referred to as the *right of indemnification.* However, if the employee is innocent of negligence, the employer is also free of liability.

Intentional Torts and *Respondeat Superior.* The agent is liable for any torts he or she commits. In the same way the principal is responsible for the negligent acts of the employee under the doctrine of *respondeat superior,* the principal may also be liable for any intentional torts of the employee. Furthermore, an employer may be responsible for any tortious acts of the employee if the employer knew or should have known that the employee had a tendency to commit such acts. Hence, a principal may be liable for negligent hiring who fails to do a background check to learn about the tendencies of potential employees.

The principal of an employee with a criminal background may be held liable for tortious acts committed by her hired agent even though the employee may not recognize the wrongfulness of his act. Therefore, employers will most likely purchase liability insurance in case particular employees engage in tortious activities.

AGENT MISREPRESENTATION

Unlike tort liability, which is based on whether the agent/employee was acting in the scope of employment, *misrepresentation liability* depends on whether the principal authorized the agent's act. If the principal authorizes the agent to engage in an act and the agent misrepresents herself intentionally or unintentionally, the principal is always liable in tort to someone who relied on the agent's misrepresentation.

If an agent has misrepresented herself, the third party has two options:

1. Cancel the contract with the principal and be compensated for any money lost.
2. Affirm the contract and sue the principal to recover damages.

Legal Principle: **As a general rule, if a principal authorizes an agent to misrepresent himself or herself, the principal is always liable.**

Principal's Liability and the Independent Contractor

As we discussed in the preceding chapter, an independent contractor is not an employee of the individual who hires him or her to do work. The individual doing the hiring does not control the details of the independent contractor's performance. Consequently, an individual who hires an independent contractor cannot be held liable for the independent contractor's tortious actions under the doctrine of *respondeat superior.*

Suppose that while working on the outside of the building he is renovating, an independent contractor accidentally injures an innocent bystander when he drops a pile of bricks. The owner of the building is not liable for the innocent bystander's injuries; the independent contractor is liable.[12] In the Case Opener, one question the court must consider is whether Janet Jackson and Justin Timberlake were independent contractors or employees of CBS. If they are employees, CBS can be responsible for the conduct of the performers through *respondeat superior.* However, if they are independent contractors, CBS cannot be held liable.

If the independent contractor engages in extremely hazardous activities, such as blasting operations, for the principal, the principal will be responsible for any damages by the independent contractor. Certain activities are held strictly liable because of their inherently dangerous nature; an employer cannot escape this liability simply by hiring an independent contractor to complete them. Nor can the employer escape liability for an independent contractor's tort if the employer directs the contractor to commit the tort.

The Case Nugget demonstrates the role of tort principles in establishing liability.

Crime and Agency Relationships

If an agent commits a crime, clearly the agent is liable for the crime. If the agent commits the crime in the scope of employment for a principal without the principal's authorization, the principal is not liable for the agent's crime. Remember, one of the elements establishing that a crime has been committed is *intent.* If a principal is unaware of or had no intent for the agent to commit a crime, there is no rationale for the principal's criminal liability. The only time the principal can be liable for the crime of an agent is when the principal has authorized the criminal act.

Legal Principle: **If an agent commits a crime in the scope of his or her employment without authorization from the principal, the principal is not liable for the crime.**

Termination of the Agency Relationship

The parties may choose to terminate an agency relationship, or it may terminate automatically by the lapse of time, fulfillment of purpose, or operation of law. (Exhibit 34-2 lists

LO3

How can an agency relationship be terminated?

---

[12] Restatement (Second) of Agency, sec. 250.

Liability When Hiring Independent Contractors

Larry S. Lawrence v. Bainbridge Apartments et al.
Court of Appeals of Missouri, Western District
957 S.W.2d 400 (1997)

In 1989, Smart Way Janitorial offered a bid to Larry Lawrence to wash the windows of Bainbridge Apartments, two seven-story buildings and four four-story buildings. Even though Lawrence could not create a safety line for the four-story buildings, the building manager insisted he wash the windows from the outside so that the residents would not be disturbed. When Lawrence started the work, he fell from one of the shorter buildings and suffered injuries. He brought suit against Bainbridge Apartments, arguing that Bainbridge was negligent on the basis of the "inherently dangerous activity" exception to the doctrine that landowners are not vicariously liable for injuries caused by the negligence of an independent contractor or his employees.

The trial court ruled that because Lawrence had received workers' compensation benefits, the injury was not covered by the inherently dangerous activity exception. The trial court granted summary judgment to Bainbridge; however, when Lawrence appealed, the decision was reversed and remanded because the court of appeals ruled that Lawrence was not a covered employee entitled to workers' compensation benefits.

The court argued that in establishing liability in this case, it would look to which party could best avoid the harm and manage the risk of loss in the inherently dangerous activity in question. An independent contractor who knows he will not be compensated by the landowner for his injuries has a strong incentive to take additional care and avoid neglect in performing his duties. As an expert, he is in a better position to understand the risks and costs in a particular job, and he may demand sufficient remuneration and safety measures to cover what he believes the risks to be. In return for his bargained-for price, he accepts the allocation of the risk. The court held that an injured independent contractor, although uninsured, cannot recover under the inherently dangerous activity exception.

---

the ways that agency relationships can be terminated.) If the relationship has ended, the agent no longer has authority to make agreements on behalf of the principal. However, the agent's apparent authority continues until the principal notifies third parties that the relationship has ended.

Notice of the termination can be actual or constructive. **Actual notice** must be given to third parties who have had business interactions with the agent; it directly informs them, orally or in writing, that the agency agreement has terminated.[13] When the agent's authority was granted in writing, actual notice also must be given in writing. Parties not directly related to an agency agreement may receive **constructive notice,** which is how the termination of an agency agreement is generally announced.[14] Constructive notice usually

Exhibit 34-2

Ways That an Agency Relationship Can Be Terminated

TERMINATION BY ACTS OF PARTIES	TERMINATION BY OPERATION OF LAW
1. Lapse of time	1. Death
2. Fulfillment of purpose	2. Insanity
3. Occurrence of specific event	3. Bankruptcy
4. Mutual agreement by the parties	4. Changed circumstances
5. Revocation of authority	5. Change in law
6. Renunciation by the agent	6. Impossibility
7. Agency coupled with an interest	7. Disloyalty of agent
	8. War

[13] Restatement (Second) of Agency, sec. 136(2).
[14] Restatement (Second) of Agency, sec. 136(3).

consists of publication in a generally circulating newspaper for the area where the agency agreement existed.

Parties forming a contract of agency in a foreign jurisdiction should include the conditions of termination within the contract. A U.S. manager conducting business in the European Union needs access to the intricacies of Chapter IV of the Agency Relationship Law that focuses on termination. Released agents in the EU receive compensation if they have brought the principal new customers from whom the principal continues to profit, if they are unable to otherwise recover costs incurred through the performance of the contract, or upon their death.

EU law prohibits the agent's receiving compensation if the principal has terminated the contract due to the agent's incapacity. EU law additionally blocks the compensation if the agent terminates the contract or assigns rights and duties under it to another person. Local legal counsel should be especially knowledgeable about such provisions and be able to help managers avoid unnecessary legal battles.

Case 34-3 highlights the potentially disastrous consequences of not understanding how an agency relationship is terminated.

CASE 34-3   ANGELA & RAUL RUIZ v. FORTUNE INSURANCE COMPANY
COURT OF APPEAL OF FLORIDA, THIRD DISTRICT
677 SO. 2D 1336 (1996)

In September 1990, Angela and Raul Ruiz purchased a homeowner's insurance policy for their mobile home from Fortune Insurance Company through Bates Hernandez Associates, an insurance broker. Bates secured the insurance through Fortune's agent, Biscayne Underwriting Management. Fortune terminated its agency relationship with Biscayne in November 1990 and notified its customers in July 1991; consequently, Fortune sent the Ruizes a notice their homeowner's insurance would not be renewed.

However, in August 1991, even though the Ruizes' insurance policy had expired, Bates sent them a renewal notice. The Ruizes paid Bates $450 to renew their insurance policy with Fortune. Bates sent this money to Biscayne, which accepted it. In August 1992, the Ruizes' mobile home was damaged by a hurricane. When the Ruizes reported the loss to Fortune, they were told they had no current insurance policy with the company. They filed suit against Fortune. In a summary judgment, the trial court ruled for Fortune. The Ruizes appealed.

OPINION PER CURIAM: Although the Ruizes contended below they never received Fortune's notice of cancellation,

Fortune produced below a copy of the notice of cancellation and proof it mailed the same to the Ruizes. The law is clear that an insurer's proof of mailing of a notice of cancellation to the insured prevails as a matter of law over the insured's denial as to its receipt.

Fortune's actual notice of cancellation to the Ruizes was legally sufficient and binding, whether the Ruizes read or understood the import of such notice. Any lack of understanding of this written notice on the part of the Ruizes only placed a duty upon them to make further inquiry of their broker, agent and/or insurer.

We further reject the Ruizes' argument on appeal that Fortune is estopped from disclaiming coverage where Biscayne accepted the Ruizes' renewal premium after Fortune's termination of its agency relationship with Biscayne. There is no evidence that Fortune engaged in any conduct or action which would reasonably lead the Ruizes to believe Biscayne had continuing actual or apparent authority to collect such premiums on behalf of Fortune.

AFFIRMED.

CRITICAL THINKING

The judge seems to think Fortune fulfilled its obligation to the Ruizes by mailing them a notice of cancellation. Why do you think the Ruizes were confused about the cancellation? How could the plaintiffs argue that they were not properly made aware that their insurance had been canceled?

ETHICAL DECISION MAKING

Explain what you think the ethical obligations were for every party in this case: Fortune, Bates Hernandez Associates, Biscayne Underwriting Management, and the Ruizes.

TERMINATION BY ACTS OF PARTIES

The agency relationship can be terminated after certain acts, as we discuss in the following sections.

Lapse of Time.   If an agency agreement specifies that the relationship will exist for a certain amount of time, it will end when that time expires.[15] An agency agreement might state that the relationship will begin on September 1 and end on September 30. While the agent and principal can agree to continue their relationship through October, they will have to make a new agreement to cover it. The agent's express authority ends when the relationship ends; thus, the principal must notify third parties that the former agent can no longer act on the principal's behalf.

Fulfillment of Purpose.   Suppose John, a homeowner, enters into an agreement with Claire, a real estate agent, to sell his house. Once Claire succeeds in selling the house, she no longer has the authority to act on John's behalf. She has fulfilled the purpose of the agency relationship.[16]

Occurrence of a Specific Event.   Depending on its purpose, an agency relationship can be terminated on the occurrence of a specific event. John employs Claire as an agent to sell his house. Once the sale is final, the agency relationship will terminate.

Mutual Agreement by the Parties.   Agency is a consensual agreement between two parties. Consequently, if John and Claire both decide they do not wish to continue in the agency relationship, they can cancel the agreement and terminate the relationship.

Revocation of Authority.   A principal can revoke an agent's authority at any time.[17] However, such revocation might constitute a breach of contract with the agent, leaving the principal liable for damages.[18] If the agent has somehow breached the fiduciary duty to the principal, however, the principal can revoke the agent's authority without liability.

Renunciation by the Agent.   An agent can terminate the agency relationship by renouncing the authority given him or her. The agent can be liable for breach of contract if the agency agreement stated a specific amount of time that the relationship is to exist.

---

[15] Restatement (Second) of Agency, sec. 105.

[16] Restatement (Second) of Agency, sec. 106.

[17] Restatement (Second) of Agency, sec. 119.

[18] Restatement (Second) of Agency, sec. 118.

COMPARING THE LAW OF OTHER COUNTRIES

Termination in the Netherlands

After a relationship of agency ends in the Netherlands, the agent is entitled to compensation if his or her duties are concluded within a "reasonable" time after termination or if the agent received orders for a certain action before the termination.

In the most interesting triggering event for mandatory compensation, the agent is entitled to "goodwill compensation" if (1) the agent brought the principal new customers, (2) the agent brought new agreements with clients who are still profitable to the principal, and (3) such payment is financially reasonable for the principal (the relationship is not being terminated due to bankruptcy).

The agent must file for goodwill compensation within five years of termination. It may not exceed the equivalent of the agent's average yearly salary.

Agency Coupled with an Interest.   An agency coupled with an interest is a special kind of agency relationship created for the agent's benefit, not the principal's. The principal may not terminate this relationship, which is also called *power given as security*. Rather, it is terminated when an event occurs that discharges the principal's obligation.

TERMINATION BY OPERATION OF LAW

Automatic termination of the agency relationship can occur when the agent is unable to fulfill his task, when the principal does not desire to continue the performance, or when further pursuit of the relationship's objectives would be illegal.

Death.   If the principal or the agent dies, the agency relationship is automatically terminated. Even if one party is unaware of the other party's death, the relationship no longer exists. Suppose an agent has authority to buy antiques on behalf of a principal and continues to purchase items without knowing the principal has died. Those transactions are not binding on the principal's estate, because as soon as the principal died, the agent's authority to act was gone.

Insanity.   If a principal or agent becomes insane, the agency relationship is finished. Some states have modified this law so that the agency contract still exists unless the person has been adjudicated insane.

Bankruptcy.   If the principal or agent files a bankruptcy petition, the agency relationship is generally no longer in existence, particularly if the agent is filing for bankruptcy and his or her credit is important to the agency relationship. Insolvency, the inability to pay debts or the condition in which liabilities outweigh assets, does not necessarily result in the termination of the agency relationship.[19]

Changed Circumstances.   If an unusual change in circumstances leads the agent to believe that the principal's instructions do not apply, the agency relationship terminates.[20] Suppose Danielle contracts Gregory to act as her agent to sell a painting she found in her great-aunt's attic and authorizes him to sell it for $5,000. However, in the course of showing the painting to several buyers, Gregory learns that the painting is a Van Gogh original. Because the painting is worth much more than $5,000, Gregory should infer that Danielle does not want the original agency to continue.

---

[19] Restatement (Second) of Agency, sec. 113.

[20] Restatement (Second) of Agency, sec. 109.

Electronic Contracts in Singapore

The possibility of e-mail and electronic fraud creates certain risks in the formation of electronic contracts. Singapore passed legislation in 1997 that attempts to combat those risks and specifies the consequences of such fraud.

Agency contracts made electronically will be valid and enforceable if the principal or a principal's designated agent sent the contract. To be legally allowed to assume that the electronic record is that of the principal, the third party either follows an agreed-on procedure of clarification or is assured that the message originated from an agent endorsed by the principal.

If an agent sends an electronic record *not* approved by the principal, the third party has the right to act as a result of it. If such actions result in injuries or damages to the third party, the principal is responsible under law and cannot claim he or she was unaware of the agent's actions. While the principal may indeed not have been aware, Singapore does not recognize lack of awareness as a defense.

Singapore's legislation intends to protect third parties from the poor judgment of principals by creating this direct link between them. Making the principal answerable and liable to the third party increases the pressure to employ reliable agents.

Change in Law. When a new law makes the commission of an existing agency agreement illegal, the agreement is terminated. LaToya hires Ryan to paint her house green. Then the city council passes a law making it illegal to paint houses green. The new law automatically terminates the agency agreement.

Impossibility. Suppose that while Gregory is trying to sell Danielle's painting, there is a fire in her house and the painting is destroyed. Because it is impossible for Gregory to sell the painting, the agency relationship cannot continue.[21]

If the agent loses qualifications needed to perform duties for the principal, the agency relationship also ends because of impossibility. Jackson hires a lawyer to serve as his agent who has unfortunately engaged in a series of illegal actions and is then disbarred. Because the lawyer can no longer fulfill the functions Jackson authorized him to perform, the agency relationship is terminated.

Disloyalty of Agent. An agency agreement is terminated whenever the agent, unknown to the principal, acquires interest against the principal's interest. It is also terminated if the agent breaches the duty of loyalty he or she has to the principal.[22] Marta is an attorney representing Lola in her suit against a pharmaceutical company. If the pharmaceutical company offers Marta a job and she accepts, the agency agreement terminates because Marta has acquired an interest opposed to Lola's interests.

War. A principal has an agent in Iran authorized to conduct business dealings on the principal's behalf.[23] If the United States goes to war with Iran, this agency relationship will no longer be in existence because there is no way to enforce the rights of the parties.

---

[21] Restatement (Second) of Agency, sec. 124.

[22] Restatement (Second) of Agency, sec. 112.

[23] Restatement (Second) of Agency, sec. 115.

CASE OPENER WRAP-UP

CBS and Janet Jackson's On-Screen Nudity

In this case, the federal appeals court found that the doctrine of *respondeat superior* does not make CBS liable for the nudity exposed by Jackson and Timberlake. Recall from the previous chapter the difference between employees and independent contractors and how agency law differentiates between the two. The court determined that CBS was not liable after finding that Jackson and Timberlake were independent contractors rather than employees. Unlike employees, independent contractors are outside the scope of *respondeat superior* as the employer has a lesser degree of control over the actions of the contractors.

As a result of the appellate court's ruling, CBS did not have to pay fees for the actions of the indecent broadcast it made during the Super Bowl. However, the FCC appealed to the Supreme Court, and in May 2009 the Supreme Court directed the court of appeals to consider reinstating the $550,000 fine that the Federal Communications Commission had imposed on CBS over Jackson's breast-baring performance. For now, uncertainty remains as to whether CBS will be held liable for the actions of its Super Bowl performers. The CBS case is an indicator that the broadcasting industry may exercise more caution and control over its agency relationships with entertainers in the future. If companies better understand liability issues related to agency relationships, they may avoid the time and costs associated with the court processes in the aftermath of broadcasting malfunctions.

Key Terms

actual notice   760

agency coupled
   with an interest   763

constructive
   notice   760

disclosed principal   753

durable power
   of attorney   751

general power
   of attorney   751

partially disclosed
   principal   754

power of attorney   751

respondeat superior   756

special power of
   attorney   751

undisclosed
   principal   754

unidentified
   principal   754

vicarious liability   756

Summary of Key Topics

Contractual Liability of the Principal and Agent	*Classification of the principal:* The principal must be classified as either disclosed, partially disclosed, or undisclosed.
	Authorized acts: These are acts within the scope of the agent's authority.
	Unauthorized acts: These acts go beyond the scope of the agent's authority.
Tort Liability and the Agency Relationship	*Principal's tortious conduct:* The law holds a principal directly responsible for his or her own tortious conduct under two conditions: (1) The principal directs the agent to commit a tortious act, and (2) the principal fails to provide proper instruments or tools or adequate instructions.

Agent misrepresentation: If an agent misrepresents himself or herself to a third party, the principal may be tortiously liable for the agent's misrepresentation.

Respondeat superior: The principal/employer is liable not because he or she was personally at fault but because he or she negligently hired an agent.

Principal's Liability and the Independent Contractor

An individual who hires an independent contractor cannot be held liable for the independent contractor's tortious actions under the doctrine of *respondeat superior* unless the contractor engages in hazardous activities.

Crime and Agency Relationships

If an agent commits a crime, clearly the agent is liable for the crime.

Termination of the Agency Relationship

Termination by acts of parties: Termination may occur by lapse of time, fulfillment of purpose, occurrence of a specific event, mutual agreement by the parties, revocation of authority, or renunciation by the agent.

Termination by operation of law: The agency relationship may be terminated automatically due to death, insanity, bankruptcy, changed circumstances, change in law, impossibility, disloyalty of agent, or war.

Point / Counterpoint

Should the Principal/Employer Be Indirectly Liable for the Actions of the Agent/Employee under the Doctrine of *Respondeat Superior?*

YES	NO
The employer should be held responsible for the actions of the employee. The employer gains the fruits of the employee's work, so a certain symmetry requires that the employer also accept the risk of fallout from the employee's possible negligence.	The employer should not be held responsible for the actions of an employee. Employees are hired to make daily choices using their competence and basic human judgment. An employee who makes a poor decision should be held individually responsible.
When a company hires an employee for a position for which she is not competent, the company should be punished for any harm the agent causes while acting in her hired capacity. The agent would not be in a position to cause harm had the company not negligently hired her in the first place. A pizza company that hires a delivery driver with a poor driving record should be held accountable for any harm that driver causes while at work delivering pizza.	Without individual responsibility, workers need never fear the full consequences of their actions. Knowing that their company will be forced to take care of them under the doctrine of *respondeat superior,* they will not exercise the same caution as they would if they were held personally accountable for every decision they make.
Harm should be compensated, and the employer is usually in a much more secure financial position to provide compensation—and to be insured against such a possibility—than is the employee.	Consider the pizza delivery driver who injures a third party while delivering pizzas for his company, perhaps because he accidentally drove through a red traffic signal. It is the driver, not the company, who ran the red light and who should be held accountable. The parent company need be responsible only for decisions it makes directly.

Questions & Problems

1. Explain when a principal is or is not contractually liable for agreements made by an agent.

2. When might a principal be liable for torts committed by an agent?

3. What terminates an agency relationship?

4. Land Transport employed Oscar Gonzalez to operate a Land Transport tractor-trailer rig. One day while working, Robert Nichols and Gonzalez were driving west on Route 9 toward Brewer, Maine. Gonzalez tried several times to pass Nichols in no-passing zones. Angered by Gonzalez's driving, Nichols made an obscene gesture to Gonzalez on two occasions. Thereafter, Gonzalez began to tailgate Nichols for several miles and continued to try to pass him. The two trucks then stopped at a traffic light. Nichols saw Gonzalez get out of his cab, and Nichols did the same. On approaching Gonzalez, Nichols attacked Gonzalez with a rubber-coated chain-linked cable. Nichols then grabbed Gonzalez, and they fell to the ground. During the scuffle, Gonzalez got up, brandished a knife, and stabbed Nichols. Nichols sued Gonzalez and Land Transport for the injuries he suffered. Land Transport moved for summary judgment. Was Land Transport successful with its motion for summary judgment? Why? [*Nichols v. Land Transport Corp.*, 103 F. Supp. 2d 25 (1999).]

5. Eleanor Schock discovered that her late father's attorney, Pat Nero, had embezzled from the estate of her father, Miller, including the sum of $23,331.72 in Miller's savings account at Old Stone Bank. At the time Nero withdrew the funds, Old Stone was being run under the conservatorship of the Resolution Trust Corporation (RTC), the FDIC's statutory predecessor. As holder of her father's estate's claims, Schock sued the FDIC, as receiver for Old Stone, for breach of contract, alleging that the bank permitted an unauthorized signatory (Nero) to withdraw funds on deposit in the Miller savings account. The FDIC receiver argued that the bank had paid Nero, a fiduciary who was authorized to receive the money in the account, in good faith and should not be held liable because Nero misappropriated the money. Schock argued that Nero's apparent authority to withdraw the money as Miller's agent ended by operation of law when Miller died. In response, the FDIC receiver argued that apparent agency terminates only when a third party has notice of the termination. Schock offered evidence that the bank had actual notice that Miller had died when it permitted the Nero savings account withdrawal. Schock's evidence included a bank employee's statement that the bank had in place a procedure for checking the obituaries in the local paper to see whether bank clients had died, as well as the fact that an obituary for Miller appeared in that paper. Was Schock successful at trial? Did the publication of an obituary constitute actual notice? [*Shock v. United States*, 254 F.3d 1 (2001).]

6. Water, Waste, & Land, Inc., is a land development and engineering company doing business under the name "Westec." Donald Lanham and Larry Clark were managers and also members of Preferred Income Investors (PII), LLC. PII is a limited liability company. Clark contacted Westec about the possibility of hiring Westec to perform engineering work in connection with a development project. In the course of preliminary discussions, Clark gave his business card to representatives of Westec. The business card included Lanham's address, which was also the address listed as PII's principal office and place of business. While PII's name was not on the business card, the letters "PII" appeared above the address on the card. However, there was no indication as to what the acronym meant or that PII was a limited liability company. Although Westec never received a signed contract, it did receive verbal authorization from Clark to begin work. Westec completed the engineering work and sent a bill for $9,183.40 to Lanham. No payments were made on the bill. Westec filed a claim against Clark and Lanham individually as well as against PII. At trial, PII admitted liability for the amount claimed by Westec. Accordingly, the court dismissed Clark from the suit, concluding that he could not be held personally liable, and entered judgment in the amount of $9,183 against Lanham and PII. Lanham appealed. On appeal, was Lanham found liable for the amount due to Westec? Why? [*Water, Waste, & Land v. Lanham*, 955 P.2d 997 (1998).]

7. Maria D., the plaintiff, alleged that she was raped by an on-duty security guard who worked for the Westec company. At approximately 2 a.m., she was driving along Pacific Coast Highway. The Westec security guard detained her by shining a spotlight from his patrol car into her moving vehicle. He asked, "How much have you been drinking tonight?" Maria D. thought the security guard was a police officer because the spotlight was shining in her face. The security guard ordered Maria D. to perform field sobriety tests and then told her to get her purse because he was going to take her to the station. Instead, Maria D. says he took her to another location where he raped her. The security guard denied that he had pulled the plaintiff over. He testified at his deposition that he saw her car on the side of the road and stopped to offer assistance and at no point did he rape her. At the time of the encounter, the security guard was on-duty, wearing a uniform and driving a Westec vehicle equipped with a spotlight, and he carried a gun and handcuffs on his belt and had a second firearm on the front passenger seat of his car. Maria D. sued Westec, claiming that the company was vicariously liable for the actions of the security guard under the doctrine of *respondeat superior*. Westec argues that the security guard was acting outside the scope of his employment when he allegedly detained and raped her. Do you think the court found that Westec should be held vicariously liable under *respondeat superior*? Why or why not? [*Maria D. v. Westec Residential Security, Inc.*, 85 Cal. App. 4th 125 (2000).]

8. Doug Hartmann Productions, L.L.C., and the Regal Riverfront Hotel, which was owned by Gateway Hotel Holdings, entered into an agreement for a professional boxing match to be held at the hotel. The contract contained a provision stating that a $5 million indemnity insurance policy was to be provided and Hartmann Productions was to provide a doctor at ringside for the match and an ambulance on stand-by at the hotel the night of the event. Maldonado was a professional boxer who participated in the match. The fight ended when Maldonado was knocked out and later lost consciousness in his dressing room. There was no ambulance on site. An ambulance was called, and Maldonado was taken to a hospital. He suffered severe brain damage as a result of his injury.

The damage could have been less severe had an ambulance been on-site for the boxing match. Maldonado sued Gateway, asserting that Hartmann Productions was an independent contractor hired by Gateway to perform an inherently dangerous activity. As such, Gateway had a duty to take special precautions to prevent injury during the inherently dangerous activity. Therefore, Maldonado argued that Gateway should be held liable for the damages resulting from the boxing match. Should the boxing match be considered an inherently dangerous activity? Did the court find Gateway liable? [*Maldonado v. Gateway Holdings, L.L.C.*, 154 S.W.3d 303 (2003).]

9. In 1989, William Petrovich's employer, the Chicago Federation of Musicians, provided health care coverage to all of its employees by enrolling them all in Share Health Plan of Illinois. Share is an HMO and pays only for medical care that is obtained within its network of physicians. To qualify for benefits, a Share member must select a primary care physician, who will provide that member's overall care and authorize referrals when necessary. Share gives its members a list of participating physicians from which to choose. Inga Petrovich, William's wife, selected Dr. Marie Kowalski from Share's list and began seeing Kowalski as her primary care physician.

In September 1990, Mrs. Petrovich saw Kowalski because she was experiencing persistent pain in her mouth, tongue, throat, and face. She also complained of a foul mucus in her mouth. Kowalski referred her to Dr. Friedman, an ear, nose, and throat specialist who had a contract with Share. When Friedman ordered that an MRI be done, Kowalski refused and instead sent a copy of an old MRI. In June 1991, after Mrs. Petrovich had made multiple visits to both doctors, Friedman found cancerous growths in Mrs. Petrovich's mouth. He performed surgery to remove the cancer later that month.

Petrovich subsequently sued Share for medical malpractice. The complaint alleges that both Kowalski and Friedman were negligent in failing to diagnose Inga Petrovich's cancer in a timely manner and that Share is vicariously liable for their negligence. Share filed a motion for summary judgment, arguing that it cannot be held liable for the negligence of Kowalski or Friedman because they were acting as independent contractors, not as

Share's agents. How should the court decide? What reasons should it give? [*Petrovich v. Share Health Plan of Illinois,* 719 N.E.2d 756 (1999).]

10. Lisa was 19 years old and pregnant when she had to seek treatment at Memorial Hospital's emergency room. The initial examining physician ordered an ultrasound for Lisa. Bruce Wayne Tripoli, the ultrasound technician, administered the examination. A third party was not present during the ultrasound.

    Tripoli asked the plaintiff if she would like to know the sex of the baby. When she said yes, Tripoli falsely explained that to determine the sex he would have to scan "much further down." Then Tripoli inappropriately touched the plaintiff. Believing that contact in that private area was part of the examination, Lisa did not stop Tripoli. After describing Tripoli's behavior to her regular obstetrician, Lisa discovered that the behavior was not necessary and was inappropriate. Lisa then brought suit against Tripoli and the hospital, among others. The issue was whether Tripoli committed the sexual assault within the scope of his employment, thereby rendering the hospital "vicariously liable." For the type of liability the plaintiff was seeking, the employment situation must create a foreseeable risk that the employee might commit an offense. Was the hospital liable? [*Lisa M. v. Henry Mayo Memorial Hospital,* 907 P.2d 358 (Supreme Court of California 1995).]

Looking for more review material?

The Online Learning Center at **www.mhhe.com/kubasek2e** contains this chapter's "Assignment on the Internet" and also a list of URLs for more information, entitled "On the Internet." Find both of them in the Student Center portion of the OLC, along with quizzes and other helpful materials.

35 Forms of Business Organization

CASE OPENER
The Dunkin' Donuts Franchise Agreement

Dunkin' Donuts Corporation operates numerous restaurants worldwide, organizing many of them as franchises. Dunkin' Donuts has the exclusive license to use and to license others to use its trademarks, service marks, and trade name. These marks and trade name have been used continuously since 1960 to identify Dunkin's doughnut shops as well as the doughnuts, pastries, coffee, and other products associated with those shops. Dipak N. Bhayani operated two Dunkin' Donuts franchises in Illinois for many years. Dunkin' Donuts later notified Bhayani that his two franchises had been violating parts of the franchise license agreement. After repeated incidents and failure to cure the violations over a substantial period of time, Dunkin' Donuts (the franchisor) demanded termination of both of Bhayani's franchises.

1. Did Dunkin' Donuts lawfully revoke Bhayani's franchises?
2. What are some potential problems that a franchisor and a franchisee might experience in their relationship?

The Wrap-Up at the end of the chapter will answer these questions.

Suppose you come up with an idea to produce a novel product you think could lead to enormous profits. But what is the best way to produce this product? Should you do it yourself by creating your own business? Do you have enough money to create your own business? What are the legal ramifications if your business is not successful? What legal responsibilities do you have with respect to your business?

Perhaps you share your idea with your best friend, who suggests that the two of you become partners in the production and sale of this product. What are the benefits associated with forming a partnership? What are the disadvantages? Are there other forms of business you should consider?

Choosing the form of business to create is one of the most important decisions an enterprise makes. The extent of liability and control the owner will have depends on the form of the business. The business world is not static, however, and businesses can and do change form over time, so this chapter relates not only to new businesses but also to existing ones. The first section introduces the major types of business organizations, describing how these forms are both created and ended. The second section considers several types of business organizations that are less well known, but important nevertheless.

Major Forms of Business Organization

SOLE PROPRIETORSHIP

If you decide to go into business on your own, you are creating a **sole proprietorship,** a business organization in which you, as the **sole proprietor,** are in sole control of the management and the profits. Thus, if you wanted to open a lawn-mowing business or a sewing shop, you would likely be creating a sole proprietorship.

Why might an entrepreneur choose to create a sole proprietorship over other forms of business organization? First, opening a sole proprietorship requires very few legal formalities. Second, a sole proprietor has complete control of the management of the organization, with freedom to hire employees, determine business hours, and expand or change the nature of the business. Third, the sole proprietor keeps all the profits from the business. These profits are taxed as the personal income of the sole proprietor.

However, sole proprietorships have disadvantages too. Suppose you are the sole proprietor of a restaurant in which a customer is injured and she sues your business. You are personally liable for any losses or obligations associated with the business. If you accrue large debts because of your business, you might have to sell your home to cover them. Moreover, because the sole proprietorship is not considered a separate legal entity, you, as the owner and sole proprietor, can be personally sued. Sole proprietorships are terminated automatically when the sole proprietor dies.

Funding for your business is limited to your personal funds and any loans you might be able to obtain. Thus, sole proprietorships often struggle in the initial stages because they have large start-up costs relative to the profits they make.

Exhibit 35-1 summarizes the advantages and disadvantages of the sole proprietorship. Sole proprietorships are by far the most popular form of business organization in the United States. As the Comparing the Law of Other Countries box illustrates, they are popular in Germany too, although Germans call them "sole traders."

An alternative form of business organization that retains many advantages of the sole proprietorship but addresses its funding drawback is the partnership.

L01

What are the major forms of business organization, and what are the differences among them?

Exhibit 35-1

Advantages and
Disadvantages of the
Sole Proprietorship

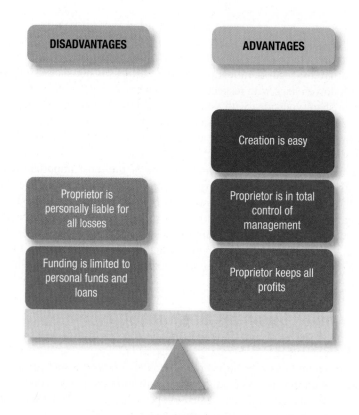

PARTNERSHIP

Suppose you and your best friend from college decide to create a business to buy and sell used books and CDs online. Both of you agree to share control of the business and split the profits equally. According to the Uniform Partnership Act (UPA), you and your friend have created a **partnership,** a voluntary association between two or more persons who co-own a business for profit. Except in a few cases, a partnership is not considered a separate legal entity and is dissolved when any partner dies. The Uniform Partnership Act governs partnerships in most states in the absence of an express agreement.

What are the advantages of a partnership? First, formation is easy. The partners, each considered an agent of the partnership, are generally not required to create an official or even a written agreement to establish it. Second, because in most cases the partnership is not considered a separate legal entity, income from the business is taxed as individual income for each partner. For that reason, partners can also deduct business losses from their taxable income.

The major disadvantage of partnerships is that partners are personally liable for the firm's debts. If you are in a partnership with your best friend, who embezzles $50,000 through the business, you will likely be held personally liable for that $50,000. Exhibit 35-2 summarizes the advantages and disadvantages of a partnership.

There are several types of partnerships (see Exhibit 35-3). In a **general partnership** the partners divide the profits (usually equally) and the management responsibilities and share unlimited personal liability for the firm's debts. Thus, in our Internet business example, you and your best friend form a general partnership by agreeing to share management responsibilities and profits as well as assuming unlimited personal liability.

Sole Traders in Germany

Germany's equivalent to the U.S. sole proprietor is the sole trader, which, while not recognized as a separate business organization, is defined quite broadly to include "anyone carrying out business under his or her own name." Sole traders are limited companies that can employ a staff but may not have partners or shareholders.

Major traders are those operating a large-scale organization. Because the organizations are large, major traders must register their companies. A sole trader who manufactures goods, trades securities, or buys and sells large quantities of goods also must register.

Minor traders who wish to elevate their status to major trader must first submit company records to the registrar. The registrar must be satisfied that elements such as the number of employees and the amount of bank credit are large enough. While being a major trader does mean being governed by more extensive regulations, for many organizations it also presents opportunities for growth and expansion.

Because by definition a sole trader must operate under his or her own name, German companies at one time had to change names when a sole trader sold the firm. Changing names presented a problem to those who wished to keep the name because of its familiarity to customers. Eventually, a stipulation was added to German law permitting the "trading name" to be included in the sale of the company.

Now imagine that your parents want to invest in your Internet business, sharing in its profits but not assuming management responsibilities or personal liability for its debts. Your parents can join your business as limited partners, and your partnership will become a **limited partnership (LP),** an agreement between at least one general partner and at least one limited partner. The general partners, you and your best friend, assume unlimited personal liability for the partnership's debts, but your parents, the limited partners, assume no liability beyond the capital they have invested in it and no part in its management. However, as limited partners, they pay taxes on their share of the profit.

If a limited partner dies, the limited partnership is usually unaffected. If a general partner dies, however, the limited partnership is usually dissolved.

A limited partnership must meet certain requirements not expected of general partnerships. First, it must use the word *limited* in its title. Second, the parties must file a certificate

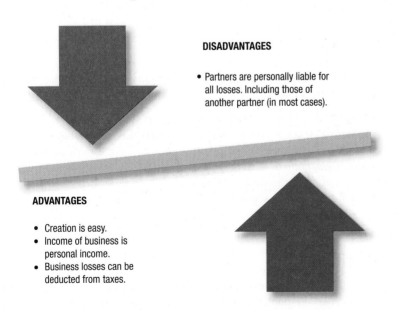

DISADVANTAGES

- Partners are personally liable for all losses. Including those of another partner (in most cases).

ADVANTAGES

- Creation is easy.
- Income of business is personal income.
- Business losses can be deducted from taxes.

Exhibit 35-2

Advantages and Disadvantages of the Partnership

773

Exhibit 35-3

Types of Partnerships

General partnership	A partnership in which the partners equally divide the profits and management responsibilities and share unlimited personal liability for the partnership's debts
Limited partnership (LP)	A partnership consisting of one general partner and at least one limited partner who does not have any part in the management of the business
Limited liability partnership (LLP)	A partnership in which all partners are liable only to the extent of the partnership's assets
Cooperative	A business organization consisting of individuals who join together to gain an advantage in the market that mutually benefits all members; can be incorporated or unincorporated
Joint venture	A relationship between two or more persons or corporations that is created for a specific business undertaking
Franchise	A business organization in which a franchisee, through a contractual agreement, sells a good or service that is trademarked by a franchisor
Business trust	A business organization controlled by a group of trustees who operate the trust, according to a written agreement, for the beneficiaries; the trustees and the beneficiaries have limited liability

of partnership with a state office to create it; otherwise, it exists as a general partnership, and all parties are personally liable for all its debts.

Suppose you are an attorney and a partner in a law firm with 30 other partners. One of your partners is sued because he was negligent in his duties as an attorney. This partner has unlimited liability for professional malpractice. But will you and the other partners also be held liable?

If the partners have created a **limited liability partnership (LLP),** all the partners assume liability for one partner's professional malpractice, but only to the extent of the partnership's assets; the other partners' personal assets cannot be taken. Moreover, each partner is liable for her own negligence *and* the negligence of those that she supervises. This distinctive feature of the LLP is the reason many professionals who do business together adopt it instead of the LP form.

Legal Principle: Every partner in a limited liability partnership has liability limited to the partnership's assets.

LLPs are fairly new; in 1991, Texas became the first state to enact a statute permitting their creation. Almost all states now have similar statutes. Like the limited partnership, the LLP has several special requirements. First, the business name must include the phrase *Limited Liability Partnership* or an abbreviation of the phrase. Second, the parties must file a form with the secretary of the state to create the LLP.

The LLP is not considered a separate legal entity. Each partner pays taxes on his or her share of the income of the business. An alternative form of business organization, the corporation, separates business ownership from business control.

CORPORATION

When you hear the word *business,* you probably think of firms like Walmart, Kmart, McDonald's, and Nike. Perhaps the most dominant form of business organization is the

corporation, a legal entity formed by selling shares of stock to investors, who then become **shareholders** and the owners of the company. These shareholders elect a board of directors, which is responsible for managing the business. The board of directors, in turn, hires officers to run the day-to-day business.

None of the other forms of business we have discussed are separate legal entities. How does a corporation become a separate legal entity? It must be created according to state law. (Chapter 38 discusses the laws governing the creation and functioning of the corporation.)

What are the consequences of being a separate legal entity? First, while the corporation can be sued and can be held liable for its debts, shareholders cannot. Their liability is usually limited to the amount they have invested in their share purchases, which supplies the company with capital. Second, the corporation is not dissolved when shareholders die. Third, the corporation must pay taxes on its profits, *and* its shareholders must pay taxes on the dividends (distributions of those profits) they receive from it. Exhibit 35-4 summarizes the advantages and disadvantages of the corporate form of business.

One way to avoid the double taxation is by forming an **S corporation,** which is a corporation under federal tax law but is taxed like a partnership as long as it follows certain regulations. For example, the S corporation cannot have more than 100 shareholders. Its income is taxed only when distributed to the shareholders, who must report the income on their personal income tax forms. S corporations are often, though not always, formed under federal law. Alternatively, other forms of corporation are created under state law.

Legal Principle: A corporation is a separate legal entity and can be sued.

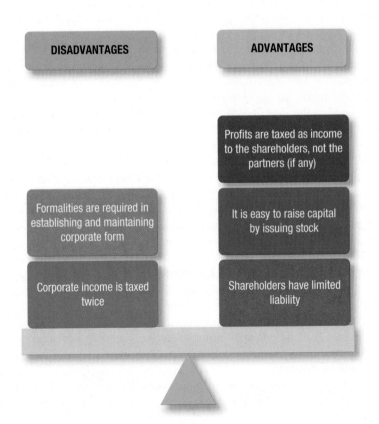

Exhibit 35-4

Advantages and Disadvantages of the Corporation

DISADVANTAGES

ADVANTAGES

Profits are taxed as income to the shareholders, not the partners (if any)

Formalities are required in establishing and maintaining corporate form

It is easy to raise capital by issuing stock

Corporate income is taxed twice

Shareholders have limited liability

LIMITED LIABILITY COMPANY

One of the newest forms of business organization in the United States is the **limited liability company (LLC),** an unincorporated form of business organization that many people see as combining the most advantageous features of partnerships and corporations. It combines the tax advantages and management flexibility of a partnership with the limited liability of a corporation.

First recognized in the United States in 1977 in Wyoming, the LLC is now recognized in every state, although the rules on LLCs have not evolved uniformly. To bring some uniformity to this area of law, the National Conference of Commissioners on Uniform State Laws drafted the Uniform Limited Liability Company Act (ULLCA) in 1995. In 2006, the commissioners revised the ULLCA. This act provides a model for states to follow, but it has not been uniformly adopted, so it is always necessary to check the specific requirements in the state in which you wish to create your LLC.

Key Reasons for the Rapid Acceptance of Limited Liability Companies.

As previously mentioned, the LLC offers its owners (referred to as **members**) the same limited liability for business debts as that offered by the corporation. But unlike the corporation, the LLC is not required to allocate profits and losses in proportion to ownership interests; nor is it required to hold an annual meeting and draft meeting minutes, so record keeping is simpler and more flexible. Unlike the case with limited partnerships, to obtain limited liability, an LLC member does not have to give up his or her right to participate in management of the LLC. In fact, an additional advantage of the LLC is the flexibility it offers members in terms of alternative ways to structure its management.

The most frequently cited advantage of the LLC is that the IRS generally treats it like a partnership or sole proprietorship. This means that members report their share of the profits and losses of the LLC on their personal tax returns. Consequently, no separate tax is assessed on the company itself, thereby allowing its members to avoid double taxation. In contrast, members of a corporation are subjected to double taxation. However, if the LLC members prefer, they may elect to have the entity taxed like a corporation. In a situation where most of the profits are going to be reinvested in the business, this option allows the profits to be taxed at the lower corporate rate. So, while we think of the opportunity to avoid double taxation as a key benefit of the LLC, more important perhaps is the fact that the members have the choice of how they wish to be taxed.

In our global environment, an increasingly important advantage of LLCs is that members need not be citizens or permanent residents of the United States. Other organizational forms, such as the subchapter S corporation, are available only when all the owners are U.S. citizens. Finally, as with a corporation, ordinary business expenses such as salaries paid to owners can be deducted from the profits of an LLC before the LLC's income is allocated to its owners for tax purposes.

Formation and Management of Limited Liability Companies.   A limited liability company is formed by filing articles of organization in the state in which members want to establish their LLC. While precise requirements vary by state, typically the articles include the name of the business, which must include the words *Limited Liability Company* or the initials *LLC,* its principal business address, the name and address of a registered agent for service, the names of the owners, and information about how the company's management will be structured.

LLCs typically want to do business in more states than just the state where they are formed, and they usually need to register in every additional state in which they intend to operate, a process referred to as *qualification*. Qualification simply entails filing a certificate of authority or some similar document, and getting a business license, in each additional state in which the business plans to operate. The LLC is usually referred to as a *foreign company* in the additional states, and under most state statutes the LLC is governed by the rules of the state where it was created, regardless of where it is transacting business.

For purposes of jurisdiction, however, an LLC is considered a citizen of every state in which its members reside. Remember that one of the reasons a party can be sued in federal court when a matter involves more than $75,000, is the existence of diversity of citizenship—no plaintiff and defendant are residents of the same state. For determining whether diversity exists, a corporation is considered a resident of the state in which it is incorporated and the state that is its primary place of business. However, this rule does not apply to LLCs, as their citizenship is determined by the residences of their members. Consequently, if parties want to increase their likelihood of having access to the federal courts, they may want to consider either limiting LLC membership to individuals of only one or a few states or using a different form of business organization.

When members form an LLC, they typically draft an operating agreement, which is the foundational contract among the entity's owners. It spells out such matters as how the company is to be managed, how the profits and losses will be allocated, how interests may be transferred, and how and when the LLC may be dissolved. Any matter not covered in the operating agreement will be resolved in accordance with the state LLC statute; if a matter is not covered by the relevant statute, the principles of partnership law are generally followed.

While there is no requirement for an LLC to have a detailed, written operating agreement, in order to ensure the smooth functioning of the company, it is a good idea to have one. Failure to have such an agreement may result in a court imposing standards on the LLC that may be very different from what the members had in mind when they formed the company.

Exhibit 35-5 compares the standard forms of business organization discussed above.

> To see an explanation of shareholder dividends and capital gains, please see the **Connecting to the Core** activity on the text Web site at www.mhhe.com/kubasek2e.

Legal Principle: As a general rule, an LLC is formed by filing articles of organization in the state in which members want to establish their LLC. Precise requirements for formation vary by state. Moreover, an LLC needs to register in every additional state in which it will do business.

Specialized Forms of Business Organization

In addition to the traditional forms of business organization we've mentioned above, some specialized forms have become important: cooperatives, joint stock companies, business trusts, syndicates, joint ventures, and franchises.

L02

What are the specialized forms of business organization?

COOPERATIVE

A **cooperative** is an organization formed by individuals who usually pool their resources to gain an advantage in the market. Farmers might pool their yields of certain crops to ensure a high market price. Usually, members of the cooperative receive dividends in proportion to how many times per year they engage in business with the cooperative.

Cooperatives may be incorporated or unincorporated. Unincorporated cooperatives are treated like partnerships, meaning members share joint liability for the cooperative's actions.

Exhibit 35-5   Traditional Forms of Business Organizations

	SOLE PROPRIETORSHIP	GENERAL PARTNERSHIP	LIMITED LIABILITY COMPANY	CORPORATION
Legal Position	Not a separate legal entity.	Not a separate legal entity in most states.	A separate legal entity.	A separate legal entity.
Creation	Creation is easy and requires very few legal formalities.	Creation is easy. The partners are generally not required to create an official or written agreement to create the partnership.	The company must file a form with a state agency and the name must include *Limited Liability Company* or an abbreviation of the phrase.	Must be created according to state law, which includes filing paperwork such as the articles of incorporation and issuing initial stock certificates to the shareholders of the corporation.
Control Considerations	Sole proprietor has total control.	Each partner is entitled to equal control.	In member-managed LLCs, all the members have control and decisions are made by majority vote. In manager-managed LLCs, the members designate a group of persons to manage the firm.	Separation of ownership and control.
Liability	Sole proprietor has unlimited personal liability.	Each partner has unlimited personal liability for partnership debts.	Each partner's liability is limited to his or her capital investments.	Liability is limited to loss of capital contribution.
Lifetime	Limited to life of proprietor.	Limited by life of partners.	Can exist beyond the illness or death of its members.	Can have unlimited life.
Taxation	Profits are taxed directly as income to the sole proprietor.	Profits are taxed as income for partners.	Profits are taxed as income for partners unless otherwise indicated on the tax form. An LLC with two or more members can choose to be taxed as a corporation or partnership.	Profits are taxed as income to the corporation and as income to the partners in the form of dividends.
Transferability of Ownership Interest	Nontransferable.	Nontransferable.	Generally unlimited transfer.	Generally unlimited transfer.
Dissolution	The business is dissolved when the proprietor dies or decides to dissolve the business.	The partnership is dissolved when one partner dies or when the partners agree to dissolve it.	The members must have a majority vote to dissolve the business. A member's dissociation does not dissolve the entire business.	The corporation is not dissolved when the shareholders die. Dissolution often involves extensive legal paperwork and approval by at least two-thirds of all voting shares.

Limited Liability Companies in Mexico

A limited liability company in Mexico is "an association of individuals who are exempt from individual responsibility to third parties, yet who own the stock separately from the owner." Limited liability companies are identifiable because their name must be followed by the phrase *Sociedad de Responsibilidad Limitada*. Without this phrase, courts assume that a partnership exists.

The LLC's important distinguishing factor is that members are an entity separate from the owners. Members, from 2 to 25 in number and referred to as *share/stockholders,* invest capital in the company. While they do not have any individual responsibility, collectively they must give their consent before the company can sell shares to new members. The decision must be unanimous; generally, members have one vote for every 100-peso share.

Mexico adopted the limited liability company model from Germany, where such companies are enormously popular, in hopes of attracting more investors to small companies by limiting their responsibilities.

Members of incorporated cooperatives, on the other hand, enjoy limited liability just as do the shareholders of a corporation.

JOINT STOCK COMPANY

A **joint stock company** is a partnership agreement in which company members hold transferable shares while all the goods of the company are held in the names of the partners. Thus, the joint stock company is a mix of corporation and partnership. As in the corporation, members who hold shares of stock own the joint stock company. As in the partnership, these shareholders have personal liability, and in most cases the company is not a separate legal entity.

BUSINESS TRUST

A **business trust** is a business organization governed by a group of **trustees,** who operate the trust for the **beneficiaries.** A written trust agreement establishes the duties and powers of the trustees and the interests of the beneficiaries. As in a corporation, the trustees and beneficiaries enjoy limited liability, and in most states business trusts are taxed like corporations.

SYNDICATE

An investment group that comes together for the explicit purpose of financing a specific large project is a **syndicate.** Syndicates are often used to purchase professional sports teams and are quite useful for their ability to raise large amounts of money in a short time. They are usually considered a type of joint venture; thus they are almost always governed by partnership law.

JOINT VENTURE

A **joint venture** is a relationship between two or more persons or corporations created for a specific business undertaking. This relationship may entail financing, producing, and selling goods, securities, or commodities. Participants in the joint venture usually share the profits and losses equally.

Joint ventures can be agreements between small or very large businesses. For example, Penske Truck Leasing Co., L.P., is a joint venture among Penske Corporation, Penske Automotive Group, and General Electric with annual revenues of more than $4 billion.

E-COMMERCE AND THE LAW

Exploring Forms of Business Organization on the Internet

If you are considering starting a business, the Internet can provide much information to help you decide which form you should create. At Business Tools (http://smallbiz.findlaw.com/book), you can read more about sole proprietorships, partnerships, and corporations.

You can also search online for laws that affect the forms of business within your state. At Texas Business Forms (www.sos.state .tx.us/corp/forms.shtml), you can read about and download the forms required to create various types of business in Texas. Thus, the Internet can make it easier to create your business by increasing the information available to you.

COMPARING THE LAW OF OTHER COUNTRIES

Types of Business Organization in China

The concept of *legal persons* is at the root of all Chinese business law. The Civil Code of China defines a legal person as "an organization which possesses civil legal capacity for civil acts and which, according to the law, independently enjoys civil rights and assumes civil obligations." The definition goes on to describe two types of legal persons.

The first is the *enterprise legal person,* any privately, collectively, or state-owned registered enterprise that meets four criteria: (1) existence of an outlined organizational structure, (2) an organization title, (3) articles governing the structure, and (4) the necessary funds and property. A foreign-owned or foreign joint venture may also acquire enterprise legal person status by applying for approval and registration.

The second type of legal persons is *other legal persons.* These include government agencies, institutions, and associations. Government agencies need not apply for registration because they are given legal-person status on their establishment. Other institutions and associations must meet the criteria above and may also be subject to approval and registration based on State Council rules specified in 1998.

This joint venture operates more than 225,000 vehicles in North America, South America, Europe, and Asia. From a legal standpoint, partnerships and joint ventures are virtually the same. Thus, courts frequently apply partnership law to joint ventures. Joint ventures differ from partnerships, however, because they are usually created for making and selling a single product, while a partnership creates an ongoing full business. The joint venture is usually terminated when all the stock has been sold or at the discretion of the members.

Also unlike a partnership, the joint venture is not automatically terminated when one of the members dies. Members of a joint venture also have less authority than general partners because they are not agents of the other members.

Joint-venture partners usually share equal management of the task for which they have come together, but they can agree to give one party greater management responsibilities. Both (or all) parties usually assume liability for the project, and each can be held responsible for the liability of the other(s).

Like a partnership, a joint venture may be formed without drawing up a formal agreement.

Case 35-1 provides a judicial discussion of the elements necessary for the establishment of a joint venture.

MMK GROUP, LLC v. THE SHESHELLS COMPANY, LLC, ET AL.
U.S. DISTRICT COURT FOR THE NORTHERN DISTRICT OF OHIO
591 F. SUPP. 2D 944 (2008)

In 2002, Tina Bruce invented Lilypadz breast shields, a device that prevents breast milk leakage from nursing mothers. To refine and commercialize this idea, Ms. Bruce joined with Charles Pawloski, her uncle, to form Me & My Kidz, L.L.C. (M&MK), an Ohio limited liability company. To produce the breast shields, M&MK contacted Thermodyn and entered into a nondisclosure agreement. This nondisclosure agreement prohibited Thermodyn and its employees from disclosing M&MK's trade secret information and from competing with M&MK. M&MK argued that despite the nondisclosure agreement, Thomas Hass (a Thermodyn employee) used M&MK's confidential information to begin launching a competing product, SheShells Breast Coverlets.

Meanwhile, James MacMillan, the president of Thermodyn, claimed the relationship between Thermodyn and M&MK was a joint venture. Because he believed the relationship was a joint venture, Mr. MacMillan threatened to stop production unless M&MK provided increased financial benefits, provided Thermodyn with all of the patent information, and indemnified Thermodyn from any lawsuits. M&MK complied with the requests until Thermodyn met all of the outstanding production orders for breast shields and then notified Thermodyn of its intention to terminate their relationship.

After the relationship was terminated, Thomas Haas began selling the knock-off SheShells Breast Coverlets in violation of the trade-secrets agreement. M&MK filed suit against Mr. Haas, his company SheShells Co., LLC, and Thermodyn. The Thermodyn defendants filed counterclaims against M&MK, claiming a breach of an alleged joint venture. M&MK disagreed, claiming the two businesses did not have a joint venture and subsequently motioned to dismiss the breach of joint venture claim.

JUDGE KATZ: Under Ohio law, a joint venture is a partnership established for the purposes of a single business enterprise. The essential elements of a partnership are as follows:

(1) an express or implied partnership contract between the parties;

(2) the sharing of profits and losses;

(3) mutuality of agency;

(4) mutuality of control; and

(5) the co-ownership of the business and of the property used for partnership purposes or acquired with partnership funds.

The essential elements of a joint venture partnership are similar:

(1) a joint contract;

(2) an intention to associate as joint venturers;

(3) community of interest and control, including contributions to the joint venture;

(4) the mutual right to direct and control the purpose of the joint venture; and

(5) an agreement for the division of profits and losses jointly, not severally.

A joint venture is distinguished from a partnership because the former relates to a single enterprise and the latter to a continuing business.

M&MK argues that Thermodyn alleges insufficient facts to establish the existence of a joint venture. The Court disagrees. Under the first element of a joint venture, Thermodyn must allege a set of facts in support of the existence of "a joint contract." M&MK argues that the November 8, 2002, letter from Pawloski to the marketing director of Thermodyn and the "Thermodyn & M&MK Relationship" document cannot be construed as a joint contract because they do not satisfy the requirements of a contract under Ohio law. However, it is not necessary for Thermodyn to submit a single written contract or document to establish a joint contract. To establish an implied contract under Ohio law, a plaintiff must prove each of the elements of a contract, i.e. an agreement, based on a meeting of the parties' minds and mutual assent, to which the parties intended to be bound. A plaintiff need not show that the parties formally exchanged promises. Instead, a "contract implied in fact may be proved by showing that the circumstances surrounding the parties' transactions make it reasonably certain that an agreement was intended."

Here, Thermodyn has alleged facts necessary to support a claim that the various documents submitted to the Court as well as the conduct of the parties establish a "joint contract." A letter from Pawloski to the marketing director of Thermodyn described Thermodyn as a "long-term strategic partner and supplier of our LilyPadz product . . . we want to see both . . . benefit from this venture." The letter goes on to set the target cost "of $3.75 per finished unit and for Thermodyn to have at least a 40% manufacturing margin." The "Thermodyn & M&MK Relationship" document states that M&MK and Thermodyn intend to have a "transparent" relationship and explains the roles of each company: which will maintain the raw materials, how inventory shall be calculated, and how profit margins shall be calculated. Furthermore, the conduct of the parties is notable. Neither party disagrees that Thermodyn did in fact manufacture Lilypadz for several years, and Thermodyn Defendants allege that over "several years" Thermodyn invested $160,000 in equipment and staffing for the project.

Under the second element of a joint venture, Thermodyn must allege a set of facts in support of "an intention to associate as joint ventures." M&MK argues that the November 8, 2002, letter does not explicitly state M&MK's intention to associate as a joint venture. However, the letter from Pawloski states a desire for M&MK and Thermodyn to both benefit from "this venture," and the Thermodyn & M&MK Relationship document delegates the duties and responsibilities that relate to the single enterprise of manufacturing and selling Lilypadz. Furthermore, some kind of business relationship existed between the companies that distributed the delegation of duties consistent with the above mentioned documents: M&MK marketed, distributed, and sold Lilypadz, while Thermodyn manufactured them.

For the Third and Fourth elements, Thermodyn must allege a set of facts in support of a "community of interest and control, including contributions to the joint venture" and "the mutual right to direct and control the purpose of the joint venture." Thermodyn alleges that Thermodyn "came up with numerous modifications to the product . . . to assist in the development of the Lilypadz project." Also, the Thermodyn and M&MK Relationship document states that "M&MK can work with Thermodyn during this startup and Thermodyn can be asked to sit in on sales meetings with major Lilypadz customers." Furthermore, one of the reasons that Thermodyn has brought this Counterclaim is because M&MK "invested no funds in the project" and Thermodyn does not believe it was sufficiently compensated for its contributions.

Fifth, Thermodyn must allege a set of facts in support of "an agreement for the division of profits and losses—jointly, not severally." Thermodyn has satisfied this element with allegations evidenced by the Thermodyn and M&MK Relationship document which states that "[b]oth companies should expect to share in the costs as well as the success of the Lilypadz product." Thus, M&MK's motion to dismiss the breach of joint venture claim is denied.

DENIED.

CRITICAL THINKING

The process of critical thinking requires that we ask critical questions about whatever reasoning we encounter, even if, as in this case, the reasoning appears very convincing. Of the five criteria Judge Katz uses to claim that the companies were in a joint venture, which do you think he provides the weakest argument and least justification for?

ETHICAL DECISION MAKING

Essentially, the court ruled in favor of Thermodyn and did not punish Thomas Haas for selling knock-off breast shields he created through stealing trade secrets. What theory or theories of ethical decision making might instead punish Haas for his actions violating the nondisclosure agreement? Explain.

L03

What is a franchise?

FRANCHISE

When you go into McDonald's to eat lunch, what type of business are you patronizing? You are likely eating at a **franchise.** This form of business organization is a business that exists because of an arrangement between the **franchisor,** an owner of a trade name or trademark, and the **franchisee,** a person who sells goods or services under the trade name or trademark. Exhibit 35-6 summarize the advantages and disadvantages of a franchise for the franchisor.

Generally, franchises fall into one of three categories. In a **chain-style business operation,** such as McDonald's and Burger King, the franchise operates under the franchisor's business name and is required to follow the franchisor's standards and methods of business operation.

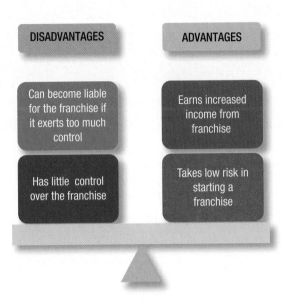

Exhibit 35-6
Starting a Franchise:
Advantages and
Disadvantages for
the Franchisor

DISADVANTAGES

Can become liable for the franchise if it exerts too much control

Has little control over the franchise

ADVANTAGES

Earns increased income from franchise

Takes low risk in starting a franchise

In the second category, **distributorships,** the franchisor manufactures a product and licenses a dealer to sell it in an exclusive territory. A car dealership is an example of a distributorship.

Finally, the third category is the **manufacturing arrangement,** in which the franchisor provides the franchisee with the formula or necessary ingredient to manufacture a product. Soft-drink companies, for example, provide the syrup used to produce the final product, and then sell it, according to the franchisor's standards.

Exhibit 35-7 indicates how important franchises are for the market economy.

Look at Case 35-2 to see how the supreme court of Arkansas determined whether a franchise agreement existed between Mary Kay Cosmetics and Janet Isbell.

Franchising is one way to spread your business across the world.

Exhibit 35-7 The Top 10 Global Franchises, 2009

1. Subway (worldwide sales of more than $12 billion)
2. McDonald's
3. Liberty Tax Service
4. Sonic Drive In Restaurants
5. Intercontinental Hotels Group
6. Ace Hardware Corp.
7. Pizza Hut
8. UPS Store
9. Circle K
10. Papa John's International. Inc.

Source: Ranked by *Entrepreneur Magazine* on the basis of financial strength and stability, growth rate, and size of the system; www.entrepreneur.com/franchise500/index.html.

MARY KAY, INC., A/K/A MARY KAY COSMETICS, INC. v. JANET ISBELL
SUPREME COURT OF ARKANSAS
338 ARK. 556; 999 S.W. 2D 669; 1999 ARK. LEXIS 443

In 1980, Janet Isbell signed an agreement to become a beauty consultant for Mary Kay. This agreement established that Isbell would sell products to customers at home demonstration parties, but she was prohibited from selling in retail establishments. In September 1981, Isbell signed her first agreement to become a unit sales director. She signed her second agreement in July 1991. In addition to serving as a beauty consultant, Isbell recruited other beauty consultants. She earned compensation in the form of commission on her sales as well as on the sales of the consultants she recruited. In 1994, she rented a space in a shopping mall to serve as a training center. In April 1994, Mary Kay's legal coordinator contacted Isbell, stating that the store space was not to be used to sell Mary Kay products. According to the agreement, Isbell's office could not look like a Mary Kay store. Furthermore, Isbell was told to cease all photo sessions of potential customers and to stop advertising "glamour tips."

In September 1995, the vice president of sales development notified Isbell that Mary Kay was terminating its agreements with her. Isbell filed suit against Mary Kay, claiming she was a franchise under Arkansas' Franchise Practices Act. She argued that Mary Kay violated the Franchise Practices Act by refusing to comply with the FPA provisions for termination of a franchise. In August 1997, the trial court granted summary judgment to Isbell, but it did not explain why Isbell's relationships with Mary Kay could be considered a franchise. The trial court ruled as a matter of law that Mary Kay's termination of Isbell had violated the Act, and a jury awarded Isbell $110,583.33.

JUDGE GLAZE: The threshold issue to be decided is whether the Arkansas Franchise Practices Act applies, because if it does, Isbell would be entitled to the designation of franchisee and permitted to invoke the protections and benefits of that Act.

To determine whether the Arkansas Franchise Practices Act applies to this case depends upon our interpretation and construction of the pertinent provisions of the Act. In this view, we turn first to Ark. Code Ann. §4-72-202 (1) (Supp. 1997), which in relevant part defines "franchise" to mean the following:

> [A] written or oral agreement for a definite or indefinite period, in which a person grants to another a license to use a trade name, trademark, service mark, or related characteristic within an exclusive

or nonexclusive territory, or to sell or distribute goods or services within an exclusive or nonexclusive territory, at wholesale, retail, by lease agreement, or otherwise.

While the Act's definition of franchise is helpful, that definition alone is not dispositive of the issue as to whether Isbell, under the parties' agreement, is or is not a franchisee. The answer, however, can be found in §§ 4-72-203 and 4-72-202 (6) of the Act. Section 4-72-203 clearly provides the Act applies only to a franchise that contemplates or requires the franchise to establish or maintain a place of business in the state. Next, § 4-72-202 (6) defines "place of business" under the Act as meaning "a fixed geographical location at which the franchisee [1] displays for sale and sells the franchisor's goods or [2] offers for sale and sells the franchisor's services."

We first should note that Isbell concedes that, as a sales director, her agreements with Mary Kay provided that she could not display for sale or sell Mary Kay products from an office, whether that office was located in her home or her training center. In fact, Isbell testified that she never displayed or sold Mary Kay products from her training center, and to have done so would have been a violation of her agreement with Mary Kay.

While conceding that the parties' agreements never contemplated that Isbell would or could sell the franchisor's goods from a fixed location, she argues no such prohibition prevented her from selling Mary Kay services from her home or training center. Specifically, Isbell suggests the facial makeovers and "Glamour Shots" photo sessions that were a part of Mary Kay's demonstration and training program constituted services that the parties contemplated could be sold by Isbell from her center.

Mary Kay's Director's Guide, which was made a part of the parties' agreements, very clearly provided that a sales director's office, albeit it her home or training center, could only be used to interview potential recruits and hold unit meetings and other training events. The Guide further provided that the office or center should not give the appearance of a cosmetic studio, facial salon or retail establishment, or give the appearance of being a "Mary Kay" store. Thus, nowhere in the parties' Guide or agreements can it be fairly said that the parties ever contemplated that Isbell could use her office or center as a fixed location to display or sell Mary Kay products or services.

[continued]

Even if we could agree with Isbell's contention that she was not prohibited from selling (or was otherwise authorized to sell) Mary Kay services, her argument must fail for another reason. Isbell simply never showed she sold Mary Kay services. She claims that because her contract requires her to provide motivational, counseling, and training services, such services should be considered part of the sale and commission when the product is actually sold. Isbell offered no proof as to what part of the commission, if any, was attributable to services. Neither Isbell nor Mary Kay was shown to have received any separate compensation for services provided to potential customers, but, to the contrary, evidence was presented showing these services, like the photographs taken at makeover sessions, were provided at cost with only the photographer receiving payment.

Finally, Isbell argues that her home constituted a place of business under the Act because as a consultant she occasionally displayed and sold products there. This argument, however, is not supported by the parties' agreement, since it never contemplated a fixed location for the display and sale of products. As previously stated, a Mary Kay consultant's location for selling products is her home or those of her potential customers.

In sum, we conclude that the agreements between Janet Isbell and Mary Kay did not contemplate the establishment of a fixed place of business as that term is defined in Ark. Code Ann. § 4-72-202 (6). As such, the business relationship entered into by Isbell and Mary Kay was not a franchise within the protection of the Arkansas Franchise Practices Act, and the court below erred in so holding.

REVERSED and DISMISSED.

CRITICAL THINKING

Outline the judge's reasoning in this case. What evidence does he use to support this reasoning?

What missing information would you call for when considering the facts of this case?

Would you interpret the Arkansas Franchise Practices Act and apply it to the facts of the case differently than Judge Glaze does? Why or why not?

ETHICAL DECISION MAKING

Consider the WPH framework. What values is Isbell promoting? What values are in conflict? Was the court fair in assessing her actions in light of these values?

Franchise Law. Because franchisors are usually larger than franchisees and have more resources, they often have the upper hand in franchise relationships. However, federal and state laws have been established to protect the franchisee.

A franchise is a contractual relationship between the franchisor and the franchisee. Thus, contract law, and the Uniform Commercial Code in particular, apply. If the terms of the contract are not met, either side can sue for breach of contract.

Creation of the Franchise. In the franchise relationship, the parties make a franchise agreement regarding payment to the franchisor, location of the franchise, restrictions the franchisee must follow, and method of termination of the franchise.

The franchise agreement usually sets out what the franchisee pays the franchisor (a large sum) for use of the trade name or trademark and what percentage of sales income will go to the franchisor. If the franchise requires a building, the agreement will specify who pays for buying or renting it or for building it if it must be constructed.

The franchisor usually includes in the agreement business practices that are forbidden and business standards, such as for cleanliness, that must be met. The franchisor can also set sales quotas and record-keeping requirements. The franchisee might be required to purchase certain supplies from the franchisor at a set price, but the franchisor cannot establish the price at which the franchisee sells the goods.

The disagreement in the opening scenario for this chapter arose because of the third factor in franchise agreements. Because many Dunkin' Donuts restaurants are owned by franchisees, Dunkin' Donuts established guidelines and policies that promote business practices that enhance the quality of food and services at each restaurant. Dunkin' Donuts also has quality, safety, and cleanliness standards for each of its franchises. The franchise agreement stipulated that Dunkin' Donuts could inspect Bhayani's restaurant at any reasonable time.

Although the franchisor has the legal authority to ensure that the franchisee maintains the quality of goods and services associated with the franchise, it must be cautious. If it exercises too much authority in the day-to-day affairs of the business, the franchisor could be held liable for the torts of the franchisee's employees.

Termination of the Franchise.

Much of the litigation associated with franchises regards wrongful termination of a franchise. The franchise agreement establishes how the franchise will be terminated. The business is usually established for a trial period, such as a year. If the franchisee does not meet the requirements in the agreement, the franchisor can terminate it but must give sufficient notice. The termination also usually must have cause. For example, good cause exists if the franchisee repeatedly violates the franchise agreement. Additionally, the franchisor needs to have documented the warnings sent to the franchisee regarding the violations. The typical agreement gives the franchisor broad authority to terminate; in recent years, however, many states have been giving the franchisee greater termination protection.

Legal Principle: **When a franchisee does not uphold the franchise agreement, the franchisor can terminate the relationship with sufficient notice.**

The courts usually rely heavily on the written agreement when determining whether a franchise was wrongfully terminated. Look at Case 35-3, which illustrates the agreement's importance.

CASE 35-3   COUSINS SUBS SYSTEMS, INC. v. MICHAEL R. McKINNEY

U.S. DISTRICT COURT FOR THE EASTERN DISTRICT OF WISCONSIN
59 F. SUPP. 2D 816 (1999)

Cousins Subs Systems entered into an agreement with Michael McKinney, whose company operates a chain of gas stations, to operate several Cousins submarine sandwich shops placed in the gas stations.

In April 1998, McKinney became disillusioned with the agreement and terminated it. He claimed Cousins had guaranteed him annual sales of $250,000 to $500,000 at each of his franchises and promised to provide advertising. McKinney also claimed Cousins guaranteed it would provide assistance in recruiting other franchises. Finally, McKinney argued Cousins enforced unrealistically *high prices of subs. McKinney alleges he terminated the agreement because Cousins failed to uphold its promises.*

In June 1998, Cousins filed suit against McKinney for wrongfully terminating the agreement with Cousins. Later in 1998, McKinney filed a counterclaim against Cousins. Cousins filed a motion to dismiss the counterclaim.

JUDGE ADELMAN: McKinney first contends that Cousins violated Minn. Stat. § 80C.13, subd. 2, which provides:

No person may offer or sell a franchise in this state by means of any written or oral communication which includes an untrue statement of a material fact or which omits to state a material fact necessary in order to make the statements made, in light of the circumstances under which they were made, not misleading.

McKinney does not clearly delineate his theory as to how this statute was violated. He appears to assert that Cousins violated this statute by making untrue oral representations to him about how much money he would make and about how much advertising and recruitment assistance it would provide. The main problem with this claim and, for that matter, with all of McKinney's claims is that the oral promises allegedly made by Cousins are directly contradicted by the written terms of the agreements that he signed and attached as exhibits to his pleadings. Where the allegations of a complaint are inconsistent with the terms of a written contract attached as an exhibit, the terms of the contract prevail over the averments differing therefrom. Unfortunately for McKinney, every oral representation that he alleges was made by Cousins is inconsistent with the written contracts he signed or the written circular he received.

McKinney alleges first that Cousins . . . orally guaranteed that annual sales at McKinney's franchises would be between $250,000 and $500,000, and that this level of sales was not realized. However, the Area Development Agreement states that McKinney "has not received any warranty or guaranty, express or implied, as to the potential volume, profits, or success of the business venture." The Franchise Agreement contains virtually identical language. Thus, McKinney's claim of guaranteed profits is directly contradicted by the written contracts. McKinney also claims that Cousins promised to provide "advertising . . . in excess of the amount paid by McKinney," and that Cousins failed to do so. But the Uniform Franchise Offering Circular states that "Cousins is not obligated to spend any specific amounts on advertising in the area where a particular franchisee is located. . . ." Thus, this claim too is directly contradicted by the written language of an exhibit. McKinney next alleges that Cousins "expressly guaranteed and promised

to provide extensive assistance in recruitment of other franchisees in the development area," but that such assistance was not forthcoming. The Area Development Agreement, however, states, with respect to the recruitment issue, "AREA DEVELOPER shall be responsible for advertising for, recruiting and screening prospects for SHOPS within the Exclusive Area." Thus, every single oral promise that McKinney asserts was made by Cousins is inconsistent with the documents appended to his complaint. Under Seventh Circuit case law the language of the exhibits prevails.

McKinney's claims are further undermined by other language in the agreements. The area development and franchise agreements each contain integration clauses which expressly disavow any promises not included in the written agreements between the parties. The Area Development Agreement, for example, states that "this Agreement . . . constitutes the entire agreement of the parties, and there are no other oral or written understandings or agreements . . . relating to the subject matter of this agreement."

McKinney cannot prevail on his claim under the Minnesota statute unless, in offering him a franchise, Cousins made an untrue statement of material fact. Cousins offered the franchises to McKinney through the written franchise documents, not through the alleged oral promises that are inconsistent with the exhibits. And the written documents do not contain untrue statements of material fact or omissions of material facts, nor does McKinney claim that they do. Therefore, McKinney's claim that the Minnesota Franchise Act was violated fails.

In sum, McKinney is an experienced businessman who made a deal which turned out to be less favorable than he anticipated. McKinney expressly acknowledged in detailed written agreements negotiated with the assistance of counsel that his purchase of a franchise was not a risk-free endeavor. He now makes allegations that are directly contrary to the agreements he signed. For the reasons stated, his claim under the Minnesota statute fails.

DISMISSED.

CRITICAL THINKING

What are the primary facts of this case? How would you word the issue of the case in your own words?

Judge Adelman repeatedly says the written terms of the contract between Cousins and McKinney are inconsistent with any alleged oral agreements they made. Do you agree that written contracts should overrule oral agreements in most instances? Why or why not?

ETHICAL DECISION MAKING

Who are the primary stakeholders affected by the court's ruling for Cousins?

The decisions of a court have implications for business ethics. While Chapter 2 distinguishes between what the law requires of a manager and what ethics requires, the relationship between the law and ethics is reciprocal. While ethical judgments lie behind various laws, law does have impacts on business ethics. In this case, the court's decision reminds us that business ethics must pay attention to the various stakeholders who feel the impacts of any business agreement.

CASE OPENER WRAP-UP

Dunkin' Donuts

Bhayani's Dunkin' Donuts franchises violated the license agreement on multiple levels. Financially, under the franchise agreements, Bhayani agreed to pay a franchise fee of 4.9 percent of gross sales to Dunkin' Donuts and an advertising fee of 5 percent of gross sales to the Franchise Owners Advertising and Sales promotion fund. However, Bhayani fell behind on both financial payments on numerous occasions. By the time Dunkin' Donuts sent notice of termination, Bhayani owed $33,189.38 in delinquent fees and failed to cure the financial default.

Furthermore, Bhayani's franchises were also in violation of health and safety standards from the license agreement. During its routine health inspections, Dunkin' Donuts found multiple health and sanitation violations such as pests and evidence of pests; improper storage, refrigeration, and cooking temperatures; improper food and chemical storage; unsanitized utensils; faulty faucets; unclean floors, walls, countertops, toilets, and sinks; insufficient employee hygiene; ill-kept trash areas; and various documentation deficiencies. While some of these were cured by the time of the next inspection, most were not. After each substandard inspection, Dunkin' Donuts sent a notice of default and notice to cure. On the basis of the perceived failure to cure these violations over a substantial period of time, Dunkin' Donuts sent Bhayani a supplemental notice of termination.

As a franchisor, Dunkin' Donuts Corporation is permitted to establish certain standards for franchisees. With regard to Bhayani's restaurants, Dunkin' Donuts established standards for cleanliness and also negotiated financial rates. In accordance with the provisions in the license agreement, Dunkin' Donuts terminated the franchises. Bhayani claimed that any breaches of the agreement by him—either financial breaches or health, sanitation, and safety violations—were directly caused by the bad-faith actions of Dunkin' Donuts. He argued that Dunkin' Donuts targeted him for his franchisee activism by classifying him as a "C" franchise and blocking his attempt to open another franchise. However, the court found that Bhayani did not show that his franchises were exceptional or that they were terminated on the basis of some sort of "pretext" of Dunkin' Donuts. Thus, Dunkin' Donuts was well within its legal rights to terminate the franchise agreement.

Disagreements regarding payments or health standards of franchises are examples of what could go wrong with a franchising agreement. Another example of potential problems between franchisors and franchisees is disagreement over the termination of the franchise. All of these problems exist in the Dunkin' Donuts case. Both parties probably would have benefited from a greater understanding of the responsibilities of the franchisor and franchisee.

Key Terms

beneficiaries 779	chain-style business	corporation 775	franchise agreement 785
business	operation 782	distributorships 783	franchisee 782
trust 779	cooperative 777	franchise 782	franchisor 782

Summary of Key Topics

**Major Forms of
Business Organization**

Sole proprietorship: The owner has total control and unlimited personal liability. Profits are taxed directly as income to the sole proprietor.

General partnership: For most purposes, the partnership is not a legal entity, and each partner has equal control and unlimited liability, with profits that are taxed as income for partners.

Limited partnership: Limited partnerships are similar to general partnerships, except that limited partners' liability is limited to the extent of their capital contributions.

Corporation: A corporation is a separate legal entity wherein the owners' liability is limited to the amount of their contributions and the profits are taxed as income to the corporation.

S Corporation: An S corporation is a corporation under federal tax law but is taxed like a partnership as long as it follows certain regulations.

Limited liability company: An LLC is an unincorporated form of business organization that combines the tax advantages and management flexibility of a partnership with the limited liability of a corporation.

**Specialized Forms of
Business Organization**

Cooperative: A cooperative is a business organization in which the members usually pool their resources together to gain some kind of advantage in the market.

Joint stock company: A joint stock company is a partnership agreement in which company members hold transferable shares while all the goods of the company are held in the names of the partners. A joint stock company is a mixture of a corporation and a partnership.

Syndicate: A syndicate is an investment group that comes together for the explicit purpose of financing a specific large project.

Business trust: A business trust is a business organization governed by a group of trustees, who operate the trust for the beneficiaries.

Joint venture: A joint venture is a relationship between two or more persons or corporations created for a specific business undertaking.

Franchise: A franchise is a business that exists because of an arrangement between an owner of a trade name or trademark and a person who sells goods or services under the trade name or trademark.

Point / Counterpoint

Should a New Restaurateur Open a Franchise Rather than Become a Sole Proprietor?	
YES	NO
A businessperson new to the restaurant business should open a restaurant as part of an existing franchise rather than encounter the substantial risks of opening a sole proprietorship. Sole proprietors have unlimited personal liability, meaning they are held solely accountable for the finances in their businesses; they often must provide their houses as collateral to obtain small-business loans. A sole proprietor can also be held personally liable for injury in the restaurant and can be sued by an employee or customer, whereas a franchisee usually is not held solely liable for an injury. A franchisor can also provide crucial guidance and supervision to a new businessperson, including clear business practices that have already proved successful, forbidden practices that would endanger the franchise, and minimum standards of cleanliness and service. This assistance eliminates the trial-and-error period sole proprietors must experience and helps the new businessperson avoid repeating others' past errors.	A new restaurateur should be a sole proprietor rather than a franchisee to enjoy greater potential for long-term success. With careful research and expert advice, sole proprietors can obtain low-risk, longer-term loans that are unlikely to jeopardize their personal assets. Sole proprietors can add a full or limited business partner later and implement additional safety measures to decrease liability. A franchise must pay the franchisor a percentage of profits. After debts are repaid, a sole proprietor keeps all profits for improvements and personal income. Franchises severely restrict creativity. A sole proprietor is truly her or his own boss and can change the look and menu of the restaurant at any time, determine which hours to be in operation, and decide whether to hire a manager or manage the restaurant directly. Perhaps most important, a sole proprietor retains flexibility if the economy changes. If need be, she or he can simply uproot the restaurant and move to a different location.

Questions & Problems

1. What is the distinction between a general partnership and a limited partnership?

2. Explain why a cooperative could not claim to be a syndicate.

3. Suppose you were asked to review and assess a franchise agreement. What responsibilities would you expect to find included in that agreement?

4. Joe Orosco, an employee of Sun-Maid Growers, Inc., lost his arm in an industrial accident with a raisin elevator in 1991. Sun-Maid was one of four members of a marketing cooperative called the Sun-Diamond Corporation. According to the cooperative agreement, Sun-Diamond was authorized to provide certain management services to Sun-Maid. Orosco sued Sun-Maid and Sun-Diamond, arguing that both corporations were liable because they were involved in a joint venture to design, manufacture, construct, repair, maintain, install, and test the processing line on which Orosco lost his arm. Were the two corporations involved in a joint venture? What additional facts would you want to know before forming your answer? If they were involved in a joint venture, should Sun-Diamond be held liable for Orosco's injuries? Why or why not? [*Orosco v. Sun-Diamond Corp.,* 51 Cal. App. 4th 1659 (1997).]

5. "YOU AND I" was a thoroughbred racehorse owned by a syndicate composed of 40 equal ownership shares. The syndicate agreement stated that if an acceptable offer was made to purchase the horse from the syndicate, each syndicate member had a "first right to purchase" under which he could sell his interest in the horse or buy the interests of the other syndicate members who had elected

to sell their interests in the horse. The syndicate agreement, however, required that if a syndicate member planned to exercise his first right to purchase, he had to notify the syndicate manager of his intent within 10 days of his receiving notification of the acceptable offer. In September 2003, Brereton Jones, a syndicate member and the syndicate manager, received an offer from Blooming Hills Farms to buy YOU AND I for $500,000. Jones sent a memo to all the syndicate members notifying them that Blooming Hills Farms had made the offer, that he believed the offer to be fair, and that he planned to sell his interest. Jones received word from 39 of the 40 syndicate members that they planned to sell their interests in YOU AND I. The following day, Never Tell Farm, a syndicate member, notified Jones that it planned to exercise its first right to purchase. Jones and Never Tell proceeded to negotiate over whether Never Tell would exercise its first right to purchase, and the 10-day window elapsed. When the negotiations fell through, Never Tell notified Jones of its intent to exercise its first right to purchase. Jones told Never Tell that it had not timely asserted its right and thus the horse had been sold to Blooming Hills Farms. Never Tell sued Jones, claiming that under the syndicate agreement it should have had the right to purchase the other syndicate members' interests in YOU AND I. With whom do you think the court sided in this case? Why? [*Never Tell Farm, LLC v. Airdrie Stud, Inc.,* 123 Fed. Appx. 194 (2005).]

6. The Garden City Boxing Club held exclusive satellite licensing rights for a live broadcast of a boxing match between Oscar De La Hoya and Fernando Vargas. Luis Dominguez owned Antenas Enterprises, the installer of a satellite account at Mundelein Burrito restaurant. However, Antenas listed Mundelein Burrito as a residence instead of a commercial location. A commercial establishment could show the boxing match only if it was contractually authorized by GCB to do so and if it paid the appropriate fee of $20 times the maximum fire code occupancy of the establishment. Mundelein Burrito showed the event to its patrons. However, because Mundelein Burrito was classified as a residence, it did not pay the proper fee for a commercial establishment. The Garden City Boxing Club filed suit against Dominguez, the sole proprietor of Antenas, to collect the lost fees from the boxing match.

As a sole proprietor, should Dominguez be held personally liable for Antenas Enterprises' actions? [*Garden City Boxing Club, Inc. v. Luis Dominguez,* 2006 U.S. Dist. LEXIS 38184 (2006).]

7. Chic Miller operated a General Motors (GM) franchise car dealership. His written franchise agreement with GM stipulated that Miller had to maintain a floor-plan financing agreement with a lender to enable him to buy new cars from GM. Initially, Miller maintained a line of credit with a GM affiliate (GMAC), but he terminated the agreement because he felt that GMAC charged him an exorbitant interest rate. Miller was able to find another line of credit from Chase Manhattan Bank, but Chase withdrew its financing agreement with Miller after one year. Miller attempted to resume the agreement with GMAC, but GMAC refused. Miller alleged *ipse dixit* (an assertion without evidence) that GMAC discouraged other lenders from providing a line of credit to Miller. GM then notified Miller that it was terminating its franchise relationship with him because he failed to satisfy the financing stipulation of the written franchise agreement. Two months after receiving this notice from GM, Miller attempted to sell his franchise to Kenneth Crowley, the owner of another car dealership. GM rejected this sale, alleging that Miller no longer had a franchise to sell because GM had terminated the franchise agreement two months earlier. Miller sued GM for failing to help his franchise obtain floor-plan financing and for rejecting the sale of his franchise to Crowley. How do you think the court ruled in this case? What requirements must GM meet to lawfully terminate a franchise? Did GM meet those requirements? [*Chic Miller's Chevrolet, Inc. v. GMC,* 352 F. Supp. 2d 251 (2005).]

8. Margaret Miller operated an H&R Block tax preparation franchise for 15 years. She hired William Hehlen as an income tax return preparer for five years, from 1997 to 2001. Each year, Miller and Hehlen signed an employment agreement drawn up by H&R Block. The 2001 agreement was between Hehlen and "Margaret Miller, doing business as H&R Block," and included stipulations prohibiting Hehlen from reproducing confidential business information and from soliciting clients away from Miller's business. Hehlen maintained on his home computer a spreadsheet of customer names that he

obtained from Miller. In April 2001, H&R Block terminated its franchise agreement with Miller, and Miller subsequently operated her business as a sole proprietorship under the name "MJM & Associates." Hehlen's employment with Miller ended after the 2001 tax season. In December 2001, Miller sent advertising postcards to clients referring to Hehlen as one of her associates. When Hehlen, who went to work for another H&R Block office, learned of the postcards, he began telephoning the customers whose names he had obtained from Miller. Miller learned of the calls in February 2002 and filed a cease-and-desist action against Hehlen, arguing that Hehlen was violating his employment contract with Miller. Hehlen argued that his employment contract was with Miller's H&R Block franchise, which ceased to exist after April 2001. Do you think Hehlen's employment contract was signed with Miller's franchise or with Miller's sole proprietorship? If you think Hehlen's contract was with Miller's franchise, should Miller have the right to enforce the contract provisions after H&R Block terminated her franchise agreement? Why or why not? [*Miller v. Hehlen,* 104 P.3d 193 (2005).]

9. Tammy Duncan began working as a waitress at a diner owned by her mother Hazel Bynum and stepfather Eddie Bynum. A few weeks later, the three created an agreement in which Tammy was to assume comanager duties for her stepfather. Tammy then began doing paperwork and bookkeeping for the diner in addition to occasionally waiting tables and performing other duties. She testified that she made no agreement to share in the diner's profits and that she understood she was going to take over her stepfather's duties as

manager. The bank account for the diner was still to remain in Eddie Bynum's name and Tammy's parents did not change any business tax information. In the course of her employment, Tammy was injured when she slipped off a ladder and fell onto both knees. The diner's insurer, Cypress, paid Tammy temporary total disability benefits. However, five months later Cypress notified Tammy that it intended to controvert her claim on the basis of alleged newly discovered evidence that she was not an employee of the diner but was a co-owner under the agreement she had made with her mother and stepfather. What are the essential elements of a partnership? Was Tammy Duncan a partner in the diner? Why or why not? [*Cypress Insurance Company v. Duncan,* 281 Ga. App. 469 (2006).]

10. Harvey Pierce was a work-release inmate from the local county jail who worked at an Arby's franchise restaurant owned by Dennis Rasmussen, Inc. (DRI). One day in June 1999, Pierce walked off the job without permission and crossed the street to wait for his former girlfriend, Robin Kerl, and her fiancé, David Jones, in the parking lot of the Walmart store where both Kerl and Jones worked. When Kerl and Jones exited the store, Pierce shot both of them in the head, killing Jones and seriously injuring and permanently disabling Kerl. Pierce then shot himself and died immediately. Kerl and Jones's estate sued Arby's and DRI for negligent supervision, hiring, and retention, arguing that Arby's, the franchisor, was vicariously liable for the negligence of DRI, the franchisee. Do you think Arby's should be vicariously liable for the negligence of its franchisee? Why or why not? [*Kerl v. DRI and Arby's, Inc.,* 682 N.W.2d 328 (2004).]

Looking for more review material?

The Online Learning Center at **www.mhhe.com/kubasek2e** contains this chapter's "Assignment on the Internet" and also a list of URLs for more information, entitled "On the Internet." Find both of them in the Student Center portion of the OLC, along with quizzes and other helpful materials.

Partnerships: Nature, Formation, and Operation

LEARNING OBJECTIVES

After reading this chapter, you will be able to answer the following questions:

1   What is a partnership?

2   What are the different ways in which a partnership can be formed?

3   What are the rights of partners as they interact with each other?

4   Are all members of a partnership liable for interactions with third parties?

CASE OPENER
Jax Restaurant Partnership

One afternoon in October 2000 Nicole Moren completed her day shift at Jax Restaurant at 4 p.m. and left to pick up her two-year-old son from day care. Moren was a partner in the restaurant. At about 5:30, Moren returned to the restaurant with her son after learning that her sister and partner, Amy Benedetti, needed help. Moren then called her husband to pick up their child. Because Moren did not want her son running around the restaurant, she brought him into the kitchen with her and put him on top of the counter until his ride arrived. While she was making pizzas, her son reached his hand into the dough-pressing machine. Unfortunately, his hand was crushed, resulting in permanent damages.

As a result of his son's debilitating accident, the child's father commenced a negligence action against the partnership. Therefore, the partnership served a third-party complaint on Nicole Moren, arguing that if the restaurant was obligated to compensate her son, the partnership was entitled to indemnity (reimbursement) from Moren for her own negligence. In other words, the partnership argued that it should not be held financially liable for the damages because the accident was Moren's own fault since she let her son enter the kitchen and play near the dough press.

1. Is the partnership as a whole liable even though it was primarily Moren's negligence that caused her son's injury?
2. What could Jax Restaurant have done to avoid this suit?

The Wrap-Up at the end of the chapter will answer these questions.

In the Jax Restaurant case, the court had to consider the laws of partnership in determining whether to find the partnership as a whole liable. The Uniform Partnership Act (UPA) is the main statute governing partnership law. If there is no express partnership agreement, UPA establishes the rules for the partnership.

This chapter discusses the creation and operation of the partnership, and the following chapter considers how partnerships are terminated as well as special types of partnerships. The first section of this chapter considers the nature of the partnership relationship, how partnerships are created, and how they function.

Nature of the Partnership

LO1

What is a partnership?

What exactly is a partnership? According to UPA Section 6, a **partnership** is "an association of two or more persons to carry on as co-owners a business for profit." Let's analyze all four parts of this definition to understand their implications. (See Exhibit 36-1.)

First, by "association," UPA means that the partnership is a voluntary and consensual relationship. No one can force someone else to enter into a partnership with him or her. Second, a partnership requires "two or more persons." UPA defines *persons* as "individuals, partnerships, corporations, and other associations." Therefore, almost any individual or group of people could serve as a partner, but these persons must have the legal capacity to be partners. Although minors can serve as partners, the resulting partnership agreement is voidable.

Third, in a partnership, the partners must operate the business for a profit. This criterion is interpreted to mean that the partners must intend to make some kind of profit from the business.

Finally, the partners must serve as co-owners. Being co-owners means that they must share its profits or losses as well as share in the management of the business.

Exhibit 36-1

Characteristics of a Partnership

A partnership is:	
An association	It is a consensual and voluntary relationship, meaning that no one was forced into the partnership.
Between two or more legal persons	It consists of two or more individuals, partnerships, corporations, or other forms of business organization.
To carry on a business for profit	Its purpose is to make several business transactions for the trade, occupation, or profession with the intention of making a profit from the business.
As co-owners	The partners share in the management and profits of the business. No party can receive a share of the profit for the purpose of payment of debt, interest, or annuity or from the sale of property.

The fourth element of the definition is that the partnership be "for profit,"
To summarize, a partnership has the following characteristics:

- *Voluntary* and *consensual* relationship.
- Between two or more *individuals, partnerships, corporations,* or other forms of business organization.
- Who engage in *numerous business transactions* over a period of time.
- Intending *to make a profit.*
- And *sharing* the *profits* and *management* of the business.

Courts look for these factors when parties dispute whether a partnership exists.

Probably the most important factor in determining whether a partnership exists is whether the profits from the business are shared. UPA has established several exceptions in which a sharing of profits does not constitute a partnership. For example, when an employer shares profits with an employee as payment for work, or when a landlord accepts shares of profits for payment of rent, there is no partnership. If a party receives a share of profits for any of the following reasons, there is no partnership:

- Payment of a debt.
- Payment of an annuity to a widow or representative of a deceased partner.
- Payment from the sale of goodwill of a business or some other property.
- Payment of interest on a loan.

> To see a description of considerations a business manager ought to have regarding whether a partnership will result in synergy, please see the **Connecting to the Core** activity on the text Web site at www.mhhe.com/kubasek2e.

Legal Principle: **Perhaps the most important factor in determining whether a partnership exists is whether the profits are shared. Furthermore, this sharing of profits must not meet one of the UPA exceptions.**

Case 36-1 illustrates the court's analysis of whether a partnership relationship indeed exists.

CASE 36-1

INGRAM v. DEERE
SUPREME COURT OF TEXAS
52 TEX. SUP. J. 1030 (2009)

Jesse Ingram, a licensed psychologist, and Louis Deere, a board certified psychiatrist, entered into an oral agreement providing that Dr. Deere would serve as the medical director for a multidisciplinary pain clinic. Dr. Deere contends that they agreed he would receive one-third of the clinic's revenues, Dr. Ingram would receive one-third, and the remaining one-third would be used to pay the clinic's expenses. Dr. Deere also claims that when he and Ingram began working together, Ingram told him their work "was a joint venture, or [they] were partners, or [they] were doing this together."

Fourteen months after Dr. Deere began working at the clinic, Dr. Ingram prepared a written agreement to memorialize their arrangement. The document stated Dr. Ingram was the "sole owner" of the clinic. Subsequently, Dr. Deere

refused to sign the document, claiming that it contradicted their initial arrangement. Immediately after Deere received the document, he ceased working at the clinic and later sued Ingram, asserting claims of common law fraud, statutory fraud, fraudulent inducement, breach of contract, and breach of fiduciary duty. The appellate court supported the jury's finding that a partnership existed between Dr. Deere and Dr. Ingram. Subsequently, the Supreme Court of Texas must determine whether Dr. Deere and Dr. Ingram indeed created a partnership for their pain clinic.

JUDGE WAINWRIGHT: The Texas Uniform Partnership Act (TUPA) was passed in 1961 and substantially adopted the major provisions of the Uniform Partnership

Act (UPA), which itself was adopted in every state except Louisiana after it was approved by the National Conference of Commissioners on Uniform State Laws in 1914. TUPA was replaced by The Revised Partnership Act (TRPA), effective January 1, 1994, the result of a project of the Partnership Law Committee of the State Bar of Texas Section on Business Law and the Texas Business Law Foundation Act of May 31, 1993. TRPA carried forward some of the common law modifications in ways relevant to this case that were promulgated in TUPA. The partnership in this case was allegedly formed in 1997. It is uncontested that TRPA governs this dispute; rather, the parties contest whether Deere has proven the existence of a partnership under TRPA.

TRPA provides that "an association of two or more persons to carry on a business for profit as owners creates a partnership." Unlike TUPA, TRPA articulates five factors, similar to the common law factors, that indicate the creation of a partnership. They are:

(1) receipt or right to receive a share of profits of the business;
(2) expression of an intent to be partners in the business;
(3) participation or right to participate in control of the business;
(4) sharing or agreeing to share:

  (A) losses of the business; or
  (B) liability for claims by third parties against the business; and

(5) contributing or agreeing to contribute money or property to the business.

The common law required proof of all five factors to establish the existence of a partnership. TRPA contemplates a less formalistic and more practical approach to recognizing the formation of a partnership.

First, TRPA does not require direct proof of the parties' intent to form a partnership. Formerly, the intent to be partners was a "prime," although not controlling, element in the creation of a partnership. Instead, TRPA lists the "expression of intent" to form a partnership as a factor to consider. Second, unlike the common law, TRPA does not require proof of *all* of the listed factors in order for a partnership to exist. Third, sharing of profits—deemed essential for establishing a partnership under the common law—is treated differently under TRPA because sharing of profits is not required. Still, TRPA comments note that the traditional import of sharing profits as well as control over the business will probably continue to be the most important factors.

Profit Sharing

Deere argues that he received or had the right to receive a share of the clinic's profits because he and Ingram had an agreement in which each of them would receive one-third of the clinic's "gross revenue" and the remainder would be used for expenses. It is true that the "receipt or right to receive a share of profits of the business" may be indicative of the existence of a partnership under TRPA, but a share of profits paid as "wages or other compensation to an employee or independent contractor" is not indicative of a partnership interest in the business. The evidence does not establish that Deere received a share of profits as contemplated under TRPA . . . [because] the agreement between Ingram and Deere cannot constitute Deere's receipt of "profits," but rather of gross revenue.

Second, Ingram wrote twenty checks to Deere as compensation from January 1997 until March 1999. These checks referred to Deere as a "medical consultant" and the payments as "contract labor." Therefore, they contradict his argument that he received profits as a partner in the clinic.

Expression of Intent to be Partners

"[E]xpression of an intent to be partners in the business" is one of five factors courts use in determining whether a partnership exists. This is different from the common law definition of a partnership that required proof that the parties intended to form a partnership at the outset of their agreement. When analyzing expression of intent under TRPA, courts should review the putative partners' speech, writings, and conduct. Evidence of expressions of intent could include, for example, the parties' statements that they are partners, one party holding the other party out as a partner on the business's letterhead or name plate, or in a signed partnership agreement.

Deere argues that he expressed his intent to be a partner with Ingram by sharing the clinic's profits and losses and having access to the clinic's records. His evidence of other factors, sharing of profits and losses and control of the business, is insufficient to establish expression of intent. Deere's evidence is also insufficient because there must be evidence that both parties expressed their intent to be partners.

Deere also testified that the clinic kept its established name after he joined as the medical director, and he and Ingram never discussed a name change. He never signed a lease agreement for the building owned by Ingram where the clinic was housed, was not named on the clinic's bank account, never signed a signature card for the clinic's bank account, and never filed taxes representing that he was co-owner of the clinic. Additionally, Deere paid his own medical malpractice insurance, which he acknowledged was his common practice when he did contract work. Deere cannot provide the content, context, or circumstances to give any of the alleged expressions of intent legal significance as evidence of a partnership.

Control

Deere argues he had an equal right to control and manage the clinic's business because, although he was never allowed to see the books and records, he repeatedly requested to see them. He also points to Ingram's testimony that "maybe" Deere viewed the clinic's books on one occasion. Furthermore, Deere argues that he had control because Ingram discussed with him how much the clinic made, the amounts paid to the staff, and the need to hire Ingram's wife as personnel director. No other evidence supports these statements and proves he participated in or had the right to control the clinic's business.

Sharing of Losses and Liability for Third Party Claims

According to Deere, he and Ingram agreed that Deere would receive one-third of the clinic's gross revenue, Ingram would receive one-third of the clinic's gross revenue, and the remainder would be used to pay clinic expenses. Deere argues that this agreement determined how losses would be shared, but he testified that there was never a discussion of how expenses in excess of one-third of the clinic's gross revenue would be divided between him and Ingram. Here, Ingram and Deere never discussed what would happen to the allocation if expenses exceeded one-third of the revenue or gross income. They never discussed losses, only expenses. There is no legally cognizable evidence to support the contention that Ingram and Deere agreed to share losses.

Contribution of Money or Property

Finally, there is no evidence that Deere "contribut[ed] or agree[d] to contribute money or property" to the clinic as a partner. Deere does not argue that there was any *agreement* that he contribute either money or property to the enterprise. Furthermore, Deere does not contend that he actually contributed money to the clinic. In fact, Deere acknowledged at trial that he did not contribute to clinic renovations or the purchase of medical equipment and supplies and that he did not agree to use his personal resources to pay for any expenses in the operation of the clinic. Rather, Deere's only argument regarding this factor is that he contributed his reputation as property to the alleged partnership.

In this case, Deere has not provided legally sufficient evidence of any of the five TRPA factors to prove the existence of a partnership. Accordingly, we reverse the court of appeals' judgment.

REVERSED.

CRITICAL THINKING

What evidence led the court to determine that the two doctors were not partners? Do you think any evidence hints at suggesting the two men could have formed a partnership?

ETHICAL DECISION MAKING

Suppose for a moment that the court did believe a partnership existed. Perhaps Ingram was objecting to the partnership because he did not want to give Deere as large a portion of the revenue or profits. Notice that business ethics requires that we think beyond ourselves. Use the universalization test to explain why one should not attempt to avoid partnership responsibilities.

In situations where there are no articles of partnership, the courts may look at other documentation to determine whether a partnership existed. Informal documentation, such as e-mails, notes, and memos, may be used to identify the existence of a partnership and/or the terms of a partnership. For example, before actress Vanessa Hudgens became famous through her recurring role in the *High School Musical* movie series, she worked with business manager Johnny Vieira. During their time together, Vieira claimed that he and Hudgens agreed to work together to launch her career and also agreed to share in the profits of her success equally. However, once Hudgens became a teen star, Vieira claims that she stopped working with him and failed to pay him his portion of the profits. Consequently, Vieira filed a lawsuit against Hudgens, asking for $5 million in punitive damages. In his lawsuit, Vieira noted a signed photograph on which Hudgens wrote "Johnny, thank you for everything, without you, I would be no where, we will make it

Forms of Partnerships in the ICT Sector in Developing Countries

In the information and communication technology (ICT) sector of developing countries, businesses use partnerships between local and multinational companies to create a support structure. Three forms of partnership are especially important: (1) industrial districts, (2) *keiretsu* (a group of businesses in which each individual business has a stake in the others), and (3) offshore partnerships.

Industrial districts are loosely structured collectives of small to medium-size firms located in a specific area and highly specialized in one or more phases of a production process. Industrial districts are coordinated through both personal relationships and marketlike mechanisms. One purpose is to pool local competencies.

Keiretsus bring foreign ICT companies into a partnership and act as "hubs" served by local ICT ventures. *Keiretsus* add the strength of a competent hub, but over time this strength could make it less likely that local firms will develop strength of their own.

Offshore partnerships combine the strengths of outside firms with those of firms in developing countries. The developing-country firms use offshore partnerships to gain international exposure and technological competence. Foreign companies, such as U.S. and European Union (EU) firms, use offshore partnerships to gain (1) access to competent, low-cost workers and (2) the opportunity to enter developing markets.

BIG—Vanessa Hudgens."[1] The case was set to go to trial; however, two weeks before trial, Hudgens and Vieira reached a settlement outside court.

Now that you know how the courts determine whether a partnership exists, what kind of legal status do partnerships have? They can be either legal entities or aggregates of the partners.

PARTNERSHIP AS A LEGAL ENTITY

In some respects, a partnership is treated as a *legal entity,* a "person" separate from the partnership with a life of its own.

First, a partnership is often considered a legal entity when it is sued or being sued. States determine when the partnership can or cannot be named in the suit. Second, under the doctrine of marshaling assets, partnership assets are arranged in a certain order to pay any outstanding debts. Partnership creditors have first priority on partnership assets, while individual personal creditors have first priority on the assets of the individual partners. Thus, partnership assets are kept separate from the individual partner assets.

Third, the partnership may hold title to property that individual partners do not hold. If the partners want to sell partnership property, all must participate in the transaction. Finally, every partner is considered an agent of the partnership, and each has a fiduciary relationship with the others.

PARTNERSHIP AS A LEGAL AGGREGATE

Sometimes a partnership is considered a legal aggregate of the partners, such as when partnership debts eventually become the debts of the individual partners. Further, the partnership is not taxed as a separate being; instead, the partners pay taxes on the income generated through the partnership. Finally, because the partnership ceases to exist when one of the partners dies (unless otherwise established by the partnership agreement), the partnership is then considered an aggregate of the individual partners.

LO2

What are the different ways in which a partnership can be formed?

Formation of the Partnership

While an explicit written agreement is not required to create a partnership, partners are advised to create one to ensure that the terms of the partnership will be upheld. Suppose that

[1] www.people.com/people/article/0,20218606,00.html.

you and your partner orally agree you will receive three-fourths of the profits because you are doing significantly more management tasks. However, when you distribute the funds, your partner sues you because you give him only one-fourth of the profits. Without a written partnership agreement, the courts will have a difficult time ruling in your favor.

A written agreement that creates a partnership is called the **articles of partnership.** What kind of information do the articles usually include? First, the partners' names, as well as the name of the partnership, should be listed. Second, the agreement should address the duration of the partnership, such as the date or event that signals the agreement's expiration, or it should make the partnership's term indefinite. Third, the agreement should state the division of profits as well as losses. Fourth, it should establish the division of management duties. Fifth, the agreement should state exactly what capital contributions each partner will make.

Legal Principle: A written agreement, although not legally mandatory, should be created when a partnership begins. This way, both parties can be protected if a dispute occurs or if an issue is brought to court.

PARTNERSHIP BY ESTOPPEL

Parties not named in partnership agreements can sometimes be partners. How? Suppose you create a partnership agreement with your best friend. You then tell your first potential customer that your parents are also partners in the business. On the basis of your parents' participation, she decides to place an order with you. Your parents discover that you have reported they are your partners, but they do not contact the customer to tell her they are not partners. When your business cannot afford to purchase the goods to sell them to the customer, the customer sues you and your parents. Because your parents were aware of the misrepresentation but did not correct it, they will be estopped from denying they are your partners. While they will not be able to claim the rights associated with being a partner (such as sharing the profits), in many states they could be held liable for damages to the customer.

Most states recognize two situations in which a partnership by estoppel exists: (1) as in the example above, when a third party is aware of and consents to a misrepresentation of partnership, and (2) when a nonpartner has represented himself or herself as a partner and a third party *reasonably relies* on this information to his or her detriment. The nonpartner can be held liable for the third party's damages.

Exhibit 36-2 summarizes how a partnership can be created.

Exhibit 36-2
Formation of a Partnership

A partnership can be formed by:	
Articles of partnership	A partnership is formed by a written agreement that states the partners' names, the name of the partnership, the duration of the partnership, the division of profits and losses, the division of management duties, and the capital contributions that will be made by each partner
Estoppel	If a third party is aware of and consents to a misrepresentation of partnership, a partnership can be formed. Or if a nonpartner acts as a partner and a third party reasonably relies on this information, the nonpartner can be considered a partner and thus be liable for the third party's damages.

Interactions between Partners

LO3

What are the rights of partners as they interact with each other?

The operation of the partnership encompasses two types of interactions: those between the partners and those between the partnership and third parties. The partners have certain rights and duties within each type.

DUTIES OF PARTNERS TO ONE ANOTHER

Most partners' duties to one another include the duty to be loyal. The duty to be loyal functions as an example of the fiduciary duty. Furthermore, most partners' duties include the duty of obedience. The duty of obedience is an example of the duty of care.

Perhaps the most important type of duty partners have toward one another is the fiduciary duty. Partners must, in good faith, work for the benefit of the partnership. They should not take any action that will undermine it, such as engaging in business that competes with it.

Partners must disclose any material facts affecting the business. A partner who derives benefit from the partnership without the consent of the other partners must notify them of this benefit. Case 36-2 considers how a partner's fiduciary duty conflicts with a partner's belief that another partner is behaving unethically.

CASE 36-2   COLETTE BOHATCH v. BUTLER & BINION
SUPREME COURT OF TEXAS
977 S.W.2D 543 (1998)

Colette Bohatch became an associate in the Washington, D.C., office of Butler & Binion in 1986. John McDonald and Richard Powers, both partners, were the only other attorneys in the office. After Bohatch was made a partner in February 1990, she became concerned that McDonald was overbilling Pennzoil, the office's main client. Bohatch met with the law firm's managing partner, Louis Paine, to report her concern. In July 1990, McDonald met with Bohatch to report that Pennzoil was dissatisfied with her work.

The next day, Bohatch spoke to Paine, as well as two other members of the law firm's management committee. Paine led an investigation of Bohatch's complaint and discussed the billed hours with the in-house counsel at Pennzoil, who concluded the bills were reasonable. In August 1990, Paine met with Bohatch, telling her that there was no basis for her claims against McDonald and that she should look for work elsewhere. The firm refused Bohatch a year-end partnership distribution for 1990. Finally, in August 1991, Bohatch was given until November to vacate her office. She filed suit in October 1991, and the firm voted to expel her from the partnership three days later.

At trial, the jury ruled the firm breached the partnership agreement and its fiduciary duty and awarded Bohatch

$57,000 for past lost wages, $250,000 for past mental anguish, $4,000,000 total in punitive damages (this amount was apportioned against several defendants), and attorney's fees. Later, the trial court reduced the punitive damages to around $237,000. The court of appeals ruled the firm's only duty to Bohatch was not to expel her in bad faith. When it found no evidence the firm had fired Bohatch for its own gain, the appeals court ruled Bohatch could not recover for breach of fiduciary duty. The case was appealed to the Supreme Court of Texas.

JUDGE ENOCH: We have long recognized as a matter of common law that "the relationship between . . . partners . . . is fiduciary in character, and imposes upon all the participants the obligation of loyalty to the joint concern and of the utmost good faith, fairness, and honesty in their dealings with each other with respect to matters pertaining to the enterprise." Yet, partners have no obligation to remain partners; "at the heart of the partnership concept is the principle that partners may choose with whom they wish to be associated." The issue presented, one of first impression, is whether the fiduciary relationship between and among partners creates an exception to the at-will nature of partnerships; that is, in this case, whether it gives rise to a duty not to expel a partner who reports suspected overbilling by another partner.

While Bohatch's claim that she was expelled in an improper way is governed by the partnership agreement, her claim that she was expelled for an improper reason is not. Therefore, we look to the common law to find the principles governing Bohatch's claim that the firm breached a duty when it expelled her.

Courts in other states have held that a partnership may expel a partner for purely business reasons. Further, courts recognize that a law firm can expel a partner to protect relationships both within the firm and with clients. Finally, many courts have held that a partnership can expel a partner without breaching any duty in order to resolve a "fundamental schism."

The fiduciary duty that partners owe one another does not encompass a duty to remain partners or else answer in tort damages. Nonetheless, Bohatch and several distinguished legal scholars urge this Court to recognize that public policy requires a limited duty to remain partners—i.e., a partnership must retain a whistleblower partner. They argue that such an extension of a partner's fiduciary duty is necessary because permitting a law firm to retaliate against a partner who in good faith reports suspected overbilling would discourage compliance with rules of professional conduct and thereby hurt clients.

While this argument is not without some force, we must reject it. A partnership exists solely because the partners choose to place personal confidence and trust in one another. Just as a partner can be expelled, without a breach of any common law duty, over disagreements about firm policy or to resolve some other "fundamental schism," a partner

can be expelled for accusing another partner of overbilling without subjecting the partnership to tort damages. Such charges, whether true or not, may have a profound effect on the personal confidence and trust essential to the partner relationship. Once such charges are made, partners may find it impossible to continue to work together to their mutual benefit and the benefit of their clients.

We are sensitive to the concern expressed by the dissenting Justices that "retaliation against a partner who tries in good faith to correct or report perceived misconduct virtually assures that others will not take these appropriate steps in the future." However, the dissenting Justices do not explain how the trust relationship necessary both for the firm's existence and for representing clients can survive such serious accusations by one partner against another. The threat of tort liability for expulsion would tend to force partners to remain in untenable circumstance—suspicious of and angry with each other—to their own detriment and that of their clients whose matters are neglected by lawyers distracted with intra-firm frictions.

We emphasize that our refusal to create an exception to the at-will nature of partnerships in no way obviates the ethical duties of lawyers. Such duties sometimes necessitate difficult decisions, as when a lawyer suspects overbilling by a colleague. The fact that the ethical duty to report may create an irreparable schism between partners neither excuses failure to report nor transforms expulsion as a means of resolving that schism into a tort.

We hold that the firm did not owe Bohatch a duty not to expel her for reporting suspected overbilling by another partner.

AFFIRMED.

CRITICAL THINKING

Think about the judge's reasoning that led to the conclusion that the firm did not owe Bohatch a duty not to expel her for reporting suspected overbilling. Is there any additional information you would have liked to know to determine whether the firm should have been allowed to dismiss Bohatch?

ETHICAL DECISION MAKING

Bohatch made a decision about ethics when she chose to report what she suspected to be overbilling by a colleague. Do you think she made a good ethical decision? Would you guess she was guided by the Golden Rule, deontology, the universalization test, or some other method of ethical reasoning?

The second type of duty the partners have is a duty of care to the other partners. Each partner must perform her management functions to the best of her abilities. A partner who makes an honest mistake in fulfilling responsibilities to the partnership will not be held liable for the mistake.

Exhibit 36-3 summarizes the primary duties of partners to one another.

Exhibit 36-3

Duties of Partners
to One Another

Fiduciary duty	The partners must work for the benefit of the partnership and not engage in any action or business that could undermine or compete with the partnership. The duty of obedience is an example of a fiduciary duty. The partners must obey the partnership agreement; if they disobey the agreement, they can be held liable for any losses.
Duty of care	The partners must perform their management functions to the best of their abilities.

RIGHTS OF THE PARTNERS IN THEIR INTERACTIONS WITH OTHER PARTNERS

According to the law, partners have certain rights regarding their interactions with other partners.

Right to Share in Management.   Unless otherwise stated in the partnership agreement, all partners have a right to participate equally in the management of the partnership. Even if one partner has an unusually large proportion of the management duties, each partner will have one vote in determining how the partnership is managed.

While most decisions are made by majority vote, some require agreement by all partners. If the partners are voting on whether to change some element of their partnership agreement, they all must agree with the change. Other decisions that require a unanimous vote include the admission of new partners and alterations in the nature of the business.

Right to Share in Profits.   If the partnership agreement does not establish another division of profits, all partners share equally in both profits and losses.

Right to Compensation.   Unless otherwise agreed, no partner will receive a salary for participation in the business regardless of the amount of time and effort put in. Of course, the partners may agree to create salaries for certain partners, but no partner enters the partnership relationship with a right to compensation for performing business activities. If a partner dies during the term of the partnership, however, the surviving partners are entitled to compensation for services in closing the partnership's business affairs.

Property Rights.   Partners have three property rights: (1) the right to participate in the management of the business, (2) the right to specific partnership property, and (3) the right to their partnership interest. (See Exhibit 36-4.) We've discussed the first right above; here we discuss the other two.

First, partners own the partnership property as *tenants in property*, which means they own it as a group. Any property brought into or acquired by the partnership is considered property of the partnership. Property in the name of an individual partner but purchased with partnership funds will be considered partnership property.

One way to determine whether specific property is a partnership asset is to determine the relationship of the asset to the partnership. If the asset is closely related to the business of the partnership, it will likely be considered a partnership asset.

Each partner has the right to possess partnership property. However, a partner cannot use this property to pay a personal debt. Similarly, the partner cannot sell or use the property if the purpose is outside the partnership interest.

Exhibit 36-4
A Partner's Property
Rights

Right to participate in the management of the business	All partners have a right to participate equally in the management of the partnership.
Right to specific partnership property	Partners own the partnership property as a group, and any property that is acquired by the partnership is considered property of the partnership. They have a right to this property but cannot use it to pay a personal debt and cannot sell or use the property if the purpose is outside the partnership interest. If a partner dies, the surviving partners receive the rights to the specific partnership property.
Right to partnership interest	Each partner has a right to the interest of the partner's share of the profits and a return on capital contributed by the partner. If a partner dies, the interest earned by the deceased partner is added to his or her estate and is not given back to the partnership.

What happens to the partnership property if a partner dies? According to the **right of survivorship,** the rights in specific partnership property pass to the surviving partners. However, the surviving partners must account to the deceased partner's estate for the value of that partner's interest in the specific property.

Second, a partner has a right to interest in the partnership. This interest, composed of a combination of the partner's share of the profits and a return of capital contributed by the partner, is part of the partner's personal property. If necessary, a partner can sell his interest in the partnership to a creditor. A partner's personal creditor cannot seize specific items of partnership property; however, the creditor can obtain a **charging order,** which entitles the creditor to the partner's profits while the partner continues to act as a partner and engage in the partnership business.

Right to Inspect Books.   Each partner has the right to receive full information regarding partnership matters. This right corresponds to the partners' fiduciary duty to disclose any information affecting the partnership. Thus, partners must have access to all partnership books and records and be allowed to make copies of them. Unless otherwise agreed, the records must be kept at the principal business office.

Right to an Account.   An **accounting** is a review and listing of all partnership assets and/or profit and typically lists the distribution of assets and profit to the partners. Each partner has a right to an accounting in four circumstances:

- Whenever the partnership agreement provides for an accounting.
- Whenever the copartners wrongfully exclude a partner from the partnership or from access to the books.
- Whenever any partner fails to disclose a profit or benefit from the partnership, thus breaching his or her fiduciary duty.
- Whenever circumstances render an accounting "just and reasonable."

Legal Principle: Unless otherwise stated in the partnership agreement, a partner's rights include the right to share in management, the right to share in profits, the right to compensation, property rights, the right to inspect books, and the right to an account.

Interactions between Partners and Third Parties

L04

Are all members of a partnership liable for interactions with third parties?

Each partner can serve as an agent for the other partners as well as for the partnership. As long as the partner has authority to act, each partner's act in performing business duties as well as making agreements with third parties is binding for the partnership. If the partner has authority to act and the partnership is bound by the act, each partner has unlimited personal liability for the obligation.

ACTUAL AUTHORITY OF THE PARTNERS

According to UPA, general agency principles establish that partners have the authority to bind a partnership in an agreement. If a partner, following normal business procedures, binds the partnership to an agreement, both the partner and the partnership are liable for the obligation in the agreement.

Suppose Brittany is a partner in a firm. While allegedly carrying on partnership business, she engages in a business transaction and binds the partnership to the agreement. Yet suppose Brittany really didn't have authority to bind the partnership to the agreement with the third party. In this case, both Brittany and the firm are liable for the obligation. However, if the third party was aware that Brittany did not have the authority to bind the partnership to the agreement, Brittany will be held liable for the obligation but the partnership will not.

IMPLIED AUTHORITY OF THE PARTNERS

Because of the nature of the partnership, partners generally have greater implied authority than do typical agents. Their implied authority is usually determined by the nature of the business, and it permits partners to enter into agreements necessary to carry on partnership business. Thus, a partner has the authority to purchase goods necessary to perpetuate the business. However, a partner does not have implied authority to sell any property without the consent of all other partners.

LIABILITY TO THIRD PARTIES

According to UPA, if a partnership is liable, each partner has unlimited personal liability. That is, all partners are **jointly liable** for the partnership's debts. To bring a claim, a party must either name all partners as defendants or simply name the partnership. If the claim is successful, each partner is liable for the judgment. If one partner pays the entire judgment, the other partners must indemnify, or reimburse, him or her. In the Case Opener, the partners in Jax Restaurant were concerned about their joint liability for the accident that occurred in their dough press. The partners argued that they should not be held jointly liable because it was the negligence of one partner that caused her own son's injury. They argued that if they were liable, Moren should have to indemnify the other partners as a result of her negligent behavior. Do you think the court made all the partners pay the damages?

When a partner commits a tort or a breach of trust, all partners are jointly and severally liable. In fact, all partners are jointly and severally liable for the entire amount of any judgment rendered. **Joint and several liability** means that a third party can choose to sue the partners separately or all partners jointly in one action. Suppose William sues your partnership, which has four partners. William might name one of the partners in the first action. If the partner is found liable, William can sue all three other partners separately. However, if in the first claim the court ruled that the partnership was not liable in any form, William cannot bring a successful claim against a second partner on the issue of the partner's liability.

If William brings a successful claim against a partner, he can collect the judgment only on the assets of one partner. The partner is required to reimburse the partnership for the damages it pays to William. Case 36-3 considers how other partners can be held liable for the negligence of one partner.

CASE 36-3   ERIC JOHNSON & LORI JOHNSON v. ST. THERESE MEDICAL CENTER
APPELLATE COURT OF ILLINOIS, SECOND DISTRICT
296 ILL. APP. 3D 341; 694 N.E.2D 1088; 1998 ILL. APP. LEXIS 301

In November 1990, Eric and Lori Johnson brought their 22-month-old daughter, Erica, to St. Therese Medical Center, where she was treated and released by Dr. Bruce Sands. Dr. Sands was a partner of Northern Illinois Emergency Physicians, Ltd. Drs. Richard Keller, Michael Oster, Thomas Braniff, Rodney Haenschen, and Phillip Gillespie were the other partners. The Johnsons filed suit against Dr. Sands and the partnership, arguing that Dr. Sands negligently caused the death of Erica and the partnership was liable because St. Therese acted on its behalf. A jury gave the Johnsons a $4 million award against Dr. Sands, St. Therese, and the partnership. Dr. Sands later filed for bankruptcy.

All the partners were issued citations to discover the assets of the partnership. At the citation hearings, all the partners (except Gillespie) admitted they were partners in the partnership at the time of the Johnson incident. In February 1997, the trial court judge ruled the Johnsons could proceed against the general partners individually if they were partners at the time of the incident. Consequently, the plaintiffs started motions to withhold the wages of all partners. Court proceedings ensued in which various partners argued they should not be held personally liable. Several were sentenced to jail time because they refused to testify regarding their personal assets. In June 1997, the trial court ruled that the assets of Keller, Haenschen, and Braniff be turned over to the Johnsons.

JUSTICE MCLAREN: We acknowledge that all partners are jointly and severally liable for everything chargeable to the partnership for the loss or injury of a third person due to any wrongful act or omission of any partner acting in the ordinary course of the business of the partnership. Further, "an unsatisfied judgment against a partnership in its firm name does not bar an action to enforce the individual liability of any partner." However, "[a] judgment entered against a partnership in its firm name is enforceable only

against property of the partnership and does not constitute a lien upon real estate other than that held in the firm name." Therefore, where judgment is entered against a partnership, but not against the individual partners, the judgment may not be satisfied by the personal assets of the individual partners.

For example, in Cook, the Department of Revenue issued a notice of tax liability to a partnership. The Department of Revenue was unable to enforce the tax liability against the partnership because the Partnership had previously filed for bankruptcy. Therefore, the Department of Revenue attempted to enforce the partnership's tax liability against the plaintiff, a general partner. The partner received a copy and was aware of the contents of the notice of tax liability issued to the partnership. However, the Department of Revenue did not issue a notice of tax liability or a final assessment to the partner in his individual capacity. Thus, the trial court granted the partner's motion for summary judgment.

This court affirmed, stating that, because a partnership can own property, it is a separate entity from its partners. Because the Department of Revenue issued notice of tax liability and the final assessment to the partnership, and not to the partner individually, and, because the Department of Revenue did not join the partner, the partner did not have notice that he could be liable personally for the partnership's tax debt. Thus, this court reasoned that the partner was denied due process.

The case at bar is closely analogous to Cook. The plaintiffs in the instant case named the Partnership, but not the individual Partners, in their complaint. The plaintiffs served the Partnership, but not the individual Partners. In addition, the Partners in this case, just like the partner in Cook, were aware of the contents of the plaintiffs' complaint against the Partnership. However, because the Partners were not named defendants and were not served in their individual capacities, they were not put on notice that their personal assets were at risk. Further, the plaintiffs in this case are unable to collect from Sands because he has filed for bankruptcy protection. Finally, judgment was entered against the Partnership, but not the individual Partners. Thus, the Partners were not judgment debtors and were not subject to citations proceedings to the extent that the plaintiffs had any claim upon the Partners' individual assets. Accordingly, the trial court erred when it attempted to enforce the judgment against the Partners by ordering the turnover of the Partners' assets and holding the Partners in contempt.

The plaintiffs argue that the Partners are judgment debtors because the partnership name is on the judgment order. However, the plaintiffs fail to recognize that "[a] judgment entered against a partnership in its firm name is enforceable only against property of the partnership." Because nothing in the record indicates that the Partners held assets which belonged to the Partnership, their argument fails.

Next, the plaintiffs argue that the Partners are judgment debtors because they are jointly and severally liable for the debts of the Partnership. We do not dispute this statement. However, the plaintiffs ignore the fact that judgment was entered against the Partnership, and not the Partners as individuals. Thus, until a judgment is entered against the Partners individually, the plaintiffs cannot recover from the Partners' personal assets.

The plaintiffs also argue that section 2-411(b) of the Code of Civil Procedure permits the enforcement of liability in supplementary proceedings against an individual partner.

Section 2-411(b) provides, "An unsatisfied judgment against a partnership in its firm name does not bar an action to enforce the individual liability of any partner." Although "action" is not defined, the plaintiffs assert that a supplementary proceeding to collect a judgment is an "action" within the meaning of section 5/2-411(b). We disagree.

Section 12-102 of the Code of Civil Procedure provides that "[a] judgment entered against a partnership in its firm name is enforceable only against property of the partnership and does not constitute a lien upon real estate other than that held in the firm name." Under the plaintiffs' interpretation of section 2-411(b), this section has no meaning. Under the plaintiffs' interpretation, a judgment against only a partnership is enforceable against the partners individually without a judgment being entered against the partners individually. Because the plaintiffs' interpretation of section 2-411(b) renders section 12-102 ineffective, it cannot be adopted by this court.

Next, the plaintiffs assert that "a judgment against a partnership, by definition, is a judgment against each partner." However, this court's decision in Cook clearly contradicts the plaintiffs' position. In Cook, we held that, although partners are liable for the debts of the partnership, to be able to collect from the partners the plaintiff must provide the partners with notice that they will be individually liable for the partnership's debt. Since the plaintiffs failed to provide such notice, their argument fails.

REVERSED.

CRITICAL THINKING

Part of the confusion in this case was based on the ambiguity in Section 2-411(b) of the Code of Civil Procedure. Can you identify the ambiguity and explain how different interpretations of the code lead to different conclusions?

ETHICAL DECISION MAKING

Suppose you were one of the partners in this case. If you were guided by duty ethics, would any of the details of the case be altered?

Legal Principle: **As a general rule, if the partnership is liable, all partners are liable for the debts of the partnership. Furthermore, all partners are liable for a tort or breach of trust committed by a single partner.**

LIABILITY OF INCOMING PARTNERS

When a partnership adds another partner, the new partner assumes limited liability for any obligations that occurred before he or she was added. The new partner cannot be held personally liable for them, but the capital the new partner adds can be used to pay them off. Clearly, because an incoming partner assumes limited liability, the dates of agreements, as well as the date the new partner was added, are extremely important.

Silent Partnerships in Germany

The original intent behind silent partnerships was to allow two people to engage in a partnership without having to inform the third party. Recently, both civil and common law countries have been moving away from this total anonymity. France permits the silent partner to choose whether to disclose the relationship. Germany, however, has held to the original intent of silent partnerships.

Under German law, a contract is formed between the silent partner (usually the financier) and the proprietor of the business. In exchange for his or her investment, the silent partner receives a designated share of the profits. Enlisting a silent partner does not require registration, and the company should continue to operate under the proprietor's name.

Because business is conducted under the proprietor's name and the partnership remains a secret to the third party, silent partners are not held personally liable for damages incurred in the course of business. This nonliability makes silent partnerships less widely used in Germany than in other countries. Nevertheless, it creates unique situations. A proprietor could enlist his or her child as a silent partner, who collects assets while remaining anonymous and ineligible for any liability claims. Nonliability guards the interests of the silent partner.

In Germany, the benefits swing in favor of the silent partner. While the proprietor transacts all the business and the third party remains unaware of the existence of the partnership relationship, silent partners enjoy minimal responsibility and no risk of personal liability.

You may be surprised that the silent partnership arrangement is legal in Germany. But as a critical thinker you have a responsibility to rethink your reasoning. Can you create a list of reasons why our own legal system should encourage silent partnerships?

The Revised Uniform Partnership Act

Just as the original Uniform Partnership Act governs partnerships in the absence of an express agreement, the Revised Uniform Partnership Act (RUPA) has significantly changed several laws that relate to partnerships. Since being approved in 1996, RUPA has been adopted in roughly half the states, so it is wise to determine whether the state in which a partnership was formed operates under UPA or RUPA. Although RUPA generally serves to expand UPA, there is some disagreement between them about the rules of partnership.

CASE OPENER WRAP-UP

Crushed Hand in the Dough Press at Jax Restaurant

Under Minnesota's Uniform Partnership Act (UPA), a partnership is liable for loss or injury caused to a person "as a result of a wrongful act or omission, or other actionable conduct, of a partner acting in the ordinary course of business of the partnership or with authority of the partnership." Thus, the key questions the court considered in the Jax Restaurant case were whether this injury occurred in the regular course of business of Nicole Moren or under the authority of the partnership.

Indeed, the court correctly concluded that Moren's conduct was in the ordinary course of business of the partnership and, as a result, that she did not need to indemnify (reimburse) the partnership for any negligence on her part. The incident happened in the ordinary course of the partnership's business because one of the cooks scheduled to work that evening did not come in and Moren's partner asked her to help in the kitchen. It was also undisputed that Moren was making pizzas for the partnership when her son was injured, and even though she was simultaneously acting in her role as a mother, her conduct remained in the ordinary course of the partnership business. Therefore, the entire partnership can be found liable for Moren's actions, and she would not need to reimburse the other partners for her own negligence.

To prevent potential lawsuits, it is important for business owners and partners to establish clear guidelines of conduct for partners to follow. The rules of the partnership did not prohibit bringing unauthorized persons back to the kitchen or establish clear protocol for family members of partners. Furthermore, another partner, Amy Benedetti, authorized Moren's conduct by calling Moren to replace a worker and by not telling her that her child must leave the kitchen. Under Minnesota law, authorization from the other partners is merely an alternative basis for establishing partnership liability. The outcome of this case might have been quite different if the partnership had rules preventing negligence or if one of the partners had not authorized Moren's son to be near the dough press. Under those circumstances, Moren would have been responsible for reimbursing the partnership for damages resulting from her own negligence.

Key Terms

accounting   803
articles of
   partnership   799

charging order   803
joint and several
   liability   804

jointly liable   804
partnership   794

right of
   survivorship   803

Summary of Key Topics

Nature of the Partnership

The Uniform Partnership Act defines a partnership as "an association of two or more persons to carry on as co-owners a business for profit."

An essential element in a partnership is the sharing of profits from the partnership.

Formation of the Partnership

A partnership is created by the articles of partnership, which should include the name of each partner and the partnership, the duration of the partnership, how profits will be divided, the division of management duties, and the contributions to be made by each partner. A partnership can also be formed by estoppel. When a person relies to his detriment on a misrepresentation by a nonpartner that he is a partner, then the nonpartner will be held liable as if he is a partner.

Interactions between Partners

Each partner has specific duties, including:

- Duty to be loyal
- Duty of obedience
- Duty of care

Each partner has specific rights, including:

- Right to share in management
- Right to inspect books
- Right to compensation
- Rights to partnership property

Interactions between Partners and Third Parties

If a partnership has a liability, each partner has unlimited personal liability. All partners are jointly and severally liable for the commission of a tort by any partner.

There is only implied liability when purchases are made to perpetuate the partnership's business.

The Revised Uniform Partnership Act

RUPA is a revised version of UPA, and its use varies from state to state.

Point / Counterpoint

Should a Minor Be Allowed to Enter into a Business Partnership?	
YES	**NO**
Individuals under the age of 18 should be allowed to enter into business partnerships. If an existing business decides that a business created by a minor is a desirable partner, the minor should be able to enter into that partnership on grounds of personal liberty.	Individuals under the age of 18 should not be allowed to enter into a business partnership. They are considered juveniles in the eyes of the law and are treated differently in court.

Individuals under the age of 18 should be allowed to enter into business partnerships. If an existing business decides that a business created by a minor is a desirable partner, the minor should be able to enter into that partnership on grounds of personal liberty.

Although the United States and other countries act as if adulthood occurs at an arbitrary point in time (age 18 in the United States), research argues differently. According to Richard Fabes and Carol Lynn Martin's *Exploring Child Development,** 18 is just one year in a five-year phase called *late adolescence* or *early adulthood.* Levels of maturity and decision-making abilities vary greatly. Some individuals over 18, who may enter into contracts and partnerships, may not be as mature as other young adults a few years their junior.

Some people say minors are not accustomed to making decisions that affect the lives of others. But young adults already make life-altering decisions. In most states, the age of consent for sexual intercourse is 16, while some states (Iowa, Missouri, and South Carolina) and other developed countries (Italy and Iceland) set it as low as 14.

Furthermore, 16- and 17-year-olds are allowed to obtain a driver's license in most states. Offenders under 18 can be tried as adults in a criminal court and be sentenced to life in prison.

If a minor has been smart and responsible enough to create a profitable business, one so successful that another business wants to create a partnership, she or he should be allowed to enter into the partnership.

Individuals under the age of 18 should not be allowed to enter into a business partnership. They are considered juveniles in the eyes of the law and are treated differently in court.

According to UPA, a partnership can be valid only when the relationship between partners is *voluntary* and *consensual.* Juveniles in the United States are not allowed to consent to participating in several activities because they are rightfully considered immature and inexperienced. They cannot consent to participate in a sexual relationship (in some states), marry or sign prenuptial agreements, purchase or smoke cigarettes or other tobacco products, gamble, or purchase or consume alcohol. They should also be considered too immature to make the life-altering decision of entering into a business.

A juvenile is a dependent of his or her parents. Parents decide how to invest their child's money, which schools their child should attend, and what time their child should be required home. Because parents play such a significant role in their child's life, juveniles are not accustomed to making major decisions.

It isn't fair to expect a juvenile partner to take an equal role in managing the partnership and making money when the juvenile is devoting most of his or her time to growing, developing, and learning in school.

* Informational Web site: http://wps.ablongman/ab_fabes_exploring_2/0,4768,225940-,00.html.

Questions & Problems

1. Explain each element of UPA's definition of a partnership.

2. What is the distinction between partnership as a legal entity and partnership as a legal aggregate?

3. What is the relationship between the obligations of a general partner and those of a limited partner?

4. Abdul Bensaid and Cynthia Brown are the sole members of Nadia's LLC, a limited liability company that owns and operates Nadia's Restaurant. After purchasing the restaurant, Bensaid discussed possible renovations for the building with the Alexander Company. Bensaid met with an architect

at the restaurant several times. Brown was present at one of those meetings, but neither she nor Bensaid stated they were or were not operating as a partnership and neither disclosed that they were part of a limited liability company. Later, Bensaid entered into a contract with Alexander Company for remodeling work. Bensaid was designated in the contract as both the owner and the owner's representative. Brown did not sign the contract, but she did issue a check from her personal checking account for the initial work at the restaurant. Furthermore, when Alexander Company asked Bensaid to provide proof of financial ability before completion of the renovations, it received a letter from the bank indicating that Brown was approved for a loan in the amount of $75,000, contingent on an appraisal of her home. However, Alexander Company was not paid any additional amounts allegedly owed and subsequently filed a complaint against Bensaid and Brown. Brown rejected the notion that she should be found liable since she was not in a partnership with Bensaid. Alexander Company alleged that on the basis of its course of dealings with Bensaid and Brown, it was led to believe that the two were partners and assumed joint responsibility for payments. Did a partnership by estoppel exist between Bensaid and Brown in their dealings with Alexander Company? [*The Alexander Company, Inc. v. Abdul Bensaid and Cynthia Brown*, 2002 WI App 165; 256 Wis. 2d 693; 647 N.W.2d 467 (2002).]

5. Paul Berkowitz is the minority shareholder of several related corporations and partnerships. He brought suit to force the appellants, Astro Moving and Storage Co., Inc., to produce certain books and records. Astro was currently in the process of voting to remove Berkowitz from his position as officer and director of the business entities. Berkowitz argued that his partner status gave him the right to inspect the books. According to Berkowitz, Astro had made an offer to buy him out, and he wanted to access the books to determine the true value of his shares. Do you think Berkowitz had a right to inspect the books? How do you think the court decided? [*Berkowitz v. Astro Moving and Storage Co., Inc.*, 658 N.Y.S.2d 425 (1997).]

6. Ian M. Starr was a partner in the law firm Fordham & Starrett. After Starr's first year of employment, the firm's profits were divided evenly among all partners.

During his second year with the firm, Starr's relationship with the other partners began to deteriorate, and he quit the firm on the last day of the year. Listing several negative factors relevant to Starr's performance, the firm paid him less than half an equal share. Starr brought an action to recover amounts to which he claimed he was entitled under the partnership agreement. He also claimed breach of fiduciary duty. Starr's former partners counterclaimed that Starr had violated his fiduciary duties to the partners and breached the partnership agreement. How do you think the court settled this conflict? [*Starr v. Fordham*, 648 N.E.2d 1261 (1995).]

7. The Vancouver Group is made up of five investors, Pietz, Wynne, Fordham, Indermuehle, and Smith. The group entered into a partnership with Robert Berry for the joint purchase of the Sundance Hotel and Casino. The group and Berry made an offer to purchase the hotel. Pietz agreed to supply $500,000 to the deal and post a $285,000 letter of credit. However, after receiving information that caused him to doubt Berry, Pietz withdrew his interests from the partnership. Berry threatened to sue Pietz for breach of contract, fraud, and tortious breach of the covenant of good faith. Pietz and Berry settled, and Pietz subsequently sued the group for the cost of the settlement. The trial court rejected Pietz's claim of breach of fiduciary duty. He appealed the decision. How do you think the court decided? Was there a breach of fiduciary duty? [*Pietz v. Indermuehle*, 949 P.2d 449 (1998).]

8. David Byker was an accountant working for Tom Mannes. The two talked about going into business together because they had complementary business skills—Mannes (defendant) could locate certain properties because of his real estate background and Byker (plaintiff) could raise money for the property purchases. Subsequently, the two agreed to engage in an ongoing business enterprise, to furnish capital, labor, and/or skill to the enterprise, to raise investment funds, and to share equally in the profits, losses, and expenses of the enterprise. To facilitate the investment of limited partners, Byker and Mannes created separate entities wherein they were general partners or shareholders for the purposes of operating each separate entity. After the two men encountered some financial difficulties with a venture, Byker approached Mannes with

regard to equalizing payments as a result of the losses incurred with the failed business opportunity. Mannes claims that this was the first time he ever received notice about any outstanding payments. After unsuccessfully seeking reimbursement from Mannes, Byker filed suit for the recovery of the money on the basis that the two men had entered into a partnership. Specifically, Byker asserted that the obligations between him and the defendant were not limited to their formal business relationships established by the individual partnerships and corporate entities but that there was a "general" partnership underlying all their business affairs. In response, Mannes asserted that he merely invested in separate business ventures with the plaintiff and that there were no other understandings between them. Did the two businessmen form a partnership, or were their business deals all separate ventures? Was there intent to make a consensual business relationship even though Mannes argues there was not? [*Byker v. Mannes*, 465 Mich.637; 641 N.W.2d 210 (2002).]

9. Richard Hunley, Nada Tas, Joseph Tas, and Kenneth Brown all became general partners of Parham-Woodman between 1986 and 1987. In 1985, Citizens Bank of Massachusetts loaned Parham-Woodman $2 million for the construction of a new office facility. When Parham-Woodman stopped making payments on the loan, the bank sold the building and sued the firm and the partners to recover the debt not paid. The partners argued that they were not liable for the debt because they had joined the firm after the loan agreement was made. Do you agree with them? Why or why not? [*Citizens Bank of Massachusetts v. Parham-Woodman Medical Associates*, 874 F. Supp. 705 (1995).]

10. Phillip Heller was a partner of the Pillsbury, Madison & Sutro law firm. The relationship between Heller and the firm was not strong, as Heller's work performance was unsatisfactory. He billed 1,000 hours fewer than he had estimated that he would produce, and he did not establish strong working relationships. Heller signed the partnership agreement in 1992. The agreement authorized the Executive Committee to expel partners. After Heller submitted a derogatory and lewd article entitled "Why I Fired My Secretary," the committee met and terminated Heller's partnership. Heller challenged the authority of the committee to expel him, regardless of whether he had signed the partnership agreement. Do you think the court agreed with him? Why or why not? [*Heller v. Pillsbury, Madison & Sutro*, 58 Cal. Rptr. 2d 336 (1996).]

Looking for more review material?

The Online Learning Center at **www.mhhe.com/kubasek2e** contains this chapter's "Assignment on the Internet" and also a list of URLs for more information, entitled "On the Internet." Find both of them in the Student Center portion of the OLC, along with quizzes and other helpful materials.

37 Partnerships: Termination and Limited Partnerships

LEARNING OBJECTIVES

After reading this chapter, you will be able to answer the following questions:

1   What are the steps in the termination of a partnership?

2   How is a limited partnership formed?

3   What are the rights and privileges of a limited partner and a general partner?

CASE OPENER
Partnership Problems of Wildmeadow Village

Christian Wyller was a partner in Wildmeadow Village partnership, which owned an office building in Juneau, Alaska. Under difficult economic circumstances, the partnership received an invitation to bid (ITB) from the state of Alaska to lease approximately 7,000 square feet of office space for five years. Wildmeadow secured the bid from the state. The partners held a partnership meeting and approved the state lease and various improvements necessary to meet the bid specifications. At the partnership meeting, it was reported that improvements of roughly $120,000 were necessary to meet the state bid. However, some of Wyller's partners authorized work on the entire building, including repairs not necessary for the state lease and not properly approved by the partnership. The total cost of repairs and improvements actually made to the building was $257,000, and the excess repairs were not authorized by the entire partnership.

After construction began, the partners discovered that their loan application to the bank was rejected and they would have to pay for the entirety of the repairs out of pocket. Wyller expressed reluctance to pledge cash or personal collateral for a loan, objected to substantial expenditures made without authorization, and said that he was at the limit of his resources. He would not pay for repairs he did not approve. Subsequently, the construction bills were not paid, and the construction company brought suit against Wildmeadow Village partnership and its individual partners. At trial, Wyller argued that he was entitled to damages because he did not authorize the repairs and he did not wrongfully cause the dissolution of the partnership. The court found Wyller partially at fault for the dissolution of the partnership and therefore not entitled to damages from the other partners. Wyller appealed to the supreme court of Alaska.

1. Should Wyller have to pay construction costs for the repairs he did not authorize?
2. How are partnerships dissolved?

The Wrap-Up at the end of the chapter will answer these questions.

Termination of the Partnership

Before any partnership can be considered completely terminated, it must go through the *dissolution stage* and the *winding-up stage.* **Dissolution** is complete when any partner stops fulfilling the role of a partner to the business (by choice or default). Partners complete the **winding-up** stage by taking account of the assets of the partner who has left and redistributing them among the other partners. The sections below explain the steps that must occur in the dissolution and winding-up stages for the termination to be complete. (Exhibit 37-1 summarizes all the stages in the life cycle of a partnership.)

LO1

What are the steps in the termination of a partnership?

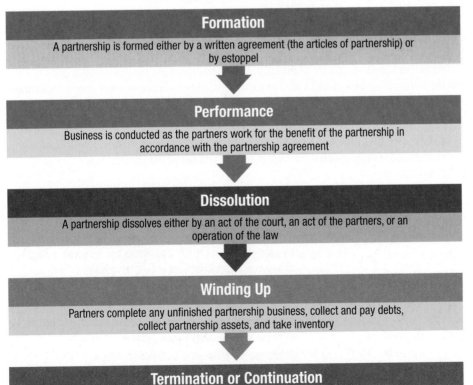

The Life of a Partnership

Formation
A partnership is formed either by a written agreement (the articles of partnership) or by estoppel

Performance
Business is conducted as the partners work for the benefit of the partnership in accordance with the partnership agreement

Dissolution
A partnership dissolves either by an act of the court, an act of the partners, or an operation of the law

Winding Up
Partners complete any unfinished partnership business, collect and pay debts, collect partnership assets, and take inventory

Termination or Continuation
The partnership is terminated   The partnership continues by creating a continuation agreement

Exhibit 37-1
The Life Cycle of a Partnership

Dissolution of the Business

Section 29 of UPA defines *dissolution* as "the change in the relation of the partners caused by any partner's ceasing to be associated with the carrying on, as distinguished from the winding up"—the activity of completing unfinished partnership business, collecting and paying debts, collecting partnership assets, and taking inventory—"of the business." It is important to note that dissolution does not necessarily mean that the business cannot continue functioning; it simply means that there is a significant change in partner relations. Indeed, a partnership can continue after dissolution.

What might cause the dissolution of the partnership? The dissolution may occur by an act of the partners, an operation of the law, or an act of the court (see Exhibit 37-2). One significant issue in the case of the Wildmeadow Village partnership was whether the dissolution of the business occurred properly. As you read this section, keep the chapter opener in mind to decide for yourself how Wyller's partnership was dissolved.

ACT OF PARTNERS

The partnership is a voluntary and consensual relationship, so the partners have the power to dissolve it at almost any time. They may simply agree that it will terminate at a certain time. Suppose Soo and Gerarldo, two partners in a college preparation business, are graduating from college. They both plan to accept jobs at other firms; neither expects to continue the college preparation business. When they created this business, they might have agreed to dissolve the partnership when one of them graduated from college. However, if the business is either a flop or an enormous success, they can agree to dissolve the partnership early or extend its term after graduation.

Alternatively, partners might agree to dissolve the partnership once they achieve a certain objective. Consider a partnership to sell homes in a housing development. Once all the homes have been sold, the partners may agree to dissolve the partnership.

When can a partnership be **rightfully dissolved,** meaning the dissolution does not violate the partnership agreement? We have established two circumstances above (after meeting an established objective and at the end of the term stated in the partnership agreement). Here are others:

1. *A partner withdraws from the partnership at will.* (A *partnership at will* is an agreement that does not specify the objective or duration of the partnership.)

Exhibit 37-2

Causes of a Partnership Dissolution

Act by a partner	A partner withdraws from the partnership at will.
	A partner withdraws or is expelled according to the partnership agreement (e.g., once the partnership has achieved a certain objective or a certain amount of time has passed).
Operation of the law	A partner dies.
	A partner is adjudicated bankrupt.
	The partnership engages in an activity that becomes illegal.
Act of the court	A partner is adjudicated insane.
	Continuing the partnership becomes impractical.
	A partner is incapable of carrying out the duties established by the agreement.
	The court dissolves the partnership for other reasons.

Partnership Dissolution

In re Leah Beth Woskob, Debtor; Alex Woskob; Helen Woskob; the Estate of Victor Woskob v. Leah Beth Woskob, Appellant
U.S. Court of Appeals for the Third Circuit
305 F.3d 177 (2002)

In 1996, Leah Beth Woskob and Victor Woskob formed a partnership, the Legends Partnership, to construct, own, and operate the Legends, an apartment building. Married when they formed the partnership, the Woskobs separated and filed for divorce the following year. During the divorce proceedings, Victor prevented Leah from receiving any of the partnership proceeds. Leah was granted a petition for special relief and awarded the exclusive right to manage and derive income from the partnership. Shortly thereafter, Victor filed for bankruptcy. Leah continued to file tax returns on behalf of the partnership, each of which listed Victor as a general partner. When Victor died in a car accident in 1999, Leah gave his estate notice that she was exercising her right to buy out Victor's interest in the partnership. Victor's estate sued, claiming the partnership had already been dissolved and requesting that someone be appointed to oversee its winding up and a full accounting of the company's assets. When Leah filed for bankruptcy, the suits were moved to the bankruptcy court. The bankruptcy court ruled in favor of Leah, finding that the partnership had dissolved on Victor's death. Victor's estate appealed to the district court, which found that the partnership had dissolved two years *before* Victor's death,

making Leah's attempt to buy out Victor's interest untimely. Leah appealed.

The task before the appeals court was to determine the timeliness of Leah's attempt to buy out Victor's interest in the partnership, which depended entirely on the date of the dissolution of the partnership. The court looked to the Uniform Partnership Act (UPA), which defined the dissolution of a partnership as "the change in the relation of the partners caused by any partner ceasing to be associated in the carrying on, as distinguished from the winding up, of the business." Victor's estate claimed that the dissolution occurred at any one of three points, each at least 18 months before Victor's death. First, Victor excluded Leah from the partnership after they separated; second, Leah excluded Victor from the partnership after seeking special relief from the Court of Common Pleas; third, Victor filed for bankruptcy.

The appeals court found that the exclusions of Leah and Victor from the partnership were not, in and of themselves, grounds for automatic dissolution of the partnership. Rather, they could have provided a *basis* for dissolution, had either Leah or Victor sought judicial decree of the dissolution after being excluded. In addition, bankruptcy in and of itself is not grounds for automatic dissolution of the partnership. If the nondebtor partner does not consent to continue the partnership with the debtor, bankruptcy may be grounds for dissolution. However, Leah continued to list Victor as a general partner on the tax returns she filed for the partnership, even after he filed for bankruptcy. Thus, the appeals court found that the partnership had not dissolved prior to Victor's death in 1999 and that Leah's attempt to buy out Victor's interest in the partnership was therefore timely.

2. *A partner withdraws in accordance with the partnership agreement.* The partnership agreement may establish specific reasons that a partner may withdraw.

3. *A partner is expelled from the partnership in accordance with the partnership agreement.* Suppose you are a partner in a law firm and you steal some type of property from the partnership. The partnership agreement will usually determine the reasons a partner may be removed from the partnership, and theft is often one of them.

If a partnership is rightfully dissolved, all partners can demand that it be wound up and can participate in that process. Moreover, if the partners unanimously agree, they can continue the business using the partnership's name.

However, a partner who dissolves the partnership in violation of the partnership agreement can be held liable for **wrongful dissolution.** That partner cannot require that the business be wound up but can be held liable for damages to the remaining partners. They can choose to continue the business under the partnership name or wind it up.

In the chapter opener, if Wyller dissolved the partnership wrongfully, he could be liable for damages resulting from the failure to pay construction costs for the renovations. Because none of the partners withdrew at will or left the partnership in accordance with the partnership agreement, it appears that the Wildmeadow Village partnership was dissolved wrongfully. Now the court must decide who was responsible for the dissolution and whether it was indeed Wyller who dissolved the partnership wrongfully. If Wyller is responsible, he cannot require the winding up of his partnership and he may be held liable for the damages to the construction company.

Legal Principle: **As a general rule, the partners have the power to dissolve the partnership at almost any time.**

OPERATION OF LAW

Several circumstances provided by law can dissolve a partnership: if a partner dies, if a partner is adjudicated bankrupt, or if the partnership business engages in an activity that suddenly becomes illegal. Suppose Congress decides cigarettes are illegal. A partnership that manufactures and sells cigarettes will be automatically dissolved.

ACT OF THE COURT

A partner may apply to the court to dissolve the partnership for any of the following reasons:

- A partner is adjudicated insane
- It becomes impractical to carry out the business of the partnership (continuing will result only in lost profits).
- A partner is incapable of carrying out his or her duties as established by the partnership agreement.
- Other special circumstances exist. Suppose partners begin bitterly disagreeing about how the business should be managed, preventing the cooperation necessary for a partnership to exist. In this instance, the court can dissolve the partnership.

Case 37-1 is one in which the court decided to dissolve a partnership.

CASE 37-1   LIEM PHAN VU v. DAVIS HA ET AL.
SUPERIOR COURT OF CONNECTICUT
1997 CONN. SUPER. LEXIS 259

Liem Phan Vu and Davis Ha had an oral agreement to create a partnership to run a new nail salon. They agreed Ha would hold 60 percent of the partnership interest while Vu would hold 40 percent. Vu was responsible for advertising as well as keeping the books and records for the salon. Ha was responsible for operating and managing the business. The salon opened in summer 1995, and the partnership ended in November 1995. In November, Vu presented Ha with a proposed agreement to make the partnership a limited liability company. Ha was unhappy with the agreement and changed the locks on the salon. Ha testified that he thought Vu had taken items from the salon and was not doing sufficient record keeping. Vu argued Ha was excluding her from the business in violation of the partnership agreement. When the dispute went to trial, each party
attempted to show he or she had invested more in the partnership. Vu brought suit for fourteen claims of relief; however, she really wanted the partnership to be dissolved and her portion of the investment returned. After reviewing her claims, the court considered the dissolution of the partnership.

JUDGE D'ANDREA: The court has the power to dissolve a partnership by judicial decree, and may do so if it finds circumstances which would render a dissolution equitable. The court cannot imagine circumstances more compelling than exist in this case for such a finding. The parties have lost faith completely in each other; they each levy charges against the other for the failure of the business; one believes the other failed to keep proper records and to keep him apprised of the state of the finances; one claims physical exclusion from the business by the other and verbal attacks upon her.

Since the court cannot affix blame for the demise of the partnership on either party, and does not find that a breach of the partnership contract has been proven, the rights of the parties are generally governed by Connecticut General Statutes 34–76.

Accordingly, the court orders dissolution of the partnership between the parties. Because the defendant Ha has continued in possession of the premises and continues to operate the business of the partnership, he is ordered to pay the plaintiff Vu the value of her interest in the partnership. No expert evidence was presented as to the value of the business, and the court can only be guided by the testimony of the defendant as to the value of the stock in trade. This figure is $2,000 and the plaintiff's interest in the partnership being forty percent; she is entitled to forty percent of that

amount, or $800. The court also views the security deposit for the lease on the premises to be an asset of the business. That amount being $10,800, the plaintiff is entitled to forty percent thereof, or $4,320. Furthermore, the plaintiff shall not be responsible for the terms of the lease or for any existing obligation of the partnership.

Therefore, the court orders:

(1) A decree of dissolution of the partnership between the parties;

(2) That the defendant pay to the plaintiff the sum of $5,120 as the value of her interest in the partnership;

(3) That the defendant indemnify and hold the plaintiff harmless from any liability under the lease of the premises at 21 High Ridge Road, Stamford, and from all liabilities for the debts and obligations of the partnership.

Finding for the plaintiff.

CRITICAL THINKING

Review the court's reasoning in *Liem Phan Vu*. What evidence would the court have needed to refuse to dissolve the partnership despite the feuding between the partners? The court provides hints about what that evidence would be.

ETHICAL DECISION MAKING

The text discusses the dissolution of the partnership and explains how partners can be penalized if they attempt to leave the partnership wrongfully. What values are upheld by the court's protection of the partnership? In other words, if the court did not hold value *X*, the demise of the partnership would not be considered such a liability.

Consequences of Dissolution

A partner who intends to dissolve or withdraw from the partnership must give the other partners notice of this intent. Once the partnership is dissolved, the partner no longer has actual authority to bind the partnership. However, if the partnership does not notify third parties of the dissolution, the partner can still have implied authority to bind the partnership. Suppose one of the partners in the college preparation business intends to dissolve the partnership. Before Soo can notify Geraldo of her intent, he makes an agreement to begin working with five new students to prepare them for college. Because Soo has not yet given notice of her intent to dissolve, she is still liable for the agreement Geraldo has made.

To ensure that a dissolving partner does not create additional liability for the partnership, firms usually take active steps to notify third parties about the dissolution, often by placing an advertisement in the newspaper. However, firms must provide direct verbal or written notice to any third party that has provided credit to the partnership.

Read the Comparing the Law of Other Countries box on Scotland. What ethical behavior does the Scottish law encourage that might not be encouraged under U.S. law?

Termination of Partnerships in Spain

In Spain, full dissolution is permitted in four situations (*full dissolution* simply means that the partnership ends without litigation or a waiting period): (1) One partner dies, (2) a partner is declared insane and unfit to manage the business, (3) a partner is declared bankrupt, and (4) a partner requests that the partnership be terminated.

Spain also allows for *provisional* (temporary) *dissolution*, followed by litigation to determine the legitimacy of the termination request. Provisional dissolution occurs when (1) a partner fails to comply with provisions of the contract, (2) a partner inexplicably abandons the partnership and does not return on request, (3) a partner fails to bring the capital he or she promised, (4) a partner is accused of fraud or mismanagement, (5) a partner exceeds the limits of his or her power, and (6) a partner uses capital belonging to the partnership in his or her own name.

During partial dissolution, the accused partner is excluded from all managerial responsibilities and profits and from any liability from business conducted during this time. Provisional dissolution prevents those unfairly accused of certain behaviors from losing their position in the partnership. But the process can be a tedious and lengthy one, whether the partial dissolution moves to complete termination or the partnership resumes.

After the dissolution of the partnership, the partners' next step is either winding up the business or continuing the partnership or business. We'll discuss winding up the business first.

Winding Up the Business

Once a partnership has been liquidated, the partners begin the process of winding up, the activity of completing unfinished partnership business, collecting and paying debts, collecting partnership assets, and taking inventory. During the process, the partners must still fulfill their fiduciary duty to one another and disclose all information about the partnership assets. However, they can engage in business that competes with the partnership business. Case 37-2 examines a partner's fiduciary duty during the winding-up period of the termination of the partnership.

Effects of Dissolution in Scotland

In many countries, a partner's ability to bind the partnership immediately ceases on the termination of the partnership. In Scotland, however, a partner may engage in business transactions in the name of the partnership for an unlimited time, provided the transactions are necessary to wind up the affairs of the former relationship. The intention behind this law is to prepare for any instances in which a partnership wants to terminate quickly but may have pending business. The partners can go ahead and cease the relationship and then tie up any loose ends.

For example, a partnership waiting to collect profits from a certain venture can dissolve before the profits have been deposited. Scottish law ensures that a bank is justified in accepting the signature of a partner wanting to deposit or withdraw money from a dissolved partnership's trust. The deposit and withdrawal are considered necessary in winding up the business of the partnership.

JACK A. KAHN AND DENISE W. KAHN v. STEWART MESHER AND LIESELOTTE MESHER

COURT OF APPEALS OF WASHINGTON, DIVISION ONE
2000 WASH. APP. LEXIS 2090 (2000)

Stewart Mesher and Jack "Alder" Kahn jointly invested in real estate for approximately 30 years. In October 1993, Mr. Kahn notified Mr. Mesher that he was dissolving the partnership. One year later, the parties entered into an agreement (the "SMAK Agreement") which governed the terms of the wind-down of the partnership, including the distribution of partnership properties. The SMAK Agreement specifically addressed the sale of a parcel of land called the Bothell property.

An outside party known as Sundquist wanted to make an offer on the Bothell property. Mr. Mesher arranged to sell the property secretly for $984,000 without informing Mr. Kahn of the offer. Mr. Mesher then went to Mr. Kahn to arrange for Mr. Kahn to sell him his shares in the Bothell property, still without telling him about the impending sale of the property. After the transfer of shares, Mr. Mesher signed a purchase and sale agreement for the Bothell property for $961,000 Subsequently, Mr. Kahn sued Mr. Mesher for breach of fiduciary duty to the partnership during the winding-up process. The trial court ruled in favor of Mr. Kahn. Mr. Mesher appeals.

JUDGE WEBSTER: Washington law has long held "that the relationship among partners is fiduciary in character and imposes upon the partners the obligation of candor and utmost good faith in their dealings with each other." There is no stronger fiduciary relationship known to the law than that of co-partners, and each partner is a trustee for all. The good faith obligation of a partner demands that the partner abstain from any and all concealment concerning matters pertaining to the partnership business.

Furthermore, Washington statutory and case law provides that the partners owe one another these fiduciary duties through the "winding-up" period of the partnership. The Washington statute provides in pertinent part:

> Every partner must account to the partnership for any benefit, and hold as trustee for it any profits derived by him without the consent of the other partners for any transaction connected with the formation, conduct, or liquidation of the partnership or from any use by him of its property.

Moreover, in *Bovy,* the Court of Appeals held that partners are "obligated to fully disclose any information

pertaining to the winding up of partnership affairs." Thus, the obligations of good faith and full disclosure continue during the winding up of the partnership and until the partnership affairs are completely settled.

The Meshers argue that *Elmore v. McConaghy* controls, and limits the scope of fiduciary duties the parties owed to one another during the winding-up of the partnership. In *Elmore,* the Supreme Court stated that:

> Whatever fiduciary relation was imposed on the partners toward each other during the continuance of the partnership, the relation ceased when they began to negotiate between themselves as to the price to be paid by one for the other's interest

The Meshers' reliance on *Elmore* is misplaced. *Elmore* was decided prior to this State's adoption of the Uniform Partnership Act, which explicitly defined the fiduciary duty of partners as continuing through the winding-up of the partnership.

In this case, the winding-up of the partnership was not complete, and fiduciary duties did not cease, until the Kahn/Mesher transaction closed on September 30, 1997. The closing of the real estate transaction represented the final settlement of the partnership affairs.

Indeed, the SMAK agreement, which delineated the terms of the winding-up of the partnership, specifically provided that the partnership would not terminate until all partnership accounts were settled. While Mesher argues that his fiduciary duties ceased upon the agreement of the parties on a price on August 22, 1997, the SMAK agreement required that Mesher pay Kahn and Kahn transfer the Kahns' interest to Mesher. This requirement was not met until the transaction closed on September 30. Thus, under the SMAK agreement, Mesher owed Kahn fiduciary duties until at least September 30, 1997.

Because Mesher owed Kahn a fiduciary duty after August 22, 1997, we must determine whether he breached that duty by not revealing the Sundquist offer to Kahn.

As noted above, partners are "obligated to fully disclose any information pertaining to the winding up of partnership affairs." Mesher admits that he never notified Kahn of the Sundquist offer, which is information pertaining to the winding up of partnership affairs. Moreover, when partners engage in transactions with each other, they are obligated to disclose all material facts. Here, the ability of the partnership to dispose of partnership property at a higher price is a material fact.

Instead of disclosing the Sundquist offer to Kahn, Mesher kept the offer to himself in order to keep the entire profit for himself. This was a breach of his fiduciary duty, and the Kahns were thus entitled to judgment as a matter of law.

AFFIRMED.

CRITICAL THINKING

The Meshers relied on the precedent of *Elmore v. McConaghy* to support their conclusion that Stewart Mesher did not owe a fiduciary duty to disclose information to Jack Kahn. Why was reliance on *Elmore* erroneous?

ETHICAL DECISION MAKING

Suppose a classmate argues that injustice occurred with the court's decision. Your classmate thinks that Mesher should not have been punished because he was just receiving the products of his labor. After all, he was the one negotiating the sale of the property, and he didn't *force* Mr. Kahn to sell his shares. How would you argue against your classmate?

Who can demand that the winding-up process begin? We've seen that if a partnership has been rightfully dissolved, any partner can do so. However, a partner who wrongfully dissolves a partnership has no such right. In Case 37-3, the court considers a demand for an accounting in the winding-up phase.

CASE 37-3

ROBERT M. TAFOYA v. DEE S. PERKINS, NO. 95CA0408
COURT OF APPEALS OF COLORADO, DIVISION FOUR
932 P.2D 836; 1996 COLO. APP. LEXIS 206; 20 BTR 1115

Robert Tafoya and Dee Perkins, brother and sister, entered into a partnership with Dee's husband, Eugene Perkins. Eugene bought an apartment complex in 1977; however, he did not want to manage it. He held the title to the land in his name and contributed all necessary capital. Dee was to keep the books and assist in the management of the complex. Finally, Robert Tafoya was to live at, manage, and maintain the complex. In 1979, the apartment complex was sold. The partnership took back a 10-year promissory note with a balloon payment due in 1989.

Ten years later, when the balloon payment was due, Eugene purchased the apartments again at a foreclosure sale. In December 1989, he issued a Notice of Termination of Partnership because of losses associated with the partnership. At the same time, Robert Tafoya ceased being associated with the partnership. In July 1990, Eugene Perkins died. The trial court ruled that his death, as well as Tafoya's

separation from the partnership, were sufficient to dissolve the partnership. Dee continued to manage the property until January 1994, when she sold it for a profit. Tafoya filed his complaint before the sale of the property, arguing Dee had breached her fiduciary duty and requesting an accounting of the partnership's assets. The trial court found no breach of fiduciary duty yet concluded Tafoya was entitled to an accounting and awarded him a share of the proceeds from the apartment complex sale. Dee Perkins appealed, arguing Tafoya's claim was barred by a statute of limitations.

JUDGE DAVIDSON: Section 7-60-129, C.R.S (1986 Repl. Vol. 3A) of the Uniform Partnership Law (the Act) provides that:

> The dissolution of any partnership is the change in relation of the partners caused by any partner

[continued]

ceasing to be associated in the carrying on as distinguished from the winding up of the business.

Under this section, when a partner withdraws from the business, the partnership is dissolved as to that party. However, the remaining partners may elect to continue operating as a partnership.

Section 7-60-143, C.R.S. (1986 Repl. Vol. 3A) of the Act states as follows:

> The right to an account of his interest shall accrue to any partner or his legal representative, as against the winding up partners, the surviving partners, or the person or partnership continuing the business at the date of dissolution, in the absence of any agreement to the contrary.

Courts have reached varying conclusions, depending on the circumstances, about when a statute of limitations begins to run on a claim seeking an accounting. However, §§ 7-60-129 and 7-60-143, taken together, provide that, absent an agreement to the contrary, at least in the circumstances of a withdrawing partner seeking an accounting against any partners winding up or continuing the business, the cause of action accrues on the date the withdrawing partner ceases to be associated with the business, resulting in dissolution of the partnership. Hence, regardless of the legal effect of the husband's notice of termination or his later death, once plaintiff himself ceased to be

associated with the partnership, not only did this dissolve any still-existing partnership, it also caused the statute of limitations to begin to run on his own claim for an accounting against plaintiff.

The Act does not set forth or specify the applicable statute of limitations. Nor does any statute of limitations specifically address an action for partnership accounting. We therefore conclude that the applicable statute of limitations is § 13-80-102(1)(i), C.R.S. (1987 Repl. Vol 6A), which sets forth a two-year "catch-all" period of limitations for "all other actions of every kind for which no other period of limitation is provided."

We do not agree with plaintiff's suggestion that, because the action is one to "recover . . . an unliquidated, determinable amount of money due" him, the appropriate statute of limitations for this action is six years under § 13-80-103.5. Because the amount due from the accounting was not capable of ascertainment by reference to the partnership agreement or by a simple computation derived from the agreement, that statute does not apply.

The trial court found that plaintiff ceased to be associated with the partnership in 1989, causing a dissolution of the then-existing partnership. That finding is not challenged on appeal. Plaintiff did not file his complaint until January of 1994. As a result, his claim for an accounting is not timely because it falls outside the two-year period of limitation in § 13-80-102(1)(i).

REVERSED.

CRITICAL THINKING

How do you react to the evidence in this case? Does it strike you as incomplete? What additional information would you like to have if you were deciding the case?

ETHICAL DECISION MAKING

What primary values did the court uphold in its decision? If you were the judge reviewing the case, which values would motivate your decision?

Once all the partnership assets have been gathered, the assets are distributed to the partners or any creditors the partnership might have. If the partnership has been successful (it has very little or no debt), the order of distribution of assets is not too important. However, if a dissolved partnership has many creditors, the order of distribution of the assets is immensely important. According to UPA, distribution of liquidated assets must take the following order:

1. Payment to creditors of the partnership.
2. Payment of refunds or loans to partners for loans made to the firm.
3. Payment to partners of the capital they invested.
4. Payment of profits distributed to partners on the basis of the partnership agreement.

See the **Connecting to the Core** feature at the text Web site at www.mhhe.com/kubasek2e for a description of allocating income among partners.

Continuing Partnership after Dissolution

Sanfurd G. Bluestein and Sylvia Krugman, Plaintiffs v. Robert Olden, Defendant
U.S. District Court for the Southern District of New York
2004 U.S. Dist. LEXIS 3631

In 1978, Bluestein, Krugman, and Olden formed a partnership, the principal asset of which is a building located in New York City. For 26 years, Olden operated Olden Camera and Lens Company, Inc., in part of the building. Olden Camera itself had been in the building for more than 60 years. In 2001, the plaintiffs sent a letter to Olden to terminate the partnership in accordance with the terms of the partnership agreement. After the letter was sent, the partnership continued to operate in dissolution. The partners agreed to sell the building, but they could not agree on whom to sell to and how much to charge. Olden offered $9 million for the plaintiff's combined interest in the partnership, but he wanted the plaintiffs to release any claims against him and his business, as well as any

claims to profits from the partnership for 2002–2003. A competing offer from a third party contained no requirements and offered $15,400,000 for the building, to be reduced by $200,000 if Olden's business remained in the building.

The plaintiffs filed an order to show cause, requesting "1) the appointment of plaintiff Bluestein as Liquidating and/or Winding Up Partner of the general partnership; 2) a direction that Olden cooperate in the liquidation of the assets of the partnership; and 3) enjoining Olden from entering into any new leases or renewing any leases for space in the building." Because the partnership was terminated in accordance with the partnership agreement, the court ruled that Olden could not prevent maximization of the partnership's assets. Bluestein was appointed the liquidating partner and given sole authority to liquidate the partnership's assets and divide the proceeds after paying the partnership's debts. Olden was ordered to cooperate in the liquidation of the assets and enjoined from entering into or renewing any leases or agreements affecting the partnership's building in New York City. The court retained jurisdiction to ensure that the partners complied with its orders.

If the partners' liabilities for the partnership are greater than their liquidated assets, the partners are liable for the losses. Each partner must contribute his or her share of the losses to pay the creditors. If one partner is unable to contribute his or her share and another partner covers the first partner's unpaid share, the second partner has a right of contribution against the partner who did not pay.

CONTINUING THE PARTNERSHIP AFTER DISSOLUTION

After a partnership has been dissolved, the remaining partners have several options, one of which is to continue the partnership. What happens to the noncontinuing partner? Regardless of why the partner is noncontinuing, this partner must receive his or her interest in the partnership. A noncontinuing partner who holds, say, 20 percent of the partnership in which the assets are valued at $10,000 must receive $2,000 after dissolution.

> Legal Principle: **After the dissolution of a partnership, the remaining partners may continue the partnership.**

Perhaps the best way that partners can preserve a partnership business is through a *continuation agreement*. This agreement states that continuing partners can keep partnership property and carry on the partnership business, particularly when a partner dies.

Limited Partnerships

L02

How is a limited partnership formed?

Limited partnerships, introduced in Chapter 35 and also known as *special partnerships*, originated in Europe more than 500 years ago and have existed in the United States for nearly 200 years. Recall that the **limited partnership** is an agreement between at least one general partner and at least one limited partner. The general partner has management responsibility for the partnership and assumes unlimited personal liability for the debts of the partnership. In contrast, the limited partner assumes no liability for the partnership beyond the capital he or she invested in the business. Limited partnerships are attractive to potential investors because of the limited liability and tax advantages they offer.

Functioning as the equivalent of RUPA, the Revised Uniform Limited Partnership Act (RULPA) is the law governing limited partnerships. Like all law, RULPA is not static; it changes as lawmakers revise it to handle new issues that arise and to better achieve social goals. RULPA was originally drafted in 1976, revised in 1985, and revised again in 2001. About one-fourth of the states have adopted the 1976 version of RULPA, and about three-fourths have adopted the 1985 version. Only a handful of states have adopted the 2001 version. Louisiana is the only state not to have adopted any version of RULPA.

FORMATION OF THE LIMITED PARTNERSHIP

How is the limited partnership created? In contrast to the often-informal partnership agreements described in the previous chapter, the formation of a limited partnership must follow very specific statutory requirements. The general and limited partners must sign a **certificate of limited partnership** and file it with the secretary of state to receive limited liability.

RIGHTS AND LIABILITIES OF THE LIMITED PARTNERS AND THE GENERAL PARTNERS

Limited partners generally have all the rights given to partners in general partnerships, as discussed in the previous chapter. Thus, the limited partner (as well as the general partner) has the right to share in the profits of the business and to receive an account of the partnership. A general partner who wants to add a partner must have the consent of all partners in the limited partnership. Finally, an additional right of limited partners is that they often recover their investment before general partners do.

However, the limited partner has a few special rights under RULPA. For example, if a general partner fails to bring a suit on behalf of the limited partnership, the limited partner can bring the suit.

What about the duties and liabilities of the partnership? The general partner has unlimited personal liability for the debts of the partnership. This broad liability is in contrast to the limited partner's liability, restricted to the amount of capital the partner has invested in the business. Thus, if you enter into a limited partnership by contributing $10,000 to it, as a limited partner you cannot be held liable for more than $10,000.

LO3

What are the rights and privileges of a limited partner and a general partner?

A limited partner's limited personal liability depends on the partner's maintaining three conditions:

1. The limited partner has complied in good faith with the requirement that a certificate of limited partnership is filed.
2. The limited partner does not participate in the control of the business.
3. The limited partner's surname is not part of the partnership name.

If any of these conditions are violated, the limited partner surrenders his or her limited liability. For example, the general partner typically has exclusive control and management of the limited partnership; the limited partner, in contrast, does not share in this control, so the courts will likely rule that the partner has forfeited his or her limited liability.

Exhibit 37-3 distinguishes several aspects of general partners and limited partners.

DISSOLUTION OF THE LIMITED PARTNERSHIP

Dissolution of the limited partnership is very similar to dissolution of the general partnership. The limited partner has no right or power to dissolve the partnership. While the death or bankruptcy of the limited partner rarely dissolves the partnership, the death of the general partner usually does (unless the agreement specifies otherwise). According to RULPA, a limited partnership can be dissolved for any of the following reasons:

1. The expiration of the term established in the certificate of limited partnership.
2. The completion of the objective established in the certificate.
3. The unanimous written consent of all partners (limited and general).
4. The withdrawal of the general partner (unless the certificate establishes that other general partners will continue).
5. An act of the court.

Exhibit 37-3

Comparison of General Partners and Limited Partners

	GENERAL PARTNER	**LIMITED PARTNER**
Control of Business	Has *all* rights associated with controlling the business	Has *no* right to participate in the management and control of the business
Liability	Has unlimited personal liability for all partnership debts	Has liability limited to the amount of capital the partner has contributed to the business
Agency of Partnership	Acts as an agent of the partnership	Is not an agent of the partnership

If the limited partnership is dissolved, the limited partnership's assets are distributed in the same format as described earlier in this chapter: payment to third-party creditors, payment to partners who have loaned the partnership money, payment to the partners according to their investments in the partnership, and payment to the partners on the basis of their shares of the profits.

Limited Liability Companies

Limited partnerships have been around for a number of years, but the *limited liability company (LLC)* is relatively new. An LLC is similar to a limited partnership in that each member has limited liability dependent on the investment he or she makes, while still receiving the tax breaks often afforded to those in a partnership. Like the limited partnership, the LLC is created with an agreement between members. Each member also gets a say in the management of the company, whereas in a limited partnership only the general partners make management decisions. Basically, in limited partnerships, for an LLC to obtain limited liability, the owner (referred to as a *member*) does not have to give up his right to participate in management of the LLC. In fact, an additional advantage of the LLC form is the flexibility it offers members in terms of alternative ways to structure its management.

However, because LLCs are new, the Uniform Limited Liability Company Act that has been drafted to govern them has not been accepted by many states. Until a uniform system has been adopted, managers should check the laws with regard to LLCs in each state to ensure that the liabilities, as well as rights and duties, of a company established in one state continue to apply when conducting business outside that state.

> To see how dissolution relates to a partnership's accounts, please see the **Connecting to the Core** activity on the text Web site at www.mhhe.com/kubasek2e.

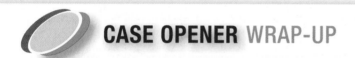

CASE OPENER WRAP-UP

Wildmeadow Village Partnership Problems

Ultimately, the supreme court of Alaska ruled against Wyller. The court determined that he was partially at fault for the wrongful dissolution of the Wildmeadow partnership, and therefore Wyller was not entitled to damages from the other partners. Even though the other partners conducted business behind Wyller's back and approved spending that Wyller did not know about, his conduct in the situation was less than ideal. Specifically, the court observed that shortly after the bank's loan refusal, Wyller informed the other partners that he did not consider himself bound to provide financing for *any* of the improvements that by then had been made to the property. This fact is important because Wyller approved some of the renovations but refused to pay his fair share of the cost. Furthermore, Wyller refused to complete the loan application process despite having previously approved the state of Alaska as a tenant and the submission of the loan application. For these reasons, Wyller was not justified in preventing the partnership from paying for any of the improvements. Nor was he justified in denying personal or partnership responsibility for the costs.

After consideration of the facts, the court found that Wyller's failure to pay for the construction contributed to the dissolution of the partnership. Wyller wrongfully denied responsibility for any of the construction costs, and his denial of authorization to pay construction costs contributed to the course of events that precipitated the dissolution. Failure to pay construction costs brought about the suit, and that suit resulted in wrongful dissolution of the partnership. Therefore, the supreme court of Alaska affirmed the lower court's decision. To avoid such partnership problems in future scenarios, it is important to stress the importance of transparency in partnerships. Had Wyller been allowed to authorize or reject the additional construction costs, the partnership would probably not have been sued in the first place. Furthermore, an understanding of the Uniform Partnership Act and how partnerships are rightly dissolved is something all partners should have before forming a business to avoid legal problems.

Key Terms

certificate of limited
   partnership   823

dissolution   813

limited partnership   822

rightfully dissolved   814

winding up   813

wrongful
   dissolution   815

Summary of Key Topics

Termination of the Partnership

Termination begins when a partnership dissolves. Once the partnership has been dissolved and the assets have been liquidated and distributed, the partnership has been terminated.

Dissolution of the Business

Dissolution refers to the ceasing of a partnership. Acts of partners, the operation of the law, and acts of the court can rightfully dissolve a partnership.

Consequences of Dissolution

A partner who wishes to dissolve or withdraw from the partnership must give notice of intent. Third parties should be contacted promptly to avoid creating additional liability for the partnership.

Winding Up the Business

Winding up is the activity of completing unfinished partnership business, collecting and paying debts, collecting partnership assets, and taking inventory.

Limited Partnerships

The limited partnership is governed by an agreement between at least one general partner and at least one limited partner. This partnership permits investors to share in the profits of a partnership but limits their liability to the amount they invest.

Limited Liability Companies

An LLC is formed by an agreement between members, each of whom has limited liability while receiving the tax breaks often afforded to those in a partnership. In addition, each member also gets a say in the management of the company.

Point / Counterpoint

Should a Partnership Be Allowed to Expel a Partner on the Basis of Illegal Conduct Unrelated to the Terms of the Partnership Agreement?	
YES	NO
A partnership should be able to expel a partner on the basis of illegal personal conduct even when the illegal conduct isn't specified in the partnership agreement.	A partnership should not be allowed to expel an individual based on his or her involvement in illegal activity.

It would be nearly impossible to create a partnership agreement that dictated every possible occasion for dissolving the partnership. Individuals are always expected to conduct themselves within the bounds of national, state, and local laws. Any illegal behavior should have implications for the partnership as an ongoing business enterprise.

A partner's personal behavior affects the entire partnership, its reputation, and its associated business in many ways. If one partner of a five-partner law firm is arrested for smoking marijuana, clients may associate this partner with the entire firm. If he participates in this illegal activity, in which other illegal activities does he partake? Does he keep faulty books? Will clients be overcharged?

Clients may begin to question the firm as a whole for allowing someone who partakes in illegal activities to remain a partner. Do *all* the attorneys participate in illegal activities?

While a partner may suffer personal legal consequences for his actions, the whole partnership suffers when one partner makes a poor personal choice. Therefore, the partnership should be able to determine the consequences.

The partners had the opportunity when formulating the partnership agreement to include a stipulation for its dissolution in such a case. If they did not, no individual can be aware of the potential impact of her actions on her status as a partner. Had she known the possible consequences, she might have acted differently. However, she cannot be expected to abide by restrictions that were not stated in the first place.

Is it logical to revoke an individual's driver's license because she looked at pornography in a state where such activity is illegal? An individual can make a poor personal choice and still be capable of performing her expected duties.

A rule allowing partnerships to expel a partner on the basis of unrelated illegal activity could also be easily abused by partnerships that want to expel a partner for other reasons, such as convenience or the desire for additional profit. The partner already suffers personal legal consequences and should not experience additional penalties for an activity that has no impact on the partnership.

Questions & Problems

1. What stages must occur for the termination of a partnership to be complete?

2. Why is the partnership's debt particularly important in the winding-up stage?

3. What are the advantages of being a limited partner rather than a general partner?

4. In June 2001, Greenfeld, Stitely, and Karstetter negotiated to merge their practices into a partnership that would provide accounting, tax, and information technology services. The partnership was profitable every year from its inception. However, Stitely felt that Greenfeld's information technology services were not generating as much revenue as his one-third share in the partnership should. So Stitely indicated to the partners that he wanted to withdraw from the partnership. Soon after, Stitely and Karstetter agreed to instead continue as partners together after Greenfeld was out of the picture. Greenfeld did not violate his partnership agreement, but the two partners forced Greenfeld out of the partnership without compensating him for his interest. They accomplished this by unlawful means, such as

purporting to withdraw from the partnership while in reality seizing control of its assets. Furthermore, they transferred the assets of the partnership to their new company, preventing Greenfeld from having computer access to the business files, software, and client records. Was the partnership terminated properly? If the dissolution was wrongful, what potential consequences could Stitely and Karstetter face? [*Wayne I. Greenfeld v. Frank L. Stitely, et al.,* 2007 Va. Cir. LEXIS 7 (2007).]

5. Jones and Hardy entered into an oral partnership agreement. They planned to develop and lease certain areas of land. Together, they formed the Bloomington Knolls Association. Jones and Hardy began to experience financial problems, and they brought in a third partner, Jackson, to arrange additional financing for the project. Jones subsequently dissolved the partnership and requested that he be given a portion of the land as his share of the partnership assets. Jackson and Hardy did not honor his request, and Jones never received any assets of the partnership. Jones moved for an accounting and winding up of partnership affairs and brought the

case to court. The district court entered judgment against Hardy and Jackson, jointly and severally, for an amount representative of Jones's interest in the partnership. Jackson and Hardy appealed the district court's decision. How do you think the court decided? [*MacKay v. Hardy,* 896 P.2d 626 (1995).]

6. Stephen Wainger is a former partner of the law firm Glasser & Glasser. According to the partnership agreement, a withdrawing partner is entitled to compensation for "any undivided profits of the firm with respect to uncollected fees which were fully earned by the firm prior to the effective date of his withdrawal, but which fees are received by the firm subsequent to such date." Before leaving the firm, Wainger worked on several asbestos compensation cases. After he left the partnership, the cases were settled and the firm received significant profits. Wainger argued that he should be compensated for his work despite the fact that he left the firm before the settlement of the cases. Do you agree? The trial court found that Wainger was entitled only to fees that had been fully earned at the time of his withdrawal. How do you think the court decided the case on appeal? [*Wainger v. Glasser & Glasser,* 462 S.E.2d 62 (1995).]

7. Astroline Company, a limited partnership, is in the investment business. Astroline heard of an opportunity to purchase the license to a television station, and the company developed a second limited partnership, Astroline Communications Company, to purchase the station. Astroline provided the funding for Astroline Communications but remained a limited partner of the company. Astroline Communications began to experience financial problems and filed for bankruptcy. Do you think the court found Astroline Company, as a limited partner, liable for Astroline Communications Company's debts? Why or why not? [*In re Astroline Communications Company Limited Partnership,* 188 BR 98 (1995).]

8. Carl Disotell and Earl Stiltner met in 1997. They discussed Stiltner's property and agreed to form an equal partnership to develop, construct, and operate a hotel on the property. They never entered into a written partnership agreement. They intended to convert the two-story commercial building on the property into a hotel. In May 1998, Disotell advised Stiltner that the property required a sewer line. Construction on the property had not yet begun. Stiltner disagreed that a sewer line was necessary; he thought there would be no increase in sewage from the property because Disotell had not yet commenced construction. He denied Disotell the building access needed to assess the mechanical, electrical, and other systems. He also refused to remove his personal property from the building. A complete breakdown in the relationship between Stiltner and Disotell then occurred. Subsequently, the partnership never produced a profit. Should the court, as a matter of law, dissolve the partnership and judicially supervise the winding up of the partnership affairs? Why or why not? [*Carl Disotell v. Earl Stiltner,* 100 P.3d 890 (2004).]

9. Mige Associates, a limited partnership, owned an apartment building. The building could have been developed into a housing cooperative. The projected profits for such a conversion were significant. The conversion required the signed agreement of one of Mige's general partners, Jon Meadow. Meadow's decision to sign the agreement was contingent on the promise that he receive more money from the deal than the other partners. After his request was denied, Meadow refused to sign the agreement. Two of the limited partners, Drucker and Schaffer, filed suit against Meadow. They claimed that he had breached his fiduciary responsibility to the general and limited partners of Mige Associates. The trial court found in favor of Meadow. How do you think the case was decided on appeal? Did the economic benefits of the conversion create a fiduciary obligation for Meadow to sign the agreement? [*Drucker v. Mige Associates,* 639 N.Y.S.2d 365 (1996).]

10. After the dissolution of a partnership formed to develop the Four Seasons Resort, TSA International Limited brought an action against Shimizu Corporation, alleging breach of fiduciary duty. TSA had approached Shimizu in 1986 with plans for developing the hotel. The two companies formed a partnership, and they began to make plans for several golf and hotel developments. The loans TSA and Shimizu had taken out soon became delinquent. The partners met to negotiate the payment of the hotel and golf course loans. At the request of Shimizu, the agreements were drafted in Japanese. TSA subsequently filed a complaint asserting, among other things, breach of fiduciary duty. When reaching the agreements, Shimizu had

discouraged TSA from hiring its own accountants or legal counsel because of "the long-term relationship of trust between Shimizu and TSA." TSA also alleged that Shimizu arranged the agreement so that Shimizu would obtain substantial tax advantages. The circuit court found in favor of Shimizu. How do you think the case was decided on appeal? Did Shimizu breach its fiduciary duty? [*TSA Intern. Ltd. v. Shimizu Corp.,* 990 P.2d 713 (1999).]

Looking for more review material?

The Online Learning Center at **www.mhhe.com/kubasek2e** contains this chapter's "Assignment on the Internet" and also a list of URLs for more information, entitled "On the Internet." Find both of them in the Student Center portion of the OLC, along with quizzes and other helpful materials.

38 Corporations: Formation and Financing

LEARNING OBJECTIVES

After reading this chapter, you will be able to answer the following questions:

1   What are the characteristics of corporations?

2   What are the powers granted to corporations by the states?

3   How are corporations classified?

4   How are corporations formed?

5   What are some potential problems with the formation of corporations?

6   How do corporations get funding?

CASE OPENER
The Formation of the Facebook Corporation

On October 28, 2003, Mark Zuckerberg was a sophomore at Harvard University when he created a Web site called Facemash that was similar to an existing Web service called Hot or Not. However, the following semester, in 2004, Zuckerberg began working on a new code for a new Web site to be called Facebook. His friends Eduardo Saverin, Dustin Moskovitz, Andrew McCollum, and Chris Hughes joined Zuckerberg to promote the new social networking site. Membership on the site quickly grew from only students at Harvard College to students at most universities in the United States. In the summer of 2004, Facebook was incorporated. As a corporation, Facebook is an "artificial person," a status with legal ramifications for both the corporate entity and its owners.

1. What are the legal implications of Facebook's status as a corporation?
2. How are corporations formed? What factors should a businessperson consider in forming a corporation?

The Wrap-Up at the end of the chapter will answer these questions.

This chapter explains the steps necessary to establish a corporate entity. Although state law generally governs corporations and each state has its own corporate regulatory statutes, the Revised Model Business Corporation Act (RMBCA) is the basis of most state statutes. More than 25 states have adopted at least part of RMBCA. This chapter refers to specific RMBCA guidelines, but remember that not all states follow them.

The first two sections of this chapter examine corporations' characteristics and powers. The third section describes different classifications of corporations. The next section explains the process of corporate formation and problems associated with it, and the final section covers corporate financing.

Characteristics of Corporations

How are corporations different from other forms of business organization? We addressed some of their characteristics in Chapter 35. Let's now take a closer look.

LO1

What are the characteristics of corporations?

LEGAL ENTITY

Under U.S. law, corporations are legal entities; in other words, they exist separately from their shareholders. Thus, corporations can sue or be sued by others.

RIGHTS AS A PERSON AND A CITIZEN

Courts consider corporations to be "legal persons." For example, in 2006 in Boston, a woman was killed when the ceiling of a tunnel collapsed over her. The ceiling was fastened with bolts that were supported by a glue distributed by the corporation Powers Fasteners. Apparently the contents of this glue were known to "creep," that is, to slowly loosen. The company never informed anyone associated with the construction of the tunnel about the hazardous characteristics of the glue. The Massachusetts attorney general decided to take the corporation to court for manslaughter, just as an individual would be taken to court on such charges. Also, like natural persons, most corporations have certain rights according to the Bill of Rights. Specifically, the Fifth and Fourteenth amendments state that government cannot deprive any "person" of life, liberty, or property without due process. Courts have held that corporations are "persons" in this case and thus have a right to due process. Courts also consider corporations to be persons with respect to the Fourth Amendment and thus protected from unreasonable searches and seizures. Finally, corporations have free speech rights protected by the First Amendment. As Chapter 5 explained, however, the First Amendment protects corporate *commercial* speech to a lesser degree than corporate *political* speech.

In Case 38-1, the Supreme Court considered whether the Federal Election Commission's regulations are unconstitutional limits on speech.

CASE 38-1   FEDERAL ELECTION COMM'N v. BEAUMONT
UNITED STATES SUPREME COURT
539 U.S. 146 (2003)

In 2003, the corporation North Carolina Right to Life, Inc. (NCRL,) sued the Federal Election Commission (FEC) claiming that two FEC regulations were unconstitutional.

Specifically, the first regulation challenged the one that stops corporations from making contributions, and the second regulation was the one that provides an exemption from the ban for corporate contributions for particular nonprofit corporations.

With respect to the second regulation, to be considered a "qualified nonprofit corporation," or one that is exempt from the ban, a nonprofit corporation must have the following characteristics: Its only purpose is the advancement of political ideas, it does not engage in business activities, no shareholders or other individuals receive benefits that could discourage anyone from disassociating from the corporation on the basis of that corporation's political standpoints, and it was not founded by a business corporation or labor organization and accepts no form of donations from business corporations.

NCRL said that it met this exemption except for the fact that it accepted small corporate donations and dealt in "minor business activities incidental and related to its advocacy of issues." NCRL further argued that its officers were subject to liability as criminals and thus, their First Amendment rights were suppressed.

Finally, NCRL contended that the Act's ban on corporate contributions to political candidates violated the organization's right to association.

JUDGE SOUTER: First, NCRL argues that on a class-wide basis "*[Massachusetts Citizens for Life]*-type corporations pose no potential of threat to the political system," so that the governmental interest in combating corruption is as weak as the Court held it to be in relation to the particular corporation considered in *Massachusetts Citizens for Life.* But this generalization does not hold up. For present purposes, we will assume advocacy corporations are generally different from traditional business corporations in the improbability that contributions they might make would end up supporting causes that some of their members would not approve. But concern about the corrupting potential underlying the corporate ban may indeed be implicated by advocacy corporations. They, like their for-profit counterparts, benefit from significant "state-created advantages," and may well be able to amass substantial "political"war chests. Not all corporations that qualify for favorable tax treatment under §501(c)(4) of the Internal Revenue Code lack substantial resources, and the category covers some of the Nation's most politically powerful organizations, including the AARP, the National Rifle Association, and the Sierra Club. Nonprofit advocacy corporations are, moreover, no less susceptible than traditional business companies to misuse as conduits for circumventing the contribution limits imposed on individuals.

Second, NCRL argues that application of the ban on its contributions should be subject to a strict level of scrutiny, on the ground that §441b does not merely limit contributions, but bans them on the basis of their source. This argument, however, overlooks the basic premise we have followed in setting First Amendment standards for reviewing political financial restrictions: the level of scrutiny is based on the importance of the "political activity at issue" to effective speech or political association. Restrictions on political contributions have been treated as merely "marginal" speech restrictions subject to relatively complaisant review under the First Amendment, because contributions lie closer to the edges than to the core of political expression. This is the reason that instead of requiring contribution regulations to be narrowly tailored to serve a compelling governmental interest, "a contribution limit involving 'significant interference' with associational rights" passes muster if it satisfies the lesser demand of being "'closely drawn' to match a 'sufficiently important interest.'"

It is not that the difference between a ban and a limit is to be ignored; it is just that the time to consider it is when applying scrutiny at the level selected, not in selecting the standard of review itself. But even when NCRL urges precisely that, and asserts that §441b is not sufficiently "closely drawn," the claim still rests on a false premise, for NCRL is simply wrong in characterizing §441b as a complete ban. As we have said before, the section "permits some participation of unions and corporations in the federal electoral process by allowing them to establish and pay the administrative expenses of [PACs]." The PAC option allows corporate political participation without the temptation to use corporate funds for political influence, quite possibly at odds with the sentiments of some shareholders or members, and it lets the government regulate campaign activity through registration and disclosure, without jeopardizing the associational rights of advocacy organizations' members.

NCRL cannot prevail, then, simply by arguing that a ban on an advocacy corporation's direct contributions is bad tailoring. NCRL would have to demonstrate that the law violated the First Amendment in allowing contributions to be made only through its PAC and subject to a PAC's administrative burdens. But a unanimous Court in *National Right to Work* did not think the regulatory burdens on PACs, including restrictions on their ability to solicit funds, rendered a PAC unconstitutional as an advocacy corporation's sole avenue for making political contributions. There is no reason to think the burden on advocacy corporations is any greater today, or to reach a different conclusion here.

REVERSAL.

CRITICAL THINKING

What is the assumption about advocacy corporations and traditional business corporations that Justice Souter makes? How does this assumption support his reasoning?

ETHICAL DECISION MAKING

While the FEC does not completely ban the participation of corporations in electoral processes, such participation is strictly regulated. What is the ethical basis for the explanation Justice Souter gives for the necessity of such regulation?

CREATURE OF THE STATE

State incorporation statutes establish the requirements for corporate formation. Each individual corporation's charter creates a contract between that corporation and the state.

LIMITED LIABILITY

Because corporations are legal entities separate from their shareholders, corporations assume liability for corporate actions. Shareholders' liability is therefore limited to their investment in the corporation. In 1977 Big O Tire Dealers sued Goodyear Tire & Rubber Company for copying its Bigfoot trademark on new tires. The court agreed and awarded Big O Tire several million dollars in damages, which the Goodyear corporation, and not individual Goodyear shareholders, paid. Although these damages may have reduced the dividends Goodyear shareholders received, the court did not hold the shareholders individually liable for any portion of the award.

FREE TRANSFERABILITY OF CORPORATE SHARES

Generally, shareholders can freely transfer their corporate shares. That is, they can sell their shares or give them to charity.

PERPETUAL EXISTENCE

If shareholders die, corporations do not dissolve. If corporate directors or officers withdraw or die, the corporation continues to exist. The **articles of incorporation,** the document a corporation files with the state explaining its organization, may include a restriction on the duration of the corporation. Otherwise, in most states, corporations can exist indefinitely. A few states, however, set a maximum length of life for corporations, after which they must formally renew their corporate existence.

To see why managers generally act in the interest of shareholders, please see the **Connecting to the Core** activity on the text Web site at www.mhhe.com/kubasek2e.

CENTRALIZED MANAGEMENT

Unless the articles of incorporation specify otherwise, shareholders do not participate in corporate management. Instead, they elect a board of directors that, in turn, selects officers to manage the day-to-day business of the corporation.

CORPORATE TAXATION

Because corporations are separate legal entities, government taxes their income directly (S corporations are an exception; we discuss them later). Corporations must pay federal and state taxes on their income, but they have control over that income. They can distribute it to shareholders in the form of **dividends,** although they do not receive tax deductions for doing so. In fact, shareholders pay taxes on dividends they receive. Since the corporation pays taxes on its income and the shareholders pay taxes on their dividends, dividends are subject to double taxation, a disadvantage for corporations. Corporations can also keep profits, or **retained earnings,** to reinvest. This can raise their stock prices, benefiting shareholders when they sell their stock.

LIABILITY FOR OFFICERS AND EMPLOYEES

Because the relationship between corporations and their directors, officers, and employees is an agency relationship, corporations are liable for torts and crimes committed by their agents during the scope of their employment. Courts refer to this liability as the doctrine of *respondeat superior* (Latin for "let the master answer"). Although in the past courts were reluctant to impose criminal liability on corporations, prosecutions today are much more common. Chapter 7, "Crime and the Business Community," discusses corporate sentencing guidelines and punishment.

Corporate Powers

LO2

What are the powers granted to corporations by the states?

Because corporations are creatures of the state, they have only those powers that states grant them through state incorporation statutes and each corporation's articles of incorporation. Exhibit 38-1 lists the powers of the corporation.

Legal Principle: **The only authority possessed by corporations is respect to the powers granted to them in their articles of incorporation.**

EXPRESS AND IMPLIED POWERS

State incorporation statutes typically grant corporations the following express powers: the power to have perpetual existence, to sue and be sued in the corporation's name, to acquire property, to make contracts and borrow money, to lend money, to make charitable donations, and to establish rules for managing the corporation. Corporations may take whatever actions are necessary to execute these express powers. Thus, they also have implied powers, usually given in the statement of corporate purpose in the articles of incorporation.

Exhibit 38-1

Powers of the Corporation

Express Powers

Power to have perpetual existence

Power to sue and be sued in the corporation's name

Power to acquire property; power to make contracts and borrow money

Power to lend money

Power to make charitable donations

Power to establish rules for managing the corporation

Implied Powers

Power to take whatever actions are necessary to execute express powers

Power given in the statement of corporate purpose in the articles of incorporation

Classification of Corporations

Corporations can be classified as public or private; profit or nonprofit; domestic, foreign, or alien; publicly held or closely held; an S corporation; or a professional organization.

L03

How are corporations classified?

PUBLIC OR PRIVATE

A **public corporation** is a corporation created by the government to help administer law. Public corporations, like the Federal Deposit Insurance Corporation (FDIC), often have specific government duties to fulfill. Conversely, private persons create **private corporations** for private purposes. Private corporations do not have government duties.

PROFIT OR NONPROFIT

Most corporations are **for-profit corporations.** Their objective is to operate for profit. Shareholders seeking to make a profit purchase the stock these corporations issue. Their profit if the firm prospers can take two forms. First, shareholders may receive dividends from the corporation. Second, the market price of the stock can increase, allowing shareholders to sell their stock at a higher price than they paid.

Nonprofit corporations may earn profits, but they do not distribute them to shareholders. In fact, nonprofit corporations do not have shareholders, their objective is not to earn profit, and they do not issue stock. Instead, nonprofit corporations provide services to their members (not shareholders) and reinvest most of their profits in the business. Churches and charitable organizations are examples of nonprofit corporations.

DOMESTIC, FOREIGN, AND ALIEN CORPORATIONS

A corporation is a **domestic corporation** in the particular state in which it is incorporated. Corporations that operate in more than one state must obtain a certificate of authority in each state in which they do business. A corporation is a **foreign corporation** in states in which it conducts business but is not incorporated. The McDonald's Corporation is incorporated in Delaware but does business in all 50 states. Thus, it is a domestic corporation in Delaware and a foreign corporation in the other 49 states.

An **alien corporation** is a business incorporated in another country. A U.S. corporation that wants to do business in Canada or Mexico is an alien corporation in those countries.

PUBLICLY HELD OR CLOSELY HELD

The stock of **publicly held corporations** is available to the public. Thus, if you wanted to invest in a corporation, you could purchase stock in a publicly held corporation. Most publicly held corporations have many shareholders, and managers of these corporations usually do not own large percentages of the corporation's stock. Shareholders wishing to sell their shares do not face many transfer restrictions.

In contrast, **closely held corporations** (also called *close, family,* or *privately held corporations*) generally do not offer stock to the general public. Shareholders are usually family members and friends, who often are active in or manage the business and maintain restrictions on the transfer of shares to prevent outsiders from gaining control. Although they account for only a small fraction of corporate assets and revenues, most U.S. corporations are closely held corporations. In fact, about 50 percent of all U.S. corporations are S corporations.

SUBCHAPTER S CORPORATION

Chapter 35 introduced S corporations (named after the subchapter of the Internal Revenue Code that provides for them), a particular type of closely held corporation that enjoys the tax status of partnerships. Thus, S corporation shareholders report their income from the corporation only once, as personal income.

S corporations offer two more tax advantages. First, shareholders may deduct corporate losses from their personal income, reducing their taxes in case of loss. Second, when the shareholder is part of a lower tax bracket than non-S corporations, the entirety of the corporation's income is taxed at the shareholder's lower rate, even if dividends are retained and not distributed. The lower rate applies because of the relationship between the corporation and the personal income of the shareholders.

An S corporation must meet certain requirements. First, it cannot have more than 100 shareholders. Second, only individuals, trusts, and (in certain circumstances) corporations can be shareholders (partnerships cannot be shareholders). Third, S corporations can issue only one class of shares, although they need not have identical voting rights. Fourth, all S corporations must be domestic corporations. Finally, no shareholder can be a nonresident alien.

PROFESSIONAL CORPORATION

If a group of dentists, doctors, or other professionals wants to practice as a corporation, all 50 states permit them to incorporate. Because of the nature of professional work, however, courts sometimes impose personal liability on doctors in professional corporations for medical malpractice performed under their oversight.

Formation of the Corporation

L04

How are corporations formed?

The creation of a corporation has two steps: general organizational activities and legal activities.

ORGANIZING AND PROMOTING THE CORPORATION

Two groups of important players are responsible for the organization of the corporation: promoters and subscribers. Promoters begin the corporate creation and organization process by arranging for necessary capital, financing, and licenses. They raise capital for the infant corporation by making subscription agreements with subscribers (investors) who agree to purchase stock in the new corporation.

Promoters.   Promoters prepare the corporation's incorporation papers. They can also enter into contracts as needed, say, to purchase or lease buildings for the corporation. Frank Seiberling was the promoter who founded the Goodyear Tire & Rubber Company. In 1898, he purchased Goodyear's first plant in Akron, Ohio, with $3,500 borrowed from his brother-in-law and established Goodyear workers' hourly wages between 13 and 25 cents.

When problems with preincorporation contracts arise, courts generally hold promoters liable and rule that these contracts do not bind infant corporations. Promoters are not agents of the infant corporation, however, because they cannot serve as such for a principal that does not yet exist.

Once incorporated, corporations can accept or reject preincorporation agreements. Even so, if a corporation accepts a preincorporation agreement, courts usually still hold promoters liable for the contract.

In two cases, however, promoters are not personally liable. They can include a clause in the contract stating that the corporation's adoption of the contract terminates their liability; or the corporation, the promoter, and a third party can enter into a **novation,** agreeing to substitute the third party for one of the two original parties in a contract and terminating the rights under it.

In Case 38-2, the Colorado appellate court considered whether a promoter was liable for a preincorporation contract.

CASE 38-2   COOPERS & LYBRAND v. GARRY J. FOX
COURT OF APPEALS OF COLORADO, DIVISION FOUR
758 P.2D 683 (1988)

In November 1981, Garry Fox met with a representative of Coopers, a national accounting firm, to request a tax opinion and other accounting services. Fox told Coopers he was acting on behalf of G. Fox and Partners, Inc., a corporation he was in the process of forming. Coopers knew the corporation did not yet exist and accepted the agreement. G. Fox and Partners, Inc., incorporated in December 1981. When Coopers finished its work, it billed Fox $10,827. Neither Fox nor his corporation paid the bill. Coopers sued Fox personally, arguing he was liable because he was the promoter. The trial court found that no agreement obligated Fox individually to pay the fee and found in favor of Fox. Coopers appealed.

JUDGE KELLY: As a preliminary matter, we reject Fox's argument that he was acting only as an agent for the future corporation. One cannot act as the agent of a nonexistent principal.

On the contrary, the uncontroverted facts place Fox squarely within the definition of a promoter. A promoter is one who, alone or with others, undertakes to form a corporation and to procure for it the rights, instrumentalities, and capital to enable it to conduct business.

When Fox first approached Coopers, he was in the process of forming G. Fox and Partners, Inc. He engaged Coopers' services for the future corporation's benefit. In addition, though not dispositive on the issue of his status as a promoter, Fox became the president, a director, and the principal shareholder of the corporation, which he funded, only nominally, with a $100 contribution. Under these circumstances, Fox cannot deny his role as a promoter.

Coopers asserts that the trial court erred in finding that Fox was under no obligation to pay Coopers' fee in the absence of an agreement that he would be personally liable. We agree.

As a general rule, promoters are personally liable for the contracts they make, though made on behalf of a corporation to be formed. The well-recognized exception to the

general rule of promoter liability is that if the contracting party knows the corporation is not in existence but nevertheless agrees to look solely to the corporation and not to the promoter for payment, then the promoter incurs no personal liability. In the absence of an express agreement, the existence of an agreement to release the promoter from liability may be shown by circumstances making it reasonably certain that the parties intended to and did enter into the agreement.

Here, the trial court found there was no agreement, either express or implied, regarding Fox's liability. Thus, in the absence of an agreement releasing him from liability, Fox is liable.

Coopers also contends that the trial court erred in ruling, in effect, that Coopers had the burden of proving any agreement regarding Fox's personal liability for payment of the fee. We agree.

Release of the promoter depends on the intent of the parties. As the proponent of an alleged agreement to release the promoter from liability, the promoter has the burden of proving the release agreement.

Fox seeks to bring himself within the exception to the general rule of promoter liability. However, as the proponent of the exception, he must bear the burden of proving the existence of the alleged agreement releasing him from liability. The trial court found that there was no agreement regarding Fox's liability. Thus, Fox failed to sustain his burden of proof, and the trial court erred in granting judgment in his favor.

It is undisputed that the defendant, Garry J. Fox, engaged Coopers' services, that G. Fox and Partners, Inc., was not in existence at that time, that Coopers performed the work, and that the fee was reasonable. The only dispute, as the trial court found, is whether Garry Fox is liable for payment of the fee. We conclude that Fox is liable, as a matter of law, under the doctrine of promoter liability.

REVERSED.

CRITICAL THINKING

What is the court's reasoning in this case? Given that reasoning, what if anything could Garry Fox have done differently to avoid liability?

ETHICAL DECISION MAKING

The doctrine of promoter liability, like most other doctrines in business law, has ethical roots. Legal doctrines are trying to advance our achievement of particular values or, in the language of the WPH model, purposes. Try to discover the value emphasis underlying adherence to the doctrine of promoter liability.

Subscribers. Subscribers offer to purchase stock in a corporation during the incorporation process. A subscriber becomes a shareholder once the corporation incorporates or accepts his or her purchase offer, whichever occurs first.

Courts interpret subscription agreements in two ways. In some states, subscription agreements are continuing offers to buy stock in the corporation that subscribers may revoke at any time. In other states, courts view subscription agreements as contracts among various subscribers. These contracts cannot be revoked unless all subscribers consent. RMBCA says that subscribers cannot revoke subscription agreements for six months unless the agreements provide otherwise or all subscribers consent.

SELECTING A STATE FOR INCORPORATION

Next, an infant corporation must select a state in which to incorporate. Each state has different laws governing the incorporation process and different corporate tax rates. Other factors corporations consider when selecting a state for incorporation include:

- How much flexibility does the state grant to corporate management?
- What rights do state statutes give to shareholders?
- What restrictions does the state place on the distribution of dividends?
- Does the state offer any kind of protection against takeovers?

Although most corporations incorporate in the state in which they are located and do most of their business, more than half of all publicly held corporations, including more than half of the Fortune 500 companies, are incorporated in Delaware. Decades ago, Delaware offered extremely low corporate tax rates and granted more extensive rights to management in the event of a takeover than did other states. Thus, in the 1940s and 1950s, many corporations changed their state of incorporation to Delaware. Although other states have made their corporate laws more attractive since then, many corporations remain incorporated in Delaware because its courts are highly experienced in corporate law. Closely held corporations and professional corporations, however, almost always incorporate in the state in which most of their stockholders live.

Although a corporation can incorporate in only one state, it can file a certificate of authority to do business in other states. Some states fine corporations that fail to obtain a certificate of authority before conducting business in the state. Other states fine directors and officers of these corporations directly and hold them personally liable for contracts made in the state.

Once a corporation chooses a state for incorporation, it can begin the formal legal process of incorporation.

Corporate Structure in Germany

German law establishes three tiers of corporate power. The board is the lowest, management makes up the second, and the supervisory board is the top tier. The supervisory board is similar to a board of directors in a U.S. corporation. The supervisors must approve managers' actions, including appointments, distribution of profits, and actions that affect the corporation's capital. Without the consent of the supervisors, managers are nearly powerless.

Supervisors cannot limit managerial authority to deal with third parties, however. Here managers enjoy considerable power and can act on their own discretion. Because supervisors cede considerable control in these situations, they have the power to appoint managers they feel will be reliable.

Although the board makes up the lowest tier of corporate power, it exercises considerable influence. Shareholders elect the board, a group of at least three members that acts as a mediator between shareholders and management. Because both managers and supervisors understand the importance of shareholders' interests, they listen to the board's recommendations.

Legal Process of Incorporation

SELECTION OF CORPORATE NAME

All states require that corporations attach *Corporation, Company, Limited, Incorporated,* or an abbreviation of one of these terms to the end of the business name to indicate the firm is incorporated. Kraft Foods Inc., The Hershey Company, Facebook Inc., and McDonald's Corporation serve as examples of corporate names. Corporations must also distinguish their names from those of all other domestic or foreign corporations licensed to do business within the state. This requirement protects third parties from confusion over similar names. Once the corporation has chosen a name, this name is subject to the approval of the state.

INCORPORATORS

An **incorporator** is an individual who applies to the state for incorporation on behalf of a corporation. RMBCA requires only one incorporator to incorporate a business, although it permits more. Although promoters frequently serve as incorporators, RMBCA does not require that incorporators be promoters or subscribers. In fact, RMBCA does not require that incorporators have an interest in the company. Generally, their only duty is to sign the articles of incorporation.

ARTICLES OF INCORPORATION

The *articles of incorporation* is a document providing basic information about the corporation. According to RMBCA, it must include (1) the name of the corporation, (2) the address of the registered office, (3) the name of the registered agent (the specific person who receives legal documents on behalf of the corporation), and (4) the names and addresses of the incorporators.

Many articles of incorporation include several additional elements, such as a clause describing the nature and purpose of the corporation. This statement of purpose grants the corporation power to engage in certain business activities. Many articles also describe the corporate capital structure and authorize the corporation to issue a certain number of shares of stock.

The incorporators must execute and sign the articles of incorporation and file the document with the secretary of state, including the required filing fee, to legally form the corporation. Once filed, the articles govern the corporation. Next, the secretary of state usually issues a **certificate of incorporation,** a document certifying that the corporation is incorporated in the state and authorized to conduct business.

FIRST ORGANIZATIONAL MEETING

After the secretary of state issues the certificate of incorporation, the shareholders usually meet to elect the corporate board of directors, pass corporate bylaws, and carry out other corporate business. Sometimes shareholders name the board members before this first organizational meeting and list them in the articles of incorporation. In these situations, the directors usually run the meeting.

At the meeting, shareholders adopt a set of corporate **bylaws,** or rules and regulations that govern the corporation's internal management. The articles of incorporation determine who has the power to amend the corporate bylaws after the first organizational meeting: shareholders, directors, or both.

Shareholders may also authorize the corporation to issue shares of stock and approve preincorporation contracts that promoters have made in the corporation's name.

Potential Problems with Formation of the Corporation

L05

What are some potential problems with the formation of corporations?

Most businesses incorporate to enjoy limited liability or perpetual existence. Shareholders benefit, however, only if the promoters and incorporator formally and correctly incorporate the business. If there is an error or omission during the incorporation process, courts may rule the organization is a **defective corporation.** Shareholders may be personally liable for a defective corporation's actions.

RESPONSES TO DEFECTIVE INCORPORATION

Suppose an incorporator incorrectly indicates the address of the corporate office in the articles of incorporation. Does the corporation still exist? Depending on the seriousness of the error, courts may disregard it by recognizing the firm as a *de jure* or a *de facto* corporation.

De Jure Corporations. A *de jure* corporation (literally, "a corporation from law," or a lawful corporation) has met the substantial elements of the incorporation process. Courts usually hold that corporations that make minor errors in the incorporation process still enjoy *de jure* corporate status. Exhibit 38-2 illustrates the process for creating a *de jure* corporation.

Thus, even if the incorporator wrote the incorrect address of the corporate office in the articles of incorporation, courts would not revoke the corporation's limited liability. No party can question a *de jure* corporation's status as a corporate entity in court.

De Facto Corporation. Suppose, however, that the incorporator makes a more serious mistake or omission, such as not filing the articles of incorporation with the secretary of state. In this case, courts may recognize the corporation as a *de facto* corporation

Exhibit 38-2

De Jure Corporation Formation

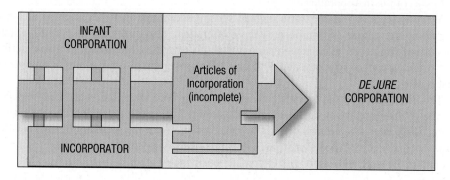

(literally, "a corporation from the fact," or a corporation in fact). A *de facto* corporation has not substantially met the requirements of the state incorporation statute, but courts recognize it as a corporation for most purposes to avoid unfairness to third parties who believed it was properly incorporated. *De facto* corporations, regardless of whether the state has a general corporation statute, must meet the following requirements:

- The promoters, subscribers, and incorporator made a good-faith attempt to comply with the incorporation statute.
- The organization has already conducted business as a corporation.

The process for recognizing a corporation as a *de facto* corporation is depicted in Exhibit 38-3.

Only the state can challenge a *de facto* corporation's existence as a corporate entity, in a suit called an action of *quo warranto* (Latin for "by what right").

Corporation by Estoppel.   Defective corporations cannot escape corporate entity status due to mistakes or omissions in their incorporation procedures. Suppose a corporation's articles of incorporation do not include the name of its registered agent and the directors, managers, and shareholders are unaware of the mistake. If the corporation conducts business with a third party who later sues for breach of contract, the corporation cannot claim it is not a corporate entity to escape liability. Courts hold that the corporation is a **corporation by estoppel;** thus, they *estop* (bar) the corporation from denying its corporate status. This ruling does not remedy the error or grant the firm corporate status for conducting future business.

If a corporation makes a significant error in the incorporation process and is not a *de jure* or *de facto* corporation, and corporation by estoppel does not apply, courts usually deny the organization corporate entity status. Thus, the organization does not enjoy limited shareholder liability.

Piercing the Corporate Veil.   In some cases, courts will deny limited liability to a corporation that would normally have *de jure* or *de facto* status because shareholders have used the corporation to engage in illegal or wrongful acts. Shareholders attempt to

Exhibit 38-3   *De Facto* Corporation Recognition Process

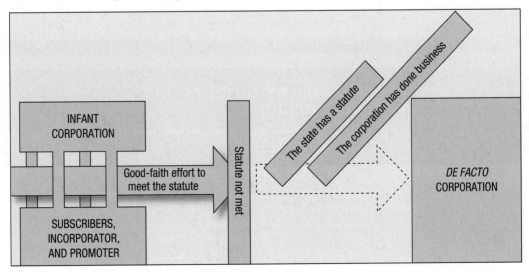

CASE NUGGET

Pharmaceutical Sales and Consulting Corporation v. J.W.S. Delavaux Co.
District Court of New Jersey
59 F. Supp. 2d 398 (1999)

Pharmaceutical Sales and Consulting sued J.W.S. Delavaux Co., alleging Delavaux failed to pay commissions due under a sales agreement between the parties. The sales agreement was signed by Pharmaceutical's president and on its behalf. The company had indicated it was a corporation, but Delavaux later discovered it was not a registered corporation and filed a motion to dismiss Pharmaceutical's complaint.

Delavaux maintained that Pharmaceutical's lack of corporate status as of the date of contract rendered the agreement invalid and unenforceable. Delavaux relied on the absence of several documents that, in its view, were essential to any claim that Pharmaceutical had attained *de facto* corporate status.

The court denied Delavaux's motion, but it also found that Pharmaceutical could not rely on the doctrine of *de facto* incorporation to demonstrate that it could sue Delavaux for breach of the parties' agreement, because Pharmaceutical had not made a bona fide attempt to incorporate before entering into the agreement with Delavaux.

---

hide behind the "corporate veil" of limited liability to protect themselves from personal liability. In these cases, courts *pierce the corporate veil,* or impose personal liability on shareholders. Shareholders of closely held and parent-subsidiary corporations frequently mix personal and corporate interests such that no separate corporate identity exists. Thus, courts often pierce the corporate veil of these corporations.

Legal Principle: **The limited liability of corporate shareholders may not exist when shareholders have acted in an illegal or wrongful manner.**

Courts are likely to pierce the corporate veil when:

- A corporation lacked adequate capital when it initially formed.
- A corporation did not follow statutory mandates regarding corporate business.
- Shareholders' personal interests and corporate interests are commingled such that the corporation has no separate identity.
- Shareholders attempt to commit fraud through a corporation.

If a corporation does not carefully maintain separate corporate and shareholder funds and records, courts may pierce the corporate veil and impose personal liability on shareholders, as Case 38-3 illustrates.

CASE 38-3 J-MART JEWELRY OUTLETS, INC. v. STANDARD DESIGN
COURT OF APPEALS OF GEORGIA
218 GA. APP. 459 (1995)

Jim Halter, the major shareholder of J-Mart Jewelry Outlets, Inc., and several other corporations, was aware J-Mart was in financial trouble. Before the firm went out of business, Halter paid off his personal credit cards using corporate funds. He also paid the corporation $1 for a corporate car *that had been purchased with corporation funds. Four of J-Mart's creditors brought suit against Halter in an attempt to recover corporate funds. The trial court jury pierced the corporate veil to hold Halter personally responsible for the debts. Halter appealed.*

JUDGE BLACKBURN: The concept of piercing the corporate veil is applied in Georgia to remedy injustices which arise where a party has over extended his privilege in the use of a corporate entity in order to defeat justice, perpetrate fraud or to evade contractual or tort responsibility. Because the cardinal rule of corporate law is that a corporation possesses a legal existence separate and apart from that of its officers and shareholders, the mere operation of corporate business does not render one personally liable for corporate acts. Sole ownership of a corporation by one person or another corporation is not a factor, and neither is the fact that the sole owner uses and controls it to promote his ends. There must be evidence of abuse of the corporate form. Plaintiff must show that the defendant disregarded the separateness of legal entities by commingling on an interchangeable or joint basis or confusing the otherwise separate properties, records or control.

In deciding this enumeration of error, we are confronted with two maxims that sometimes conflict. On the one hand, we are mindful that great caution should be exercised by the court in disregarding the corporate entity. On the other, it is axiomatic that "when litigated, the issue of 'piercing the corporate veil' is for the jury[,]" unless there is no evidence sufficient to justify disregarding the corporate form. Our examination of the trial transcript convinces us that there is evidence in this case rising to such level.

Halter knew as early as late April but not later than June 1991 that J-Mart would have to cease operations as a result of its financial difficulties. There was direct evidence that the $6,902.87 balance on Halter's American Express personal account was paid by J-Mart on December 23, 1991, eight days before it ceased doing business. The check was marked "PAYMENT IN FULL: JIM'S PERSONAL[,]" indicating that a material question of fact existed as to whether Halter used corporate funds to pay a personal debt. The evidence also established that J-Mart, with knowledge that it would soon cease doing business, purchased a new Cadillac for Halter's use. It thereafter made three payments on the vehicle before transferring it to Halter for $1 and allowing him to assume the remaining payments, indicating the presence of further questions of material fact relative to a de facto unauthorized payment for Halter's personal benefit. In light of the evidence presented, the trial court properly denied the motion for a directed verdict upon the claim of Halter's personal liability for violation of the corporate form.

Evidence raising material questions of fact as to Halter's possible abuse of the corporate form were thus properly before the jury. On appeal, we construe all the evidence most strongly in support of the verdict, for that is what we must presume the jury did; and if there is evidence to sustain the verdict, we cannot disturb it. So viewing the evidence, we conclude that the jury's verdict was proper and must stand. **AFFIRMED.**

CRITICAL THINKING

Given what you know of the facts of the case, could Halter have provided any information that would lead you to believe he was not responsible for the debts? What would it be?

ETHICAL DECISION MAKING

Describe the ethical conflict Halter was facing. For what purpose, or value, was he acting? Had Halter followed the Golden Rule, would he have acted as he did? What might have convinced Halter to refrain from using corporate funds to pay off his personal credit cards?

Corporate Financing

Corporations, like other businesses, need a source of funding. They most commonly obtain financing by issuing and selling corporate securities: debt securities, which represent loans to a corporation, and equity securities, which represent ownership in a corporation.

LO6

How do corporations get funding?

DEBT SECURITIES

Debt securities, or **bonds,** represent loans to a corporation from another party. Bonds are usually long-term loans on which the corporation promises to pay interest. They frequently list a maturity date on which the corporation must repay the face amount of the loan.

Before the maturity date, however, corporations usually pay bond holders fixed-dollar interest payments on a scheduled basis. Hence, bonds are sometimes called *fixed-income securities.*

Corporations can issue the following types of bonds:

- *Unsecured bonds (debentures):* No assets support corporations' obligation to repay the face value of unsecured bonds.
- *Secured bonds (mortgage bonds):* Specific property supports corporations' obligation to repay secured bonds.
- *Income bonds:* A corporation pays interest on income bonds in proportion to its earnings.
- *Convertible bonds:* Shareholders may exchange their convertible bonds for shares of company stock.
- *Callable bonds:* Corporations may call in and repay the bonds at specific times.

EQUITY SECURITIES

While bond owners have loaned money to a corporation, stock owners actually own part of the corporation, in the form of shares of stock called **equity securities.** Stockholders thus have a voice in the firm's control. Not all corporations issue bonds, but all issue stock. Common stock and preferred stock are the two major types.

Preferred Stock.   Owners of **preferred stock,** or *preferred shares,* enjoy preferences in the distribution of assets and dividends. They usually receive a percentage of dividends associated with the face value of their preferred stock, and they will receive dividends before owners of common stock do. Some corporations limit preferred stock owners' voting rights.

Cumulative preferred stock requires that if a corporation cannot pay the required dividends in a given year, it must pay them in the next year before it pays any common stock dividends. *Convertible preferred stock* allows its owner to convert shares into common stock at any time. *Redeemable preferred stock* (also known as *callable preferred stock*) permits the issuing corporation to buy shares back from shareholders in certain circumstances. *Participating preferred stock* entitles its owner to both preferred stock dividends and, after the corporation has paid common stock dividends, additional dividends.

Common Stock.   Owners of **common stock,** or *common shares,* own a portion of a corporation but do not enjoy any preferences. A common stock owner is entitled to corporate dividends in proportion to the number of shares he or she owns and has the right to vote in corporate elections. Each share is usually worth one vote. Thus, if you own 20,000 common shares of a corporation, you have 20,000 votes. In some cases, however, most notably the election of the board of directors, corporations use a method called *cumulative voting* to increase the influence of shareholders who own a small number of shares. (The next chapter discusses cumulative voting in more detail.)

Common stock owners have the lowest priority when a corporation distributes dividends. Creditors and preferred stock owners receive dividends first. Once a corporation pays these groups, however, common stock owners have a claim to the remainder of the corporate earnings.

Company Law in France

French law categorizes companies into two types: Société Anonymes (SA) and Société Responsabilité Limitée (SARL). Several factors determine a company's category, including its relationship to shareholders, its management hierarchy, and the extent of its liabilities.

SA companies offer shares to the public and must have at least seven shareholders. SARL companies, on the other hand, sell shares exclusively to company members. They must have at least 2 but no more than 50 shareholders. Their shares are nonnegotiable and freely transferable among company members.

One managing director, with as many as 14 subordinate directors, runs SA companies; at least one director must be a shareholder. SARL companies, in contrast, have one or two managers and allow nonmembers to serve. French law also requires that all SA companies appoint an independent auditor to verify the legality of their accounts. The auditor must report to the French government any irregularities she or he suspects to be criminal in nature. French law does not require that SARL companies appoint an auditor.

Member liability is closely related to the managerial structure of SA and SARL companies. Members of SARL companies are liable only to the extent of their contributions to the company. If the manager of a SARL company makes a transaction with a third party, all members are liable for the manager's action, regardless of whether he is a member of the company. Liability to third parties does not rest on all members in SA companies. Rather, in most cases the managing director is liable for damages caused by her actions, regardless of whether she benefited personally.

CASE OPENER WRAP-UP

Facebook

Zuckerberg's actions in 2004 were instrumental in creating what is now Facebook today. There are currently over 250 million users on the Web site from all over the world. In 2007, Microsoft bought a 1.6 percent share of the corporation for $240 million. Facebook gained another investor in November of that year, a billionaire from Hong Kong, Li Ka-shing, for $60 million. Estimates put the corporation's value around $4 billion to $5 billion. Ultimately, its corporate status allows Facebook to enjoy perpetual existence; to sue and be sued; to acquire property; to make contracts; to borrow and lend money; to make charitable donations; and to establish rules for managing the corporation. Moreover, Facebook's shareholders enjoy limited liability.

Key Terms

alien corporation   835
articles of
    incorporation   833
bonds   843
bylaws   840
certificate of
    incorporation   839
closely held
    corporations   835

common stock   844
corporation by
    estoppel   841
de facto corporation   840
de jure corporation   840
debt securities   843
defective corporation   840
dividends   834
domestic corporation   835

equity securities   844
for-profit corporations   835
foreign corporation   835
incorporator   839
nonprofit corporations   835
novation   837
preferred stock   844
private corporations   835
promoters   836

public corporation   835
publicly held
    corporations   835
retained earnings   834
S corporations   836
subscribers   836
subscription
    agreements   836

Summary of Key Topics

Characteristics of Corporations	A corporation is a legal entity, and it has rights, just as a person and citizen has rights.
	A corporation is a creature of the state.
	There is limited liability of shareholders.
	There is unrestricted transferability of corporate shares.
	A corporation has perpetual existence and centralized management.
	There is corporate taxation and liability for corporate agents.
Corporate Powers	Corporations have both express and implied powers.
Classification of Corporations	Corporations can be classified as public or private.
	Corporations can be for profit or can be classified as nonprofit.
	A corporation can be domestic, foreign, or alien.
	A corporation can be publicly held or closely held.
	A corporation can be classified as an S corporation.
	A corporation can also be classified as a professional corporation.
Formation of the Corporation	Promoters organize corporate formation.
	Subscribers offer to purchase stock in corporations in the formation process.
	A state is selected for incorporation.

Legal Process of Incorporation

The incorporation process consists of:

- Selection of a corporate name.
- Drafting and filing of articles of incorporation.
- First organizational meeting.

Potential Problems with Formation of the Corporation

Remedies for defective incorporation include:

- *De jure* corporations
- *De facto* corporations
- Corporations by estoppel
- Piercing the corporate veil

Corporate Financing

Corporate financing can consist of:

- Debt securities (bonds)
- Equity securities (preferred stock, common stock)

Point / Counterpoint

Should Corporations Be Allowed the Status of "Legal Personhood" and Be Given Full Protection under the Bill of Rights?	
YES	NO
On May 10, 1886, in the case of *Santa Clara County v. the Southern Pacific Railroad Company*, the Supreme Court clearly decided "other corporations" deserved "equal protection of the laws," specifically the Fourteenth Amendment.	Clearly, the creators of the Bill of Rights were aware that corporations existed at the time. Yet corporations were not mentioned as having rights independent of the natural persons associated with them, so the Bill of Rights was not designed to protect corporations as "legal persons."
A corporation is created by and composed of natural persons directly affected by its actions. Their rights cannot be violated, and violating the rights of the corporation indirectly does that. We should not place limitations on a group of people simply because they have pooled their efforts and formed a corporation.	Further, classifying corporations as "legal persons" and allowing them protection under the Bill of Rights, though advantageous for corporate interests, is harmful to human interests. For example, corporate money speaks much louder than one person's letter when influencing politicians.
Logical limitations are in place to restrict corporations' existence as "persons." Corporations cannot become official citizens and cannot vote; the natural citizens involved with the corporation are expected to vote with its best interest in mind.	If corporations are given rights as a natural person, the individuals making decisions behind the corporation are not being held accountable to the larger community. The corporation is punished for a poor decision rather than the individual, who used poor judgment but who may not suffer much, if any, of the consequences.
Finally, corporations deserve the same rights as natural persons because they fulfill the same obligations, only as entities separate from the natural persons associated with them. Shareholders pay taxes, for instance, and so do corporations.	Corporations also do not face the same restrictions as a natural person. A natural person's life must end, while a corporation is allowed perpetual existence.
	Lastly, corporations do not face the same potential consequences as natural persons. A corporation cannot be sent to jail for its actions. It cannot be rehabilitated and changed into a profitable member of society if it breaks the law.

Questions & Problems

1. Name at least three characteristics that distinguish corporations from other forms of business organization.

2. Distinguish between a closely held corporation and a publicly held corporation.

3. The Metacon Gun Club operated an outdoor shooting range adjacent to a river, a golf course, a riding stable, several private homes, and a state park. The Simsbury-Avon Preservation Society, a corporation composed of homeowners who live adjacent to the gun club, sued Metacon, alleging that the discharge of chromium, lead, lead shot, lead bullets, ammunition fragments, and ammunition wadding had contaminated groundwater. The members of the society depended on water resources in the vicinity of the gun club. Metacon argued that the society was not a corporation at the time it filed the suit because the state returned its paperwork several days later due to a missing address. Thus, Metacon argued, the society was not a legal entity and did not have standing to sue. How do you think the court ruled in this case? Why? [*Simsbury-Avon Pres. Soc'y, L.L.C. v. Metacon Gun Club, Inc.*, 2005 U.S. Dist. LEXIS 11699 (2005).]

4. In 2009, Mark McEwen, a personality from the *Early Show* on CBS, brought a lawsuit against the

Baltimore Washington Medical Center. McEwen went to the emergency room at the hospital with symptoms of a stroke, and a doctor told him he had the stomach flu and sent him away. On the plane heading home, McEwen suffered a stroke. Subsequently, McEwen filed a claim against the medical center, stating that his stroke could have been avoided if the doctor had prescribed aspirin and anticoagulants. How do you think the court decided the case? Do you think the court should hold the doctor responsible, or should the medical center be held accountable for the doctor's actions? [*McEwen et al v. Baltimore Washington Medical Center, Inc. et al* (2009)].

5. Attorney Nicholas Kepple, the president of M&K Realty, drew up a contract for the sale of a parcel of land (Lot 5) from Howard Engelsen to M&K. To establish a purchase price for the sale, Engelsen had Lot 5 appraised. The appraisers based their appraisal of Lot 5 on several facts that Kepple and Engelsen learned were incorrect after they signed the contract. These facts included the total acreage of Lot 5 and whether Lot 5 could be divided into two separate lots without the need for a subdivision approval from the planning and zoning commissioner. After learning that these facts were in error, Kepple saw that the original purchase price was well below the market price for Lot 5, and he attempted to complete the sale for the original purchase price. Engelsen informed Kepple that he would not complete the sale of Lot 5 because M&K had never legally formed as a corporation under the state incorporation statutes and thus lacked the capacity to enter the contract in the first place. Do you think the court agreed with Engelsen's argument? Why or why not? [*BRJM LLC v. Output Systems, Inc., et al.*, 2005 Conn. Super. LEXIS 1699 (2005).]

6. Richard Schoon was elected to the board of directors at the Troy Corporation, a private corporation in Delaware. There are three stock series of stock options. A series A share allows someone to elect four of five directors on the corporation's board. A series B share allows a stockholder to elect the fifth member of the board. Anyone who has a series C share has no voting rights. The CEO of Troy, Daryl Smith, owns the majority of the A shares, and thus he elected four directors of the board. Schoon was elected as the fifth director, although he owned no shares. Schoon claimed that Smith "dominated the board" because he elected the other four directors and they were compliant to his wishes. Schoon believed that in several instances, Smith took actions that benefited him personally yet harmed the corporation's finances. In 2008, Schoon filed a derivative suit that shareholders typically file. However, Schoon was not a shareholder and owned no stock in the company. Do you think the court accepted his suit? Why or why not? [*Schoon v. Smith*, Del. Supr. (2008).]

7. Citicorp, the owner of both Diners Club and Carte Blanche, merged the two credit card firms into one firm, giving Diners Club the dominant voice. Diners Club then ceased Carte Blanche's long-standing assistance to Carte Blanche Singapore (CBS). CBS sued Diners Club, claiming that it owed CBS a duty to continue providing services. CBS argued that because Carte Blanche and Diners Club were essentially the same firm, the court should pierce the corporate veil and hold Diners Club responsible for Carte Blanche's failure to provide services to CBS. How do you think the court ruled in this case? Why? [*Carte Blanche (Singapore) v. Diners Club International*, 2 F.3d 24 (1993).]

Looking for more review material?

The Online Learning Center at **www.mhhe.com/kubasek2e** contains this chapter's "Assignment on the Internet" and also a list of URLs for more information, entitled "On the Internet." Find both of them in the Student Center portion of the OLC, along with quizzes and other helpful materials.

Corporations: Directors, Officers, and Shareholders

LEARNING OBJECTIVES

After reading this chapter, you will be able to answer the following questions:

1   Why is it important to regulate the interactions among directors, officers, and shareholders within a corporation?

2   What is the role of a director, an officer, and a shareholder?

3   What are the duties of directors, officers, and shareholders?

4   In what ways can a director, officer, and shareholder be held liable?

5   What are the rights of directors, officers, and shareholders?

CASE OPENER
Roles of Directors, Officers, and Shareholders of Bank of America

In 2009, the Securities and Exchange Commission (SEC) alleged that the Bank of America Corporation misled shareholders about bonuses (amounting to billions of dollars) being paid to Merrill Lynch & Co. executives. The bonuses were distributed when Bank of America was acquiring the firm for $50 billion. The SEC decided to fine Bank of America $33 million. The corporation said that refusing to disclose details about the Merrill bonuses to shareholders during a vote regarding the merger was the right course of action. However, Bank of America also agreed to the penalty fine.

Bank of America claimed that the acceptance of the penalty fine was no admission of guilt but, rather, a way to avoid a costly court battle. The SEC worried that court costs would come from the government bailout money that the corporation had received in 2009.

1. If you were a shareholder in Bank of America would you think that the corporation's officers and directors breached their fiduciary duty to disclose?

2. What rights do shareholders have within a corporation? What responsibilities do the officers and directors of a corporation have to the shareholders?

The Wrap-Up at the end of the chapter will answer these questions.

As the opening scenario demonstrates, many groups of individuals within a corporation have their priorities and agendas. Not surprisingly, these often come into conflict. To ensure that such conflicts are equitably resolved, statutory laws delegate particular roles, duties, and rights to each group.

The statutory law governing corporations has a long and dynamic history. In 1946, the American Bar Association (ABA) drafted the first version of the Model Business Corporation Act (MBCA). Like almost all new laws, MBCA met with varying degrees of success, and over time legislatures have molded it to achieve certain objectives. The ABA has amended the act numerous times since 1946, and more than 25 states adopted at least part of it.

When the law changes, however, it often changes at an uneven pace. A sudden reformation sometimes interrupts a trend of incremental change. Thus, after nearly 40 years of minor revisions, the ABA in 1984 discontinued its revisions of MBCA and drafted the Revised Model Business Corporation Act (RMBCA). More than half the states have adopted all or part of RMBCA. This chapter explains the duties and rights set forth in RMBCA and common law.

Importance of Regulating Interactions among Directors, Officers, and Shareholders within a Corporation

LO1

Why is it important to regulate the interactions among directors, officers, and shareholders within a corporation?

The three major groups of individuals within a corporation are *directors, officers,* and *shareholders.* Each has different interests, and in many situations their interests conflict. Statutory law ensures that the directors, officers, and shareholders work together to the benefit of all.

Although directors and officers play different roles within the corporation, they share the same goal. Both attempt to ensure that their institution survives and they keep their jobs. Shareholders, on the other hand, want to raise the value of the company's stock.

These differences can lead to conflict. If a corporation has an opportunity that can quickly raise the value of its stock, shareholders will push the directors and officers to take it. But if the directors and officers believe that the decision might jeopardize their jobs, they will resist. To resolve conflicts, the law gives each group legal duties and rights.

Roles of Directors, Officers, and Shareholders

LO2

What is the role of a director, an officer, and a shareholder?

The duties and rights of directors, officers, and shareholders depend on the specific roles they play. These roles are discussed below and outlined in Exhibit 39-1.

DIRECTORS' ROLES

When a corporation faces an important decision, the board of directors meets to decide what course of action it will take. Although their vital role gives directors considerable power, no one director wields much by himself or herself. A director who wants the company to move in a certain direction must solicit the approval of other directors on the board before the company will begin to shift.

Elections.   Typically, shareholders use a majority vote to elect directors. The only exception occurs during incorporation. Because there are no shareholders in the beginning, either the incorporators appoint board members or the corporate articles name them.

Exhibit 39-1   Roles of Directors, Officers, and Shareholders

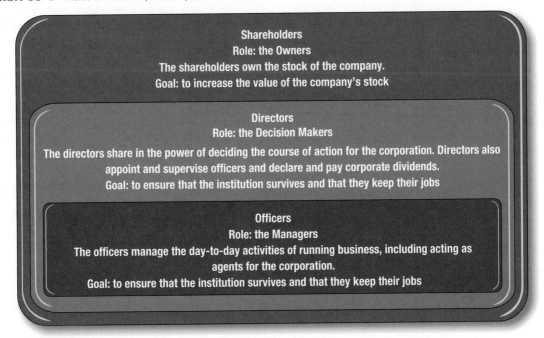

Shareholders
Role: the Owners
The shareholders own the stock of the company.
Goal: to increase the value of the company's stock

Directors
Role: the Decision Makers
The directors share in the power of deciding the course of action for the corporation. Directors also appoint and supervise officers and declare and pay corporate dividends.
Goal: to ensure that the institution survives and that they keep their jobs

Officers
Role: the Managers
The officers manage the day-to-day activities of running business, including acting as agents for the corporation.
Goal: to ensure that the institution survives and that they keep their jobs

This first board serves until the first shareholder meeting, at which the shareholders elect a new board. The corporate articles or bylaws specify the number of corporate directors. In the past, the minimum required was three, but today many states allow fewer. In fact, if a corporation has fewer than 50 shareholders, Section 7.32 of RMBCA allows companies to eliminate the board of directors altogether. This change illustrates how the need for practicality can stimulate change in the law. The benefits of the corporate form of business organization have drawn an enormous number of businesses, especially small businesses, to incorporate in recent years. The requirement of at least three directors, however, burdened small corporations that did not generate sufficient business to warrant three directors. Thus, many states eased or removed the three-director requirement.

Interestingly, almost anyone can become a director. The legal requirements are lax, and in most states directors are not even required to own stock in the corporation. In some cases, however, statutory law and corporate bylaws require not only ownership but also a minimum age.

Directors typically serve for one year, but most state statutes allow longer terms if they are staggered. Directors can be removed *for cause*—for failing to perform a required duty. Removal is typically a result of shareholder action, but in some cases directors can remove other directors for cause. Directors removed for cause can ask the courts to review the legality of their removal. Only a few states allow removal without cause, and then only if shareholders reserve that right at the board election.

Meetings and Voting.   A minimum number of directors, or a *quorum,* must be present at each directors' meeting for decisions to be valid. Quorum requirements are different in each state, but most states leave the decision up to the corporation itself. Because a quorum is required at each meeting, directors are notified whenever special meetings are called. Directors vote in person, and each has one vote. While ordinary decisions require a majority vote, more important decisions sometimes require a two-thirds vote.

Although directors' meetings are usually held in a central location, Section 8.20 of RMBCA permits them to be held via telephone conference.

Directors as Managers.   Although directors vote on major decisions about the corporation, they are also responsible for many day-to-day managerial activities. They appoint, supervise, and remove corporate officers as they see fit, and they declare and pay corporate dividends to shareholders. They are also responsible for making financial decisions and authorizing corporate policy decisions. Some directors are also officers or employees of the corporation; they are *inside directors.* Directors who are not officers or employees are *outside directors.* Outside directors are further divided into *affiliated directors* and *unaffiliated directors.* Affiliated directors have business contacts with the corporation, while unaffiliated directors do not.

Because the day-to-day tasks of a corporation can be overwhelming for a small board that has larger issues to address, directors often appoint an executive committee to handle day-to-day responsibilities.

OFFICERS' ROLES

Officers are executive managers whom the board of directors hires to run the day-to-day business of the corporation. Their decisions influence the corporation immensely. Officers act as agents of the corporation, and thus the rules of agency apply to their work. (Refer to Chapter 33 for the rules of agency.)

Qualifications required of officers are set forth in the corporate articles and bylaws of each corporation, but in most cases an individual may serve as both a director and an officer. Many corporations find it beneficial to include an officer on the board so that the directors can stay in touch with day-to-day operations.

SHAREHOLDERS' ROLES

Shareholders own the firm. As soon as an individual purchases the stock of a particular corporation, he or she becomes an owner of the corporation. However, there is a major division between shareholders within a corporation. There are majority shareholders and minority shareholders. A majority shareholder is a shareholder who controls more than half of the outstanding shares of a corporation, or at least 51 percent. A minority shareholder is one who controls fewer than half of the outstanding shares of a corporation.

While a shareholder is not legally recognized as an owner of corporate property, every shareholder has an *equitable,* or ownership, interest in the company. Shareholders are not directly responsible for the daily management of the corporation, but they elect the directors who are.

Power of Shareholders.   The articles of incorporation established within each corporation, and general incorporation law in each state, grant shareholders certain powers. Because shareholders must approve major board decisions, they are in some sense empowered to make decisions for the corporation. Their most influential power, however, is to elect and remove directors.

For example, in 2008 and 2009, Bank of America chairman and CEO Ken Lewis approved the questionable acquisitions of two financially troubled companies, Countrywide Financial and Merrill Lynch. Many shareholders disagreed with Lewis's decisions and lost confidence in his ability to lead the company. Consequently, to remedy the situation, Bank of America shareholders voted to remove Lewis from his chairman of the board position and opted to find a new leader. Lewis was able to retain his position as CEO but was no longer permitted to head the board of directors.

Shareholders also have the power to propose ideas for the corporation. The Securities and Exchange Commission has established that any shareholder who owns more than $1,000 worth of stock in the corporation can submit proposals to be included in *proxy materials* sent to the shareholders before their annual meeting.

Meetings.   Shareholders typically meet once a year, but in emergencies they can meet more often. The board of directors, shareholders who own at least 10 percent of the corporation's outstanding shares, and others authorized in the articles of incorporation may call a special shareholder meeting.

Like directors' meetings, shareholder meetings require a quorum, generally the presence of shareholders holding more than 50 percent of the outstanding shares. A majority vote of the shares represented is then required to pass resolutions. Occasionally, however, articles of incorporation include supermajority provisions, which state that more than a majority is needed to pass major corporate proposals, such as those for corporate merger or dissolution.

Because shareholders cannot always attend shareholder meetings, they can authorize a third party to attend and vote in their place. This authorization is called a **proxy.** Under Section 7.22(c) of RMBCA, proxies last for 11 months and can be withdrawn at any time unless specifically designed to be irrevocable.

An individual shareholder can also enter a voting trust by transferring his or her share titles to a trustee in exchange for a *voting trust certificate.* The trustee is then responsible for voting for those shares, either as directed in the trust or at the trustee's discretion. The shareholder, however, retains all other shareholder rights (discussed below).

Before a meeting, shareholders can sign a *shareholder voting agreement* in which they agree to vote together in a certain manner. These agreements are usually legally enforceable.

Voting.   Like directors, each shareholder is entitled to one vote per share in most instances. Corporations practice unique voting processes, however, that alter the influence of each shareholder's votes and are especially important for minority shareholders. One such process required in most states, *cumulative voting,* ensures that minority shareholders have a voice in electing the board of directors. It gives each group, majority and minority shareholders, a certain number of votes to cast by multiplying the number of shares the group owns by the number of open director positions. If a company is electing eight directors and the minority shareholders own 2,000 shares, the minority shareholders get 16,000 votes to cast in the election. If the majority shareholders in the same corporation own 8,000 shares, they get 64,000 votes.

Although it may seem that minority shareholders still have little influence in the election, cumulative voting permits them to vote at least one director onto the board because they can cast all their votes for one candidate. If the majority shareholders want to elect all eight directors from their nominees, each nominee must receive more than 16,000 votes in order to beat the 16,000 votes of the minority nominee. But because the majority shareholders have only 64,000 votes to cast, they cannot cast more than 16,000 votes for each of eight candidates (16,000 $\times$ 8 = 128,000). Thus, if the minority shareholders cast all their 16,000 votes for one candidate, they can guarantee that candidate's election.

Cumulative voting is more egalitarian than simple majority voting because it ensures that every voice within the corporation is heard, not just the voices of those with the most power. Without it, majority shareholders could monopolize control of the company and disregard the interests of the minority shareholders. Cumulative voting is not guaranteed in RMBCA, however; rather, it occurs only if the corporation's articles of incorporation provide for it.

Duties of Directors, Officers, and Shareholders

LO3

What are the duties of directors, officers, and shareholders?

Because all individuals within a corporation depend on one another, the law gives them specific legal responsibilities called *fiduciary duties.*

DUTIES OF DIRECTORS AND OFFICERS

Shareholders have little input in the day-to-day operations of the corporation; they trust the directors and officers to run the company to the best of their ability. Thus, directors and officers have duties to the shareholders and to the corporation. Their two primary fiduciary duties are the duty of care and the duty of loyalty.

Duty of Care.   The fiduciary *duty of care* means that directors and officers must exercise due care when making decisions for the corporation. The phrase *due care* is ambiguous, and various courts have interpreted it differently over time. In general, however, it requires exercising the care that an ordinary prudent person would exercise in the management of his or her own assets. In other words, a person acting with due care acts in good faith and in the best interest of the company.

Legal Principle: **The directors and officers bear liability for failure to exercise a duty of care with respect to the management of shareholder assets.**

Given their duty to act in the best interest of the company, directors and officers must supervise employees who work for the corporation to a reasonable extent. They also have a duty to attend director and corporate business meetings. Most important, however, they have a fiduciary duty to make informed and reasonable business decisions.

The directors and officers of Enron Corp. failed in their duty of care with regard to their shareholders by not acting in the best interest of the company. They continued to advocate that employees invest in the employee stock-sharing options, even though it appears that they knew the stock was drastically overpriced. Furthermore, they failed in their duty of care regarding oversight. The directors and officers either did not pay enough attention to see the collapse of their stock coming or they purposely kept the information secret. Either way, they breached their fiduciary duty of care and therefore are liable to their shareholders, many of whom were Enron employees.

In February 2009, shareholders of the company Citigroup brought action against the company's current and former directors. One of the alleged liabilities of the directors was a failure to obey fiduciary duties. Shareholders claimed that substantial risks the company faced in the subprime lending market were not properly managed or monitored. The shareholders explained that there were signs of severe problems in the credit and real estate markets beginning in 2005 that should have put the Citigroup directors on heightened alert. Essentially, what the Citigroup shareholders were claiming was that the directors failed in their duty of care regarding oversight. The directors did not seem to pay enough attention to problems within the subprime lending market that were going to directly affect the company.

Directors and officers are expected to stay abreast of all important corporate matters and obtain information about business transactions, review contracts, read reports,

E-COMMERCE AND THE LAW

When a B2B Company Cooks the Books

When you hear the phrase "cook the books," you likely think of companies like Enron, Tyco, and Adelphia. Why did the officers and directors of these companies fail to realize that accountants were cooking company books? Were any officers or directors involved in the fraud?

E-commerce firms have cooked their books too. PurchasePro, a business-to-business software firm that gave companies access to an online marketplace, was allegedly engaged in "overstating revenues, engaging in aggressive accounting practices and mismanaging corporate assets." Basically, the company manipulated its financial records to make itself look far more successful than it really was. It went bankrupt in September 2002.

Federal prosecutors charged company officers and directors with conspiracy, securities fraud, and obstruction of justice, a breach of their duty of care. Two senior officers, Jeffrey R. Anderson and Scott H. Miller, pleaded guilty to federal crimes in 2003. Their behavior was similar to that of officers of other, more well-known companies that have cooked the books—they had secret side deals with purchasers that gave the appearance of sales that did not really exist; they misrepresented the company's financial health so that investors could not make informed decisions; and, when news of alleged fraud surfaced, they used their energy to shred incriminating documents.

and attend presentations. After all, if directors and officers are uninformed, they cannot make decisions in the best interest of the company. RMBCA does allow directors to make decisions based on information gathered by other employees. Interestingly, however, most corporations do not allow directors' decisions to be based on secondhand information.

The decisions corporate directors and officers make must not only be informed; they must also be reasonable. If a director or officer is taken to court for breaching the duty of care by making an unreasonable decision, the court typically inquires whether the decision had any rational business purpose. In other words, was there good reason to think the decision *could* have helped the company?

Part of the duty of care is to voice dissent when the corporation is doing something a director or officer does not think is in its best interest. It is unusual for a dissenting director to be held personally liable for decisions made by the corporation that entail mismanagement.

Duty of Loyalty.   Because directors and officers have great decision-making freedom, they have the power to make business decisions that will benefit themselves while harming the company. Thus, to protect shareholders, directors and officers have a fiduciary *duty of loyalty,* which puts the corporation's interest above their own when making business decisions.

When directors or officers violate their duty of loyalty, they are **self-dealing.** There are two types of self-dealing. The first, *business self-dealing,* occurs when a director or officer makes decisions that benefit other companies with which she has a relationship. The second, called *personal self-dealing,* occurs when a director or officer makes business decisions that benefit him personally.

When Citigroup shareholders brought the company directors to court in 2009, a second complaint was that the directors and other defendants authorized a multimillion-dollar benefit and payment package for the CEO of Citigroup in 2007. Those in charge of a company are not supposed to engage in self-dealing activities that benefit them before the rest of the company.

A director or officer who is self-dealing often forces the corporation into unfair business deals. Directors and officers can also breach their fiduciary duty of loyalty, however, by *preventing* corporate opportunity. This breach usually happens when directors or officers own other companies that compete with their corporation without the consent of the board of directors or the shareholders. If a director or officer uses corporate assets to start another

Duty of Care

In re Caremark Int'l
698 A.2d 959 (1996)

Caremark, a corporation headquartered in Illinois, provided patient care and managed health care services. It was indicted by a grand jury for paying a doctor to distribute a drug produced by the corporation and for making inappropriate referral payments to another doctor. Several Caremark shareholders filed a derivative suit (discussed below) alleging that Caremark's directors breached their fiduciary duty of care by allowing situations to develop that exposed the corporation to enormous legal liability.

The Court of Chancery of Delaware ruled:

[C]ompliance with a director's duty of care can never appropriately be judicially determined by reference to the content of the board decision that leads to a corporate loss, apart from consideration of the good faith or rationality of the process employed. That is, whether a judge or jury considering the matter after the fact, believes a decision substantively wrong, or degrees of wrong extending through "stupid" to "egregious" or "irrational," provides no ground for director liability, so long as the court determines that the process employed was either rational or employed in a good faith effort to advance corporate interests. To employ a different rule—one that permitted an "objective" evaluation of the decision—would expose directors to substantive second guessing by ill-equipped judges or juries, which would, in the long-run, be injurious to investor interests.

business, goes into the same line of business, or uses her position to develop a new business that the company might have pursued, she is preventing corporate opportunity and can be held liable for violating the fiduciary duty of loyalty.

A director or officer convicted of breaching the duty of loyalty is required to cede to the corporation all profits earned as a result of the breach. The corporation need not have been able to earn those profits in the absence of the breach. The goal of the rule is to discourage breaches of the duty of loyalty by taking all profits so made.

The fiduciary duties of care and loyalty are rooted in ethics. Without them, directors and officers could pursue their own interests at the expense of others. Think back to Chapter 2 and the different ethical guidelines used to make ethical decisions. Which ethical guideline is the legal system using when it delegates fiduciary duties?

Duty to Disclose Conflict of Interest.   Because individual directors and officers can frequently benefit personally from decisions made by the board, they have a fiduciary duty to fully disclose conflicts of interest that arise in corporate transactions. If the board addresses an issue that might personally benefit a particular director, that director is required not only to disclose the self-interest but also to abstain from voting on that issue. Decisions can be made that will personally benefit one director or officer as long as (1) there is full disclosure of the interest and (2) the disinterested board members and/or disinterested shareholders approve it.

DUTIES OF SHAREHOLDERS

Although shareholders typically have few legal duties, in rare instances majority shareholders have fiduciary duties to the corporation and to minority shareholders. In some corporations, the majority shareholder owns such a significant portion of the corporation's stock as to essentially control the firm. When that individual sells his shares, control of the company shifts to another individual. Thus, the majority shareholder in this situation has a fiduciary duty to act with care and loyalty when selling the shares. In closely held corporations, a breach of this fiduciary duty is known as *oppressive conduct.*

CASE NUGGET

Duty of Loyalty

Patrick v. Allen
355 F. Supp. 2d 704 (2005)

RPO, a privately traded corporation, rented land to a private golf course, of which several of RPO's directors were members. The directors charged the golf course enough rent to cover only the property taxes on the land. Patrick, a shareholder of RPO, brought a suit against the directors of RPO, alleging that they breached their fiduciary duty of loyalty to the corporation by failing to maximize the value of the corporation for shareholders. The directors argued that they were exempt from liability under the business judgment rule (covered below).

The U.S. District Court for the Southern District of New York ruled against the RPO's directors, holding:

The business judgment rule will not protect a decision that was the product of fraud, self-dealing, or bad faith. Directors may benefit from the rule only if they possess a disinterested independence and do not stand in a dual relation which prevents an unprejudicial exercise of judgment. It is black-letter, settled law that when a corporate director or officer has an interest in a decision, the business judgment rule does not apply. . . . A director is considered interested in a transaction if the director stands to receive a direct financial benefit from the transaction which is different from the benefit to shareholders generally. . . . The duty of loyalty requires a director to subordinate his own personal interests to the interest of the corporation.

More than half of U.S. publicly traded corporations are incorporated in Delaware. Thus, when Delaware courts rule on the duties of majority shareholders to minority shareholders, for example, the courts' rulings have a far-reaching impact. In Case 39-1, brought before the supreme court of Delaware, minority shareholders sued the majority shareholder for violating its fiduciary duties.

CASE 39-1
FRIEDA H. RABKIN v. PHILIP A. HUNT CHEMICAL CORP.
SUPREME COURT OF DELAWARE
498 A.2D 1099 (1985)

On March 1, 1983, Olin Corporation bought 63.4 percent of the outstanding shares of Hunt Chemical Corporation from Turner and Newall Industries, Inc., at $25 per share, which made Olin the majority shareholder. Before Turner and Newall Industries sold the shares to Olin, it insisted Olin agree to pay $25 per share if Olin acquired the remaining Hunt stock within one year. On July 5, 1984, Hunt merged into Olin by buying the remaining stock for $20 a share. The minority shareholders of Hunt challenged the Olin-Hunt merger, on the grounds that the price offered was grossly inadequate because Olin had unfairly manipulated the timing of the merger to avoid the one-year commitment, and that specific language in Olin's Schedule 13D, filed when it purchased the Hunt stock, constituted a price commitment by which Olin failed to abide, contrary to its fiduciary obligations to the minority shareholders. The trial judge dismissed the complaint on grounds that the only remedy legally available to the minority shareholders was an appraisal. The plaintiffs then sought and were denied leave to amend their complaints. They appealed.

JUDGE MOORE: The plaintiffs have charged that the merger does not meet the entire fairness standard required. They offer specific acts of unfair dealing constituting breaches of fiduciary duties which, if true, may have substantially affected the offering price. These allegations, unrelated to judgmental factors of valuation, should survive a motion to dismiss.

Olin's alleged attitude toward the minority, at least as it appears on the face of the complaints and their proposed amendments, coupled with the apparent absence of any meaningful negotiations as to price, all raise unanswered questions about the undiminished duty of loyalty to Hunt.

In our opinion, the facts alleged by the plaintiffs regarding Olin's avoidance of the one-year commitment support a claim of unfair dealing sufficient to defeat dismissal at this stage of the proceedings. At the very least, the facts alleged import a form of overreaching, and in the context of entire fairness they deserve more considered analysis than can be accorded them on a motion to dismiss.

REVERSED.

CRITICAL THINKING

What reasons does the court give for its conclusion? Are you persuaded by those reasons?

ETHICAL DECISION MAKING

Clearly, the court emphasizes a particular value in its ruling. What is this value? The court's emphasis on this particular value makes it difficult to emphasize other values. Which value(s) does this ruling de-emphasize?

L04

In what ways can a director, officer, and shareholder be held liable?

Liabilities of Directors, Officers, and Shareholders

Because almost all individuals within a corporation have legal fiduciary duties to it, they can be held liable for harming the business by violating these duties. There are, however, certain instances in which directors, officers, and shareholders cannot be held liable for harming the business.

LIABILITY OF DIRECTORS AND OFFICERS

Liability for Torts and Crimes. Although corporations themselves are liable for the torts and crimes of their directors and officers, directors and officers can be held personally responsible for their own torts and crimes and even for those of other employees whom they have failed to adequately supervise.

According to the responsible person doctrine, a court may find a corporate officer criminally liable regardless of the extent to which the officer took part in the criminal activity. Even an officer who knew nothing about the criminal activity can be held criminally liable if the court determines that a responsible person would have known about and could have prevented it.

Directors and officers who use inside information to trade the corporation's stock for personal profit can be held liable for breaching their fiduciary duty to the shareholders from whom they purchase or to whom they sell the stock.

Legal Principle: **As a general rule, directors and officers are held liable for many of the same actions because they have nearly identical fiduciary duties to the corporation.**

Business Judgment Rule. Although directors and officers are expected to make decisions in the best interest of the corporation, they are not expected to make perfect decisions all the time. Many decisions harm the corporation inadvertently.

The Business Judgment Rule

**Auerbach v. Bennett
393 N.E.2d 994 (1979)**

An internal audit of the GTE Corporation suggested that the corporation's management had paid more than $11 million in bribes and kickbacks both in the United States and abroad over a four-year period. Auerbach, a GTE shareholder, immediately initiated a shareholder derivative action (discussed below) against GTE's directors.

The Court of Appeals of New York, however, held that the business judgment rule exempted the GTE directors from liability for their poor business decisions. The court stated:

[The business judgment doctrine] bars judicial inquiry into actions of corporation directors taken in good faith and in the exercise of honest judgment in the lawful and legitimate furtherance of corporate purposes. Questions of policy of management, expediency of contracts or action, adequacy of consideration, lawful appropriation of corporate funds to advance corporate interests, are left solely to their honest and unselfish decision, for their powers therein are without limitation and free from restraint, and the exercise of them for the common and general interests of the corporation may not be questioned, although the results show that what they did was unwise or inexpedient.

Although shareholders may want to hold their directors and officers liable for these decisions, the *business judgment rule* does not allow them to do so. This rule says that directors and officers are not liable for decisions that harm the corporation if they were acting in good faith at the time. In other words, if there was reason to believe that the decision was a good one at the time, the directors and officers are not liable for the resulting harm.

Exhibit 39-2 summarizes the liability of directors and officers.

Although the business judgment rule is not a statute, it is common law recognized by almost every court in the country. The rule is practical because it grants directors freedom to work without constant fear of personal liability. It also encourages individuals to serve as directors by removing the threat of personal liability for inadvertent mistakes. Case 39-2 illustrates how the courts interpret and apply the business judgment rule.

> Can be held personally liable for their own torts and crimes

> Can be held personally liable for the torts and crimes of other employees that they supervise

> Can be held liable for wrongful transactions involving company stock

> Cannot be held liable for decisions that harm the company if they were acting in good faith at the time of the decision

Exhibit 39-2

Liability of Directors and Officers

STATE OF WISCONSIN INVESTMENT BOARD v. WILLIAM BARTLETT
COURT OF CHANCERY OF DELAWARE, NEW CASTLE
C.A. NO. 17727 (2000)

The State of Wisconsin Investment Board (SWIB) owned 11.5 percent of the outstanding shares of common stock in the pharmaceutical company Medco Research, Inc. In 1996, Medco began searching for a merger partner. In a proxy statement on January 5, 2000, Medco recommended shareholders vote for a merger between Medco and King Pharmaceuticals, Inc. On January 11, 2000, SWIB filed a request for injunctive relief on the grounds that the board of directors breached their fiduciary duties of care, loyalty, and disclosure in negotiating the merger. SWIB argued that the majority of Medco's directors were self-interested, and that no reasonably prudent businessperson of sound judgment would have negotiated the merger as Medco had. SWIB alleged Medco failed to disclose all information material to the shareholders, did not adequately inform themselves of all information available about the merger, and failed to adequately supervise a self-interested director. Medco refutes all claims.

JUDGE STEELE: Unless this presumption [that a board of directors acted with care, loyalty, and in good faith] is sufficiently rebutted, raising a reasonable doubt about self-interest or independence, the Court must defer to the discretion of the board and acknowledge that their decisions are entitled to the protection of the business judgment rule.

In order to require application of the entire fairness standard, the plaintiff has to show that a majority of directors has a financial interest in the transaction or a motive to entrench themselves in office through the merger. Plaintiff's allegations of self-interest do not meet the threshold necessary to rebut the presumption of the business judgment rule.

The plaintiff's allegations do not demonstrate that the Medco board failed to inform itself of all material facts concerning the proposed merger with King. I conclude that Medco's board met its duty of care in proceeding with the King merger. Despite the material disputes of fact, I am confident that Medco's board adequately informed themselves of all material information necessary to execute the merger agreement.

I cannot, on the basis of these allegations, find that the board either willfully left itself uninformed in order to serve its "self-interest" or failed to act in "good faith and in the honest belief that the merger was in the best interests of the company." It is equally apparent to me that the board sufficiently complied with the "good-faith" standard set forth by this Court in Aronson. I have also been led to conclude that the directors were acting to benefit the economic interest of the shareholders.

Plaintiff's request for preliminary injunction is hereby denied with respect to the shareholder vote and denied with respect to the merger.

Judgment for defendant.

CRITICAL THINKING

What words or phrases in the court's argument are ambiguous? Why are these ambiguous words important?

ETHICAL DECISION MAKING

Suppose you were on the board of directors in this case. The universalization test guides your ethical decisions. Would you have made a different decision?

LIABILITY OF SHAREHOLDERS

Because shareholders are the owners of the corporation, their main liability is for the extent of their investment when the company loses money. In rare instances, however, shareholders are personally liable. For example, individuals sometimes sign stock subscription agreements before incorporation that contractually obligate them to purchase shares in the corporation. For **par-value shares,** or shares that have a fixed face value noted on the stock certificate, the shareholder must pay the corporation at least the par value of the stock. For **no-par shares,** or shares without a par value, the shareholder must pay the fair market value. A shareholder who does not buy the shares is personally liable for breach of contract.

A shareholder who receives **watered stock,** or stock issued below its fair market value, is also individually liable for the difference between the price she paid for the shares and their stated corporate value.

Finally, a shareholder can also be held personally liable for receiving illegal dividends. State statutes mandate that corporations pay dividends from only certain funds. Also, dividends are always illegal if they are paid when the corporation is insolvent or if they cause the corporation to become insolvent. A shareholder who knew that a dividend was illegal when he received it is personally liable and must return the funds to the corporation.

Exhibit 39-3 summarizes the liability of shareholders.

Rights of Directors, Officers, and Shareholders

Because shareholders are in a position of limited decision-making power, they have rights that allow them to participate within the corporation. Directors and officers also have specific rights that allow them to perform their duties to the best of their abilities.

DIRECTORS' RIGHTS

The unique responsibilities of corporate directors call for unique rights. There are four: the rights of compensation, participation, inspection, and indemnification.

All corporate directors have a right to *compensation* for their work, which different corporations grant in different ways. Most directors hold other managerial positions within their companies and receive their compensation through those positions. Another common solution is to pay directors nominal sums as honorariums for their contributions. In some corporations, directors can determine their own compensation.

Because directors are required to make informed business decisions, they have the rights of *participation* and *inspection.* They can get involved in and understand every aspect of the business. A corporate director has the right to be notified of all meetings and has access to all books and records.

L05

What are the rights of directors, officers, and shareholders?

Exhibit 39-3

Liability of Shareholders

Are liable for the debts of the corporation, to the extent of their investment

Are liable for a breach of contract if a stock subscription agreement was signed and yet no stock was purchased

Are liable for watered stock

Can be held personally liable for receiving illegal dividends

Assigned Directors in Japan

A common corporate practice in Japan is for multiple corporations, banks, and companies to form hierarchical conglomerates known as *keiretsu*. There are two types. The first is a horizontal *keiretsu*, in which a powerful bank acts as the unifying agent under which several large corporations come together. With the exception of the bank, the members share equal power. The second type is a vertical *keiretsu*, hierarchically ordered with an unequal distribution of power, in which large corporations often control several hundred subordinate companies.

Power distribution within *keiretsus* plays a key role in determining the board of directors. Usually the main bank or parent corporation assigns its own executives to serve on the boards of the less powerful companies. The prosperity of these companies is important to the main banks and parent corporations. The assigned directors act as overseers, consultants, and mentors. They want to promote simultaneously the interests of the parent corporation and the growth of the subordinate ones. Thus, the subordinate companies do not view the assignment of directors as a sign of mistrust. To the Japanese the logic is patent: If the success of the *keiretsu* and the success of each company are reciprocal, all parties should work together to achieve the collective goal.

Finally, because of their great legal vulnerability, directors have the right to *indemnification*. In other words, they can be reimbursed for any legal fees incurred in lawsuits against them.

OFFICERS' RIGHTS

Corporate officers are technically employees of the corporation, so their rights are defined by employment contracts drawn up by the board of directors or the incorporators. Officers are in a contractual relationship with the corporation, and if they are removed in violation of the contract terms, the corporation may be liable for breach of contract.

SHAREHOLDERS' RIGHTS

Although shareholders' most powerful right is the right to vote at shareholders' meetings, they also possess many other rights.

Stock Certificates. Some corporations issue stock certificates to shareholders as proof of ownership in the corporation. Each certificate includes the corporation's name and the number of shares it represents. A sample stock certificate is shown in Exhibit 39-4. A shareholder's ownership in the corporation, however, does not depend on possession of the physical stock certificate. If the certificate is destroyed in a fire, the shareholder's ownership in the corporation is not destroyed. The shareholder can request a reissued certificate, although she may be required to guarantee payment to the corporation if the original certificate should reappear at a later date.

In most states, however, shares may be *uncertificated*, meaning that the corporation does not issue physical stock certificates. In this case, shareholders usually have a right to receive a letter from the corporation giving the information typically included on the face of a stock certificate.

Preemptive Rights. Under common law, shareholders have *preemptive rights*, which give preference to shareholders to purchase shares of a new issue of stock. Each shareholder receives preference in proportion to the percentage of stock he already owns.

Suppose Manuela owns 1,500 shares in a corporation with 5,000 outstanding shares, or 30 percent of the outstanding stock. The corporation decides to issue an additional 10,000 shares. If it does not grant preemptive rights, the degree of Manuela's control of

Exhibit 39-4   Example of a Stock Certificate

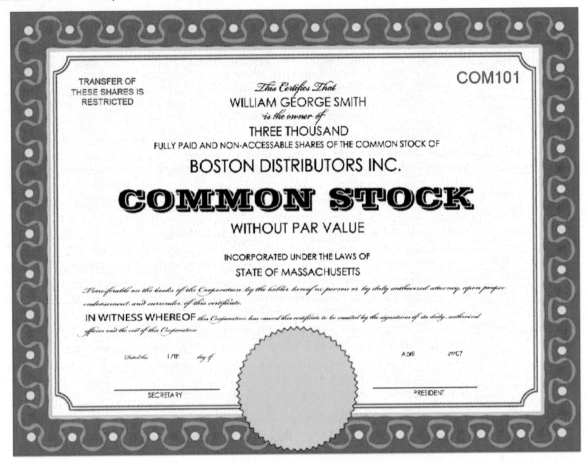

the corporation will fall because she now owns 1,500 of 15,000 shares, or only 10 percent of its stock. With preemptive rights, if Manuela elects to purchase 3,000 shares of the newly issued stock, she owns 4,500 of 15,000 shares and retains her 30 percent control.

In most states, a corporation's bylaws can negate preemptive rights, so the corporation determines whether to grant them. Preemptive rights are especially important for individuals who own stock in close corporations due to the relatively small number of issued shares. If a close corporation issues additional shares, an individual shareholder may lose proportional control over the firm if he does not buy newly issued shares. But if preemptive rights exist, all shareholders receive **stock warrants,** which they can redeem for a certain number of shares at a specified price within a given time period. Like shares of stock, stock warrants are often traded publicly on securities exchanges.

Dividends.   If directors fail to declare and distribute dividends, shareholders have the right to take legal action to force them to do so. In many cases, however, directors have good reason to hold dividends for a limited amount of time to finance major undertakings such as research or expansion. Thus, shareholders must show that the directors are acting unreasonably and abusing their discretion in withholding the dividend.

To see the reasons for declaring stock dividends, please see the **Connecting to the Core** activity on the text Web site at www.mhhe.com/kubasek2e.

Inspection Rights.　All shareholders have the right to inspection in both statutory and common law. A shareholder can, moreover, appoint an agent to conduct the inspection on her behalf. To prevent abuse, however, this right has many limitations. Shareholders can inspect records and books only if they ask in advance and have a *proper purpose.* Some states allow only shareholders with a minimum number of shares to inspect; others require that shareholders own stock for a minimum amount of time before inspection. Corporations can deny shareholders the right to inspect confidential corporate information, such as trade secrets. A shareholder who feels his right of inspection has been wrongly denied can take the issue to court.

Share Transfer.　The law generally permits property owners to transfer their property to another person, and in most cases stock is considered transferable property. In closely held corporations, however, transfer of stock is usually restricted so that shareholders can choose the corporation's other shareholders; they enjoy the corporate equivalent of the right of *delectus personae* (this allows partners to choose the individuals with whom they will go into business). Restrictions on transferability must be included on the face of the stock certificate.

One method of restricting stock transferability is the **right of first refusal.** If a corporation establishes this right in its bylaws, the corporation or its shareholders have the right to purchase any shares of stock offered for resale by a shareholder within a specified period of time.

Corporate Dissolution.　Shareholders have the right to petition the court to dissolve their corporation if they feel that it cannot continue to operate profitably. According to Section 14.30 of RMBCA, if a corporation engages in any of the following behaviors, shareholders have a legal right to initiate dissolution:

1. Directors are deadlocked in managerial decisions and harming the corporation.
2. Directors are acting in illegal, oppressive, or fraudulent ways.
3. Assets are being wasted or used improperly.
4. Shareholders are deadlocked and cannot elect directors.

Once dissolution has taken place and the corporation has settled its debts with its creditors, shareholders have a right to receive the remaining assets of the company in proportion to the number of shares they own. Case 39-3 provides an illustration of a case seeking dissolution.

CASE **39-3**　**MOUZAKITIS v. PEARL NIGHTLIFE, INC., ET AL.**
NEW YORK SUPREME COURT, QUEENS COUNTY
AVAILABLE AT http://decisions.courts.state.ny.us/fcas/fcas_
docs/2009mar/4000284202008100sciv.pdf (2009)

Marianthi and Leonidas Mouzakitis, husband and wife, own fifteen of the hundred shares that were issued in the operation of a restaurant in New York. The operator is Pearl　*Nightlife, Inc., and the restaurant is situated at 45-30 Bell Boulevard in Bayside, New York. The corporation's president, Nicholas Kiriakis, owns thirty shares and manages the restaurant. The Mouzakitises alleged that those in control of the corporation, including Kiriakis, did not fulfill the needs of the corporation. Specifically, Kiriakis was said to neglect paying salaries and dividends, block an inspection of corporate records and books, and mismanage and divert the corporation's funds and assets.*

JUDGE KITZES: In *Leibert,* the Court of Appeals recognized a common-law right to dissolution of a corporation where the officers or directors of the corporation are engaged in conduct which is violative of their fiduciary duty to shareholders. Dissolution is appropriate if the directors or those in control of the corporation are looting the corporate assets to enrich themselves at the expense of the minority shareholders; continuing the corporation solely to benefit those in control; or that the actions of the directors or those in control has been calculated to depress the capital of the corporation in order to coerce the minority shareholders to sell their stock at a depressed price.

[The petitioners] have set forth sufficient allegations and support to raise an issue that the majority shareholders are enriching themselves at the expense of the minority. The sworn statements of the petitioners are sufficient to warrant a hearing to determine the validity of these allegations.

AFFIRMED.

CRITICAL THINKING

What reasons did the court offer to support its conclusion? What do you think about the quality of those reasons?

ETHICAL DECISION MAKING

Recall the WPH framework. Suppose that your decision is guided by the Golden Rule. Why is application of the Golden Rule more complex than it may seem at first glance? *Clue:* Are humans so similar that what one person would want to happen in a particular situation is identical to what every other person would want to happen?

Shareholder's Derivative Suit. If corporate directors fail to sue when the corporation has been harmed by an individual, another corporation, or a director, individual shareholders (who held stock at the time of the alleged wrongdoing) can file a **shareholder's derivative suit** on behalf of the corporation. Before filing, the shareholders must file a complaint with the board of directors. If there is no response, they can proceed with the suit. Enron shareholders have brought shareholder's derivative suits against various directors and officers. The Case Opener presented an example of a shareholder's derivative suit. The Bank of America shareholders had the right to bring suit against the Bank of America corporation because information regarding the controversial Merrill Lynch bonuses was never disclosed. Such information should have been disclosed to the shareholders at a meeting where the shareholders were to vote over whether to acquire Merrill Lynch.

It seems highly unlikely that directors will sue themselves for damages they caused. Thus, the shareholder's derivative suit is an important way for shareholders to hold directors accountable for their behavior. Because the suit is filed on the corporation's behalf, all damages recovered are given to the corporation, not the individual shareholder.

Shareholder's Direct Suit. Shareholders can also bring a direct suit against the corporation. In a *shareholder's direct suit,* the shareholder alleges damages caused by the corporation. For example, a shareholder may allege that the board of directors is improperly withholding dividends or wrongly denying the shareholder's right to inspect corporate records. However, in some instances a direct suit it not appropriate. For example, a shareholder may not file a direct suit alleging that an officer has violated a fiduciary duty. In such a circumstance, the violation would engage all shareholders. If a court awards damages as a result of a shareholder's direct suit, they go to the shareholder personally.

Legal Principle: Damages recovered from a derivative suit go to the corporation. In contrast, damages recovered from a direct suit go only to the shareholder.

If more than one shareholder has suffered damages caused by the same act of the corporation, the shareholders may bring a class action suit against the corporation. A *class action suit* is brought by one shareholder on behalf of a group of shareholders to recover damages for the entire group.

 # CASE OPENER WRAP-UP

Bank of America

The shareholders in Bank of America had the right to bring suit against the corporation because the information regarding the Merrill Lynch bonuses was never disclosed, even at a meeting where the shareholders were to vote over whether to acquire the firm. In this case, the SEC decided only to fine the corporation, hoping that the government bailout money would not be used in a court battle. Although both the SEC and Bank of America agreed to a fine of $33 million, the judge was not inclined to agree to such a penalty.

Instead, Judge Rakoff said that the $33 million penalty, agreed to by both parties, was "strangely askew." Of Bank of America's refusal to disclose information about Merrill's bonuses, Judge Rakoff said, "I cannot ignore issues of responsibility; was there some sort of ghost that performed those actions?" Judge Rakoff ultimately decided that the corporation "effectively lied to their shareholders."

So, instead of determining the fine to be a just penalty, the judge instructed Bank of America to release the names of anyone who had been involved with the decision to not disclose the bonuses the year before. In addition, the judge told the corporation to supply more information, specifically the "who, what, where" regarding the proxy statement or the document given to shareholders before the merger vote.

Key Terms

no-par shares 861	proxy 853	self-dealing 855	stock certificates 862

par-value
    shares   861
	right of first
	    refusal 864
		shareholder's
		    derivative suit 865
			stock warrants 863
			watered stock 861

Summary of Key Topics

Roles of Officers, Directors and Shareholders	The board of directors meets to decide important issues faced by the corporation. Directors also supervise officers of the corporation, as well as declaring dividends for the shareholders. A corporate directors meeting is valid only when a minimum number of directors is present at the meeting; that minimum number is called a quorum.

Officers are executives hired by the directors to manage the daily actions of the corporation.

Shareholders are the owners of the firm. They elect the members of the board of directors. Usually they gather at an annual meeting to propose ideas and to listen to reports from the corporate officers. When they cannot attend, they can authorize a third party, a proxy, to vote on their behalf. Proxy materials are often sent out to the shareholders before their annual meeting; these proxy materials detail shareholders' ideas for the company. |
| **Duties of Directors, Officers, and Shareholders** | The shareholders do not generally have duties, but the directors and officers have duties to the shareholders and to the corporation. Their primary fiduciary duties are the duty of care and the duty of loyalty. In terms of the duty of care, officers and directors must act in good faith and in a manner consistent with the best interests of the shareholders. The duty of loyalty requires the directors and officers to put the interests of the shareholders above their personal interests. |
| **Liabilities of Directors, Officers, and Shareholders** | Officers and directors are liable for their own actions, as well of those of the employees of the firm that they had reason to be aware of. The business judgment rule provides that directors and officers are not liable for decisions that harmed the corporation if they were acting in good faith at the time of the decision.

The main liability for shareholders is the total extent of their investment in the corporation when the firm loses money. |
Rights of Directors, Officers, and Shareholders	The rights of directors are the following: the rights of compensation, participation, inspection, and indemnification. Officers' rights are determined by the terms of their employment contract. Shareholders have many rights including the following: the right to vote at shareholders' meetings, occasional preferential or preemptive rights to purchase shares of a new issue of stock, a right of first refusal to buy shares offered for resale by a shareholder, a right of inspection of corporate books and records when they have a proper purpose, and the right to request dissolution.
Stock warrants	Stock warrants are vouchers issued to shareholders entitling them to a given number of shares at a specified price.
Shareholder's derivative suit	A shareholder's derivative suit is filed by a shareholder of a corporation when corporate directors fail to sue in a situation where the corporation has been harmed by an individual or another corporation. Before the suit can be filed, the shareholder must file a complaint with the board of directors; the shareholder can proceed with the suit only if nothing is done in response to the complaint.

Point / Counterpoint

Should Both Majority and Minority Shareholders Have a Fiduciary Duty to Sell Their Shares in Ownership of the Corporation "with Care"?	
YES	NO
Both majority and minority shareholders should sell their shares in ownership of the corporation "with care." All shareholders have the potential to benefit from a successful corporation. Thus, all are obligated to practice care when selling shares. Majority shareholders need to act with care because one purchase of a majority shareholder's stock could give the new majority shareholder sufficient power to dismantle the corporation. However in some corporations, a potential shareholder could also easily obtain enough minority-shareholder stock to become the majority shareholder—and potentially harm or dismantle the corporation. Thus, minority shareholders should also be aware that their decisions to sell shares (and to whom) influence other shareholders, directors, officers, employees, customers, associated businesses and corporations, and the outside community. All these people trust the shareholders to keep their interests in mind when making decisions. The future of a corporation depends on everyone associated with it, from the largest consumer to the newest employee, and from the majority to the minority shareholder.	While majority shareholders obviously need to act with care when selling their shares of a corporation, minority shareholders do not. Minority shareholders are significantly less influential than the majority shareholder in a corporation. When a minority shareholder sells his stock, the new shareholder does not have the power to immediately dismantle the corporation or enact drastic changes without the support of other shareholders. The exception, of course, is a minority shareholder who sells her shares to the majority shareholder. Minority shareholders also are not as heavily invested in the corporation. The majority shareholder holds the potential to benefit significantly more than the minority shareholders. Hence, the care taken by the majority shareholder should be proportionally greater than the care taken by minority shareholders. Because minority shareholders are not as heavily invested in the corporation, their burden and obligation to the corporation should also be less.

Questions & Problems

1. Explain the primary duties of officers and directors.

2. Explain the primary duties of shareholders.

3. What is the business judgment rule?

4. XL America, Inc., acquired Intercargo Corporation for $12 a share on May 7, 1999. Before this date, several stockholders of Intercargo requested an injunction against the merger. The court denied this request, and the stockholders amended their complaints. The stockholders sued the directors of Intercargo for breach of fiduciary duty in connection with the merger. They alleged that the directors failed to ensure that the Intercargo stockholders would receive the highest value reasonably attainable and thus did not live up to their duties.

   They also alleged that the directors failed to disclose material information to the Intercargo stockholders that bore on the stockholders' decision of whether to approve the merger. What do you think the court decided in this case? What facts would the stockholders have to present to convince the judge that the directors had in fact breached their fiduciary duties? [*McMillan v. Intercargo Corporation,* C. A. No. 16963 (2000).]

5. Sharon Dowell and P&A Irrigation, Inc. sued Steven Bitner for breaches of fiduciary duty owed to Dowell and P&A. Bitner, Dowell's former partner, left P&A to start a competing company. Bitner served as an officer, director, and employee of P&A

prior to his departure. After he left P&A, Bitner entered into a contract with a competing supplier and solicited an employee of P&A to join the new business. Bitner established Central Illinois Irrigation on March 20, 1989. He stopped working for P&A on March 18, 1989, and his activities with respect to Central prior to that date were limited to planning and formation. Bitner subsequently contacted customers and notified them that P&A no longer employed him. He explained to the customers that he had started his own business and would appreciate their patronage. Do you think Bitner breached his fiduciary duty to P&A? Why or why not? *Dowell v. Bitner,* 652 N.E. 2d 1372 (1995).

6. Performance Nutrition, Inc. (PNI), developed, marketed, and sold nutritional supplements. In 1996, Kennedy Capital Management, a major stockholder of PNI, organized an election of the board of directors to put in new management. Anthony Roth, a member of the board of directors, took over as the CEO of PNI. PNI faced financial difficulties, and Naturade, PNI's primary vendor, was interested in buying the company. Roth and officials at Naturade began negotiations, and Naturade assured Roth that a position would be created for him if the takeover was successful. According to the plan, PNI would file for bankruptcy, and Naturade would purchase its assets. Roth did not share the plan with any other shareholders or members of the board of directors. Although Naturade's offer was unreasonably low, Roth did not make any efforts to sell PNI's assets to any company other than Naturade. Before PNI filed for bankruptcy in 1997, Roth signed a letter of intent to sell PNI's assets to Naturade. Despite the obvious conflict of interest, Roth never included other PNI directors in the decision making. Do you think Roth breached his fiduciary duties to the company? Why or why not? [*In re Performance Nutrition, Inc.,* 239 B.R. 93 (1999).]

7. Boston Children's Heart Foundation (BCHF) is a nonprofit corporation organized for the purposes of conducting medical research and providing medical services to patients at Boston Children's Hospital. Nadal-Ginard was the president and a member of the board of directors of BCHF. He also served as an investigator for the Howard Hughes Medical Institute (HHMI), where he was paid a substantial salary and was involved in similar research. Nadal-Ginard did not disclose his employment with HHMI to the other members of the board of directors. He determined his own salary with BCHF, established a severance benefit plan, and used BCHF funds for personal expenses. After learning that Nadal-Ginard was a salaried employee of HHMI, BCHF filed suit, claiming that Nadal-Ginard breached his fiduciary duties to the corporation. The district court agreed with BCHF and awarded damages. Nadal-Ginard appealed the court's decision, arguing that he did not breach his fiduciary duty and that no conflict of interest existed. Do you think the court affirmed the district court's decision? Why or why not? [*Boston Children's Heart Foundation, Inc. v. Bernardo Nadal-Ginard,* 73 F.3d 429 (1996).]

8. The Oakland Raiders filed suit against the National Football League. The Raiders claimed that NFL management's wrongful control of the NFL entities resulted in a breach of fiduciary duty and adverse treatment of the Raiders. As part of its investigation, the Raiders wanted to inspect the corporate documents of National Football League Properties, Inc. (NFLP). Each of the 30 NFL teams is an equal shareholder of NFLP and has a licensing agreement with it. NFLP acknowledged that the Raiders club was a shareholder but refused to produce certain documents. According to NFLP, the Raiders did not have the right to inspect corporate documents protected by the attorney-client privilege. The court found that, as a member, director, and shareholder of NFLP, the Raiders had the right to examine privileged documents. NFLP challenged the court's decision. How do you think the court of appeals decided? Should NFLP be compelled to produce the privileged documents? Why or why not? [*National Football League Properties, Inc. v. The Superior Court of Santa Clara County,* 65 Cal. App. 4th 100 (1998).]

9. In February 2009, the SEC accused Texas billionaire P. Allen Stanford and two additional senior executives of committing a "massive Ponzi scheme," or substantial fraud. Subsequently, all of Stanford's financial operations were shut down, and a civil suit was filed against him. The SEC alleged that Stanford and the executives were pulling in investors and sold about $8 billion worth of "certificates of deposit." The certificates then seemed to be invested in real estate and other operations associated with Stanford's own personal dealings. Basically, the

SEC alleged that investors were pulled in to invest in fake financial products and ventures. How do you think the court decided? Why? [*SEC v. Stanford International Bank, LTD., et al.,* available at http://www.insuranceinsider.com/sec-v-stanford-international-bank-order (2009).]

10. Amalgamated Bank, a shareholder of UICI, a Delaware corporation, asked to inspect UICI's books and records to determine whether UICI's directors breached their fiduciary duties or otherwise harmed shareholders by acting illegally. Amalgamated also wanted to determine whether sufficient evidence existed to bring a shareholder action suit against UICI's directors, who had done business with the corporation and had profited handsomely. UICI denied Amalgamated's request for three reasons. First, the statute of limitations for bringing suit against the corporation had expired. Second, some of the meeting minutes requested by Amalgamated did not directly concern the transactions in question. Third, UICI wanted to require that Amalgamated maintain the confidentiality of the information it reviewed. The bank brought suit against UICI, alleging that it ought to be able to review the documents in question because it provided a proper purpose in its letter of request. How do you think the court ruled in this case? Why? [*Amalgamated Bank v. UICI,* 2005 Del. Ch. LEXIS 82 (2005).]

Looking for more review material?

The Online Learning Center at **www.mhhe.com/kubasek2e** contains this chapter's "Assignment on the Internet" and also a list of URLs for more information, entitled "On the Internet." Find both of them in the Student Center portion of the OLC, along with quizzes and other helpful materials.

Corporations: Mergers, Consolidations, Terminations

LEARNING OBJECTIVES

After reading this chapter, you will be able to answer the following questions:

1 What are mergers and consolidations?

2 What are the procedures for mergers and consolidations?

3 What are asset purchases?

4 What are stock purchases?

5 What is a takeover?

6 In what ways could the termination of mergers and consolidations occur?

CASE OPENER
The Merger between the Cable Channels Lifetime and A&E

On August 27, 2009, the cable channels Lifetime and A&E completed their merger. Previously, there were three companies that had jointly owned the two channels: the Hearst Corporation, the Walt Disney Company, and NBC Universal. The new company that resulted from the merger covered 10 television channels and 20 Web sites. After the merger, numerous business law questions emerged. Which corporation's board would govern the new corporation? What would happen to the stock previously associated with the two channels? How would antitrust laws affect the legality of the merger?

1. If you were a leader in the planned merger, what are some issues you should anticipate? Think about this question from the perspective of shareholders, federal regulatory agencies, and the general public.

2. What methods would you implement to ease these three groups' concerns?

The Wrap-Up at the end of the chapter will answer these questions.

LO1

What are mergers and consolidations?

Introduction to Mergers and Consolidations

Although many people believe that mergers and consolidations are synonymous, they are in fact two legally distinct procedures. Nevertheless, in both mergers and consolidations, corporations, shareholders, and creditors have the same rights and liabilities.

MERGERS

A **merger** occurs when a legal contract combines two or more corporations such that only one of the corporations continues to exist. A useful way to understand a merger is to think of one corporation absorbing another corporation (called an *absorbed corporation* or a *disappearing corporation*), yielding a single *surviving corporation.*

The surviving entity remains a single corporation, but it changes in several ways after the merger. First, its shareholders must amend its articles of incorporation according to the specific conditions of the merger. Second, the surviving corporation becomes liable for all debts and obligations of the absorbed corporation.

The surviving corporation also grows from the merger because it obtains the absorbed corporation's property and assets. Additionally, it acquires the absorbed corporation's rights, powers, and privileges. This acquisition can be complicated if the absorbed company had a legal right to sue third parties. The surviving corporation's right to sue for debt and damages on behalf of the absorbed corporation is called a **chose in action** (*chose* is French for "thing"). Although a few states do not allow corporations to transfer their rights, powers, and privileges in a merger, most states agree that if a corporation had a right to sue third parties before a merger, then the surviving corporation retains that right.

The union of Lifetime and A&E was a merger because it resulted in a single corporation that took the names of the former corporations. The surviving corporation holds all the liabilities and assets each firm possessed before the merger.

Legal Principle: **In most states, corporations who merge may transfer their rights, powers, and privileges to the new corporation formed by the merger.**

CONSOLIDATIONS

Like mergers, **consolidations** legally combine two or more corporations. In a consolidation, however, neither of the original corporations continues to exist legally. Rather, they form an entirely new corporation with its own legal status.

Because the new corporation has independent legal status, the articles of incorporation of the original companies are void. The shareholders of the new corporation create new articles of incorporation, called *articles of consolidation,* according to the details of the consolidation.

Consolidated entities assume the liabilities, debts, and obligations of the original corporations. The new corporation also acquires the original corporations' property and assets. Finally, the consolidated corporation takes on the rights, privileges, and powers of the original companies.

Today, consolidations are very rare. As Section 11.01 of RMBCA reads, "In modern corporate practice consolidation transactions are obsolete since it is nearly always advantageous for one of the parties in the transaction to be the surviving corporation."

To see a description of the general changes in day-to-day business after a consolidation occurs, please see the **Connecting to the Core** activity on the text Web site at www.mhhe.com/kubasek2e.

Procedures for Mergers and Consolidations

Whether corporations combine through merger or consolidation, the procedures governing the transition are identical. Exhibit 40-1 explains the process of mergers and consolidations.

State statutes govern mergers and consolidations. In most states, corporations can merge or consolidate with either domestic (in-state) or foreign (out-of-state) corporations. Because acquisitions between domestic corporations are very different from acquisitions between corporations from different states, different laws govern acquisitions between domestic corporations and acquisitions between foreign corporations. Although these laws vary across states, several requirements apply universally:

1. The boards of directors of all involved corporations must approve the merger or consolidation plan.
2. The shareholders of all involved corporations must approve the plan by a vote at a shareholder meeting. Most states require the approval of two-thirds of the outstanding shares of voting stock. If, however, a merger increases the number of the surviving corporation's shares by no more than 20 percent, most states do not require the approval of the surviving corporation's shareholders.
3. The involved corporations must submit the merger or consolidation plan to the secretary of state.
4. After reviewing the plan to ensure that the corporations have satisfied all legal requirements, the secretary of state issues a certificate to grant approval for the merger or consolidation.

LO2

What are the procedures for mergers and consolidations?

Exhibit 40-1   Process for Mergers and Consolidations

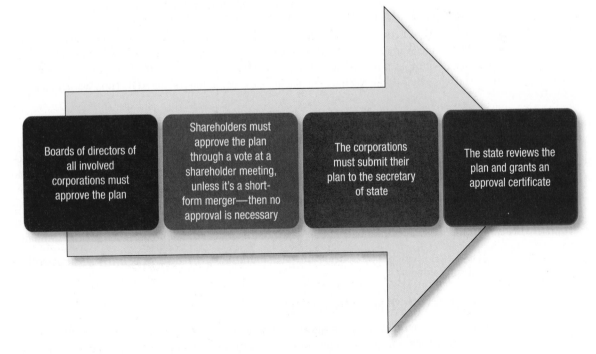

Boards of directors of all involved corporations must approve the plan

Shareholders must approve the plan through a vote at a shareholder meeting, unless it's a short-form merger—then no approval is necessary

The corporations must submit their plan to the secretary of state

The state reviews the plan and grants an approval certificate

Merger Control in France

The aim of merger control statutes in France is not to discourage mergers but to ensure that the combination of businesses does not impede competition. The creation of the Commission for Competition helps foster this goal. The commission, composed of members of the Council of State, magistrates of the administrative or judicial order, and several part-time reporters, is available to offer advice to businesses seeking to merge. The French government, specifically the minister for the economy, also uses the commission as a resource when determining whether a proposed merger will benefit the French economy or whether the resulting concentration

of power will decrease competition. After learning of a proposed merger, the minister has three months to issue an opinion. During this period, the minister employs the expertise of the commission. If the commission decides that a proposed merger exceeds reasonable concentration of power, the minister for the economy must intervene with an injunctive option depending on the particular circumstances of the merger. The minister can (1) enjoin the companies from completing the merger, (2) alter the merger's value, (3) make provisions to ensure higher degrees of competition in the market, or (4) arrange compensatory contributions to social or economic welfare if the merger will necessarily reduce competition.

In addition, the surviving or consolidated corporation issues shares or otherwise compensates shareholders of the corporation that no longer exists.

In 1998, federal regulators determined that a merger between Daimler-Benz and Chrysler did not violate antitrust laws because the two corporations competed in very different markets. Other mergers, however, often present antitrust issues and thus require the approval of federal regulators.

For example, in December 2000, approximately a year after AOL and Times Warner first announced their proposed merger, the Federal Trade Commission (FTC) unanimously approved the merger because the new company pledged to protect consumers' choice of services offered by competitors. Following the FTC's decision, the Federal Communications Commission (FCC) approved the merger in early January, imposing similar conditions on the new company to promote a competitive Internet services market. For example, the FCC required that AOL Time Warner work with EarthLink, an Internet service provider (ISP) and AOL's biggest competitor, as well as with Microsoft and Juno. The FCC also demanded that AOL Time Warner allow subscribers to use its software (i.e., instant messaging) to communicate with subscribers of other ISPs. (Can you see what values the FCC is trying to advance and whom it is trying to protect in placing these conditions on the AOL Time Warner merger?)

THE RIGHTS OF SHAREHOLDERS

When shareholders invest in corporations, they expect the board of directors to handle daily business issues. They also expect, however, to vote on exceptional matters, including mergers, consolidations, changes in partners, sales or leases of the corporation, and exchanges of assets. Because shareholders have a vested interest in the survival and prosperity of the corporation, these matters are of great significance to them. Thus, the merger and consolidation procedures require shareholder approval. In Case 40-1, the Delaware Supreme Court examined whether a shareholder vote in favor of a merger was legitimate.

Legal Principle: **Merger and consolidation procedures require the approval of shareholders.**

SHORT-FORM MERGERS

Although most mergers require shareholder approval, short-form mergers do not. A **short-form merger,** or a **parent-subsidiary merger,** occurs when a parent corporation merges with a subsidiary corporation. The procedure for short-form mergers, detailed in

HARTLEIB v. SIRIUS SATELLITE RADIO ET AL.

UNITED STATES DISTRICT COURT, CENTRAL DISTRICT OF CALIFORNIA

AVAILABLE AT http://digitaldaily.allthingsd.com/files/2008/12/hartleib_v_siri-order.pdf (2008)

In 2008, the shareholders of Sirius, the satellite radio provider, sued Sirius XM after the merger between Sirius and XM. The shareholders allege that Sirius executives damaged the prices of stock for the corporation because they created and maintained agreements with XM that both companies would refrain from looking at other merger deals and canceling the merger completely. The shareholders stated that these agreements were made so that while the FCC considered approval of the merger for sixteen months, the merger would still happen with 100% certainty. Basically, the shareholders stated that Sirius executives wanted the merger to occur at "any and all costs."

JUDGE CARNEY: Although the complaint identifies alleged fraud and wrongdoing committed by Defendants, it does not state how each specific Sirius director was responsible for those actions. For instance, it would be helpful if Mr. Hartleib could show how a majority of the current directors, as individuals, approved of an allegedly fraudulent statement or action or committed some wrongdoing that would make them unable to exercise independent judgment in this case. Generalized statements alleging that "each board member" knew of some wrongdoing will not suffice to meet the heightened standards of Rule 23.1. Such generalized allegations are even more ineffective in situations, like this one, where the majority of the board was not empanelled at the time of the alleged wrongdoing. The changeover in board membership further undermines the relevance of Mr. Hartleib's argument that Sirius's lukewarm response to his shareholder activism before the merger shows that its current board cannot be trusted to exercise independent judgment. The Court also fails to see the relevance of directors' membership on the audit committee. Furthermore, Mr. Hartleib cannot escape the demand requirement simply by asserting that the majority of the board bears liability in the action because a majority of board members are named as defendants in his suit.

DISMISSED.

CRITICAL THINKING

What problems does Judge Carney have with the way that the plaintiff presented his argument?

Had the plaintiff adjusted the argument as the judge advised, do you think the judge would have ruled in his favor?

ETHICAL DECISION MAKING

If you were in the position of the Sirius executives in this case, would you have threatened the stock process in an effort to create a merger with another satellite radio corporation? If your decision was guided by the Golden Rule, how would you have behaved?

Section 11.04 of RMBCA, is simpler than the procedure for mergers between unrelated corporations because short-form mergers can occur without shareholder approval.

Short-form mergers have other requirements, however. The parent corporation must own at least 90 percent of the outstanding shares of each class of the subsidiary's stock. If the proposed short-form merger satisfies this condition, the board of directors of the parent corporation can vote to approve the merger plan. The board must also submit the plan to the subsidiary's shareholders, even though they do not have veto power. Finally, the state must approve the merger proposition.

Merger Control in South Africa

South Africa, like many other countries, takes measures to secure a competitive but fair environment for mergers. Specifically, the Companies Act and the rules of the Johannesburg Stock Exchange control mergers. The Companies Act provides protection for minority shareholders. For instance, shareholders cannot approve a merger unless 90 percent of all shareholders vote to accept the offer. Additionally, minority shareholders have access to South African courts and may employ them when disputes arise. The Companies Act also establishes a panel to inquire about mergers or takeovers.

The Johannesburg Stock Exchange has established rules that govern the treatment of shareholders in mergers and takeovers. For example, if a change of corporate control takes place outside the stock exchange, the initiator of the merger must extend the offer to the shareholders and disclose all pertinent information to them within a reasonable amount of time.

Although short-form mergers are legal, to protect shareholders from directors, courts often require that directors seek and adhere to shareholders' opinions.

APPRAISAL RIGHTS

The law protects shareholders as a group from corporations, but it also protects individual shareholders from one another. Suppose that although an overwhelming majority of shareholders vote to approve a merger, a single shareholder dissents. In this situation, the law does not force the dissenting shareholder to become a shareholder in a corporation different from the one in which she originally invested. Thus, the law permits dissenting shareholders to exercise their appraisal rights. An **appraisal right** is a dissenting shareholder's right to have his or her shares appraised and to receive monetary compensation from the corporation for their value.

Strict procedures govern appraisal rights. Before a shareholder vote, dissenting shareholders must submit a notification of dissent. By conveying their disapproval before the vote, the dissenting shareholders may sway other shareholders to reconsider their decision. If, however, the shareholder vote approves the transaction, the dissenting shareholders must issue another statement demanding adequate compensation for their shares.

The corporation must then present the dissenting shareholders with a document stating the value of their shares. Shareholders and corporations often clash when determining the value of these shares. Generally, however, they use the value of the shares on the day before the shareholder vote. The language of the law is of little help; it ambiguously calls for the "fair value of shares" (RMBCA 13.01). If the dissenting shareholders and the corporation cannot reach an agreement, courts intervene to establish the shares' value, as Case 40-2 illustrates.

CASE 40-2   CHARLAND v. COUNTRY VIEW GOLF CLUB, INC.
SUPREME COURT OF RHODE ISLAND
588 A.2D 609 (1991)

Gilbert Charland owned fifteen percent of the shares of the Country View Golf Club. Believing that the club's management was engaged in illegal activities, Charland petitioned *for the dissolution of the corporation. The other shareholders, some of whom Charland suspected had been involved in the illegalities, did not want the corporation to be dissolved.*

The remaining shareholders enacted the section of Rhode Island's corporate code that allows shareholders to avoid dissolution by purchasing the dissenter's shares at "a price equal to their fair value . . . as of the close of the business on the day on which the petition for dissolution was filed."

Charland and the golf course's management bickered over the fair value of the shares. Eventually, they hired an outside appraiser to determine the shares' value. The appraiser concluded that Charland's shares were subject to a "minority discount." A minority discount means that the value of the shares is lower because they constitute only a minority of the total shares, and thus their owner lacks decision-making power. Moreover, the other shareholders considered applying a lack of marketability discount to Charland's shares.

Charland believed the discounted price was unfair. He claimed that it punished him, for if the dissolution were successful, he would be entitled to the same amount per share as all the other shareholders, regardless of how many shares he owned. Thus, by giving him the discounted value, the court would have rewarded the suspect ownership.

The district court ruled that the discounted value should stand. The appeals court, however, reversed the decision. The golf club appealed.

JUSTICE KELLEHER: We shall consider only one issue: whether Charland received fair value for his shares.

Three separate issues must be resolved in determining fair value. The first issue is whether this court should apply a minority discount to Charland's shares. The second issue is whether this court should apply a discount for lack of marketability. The third issue is whether any discount was, in fact, applied to Charland's shares with the result that Charland received less than the fair value.

A minority discount has been described as a second-stage adjustment for valuing minority shares. That is, after a minority shareholder's stock is initially discounted for the minority percentage owned, the pro rata [Latin for "in proportion"; refers to the amount the corporation must pay Charland based on the fractional share of his ownership] value is determined. Then, an additional discount is applied to the pro rata value because the minority shareholder lacks corporate decision-making power. This second calculation is called a minority discount.

The issue of whether to apply a minority discount in a situation in which a corporation elects to buy out a shareholder who has filed for dissolution has never been resolved by this court. In fact, few jurisdictions have decided this question.

Most courts that have considered this question have agreed that no minority discount should be applied when a corporation elects to buy out the shareholder who petitions for dissolution of the corporation.

Brown v. Allied Corrugated Box Co. is an often-cited case in this area of law. In *Brown* a minority shareholder in a closely held corporation initiated an action for involuntary dissolution. The majority shareholder asked to purchase the minority shareholder's stock. The two parties could not reach an agreement regarding the value of the minority shares. A commission comprising three appraisers valued the shares, and two of the three commissioners (majority commissioners) devalued the shares for their noncontrolling status.

On appeal the court reversed the judgment confirming the report of the majority commissioners. The court conceded that if the shares were placed on the open market, their minority status would substantially decrease their value. The court, however, went on to note that this devaluation has little validity when the shares are to be purchased by the corporation. When a corporation elects to buy out the shares of a dissenting shareholder, the fact that the shares are noncontrolling is irrelevant.

In addition, the court in *Brown* observed that had the plaintiffs proved their case and had the corporation been dissolved, each shareholder would have been entitled to the same amount per share. There would be no consideration given to whether the shares were controlling or noncontrolling. Furthermore an unscrupulous controlling shareholder could avoid a proportionate distribution under dissolution by buying out the shares, and the very misconduct and unfairness that incited the minority shareholders to seek dissolution could be used to oppress them further.

We agree with the rationale of *Brown* and hereby adopt the rule that in circumstances in which a corporation elects to buy out a shareholder's stock, we shall not discount the shares solely because of their minority status.

A second and more difficult issue to resolve is whether a lack of marketability discount should be applied to Charland's shares. This discount is separate from and bears no relation to a minority discount. The courts that have addressed this question are divided.

[W]e believe . . . a lack of marketability discount is inapposite when a corporation elects to buy out a shareholder who has filed for dissolution of a corporation. As a recent law review article noted:

> In dissolution cases, strong reasons support the use of pro rata value without a discount. A minority shareholder seeking dissolution claims that majority shareholders have engaged in some unfair, possibly tortious, action. If the minority shareholder succeeds in having the company dissolved, all shareholders will receive their pro rata share of the assets, with no account given to the minority [or illiquidity] status of their shares. Minority shareholders should not receive less than this value if, instead of fighting the dissolution action, the majority decides to seek appraisal of minority shares in order to buy out the minority and reduce corporate discord.

We therefore today adopt the rule of not applying a discount for lack of marketability.

We therefore remand this case to the Superior Court to determine the fair value of Charland's shares as of September 4, 1984, without applying a discount for either minority status or lack of marketability of his shares in Country View in conformity with the rules set forth herein.

REMANDED.

CRITICAL THINKING

Justice Kelleher's reasoning relies heavily on an analogy between the case at hand and *Brown v. Allied Corrugated Box Co.* Do you find this analogy to be persuasive? If *Brown v. Allied Corrugated Box Co.* never happened, what reasons do you think the court would use to support its conclusion?

ETHICAL DECISION MAKING

Think about the WPH process of ethical decision making. Which stakeholders are particularly affected by the court's ruling? Why?

Procedures for Appraisal Rights. The procedures governing appraisal rights are extensive. If the dissenting shareholders hope to receive compensation, they must follow the procedures accurately.

Dissenting shareholders who properly exercise their appraisal rights experience changes in their legal status as shareholders and in corresponding rights, depending on the jurisdiction. In some states, the law strips dissenting shareholders of their rights, including the right to vote and receive dividends. Shareholders who lose their legal status, however, retain the right to sue on the basis of evidence of illegal conduct associated with the merger or consolidation. Some states that revoke dissenting shareholders' legal status reinstate their status during the appraisal process. Thus, shareholders can withdraw from the appraisal process, contingent on corporate approval. Other jurisdictions do not reinstate status until after the appraisal is finished.

The issue of legal status and rights arises only if dissenting shareholders properly invoke their appraisal rights. If dissenting shareholders do not properly invoke these rights, courts force them to comply with the decision of the majority of the corporations' shareholders. If you were to operate within the WPH framework, would you find these procedures adequate, restrictive, or overly simplistic?

Purchase of Assets

LO3

What are asset purchases?

In addition to engaging in mergers and consolidations, corporations can extend their business operations by purchasing all or a substantial amount of another corporation's assets. *Assets* include intangible items (such as goodwill, a company name, and a company logo) and tangible items (such as buildings and other property). When an asset purchase occurs, the acquiring corporation (the one purchasing the assets) assumes ownership and control over tangible and intangible assets of the selling corporation.

The selling corporation needs the approval of both its board of directors and its shareholders before it can sell its assets. Shareholders of the acquired corporation who disagree with the transfer can demand appraisal rights in most states. Whether the acquiring corporation needs shareholder approval depends on the extent to which the merger alters the corporation's business position. Asset purchases normally do not change a corporation's legal status; thus, acquiring corporations do not usually need shareholder approval.

Although asset purchases seem similar to mergers and consolidations, they are significantly different because a corporation that purchases the assets of another corporation generally does not acquire its liabilities. In contrast, mergers and consolidations transfer all obligations.

In three circumstances, however, the acquiring corporation does assume the liabilities of the selling corporation. First, the contract governing the purchase may expressly or impliedly state that the acquiring corporation takes on the selling companies' liabilities in addition to its assets.

Second, although the two corporations may intend that the transaction be a purchase of assets, it may fall within the legal framework of a merger or consolidation. Thus, the acquiring corporation receives both the assets and the liabilities of the selling corporation.

Third, the purchaser does not avoid the selling corporation's liabilities if the corporations execute the sale under fraudulent circumstances. The U.S. Department of Justice and the Federal Trade Commission have stringent guidelines to ensure that the directors and shareholders of the acquired corporation have not used the asset sale to escape payment of obligations or pending lawsuits. These guidelines make it difficult, and sometimes impossible, for corporations to acquire other corporations through asset purchases. Thus, a corporation seeking to extend its business by purchasing another corporation's assets must be familiar with these guidelines to ensure that the sale is legal.

Legal Principle: Asset purchases are significantly different from mergers and consolidations because a corporation that purchases the assets of another corporation generally does not acquire its liabilities.

Purchase of Stock

Besides engaging in mergers, consolidations, and asset purchases, corporations can extend their operations by purchasing another corporation's stock. As with asset purchases, an acquiring corporation, or *aggressor,* can buy any or all of another corporation's voting shares. Through such a stock purchase, the purchasing corporation gains control of the selling corporation in a corporate takeover.

LO4

What are stock purchases?

The Nature of Takeovers

During the 1980s, not only did the number of corporate takeovers increase, but so too did the number of hostile takeovers. **Hostile takeovers** are takeovers to which the management of the target corporation objects. When a hostile takeover succeeds, the target corporation's management frequently compares the transition to a full-scale invasion characterized by layoffs and dramatic changes in company policy.

In the 1980s, corporations afraid of a hostile takeover concealed financial difficulties so as not to appear vulnerable to other corporations. Thus, they maintained a strong profile within the business community while their directors secretly sought a way out of their financial troubles.

LO5

What is a takeover?

TYPES OF TAKEOVERS

To initiate a stock purchase, the aggressor must appeal directly to the shareholders of the corporation it hopes to buy, known as the *target corporation.* The aggressor can offer several types of deals to the target shareholders (see Exhibit 40-2). It can make a **tender offer,**

Exhibit 40-2

Types Of Takeovers

Tender offer	The aggressor offers target shareholders a price above the current market value of the stock.
Exchange offer	The aggressor offers to exchange the target corporation's current stock for stock in the aggressor's corporation.
Cash tender offer	The aggressor offers to pay cash for the target corporation's stock.
Beachhead acquisition	The aggressor gradually accumulates a substantial number of the target corporation's shares and then initiates a proxy fight.
Hostile takeover	The management of the target corporation objects to the takeover.

in which it offers target shareholders a price above the current market value of the stock. Aggressors, however, often require that they receive a certain number of shares within a certain time frame.

Alternatively, the aggressor may make an exchange tender offer. In an **exchange tender offer,** the aggressor offers to exchange target shareholders' current stock for stock in the aggressor's corporation. The aggressor may also make a **cash tender offer** to the target shareholders in which it pays them cash for their stock.

Other types of takeovers are more covert than these tender offers. For example, a **beachhead acquisition** occurs when an aggressor gradually accumulates the target company's shares. (The accumulated bloc of shares is analogous to a beachhead, an initial area of control from which the aggressor can launch later attacks.)

After acquiring a substantial number of the target corporation's shares, the aggressor initiates a proxy fight by fighting for control over target shareholders' proxies. (Chapter 39 discusses proxies in more detail.) Because the holder of a proxy has the right to vote at shareholder meetings, if an aggressor can control a majority of proxies, it can outvote the other shareholders. The aggressor can then use the proxies it controls to elect a board of directors that supports the acquisition.

Before an aggressor can gain control of the target corporation through proxies, it needs a key piece of information: a list of target shareholders. Although resistant target corporations often want to conceal this information, federal securities law requires that target corporations assist aggressors in some ways. Thus, to avoid lengthy and expensive lawsuits, target corporations often provide a list of shareholders voluntarily. Providing the list does not guarantee that the aggressor will succeed, especially because federal regulations protect the target corporation. For instance, federal regulations permit the management of target companies to use corporate funds to educate shareholders on the disadvantages of a takeover.

Proxy solicitation, or fighting, doesn't always take place between an aggressor and a target corporation. In fact, proxy solicitation can occur within a company. For example, when Hewlett-Packard (HP) announced its intention to take over fellow computer company Compaq, Walter Hewlett, an HP board member and the son of HP cofounder William Hewlett, was strongly opposed. Convinced that the $22 billion HP-Compaq merger would be a failure, Walter Hewlett initiated a proxy fight within the company.

In an attempt to discourage HP voters from approving the takeover, Walter Hewlett sent out mailings to shareholders, took out advertisements in major papers, and blasted the merger, calling it a "mistake." After months of proxy fighting, HP shareholders voted to approve the merger, 838 million votes to 793 million votes. Additionally, Walter Hewlett's lawsuit was dismissed, and HP moved forward with its acquisition of Compaq.[1]

Those seeking to acquire corporations have developed tactics to overcome the law's rules encouraging cooperation from target corporations. Because contacting each individual target shareholder is expensive, aggressors often try to win the favor of a few institutional investors that own a large bloc of shares. If an aggressor can obtain the proxies of these investors, it can win control of the target corporation.

RESPONSE TO TAKEOVERS

Once an aggressor has presented its offer to the target corporation's shareholders, the target corporation's board of directors must inform shareholders of all facts pertinent to shareholders' votes. After reviewing these material facts, the directors vote to accept or reject the offer and advise shareholders accordingly.

If the directors conclude that a takeover is not in the company's best interest, the company may employ many methods of resistance. One common method is a **self-tender offer,** in which the target corporation offers to buy its shareholders' stock. If the shareholders accept the offer, the target corporation maintains control of the business.

Alternatively, target corporations may defend themselves using leveraged buyouts. A **leveraged buyout (LBO)** occurs when a group within a corporation (usually management) buys all outstanding corporate stock held by the public. Thus, the group gains control over corporate operations by "going private," or becoming a privately held corporation.

LBOs are usually high-risk endeavors, however, because the target corporation must borrow money to purchase the outstanding stock. It may have to borrow money from an investment bank or issue corporate bonds.

Illustrative jargon describes many methods of resistance to corporate takeovers. In Case 40-3, the Georgia court of appeals considers the legality of a "golden parachute."

---

[1] http://news.cnet.com/Costs-mount-in-HP-proxy-fight/2100-1003_3-859261.html and www.pcworld.com/article/97944/its_official_hp_acquires_compaq.html.

CASE 40-3   ROYAL CROWN COMPANIES, INC. v. MCMAHON
COURT OF APPEALS OF GEORGIA
183 GA. APP. 543 (1987)

McMahon was the president of Arby's Inc., a subsidiary of Royal Crown Companies, Inc. It appeared that another corporation was positioning itself to buy Royal Crown. To reassure its top managers, Royal Crown enacted agreements stipulating that management would receive severance pay in the event of termination of employment or resignation after change of corporate control. McMahon resigned after the aggressor bought Royal Crown, but he did not receive his severance pay. He sued the corporation, and the trial court found in his favor. Royal Crown appealed.

JUDGE POPE: Royal Crown seeks to distinguish the agreement under consideration from the typical severance agreement because it is a special type of contract, which is commonly referred to as a "golden parachute." We are unpersuaded by Royal Crown's attempt, largely without legal support, to defeat this otherwise enforceable severance agreement simply because it is contingent upon a change in corporate control. The term "golden parachute" is not by itself legally significant. A severance contract by any other name would be just as enforceable.

Royal Crown argues that golden parachute agreements, in general, bear the taint of a conflict of interest in favor of the management beneficiaries to the detriment of the shareholders. We find no such conflict here. Plaintiff was not a member of the board of directors which approved this agreement. Moreover, the agreement was offered for the express purpose of protecting the shareholders by inducing the continued employment of plaintiff during a time of uncertainty when he might otherwise have been distracted by concerns for his own financial security to seek employment elsewhere.

Neither is the agreement void for failure of consideration. In the case at hand, plaintiff's employment was terminable at will and he was under no obligation to continue. The agreement was offered for the express purpose of inducing plaintiff to remain in his position during merger negotiations. Continued performance under a terminable-at-will contract furnishes sufficient consideration for the promise of additional severance pay. "We therefore reject any argument by the [employer] that any contract for severance pay is void as being without consideration."

AFFIRMED.

CRITICAL THINKING

Is there any missing information you would ask for when considering the facts of this case? If you were to argue to reverse the trial court's decision, what reasons would you offer? In your opinion, which of these reasons is the most persuasive? Do you find the court's reasons to affirm the trial court's decision to be equally persuasive?

ETHICAL DECISION MAKING

Think about the WPH process of ethical decision making. What is the purpose of the court's decision? In other words, which value is upheld? What value is in conflict with the reasoning of the court?

Response to Termination

L06

In what ways could the termination of mergers and consolidations occur?

The "death" of a corporation occurs in two phases: *dissolution,* the legal termination of the corporation, and *liquidation,* the process by which the board of directors converts the corporation's assets into cash and distributes them among the corporation's creditors and shareholders.

DISSOLUTION

Dissolution may be voluntary or involuntary, depending on who initiates and compels the dissolution. *Voluntary dissolution* occurs when the directors or shareholders trigger the dissolution procedures. The directors can initiate the proposal and submit it to the shareholders for a vote, or the shareholders can begin dissolution procedures. Either way, for dissolution to be successful, shareholders must unanimously vote for the proposal.

Regardless of whether the directors or shareholders initiate dissolution procedures, the corporation must follow specific procedures. First, the directors must file articles of dissolution with the secretary of state. These articles must include the company name, the date of dissolution, and the method of authorization of dissolution. Next, the directors must notify the shareholders. If shareholders or creditors have claims against the corporation, they must make them known within a stipulated time frame. Although the corporation establishes the time frame, the period must extend at least 120 days after the date of dissolution.

In an *involuntary dissolution,* the state forces the corporation to close. The state can initiate dissolution procedures, or individual shareholders can petition the state to order dissolution if they believe sufficient reason exists to terminate business operations. In some states, an individual shareholder of a closely held corporation can dissolve the corporation at will or after an event specified in the articles of incorporation occurs.

The secretary of state can compel involuntary dissolution for five reasons (RMBCA 14.20):

1. The corporation failed to pay taxes within 60 days of the due date.
2. The corporation failed to submit its annual report to the secretary of state within 60 days of the due date.
3. The corporation did not have a registered agent or office in the state for 60 days or more.
4. The corporation failed to notify the secretary of state within 60 days that its registered agent or registered office had changed.
5. The corporation's duration as specified in its articles of incorporation has expired.

In addition, courts can force involuntary dissolution for three reasons (RMBCA 14.30):

1. The corporation obtained its articles of incorporation fraudulently.
2. The directors have abused their power.
3. The corporation is insolvent.

Courts can also enforce involuntary dissolution if gridlock over an issue persists among the directors. Before ordering dissolution, however, courts usually urge shareholders to attempt to resolve the differences. If shareholders are unsuccessful, courts consider the extent to which the deadlock will result in irreversible damage to the corporation. If the disagreement will likely cause significant damage, courts will order the corporation to dissolve.

LIQUIDATION

The liquidation phase of termination begins once dissolution has occurred. In cases of voluntary dissolution, liquidation duties fall on the board of directors. The members of the board also become trustees of the corporate assets. As trustees, board members hold title to the corporation's property and become personally liable for breaches of fiduciary trustee duties.

Due to the heavy responsibilities trustees bear, some board members do not want to act as trustees. In other situations, shareholders do not want to entrust directors with the distribution of corporate assets. In these situations, the objecting party can petition the court to appoint a receiver not affiliated with the corporation to take over liquidation duties.

In cases of involuntary dissolution, courts automatically appoint a receiver to handle liquidation duties. Like the law in general, the law governing corporate terminations is dynamic; it changes in response to a host of external factors. Hence, although a company is legally terminated after it completes dissolution and liquidation, the law's view of the extent of the company's posttermination responsibilities has changed over time in response to scientific and technological developments. In the past, a corporation's liabilities dissolved when the corporation dissolved. Recently, however, scientists have discovered that companies' actions can have environmental effects that do not appear until many years later. Thus, stimulated by these scientific developments, courts have held that dissolved corporations remain responsible for their liabilities.

Exhibit 40-3 summarizes the life stages of a corporation.

Exhibit 40-3
Life Stages of a
Corporation

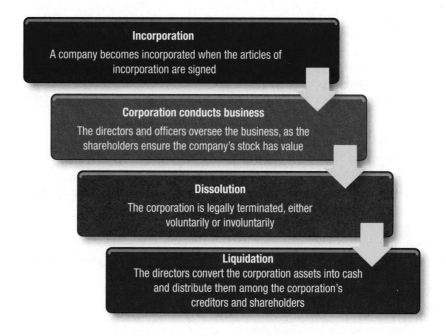

Incorporation
A company becomes incorporated when the articles of incorporation are signed

Corporation conducts business
The directors and officers oversee the business, as the shareholders ensure the company's stock has value

Dissolution
The corporation is legally terminated, either voluntarily or involuntarily

Liquidation
The directors convert the corporation assets into cash and distribute them among the corporation's creditors and shareholders

CASE OPENER WRAP-UP

A&E Television Networks

The merger between Lifetime and A&E went smoothly because the directors of the Hearst Corporation, the Walt Disney Company, and NBC Universal negotiated terms agreeable to shareholders of all the companies. The president of A&E, Abbe Raven, was to be placed in charge of the new corporation. Andrea Wong, the chief executive of Lifetime Network, was to report to Raven. The new entity would be called A&E Television Networks, and Lifetime Entertainment Services would be a subsidiary. Although the two channels produced a fair amount of the reality television available to viewers, the two networks did not encompass enough channels and Web sites to pose an antitrust problem in the eyes of federal regulators.

Key Terms

appraisal right   876

beachhead
   acquisition   880

cash tender
   offer   880

chose in action   872

consolidations   872

exchange tender
   offer   880

hostile takeovers   879

leveraged buyout
   (LBO)   881

merger   872

parent-subsidiary
   merger   874

self-tender offer   881

short-form merger   874

tender offer   879

Summary of Key Topics

Introduction to Mergers and Consolidations	*Merger:* A legal contract combining two or more corporations such that only one of the corporations continues to exist.
	Consolidation: A legal contract combining two or more corporations and resulting in an entirely new corporation.
Procedures for Mergers and Consolidations	1. Boards of directors of all involved corporations must approve the plan.
	2. Shareholders must approve the plan through a vote at a shareholder meeting.
	3. The corporations must submit their plan to the secretary of state.
	4. The state reviews the plan and grants an approval certificate.
	Short-form merger: The parent corporation merges with a subsidiary corporation. Short-form mergers do not require shareholder approval.
	Rights of shareholders: Shareholders vote only on exceptional matters regarding the corporation.
	Appraisal right: An appraisal right is the shareholder's right to have his or her shares appraised and to receive monetary compensation for their value.
Purchase of Assets	One corporation can extend its business operations by purchasing the assets of another company.
Purchase of Stock	An acquiring corporation can take control of another corporation by purchasing a substantial amount of its voting stock.
The Nature of Takeovers	A corporation can expand its size and operations by purchasing the stock of another firm.
	A *hostile takeover* is a takeover to which the management of the target corporation objects.
	Types of takeovers:
	1. Tender offers
	2. Exchange offers
	3. Cash tender offers
	4. Beachhead acquisitions
Response to Termination	*Response to takeovers:* Directors declare whether they accept or reject the offer. If they object to the offer, they can engage in methods of resistance.
	Dissolution is the legal death of a corporation.
	In *liquidation,* a corporation sells all of its assets and distributes them to repay its outstanding debts.

Point / Counterpoint

Is the Beachhead Acquisition Takeover Method Superior to the Tender Offer Takeover Method?	
YES	**NO**
The best type of corporate takeover is easily a beachhead acquisition. First, an aggressor becomes gradually involved in the operations of a target company when preparing for a beachhead acquisition. In tender offers, the aggressor just buys out key shareholders at market value and forces the company to sell. Although tender offers are sometimes faster than beachhead acquisitions, the advantages of the beachhead acquisition far outweigh the speed of the tender offer. For example, gradually becoming involved in the company lessens suspicions of and increases trust in the aggressor. Dealing with fewer initial suspicions gives the aggressor time to gain support from within the company.	The beachhead acquisition is the most hostile takeover method and is inferior to the tender offer method.
	The beachhead acquisition is excessively hostile. In performing the beachhead acquisition, aggressors "sneak" into the company and manipulate shareholders. Rather than being up front about intentions, aggressors try to convince shareholders that the aggressor company has the shareholders' best interests at heart.
Second, taking over from "inside" the corporation, rather than just buying out the company directly, allows the aggressor to appear united with part of the target company. The rest of the target company is less likely to resist a takeover if part of the company has already united with the aggressor.	Even after the takeover, the target company morale may be damaged due to the methods used in the beachhead acquisition. As a result, the aggressor company could be left with poor worker-management-shareholder relations in the remaining company.
Further, inside support shows the public that the aggressor is strong. Additionally, inside support shows that after the takeover is complete, the acquisition of the target company will likely be smooth.	Additionally, the hostile appearance of the beachhead acquisition may cause a strong defense against the aggressor company. The shareholders in the target company would be fighting a sneaky, "mean" company to protect their "pet" company. It is highly unfortunate for the aggressor if the target company fears the aggressor because the fear will make the process of taking over the target company lengthier and much more difficult overall.
Some shareholders have a high personal investment in the target company. Hence, these shareholders would be extremely resistant to simply selling off their shares and allowing the aggressor to do as it pleases to the company. The shareholders would like to remain involved in their "pet" company. These shareholders may be more willing to vote *with* the aggressor if they feel their interests will continue to be protected.	The tender offer method is superior because buying out shareholders is often easier than convincing shareholders to change their opinion in support of a competitor. Quite frankly, people are persuaded by cold, hard cash. Cash-for-stock and stock-for-stock options are tangible and immediate. Promises-for-votes arrangements are intangible and not guaranteed. Money and stock are much more appealing because they are much more secure. Hence, the tender offer takeover is superior to the beachhead acquisition method.

Questions & Problems

1. What are the primary differences between mergers and consolidations?
2. Distinguish the various types of takeovers.
3. River Cities Investment Co.'s shareholders voted to amend the articles of incorporation to limit common stock to a total of 200 shares, reducing the existing 496,507 shares into the 200 shares. River Cities' board of directors determined that the value of the stock before the reduction was $33.23 per share, and the board offered to buy the

fractions of stock the minority shareholders owned for this amount. Meanwhile, Northwest Bank Holding Company purchased River Cities and then paid the River Cities minority shareholders for their stock, in addition to notifying the stockholders of their appraisal rights. The stockholders sued, arguing that a "fair value" market price for their shares should include an additional amount per share because, by buying the shares, Northwest gains a controlling interest in the company. Does "fair value" include paying for the benefit of having a controlling interest? How would various reasonable definitions of "fair" sway the judges' opinions? [*Northwest Investment Corp. v. Wallace*, 741 N.W.2d 782 (Iowa 2007).]

4. Hilton Hotels Corporation announced a $55-per-share tender offer for the stock of ITT. When Hilton announced plans for a proxy contest at ITT's 1997 annual meeting, ITT formally rejected Hilton's tender offer and began to sell some of its assets. Hilton learned that ITT was not planning on conducting its annual meeting, and it sought an injunction to compel ITT to conduct the meeting. The court, however, denied Hilton's motion. Intent on avoiding Hilton's purchase effort, ITT announced a "Comprehensive Plan" to split ITT into three new entities. The members of ITT's board of directors would be the directors of the new ITT entities. ITT planned to implement the Comprehensive Plan without obtaining shareholder approval. ITT argued that its Comprehensive Plan was a more attractive option than Hilton's tender offer. Do you think the court allowed ITT to complete its plan? Why or why not? [*Hilton Hotels Corporation v. ITT Corporation*, 978 F. Supp. 1342 (1997).]

5. In January 2003, Motorola began a hostile tender offer to obtain the 26 percent of Next Level Communications, Inc., that it did not own. It offered Next Level shareholders $1.04 per share. After Next Level shareholders petitioned to stop the takeover, Motorola increased its offer to $1.18 per share. After four months, Motorola had acquired 88 percent of Next Level's outstanding stock. It then converted some of its preferred stock into common stock, increasing its common stock ownership of Next Level to more than 90 percent. Motorola then initiated a short-form merger with Next Level, cashing out Next Level's minority shareholders. One of these shareholders, Nick

Gilliland, sued Next Level and Motorola for breach of their fiduciary duty to disclose information about Next Level's financial condition to Next Level minority shareholders. Gilliland argued that minority shareholders needed this information to decide whether to accept Motorola's cash-out offer or to exercise their appraisal rights. Motorola and Next Level argued that they sent minority shareholders information about Next Level's financial situation when Motorola made its initial tender offer. Moreover, they argued that the notice of the short-form merger they sent to minority shareholders met statutory requirements. Do you think the court sided with the corporations or with the minority shareholders in this case? Why? If you think the court sided with the shareholders, what remedies do you think should be available to them? [*Gilliland v. Motorola, Inc.*, 873 A.2d 305 (2005).]

6. Two brothers, Alex and John, served as directors of Atlas Corporation, a closely held corporation. Alex was responsible for financial matters, and John handled the company's day-to-day operations. The relationship between the two brothers began to deteriorate in 1995. On several occasions, Alex used his position as majority shareholder to overrule the board's decisions. The conflict culminated when John learned that Alex had made decisions contrary to the majority and without informing John. The following morning, John found out that Alex no longer intended that John be president of Atlas. Alex subsequently offered John a position as a consultant. John refused and filed a complaint seeking judicial dissolution. He argued that Alex, as majority shareholder, "froze him out" of the corporation. Do you agree with John? Why or why not? [*Kiriakides v. Atlas Food Systems & Services, Inc.*, 2000 S.C. App. LEXIS 32 (2000).]

7. Greatland Directional Drilling voluntarily dissolved as a corporation and received a certificate of dissolution on October 19, 1993. Anadrill, a division of Schlumberger Technology Corporation, acquired Greatland's assets and assumed Greatland's corporate interest and liabilities. A faulty drill bit rack injured Timothy Gossman, an employee of Anadrill, while he was working at a storage facility formerly owned by Greatland. In 1984, one of Greatland's employees incorrectly modified the rack, forgetting to remount a device designed to prevent drill bits from rolling off the rack. Gossman sued Greatland

for negligence. Anadrill argued to dismiss the claim because Greatland had dissolved. The superior court agreed with Anadrill, holding that, as a dissolved corporation, it could not hold Greatland liable. Do you agree with the court's decision? How do you think the appellate court decided the case on appeal? [*Gossman v. Greatland Directional Drilling, Inc.,* 973 P.2d 93 (1999).]

8. The City of Herriman, Utah, decided that it would provide water to its residents through a municipal water system. At the time, Herriman did not own any water, wells, or delivery infrastructure, but the Herriman Pipeline and Development Co. did. The city began to acquire the company's assets. It succeeded, much to the distress of a number of the company's shareholders. The shareholders sued the city, arguing that their shares entitled them to access to water and to an ownership interest in the company's assets. The court dismissed the case, and the shareholders appealed. Did the shareholders have a valid ownership interest in the company's assets? Why? [*Dansie v. City of Herriman,* 2006 UT 23.]

9. The directors of Lone Star Steakhouse & Saloon, Inc., set up a corporate provision that granted them significant retirement benefits if another company took over Lone Star and installed new directors. The corporate provision, however, held that the directors were not entitled to these golden-parachute benefits if they approved the new directors. The California Public Employees' Retirement System (CalPERS), a Lone Star shareholder, challenged the golden-parachute provision, arguing that it granted the existing directors undue voting power in director elections. Moreover, CalPERS argued that the golden-parachute provision discouraged potentially beneficial takeovers because the provision made it costly for potential aggressors to alter Lone Star's management. Lone Star argued that the provision was a legitimate defense to hostile takeovers. With whom do you think the court sided in this case? Why? [*Cal. Pub. Emples. Ret. Sys. v. Coulter,* 2005 Del. Ch. LEXIS 54 (2005).]

10. James Simmons was injured in a work-related accident at a construction site when an elevated scissorlift aerial work platform collapsed. Mark Industries designed, manufactured, and sold the scissorlift. Mark filed for bankruptcy in federal bankruptcy court and sold its assets to Terex. The agreement between Mark and Terex, which the bankruptcy court approved, included a provision stating that Terex was not responsible for any of Mark's liability. Only three Mark employees, none of whom were officers or directors, continued with Terex after Terex closed the factory it received as part of Mark's assets. Terex did not have any business relationship with Mark until purchasing its assets in the bankruptcy court auction. There has never been any commonality of officers, directors, or stockholders between Mark and Terex. Simmons sued Terex under a theory of successor liability. Was Terex a proper successor to Mark? What does Simmons need to prove to win his case? [*Simmons v. Mark Lift Industries, Inc.,* 622 S.E.2d 213 (S.C. 2005).]

Looking for more review material?

The Online Learning Center at **www.mhhe.com/kubasek2e** contains this chapter's "Assignment on the Internet" and also a list of URLs for more information, entitled "On the Internet." Find both of them in the Student Center portion of the OLC, along with quizzes and other helpful materials.

Employment and Labor Law

LEARNING OBJECTIVES

After reading this chapter, you will be able to answer the following questions:

1 What are wage and hour laws?

2 What are the rights of employees and obligations of employers under the Family and Medical Leave Act?

3 What is FUTA?

4 What are the rules regarding workers' compensation?

5 What is COBRA?

6 What is ERISA?

7 What is OSHA?

8 What does it mean to be an "at-will" employee?

9 What are the rights of employees and obligations of employers with regard to privacy in the workplace?

10 What are the three major pieces of labor law legislation?

CASE OPENER
Madison and Save Right Pharmacy

For the last five years, Madison has worked 20 hours per week at Save Right Pharmacy. She has always been a reliable and efficient employee. When her mother became seriously ill, Madison notified Save Right Pharmacy that under the Family and Medical Leave Act (FMLA) she planned to take up to 12 weeks off to care for her. Save Right Pharmacy denied Madison's request. When Madison left work anyway, Save Right Pharmacy terminated her employment. Madison then applied for unemployment compensation so she would have income to live on while caring for her mother. Madison also applied, under COBRA (see below), for continued insurance coverage through her former employer. If you were the CEO of Save Right Pharmacy, how would you handle the employment situation with Madison?

1. Is Madison eligible for time off from work under the FMLA?
2. May Save Right Pharmacy legally terminate Madison's employment?
3. Given that Madison was fired by Save Right Pharmacy, is she eligible to collect unemployment compensation?
4. May Madison continue her insurance coverage through Save Right Pharmacy even though she has been fired from her job?

The Wrap-Up at the end of the chapter will answer these questions.

Introduction to Labor and Employment Law

The employment relationship is a contractual relationship between the employer and the employee: The employer agrees to pay the employee a certain amount of money in exchange for the employee's agreement to render specific services. Until about the middle of the 20th century, workers had virtually no rights. There were no safety standards, and a worker injured on the job could be fired. Workers of all ages often toiled in unspeakable conditions.

Today, federal and state governments impose a number of conditions on the employment relationship. The first half of this chapter covers wages, benefits, health and safety standards, and employee rights, including the right to privacy. Exhibit 42-1 lists the major relevant state and federal laws. The remainder of this chapter covers labor unions.

Fair Labor Standards Act

L01

What are wage and hour laws?

Employers may not unilaterally determine how much to pay employees or how many hours to require them to work. They must follow federal minimum-wage and hour laws. The **Fair Labor Standards Act (FLSA)**[1] covers all employers engaged in interstate commerce or the production of goods for interstate commerce.

FLSA requires that a minimum wage of a specified amount be paid to all employees in covered industries. The specified amount is periodically raised by Congress to compensate for increases in the cost of living caused by inflation. The most recent increase took effect on July 24, 2009. The federal minimum wage increased from $6.55 to $7.25.

FLSA mandates that employees who work more than 40 hours in a week be paid no less than one and one half times their regular wage for all the hours they work beyond 40 during a given week. Four categories of employees are excluded:

- Executives
- Administrative employees
- Professional employees
- Outside salespersons

[1] 29 U.S.C. §§201–260.

Exhibit 42-1
Selected Laws Affecting
Working Conditions in
the United States

Wage and hour laws	Federal and state laws that impose minimum wage and hour requirements for employees.
Family and Medical Leave Act (FMLA)	Federal act requiring that certain employers establish a policy that provides all eligible employees with up to 12 weeks of leave during any 12-month period for several family-related occurrences (e.g., birth of a child or to care for a sick spouse).
Unemployment compensation	State system, created by the Federal Unemployment Tax Act (FUTA), that provides unemployment compensation to qualified employees who lose their jobs.
Workers' compensation laws	State laws that provide for financial compensation to employees or their dependents when the covered employee is injured on the job.
Consolidated Omnibus Budget Reconciliation Act (COBRA)	Federal law ensuring that when employees lose their jobs or have their hours reduced to a level at which they would not be eligible to receive medical, dental, or optical benefits from their employer, they can continue receiving benefits under the employer's policy for up to 18 months by paying the premiums for the policy.
Employee Retirement Income Security Act (ERISA)	Federal law that sets minimum standards for most voluntarily established pension and health plans in private industry.
The Occupational Safety and Health Act of 1970 (OSHA)	Federal law that established the Occupational Safety and Health Administration, the agency responsible for setting safety standards under the act, as well as enforcing the act through inspections and the levying of fines against violators.
Employment-at-will doctrine (and wrongful discharge)	Doctrine under which an employer can fire an employee for any reason at all. The three exceptions are *implied contract, violations of public policy,* and *implied covenant of good faith and fair dealing.* In states that have adopted any of these three exceptions, employees may be able to sue for wrongful discharge.
Employee privacy laws	Federal and state laws that govern privacy policies on matters such as employer surveillance, control of and access to medical and personnel records, drug testing, and e-mail.

Employees must earn at least a minimum income and spend a certain amount of time engaged in specified activities before they become exempt. If employers try to evade the overtime rule, their employees may sue. Taco Bell felt the full impact of FLSA when several groups of its employees brought class action suits against it for allegedly shaving hours off time cards to avoid paying overtime. One suit was settled for $13 million.[2] More recently, in a class action lawsuit against Walmart by 187,000 employees who worked there from 1998 through May 2006, the firm was ordered to pay $78 million for violating Pennsylvania state labor laws by forcing employees to work through rest breaks and off the clock.[3]

Legal Principle: Employers in covered industries are required to pay a federal minimum wage.

---

[2] "Taco Bell Loses Second Big Back-Pay Case as Ore. Jury Affirms Time-Card Tampering Charge," *Nation's Restaurant News,* March 26, 2001, p. 3.

[3] "Jury Orders Pa. Walmart to Pay $78 Million," http://cbs3.com/topstories/local_story_286145532.html, October 13, 2006.

Paid Vacations in Other Countries

In Ireland, the Holiday Act of 1973 guarantees every worker, regardless of how long he or she has been with a company, three weeks of paid vacation time and nine additional days off for public holidays. In Luxembourg, regardless of age, employees are given 25 days of holiday, 12 of which they must take in succession, as well as 10 paid public holidays. Swedish law gives employees 5 weeks of vacation time and gives them 10 weeks after five years of employment. Denmark mandates no fewer than five weeks of paid vacation a year, and Spain no fewer than 30 days in addition to the country's 14 paid public ones.

The United Kingdom is like the United States in having no laws requiring paid or even unpaid holidays. The United States does not mandate any minimum annual vacation time for employees.

Family and Medical Leave Act

LO2

What are the rights of employees and obligations of employers under the Family and Medical Leave Act?

When the **Family and Medical Leave Act (FMLA)** went into effect in 1993, it was hailed by its supporters as a "breakthrough" and feared by its opponents as an unwieldy encumbrance on business. FMLA covers all public employers, as well as private employers with 50 or more employees (see Exhibit 42-2). It guarantees all eligible employees (those who have worked at least 25 hours a week for each of 12 months before the leave) up to 12 weeks of *unpaid* leave during any 12-month period for any of the following family-related occurrences:

- The birth of a child.
- The adoption of a child.
- The placement of a foster child in the employee's care.
- The care of a seriously ill spouse, parent, or child.
- A serious health condition that renders the employee unable to perform any of the essential functions of his or her job.

Exhibit 42-2

Who Is Covered under FMLA?

	YES	NO	DEPENDS
Public employers?	√		
Private employers?	√		
Employers with 50 or more employees?	√		
Employers with fewer than 50 employees?		√	
Full-time employees for at least one year?	√		
Part-time employees for at least one year? (must work at least 25 hours per week for 12 months before taking leave)			√
The leave is paid?		√	
The leave is for up to 12 weeks in a 12-month period?	√		
The employee may take more than 12 weeks off in 12 months?		√	

Madison, at the beginning of the chapter, worked for Save Right Pharmacy for five years but worked only 20 hours per week. Under FMLA, she would not be eligible to take leave to care for her mother.

FMLA is a highly complex piece of legislation, containing six titles divided into 26 sections, as well as regulations designed to guide implementation that are eight times longer than the statute itself! Many employers were still not in full compliance a year after it became effective.

To exercise rights under FMLA, an employee whose need is foreseeable (such as for childbirth) must advise the employer at least 30 days before the leave needs to begin. If the leave is unforeseeable, the employee must give notice as soon as practicable, defined as within one or two business days after the need becomes known. FMLA does not define the type of notice necessary, but the employee must state the reason for the leave and, if possible, the length of time needed. FMLA does not have to be specifically mentioned in the request.

When their FMLA leaves terminate, employees must be restored to the same position they held, or one with substantially equivalent skills, effort, responsibility, and authority. If an employee is unable to return at the end of the 12-week period, the employer need not hold the position open any longer.

While FMLA does not require that leave be paid, the employer must continue health insurance benefits. The employer may also require that an employee substitute paid time off for unpaid leave. For example, an employee with 4 weeks' accrued sick leave and 2 weeks' vacation who wishes to take a 12-week leave may be required to take the paid vacation and sick leave for that purpose, plus 6 weeks' unpaid leave.

REMEDIES FOR VIOLATIONS OF FMLA

If an employer fails to comply with FMLA, the plaintiff may recover damages for unpaid wages or salary, lost benefits, denied compensation, and actual monetary losses up to an amount equivalent to the employee's wages for 12 weeks, as well as attorney fees and court costs. If the plaintiff can prove bad faith on the part of the employer, double damages may be awarded. An employee may also be entitled to reinstatement or promotion. Although most awards under FMLA have not been large, a California worker demoted and then fired for taking time off to have surgery for a brain tumor in 1996 sued and was awarded $313,000.[4] In 1999, a state trooper denied time off to care for his pregnant wife, and subsequently his daughter, when his wife became ill during and after the pregnancy was awarded $375,000.[5] Many employment law specialists are now seeing FMLA as an act employers must carefully follow.

Unemployment Compensation

What happens if employees lose their jobs? The **Federal Unemployment Tax Act (FUTA)**,[6] passed in 1935, created a state system to provide **unemployment compensation** to qualified employees who lose their jobs. Under this law, employers pay taxes to the states, which deposit the money into the federal government's Unemployment Insurance Fund. Each state has an account from which it can access money in accordance with state eligibility rules. States have different minimum standards for qualifying for unemployment compensation, although most require that the applicant did not voluntarily quit or get fired

L03

What is FUTA?

---

[4] *Lawyer's Weekly* 6 (1996), p. 973.
[5] *Knussman v. State of Maryland et al.,* 65 F. Supp. 353 (1999).
[6] 26 U.S.C. §§ 3301–3310.

for cause. Because Madison did not qualify for leave under FMLA and stopped going to work even though Save Right Pharmacy denied her request, Save Right was legally within its rights to fire her. Whether she was fired or voluntarily quit her job, she would not be entitled to unemployment compensation in most states.

Most states fund benefits through a tax on employers; only three states require minimal employee contributions.[7] The amount of the benefit may also vary.

Workers' Compensation Laws

LO4

What are the rules regarding workers' compensation?

Workers' compensation laws came about as a result of the abuses that injured employees often suffered on the job. Before workers' compensation, an injured employee's only recourse was to sue the employer for negligence. In return for the right to recover for injuries incurred on the job, the employee gives up the right to bring negligence claims.

Unlike many other laws affecting the employment relationship, workers' compensation legislation is purely state law. Our coverage of this topic must therefore be rather generalized. Prudent businesspeople will familiarize themselves with the workers' compensation statutes of the states within which their companies operate.

Workers' compensation laws ensure that covered workers injured on the job can receive financial compensation through an administrative procedure, rather than having to sue their employer. For administrative convenience, most states exclude certain types of businesses and small firms from coverage. Some also allow businesses with sufficient resources to be self-insured, rather than participating in the state program.

Legal Principle: **Under workers' compensation laws, an employee is guaranteed the right to recover for injuries that occurred on the job without having to sue his or her employer.**

BENEFITS UNDER STATE WORKERS' COMPENSATION

To recover benefits, the injured party must demonstrate that (1) he or she is an employee, (2) both employer and employee are covered by the state workers' compensation program, and (3) the injury occurred on the job.

As a general rule, the accident leading to the injury must have taken place during the time and within the scope of the claimant's employment. Using the *premises rule,* if an employee is on company property, the courts generally find that she was on the job. If an employee who travels for work is injured on a business trip, many states will find that he is entitled to compensation for reasonable injuries suffered. A New York typist who traveled to Canada to transcribe depositions fell while showering in her hotel. She filed a successful workers' compensation claim.

An employee injured on the job must notify the employer of the injury and file a claim with the state workers' compensation board, usually within 30 to 60 days. The board will verify the claim and determine the appropriate benefits. If the employer contests the claim, a hearing takes place before the state workers' compensation board. If the claim is denied, most states provide an agency appeals process followed by a provision for appeal to the courts. Most statutes cover medical, hospital, and rehabilitation expenses and generally lost wages. In Case 42-1, the court had to decide whether workers' compensation should be the exclusive remedy for accidental injuries caused by the gross, wanton, willful, deliberate, intentional, reckless, culpable or malicious negligence, breach of statute, or other misconduct of the employer; short of a conscious and deliberate intent directed to the purpose of inflicting an injury.

---

[7] U.S. Department of Labor, http://workforcesecurity.doleta.gov/unemploy/uifactsheet.asp. The states that require employee contribution are Alaska, New Jersey, and Pennsylvania.

Reynaldo Delgado died following an explosion at a smelting plant in Deming, New Mexico, after a supervisor ordered him to perform a task that, according to Delgado's widow, was virtually certain to kill him or cause him serious injury. Phelps Dodge allegedly chose to subject Delgado to the risk despite knowing this. His widow brought a number of tort claims against Phelps Dodge and the individual supervisors. The trial court dismissed the case on grounds that the Workers' Compensation Act provided the exclusive remedy, leaving Phelps Dodge immune from tort liability. The Court of Appeals upheld that ruling in a memorandum opinion. The Supreme Court of New Mexico agreed to hear the case to determine whether Phelps Dodge was indeed immune.

JUDGE GENE E. FRANCHINI: In the summer of 1998, thirty-three-year-old Reynaldo Delgado resided in Deming, New Mexico, with his wife, Petitioner Michelle Delgado, and two minor children. Mr. Delgado had been working at the Phelps Dodge smelting plant in Hurley, New Mexico, for two years. The smelting plant distills copper ore from unusable rock, called "slag," by superheating unprocessed rock to a temperature in excess of 2,000 degrees Fahrenheit. During the process, the ore rises to the top, where it is harvested, while the slag sinks to the bottom of the furnace where it drains through a valve called a "skim hole." From there, the slag passes down a chute into a fifteen-foot-tall iron cauldron called a "ladle," located in a tunnel below the furnace. Ordinarily, when the ladle reaches three-quarters of its thirty-five-ton capacity, workers use a "mudgun" to plug the skim hole with clay, thus stopping the flow of molten slag and permitting a specially designed truck, called a "kress-haul," to enter the tunnel and lift and remove the ladle.

On the night of June 30, Delgado's shorthanded work crew, under the supervision of Mike Burkett and Charlie White, was being pressured to work harder in order to compensate for the loss of production and revenue incurred after a recent ten day shut down. Suddenly, the crew experienced an especially dangerous emergency situation known as a "runaway." The ladle had reached three-quarters of its capacity but the flowing slag could not be stopped because the mudgun was inoperable and manual efforts to close the skim hole had failed. To compound the situation, the consistency of the slag caused it to flow at a faster rate than ever, thus resulting in the worst runaway condition that many of the workers on the site had ever experienced. Respondents could have shut down the furnace, thereby allowing the safe removal of the ladle of slag. However, in order to avoid

economic loss, Respondents chose instead to order Delgado, who had never operated a kress-haul under runaway conditions, to attempt to remove the ladle alone, with the molten slag still pouring over its fifteen-foot brim. In doing so, Respondents knew or should have known that Delgado would die or suffer great bodily harm.

When Delgado entered the tunnel, he saw that the ladle was overflowing and radioed White to inform him that he was neither qualified nor able to perform the removal. White insisted. In response to Delgado's renewed protest and request for help, White again insisted that Delgado proceed alone. Shortly after Delgado entered the tunnel, the lights shorted out and black smoke poured from the mouth of the tunnel. Delgado's co-workers watched as he emerged from the smoke-filled tunnel, fully engulfed in flames. He collapsed before co-workers could douse the flames with a water hose. "Why did they send me in there?" Delgado asked co-workers, "I told them I couldn't do it. They made me do it anyway. Charlie sent me in." Delgado had suffered third-degree burns over his entire body and died three weeks later in an Arizona hospital.

When a worker suffers an accidental injury and a number of other preconditions are satisfied, the Act provides a scheme of compensation that affords profound benefits to both workers and employers. The injured worker receives compensation quickly, without having to endure the rigors of litigation or prove fault on behalf of the employer. The employer, in exchange, is assured that a worker accidentally injured, even by the employer's own negligence, will be limited to compensation under the Act and may not pursue the unpredictable damages available outside its boundaries. The Act represents the "result of a bargain struck between employers and employees. In return for the loss of a common law tort claim for accidents arising out of the scope of employment, [the Act] ensures that workers are provided some compensation."

. . . [T]he Act limits its scope to accidents, barring both compensation and exclusivity when the worker sustains a nonaccidental injury. Because the basis for limiting exclusivity depends on the nonaccidental character of the injury, Professor Larson argues:

> [T]he common-law liability of the employer cannot, under the almost unanimous rule, be stretched to include accidental injuries caused by the gross, wanton, willful, deliberate, intentional, reckless, culpable or malicious negligence, breach of statute, or other misconduct of the employer short of a conscious and deliberate intent directed to the purpose of inflicting an injury.

We hold that when an employer intentionally inflicts or willfully causes a worker to suffer an injury that would otherwise be exclusively compensable under the Act that employer may not enjoy the benefits of exclusivity, and the injured worker may sue in tort.

REVERSED and REMANDED in favor of plaintiff.

CRITICAL THINKING

What are the key words in determining whether an injury falls under the Workers' Compensation Act? Is it clear when anyone acts intentionally? What factors would make a court see a defendant's act as having "intentionally or willfully caused" a worker's injury?

ETHICAL DECISION MAKING

Delgado's widow and children are important stakeholders in the court's decision, as is Phelps Dodge. But ethical decisions require consideration of stakeholders who are often invisible at first glance. Who are other relevant stakeholders in this case?

ADVANTAGES AND DISADVANTAGES OF WORKERS' COMPENSATION

> To see a description of the tax treatment of workers' compensation benefits, please see the **Connecting to the Core** activity on the text Web site at www.mhhe.com/kubasek2e.

Employees benefit from workers' compensation laws because with very little effort they receive an almost certain recovery when injured, although the amount is less than they would have received from a successful negligence case against their employers. Employers must pay into the workers' compensation fund every year, but they thereby ensure that their employee injury costs are fixed and they will not have to pay a huge negligence award to an injured employee.

Consolidated Omnibus Budget Reconciliation Act of 1985

LO5

What is COBRA?

The **Consolidated Omnibus Budget Reconciliation Act (COBRA)** ensures that employees who lose their jobs or have their hours reduced to a level at which they are no longer eligible to receive medical, dental, or optical benefits can continue receiving benefits for themselves and their dependents under the employer's policy. The employee must pay the premiums for the policy, plus up to a 2 percent administration fee, to maintain coverage up to 18 months, or 29 months if disabled. Premiums are often quite expensive. An employee has 60 days after coverage would ordinarily terminate to decide whether to maintain it.

COBRA benefits do *not* arise under either of two conditions:

1. The employee is fired for gross misconduct.
2. The employer decides to eliminate benefits for all current employees.

Madison, in our opening scenario, applied to retain her insurance benefits under COBRA, but if her failure to come to work is deemed "gross misconduct," her benefits may be terminated. In most cases, however, when an employee voluntarily quits a job, or even is fired (but not for gross misconduct), insurance benefits may be continued (although the *employee* must pay the full cost). Employers who fail to comply with the law may be required to pay up to 10 percent of the annual cost of the group plan or $500,000, whichever is less.

Employee Retirement Income Security Act of 1974

The **Employee Retirement Income Security Act (ERISA)** is "a federal law that sets minimum standards for most voluntarily established pension and health plans in private industry to provide protection for individuals in these plans."[8] Under ERISA, employers must provide participants with all the following:

1. Plan information (features and funding).
2. Assurances that those in charge of managing plan assets have fiduciary responsibility.
3. A grievance and appeals process for participants to get benefits from their plans.
4. The right to sue for benefits and breaches of fiduciary duty.[9]

ERISA has been amended several times. Some of the most important amendments are COBRA (discussed above) and HIPAA (Health Insurance Portability and Accountability Act), "which provides important new protections for working Americans and their families who have preexisting medical conditions or might otherwise suffer discrimination in health coverage based on factors that relate to an individual's health."[10] ERISA does not apply to health plans for government or church employees or to plans maintained to comply with disability, workers' compensation, or unemployment laws.

Legal Principle: **ERISA requires that private employers keep employees informed about voluntarily established pension and health plans.**

LO6

What is ERISA?

Occupational Safety and Health Act of 1970

The federal government regulates workplace safety primarily through the **Occupational Safety and Health Act (OSHA),** which requires that every employer "furnish to each of his employees . . . employment . . . free from recognized hazards that are likely to cause death or serious physical harm." The Occupational Safety and Health Administration (abbreviated *OSHA,* the same as the act) promulgates workplace safety standards, inspects facilities for compliance, and brings enforcement actions against violators.

Under the law, employers must prominently display in the workplace either the federal or a state OSHA poster with information about employees' safety and health rights. Employers with 11 or more employees (20 percent of the establishments OSHA covers) must keep records of work-related injuries and illnesses except in low-hazard industries such as retail, service, finance, insurance, and real estate.

LO7

What is OSHA?

PENALTIES UNDER OSHA

If OSHA inspectors find violations in the workplace, they may issue citations. Penalties for violations may range from $0 to $70,000 per violation, depending on the likelihood that the violation would lead to serious injury to an employee. Penalties may be reduced if an employer has a small number of employees, has demonstrated good faith, or has few or no previous violations. If a willful violation results in the death of a worker, criminal penalties may be imposed.

---

[8] Department of Labor, Employee Retirement Income Security Act, www.dol.gov/dol/topic/health-plans/erisa.htm.

[9] Ibid.

[10] Ibid.

Occupational Safety and Health Act

Irving v. United States
162 F.3d 154 (1998)

Somersworth Shoe Company operated a manufacturing plant in New Hampshire. In 1979, when employee Gail Irving bent to retrieve a work glove behind her bench, her hair was drawn into the vacuum created by the high-speed rotation of a nearby drive shaft. Irving was very seriously injured. After nearly two decades of litigation, she won a $1 million judgment. The United States appealed.

At issue was whether OSHA inspectors were required to inspect every machine in a facility or could use their discretion in deciding what to inspect. OSHA's purpose is to provide a satisfactory standard of safety, not to guarantee absolute safety. The United States demonstrated that permitting inspectors discretion was grounded in its policies; therefore, it was not negligent and the award was reversed.

Employment-at-Will Doctrine and Wrongful Termination

LO8

What does it mean to be an "at-will" employee?

Unless an employee belongs to a union or has an employment contract with his or her employer, the employment relationship is governed by the **employment-at-will doctrine.** This doctrine provides that a contract of employment for an indeterminate period of time may be terminated at will by either party, at any time, for any reason. The traditional employment-at-will doctrine has been restricted over the past few decades, mainly by civil rights legislation (Chapter 43). States have also created exceptions that allow an employee to sue for wrongful discharge. They fall into three primary categories (not all states accept all three). The most common exception, the **implied-contract exception,** provides that an implied employment contract may arise from statements the employer makes in an employment handbook or materials advertising the position. For instance, an implied contract can arise if:

1. The employment handbook contains the steps for progressive discipline leading to discharge.
2. The handbooks makes no mention of the words *employment at will.*
3. The employee relies on that handbook.

If the employer does not follow the policies in its own handbook, a fired employee may sue for wrongful discharge.

The **public policy exception** prohibits employers from firing employees engaged in activities that further the public interest. Protected activities vary among states and include, but are not limited to, serving on jury duty, doing military service, filing for or testifying at hearings for workers' compensation claims, and whistle-blowing.

The least common exception to at-will employment is the **implied covenant of good faith and fair dealing exception.** This exception assumes that every employment contract contains an implicit understanding that the parties will deal fairly with one another. Because there is no clear agreement on what constitutes fair treatment of an employee, most states do not use this exception.

Exhibit 42-3 highlights some of the limits to the coverage of the employment-at-will doctrine.

Legal Principle: **Under the employment-at-will doctrine, a contract of employment for an indeterminate period of time may be terminated at will by either party at any time and for any reason.**

Exhibit 42-3
At-Will Employment

	YES	NO
May an employer fire an at-will employee on the basis of:		
Gender?		√
Race?		√
Political party?	√	
No reason?	√	

Employee Privacy in the Workplace

Technology brings new privacy issues to the workplace. It allows employers to gather information about employees; but it also provides more temptations for employees to be "off the job" at work, thus stimulating a need for more employer monitoring.

According to a 2006 study, 93 percent of employees with Internet access at work look at nonwork-related Web sites.[11] Employers naturally want to monitor what employees are doing when they are supposed to be on the job, but some go too far, such as monitoring keystrokes for words such as *union* and *strike*.[12] Once employers monitor employees and discover wrongdoing, the issue of employers' right to fire at will becomes relevant.

In *Michael A. Smyth v. The Pillsbury Company*,[13] Smyth alleged that his employer, the Pillsbury Company, violated his privacy rights by reading his e-mail and then illegally firing him on the basis of the content of some of his messages. Smyth had transmitted a message to his supervisor about the company's sales management team in which he threatened to "kill the backstabbing bastards" and referred to an upcoming company party as the "Jim Jones Koolaid affair."[14]

The court granted Pillsbury's motion to dismiss, ruling that Smyth did not have a reasonable expectation of privacy in e-mail communications he made voluntarily over the company system. The court was unimpressed with Smyth's assertion that management repeatedly assured employees that it would not intercept e-mail. Ultimately, the court ruled that the employer's right to prevent inappropriate, unprofessional, and possibly illegal comments over its e-mail system outweighed an employee's privacy rights.

Legal Principle: **Employees do not have a reasonable expectation of privacy when using their employers' e-mail system, even during nonworking hours.**

ELECTRONIC MONITORING AND COMMUNICATION

Questions about employer monitoring of phone conversations, e-mail, and voice mail invoke the common law tort of invasion of privacy and the federal **Omnibus Crime Control and Safe Streets Act of 1968**,[15] as amended by the **Electronic Communications Privacy Act (ECPA) of 1986**.[16]

L09

What are the rights of employees and obligations of employers with regard to privacy in the workplace?

---

[11] "The Productivity Challenge: Working with the iPod Generation," http://infoacrs.com/wri/work.html, January 17, 2007.

[12] Stephen Lesavich, "Keystroke Spies: Conflicting Rights," *National Law Journal*, May 22, 2000, p. A23.

[13] 914 F. Supp. 97 (1996).

[14] Jim Jones is the cult leader whose followers committed mass suicide by drinking a poisoned drink in Jonestown, Guyana, in 1978.

[15] 18 U.S.C. § 2210 et seq.

[16] 18 U.S.C. §§ 2510–2521.

Dear Employee,

We searched your email, so now you're fired.

stus.com

Under the first statute, employers cannot listen to or disclose the contents of private telephone conversations of employees. They may ban personal calls and monitor for compliance, as long as they discontinue listening to any conversation once they determine it is personal. Violators may be subject to fines of up to $10,000. Under ECPA, employees' privacy rights were extended to electronic forms of communication including e-mail and cellular phones. ECPA outlaws the intentional interception of electronic communications and intentional disclosure or use of the information so obtained.

The key question is whether the employee had a **reasonable expectation of privacy** with respect to the communication in question. The ECPA protects individuals' communications against government surveillance conducted without a court order, from third parties without legitimate authorization to access the messages, and from carriers such as Internet service providers. It provides employees little privacy protection with respect to communications conducted on the employer's equipment.

Employers are in the strongest position when they have a clear policy preventing any reasonable expectation of privacy. Employment law experts advise having a written policy that employees sign. At a minimum, employer privacy policies should cover the following issues:

1. Employer monitoring of telephone conversations.
2. Employer surveillance policies.
3. Employee access to medical and personnel records.
4. Drug testing policies.
5. Lie detector policies.
6. Ownership of computers and all issues unique to the electronic workplace.

DRUG TESTING IN THE WORKPLACE

Because they can be liable for employees' actions, employers are increasingly testing employees for the use of illegal drugs. Under the Drug-Free Workplace Act, employers that receive federal financial assistance or have federal contracts worth over $25,000 must develop an antidrug policy for employees, provide drug-free awareness programs for them, and warn them of penalties for violating company drug policies.

Private employers engaged in drug testing are not limited by the U.S. Constitution as are public employers, but they still need to be aware of state statutory and constitutional limits. In most states, private companies have virtually unfettered discretion to test employees for drug usage. One exception is California, whose state constitution grants an explicit right to privacy that applies to the actions of private businesses.[17] Seven additional states

---

[17] Lectic Law Library, "Drug Testing in the Workplace," ACLU Briefing Paper No. 5, www.lectlaw.com/files/emp02.htm.

CASE NUGGET

Lie Detector Tests

Polkey v. Transtrecs Corp.
404 F.3d 1264 (11th Cir. 2005)

Polkey was a supervisor in the mailroom at Pensacola Naval Air Station run by a company called Transtrecs. After discovering that some mail had been tampered with, Polkey reported it to her supervisor. Transtrecs asked all six employees, including Polkey, to take a lie detector (polygraph) test. The employee most suspected was tested first, and the test indicated he might have been the one who tampered with the mail. Polkey and the remaining employees then refused to take the test. Transtrecs fired Polkey, who sued for violation of the Employee Polygraph Protection Act (EPPA). The

district court granted summary judgment for Polkey. Transtrecs appealed.

On appeal, the district court's judgment was affirmed. The court held that Transtrecs violated EPPA by requesting and even suggesting that the employees take a polygraph test. Transtrecs had argued that it was exempt from EPPA for national security reasons, but the appellate court said that this exemption applies only to the government, for which Transtrecs was merely a contractor. Transtrecs also argued that the polygraph was part of an ongoing investigation of Polkey and that she was under suspicion. But for this exemption to apply, Transtrecs needed an articulable basis in fact to indicate that Polkey was involved in or responsible for an economic loss. Transtrecs could make no such showing, and Polkey prevailed.

have enacted at least some restrictions on drug testing in the workplace: Montana, Iowa, Vermont, Rhode Island, Minnesota, Maine, and Connecticut.[18] Some collective bargaining agreements may restrict the employer's ability to test for drugs or may mandate specific testing procedures.

Labor Law

Workers first achieved the right to organize (join unions) during the Great Depression. During the post-World War II period, over one-third of U.S. workers were organized. Yet by 2008, only 12.4 percent were.[19] Education, training, and library occupations and protective service workers such as police and firefighters had the highest unionization rates of all occupations during 2008: 38.7 percent and 35.4 percent, respectively.[20]

Labor-management relations in the United States today are governed by three major pieces of legislation. Exhibit 42-4 summarizes this legislation.

LO10

What are the three major pieces of labor law legislation?

LEGISLATION	PURPOSE OF LEGISLATION
Wagner Act of 1935	Adopted explicitly to encourage the formation of labor unions and provide for collective bargaining between employers and unions
Taft-Hartley Act of 1947	Amended the Wagner Act and was designed to curtail some of the powers the unions had acquired under the Wagner Act [The Wager Act and the Taft-Hartley Act are jointly referred to as the National Labor Relations Act (NLRA).]
Landrum-Griffin Act of 1959	Governs the internal operations of labor unions and contains "Labor's Bill of Rights" to protect employees from their own unions

Exhibit 42-4
Federal Labor Law Legislation

[18] Ibid.

[19] Bureau of Labor Statistics, http://www.bls.gov/news.release/pdf/union2.pdf.

[20] Ibid.

E-COMMERCE AND THE LAW

THE WAGNER ACT OF 1935

The first major piece of federal legislation adopted explicitly to encourage the formation of labor unions and provide for **collective bargaining** between employers and unions as a means of obtaining the peaceful settlement of labor disputes was the **Wagner Act.** Collective bargaining "consists of negotiations between an employer and a group of employees so as to determine the conditions of employment."[21] The key sections of the Wagner Act are:

1. *Section 7,* which provides, "Employees shall have the right to self-organization, to join, form or assist labor organizations, to bargain collectively through representatives of their own choosing, and to engage in concerted activities for the purpose of collective bargaining or other mutual aid and protection."
2. *Section 8(a),* which specifies the actions that are prohibited as employer unfair labor practices.

The Wagner Act also created an administrative agency, the *National Labor Relations Board (NLRB),* to interpret and enforce the NLRA. Finally, it provides for judicial review in designated federal courts of appeal.

THE TAFT-HARTLEY ACT OF 1947

The 12 years between passage of the Wagner Act and that of the Taft-Hartley Act saw a huge growth in unionization, which resulted in an increase in workers' power. Public perception of this trend led to the passage of the **Taft-Hartley Act,** also known as the *Labor-Management Relations Act,* designed to curtail some of the powers the unions had acquired under the Wagner Act. Just as Section 8(a) of the Wagner Act designated certain employer actions as unfair, Section 8(b) of the Taft-Hartley Act designated certain union actions as unfair.

THE LANDRUM-GRIFFIN ACT OF 1959

The **Landrum-Griffin Act** primarily governs the internal operations of labor unions. This act, a response to evidence of certain undesirable internal labor union practices, requires financial disclosures by unions and establishes civil and criminal penalties for financial abuses by union officials. "Labor's Bill of Rights," contained in the act, protects employees from their own unions.

---

[21] Legal Information Institute, www.law.cornell.edu/topics/collective_bargaining.html.

THE NATIONAL LABOR RELATIONS BOARD

The **National Labor Relations Board (NLRB)** interprets and enforces the **National Labor Relations Act (NLRA)**. The NLRB's three primary functions are to:

1. Monitor the conduct of the employer and the union during an election to determine whether workers want to be represented by a union.
2. Prevent and remedy unfair labor practices by employers or unions.
3. Establish rules interpreting the act.

The NLRB has jurisdiction over all employees *except* those who work in federal, state, and local government and those covered by the Railway Labor Act (employees in the transportation industry); independent contractors; agricultural workers; household domestics; persons employed by a spouse or parent; and supervisors, managerial employees, and confidential employees.

The stimulus for forming a union is typically employee dissatisfaction with some policy of or treatment by their employer. A union representative then assists the employees in a campaign to persuade a majority of the workers to accept the union as their exclusive representative. Once a majority of workers sign authorization cards indicating an interest in being represented by the union, they present these to the employer, who decides whether to formally recognize the new local union.

If the employer refuses, the union organizers can petition the NLRB for a representation election. The NLRB will supervise the election, and if the union receives a majority of the votes in the secret-ballot election, the union will be certified as the bargaining representative. During the course of the organizing campaign, certain activities of both employers and employees are prohibited by the NLRA and by rules of conduct developed by the NLRB. The constraints on employers' behavior under the NLRA are found primarily in Section 8(a)1, which prohibits interference in employees' exercise of their Section 7 rights. If an employer engages in prohibited activity during the organizing campaign, the NLRB may set aside the results of an election and order a new election. In an extreme case where the employer's conduct was so egregious as to make it impossible to hold a fair election, and the union had previously collected authorization cards signed by a majority of the employees, the NLRB may order the employer to bargain with the union without a new election.

Employers should be sure their speech and conduct during an organizing campaign do not rise to the level of coercion, restraint, or interference. Employers may express views, arguments, or opinions as long as they do not contain any threats of reprisals or promises of benefits. Finally, employers may prohibit union solicitation and the distribution of literature during work time. However, during nonwork time, such as lunch and coffee breaks, employers may prohibit organizing activity on company property *only* if there are legitimate safety or efficiency reasons for doing so and the restraint is not manifestly intended to thwart organizing efforts. The burden of proof is on the employer to demonstrate these safety or efficiency concerns.

THE COLLECTIVE BARGAINING PROCESS

Once the union has been certified, union and management must begin to bargain in good faith about wages, hours, and other terms and conditions of work. The NLRB can order the parties only to bargain in good faith; it cannot order them to reach an agreement with respect to any contract term.

Bargaining collectively in good faith means that the parties must:

1. Meet at reasonable times and confer in good faith.
2. Sign a written agreement if one is reached.
3. When intent on terminating or modifying an existing contract, give 60 days' notice to the other party, with an offer to confer over proposals, and give 30 days' notice to the federal or state mediation services in the event of a pending dispute over the new agreement.
4. Neither strike nor engage in a lockout during the 60-day notice.

An employer who fails to bargain in good faith is committing an unfair labor practice under Section 8(a)5. The most common violation by a union is bargaining for clauses that fall outside the scope of mandatory bargaining.

Legal Principle: **The parties to a union contract must bargain collectively and in good faith.**

STRIKES, PICKETING, AND BOYCOTTS

Three other activities employers may confront are strikes, picketing, and boycotts. The NLRA offers management guidance on how to respond to these activities.

Strikes are one of the most powerful tools unions have.

A **strike** is a temporary, concerted withdrawal of labor. It is the most powerful weapon employees use to secure recognition and improve their working conditions, but it is also potentially the most dangerous. Delta Air Lines' Comair pilots struck in 2001 to obtain better pay. After an eight-week work stoppage and a loss to Delta of $1.5 to $2 million per day, an agreement was reached.

A refusal to deal with, purchase goods from, or work for a business is a **boycott.** Like a strike, it is a technique for prohibiting a company from carrying on its business so that it will accede to union demands. **Primary boycotts,** against an employer with whom the union is directly engaged in a labor dispute, are lawful. However, **secondary boycotts** are illegal. These occur when employees have a labor dispute with their employer and boycott another company to force it to cease doing business with the employer.

Individuals who place themselves outside an employer's place of business for the purpose of informing passers-by of the fact(s) of a labor dispute are engaged in **picketing.** Picketing may occur as part of a strike or independently. If off-duty employees picket without a strike, they can continue to work and get paid while still getting their message across. Picketing designed to truthfully inform the public of a labor dispute between an employer and the employees is called **informational picketing** and is protected by law. However, **signal picketing,** which prevents deliveries or services to the employer, is unprotected behavior.

CASE OPENER WRAP-UP

Madison and Save Right Pharmacy

By now you should be able to answer all the questions asked at the beginning of the chapter.

Madison worked for Save Right Pharmacy for five years, but she worked only 20 hours per week so she was not eligible to take leave to care for her mother. Under FMLA, an employee must work a minimum of 25 hours per week.

Because Madison did not qualify to take leave under FMLA and simply stopped coming to work, Save Right Pharmacy was legally within its rights to fire her. Moreover, whether she was fired or voluntarily quit her job, she would not be entitled to collect unemployment compensation in most states.

If Madison's failing to come to work is deemed "gross misconduct," her insurance benefits may be terminated. In most cases, however, when an employee voluntarily quits his or her job or even is fired (but not for gross misconduct), insurance benefits may be continued (although the *employee* must pay the full cost of the insurance).

Key Terms

boycott   928

collective bargaining   926

Consolidated
   Omnibus Budget
   Reconciliation Act
   (COBRA)   920

Electronic Communications
   Privacy Act (ECPA)
   of 1986   923

Employee Retirement
   Income Security
   Act (ERISA)   921

employment-at-will
   doctrine   922

Fair Labor Standards
   Act (FLSA)   914

Family and Medical
   Leave Act
   (FMLA)   916

Federal Unemployment
   Tax Act (FUTA)   917

implied covenant of good
   faith and fair dealing
   exceptions   922

implied-contract
   exception   922

informational
   picketing   928

Landrum-Griffin Act   926

National Labor Relations
   Act (NLRA)   927

National Labor Relations
   Board (NLRB)   927

Occupational Safety
   and Health Act
   (OSHA)   921

Omnibus Crime
   Control and
   Safe Streets
   Act of 1968   923

picketing   928

primary boycotts   928

public policy
   exception   922

reasonable expectation
   of privacy   924

secondary boycotts   928

signal picketing   928

strike   928

Taft-Hartley Act   926

unemployment
   compensation   917

Wagner Act   926

workers' compensation
   laws   918

Summary of Key Topics

Introduction to Labor and Employment Law	Both the federal and state governments impose a number of conditions on the employment relationship. The purpose of this chapter was to explain many of the laws that created those constraints on the employer's ability to determine terms and conditions of employment and termination. The first half of this chapter covered wages, benefits, health and safety standards, and employee rights, including the right to privacy. The second half of this chapter covered labor unions.

Fair Labor Standards Act

Employers must follow federal minimum-wage and hour laws. FLSA covers all employers engaged in interstate commerce or the production of goods for interstate commerce and requires that a "minimum wage" of a specified amount be paid to all employees in covered industries. The specified amount is periodically raised by Congress to compensate for increases in the cost of living caused by inflation. The most recent increase took effect on July 24, 2009, when the minimum wage rose to $7.25 per hour.

Family and Medical Leave Act

FMLA requires that certain employers establish a policy that provides all eligible employees with up to 12 weeks of leave during any 12-month period for several family-related occurrences (birth of a child, to care for a sick spouse, etc.)

Unemployment Compensation

The Federal Unemployment Tax Act (FUTA) created a state system that provides unemployment compensation to qualified employees who lose their jobs.

Workers' Compensation Laws

Workers' compensation legislation consists of state laws that provide financial compensation to employees or their dependents when a covered employee is injured on the job.

Consolidated Omnibus Budget Reconciliation Act of 1985

COBRA ensures that when employees lose their jobs or have their hours reduced to a level at which they would not be eligible to receive medical, dental, or optical benefits from their employer, the employees will be able to continue receiving benefits under the employer's policy for up to 18 months by paying the premiums for the policy.

Employee Retirement Income Security Act of 1974

ERISA is a federal law that sets minimum standards for most voluntarily established pension and health plans in private industry to provide protection for individuals in these plans.

Occupational Safety and Health Act of 1970

The Occupational Safety and Health Administration is responsible for setting safety standards under OSHA, as well as enforcing the act through inspections and the levying of fines against violators.

Employment-at-Will Doctrine and Wrongful Termination

Under the employment-at-will doctrine, the employer can fire the employee for any reason at all. The three exceptions to the doctrine are *implied contract, violations of public policy,* and *implied covenant of good faith and fair dealing.* In states that have adopted any of these three exceptions, employees may be able to sue for wrongful discharge.

Employee Privacy in the Workplace

Privacy issues are of increasing importance in the workplace. Privacy policies should cover matters such as employer surveillance, control of and access to medical and personnel records, drug testing, and e-mail.

Omnibus Crime Control and Safe Streets Act of 1968: Employers cannot listen to the private telephone conversations of employees or disclose the contents of these conversations. They may, however, ban personal calls and monitor calls for compliance as long as they discontinue listening to any conversation once they determine it is personal. Violators may be subject to fines of up to $10,000.

Electronic Communications Privacy Act (ECPA) of 1986: Under ECPA, employees' privacy rights were extended to electronic forms of communication including e-mail and cellular phones. ECPA outlaws the intentional interception of electronic communications and the intentional disclosure or use of the information obtained through such interception.

Labor Law

The Wagner Act of 1935: The Wagner Act was the first major piece of federal legislation adopted explicitly to encourage the formation of labor unions and provide for *collective bargaining* between employers and unions as a means of obtaining the peaceful settlement of labor disputes.

Collective bargaining: Collective bargaining consists of negotiations between an employer and a group of employees to determine the conditions of employment.

National Labor Relations Board (NLRB): The Wagner Act created the NLRB, an administrative agency, to interpret and enforce the National Labor Relations Act (NLRA) and to provide for judicial review in designated federal courts of appeal.

The Taft-Hartley Act of 1947: Also known as the *Labor-Management Relations Act,* the Taft-Hartley Act is designed to curtail some of the powers the unions had acquired under the Wagner Act. Just as Section 8(a) of the Wagner Act designated certain employer actions as unfair, Section 8(b) of the Taft-Hartley Act designated certain union actions as unfair.

The Landrum-Griffin Act of 1959: The Landrum-Griffin Act primarily governs the internal operations of labor unions. It requires certain financial disclosures by unions and establishes civil and criminal penalties for financial abuses by union officials. "Labor's Bill of Rights," contained in the act, protects employees from their own unions.

Point / Counterpoint

In 2007, the federal minimum wage was raised for the first time in a decade as part of a three-year series of increases.

Do You Believe It Was Time for an Increase?	
YES	NO
A 2006 poll indicated that 83 percent of the U.S. public supports raising the federal minimum wage from $5.15 to $5.85 starting in 2007.[*] This was the first of a series of three increases. The final increase took place on July 24, 2009, when the federal minimum wage was increased to $7.25.[**] There has been strong bipartisan support for raising the federal minimum wage. The purchasing power of the pre-2007 federal minimum wage had significantly declined since 1997. Hardworking employees deserve a living wage. Everyone benefits when the lowest-paid have more spending power.	An increase in the federal minimum wage hurts business owners and lowers their profit margin. Business owners may pass the increased cost on to consumers or let workers go whom they can no longer afford. Many states have already passed laws requiring that employers pay a state minimum wage higher than the federal minimum wage. We should let each state decide what it wants to do on the basis of the cost of living in that state. Increasing the minimum wage during a recession is particularly harmful to small businesses.

[*] "Poll: Maximum Support for Raising the Minimum: Most Americans Now Live in States That Have Raised the Wage Floor," www.pewtrusts.org/ideas/ideas_item.cfm?content_item_id=33, April 16, 2006.

[**] www.newsitem.com/opinion/minimum_wage_hike_necessary.

Questions & Problems

1. What is required for an employee to be eligible for benefits under the Family and Medical Leave Act (FMLA)?

2. If an employee voluntarily quits his job, may the employee collect unemployment compensation? What if the employee is fired?

3. May an employee who is injured on the job collect workers' compensation and also sue the employer for negligence?

4. List and explain the exceptions to the employment-at-will doctrine.

5. What is the purpose of COBRA?

6. Safeway operates a bread-baking facility in Denver, Colorado. Safeway periodically holds company-sponsored outdoor barbecues for its employees, and it purchased a gas grill equipped with a 20-pound propane tank for the barbecues. To ensure that the grill had sufficient gas for the

barbecues, Safeway purchased a 40-pound tank. The larger tanks have a warning label stating that they should not be used with a grill ordinarily equipped with a 20-pound tank. Safeway planned to hold an employee barbecue on July 17, 1998. The plant superintendent, Edward Boone, instructed the plant engineer, Jerry Lewis, to set up the grill for the barbecue. On being informed that the grill was not adequately cooking the meat, the plant manager, Jim Kirk, again summoned Lewis. Lewis and the day-shift maintenance foreman, Fred Lake, attempted to improve the flow of gas to the grill by checking the regulator and repositioning the tank. While Lewis and Lake were working on the grill, fuel escaped and a "ball of fire" erupted. Lewis suffered severe burns to his hand and Lake's facial hair was singed. After an investigation, an OSHA inspector issued a citation to Safeway. Safeway appealed the decision. Was this a workplace safety violation? Why or why not? [*Safeway, Inc. v. Occupational Safety & Health Rev. Comm.,* 382 F.3d 1189 (10th Cir. 2004).]

7. Baxter Pharmacy paid its pharmacists a salary but no overtime pay. Under the Fair Labor Standards Act (FLSA), employers must pay employees overtime for hours worked in excess of 40 hours per week. Baxter Pharmacy believes that the pharmacists are exempt under FLSA because they are "professionals." The pharmacists disagree. Is being a professional an exemption from the requirement to pay overtime under FLSA? Are pharmacists professionals? How do you think the court ruled? [*De Jesus-Rentas v. Baxter Pharmacy Services Corp.,* 400 F.3d 72 (1st Cir. 2005).]

8. Antonucci worked as a dental assistant. She was stuck in the thumb with an instrument twice during a period of two months. Antonucci claimed that she feared for her health and safety. She quit her job and applied for unemployment compensation. Did Antonucci have "good cause" to quit her job? Should Antonucci be permitted to collect unemployment compensation? How do you think this matter was decided by the court? [*Antonucci v. State of Florida,* 793 So.2d 1116 (Fla. Dist. Ct. App. 2001).]

9. Meadows worked as an assistant manager at a Dollar General store. While she was ringing up an order for a customer, he became verbally abusive.

After she finished ringing up the sale, the customer threw the bag, containing a can of motor oil, at Meadows, hitting her in the eye. Meadows suffered a detached retina. The trial court awarded Meadows permanent partial disability under workers' compensation for her injury. Dollar General appealed the decision, arguing that the injury did not occur in the "course of employment." Do you believe that Meadows's injury occurred during the course of her employment? Why or why not? Was the trial court correct in granting her permanent partial disability, or did the appeals court overturn that decision? [*Dollar General Corp. v. Meadows,* 63 P.3d 548 (2002 WL 31991909, Okla. Ct. Civ. App. 2002).]

10. In 1990, the plaintiff, Susan Hamilton, became employed as a licensed practical nurse at the National Park Medical Center, which is owned and operated by Tenet, Inc. After more than 10 years of at least satisfactory service, Hamilton was fired in November 2000. At the time Hamilton was fired, her employer had a handbook in place that explained the mutual expectations of the employer and employees. On November 23, 2000, Hamilton worked a 7 p.m. to 7 a.m. shift. She was busy, and at 10 p.m. a patient complained that he had not received pain medication promptly enough. Hamilton's direct supervisor agreed to trade patients with her, and the supervisor took the complaining patient. Hamilton continued to care for patients until 8 a.m. when she began her charting. Later that morning, her supervisor informed her that a patient had accused her of drug use and the supervisor requested that she take a drug test. Hamilton thought that since she had been permitted to work a full shift, it was nonsensical to drug-test her, and she refused to take the test. Hamilton was sick on Friday, November 24. On Monday, November 27, she spoke to a supervisor and offered to take the drug test. She was advised that a test was no longer necessary and that she had been terminated. According to the handbook, termination was not the policy for a positive test for drug use. Hamilton's termination came despite the lack of a drug test or of a serious incident or accident, and it followed an uncorroborated accusation by a heavily medicated patient. Neither side objects to the inclusion of the handbook, which contains numerous admonishments that employment was at will. The handbook

contained a drug testing policy that laid out three situations that might subject a current employee to a drug test:

Post Accident Testing: Any current employee who is involved in a serious incident or accident while on duty, whether on or off the employer's premises, may be asked to provide a body substance sample.

Fitness-For-Duty or Reasonable Suspicion Testing: This test may be required if significant and observable changes in employee performance, appearance, behavior, speech, etc. provide reasonable suspicion of his/her being under the influence of drugs and/or alcohol. A fitness-for-duty evaluation may include the testing of a body substance sample.

Random Testing: An employee who tests positive and who successfully completes a rehabilitation program may be subject to unscheduled testing for a twelve (12) month period following reinstatement.

Subject to any limitations imposed by law, a refusal to provide a body substance sample, under the conditions described above, is considered insubordination and may result in corrective action, up to and including termination of employment.

[National Park Medical Center Employee Handbook 42-43 (1996).]

On the basis of the handbook provisions set out above, may Hamilton be fired for refusing to take the drug test? May she be fired for no reason at all (i.e., as an at-will employee)? Explain your reasoning for your answers. [*Hamilton v. Tenet Corp.*, 2008 U.S. Dist. LEXIS 69194.]

Looking for more review material?

The Online Learning Center at **www.mhhe.com/kubasek2e** contains this chapter's "Assignment on the Internet" and also a list of URLs for more information, entitled "On the Internet." Find both of them in the Student Center portion of the OLC, along with quizzes and other helpful materials.

43 Employment Discrimination

LEARNING OBJECTIVES

After reading this chapter, you will be able to answer the following questions:

1 When may an employee be legally fired?

2 What are the federal laws governing employment situations?

3 What are the legal requirements for a charge of sex discrimination?

4 What is the difference between discrimination based on disparate treatment and discrimination based on disparate impact?

5 What are the legal requirements for a charge of sexual harassment?

6 What is Title VII, and what are the employers' defenses to a charge under Title VII?

7 What are the legal requirements for a charge of age discrimination?

8 What is the Equal Pay Act?

9 May an employer discriminate on the basis of sexual orientation?

10 May employers discriminate against smokers?

CASE OPENER

Brad Gets Fired from "So Clean!"

Brad has worked in the marketing department of "So Clean!" for the last five years. So Clean is a company that produces household cleaners. Brad is an excellent employee and was recently promoted. Shortly after his promotion, Brad decided to reveal publicly that he is a homosexual. His family and most of his co-workers have been very supportive.

Soon after his promotion and announcement that he is gay, Brad began having problems with his female boss, Jennifer. She began asking Brad questions about his personal life. At first it was small things, such as asking Brad if he was a smoker (he is, although only outside the workplace). Jennifer then began asking Brad very personal questions about his sexuality and told him she did not like weak men. The final straw for Brad occurred when Jennifer announced that she would "cure" his homosexuality and told him to come home with her that night after work or be fired. Jennifer was careful that there were never any witnesses around when she asked Brad personal questions or propositioned him.

Brad refused Jennifer's advances and was fired. He filed an administrative complaint with the Equal Employment Opportunity Commission (EEOC), alleging wrongful termination, retaliation, sexual harassment, and sexual discrimination. Jennifer's response was that she fired Brad because of "creative" differences about how to run the marketing department and because he is a smoker. Jennifer has denied Brad's accusations about sexual discrimination and harassment.

1. May an employer fire an employee because that employee is gay?
2. May an employer fire an employee because the employee smokes outside the workplace?
3. May a man file a claim of sexual discrimination? Sexual harassment?
4. What rights does an employee have in the workplace?
5. What defenses does an employer have to allegations of discrimination?

The Wrap-Up at the end of the chapter will answer these questions.

When May an Employee Be Fired?

During the 18th and 19th centuries in the United States, employees had no protection in the workplace. An employee who was injured could be fired. In fact, an employer could fire a worker for no reason at all. This concept came to be known as *at-will employment*.[1] At-will employment applied in all states with no exceptions until 1959.[2]

Today, any employee who is not employed under a contract or a collective bargaining agreement[3] is considered to be an at-will employee. This means that the employee may quit at any time for any reason or no reason at all, with no required notice to the employer.[4] Similarly, an employer may fire the employee at any time, with no notice, for almost any reason. For example, your employer could decide he doesn't like the color of your shirt and fire you on the spot! The exception to the at-will rule is that an employer may not fire an employee for an illegal reason. What is an illegal reason? Broadly, any termination based on a violation of a state statute, a state constitution, a federal law, the U.S. Constitution, or public policy is illegal. (An in-depth discussion of at-will employment can be found in Chapter 42.) Exceptions to at-will employment have also been found through breaches of implied contracts with employees on the basis of employee handbooks.[5]

LO1

When may an employee be legally fired?

---

[1] See *Toussaint v. Blue Cross & Blue Shield of Mich.*, 408 Mich. 579, 600, 292 N.W.2d 880, 885 (1980) (for an extended discussion on the at-will rule).

[2] BambooWeb Dictionary, www.bambooweb.com/articles/a/t/At-Will_Employment.html. The first judicial exception to the at-will rule was created in *Peterman v. Intl. Bhd. of Teamsters, Chauffeurs, Warehousemen, and Helpers of Am., Local 396*, 174 Cal. App. 2d 184, 344 P.2d 44 (1959).

[3] Union employees are covered by collective bargaining agreements.

[4] Most employees do give an employer notice before leaving a job as a matter of professional courtesy. Such action, however, is not required under the law.

[5] "Some challenges and exceptions to at-will employment include: breach of implied contracts through employee handbooks, public policy violations, reliance on an offer of employment, and intentional infliction of emotional distress" (Legal Database, www.legal-database.net/at-will.htm).

Federal Laws Governing Employers

LO2

What are the federal laws governing employment situations?

Employees are protected in the workplace by a number of both federal and state laws. Federal laws apply to everyone in the United States. Federal law may be described as a "minimum" level of protection for all workers. State laws may give employees more, but not less, protection than federal laws. Exhibit 43-1 is an overview of some of the most important federal employment discrimination laws.

Civil Rights Act—Title VII

LO3

What are the legal requirements for a charge of sex discrimination?

During the 1960 presidential election, candidate John F. Kennedy (JFK) proposed that the United States pass national civil rights legislation. After winning the presidency, JFK began work with Congress on just such legislation. On November 22, 1963, JFK was assassinated. His vice president, Lyndon B. Johnson (LBJ), became president and saw JFK's quest for national civil rights legislation through to completion. The **Civil Rights Act (CRA) of 1964** was signed by LBJ and became federal law, assuring everyone in the nation of certain basic rights. The act is divided into sections, called *titles*. **Title VII** deals with discrimination in employment.

Title VII prohibits employers from hiring, firing, or otherwise discriminating in terms and conditions of employment and prohibits segregating employees in a manner that would affect their employment opportunities on the basis of their race, color, religion, sex, or national origin.

Title VII of the Civil Rights Act applies to employers who have 15 or more employees for 20 consecutive weeks within one year and who are engaged in a business that affects commerce. The U.S. government, corporations owned by the government, agencies of the District of Columbia, Indian tribes, private clubs, unions, and employment agencies are also covered by Title VII.

Exhibit 43-1

Federal Discrimination Laws

LEGISLATION	PURPOSE
Civil Rights Act of 1964 (CRA)—Title VII (as amended by the Civil Rights Act of 1991)	Protects employees against discrimination based on race, color, religion, national origin, and sex. Also prohibits harassment based on the same protected categories.
Pregnancy Discrimination Act of 1987 (PDA)	Amended Title VII of the CRA to expand the definition of sex discrimination to include discrimination based on pregnancy.
Age Discrimination in Employment Act of 1967 (ADEA)	Prohibits employers from refusing to hire, discharging, or discriminating in terms and conditions of employment on the basis of an employee's or applicant's being age 40 or older.
Americans with Disabilities Act (ADA)	Prohibits discrimination against employees and job applicants with disabilities.
Equal Pay Act of 1963 (EPA)	Prohibits an employer from paying workers of one gender less than the wages paid to employees of the opposite gender for work that requires equal skill, effort, and responsibility.

There are two ways to prove discrimination under Title VII: disparate treatment and disparate impact (see Exhibit 43-2). **Disparate treatment** is sometimes referred to as *intentional discrimination*. It occurs when an employee is treated differently on the basis of being a member of a protected class (i.e., race, religion, sex, national origin, or color). **Disparate impact** is often referred to as *unintentional discrimination*. It occurs when an employer sets a requirement for employment that inadvertently precludes large numbers of a protected class from employment in a particular job.

PROVING DISPARATE-TREATMENT DISCRIMINATION UNDER TITLE VII

To sue for disparate treatment under Title VII, the plaintiff must be a member of a protected class as listed in the act. In other words, the employee must have been discriminated against on the basis of race, color, national origin, religion, or sex (i.e., gender). If the employee has been hired, fired, denied a promotion, or the like, on the basis of membership in a protected class, this is a form of intentional discrimination and qualifies the employee to sue for disparate-treatment discrimination. Proving disparate-treatment discrimination in employment under Title VII is a three-step process:

1. Plaintiff (the employee) must demonstrate a prima facie case of discrimination.
2. Defendant (the employer) must articulate a legitimate, nondiscriminatory business reason for the action.
3. Plaintiff (the employee) must show that the reason given by the defendant (the employer) is a mere pretext.

To illustrate more clearly, let's break down each step. First, the plaintiff-employee has the burden of proving a prima facie case of discrimination. *Prima facie* is Latin for "at first view"[6] and means that the evidence is sufficient to raise a presumption that discrimination occurred. In the chapter opening scenario between Brad and Jennifer, Brad has alleged that Jennifer discriminated against him on the basis of sex. Brad's prima facie case may be summed up as follows: Brad was a good employee for five years. After being promoted

L04

What is the difference between discrimination based on disparate treatment and discrimination based on disparate impact?

TYPE OF DISCRIMINATION	BURDEN ON PLAINTIFF (EMPLOYEE)	BURDEN ON DEFENDANT (EMPLOYER)	BURDEN ON PLAINTIFF (EMPLOYEE)
Disparate Treatment (intentional discrimination)	Demonstrate a prima facie case of discrimination	Articulate a legitimate, non-discriminatory business reason for the action	Show that the reason given by the employer is a mere pretext
Disparate Impact (unintentional discrimination)	Establish statistically that a rule restricts employment for those in a protected class	Articulate why the policy or practice is a "business necessity"	Show that the alleged "business necessity" is a mere pretext

Exhibit 43-2

Disparate Treatment and Disparate Impact: Burden Shifting

[6] Lectic Law Library, www.lectlaw.com/def2/p078.htm.

Title VII Championship

stus.com

In the first round, the plaintiff established a prima facie case of discrimination. In the second round, the defendant rebutted with a nondiscriminatory rationale. Now, in the third round, we'll see whether the plaintiff can show the defendant's reason to be mere pretext.

and transferred to Jennifer's department, Jennifer began treating him differently than she did the females in the department. Jennifer told Brad that she did not like "weak males," asked him to come home with her (he refused), and eventually fired him. This is likely sufficient to satisfy the prima facie requirement.

Once Brad (the employee) has set forth his prima facie case (step 1), the burden shifts to Jennifer and So Clean (the employer) to articulate a legitimate, nondiscriminatory reason for firing Brad (step 2). Jennifer and So Clean could meet this requirement by arguing that Brad was not fired on the basis of his sex (because he is a male) but rather because of his "creative" differences with Jennifer in the marketing department (remember, Brad has no contract and therefore is an at-will employee).

Once Jennifer and So Clean (the employer) set forth their nondiscriminatory reason for terminating Brad (the employee), the burden shifts back to Brad one last time. Brad must demonstrate that the employer's given reason for terminating him was a mere pretext (step 3). This last step requires that Brad show that "despite his qualifications," he was fired.[7]

After all the evidence has been presented, the trier of fact (a jury in most cases)[8] must decide whether discrimination has occurred. The burden of proof in a civil case is

---

[7] *McDonnell Douglas v. Green,* 411 U.S. 792, 802 (1973).

[8] In a bench trial, the judge becomes the trier of fact as no jury is impaneled. A discrimination case could also be decided by a judge on motion for summary judgment.

preponderance of the evidence (i.e., more likely than not). If the jury finds in favor of the plaintiff-employee, damages must be assessed. Damages under Title VII include up to two years of back pay, compensatory damages, punitive damages (limited in some cases), attorney fees, court costs, court orders (including reinstatement), and remedial seniority. If the jury finds in favor of the defendant-employer, the plaintiff-employee receives nothing.

Legal Principle: **Under Title VII, an employer may not intentionally discriminate against an employee on the basis of race, color, national origin, sex, or religion.**

PROVING DISPARATE-IMPACT DISCRIMINATION UNDER TITLE VII

Disparate-impact cases are sometimes called unintentional-discrimination cases. While it is very difficult to prove disparate treatment, it is even more difficult to prove disparate impact. Disparate-impact cases arise when a plaintiff attempts to establish that while an employer's policy or practice appears to apply to everyone equally, its actual effect is that it disproportionately limits employment opportunities for a protected class.

The plaintiff proves a case based on disparate impact by first establishing statistically that the rule disproportionately restricts employment opportunities for a protected class. The burden of proof then shifts to the defendant, who can avoid liability by demonstrating that the practice or policy is a business necessity. The plaintiff, at this point, can still recover by proving that the "necessity" was promulgated as a pretext for discrimination.

The initial steps for proving a prima facie case of disparate impact were set forth in *Griggs v. Duke Power Co.*[9] In that case, the employer-defendant required that all applicants have a high school diploma and a successful score on a professionally recognized intelligence test for all jobs except laborer. The stated purpose of these criteria was to upgrade the quality of the workforce.

The plaintiff statistically demonstrated the discriminatory impact by showing that 34 percent of the white males in the state had high school diplomas, whereas only 12 percent of the black males did, and by introducing evidence from an EEOC study showing that 58 percent of the whites, compared to 6 percent of the blacks, had passed tests similar to the one given by the defendant. Because the defendant could not demonstrate any business-related[10] justification for either employment policy, the plaintiff was successful. Requiring a high IQ or high school or college diploma may be necessary for some jobs but not for all jobs at Duke Power.

Legal Principle: **Under Title VII, an employer may not unintentionally discriminate against an employee on the basis of race, color, national origin, sex, or religion.**

SEXUAL HARASSMENT UNDER TITLE VII

Harassment is a relatively new basis for discrimination. It first developed in the context of discrimination based on sex, and it evolved to become applicable to other protected classes. The definition of **sexual harassment** stated in the Equal Employment Opportunity Commission (EEOC) guidelines and accepted by the U.S. Supreme Court is "unwelcome sexual advances, requests for sexual favors, and other verbal or physical conduct of a sexual nature" that implicitly or explicitly makes submission a term or condition of employment; makes employment decisions related to the individual dependent on submission

L05

What are the legal requirements for a charge of sexual harassment?

---

[9] 401 U.S. 424 (1971).

[10] If the employer can demonstrate that the imposition of a job qualification is reasonably necessary to the legitimate conduct of the employer's business, the employer will prevail in a disparate-impact case.

to or rejection of such conduct; or has the purpose or effect of creating an intimidating, hostile, or offensive work environment. Did the actions of Jennifer create a sexually hostile environment for Brad?

Two distinct forms of sexual harassment are recognized. The first, and generally easiest to prove, is *quid pro quo*, which occurs when a supervisor makes a sexual demand on someone of the opposite sex and this demand is reasonably perceived as a term or condition of employment. The basis for this rule is that the supervisor would not make similar demands on someone of the same sex. In the opening scenario, Jennifer demanded that Brad come home with her so that she could "cure" his homosexuality. When Brad refused, Jennifer fired him. Brad likely has a cause of action for quid pro quo sexual harassment.

The second form of sexual harassment involves the creation of a *hostile work environment*. Case 43-1 demonstrates the standard used by the U.S. Supreme Court to determine whether an employer's conduct has created a hostile work environment.

CASE 43-1   TERESA HARRIS v. FORKLIFT SYSTEMS, INC.
UNITED STATES SUPREME COURT
510 U.S. 17, 114 S. CT. 367 (1994)

During her tenure as a manager at defendant Forklift Systems, Inc., plaintiff Harris was repeatedly insulted by defendant's president because of her gender and subjected to sexual innuendos. In front of other employees, the president frequently told Harris, "You're just a woman, what do you know?" He sometimes asked Harris and other female employees to remove coins from his pockets and made suggestive comments about their clothes. He suggested to Harris in front of others that they negotiate her salary at the Holiday Inn. He said that he would stop when Harris complained, but he continued behaving in the same manner, so Harris quit. She then filed an action against the defendant for creating an abusive work environment based on her gender.

The district court found in favor of the defendant, holding that some of the comments were offensive to the plaintiff, but were not so serious as to severely affect Harris' psychological well-being or interfere with her work performance. The court of appeals affirmed. Plaintiff Harris appealed to the U.S. Supreme Court.

JUSTICE O'CONNOR: As we made clear in *Meritor Savings Bank* v. *Vinson,* this language [of Title VII] "is not limited to 'economic' or 'tangible' discrimination. The phrase 'terms, conditions, or privileges of employment' evinces a congressional intent 'to strike at the entire spectrum of disparate treatment of men and women' in employment," which includes requiring people to work in a discriminatorily hostile or abusive environment. When the workplace is permeated with "discriminatory intimidation, ridicule, and insult," that is "sufficiently severe or pervasive to alter the conditions of the victim's employment and create an abusive working environment."

This standard, which we reaffirm today, takes a middle path between making actionable any conduct that is merely offensive and requiring the conduct to cause a tangible psychological injury. As we pointed out in *Meritor,* "mere utterance of an . . . epithet which engenders offensive feelings in an employee," does not sufficiently affect conditions of employment to implicate Title VII. . . . Likewise, if the victim does not subjectively perceive the environment to be abusive, the conduct has not actually altered the conditions of the victim's employment, and there is no Title VII violation.

But Title VII comes into play before the harassing conduct leads to a nervous breakdown. A discriminatorily abusive work environment, even one that does not seriously affect employees' psychological well-being, can and often will detract from employees' job performance, discourage employees from remaining on the job, or keep them from advancing in their careers. Moreover, even without regard to these tangible effects, the very fact that the discriminatory conduct was so severe or pervasive that it created a work environment abusive to employees because of their race, gender, religion, or national origin offends Title VII's broad rule of workplace equality. The appalling conduct alleged in *Meritor,* and the reference in that case to environments "so heavily polluted with discrimination as to destroy completely the emotional and psychological stability of minority group workers," merely presents some especially egregious examples of harassment. They do not mark the boundary of what is actionable.

. . . Certainly Title VII bars conduct that would seriously affect a reasonable person's psychological well-being, but the statute is not limited to such conduct. So long as the environment would reasonably be perceived, and is perceived, as hostile or abusive, there is no need for it also to be psychologically injurious.

This is not, and by its nature cannot be, a mathematically precise test. But we can say that whether an environment is "hostile" or "abusive" can be determined only by looking at all the circumstances. These may include the frequency of the discriminatory conduct; its severity; whether it is physically threatening or humiliating, or a mere offensive utterance; and whether it unreasonably interferes with an employee's work performance. The effect on the employee's psychological well being is, of course, relevant to determining whether the plaintiff actually found the environment abusive. But while psychological harm, like any other relevant factor, may be taken into account, no single factor is required.

REVERSED and REMANDED in favor of plaintiff.

CRITICAL THINKING

Identify the Court's reasons. Do you think these reasons were sufficient to overturn the previous ruling? Why or why not?

ETHICAL DECISION MAKING

Imagine that Justice O'Connor is operating under a duty-based system of ethics. What duty is she advocating in terms of employer-employee relationships? Would this ruling serve well as a universal standard?

The definition of hostile-environment sexual harassment has evolved over the years through a series of statutes and cases. To prove such harassment, a plaintiff must demonstrate the following: (1) He or she suffered intentional, unwanted discrimination because of his or her sex; (2) the harassment was severe *or* pervasive; (3) the harassment negatively affected the terms, conditions, or privileges of his or her work environment; (4) the harassment was both subjectively and objectively unwelcome; and (5) management knew about the harassment, or should have known, and did nothing to stop it.

Sexual harassment cases were not filed in large numbers immediately after Title VII's passage, with only 10,532 sexual harassment cases filed with the EEOC or state and local agencies in the year ending on October 1, 1992. Then the number of claims increased steadily until 1995, when 15,549 cases were filed. Since 1995, the number of claims has steadily declined, with only 12,025 complaints in fiscal year 2006.[11] While the likelihood of being sued for sexual harassment is not great, once a business is sued, its reputation may be tarnished and payment of damages is a real possibility. It is therefore critically important that businesspersons be able to recognize sexual harassment and prevent its occurrence in the workplace. As a business owner or manager, how would you prevent sexual harassment claims? According to one bar association article:

> There are four essential steps that managers can take to protect their businesses from being involved in sexual harassment litigation. They are: (1) implement a policy against sexual harassment; (2) require supervisory training; (3) provide a mechanism for receiving complaints; and (4) create a method for conducting prompt and thorough investigations.[12]

---

[11] U.S. EEOC, "Sexual Harassment Charges: EEOC & FEPAs Combined: FY 1992–FY 2000," www.eeoc.gov/stats/harass.html, January 18, 2001 (accessed May 1, 2001); and U.S. EEOC, "Sexual Harassment Charges: EEOC & FEPAs Combined: FY 1997–FY 2006," January 31, 2007.

[12] Laura Smith, "Avoiding Sexual Harassment Lawsuits," www.dcba.org/brief/profresp/0299.htm.

Under California state law, managers are required to undergo training to prevent sexual harassment in the workplace.

Legal Principle: Under Title VII there are two types of sexual harassment: quid pro quo and hostile environment.

Harassment in Cyberspace.

Unfortunately, new forms of technology have provided new opportunities for harassment. Consider, for example, the possibilities for online harassment. A New Jersey appellate court has ruled that employers have a duty to remedy online harassment when they have notice that employees are engaged in a pattern of retaliatory harassment using a work-related online forum.[13] Airline pilot Tammy Blakey sued her former employer, Continental Airlines, for sexual harassment, and part of her claim focused on retaliatory harassment that took place on an electronic bulletin board, the "Crew Members Forum." In particular, Blakey's fellow pilots posted information on the bulletin board that suggested that Blakey was a poor pilot and a "feminazi" and that, by filing a sexual harassment lawsuit, she was using the legal system "to get a quick buck."[14]

In ruling on the bulletin board issue, the court stated that although an electronic bulletin board did not have a physical location within an airport terminal, hangar, or aircraft, it might nonetheless have been so closely related to the workplace environment and beneficial to the employer that continuation of harassment on the forum should be regarded as part of the workplace.

This case shows that, in some situations, employers have a duty to monitor their employees' use of e-mail and the Internet. They cannot allow harassment, including retaliatory harassment on an online bulletin board. Employers can reduce their liability exposure by conducting sexual harassment training and outlining clear workplace policies that prohibit harassing behavior, including behavior that takes place in cyberspace.

Same-Sex Harassment—the Supreme Court Speaks.

Initially, same-sex harassment was not covered by Title VII. By 1997, however, the courts were split on the issue. This issue was resolved in 1998 (see Case 43-2).

[13] *Blakey v. Continental Airlines*, 751 A. 2d 538 (N.J. 2000).
[14] *Blakey v. Continental Airlines, Inc.*, 2000 WL 703018.

CASE 43-2   ONCALE v. SUNDOWNER OFFSHORE SERVICES, INC.
UNITED STATES SUPREME COURT
523 U.S. 75, 118 S. CT. 998 (1998)

On several occasions, the employee was forcibly subjected to sex-related, humiliating actions against him by fellow employees in the presence of the rest of the oil-platform crew. He was also physically assaulted in a sexual manner and was threatened with rape. When his complaints to supervisory personnel produced no remedial action, the employee filed a complaint against his employer, *alleging that he was discriminated against in his employment because of his sex.*

The district court granted the employer's motion for summary judgment, which the appellate court affirmed, holding that the employee, who was a male, had no cause of action under Title VII for harassment by male co-workers. On certiorari, the Court held that nothing in Title VII necessarily barred a claim of discrimination because of sex merely because the plaintiff and the defendant, or the person charged with acting on behalf of the defendant, were of the same sex. In reversing the judgment, the Court concluded that sex discrimination consisting of same-sex sexual harassment is actionable under Title VII. The Court reversed the appellate court's order and remanded the case for further proceedings.

JUSTICE SCALIA: This case presents the question whether workplace harassment can violate Title VII's prohibition against "discrimination . . . because of . . . sex," *42 U.S.C. § 2000e-2*(a)(1), when the harasser and the harassed employee are of the same sex.

Title VII of the Civil Rights Act of 1964 provides, in relevant part, that "it shall be an unlawful employment practice for an employer . . . to discriminate against any individual with respect to his compensation, terms, conditions, or privileges of employment, because of such individual's race, color, religion, sex, or national origin." We have held that this not only covers "terms" and "conditions" in the narrow contractual sense, but "evinces a congressional intent to strike at the entire spectrum of disparate treatment of men and women in employment."

"When the workplace is permeated with discriminatory intimidation, ridicule, and insult that is sufficiently severe or pervasive to alter the conditions of the victim's employment and create an abusive working environment, Title VII is violated." *Harris v. Forklift Systems, Inc., 510 U.S. 17, 21, 126 L. Ed. 2d 295, 114 S. Ct. 367 (1993)*

Title VII's prohibition of discrimination "because of . . . sex" protects men as well as women . . . and in the related context of racial discrimination in the workplace we have rejected any conclusive presumption that an employer will not discriminate against members of his own race. "Because of the many facets of human motivation, it would be unwise to presume as a matter of law that human beings of one definable group will not discriminate against other members of that group."

If our precedents leave any doubt on the question, we hold today that nothing in Title VII necessarily bars a claim of discrimination "because of . . . sex" merely because the plaintiff and the defendant (or the person charged with acting on behalf of the defendant) are of the same sex.

We see no justification in the statutory language or our precedents for a categorical rule excluding same-sex harassment claims from the coverage of Title VII. As some courts have observed, male-on-male sexual harassment in the workplace was assuredly not the principal evil Congress was concerned with when it enacted Title VII. But statutory prohibitions often go beyond the principal evil to cover reasonably comparable evils, and it is ultimately the provisions of our laws rather than the principal concerns of our legislators by which we are governed. Title VII prohibits "discrimination . . . because of . . . sex" in the "terms" or "conditions" of employment. Our holding that this includes sexual harassment must extend to sexual harassment of any kind that meets the statutory requirements.

Courts and juries have found the inference of discrimination easy to draw in most male-female sexual harassment situations, because the challenged conduct typically involves explicit or implicit proposals of sexual activity; it is reasonable to assume those proposals would not have been made to someone of the same sex. The same chain of inference would be available to a plaintiff alleging same-sex harassment, if there were credible evidence that the harasser was homosexual. But harassing conduct need not be motivated by sexual desire to support an inference of discrimination on the basis of sex. A trier of fact might reasonably find such discrimination, for example, if a female victim is harassed in such sex-specific and derogatory terms by another woman as to make it clear that the harasser is motivated by general hostility to the presence of women in the workplace. A same-sex harassment plaintiff may also, of course, offer direct comparative evidence about how the alleged harasser treated members of both sexes in a mixed-sex workplace. Whatever evidentiary route the plaintiff chooses to follow, he or she must always prove that the conduct at issue was not merely tinged with offensive sexual connotations, but actually constituted *"discrimination . . . because of . . . sex."*

Because we conclude that sex discrimination consisting of same-sex sexual harassment is actionable under Title VII, the judgment of the Court of Appeals for the Fifth Circuit is reversed, and the case is remanded for further proceedings consistent with this opinion.

REVERSED and REMANDED in favor of plaintiff.

CRITICAL THINKING

What assumptions would the Court have had to make for it to rule against the plaintiff in this case? Did the reasoning explicitly reject these assumptions?

ETHICAL DECISION MAKING

What stakeholders are affected by this decision? In answering the question, push yourself to go beyond the direct and obvious stakeholders.

Harassment by Nonemployees under Title VII.   Employers may be held liable for harassment of their employees by nonemployees under very limited circumstances. If an employer knows that a customer repeatedly harasses an employee yet the employer does nothing to remedy the situation, the employer may be liable. For example, in *Lockhard v. Pizza Hut, Inc.,*[15] the franchise was held liable for the harassment of a waitress by two male customers because no steps had been taken to prevent the harassment.

HARASSMENT OF OTHER PROTECTED CLASSES UNDER TITLE VII

Hostile-environment cases have also been used in cases of discrimination based on religion and race. For example, in a 1986 case, *Snell v. Suffolk County,*[16] Hispanic and black corrections workers demonstrated that a hostile work environment existed by proving that they had been subjected to continuing verbal abuse and racial harassment by co-workers and that the county sheriff's department had done nothing to prevent the abuse. The white employees had continually used racial epithets and posted racially offensive materials on bulletin boards, such as a picture of a black man with a noose around his neck, cartoons favorably portraying the Ku Klux Klan, and a "black officers' study guide," consisting of children's puzzles. White officers once dressed a Hispanic inmate in a straw hat, sheet, and sign that said "spic." Such activities were found by the court to constitute a hostile work environment.

PREGNANCY DISCRIMINATION ACT OF 1987—AN AMENDMENT TO TITLE VII

In 1987, Title VII was amended by the **Pregnancy Discrimination Act (PDA) of 1987.** This law expanded the definition of discrimination based on gender to include discrimination based on pregnancy. "Discrimination on the basis of pregnancy, childbirth or related medical conditions constitutes unlawful sex discrimination under Title VII."[17] Under the act, temporary disability caused by pregnancy must be treated the same as any other temporary disability.

Business owners and human resource professionals must be highly attuned to what questions may and may not be asked of potential employees. Examples of illegal questions include these: How many children do you have? Are you pregnant? What are your child care arrangements?[18] Once an employee has been hired, it is illegal to change the terms and conditions of employment on the basis of pregnancy. Moreover, an employer may not force a woman to take time off work during her pregnancy.

DEFENSES TO CLAIMS UNDER TITLE VII

As a business owner or manager, how would you respond if one of your employees filed a lawsuit under Title VII? Are there any legal exceptions for discriminating against a protected class? The answer, surprising to many business owners and managers, is yes. The three most important defenses available to defendants in Title VII cases are the bona fide occupational qualification, merit, and seniority system defenses. These defenses are raised

L06

What is Title VII, and what are the employers' defenses to a charge under Title VII?

---

[15] 162 F.3d 1062 (10th Cir. 1998).

[16] 782 F.2d 1094 (1986).

[17] EEOC, "Facts about Pregnancy Discrimination," www.eeoc.gov/facts/fs-preg.html.

[18] "Illegal Interview Questions," www.jobinterviewquestions.org/questions/illegal-questions.asp.

by the defendant after the plaintiff has established a prima facie case of discrimination based on either disparate treatment or disparate impact. They would obviously not be applicable to a claim based on harassment.

The Bona Fide Occupational Qualification Defense.

The *bona fide occupational qualification (BFOQ)* defense allows an employer to discriminate in hiring on the basis of sex, religion, or national origin (but not race or color) when doing so is necessary for the performance of the job. Exhibit 43-3 highlights the bases for claiming a bona fide occupational qualification. Necessity must be based on actual qualifications, not stereotypes about one group's abilities. For example, being a male cannot be a BFOQ for a job because it is a dirty job. Conversely, there may be a valid requirement that an applicant be able to lift a certain amount of weight if such lifting is a part of the job. Moreover, being a female may be a BFOQ for modeling female clothing. An employer would not be required or expected to hire a male for such a job. Employer arguments about inconvenience to the employer, such as having to provide two sets of restroom facilities, have not been persuasive in the courts. Nor have customer preferences to be served by a particular gender or nationality. The only exception to customer preference is sexual privacy (e.g., female restroom attendants in the women's restroom and male attendants in the men's room).[19]

The Merit Defense.

The merit defense is usually raised when hiring or promotion decisions are partially based on test scores. Professionally developed ability tests that are not designed, intended, or used to discriminate may be used. While these tests may have an adverse impact on a class, as long as they are manifestly related to job performance, they do not violate the act. Since 1978, the Uniform Guidelines on Employee Selection Procedures (UGESP) have guided government agencies charged with enforcing civil rights, and they provide guidance to employers and other interested persons about when ability tests are valid and job-related. Under these guidelines, tests must be validated in accordance with standards established by the American Psychological Association.

Three types of validation are acceptable: (1) *criterion-related validity,* which is the statistical relationship between test scores and objective criteria of job performance; (2) *content validity,* which isolates some skill used on the job and directly tests that skill; and (3) *construct validity,* wherein a psychological trait needed to perform the job is

	YES	NO
May a BFOQ be based on:		
Race?		√
Sex (i.e., gender)?	√	
Religion?	√	
Color?		√
National Origin?	√	
Customer preference? (exception: sexual privacy)		√

Exhibit 43-3
Bona Fide Occupational Qualification

---

[19] *In the Matter of the Accusation of the Department of Fair Employment and Housing v. San Luis Obispo Coastal Unified School District, Respondent; Marlene Anne Mendes, Complainant,* Case No. E95-96 L-0725-00s, 98-14 (October 7, 1998). See www. dfeh.ca.gov/PrecedentialD/1998-14.html.

measured. A test that required a secretary to use a computer would be content-valid. A test of patience for a teacher would be construct-valid.

The Seniority System Defense.   A bona fide seniority system is a legal defense under Title VII. Even though a seniority system, in which employees are given preferential treatment based on their length of service, may perpetuate past discrimination, such systems are considered bona fide and are thus not illegal if (1) the system applies equally to all persons; (2) the seniority units follow industry practices; (3) the seniority system did not have its genesis in discrimination; and (4) the system is maintained free of any illegal discriminatory purpose.

Legal Principle: **The three main defenses to claims under Title VII are BFOQ, merit, and seniority system.**

REMEDIES UNDER TITLE VII

A plaintiff may seek both equitable and legal remedies for violations of Title VII. Courts have ordered parties to engage in diverse activities ranging from publicizing their commitment to minority hiring to establishing special training programs for minorities. A successful plaintiff may recover back pay for up to two years from the time of the discriminatory act. *Back pay* is the difference between the amount of money the plaintiff earned since the discriminatory act and the amount of money she would have earned had the discriminatory act never occurred. For example, if one year before the case came to trial the defendant refused a promotion to a plaintiff on the basis of her sex, and the job for which she was rejected paid $1,000 more per month, she would be entitled to recover back pay in the amount of $1,000 per month multiplied by 12 months. (If the salary increased at regular increments, these are also included.) The same basic calculations are used when plaintiffs are not hired because of discrimination. Such plaintiffs are entitled to the back wages that they would have received minus any actual earnings during that time. Defendants may also exclude wages for any period during which the plaintiff would have been unable to work.

A plaintiff who was not hired for a job because of a Title VII violation may also receive remedial seniority dating back to the time when the plaintiff was discriminated against; compensatory damages, including those for pain and suffering; and, in some cases, punitive damages. In cases based on discrimination other than race, however, punitive damages are capped at $300,000 for employers of more than 500 employees; $100,000 for firms with 101 to 200 employees; and $50,000 for firms with 100 or fewer employees. An employer will not be held vicariously liable for punitive damages as long as it made "good-faith efforts" to comply with federal law.

Attorney fees may be awarded to a successful plaintiff in Title VII cases. They are typically denied only when special circumstances would render the award unjust. If it is determined that the plaintiff's action was frivolous, unreasonable, or without foundation, the courts may award attorney fees to the prevailing defendant. For more information on Title VII, visit the EEOC Web site at www.eeoc.gov.

PROCEDURE FOR FILING A CLAIM UNDER TITLE VII

Filing a claim under Title VII is much more complicated than simply filing a lawsuit. Failure to follow the proper procedures within the strict time framework may result in a plaintiff's losing his or her right to file a lawsuit under Title VII. Exhibit 43-4 spells out the steps for filing a claim under Title VII.

Exhibit 43-4   Filing a Title VII Claim of Employment Discrimination

STEP 1	STEP 2	STEP 3
File a charge with the EEOC: • Employee must file a charge with the EEOC within 180 days of the alleged discriminatory act. • Alternatively, employee may file a charge with a state agency (assuming one exists).	EEOC conciliation attempts: • EEOC notifies the employer of the charge within 10 days. • EEOC investigates and attempts to negotiate a settlement between employer and employee. • EEOC may file a lawsuit in federal court on behalf of the employee. • If no settlement is reached and no lawsuit is filed by EEOC, the commission issues a "right-to-sue" letter to the employee.	Employee may file a lawsuit.

Filing a Charge with the EEOC.   The first step in initiating a Title VII action is the aggrieved party's filing of a charge with the state Equal Employment Opportunity Commission or, if no such agency exists, the federal EEOC. A *charge* is a sworn statement that states the name of the charging party, the name(s) of the defendant(s), and the nature of the discriminatory act. In states that do *not* have state EEOCs, the aggrieved party must file the charge with the federal EEOC within 180 days of the alleged discriminatory act. In states that *do* have such agencies, the charge must be filed either with the federal EEOC within 180 days of the discriminatory act or with the appropriate state agency within the time limits prescribed by local law, which cannot be less than 180 days. If initially filed with the local agency, the charge must be filed with the federal EEOC within 300 days of the discriminatory act or within 60 days of receipt of notice that the state agency has disposed of the matter, whichever comes first.

EEOC Conciliation Attempts.   Within 10 days of receiving the charge, the EEOC must notify the alleged violator of the charge. Then the EEOC investigates the matter to determine whether there is "reasonable cause" to believe that a violation has occurred. If the EEOC does find reasonable cause, it attempts to eliminate the discriminatory practice through conciliation, that is, by trying to negotiate a settlement between the two parties. If unsuccessful, the EEOC *may* file suit against the alleged discriminator in federal district court. Failure to file suit does not necessarily mean that the EEOC does not think the plaintiff does not have a valid claim; it may be that the EEOC simply feels that it is not the type of claim the commission wishes to use its limited resources to pursue.

The EEOC Right-To-Sue Letter.   If the EEOC decides not to sue, it notifies the plaintiff of his or her right to file an action and issues the plaintiff a *right-to-sue letter,* which is not intended to be anything other than a statement that the plaintiff has followed the proper initial procedures and therefore may file a lawsuit. The plaintiff must have this letter in order to file a private action. The letter may be requested at any time after 180 days have elapsed since the filing of the charge. As long as the requisite time period has passed, the EEOC will issue the right-to-sue letter regardless of whether or not the EEOC members find a reasonable basis to believe that the defendant engaged in discriminatory behavior. In reality, due to the number of complaints, the EEOC and state EEOCs routinely issue right-to-sue letters without filing a lawsuit on the aggrieved party's behalf. Once an employee receives a right-to-sue letter, he or she is free to hire an attorney and file a lawsuit against the employer.

Age Discrimination in Employment Act of 1967

L07

What are the legal requirements for a charge of age discrimination?

The **Age Discrimination in Employment Act (ADEA) of 1967** was enacted to prohibit employers from refusing to hire, discharging, or discriminating in terms and conditions of employment against employees or applicants age 40 or older. The language describing the prohibited conduct is virtually the same as that of Title VII, except that age is the prohibited basis for discrimination. ADEA applies to employers having 20 or more employees. It also applies to employment agencies and to unions that have at least 25 members or that operate a hiring hall. As a consequence of the Supreme Court ruling in *Kimel v. Florida Board of Regents,*[20] ADEA does not apply to state employers.

It is important that business owners and managers understand ADEA because the number of claims under this act have increased, perhaps in response to a weakening economy since early 2000 and the aging of the baby-boomer generation. In 1999, approximately 1,400 age discrimination claims were filed under ADEA. Conversely, in 2001, 17,405 age discrimination claims were filed.

PROVING AGE DISCRIMINATION UNDER ADEA

Remember, ADEA does not protect *all* individuals from discrimination based on age but protects only those age 40 or over. Thus, an employer can refuse to promote an employee under 40 because he or she is too old or too young. Once a person is in the protected class, discrimination under ADEA may be proved in the same ways that discrimination is proved under Title VII: by the plaintiff's showing disparate treatment or disparate impact.

Termination is the most common cause of ADEA cases. To prove a prima facie case of age discrimination involving a termination, the plaintiff must establish facts sufficient to create a reasonable inference that age was a determining factor in the termination. The plaintiff raises this inference by showing that he or she:

- Belongs to the statutorily protected class (those age 40 or older).
- Was qualified for the position held.
- Was terminated under circumstances giving rise to an inference of discrimination.

The plaintiff need not prove replacement by someone outside the protected class.[21]

Once the plaintiff sets forth the facts that give rise to an inference of discrimination, the burden of proof shifts to the defendant to prove there was a legitimate, nondiscriminatory reason for the discharge. If the employer meets this standard, the plaintiff may recover only if he or she can show by a preponderance of the evidence that the employer's alleged legitimate reason is a pretext for discrimination. Case 43-3 demonstrates how some employers will use a pretext for discriminating against older employees.

---

[20] 120 S. Ct. 631 (2000).
[21] *O'Conner v. Consolidated Caterers Corp.,* 517 U.S. 308, 116 S. Ct. 1307 (1996).

CASE **43-3**

JAMES v. SEARS, ROEBUCK & CO.
UNITED STATES COURT OF APPEALS FOR THE TENTH CIRCUIT
21 F.3D 989, 1994 U.S. APP. LEXIS 7073 (1994)

The facts before the jury presented either an ill-conceived and poorly executed corporate efficiency move or a deliberate corporate attempt to reduce payroll costs by replacing experienced and well-paid workers forty years of age or older with lesser experienced and lower-paid, younger workers. The jury decided it was the latter and rendered judgment in favor of Plaintiffs.

JUDGE BRORBY: Sears decided to cut costs in its service centers. Sears transferred some of the clerical functions formerly performed at its Ogden, Utah, service center to a larger center in Salt Lake City, Utah, even though at the time the Ogden center was the more profitable of the two centers. Sears then eliminated the jobs of the two oldest full-time clerical employees of its Ogden service center. One of those terminated service center employees is a plaintiff in this suit. Sears did not allow the service center plaintiff to transfer to the Salt Lake center where her former work had been transferred. Sears then hired predominately younger, part-time employees to work in the Ogden and Salt Lake service centers.

Simultaneous with the service center cuts, Sears offered the employees in its Ogden retail store and service center a buy-out. Five of the Plaintiffs worked at the retail store. Under the buy-out, employees leaving Sears' employment would receive a week of severance pay for each year they worked for Sears, with a cap of twenty-six weeks. The purpose of the buy-out was to provide the cut service center employees "comparable jobs" in the retail store. However, the turnover at the Ogden and Salt Lake City service centers was so high the cut service center employees could have been easily reabsorbed within three months.

A form of the buy-out called early retirement was offered to employees fifty years of age or older. As offered by Sears, Plaintiffs accepting early retirement lost thirty-five percent of their accrued pension because they were under sixty-two years of age. Further, plaintiffs between ages fifty and fifty-four had to wait until reaching age fifty-five before their pension payments could begin.

Sears pressured Plaintiffs to accept the buy-out/early retirement in order to achieve its predetermined quota for older employees leaving. Sears' internal document shows it planned on thirteen older, full-time employees leaving under the buy-out. There were twenty full-time employees under the age of forty who were eligible for the buy-out. Sears did not plan for any of the eligible younger employees to accept.

Sears obtained the acceptances of the five retail store Plaintiffs by conduct that constituted their constructive discharge. Sears' treatment of Plaintiffs included negative job reviews and threatening them with transfers to less desirable and lower paying positions if they did not accept the buy-out/early retirement. Sears' internal document shows that the retail store was not being reorganized and none of the retail employees were to be moved or lose their jobs as a result of the changes in the service centers or the buy-out.

The Age Discrimination in Employment Act ("ADEA") provides it is unlawful for any employer "to fail or refuse to hire or to discharge any individual . . . because of such individual's age." *29 U.S.C. 623* (a)(1). The protected class under the ADEA includes individuals "who are at least 40 years of age."

Plaintiffs had the burden of establishing age discrimination by a preponderance of the evidence. The often repeated elements of a prima facie case of age discrimination are met when an employee shows "(1) [employee] was within the protected age group, (2) [employee] was doing satisfactory work, (3) [employee] was discharged, and (4) [employee's] position was filled by a younger person." Once the employee establishes these elements, the employer can offer evidence to show it was motivated by a legitimate nondiscriminatory reason for the challenged action. The employee need not prove the employer's justifications were false, id., or "that age was the sole motivating factor in the employment decision." Instead, the employee must show age was also a reason for the employer's decision, and "age was the factor that made a difference."

The evidence demonstrated Sears forced the retail Plaintiffs to accept the buy-out or early retirement in several ways. During the months before the offer, two Plaintiffs working as salespersons were singled out among similarly situated employees and pressured about quotas in a way younger employees were not. Although they were top sellers, they were threatened, pressured and systematically "written up" over quotas even though the quotas were almost never met by other salespersons. Sears then used these reviews as a pretext for telling those two salespersons Plaintiffs they would be fired or transferred to lower paying positions if they did not accept. Sears threatened to move the remaining three retail store Plaintiffs from their current jobs into high pressure sales jobs involving unreachable quotas for the sales of maintenance agreements. The record viewed in the light most favorable to Plaintiffs as prevailing parties supports the jury verdict.

REVERSED in favor of plaintiffs.

CRITICAL THINKING

The one-sided nature of this case makes it difficult to see how unclear causation often is. But to help you see exactly that potential lack of clarity, suppose this case had been tried without any of the internal documents from Sears. Under those conditions, how would the behavior of Sears be more difficult to attribute to age discrimination?

ETHICAL DECISION MAKING

The laws in this chapter are stimulated by what particular value preference? Would it be possible to argue in any fashion that Sears shares this value preference?

DEFENSES UNDER ADEA

As under Title VII, decisions premised on the operation of a bona fide seniority system are not unlawfully discriminatory despite any discriminatory impact. Likewise, employment decisions may also be based on "reasonable factors other than age." Another defense available in both Title VII and ADEA cases is the bona fide occupational qualification (BFOQ) defense. To succeed with this defense, the defendant must establish that he or she must hire employees of only a certain age to safely and efficiently operate the business in question. The courts generally scrutinize very carefully any attempt to demonstrate that age is a BFOQ.

One example of an employer's successful use of this defense is provided by *Hodgson v. Greyhound Lines, Inc.,*[22] a case in which the employer refused to hire applicants age 35 or older. Greyhound demonstrated that its safest drivers were those between the ages of 50 and 55, with 16 to 20 years of experience driving for Greyhound. Greyhound argued that this combination of age and experience could never be reached by those who were hired at age 35 or older. Therefore, in order to ensure the safest drivers, Greyhound should be allowed to hire only applicants younger than 35. In this case, the court accepted the employer's rationale.

Even if none of the foregoing defenses are available to the employer, termination of an older employee may be legal because of the *executive exemption.* Under this exemption, an individual may be mandatorily retired after age 65 if two conditions are met:

- He or she has been employed as a bona fide executive for at least two years immediately before retirement.
- On retirement, he or she is entitled to nonforfeitable annual retirement benefits of at least $44,000.

Remember, however, that federal laws are a minimum level of protection. If a state wishes, it may pass laws granting employees in its state more rights than those under federal law.

Americans with Disabilities Act

The goal of the Americans with Disabilities Act (ADA) is preventing employers from discriminating against employees and applicants with disabilities. ADA attempts to attain this objective by requiring that employers make reasonable accommodations to the known physical or mental disabilities of an otherwise qualified person with a disability unless the necessary accommodation would impose an undue burden on the employer's business.

---

[22] 499 F.2d 859 (7th Cir. 1974).

When the ADA was before Congress, some members predicted a flood of lawsuits that would bankrupt or at least overburden business. . . . Studies have shown, however, that businesses have adapted to the ADA much more easily—and inexpensively—than the doomsayers predicted. . . . Law Professor Peter Blanck of the University of Iowa has studied business compliance with the ADA, including Sears Roebuck and many other large businesses, and found that compliance was often as easy as raising or lowering a desk, installing a ramp, or modifying a dress code. Another survey found that three-quarters of all changes cost less than $100. Moreover, the predicted flood of lawsuits proved to be imaginary. Almost 90 percent of the cases brought before the Equal Employment Opportunity Commission are thrown out. And only about 650 lawsuits were filed in the ADA's first five years—a small number compared to 6 million businesses, 666,000 public and private employers, and 80,000 units of state and local governments that must comply. The American Bar Association recently conducted a survey and learned that, of the cases that actually go to court, 98 percent are decided in favor of the defendants, usually businesses.[23]

WHO IS PROTECTED UNDER ADA?

A disabled individual, for purposes of ADA, is defined as a person who meets one of the following criteria:

- Has a physical or mental impairment that substantially limits one or more of the major life activities of such individual.
- Has a record of such impairment.
- Is regarded as having such an impairment.

Employers often find it difficult to know how ADA applies to those who have mental disabilities. From 1992 to 1998, emotional/psychiatric impairment claims were 12 percent of all claims.[24] Psychiatric disorders constituted about 9 percent of the ADA lawsuits brought by the EEOC to court in 1998.[25] Typical accommodations for those with mental disabilities include providing a private office, flexible work schedule, restructured job, or time off for treatment. Despite the years of experience we have had in defining covered individuals, the issue of whether someone is a disabled person under the act is still frequently litigated.

ENFORCEMENT PROCEDURES UNDER ADA

ADA is enforced by the EEOC in the same way that Title VII is enforced. To bring a successful claim under ADA, the plaintiff must show that he or she meets all of the following:

- Had a disability.
- Was otherwise qualified for the job.
- Was excluded from the job solely because of that disability.

Under ADA, the plaintiff may file a charge with the appropriate state agency or with the EEOC within 180 days of the discriminatory act. If a charge has been filed with the state agency, an EEOC charge must be filed within 300 days of the discrimination or within 30 days of receiving notice of the termination of state proceedings, whichever comes first.

---

[23] Center for an Accessible Society, "Disability Issues Information for Journalists," www.accessiblesociety.org/topics/ada.

[24] National Council on Disability, "Equal Employment Opportunity Commission—Promises to Keep: A Decade of Federal Enforcement of the Americans with Disabilities Act," www.ncd.gov/newsroom/publications/promises_3.htm/#6, June 27, 2000 (accessed May 1, 2001).

[25] Sheryl J. Powers and Carolyn L. Wheeler, "Docket of Americans with Disabilities Act (ADA) Litigation," www.eeoc.gov/docs/ada-98.html, September 30, 1998 (accessed May 1, 2001).

The charge must identify the defendant and specify the nature of the discriminatory act. On receipt of a charge, the EEOC must notify the accused and attempt to conciliate the matter. If conciliation fails, the EEOC may then bring a civil action against the violator.

REMEDIES FOR VIOLATIONS OF ADA

Remedies for ADA violations are similar to those available under Title VII. A successful plaintiff may recover reinstatement, back pay, and injunctive relief. In cases of intentional discrimination, limited compensatory and punitive damages are also available. An employer who has repeatedly violated the act may be subject to fines of up to $100,000.

Equal Pay Act of 1963

LO8

What is the Equal Pay Act?

When the **Equal Pay Act (EPA) of 1963** was passed, the average wages of women were less than 60 percent of those of men. The primary purpose of the law was to eliminate situations where women, working alongside men or replacing men, would be paid lower wages for doing substantially the same job. The EPA prohibits any employer from discriminating within any "establishment . . . between employees on the basis of sex by paying wages to employees in such establishment at a rate less than the rate at which he pays wages to employees of the opposite sex . . . for equal work on jobs the performance of which requires equal skill, effort, and responsibility, and which are performed under similar working conditions, except where payment is made pursuant to (i) a seniority system; (ii) a merit system; (iii) a system which measures earnings by quantity or quality of production; or (iv) differential based on any factor other than sex."[26]

DEFINING *EQUAL WORK* UNDER EPA

The burden of proof in an EPA claim is on the plaintiff to show that the defendant-employer pays unequal wages to men and women for doing equal work at the same establishment. The courts have interpreted *equal* to mean substantially the same in terms of all four factors listed in the act:

- Skill
- Effort
- Responsibility
- Working conditions

The factors are looked at individually. If one job requires greater effort, whereas the other requires greater responsibility, and the other two factors are exactly the same, the jobs are not equal. Thus, a sophisticated employer could vary at least one duty and then pay men and women different wages or salaries. However, to warrant different pay, the differences must be real and not just some minor change added to make the jobs appear different.

The legal standard is that the jobs must be "substantially similar," not perfectly equal. A good illustration of this is the 2002 case of *Hunt v. Nebraska Public Power District*.[27] Lynda Hunt had been a clerk for 17 years in the district office, where she had various clerical duties. The office also employed two other clerks, a district supervisor, a district superintendent, and an office manager. When the district supervisor retired, Lynda Hunt

[26] 29 U.S.C.A. § 206(d)1.
[27] 282 F.3d 1021 (8th Cir. 2002).

was asked to take on most of his duties, in addition to her old duties, and was told she would receive a pay raise and title change. The former supervisor was earning $3,138 per month when he retired, compared to Hunt's $1,739, which did not change. The duties Hunt took on after her supervisor retired included training, disciplining, and evaluating the performance of other employees, although the actual performance forms were filled out by the remaining office manager. Other office employees testified that after the old supervisor retired, Hunt assumed the retiree's tasks and "ran the office." Hunt prevailed at trial. On appeal, the court found that the minor differences between what Hunt did and what the male supervisor had done were not significant enough to overturn the jury's finding that the jobs were substantially similar.[28]

THE IMPACT OF EXTRA DUTIES UNDER EPA

Another way to attempt to legitimize pay inequities is to give members of one sex additional duties. The courts scrutinize these duties very closely, and require that:

- The extra duties are *actually performed* by those receiving the extra pay.
- The extra duties *regularly* constitute a *significant* portion of the employee's job.
- The extra duties are *substantial,* as opposed to inconsequential.
- The extra duties are commensurate with the pay differential.
- The extra duties are available on a nondiscriminatory basis.

The courts will also make sure that different, comparable additional duties are not imposed on the parties not receiving the additional pay.

DEFENSES UNDER EPA

As a business owner or manager, what happens if you are accused of violating EPA? There are four defenses available to the employer:

- A bona fide seniority system.
- A bona fide merit system.
- A pay system based on quality or quantity of output.
- Factors other than sex.

> To see more on personal taxation and taxable damages, please see the **Connecting to the Core** activity on the text Web site at www.mhhe.com/kubasek2e.

Seniority, merit, and productivity-based wage systems must be enacted in good faith and must be applied to both men and women. At a minimum, employers should have written documentation of these policies. They should also be sure these policies are enforced. In one case, a former employee alleged that she was discriminated against because men of the same ability and ranking were consistently given higher merit raises. The employee won, despite the fact that the employer had a written merit system, because she was able to demonstrate that the merit policy was not enforced. By not considering attendance records and positions within the salary grade when giving raises, the employer had violated its own merit-raise policy.[29]

Proving that a factor other than sex resulted in the pay differential often presents great problems. The greater availability of females and their willingness to work for lower wages do *not* constitute factors other than sex. Training programs often fall into this category. A training program that requires that trainees rotate through jobs that are normally paid

---

[28] Ibid.

[29] *Ryduchowski v. Port Authority,* 203 F.3d 135 (2d Cir. 2000).

lower wages will be upheld as long as it is a bona fide training program and not a sham for paying members of one sex higher wages for doing the same job.

REMEDIES FOR VIOLATIONS OF EPA

Plaintiffs may recover back pay in the amount of the difference between what they make and what is paid to members of the opposite sex, plus attorney fees. If the employer was not acting in good faith in paying the discriminatory wage rates, the court will also award the plaintiff damages in an additional amount equal to the back pay.

Discrimination Based on Sexual Orientation—Actionable?

L09

May an employer discriminate on the basis of sexual orientation?

There is currently no federal legislation that prohibits discrimination based on sexual orientation. What does exist are individual state laws that prohibit such discrimination. Twelve states and the District of Columbia prohibit discrimination based on both sexual orientation and gender identity: California, Colorado, Illinois, Iowa, Maine, Minnesota, New Jersey, New Mexico, Oregon, Rhode Island, Vermont, and Washington.[30] An additional nine states prohibit discrimination based solely on sexual orientation. Those states are Connecticut, Delaware, Hawaii, Maryland, Massachusetts, Nevada, New Hampshire, New York, and Wisconsin.[31]

When the issue is narrowed to relationship recognition (i.e., marriage licenses, civil unions, and spousal rights for unmarried couples), the number of states recognizing such rights becomes much smaller. There are now five states that issue marriage licenses to same sex couples: Connecticut (2008), Iowa (2009), Massachusetts (2004), New Hampshire (2010), and Vermont (2009).[32] The District of Columbia began permitting same-sex marriages on March 3, 2010.[33] Two states provide some spousallike rights to unmarried couples: Hawaii (reciprocal beneficiaries, 1997) and Wisconsin (domestic partnerships, July 2009). Five states and the District of Columbia provide almost all the state-level spousal rights to unmarried couples: California, Nevada, New Jersey, Oregon, and Washington.[34] Finally, one state recognizes marriage by same-sex couples that is legally entered into in another jurisdiction: New York (2008).[35]

What do these laws mean to Brad, the employee in our opening scenario? It depends on where Brad lives. If Brad lives in Texas, and he is fired for being gay, he has no legal rights and cannot sue his employer. Conversely, if Brad lives in California (or one of the above-mentioned states), Brad may sue Jennifer and So Clean, his employer, for discrimination based on sexual orientation.

Legal Principle: **Only 21 states have laws protecting against discrimination based on sexual orientation.**

May an Employer Discriminate against a Smoker?

L010

May employers discriminate against smokers?

In the opening scenario, Jennifer discovered that Brad was a smoker. Later, she fired him. One of Jennifer's given reasons for terminating Brad's employment was that he was

---

[30] "Human Rights Campaign: Statewide Employment Laws & Policies," www.hrc.org, updated February 17, 2010.

[31] Ibid.

[32] "Human Rights Campaign: Marriage Equality & Other Relationship Recognition in the U.S.," www.hrc.org, updated March 3, 2010.

[33] "D.C. Law Permitting Same-Sex Marriages Takes Effect! Nation's Capital Is Sixth U.S. Jurisdiction to Permit Same-Sex Marriage," http://blog.buzzflash.com/alerts/799, March 3, 2010.

[34] Ibid.

[35] Ibid.

a smoker. May Jennifer and So Clean legally fire an employee for smoking outside the workplace? The answer is, "It depends!"

A recent trend has been for employers to consider a potential-employee's lifestyle when deciding whether to hire that person. Employers argue that smokers have higher health care costs and miss more work, lowering productivity.

> The Centers for Disease Control and Prevention estimated that $75 billion is spent annually on medical expenses attributed to smoking. Businesses lose $82 billion in lost productivity from smokers. And smokers take about 6.5 more sick days a year than nonsmokers. About one in five Americans—or 46 million people—smoke.[36]

As a result, some companies either won't hire smokers or are threatening to fire current employees who will not or are unable to quit smoking. In 2005, Michigan-based Weyco, Inc., announced that it would terminate all workers who did not stop smoking.[37] Many states have passed laws preventing companies from engaging in such action.

> Michigan, with 1.9 million smokers and one of the highest cigarette taxes in the nation, has no "smoker's rights law" found in 29 other states, so there isn't much that employees can do. Weyco terminated four of its employees this month after they refused to submit to a smoking breath test in light of the company's new policy that bans tobacco use among its 200 employees during work and even when they are off the clock. "We are saying people can smoke if they choose to smoke. That's their choice," said Gary Climes, Weyco's chief financial officer. "But they just can't work for us."[38]

If Brad lives in Michigan, Jennifer and So Clean may legally terminate him for smoking outside the workplace. Conversely, if Brad works in a state with "smoker's rights laws," he could not be legally terminated for smoking outside the workplace.[39] Employers should be aware that giving breaks on health care plans to employees who are nonsmokers could be in violation of smoker's rights law.

Legal Principle: Thirty states plus the District of Columbia protect a smoker's right to smoke outside the workplace.

Employment Discrimination Internationally

With many American firms having operations overseas, the question of the extent to which the U.S. laws prohibiting discrimination apply in foreign countries naturally arises. The Civil Rights Act of 1991 extended the protections of Title VII and ADA to U.S. citizens working abroad for American employers or for foreign corporations controlled by a U.S. employer. An exception is made if enforcement of Title VII would violate foreign law. In such cases, Title VII does not apply.

It is not always easy to determine whether a multinational corporation will be considered "American" enough to be covered by U.S. antidiscrimination laws. According to guidelines issued by the EEOC in October 1993, the EEOC will first consider where the company is incorporated. If the company is not incorporated, the EEOC will evaluate factors such as the company's principal place of business, the nationality of the controlling shareholders, and the nationality and location of management. No one factor is considered determinative, and the greater the number of factors linking the employer to the United States, the more likely the employer is to be considered "American."

---

[36] "Workers Fume as Firms Ban Smoking at Home," www.detnews.com/2005/business/0501/27/A01-71823.htm.

[37] Ibid.

[38] Ibid.

[39] For a list of states with smoker protection laws, see American Lung Association, "State 'Smoker Protection' Laws," http://slati.lungusa.org/appendixf.asp, updated June 15, 2009.

Legal Discrimination against Women in Saudi Arabia

In Saudi Arabia, not only are women not entitled to pay equal to that of men, but there are actual legal statutes sanctioning discrimination against women in both public and private situations. Women, who are not even allowed to drive, constitute only 5 percent of Saudi Arabia's workforce. This number may not be surprising considering the limited labor opportunities for women. The law severely limits the industries in which women can be employed. Women are forbidden to receive business licenses if they may have to interact with males or government officials. If a woman is fortunate enough to find a job, it will probably be in education or health care. Some women can be found in various retail businesses or the banking industry.

Despite its difficulties, finding a job may be easy in comparison to the discrimination Saudi Arabian women will face at work. For instance, all places of employment are segregated by sex. The only way women can be in contact with a man is by telephone or electronic exchange. Many women complain of sexual and physical abuse while on the job. These complaints come from women at all levels in the workforce, from sweatshops to hospitals. And their situation is made worse because they have basically no legal redress. The courts have unreasonably strict evidentiary rules for harassment and discrimination cases. These rules, as well as the social shame that would arise from trying to challenge a man in public, deter women from seeking a legal solution to discriminatory treatment.

To determine whether a foreign corporation is controlled by an American employer, the EEOC will again look at a broad range of factors. Some such factors include the interrelation of operations, common management, centralized labor relations, and common ownership or financial control over the two entities. A corporation that is clearly a foreign corporation and not controlled by an American entity is not subject to U.S. equal employment laws.

CASE OPENER WRAP-UP

Brad versus So Clean and Jennifer

At the beginning of this chapter, you were confronted with the situation between Brad and Jennifer. By now you should be able to answer all the questions presented to you.

In many states, an employee can legally be fired on the basis of sexual orientation. Discrimination in this area is based solely on state law. There is no federal protection against discrimination based on being gay. Similarly, firing an employee for smoking (including off the job) is also a state law issue. In Michigan, for example, such a firing would be legal. Many states are now passing laws preventing employers from firing those who smoke outside the workplace.

Brad is an at-will employee, but that does not mean that he can be fired for an illegal (i.e., discriminatory) reason. Laws protecting employees against sex discrimination and sexual harassment are just as applicable to men as they are to women. Anyone who is treated in a discriminatory way "based on sex" may sue under the appropriate state or federal antidiscrimination laws. Most, though not all, states have their own state laws against discrimination and harassment. States may give more protection than federal laws but not less protection. There are still a few states that have no state laws against employment discrimination.[40]

These are basic issues that every employer and employee should be familiar with. Remember, knowledge is power. The more you know, the better off you and your business will be.

[40] Alabama, Arkansas, Georgia, and Mississippi have no state employment antidiscrimination laws; see WAGE, "State-by-State Anti-Discrimination Laws," www.wageproject.org/content/statelaw/index.php).

Key Terms

Summary of Key Topics

When May an Employee Be Fired?	*At-will employment* means that any employee who is not employed under a contract or a collective bargaining agreement may quit at any time for any reason or no reason at all, with no required notice to the employer. Moreover, the employer may fire the employee at any time, with no notice, for almost any reason.
Federal Laws Governing Employers	Federal employment laws provide a minimum level of protection for employees. The states may give employees more rights, but not less rights, than they have under federal law.
Civil Rights Act— Title VII	Title VII of CRA (1964, as amended by the Civil Rights Act of 1991) protects employees against discrimination based on race, color, religion, national origin, and sex. It also prohibits harassment based on the same protected categories. Defenses to a charge of discrimination under Title VII include, but are not limited to, *merit, seniority,* and *bona fide occupational qualification (BFOC).*
	Disparate treatment: If the employee has been hired, fired, denied a promotion, or the like, on the basis of membership in a protected class under Title VII, this is a form of intentional discrimination and qualifies the employee to sue for disparate-treatment discrimination.
	Disparate impact: Disparate-impact cases arise when a plaintiff attempts to establish that while an employer's policy or practice appears to apply to everyone equally, its actual effect is that it disproportionately limits employment opportunities for a protected class.
	Sexual harassment: Sexual harassment includes unwelcome sexual advances, requests for sexual favors, and other verbal or physical conduct of a sexual nature that implicitly or explicitly makes submission a term or condition of employment; makes employment decisions related to the individual dependent on submission to or rejection of such conduct; or has the purpose or effect of creating an intimidating, hostile, or offensive work environment. Two recognized forms are *hostile-environment* and *quid pro quo* harassment.
	Pregnancy Discrimination Act of 1987: PDA amended Title VII of CRA to expand the definition of sex discrimination to include discrimination based on pregnancy.
Age Discrimination in Employment Act of 1967	ADEA prohibits employers from refusing to hire, discharging, or discriminating in terms and conditions of employment on the basis of an employee's or applicant's being age 40 or older.
Americans with Disabilities Act	ADA prohibits discrimination against employees and job applicants with disabilities.
Equal Pay Act of 1963	EPA prohibits an employer from paying workers of one gender less than the wages paid to employees of the opposite gender for work that requires equal skill, effort, and responsibility.
Discrimination Based on Sexual Orientation— Actionable?	In many states, an employee can legally be fired on the basis of sexual orientation. Discrimination in this area is based solely on state law. There is no federal protection against discrimination based on sexual orientation.

May an Employer Discriminate against a Smoker?

In many states, an employer may fire or refuse to hire an employee who smokes, even outside the workplace. Approximately 30 states and the District of Columbia, however, have "smoker's rights" laws that prohibit such employment action.

Employment Discrimination Internationally

The Civil Rights Act of 1991 extended the protections of Title VII and ADA to U.S. citizens working abroad for American employers or for foreign corporations controlled by a U.S. employer (unless such enforcement would violate foreign law).

Point / Counterpoint

Should Employers Be Permitted to Fire Employees for Activities, Such as Smoking, That They Do Outside Working Hours?

YES	NO
The Centers for Disease Control and Prevention estimated that $75 billion is spent annually on medical expenses attributed to smoking. Businesses lose $82 billion in lost productivity from smokers. Smokers take about 6.5 more sick days a year than nonsmokers.	Employers should have no say in what employees do outside the workplace. Forcing employees to take tests to reveal whether they are smokers is an invasion of the employees' privacy. Many employees are addicted to cigarettes and would unfairly lose badly needed employment if unable to quit smoking.

Questions & Problems

1. Name five statutes that prohibit discrimination in employment.

2. How is *equal work* defined under the Equal Pay Act?

3. Why is a disparate-impact case more difficult to establish than a disparate-treatment case?

4. Does Title VII apply to same-sex harassment?

5. List the protected classes under the Civil Rights Act of 1964 (as amended in 1991).

6. Machinchick worked for PB Power for six years. He received excellent reviews. Two years after beginning work, he was promoted to vice president. Four years after his promotion, Machinchick got a new supervisor and the company adopted a new management approach. The new supervisor, Knowlton, stated his plan to "hand-pick employees whose mindset resides in the 21st Century." On April 7, 2002, Knowlton sent an e-mail in which he stated that he wanted to "strategically hire some younger engineers and designers." Two days later, Knowlton sent an e-mail to the Human Resources Department criticizing Machinchick's performance. A short time later, Machinchick, age 63, was fired. He was told to turn over his client base to Betz, age 42. Machinchick sued PB Power, alleging it had violated the Age Discrimination in Employment Act. The trial court granted motion for summary judgment in favor of PB Power. Machinchick appealed. How should the appellate court decide? Has Machinchick shown enough evidence of age discrimination to warrant allowing the case to be heard by a jury? Explain your decision. [*Machinchick v. PB Power, Inc.,* 398 F.3d 345 (5th Cir. 2005).]

7. In late 2000, Stacy Hegwine applied for a clerk/order checker position in Fibre's customer service department. The ad mentioned no lifting or other physical requirement. Hegwine interviewed for the position with Fibre employees Carlene Cox and Ron Samples on February 16, 2001. Fibre had

no documented job description for the position at that time. During the interview, Samples told Hegwine that the position had a 25-pound lifting requirement. After watching a series of videos and receiving documents outlining Fibre's employment policies, Hegwine met with Cox. During this meeting, Hegwine disclosed her pregnancy. Cox called Hegwine and offered her the position on February 21, 2001, contingent on Hegwine's successful completion of a physical exam. Hegwine accepted the offer and was given a start date of March 1, 2001. Two days later, Hegwine completed her physical at the office of Dr. Ostrander, Fibre's medical director. As part of the exam, Hegwine was required to complete a medical history form that inquired as to her pregnancy status. Hegwine truthfully disclosed that she was pregnant. In response, Ostrander gave Hegwine a medical release form and told her that she must have it completed by her personal physician as a condition of her employment. Hegwine took this form to her physician, Dr. Herron, who completed it without being aware of any physical requirements related to Hegwine's prospective position at Fibre. Herron indicated on the form that Hegwine could lift between 20 and 30 pounds and could pull or push up to 40 pounds. On March 16, 2001, Cox called Hegwine and informed her that Fibre was "withdrawing [its] offer of employment" because her "availability" did not permit her "to perform the job." May an employer inquire about pregnancy status during a preemployment medical examination? Do you believe that Fibre retracted it's offer of employment because Hegwine was pregnant? How should the court rule? [*Stacy L. Hegwine v. Longview Fibre Company, Inc.,* 172 P.3d 688 (2007).]

8. Patricia Corley and Joseph Smith were employed by the Detroit Board of Education to work in its adult education program. Corley was employed part-time as a counselor, and Smith was her supervisor. During the course of their employment, Corley and Smith became romantically involved in a relationship that lasted three or four years. The relationship ended when Smith started dating another employee, Barbara Finch. Corley alleged that after Smith and Finch became involved, Smith repeatedly threatened her with adverse employment action if she said or did anything that interfered with his relationship with Finch. Corley also alleged that Finch taunted, embarrassed, and humiliated her by causing her workstation to be moved and by engaging in "catty" conversations with others that were about her and intended to be overheard by her. According to Corley, the alleged harassment culminated when she was discharged at the conclusion of the 1995–1996 school year. Does Corley have a claim for sexual harassment? Explain your reasoning. [*Corley v. Detroit Bd. of Ed.,* 470 Mich. 274 (Mich. Sup. Ct. 2004).]

9. Danilo Peralta began working for Avondale Industries in 1990 as an outside machinist in the ship-building department. On July 30, 2001, he sustained "severe personal injury" when his supervisor struck him with a metal chair. Peralta was unable to work and was placed on temporary total disability. Peralta attempted to return to work on August 1, 2002, and October 1, 2002, but could not be medically cleared. Peralta was found to be permanently disabled by an administrative law judge in a longshoremen's proceeding. Avondale fired Peralta on February 4, 2003, for failure to return from a leave of absence. Peralta then sued Avondale, alleging violation of the Americans with Disabilities Act. In his deposition, Peralta explained that his knee injury is his only claimed disability. He explained that he is able to walk, although not for long. He does not use crutches or a wheelchair, although he does use a velcro-type wrap brace. Peralta is able to feed himself, bathe, dress, cook, carry small items, and drive a car, although his knee bothers him when he drives. He admitted that he drives for himself and his parents notwithstanding that his medication blurs his vision and makes him dizzy. Peralta repeatedly identified his inability to work as the only major life activity that he is now unable to do as a result of his impairment, that is, his injured knee. Does Peralta have a claim for disability under ADA? Explain your reasoning. [*Peralta v. Avondale Industries,* 2004 U.S. Dist. LEXIS 22640 (16 Am. Disabilities Cas (BNA) 889; 2004).]

10. Following separate lawsuits by female prisoners in Michigan and by the Civil Rights Division of the U.S. Department of Justice, both of which alleged rampant sexual abuse of female prisoners in Michigan, the Michigan Department of Corrections (MDOC) barred males from working in certain positions at its female prisons. Specifically, the MDOC designated approximately 250 correctional officer

and residential unit officer positions in housing units at female prisons as "female only." A group of MDOC employees, both males and females, sued the MDOC, alleging that the MDOC's plan violated Title VII of the Civil Rights Act of 1964.

The issue before the court was whether gender was a bona fide occupational qualification for the positions in question. How do you think the court should rule? Why? [*Everson v. Michigan Dept. of Corrections*, 391 F.3d 737 (6th Cir. 2004).]

Looking for more review material?

The Online Learning Center at **www.mhhe.com/kubasek2e** contains this chapter's "Assignment on the Internet" and also a list of URLs for more information, entitled "On the Internet." Find both of them in the Student Center portion of the OLC, along with quizzes and other helpful materials.

The Nature of Property, Personal Property, and Bailments

LEARNING OBJECTIVES

After reading this chapter, you will be able to answer the following questions:

1   What are the classifications of property?

2   How is personal property transferred?

3   What are the rights and responsibilities of parties to a bailment?

CASE OPENER
Prisoners and Personal Property

Warner Melvin, a prisoner at a U.S. penitentiary, was required to move to a new cell. Melvin was able to move most of his belongings to his new cell before his work shift. A few items remained in his old cell: a pair of Adidas shoes, some electronic equipment, and some food. Melvin hid the property and asked the guard to deadlock the cell. The guard, Richard, looked in the cell and determined it was empty. He did not lock the cell.

When Melvin returned from work, he noticed that his property was missing. There are conflicting claims as to whether Richard knowingly allowed the other prisoners to take Melvin's property, but it is known that the cell was not locked. Melvin argued that Richard was a bailee and Richard was responsible for the lost property. Clearly the relationship between a prisoner and a prison guard is unique and different from more standard relationships, such as the relationship between a boarder and an innkeeper. However, whether this difference was strong enough to diminish any duty owed by Richard to Melvin was the question the court confronted.

Although it is often difficult for prisoners to bring litigation, several cases across the country illustrate that the loss of their personal property is not uncommon. In *Sellers v. United States,* a frequently cited case, the prison restricted the amount of personal items inmates could keep in their cells. In accordance with the restriction, the prison authorities took from Sellers an oil painting of his wife, 41 law books, an almanac, and other personal items. Sellers' items were subsequently lost. The Seventh Circuit held that once a prisoner establishes a bailment relationship and loss of property, the government is liable for conversion.[1]

1. Do you think a bailment relationship existed between Richard and Melvin?
2. Pretend that Melvin was a guest at a hotel. The hotel manager asked Melvin to move to another room. Melvin was able to transfer most of his belongings to the new room, but he then had to rush to an appointment. He requested that the front-desk attendant lock his old room. Do you think this scenario is easier to resolve? Why or why not?

The Wrap-Up at the end of the chapter will answer these questions.

[1] *Melvin v. United States,* 963 F. Supp. 1052 (1997); *Sellers v. United States,* 1996 U.S. App. LEXIS 24353. For other cases involving prisoners and lost property, see *Moore v. United States,* 1996 U.S. Dist. LEXIS 16900; *Jungerman v. City of Raytown,* 925 S.W.2d 202 (1996); and *Bacote v. Ohio Dept. of Rehabilitation and Correction,* 578 N.E.2d 565 (1988).

The Nature and Classifications of Property

LO1

What are the classifications of property?

When people hear the word *property,* they generally think of physical objects: land, houses, cars. However, this pattern of thought reflects an incomplete understanding of the concept of property. Property is a set of rights and interests in relation to others with reference to a tangible or intangible object. The essence of the concept of property is that the state provides the mechanism to allow the owner to exclude others. A less technical way to think about property is that it is anything you can own.

Those with great amounts of property have an especially significant amount of power. Because possessing property facilitates the acquisition of even more property, the identification of those who possess a disproportionate amount of property provides insight into the dynamics of influence and authority in our society.

Property is generally divided into two basic categories, real property and personal property, as shown in Exhibit 48-1. *Real property,* land and anything permanently attached to the land, is the focus of the next chapter. In this chapter, we will examine the laws governing *personal property,* which is generally defined as property that is not attached to the land, or movable property. Sometimes property is initially movable but then becomes attached to the land. In such a situation, the property is called a *fixture.* Fixtures are treated like real property, and so they are discussed in the next chapter.

Personal Property

All property that is not land or not permanently affixed to land is **personal property.** Personal property may be either tangible or intangible. *Tangible property* is property that can be identified by the senses. It is property that you can see or touch. Tangible property includes items such as furniture, cars, and other goods.

Books are typically thought of as personal property. The owner of a book may write in it and generally do what he or she wants with it, and the law protects the owner against having the book taken by someone else. However, the growing popularity of e-books has raised questions about what rights e-book users have to their e-books. In July 2009, Amazon deleted copies of George Orwell's *1984* and *Animal Farm* directly off people's Kindles (Amazon's e-book reader) and refunded their money.[2] This action sparked

[2] Brad Stone, "Amazon Erases Orwell Books from Kindle," *NYTimes.com,* July 17, 2009 www.nytimes.com/2009/07/18/technology/companies/18amazon.html.

Exhibit 48-1   Types of Property

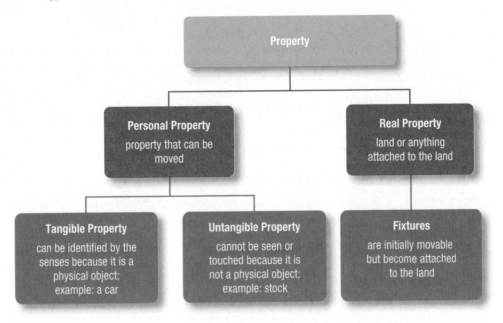

massive controversy over whether Amazon has the right to remove content that customers had bought from their Kindles.[3] At least one lawsuit has already been filed as a result of this incident.[4] Much of the outrage has been due to the fact that people do not see e-books and physical books as different types of property.[5] Businesses that offer digital content should be clear about what rights customers have to the content, and they should make that information well known and visible to avoid problems like the one Amazon is currently facing.

Intangible property includes such items as bank accounts, stocks, and insurance policies. Because most intangibles (with the exception of some classified as intellectual property and discussed in Chapter 12) are evidenced by writings, most of the following discussion applies to both tangible and intangible property. The primary issues that arise in conjunction with personal property involve (1) the means of acquiring ownership of the property and (2) the rights and duties arising out of a bailment. Both are discussed in this chapter in detail.

VOLUNTARY TRANSFER OF PROPERTY

Voluntary transfer, as a result of either a purchase or a gift, is the most common means by which property is acquired. Ownership of property is referred to as *title*, and title to property passes when the parties so intend. When transfer of the property is by purchase, the acquiring party gives some consideration to the seller in exchange for title to the property.

LO2

How is personal property transferred?

[3] Ibid.

[4] Alexandria Sage, "Amazon.com Sued over Deleted Digital Book Copies," *Reuters,* July 31, 2009 www.reuters.com/article/internetNews/idUSTRE56U72A20090731.

[5] Bobbie Johnson, "Why Did Big Brother Remove Paid-For Content from Amazon's Kindles?" *The Guardian,* July 22, 2009 (www.guardian.co.uk/technology/2009/jul/22/kindle-amazon-digital-rights).

Distinctions in Italian Property Law

In Italian law, there is a significant distinction between physical possession and a mental intention to possess. The term to describe the latter is *usucapione.* Instances of *usucapione* are characterized by persons having legal possession equivalent to that of the owner but only for a certain length of time.

Before a transition from legal possession to full ownership can occur, several requirements must be satisfied. These requirements differ depending on whether the property is classified as immovable or movable. For immovable property, the potential owner must possess the property for no less than 20 years. Movables require a 10-year period of possession. These periods of possession must

be uninterrupted. If possession of the property is lost, the individual has one year to regain it before having to start the term of possession over.

Understanding the distinction between immovable and movable property is thus important to determining the required length of possession before ownership. Immovable property includes anything attached to the ground, such as trees, buildings, homes, and arenas. Movables, therefore, include any property not attached to the ground. Movables are further divided into those that require registration and those that do not. Registration is necessary for the transference, sale, or termination of certain movable property.

Such a transfer of ownership usually requires no formalities, but in a few cases changes of ownership must be registered with a government agency. Sales of motor vehicles, watercraft, and airplanes are among the primary transfers requiring registration. To transfer such property, a certificate of title must be signed by the seller, taken to the appropriate government agency, and then reissued in the name of the new owner.

Gifts are another voluntary means of transferring ownership. They differ from purchases in that there is no consideration given for a gift. As you know from your previous reading, a promise to make a gift is therefore unenforceable. Once properly made, however, a gift is irrevocable.

To see how marketing decisions affect voluntary transfers of property, please see the **Connecting to the Core** activity on the text Web site at www.mhhe.com/kubasek2e.

Three elements are necessary for a valid gift (see Exhibit 48-2). First, there must be a *delivery* of the gift. Delivery may be actual, which is the physical presentation of the gift itself, or constructive, which entails the delivery of an item that gives access to the gift or represents it, such as the handing over of the keys to a car. Second, the delivery must be made with *donative intent* to make an immediate gift. The donor makes the delivery with the purpose of turning over ownership at the time of delivery. Third, there must be *acceptance,* a willingness of the donee to take the gift from the donor. Usually, acceptance is not a problem, although a donee may not want to accept a gift because of a desire to not feel obligated to the donor or because of a concern that ownership of the gift may impose some unwanted legal liability.

Sometimes, however, it can be difficult to determine whether something is a gift or a loan, especially when proper documentation is not filed at the time of the transaction. This was the scenario faced by Don Whittington when he disputed ownership of a 1979 Kremer Porsche displayed at the Indianapolis Motor Speedway Hall of Fame Museum. Whittington believed that he was the owner of the Porsche and that he had merely loaned it to the museum in 1980. The Indianapolis Motor Speedway Foundation believed that Whittington had given the car as a gift to the museum, and the foundation had even applied for and been granted a title to the car in 2001. In 2004, when Whittington requested the return of the car, he had to prove that he had a possessory interest in the car. Although the museum did not have a record of receiving the car as a gift or a loan, and Whittington had never applied for a tax reduction for giving the car as a gift and was able to produce one document in which he listed the car as an asset, the trial court found in favor of the foundation. The court

E-Businesses and Their Customers Benefit from New Labeling and Shipping Options

Within the past few years, the boom in e-commerce has inspired improvements in Internet postal technology. Now, e-businesses can use Internet postal technology to print labels and pay for shipping postage using accounts such as PayPal accounts.

For a small business that operates through eBay, for instance, this means the business can operate more efficiently. Before improvements in Internet postal technology, it was likely that a small business would print mailing labels by hand and make multiple trips to the post office. Now, it is possible for small businesses to print out labels and arrange for pickups from carriers.*

An additional benefit to both buyers and sellers is that they can track packages. Claims that the postal service "lost" a package are now less likely. Consequently, small businesses save money by not having to replace the package contents. Litigation over lost packages should go down too. Or at least the new technology will help plaintiffs determine what went wrong in the shipping process and which party was negligent.

*Beth Cox, "The Online Auction Site's New Integrated Labeling and Shipping Payment Options Can Improve Sellers' Operations—But They Are Not without Hitches," *ecommerce.internet.com,* March 25, 2004 (accessed July 29, 2005).

---

determined that Whittington's behavior after the museum took possession of the car was more consistent with giving the car as a gift rather than as a loan.[6]

Legal Principle: A gift made by a person during her or his lifetime requires delivery, donative intent, and acceptance.

The gifts we have been discussing so far have been what are called *inter vivos* gifts, gifts that are made by a person during his or her lifetime. Another type of gift that can be made is a gift *causa mortis,* a gift that is made in contemplation of one's immediate death. It can be revoked any time before the death of the donor, and it is automatically revoked if the donor recovers.

Litigation over gifts *causa mortis* often arises because the three elements of delivery, donative intent, and acceptance still have to occur before the gift is complete and that means before the death of the donor. Case 48-1 illustrates how difficult it can sometimes be to determine whether in fact all the elements of a gift *causa mortis* have been met.

Exhibit 48-2   Proper Property Transfer by *Inter Vivos* Gifts

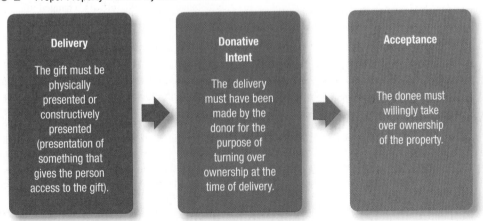

Delivery	Donative Intent	Acceptance
The gift must be physically presented or constructively presented (presentation of something that gives the person access to the gift).	The delivery must have been made by the donor for the purpose of turning over ownership at the time of delivery.	The donee must willingly take over ownership of the property.

[6] *Whittington v. Indianapolis Motor Speedway Found. Inc.,* 2008 U.S. Dist. LEXIS 62760.

STEPHEN LABATT PORTER, ET AL., APPELLANT v. BLACK WARRIOR FARMS, L.L.C., ET AL.

SUPREME COURT OF ALABAMA
976 SO. 2D 984 (2006)

Donald R. Porter, Sr., and Olga Porter had seven children: Donald, Teddy, Cecil, Shari, Stephen, Marc, and Andrew. Donald Sr. died in 1976. Under his will, part of the real estate was to become subject to a trust for the life of Olga, and at her death the remainder was to pass to the seven children. Olga died on June 27, 2001. By her will, her portion of the real estate passed to the seven children. Another provision of her will addressed her children's indebtedness to her. The will states that, upon her death, any indebtedness her children or their estate have against her will be forgiven, but that amount will be subtracted from their share of the Porter Family Trust.

In March 2000, Olga sold the family beach house. Of the proceeds from the sale, Olga sent $160,000 to Stephen and $140,000 to Marc to invest for her. Stephen had invested Olga's money in land, which at the time of her death was worth $346,000. After Olga's death, Marc returned Olga's $140,000 investment to her estate. However, Stephen did not return Olga's original investment or the appreciated amount. As justification for keeping the money, he produced a handwritten letter Olga had sent to him:

> Mrs. Olga L. Porter
> Black Warrior Farms
> Gallion, AL 36742
> September 26, 2000
> Dear Steve—
> Just a note to let you know I appreciate your investing the money for me and know you will take care of it for me—
> However, should any thing happen to me I want you to keep the balance for all you have done for me in the past—
> Will check with you after October 7th—
> My love to all,
> Olga Porter

The reference to October 7 apparently related to a cruise she was taking between September 26 and October 7, 2000. Olga's other children, besides Stephen, argue that the letter related only to the cruise, and not to anything occurring after that. Olga's will was enforced, and her children created an LLC, Black Warrior Farms, for the purpose of liquidating and distributing the estate. Each of Olga's children is a member of Black Warrior Farms, except that because Stephen has disclaimed his 1/7 interest in the estate, Stephen's three

children each hold a 1/21 interest in Black Warrior Farms. The funds held by Black Warrior Farms were distributed. Stephen's three children each received an amount less than their 1/21 share because of Stephen's alleged failure to pay into Olga's estate the money Olga had entrusted to him for investment. Black Warrior Farms and Marc sued Stephen, alleging that Stephen had not returned to the estate the $160,000 Olga had given him. Stephen responded that the September 26, 2000, letter from Olga entitled him to keep the $160,000. The trial court held that at the time of her death the value of the money Olga had entrusted to Stephen was $346,000 and further stated that a reasonable interpretation of the letter indicates that the money was not a gift, and that "should anything happen to me" in the letter refers only to the time of the cruise. The court ruled that Stephen owed the trust the money Olga gave him for investment, plus interest. Stephen and his children appealed.

JUSTICE PARKER: Olga's 1986 will clearly stated that her children's indebtedness to her was to be forgiven upon her death but that any indebtedness was to be offset against the share of her estate each child was to receive. When Olga entrusted $160,000 to Stephen in 2000, it is clear that it was not a gift but was an investment that Stephen was to handle on her behalf.

Stephen and his children argue that Olga's letter of September 21, 2000, clearly changed the status of the $160,000 Olga had given Stephen from an investment to a gift or bequest. . . . Rather, the trial court said: "A reasonable interpretation of the letter is that it expressed her wishes to deal with the money held by each son if she did not return from a cruise on which she was embarking." However, she did return. Although the trial court did not use the term *causa mortis*, it seems to be saying that the letter was, at most, either a gift conditioned upon Olga's failure to return from the cruise or a *gift causa mortis* that became void when she returned from the cruise. In *Smith v. Eshelman*, this Court held that "such a gift [*causa mortis*] . . . is revoked by law, if he [the donor] gets well of the sickness with which he was then afflicted."

As to whether Olga's letter constituted an *inter vivos* gift, this Court noted in *Ford v. Stinson*, the three elements that are necessary to establish an *inter vivos* gift: "(1) donative intent on the part of [the donor], (2) effective delivery to . . . the donee, and (3) acceptance by [the donee]."

The second and third elements are clearly established. Olga delivered the $160,000 to Stephen in March 2000. Stephen received, accepted, and invested the money.

The first element is more problematic. Olga did not show donative intent in March 2000 when she transferred the $160,000 to Stephen. Her purpose in transferring it to him was so that he could invest it on her behalf. The donative intent, if any, must be based on the September 26, 2000, letter. In that letter she clearly states a desire and intent that Stephen should have the money: "I want you to keep the balance for all you have done for me in the past—." But the portion of the sentence quoted above is preceded by a subordinate clause: "should any thing happen to me. . . ." This subordinate clause appears to qualify the independent clause by placing a condition on it. Furthermore, in the first paragraph of the letter Olga says: "I appreciate your investing the money *for me* and know you will take care of it *for me*" (emphasis added). The phrase "for me," especially its second appearance where it follows a future-tense verb "will take care," indicates that Olga contemplated continued ownership of the investment. Thus, the transfer of the $160,000 to Stephen, even after the September 2000 letter, cannot be considered an *inter vivos* gift, because it is conditional and to be effective only at a future time. In other words, Olga's letter does not show the requisite donative intent. . . .

We could all wish that Olga had been more explicit concerning the disposition of this property. But there are clear and legal ways to make a gift, and there are clear and legal ways to change a will or to make a new will. Olga did none of these; therefore, her 1986 will must stand as the last clear expression of her intent concerning her estate, including the $160,000 Stephen invested for her. . . .

Because we have ruled that Olga's letter to Stephen did not constitute a gift or a bequest to him of the $160,000, we conclude that the trial court's ruling that Black Warrior Farms and Stephen's siblings properly withheld that portion of the distribution of the funds in Black Warrior Farms from Stephen and his children was correct. . . .

Judgment AFFIRMED in favor of defendant.

CRITICAL THINKING

What ambiguity did the court have to decide to render a decision in this case? How did the court resolve this ambiguity?

ETHICAL DECISION MAKING

What ethical norm is being followed by the decision in this case?

Legal Principle: **For a gift *causa mortis,* you must have the three elements of a gift: delivery, donative intent, and acceptance before the death of the donor.**

You should remember from the chapter on contracts that sometimes a contract is drafted so that one person's obligations under a contract do not arise until the happening of a certain event. These contracts are called *conditional contracts*. Gifts can also be conditional. Case 48-2 illustrates how courts tend to handle one of the most common conditional gifts, the engagement ring.

CASE 48-2

BARRY MEYER v. ROBYN MITNICK
COURT OF APPEALS OF MICHIGAN.
244 MICH. APP. 697, 625 N.W.2D 136 (2001)

On August 9, 1996, plaintiff Barry Meyer and defendant Robyn Mitnick became engaged, at which time Barry gave

Robyn a custom-designed $14,900 engagement ring. On November 8, 1996, Barry asked Robyn to sign a prenuptial *agreement and Robyn refused. The engagement was broken during that meeting, but both parties contended that the other party caused the breakup.*

The defendant did not return the engagement ring, and the plaintiff sued, claiming it was a conditional gift, and since the condition did not occur, she should return the ring. The trial court ruled in favor of the plaintiff, finding the ring to be a conditional gift, and the defendant appealed.

CIRCUIT JUDGE P. J. FITZGERALD: . . . The issue presented is whether fault must be considered in determining ownership of an engagement ring following termination of the engagement. We conclude that determination of who owns the engagement ring following termination of the engagement does not require a determination of which party was at fault. . . .

Although Robyn does not challenge the trial court's finding that an engagement ring is a conditional gift given in contemplation of marriage, an analysis of the conditional nature of the gift is essential to a complete analysis of the issue presented. . . .

While there is no Michigan law regarding ownership of engagement rings given in contemplation of marriage where the engagement is broken, the jurisdictions that have considered cases dealing with the gift of an engagement ring uniformly hold that marriage is an implied condition of the transfer of title and that the gift does not become absolute until the marriage occurs. Most courts recognize that engagement rings occupy a rather unique niche in our society. One court explained:

> Where a gift of personal property is made with the intent to take effect irrevocably, and is fully executed by unconditional delivery, it is a valid gift inter vivos. . . . Such a gift is absolute and, once made, cannot be revoked. . . . A gift, however, may be conditioned on the performance of some act by the donee, and if the condition is not fulfilled the donor may recover the gift. . . . We find the conditional gift theory particularly appropriate when the contested property is an engagement ring. The inherent symbolism of this gift forecloses the need to establish an express condition that marriage will ensue. Rather, the condition may be implied in fact or imposed by law in order to prevent unjust enrichment. . . .

Like the courts in other states, we find that engagement rings should be considered, by their very nature, conditional gifts given in contemplation of marriage.

Once we recognize an engagement ring is a conditional gift, the question still remains: who gets the gift when the condition is not fulfilled? The general principles of law concerning a donor's right to the return of an engagement ring or its value when the marriage does not occur are contained in a collection of cases from multiple jurisdictions. Generally, courts have taken two divergent paths. The older one rules that when an engagement has been unjustifiably broken by the donor, the donor shall not recover the ring. However, if the engagement is broken by mutual agreement, or unjustifiably by the donee, the ring should be returned to the donor. The critical inquiry in this fault-based line of cases is who was at "fault" for the termination of the relationship. The other rule, the so-called "modern trend," holds that because an engagement ring is an inherently conditional gift, once the engagement has been broken the ring should be returned to the donor. Thus, the question of who broke the engagement and why, or who was "at fault," is irrelevant. This is the no-fault line of cases.

We find the reasoning of the no-fault cases persuasive. Because the engagement ring is a conditional gift, when the condition is not fulfilled the ring or its value should be returned to the donor no matter who broke the engagement or caused it to be broken. As stated by the court . . . in concluding that fault is irrelevant in an engagement setting:

> What fact justifies the breaking of an engagement? The absence of a sense of humor? Differing musical tastes? Differing political views? The painfully-learned fact is that marriages are made on earth, not in heaven. They must be approached with intelligent care and should not happen without a decent assurance of success. When either party lacks that assurance, for whatever reason, the engagement should be broken. No justification is needed. Either party may act. Fault, impossible to fix, does not count.

In sum, we hold that an engagement ring given in contemplation of marriage is an impliedly conditional gift that is a completed gift only upon marriage. If the engagement is called off, for whatever reason, the gift is not capable of becoming a completed gift and must be returned to the donor. **AFFIRMED**.

CRITICAL THINKING

Do you agree with the outcome of this case? Why or why not?

ETHICAL DECISION MAKING

What role do you think the public disclosure rule played in influencing either the plaintiff's or the defendant's behavior in this case?

INVOLUNTARY TRANSFER OF PERSONAL PROPERTY

Involuntary transfers of ownership occur when property has been abandoned, lost, or mislaid. The finder of such property *may* acquire ownership rights to such property through possession.

Property that the original owner has discarded is *abandoned* property. Anyone finding such property becomes its owner by possessing it. Recall the opening scenario. Assume that Richard, the prison guard, believed that Melvin had moved all of his property to the new cell. While cleaning out the cell, Richard came across the shoes, food, and electronic equipment. Does he now possess the property? The court did not address this hypothetical, but it illustrates, as does Case 48-3, that it is not always easy to determine whether property has in fact been abandoned.

CASE 48-3 OMNI HOLDING AND DEVELOPMENT CORP. v. C.A.G. INVESTMENTS, INC.
SUPREME COURT OF ARKANSAS
370 ARK. 220 (2007)

Bob Herren and Tom Papachristou met through a lawyer who represented them both. The men developed a business plan whereby Herren would provide financing and facilities for a crop-dusting service and a farm-equipment export business to be run by Papachristou. Although the business, Omni, was incorporated by Herren in Louisiana, it was to be located in Crittenden County, Arkansas. Subsequently, Herren persuaded Sherlee Despot, with whom he lived in Shreveport, to use money from her personal funds, bank loans, and Trust funds to purchase land in Crittenden County. With Herren's assistance, Despot organized C.A.G. as a Louisiana corporation. C.A.G. purchased an 80-acre tract of land outside of Marion, Arkansas, to serve as Omni's headquarters. Additionally, C.A.G. purchased a home for Papachristou and Crockett, his girlfriend, who was also employed by Omni. Over the next several years, C.A.G. intermittently advanced funds to Omni.

To consolidate Omni's outstanding indebtedness to C.A.G., Herren, in his capacity as president of Omni, prepared and signed a promissory note in favor of C.A.G. in the sum of $175,000. The note was secured with an aircraft owned by Omni. Omni borrowed $150,000 from Textron Financial Corporation, which loan was personally guaranteed by Despot. The $150,000 note was also secured by the identical aircraft that secured the earlier $175,000 note from Omni to C.A.G.

Omni's financial difficulties continued over the next three years, resulting in the deterioration of the business relationship among the parties. In late summer 2003, Despot and Herren learned that Omni was contemplating bankruptcy

and that Papachristou was out of the country, in Greece. Upon becoming aware of that information, Despot and Herren promptly traveled to Arkansas and discovered that the aircraft designated as security on both the Textron and C.A.G. notes had crashed in 2002. C.A.G. demanded that Omni immediately remove all personal property it owned or possessed from the real property owned by C.A.G. and surrender possession of the real property.

When Omni refused to comply, C.A.G. filed a complaint against Omni. Following a hearing, the court entered an order stating that Omni had committed an unlawful detainer of the property and that C.A.G. was entitled to a writ of possession of the property. In addition to its failure to vacate, equipment remained on the property, most of which had been "stripped," and Papachristou continued to reside on the premises. C.A.G. amended its complaint, seeking a judgment for the amount due and owing on the promissory note and a finding of abandonment with regard to Omni's personal property. Ultimately, the case was tried and the circuit court entered its order and judgment, finding, among other things, that Omni had abandoned all personal property it left on the premises following its failure to post the requisite bond to retain possession. Omni appealed.

JUSTICE IMBER: . . . Omni . . . asserts that the circuit court erred in ruling that Omni had abandoned personal property when the court ordered Omni to remove itself from the property. . . .

As to Omni's argument concerning the abandonment of its personal property, this court held in *Terry v. Lock* that the rights of a finder of property depend on how the found property is classified, with the character of the property determined by evaluating all the facts and circumstances present in the particular case. Additionally, we explained that,

> [p]roperty is said to be "abandoned" when it is thrown away, or its possession is voluntarily forsaken by the owner, in which case it will become the property of the first occupant; or when it is involuntarily lost or left without the hope and expectation of again acquiring it, and then it becomes the property of the finder, subject to the superior claim of the owner.

With that definition in mind, we now turn to Omni's argument that it did remove some property from the location, but was forced to leave behind a considerable number of items due to the size of the items, the number of items, the difficulty in removing the items, the absence of a suitable location to place the property, the short time involved, and the non court-ordered demands placed upon it by C.A.G.'s attorney. In sum, Omni claims that at no time did it voluntarily forsake its interest in its property, and that it never relinquished its hope or expectation of again acquiring its property as it vigorously defended its position during litigation. We disagree.

According to testimony elicited from Crockett, she removed files, furniture, computers, books, and office equipment from Omni's offices. Omni also removed several pieces of large equipment from the premises. The circuit court gave Omni a period of one week to remove all of its property, but Omni failed to take full advantage of that opportunity. Instead, Papachristou traveled to Greece when he could have stayed in Arkansas and used the time to retrieve Omni's property. Based upon the facts and circumstances as reflected in the record before us, and our standard of review, which is highly deferential to the credibility findings of the trial court, we cannot say that the circuit court clearly erred in finding that Omni abandoned the property it left on the premises after being afforded ample opportunity to accomplish its removal. In any event, with the termination of Omni's right as a lessee in a tenancy at will to remain on the property after the circuit court ordered the issuance of a writ of possession, any property left behind was abandoned. . . .

AFFIRMED in favor of appellee.

CRITICAL THINKING

What could Omni have done that would have led the court to come to a different decision?

ETHICAL DECISION MAKING

While C.A.G. had the legal right to take the property, would any ethical principle suggest that C.A.G. should not have taken it?

Lost property is property that the true owner has unknowingly or accidentally dropped or left somewhere. He or she has no way of knowing how to retrieve it. In most states, the finder of lost property has title to the lost good against all except the true owner.

Mislaid property differs from lost property in that the owner has intentionally placed the property somewhere but has forgotten its location. The person who owns the realty on which the mislaid property was placed has the right to hold the mislaid property. The reason is that it is likely that the true owner will return to the realty looking for the mislaid property.

In some states, the law requires that before becoming the owner of lost or mislaid property, a finder must place an ad in the paper that will give the true owner notice that the property has been found and/or must leave the property with the police for a statutorily established reasonable period of time.

Legal Principle: **The finder of lost or mislaid property acquires title to the property against all except the true owner.**

OTHER MEANS OF ACQUIRING OWNERSHIP OF PROPERTY

There are additional means by which people acquire title to property. One such means is by creation: If a person creates a piece of property, then he or she owns that property. One exception to this rule occurs when a person is paid to create property for someone else, in which case the property is owned by the person who paid for its creation. Another means of acquiring ownership is by court order. In a number of different types of cases, the court will determine who is entitled to ownership of property. For example, in a divorce case the court may award ownership of certain property to different parties, or in a bankruptcy case the court may award ownership of certain property to a creditor.

A far less common means of acquiring ownership is confusion, which involves only fungible goods. Fungible goods are goods for which one unit of the good is essentially the same as every other unit, such as grains of wheat or gallons of oil. If two people accidentally comingle their fungible goods, or if the goods are comingled because of the actions of a third party, each party is entitled to the percentage of the fungible goods that he contributed.

However, if one of the parties was responsible for the comingling, and that person cannot prove what percentage of the comingled goods she contributed, then the innocent party acquires title to all the goods. For example, if a farmer had stored grain in a rented storage elevator, and another farmer wrongfully added his grain to the elevator, the innocent farmer would be entitled to the entire amount in the silo.

Bailment

A **bailment** of personal property is a relationship that arises when one party, the *bailor,* transfers possession of personalty to another, the *bailee,* to be used by the bailee in an agreed-on manner for an agreed-on time period.

The most common illustration of a bailment occurs when a woman leaves her coat in a coat-check room. She hands her coat to the clerk and is given a ticket identifying the object of the bailment so that it can be reclaimed.

The bailment may be gratuitous or for consideration and may be to benefit the bailor, the bailee, or both. Determining who benefits from the bailment is important for determining the standard of care owed by the bailee. If the bailment is intended to benefit only the bailor, the bailee is liable for damage to the property caused by the bailee's gross negligence. An example of such a bailment occurs when you agree to keep a friend's houseplants for a week for no compensation while the friend is gone on a business trip. While there would be some debate over what constitutes gross negligence, most courts would probably agree that if one of the plants died because you misunderstood the watering instructions and gave it a little too much water, you probably would not be liable. However, if you lived in Arizona, and you took the plants home and placed them in front of a south-facing window and never watered them or checked to see whether they needed watering, and they all died, a court is likely to see that behavior as gross negligence and require that you compensate the owner.

If the bailment is solely for the bailee's benefit, the bailee is responsible for harm to the property caused by even the slightest lack of due care on the part of the bailee. An illustration of this type of bailment would occur if Jim borrowed his roommate's bike to go to the library. Even if he carefully parked the bike far away from other bikes, if someone scratched the bike while he was in the library, Jim would have to compensate his roommate for the harm done to the bike.

Finally, if the bailment is for the mutual benefit of bailee and bailor, the bailee is liable for harm to the bailed property arising out of the bailee's ordinary or gross negligence. If the property is harmed by an unpreventable "act of God," there is no liability on the part of the bailee under any circumstances.

Despite the existence of these general rules, the parties to a bailment contract can limit or expand the liability of the bailee by contract. Also, conspicuous signs have been held sufficient to limit liability. For example, a health club may have lockers with a huge sign saying, "Rent a lock for a locker for $1.00. Health Club not responsible for items stolen from unlocked lockers." If a person leaves a jacket in an unlocked locker, the health club will not be liable.

RIGHTS AND DUTIES OF THE BAILOR

L03

What are the rights and responsibilities of parties to a bailment?

The bailor has certain rights and duties in the bailment relationship (see Exhibit 48-3). Some of these rights and duties may change depending on whom the relationship primarily benefits and whether the bailment is gratuitous. This section highlights some of these important rights and duties.

In general, the bailor has the right to expect the bailee to (1) take reasonable care of the bailed property, repairing and maintaining it as necessary; (2) use the bailed property only as stipulated in the bailment agreement; (3) not alter the bailed property in any unauthorized manner; and (4) return the bailed property in good condition at the end of the bailment.

The bailor has two fundamental duties. One is the duty of compensation and reimbursement. This duty requires that the bailor provide the bailee with any agreed-on compensation for the bailment. Obviously, this aspect of the bailment has no application in a gratuitous bailment. However, in all bailments, the bailor must reimburse the bailee for any necessary costs incurred by the bailee in keeping and maintaining the bailed property, unless the bailment contract provides otherwise.

The bailor's other duty is to provide the bailee with property that is free from hidden defects that could harm the bailee. If the bailment is for the mutual benefit of both parties, the bailor must warn the bailee of any known defects or any that could have been discovered through reasonable investigation. If, however, the bailment is solely for the benefit of the bailee, the standard is slightly lower, and the bailor must warn of only known defects. If the bailor fails to live up to this duty, he may be sued for negligence by the bailee or any reasonably foreseeable third party who is injured as a result of the defect.

Exhibit 48-3

Rights and Duties of the Bailor

Rights of the Bailor

1. Right to expect that the bailee take reasonable care of the bailed property, repairing and maintaining it as necessary.
2. Right to expect that the bailee use the bailed property only as stipulated in the bailment agreement.
3. Right to expect that the bailee will not alter the bailed property in any unauthorized manner.
4. Right to expect that the bailee will return the bailed property in good condition at the end of the bailment.

Duties of the Bailor

1. Bailor must provide the bailee with any agreed-on compensation for the bailment.
2. Bailor must reimburse the bailer for any necessary costs incurred by the bailee during the bailment.

RIGHTS AND DUTIES OF THE BAILEE

The rights of the bailee generally complement the duties of the bailor, and the duties of the bailee complement the rights of the bailor. As with the bailor's rights and duties, those of the bailee also vary depending on the purpose of the bailment. The bailee's rights and duties are listed in Exhibit 48-4.

Foremost among the bailee's rights is the right to possess the bailed property during the term of the bailment. If anyone steals the bailed property from the bailee, the bailee may take legal action to recover the bailed property and may even seek compensation for the loss of the property or damage to it.

The bailee has the right to use the property in a manner consistent with the terms and purpose of the bailment. For example, if you are borrowing your friend's car while yours is being repaired, driving to work and to the grocery store would be consistent with the bailment. However, if you own an auto repair shop and you have possession of Smith's car to repair it, you cannot use the car to go on a date.

The bailee, unless the bailment is gratuitous, has the right to be compensated in accordance with the terms of the bailment. Regardless of the type of bailment, he or she has the right to be reimbursed for expenses that were necessary to maintain the bailed property.

If the bailee is to receive compensation for the bailment, the bailee may retain possession of the bailed property until payment is made. In most states, when the bailor refuses to provide the agreed-on compensation to the bailee, the bailee may ultimately sell the property after proper notice and a hearing. To enforce this right to sell the property, the bailee is given a *bailee's lien,* or a possessory lien on the property. Then, when it is sold, the proceeds are first used to pay the bailee and to cover the costs of the sale. The remaining proceeds go to the bailor.

In the opening scenario, Melvin argued that he entered into an implied bailment relationship with Richard. Although Melvin did not explicitly ask Richard to watch his property, he argued that Richard should have known that his request was made because his property was still in the cell. As the bailee, Richard became responsible for exercising a reasonable duty of care of Melvin's personal property.

DOCUMENTS RELATED TO BAILMENTS

Bailment Agreements. Bailments may be either express or implied. When a bailment is express, there is no need for a written agreement unless the statute of frauds applies

---

Exhibit 48-4

Rights and Duties of the Bailee

Rights of the Bailee
1. Right to possess the bailed property during the term of the bailment.
2. Right to use the property in a manner consistent with the terms and purpose of the bailment.
3. Right to receive compensation for the bailment unless the bailment is gratuitous.
4. Right to retain the bailed property until payment is received.

Duties of the Bailee
1. Bailee must take reasonable care of the bailed property, repairing and maintaining it as necessary.
2. Bailee must use the bailed property only as stipulated in the bailment agreement.
3. Bailee must not alter the bailed property in any unauthorized manner.
4. Bailee must return the bailed property in good condition at the end of the bailment.

Ziva Jewelry, Inc. v. Car Wash Headquarters, Inc.

Supreme Court of Alabama
897 So. 2d 1011; 2004 Ala. LEXIS 238

A bailee can be liable only for the property he possesses. In this case, Smith left his car and his keys with a car-wash employee. A case full of jewelry was locked in the trunk, but Smith did not tell any of the car-wash employees that it was in the trunk. Smith watched the car go through the car-wash tunnel and watched the employees dry the vehicle. As he was standing at the counter waiting to pay the cashier, he saw the employee wave a flag, indicating that his car was ready to be driven away. Smith then saw the employee walk away from his vehicle. While Smith was still at the counter, someone jumped into Smith's vehicle and sped off the car-wash premises. The police were called, and Smith's car was recovered 15 minutes later. The car was not damaged, but the jewelry, valued at $851,935, was missing from the trunk and never recovered.

Smith sued for negligent failure to safeguard the jewelry, but the trial court granted the defendant a summary judgment on the grounds that a bailment for the jewelry had never been established. The Supreme Court of Alabama affirmed on grounds that a bailee is not liable for the loss of the contents of a bailed vehicle when the bailee did not have actual or implied knowledge of the contents of the vehicle. In this case, there was no evidence that the car wash knew or should have reasonably foreseen or expected that it was taking responsibility for over $850,000 worth of jewelry when it accepted Smith's vehicle for the purpose of washing it.

to the bailment. As you should recall from Chapter 18, the statute of frauds requires a writing for any contract that cannot be performed within a year, so any bailment relationship that will last more than a year requires a writing to be enforceable. It is probably a good idea to put all bailments in writing, especially when the property involved is valuable. If the agreement is in writing, there will be far fewer disputes over each party's responsibilities and rights.

Documents of Title. When a bailment is for the purpose of transportation or storage of goods, certain documents of title, governed by Article VII of the Uniform Commercial Code, may be issued in conjunction with the bailment. The UCC defines a document of title as one that "must purport to be issued by or addressed to a bailee and purport to cover goods in the bailee's possession which are either identified or are fungible portions of an identified mass."

The three types of documents of title governing bailments are bills of lading, warehouse receipts, and delivery orders. A bill of lading is a document issued by a person engaged in the business of transporting goods that verifies receipt of the goods for shipment. A warehouse receipt is a receipt issued by one who is engaged in the business of storing goods for compensation. A *delivery order* is a written order to deliver goods directed to a party who, in the ordinary course of business, issues warehouse receipts or bills of lading.

Negotiability of Documents of Title. As you should recall from Chapter 26, if an instrument contains the word *bearer* or the phrase *to the order of,* it is negotiable. Thus, if a document of title specifies that the goods are to be delivered to the bearer or to the order of a named person, the person who possesses that document of title is entitled to receive, hold, and dispose of the goods it covers. Further, a good-faith purchaser of such a document of title may actually have greater rights to the document and goods than the transferor had or had the right to convey.

SPECIAL BAILMENTS

Certain bailments impose additional obligations on the bailee. These bailments will be discussed in detail in the following sections.

Innkeepers' Liability

GNOC Corp. v. Powers
2006 WL 560687 (Sup. Ct. N.J. 2006)

New Jersey's State Innkeeper's Act is a law that protects hotels from being liable for losses to their guests, as Powers unfortunately discovered. He was gambling in town and staying at a Hilton Hotel. While Powers was asleep one night, the hotel issued a second key to his room to an unknown person, who allegedly entered Powers's room and stole over $75,000 in cash winnings and chips. Powers sued, claiming negligence by the hotel. The trial court ruled in favor of the Hilton Hotel, and Powers appealed. The appeals court affirmed, holding that under New Jersey law, a hotel could not be held liable for the loss of valuables that could have been deposited in the hotel safe. Both the cash and the chips fell into the category of such valuables.

Common Carriers. Common carriers are licensed to provide transportation services to the public, as opposed to private carriers, which provide transportation services to a select group. Common carriers are subject to regulation by agencies and may be limited in the scope of services they provide by geographic region or type of goods they carry, but as long as a party seeking their services does not ask them to make any deliveries outside the scope of their ordinary course of business, common carriers cannot refuse to provide the service.

When a common carrier accepts a package for transport, a mutual-benefit bailment is created. But because the bailee is a common carrier, he or she is held to a higher standard of care: the standard of strict liability in protecting the bailed property. In other words, the common carrier is absolutely liable for any harm done to the property, even if there was no negligence on the part of the common carrier.

The only situations in which the common carrier will not be liable for harm to the bailed property are those in which the injury was caused by an act of God, an act of a public enemy, an act of the shipper, or the inherent nature of the good. These exceptions are interpreted narrowly. For example, the common carrier is still liable when the harm to the property was caused by an accident or by intentional acts of a third party. Thus, if the bailed property is stolen from the common-carrier truck that was transporting it, or if the truck gets into an accident and the contents are damaged as a result, the trucking firm is liable. However, if the fragile glass property being shipped gets broken because it was improperly crated by the owner, or if a tornado picks up the truck and drops it, demolishing the truck and its contents in the process, the common carrier will not be liable.

Sometimes a party will transport property using two or more connecting carriers. In such cases, a *through bill of lading* is used, which lists all carriers. Under this document, the shipper can recover from the original carrier or any of the connecting carriers. However, there is a presumption that the last carrier received the property in good condition.

To see how management and marketing considerations affect the choice of a common carrier, please see the **Connecting to the Core** activity on the text Web site at www.mhhe.com/kubasek2e.

Innkeepers' Liability. At common law, innkeepers, as well as anyone else who provided lodging to others, were held to the same strict-liability standard of care for their guests' property as were common carriers. However, today this standard applies only to those who are regularly in the business of making lodging available to the public. The standard also applies only to guests, or travelers, as opposed to lodgers, who are defined as permanent residents of the facility.

Some states further allow that innkeepers can avoid strict liability for their guests' personal property by providing them with a safe in which they may keep their valuables. Guests must be clearly notified of the existence of the safe and the limitation on the innkeeper's liability in the event that the guests fail to take advantage of the safe. Under some statutes, failure to use the safe will merely limit the innkeeper's liability; under others, it will relieve the innkeeper from liability other than that caused by his or her ordinary negligence.

Generally, the innkeeper does not have any responsibility for a guest's automobile. However, if the innkeeper provides parking facilities, a bailment exists and the innkeeper is held to the standard of reasonable care.

CASE OPENER WRAP-UP

Prisoners and Personal Property

The court determined that a bailment relationship existed between Melvin and Richard. Further, the court explained that the relationship between an inmate and a prison official is more substantial than that between a boarder and his host. Inmates do not pay prison officials to safeguard their personal belongings; thus, the relationship cannot constitute a bailment for hire. However, the restrictions on an inmate's property and his or her ability to control access to the property are imposed for the benefit of prison officials of the United States and for the protection of inmates. Although Melvin did not tell Richard that there was property in his cell, Richard did not suggest any other reason as to why Melvin would desire to have his cell locked other than to secure his property. Once Richard agreed to lock the cell, he had the duty, as a bailee, to act with reasonable care. The court took the majority position in holding that the personal property of inmates is protected.

Key Terms

bailment 1069	documents of title 1072	*inter vivos*	warehouse receipt 1072
bill of lading 1072	gift *causa mortis* 1063	gifts 1063	
common carriers 1073	innkeepers 1073	personal property 1060	

Summary of Key Topics

The Nature and Classifications of Property

Property is a set of rights in relation to a tangible object, the most significant of which is probably the right to exclude others.

Property can be divided into three categories:

Real property: Land and anything permanently attached to it.

Personal property: Tangible movable objects and intangible objects.

Intellectual property: Property that is primarily the result of one's mental rather than physical creativity.

Personal Property   Personal property can be transferred voluntarily through a gift or sale. It may also be transferred involuntarily if it is lost or mislaid.

Bailment   A bailment is a special relationship in which one party, the *bailor,* transfers possession of personalty to another, the *bailee,* to be used by the bailee in an agreed-on manner for an agreed-on time period.

Point / Counterpoint

What Constitutes "Possession" of Personal Property?

Barry Bonds, the San Francisco Giants slugger, stepped up to the plate in the first inning with 72 home runs for the season. With the bases empty and a full count, Bonds connected with a slow knuckleball, sending it over the right-field wall and into the baseball glove of a fan named Alex Popov. Before Popov could establish secure possession of the ball, however, a crowd of fans mobbed him, jarring the ball loose. Patrick Hayashi, a nearby fan who was not part of the crowd that mobbed Popov, picked up the ball on the ground nearby. Popov sued Hayashi for the property rights to the ball.

| Should Popov Win? ||
YES	NO
Popov asserted as much control over the ball as the nature of the situation permitted. If the unruly mob of fans had not descended on him as he caught the ball and jarred it loose, he likely would have been able to exercise complete and secure control over it. The court should be wary of establishing a rule that sanctions mob rule in the stands. A ruling for Hayashi would signal to fans everywhere that a ball is fair game as long as no one exercises complete control over it. As a result, fans would have a strong incentive to assault other fans right before they could gain possession of a ball. This form of competition is not socially beneficial. Hence, the court should establish a clear rule that interference from other fans cannot deprive the original possessor of his property rights in the ball. Allowing Popov to bring suit against the mob that jarred the ball loose from his glove is unsatisfactory for several reasons. First, it is impossible for Popov to show that but for the actions of the mob, he would have established complete control over the ball. Second, because the mob was quite large, it is impossible to determine which fans were acting maliciously and which fans were inadvertently pulled into the mix. Hence, even though Hayashi is not guilty of any wrongdoing himself, he should not be able to profit from the wrongdoing of others.	The standard rule in property law is that an individual must demonstrate full control over an object before he is deemed to have possession of that object. Popov did not have complete possession of the ball before it came loose. If the ball had been jarred loose because Popov collided with an inanimate wall, he could not argue that he had possession of the ball. This case is no different, because Hayashi did not cause the ball to fall out of Popov's glove. A ruling for Hayashi would not tend to encourage physical fighting for the ball because Hayashi was an innocent bystander, not a part of the mob that attacked Popov. The law should not allow those who use force to take baseballs from other fans to profit from their force. But if the ball comes loose before any fan establishes certain possession of it, any other fan who did not intentionally cause the ball to come loose may capture the rights to the ball by gaining possession of it. A ruling for Hayashi does not leave Popov without a remedy. He is free to bring suit against the fans who mobbed him and caused the ball to come loose from his glove. If he can demonstrate that they deprived him of control over the ball, he can recover the value of the ball from them. That result is the most fair because the unruly fans were the wrongdoers in this case, not Hayashi.

Questions & Problems

1. Explain which type of property each of the following is:
   a. A tree
   b. Lumber
   c. A car
   d. A built-in oven

2. What is the difference between a gift *causa mortis* and an *inter vivos* gift?

3. How is lost property different from mislaid property, and why is that distinction important?

4. What is the relationship between the rights of the bailee and the duties of the bailor?

5. The Daisy Keith Trust (of which Thomas Max Nygaard was trustee) obtained title to royalty interest in certain oil and gas wells. Sometime in the early 1980s, Getty Oil Company, later succeeded by Chevron Texaco, began oil and gas production from the wells. Nygaard received a letter from Texaco informing him that the production from the wells had yielded royalties which were due to the Daisy Keith Trust. Nygaard received a check for the amount Texaco claimed was due. In July 1996, Nygaard contacted Texaco, claiming that additional royalties were due. The claim was supported by an "independent study." Texaco responded by sending Ronnie Martin and Daniel P. Loughry to meet with Nygaard on December 3, 1998. No agreement was reached. On June 4, 2002, Nygaard, in his capacity as trustee, filed suit for unpaid royalties. The defendants filed motions for summary judgment, asserting that the statute of limitations barred Nygaard's claims. The trial court granted summary judgment. Nygaard appealed, alleging that the trial court applied an incorrect statute of limitations, as it applied the statute for personal property (with a three-year statute of limitation), but Nygaard argues that the mineral interests are actually real property (with a 10-year statute of limitation). Are mineral rights personal property or real property? Why? [*Nygaard v. Getty Oil Co.,* 918 So. 2d 1237 (Miss. 2005).]

6. Ellen Brin filed an action against Roger Stutzman to recover several articles of personal property. Brin and Stutzman had previously been involved in a relationship, but the relationship had since been completely terminated. Brin demanded that Stutzman return several pieces of personal property, including a computer and a treadmill. The trial record indicated that Brin transferred the computer to Stutzman "on the condition that [Stutzman] would eventually marry her, as this was her perception." In her testimony, Brin indicated that she had lent the treadmill to Stutzman for his personal use. Brin claims that the computer and treadmill were not intended as gifts. Do you think the court agreed? Should the property be returned to Brin? Why or why not? [*Brin v. Stutzman,* 951 P.3d 291 (1998).]

7. Defendant Tubbs met her fiancé, Church, over the Internet. After several years of correspondence and visits, they became engaged in February 2000. Church and Tubbs planned to be married in Las Vegas in July 2000. Two months before the engagement, Church paid off $4,100 of Tubbs's credit card debt. He also gave Tubbs an engagement ring that he purchased for $7,274.42. On March 15, 2000, he deposited $194,852.56 in Tubbs's bank account to fund the purchase of land and a residential home in Michigan. Tubbs purchased the home in both of their names as joint tenants, on Church's instructions, and in April she moved in. Church moved some personal property to the residence, including a family heirloom diamond ring. On June 5, 2000, Tubbs e-mailed Church stating that their relationship was over because she was horrified after seeing his "bizarre and abnormal behavior" on the Internet and because she had discovered that he led a "risqué lifestyle as a cross-dresser and bi-sexual." Tubbs rejected Church's demands to repay the $4,100 and to return the engagement ring, his personal property, and her interest in the Michigan home. On July 24, 2000, Church died in England.

   Church's estate subsequently filed suit to recover the property. The court entered a final judgment entitling the estate to the rings or a money judgment for their values; the real property, partitioned as a matter of law to account for its appreciation; complete right, title, interest, and possession of the land and residential home, free and clear of any claim, right, title, or interest of Tubbs; and a money judgment in the amount of $75,000 (the amount of Tubbs's home equity mortgage), less credits to Tubbs of $13,000 for property taxes she paid from 2000 through 2005, or a modified money judgment in the amount of $62,000. Tubbs appealed. What arguments might she have made on appeal? How do you think the appellate court ruled in this case, and why? [*Salens v. Tubbs,* 2008 WL 4072342 (C.A.6 Mich.).]

8. Davis and Hansen own adjacent lots. When Davis bought his lot in 1984, the warranty deed contained an easement across the lot he was purchasing to the property now owned by Hansen. The easement in the deed to Davis from the seller, Rodgers, stated that the easement on the land "shall be only for the benefit of Grantor [Rodgers], his grantees, heirs and assigns." Davis had been advised by a lawyer that the easement was not legally enforceable, so Davis put a garden on the easement area. Hansen bought his lot in 2006 and offered Davis $5,000 for an easement to access the property. Davis said no. Hansen then purchased the easement written in 1984 from Rodgers' widow, who had inherited Rodger's property.

Once he had bought the easement, Hansen told Davis he was going to use his easement and he immediately cleared the easement on Davis's property for a road and water and sewer lines. Davis then sued Hansen for trespass. Hansen counter-sued, seeking to prove ownership of the easement. The trial court ruled in favor of Davis, holding that Hansen had engaged in adverse possession of the easement by planting a garden over the easement, which extinguished it, and ordered Hansen to pay $13,345 in "restoration" damages. Hansen appealed. What do you believe happened on appeal? Why? *Hansen v. Davis,* 220 P.3d 911 (Sup. Ct., Alaska, 2009)

9. Sherman Hawkins is an inmate at Montana State Prison. Hawkins escaped from prison on July 12, 1997. After his escape, the prison officials placed Hawkins's personal property in a box and removed it from his cell. Two days later, Hawkins was caught and returned to the prison. Though he requested the return of his personal property, prison officials allowed him to retain only his legal papers and legal materials. Hawkins was informed that his property was considered abandoned and would be destroyed. The property included a television, a stereo, a word processor, glasses, and books. Hawkins argued that his personal property was not abandoned. Because he was returned to the prison within two days and the prison officials had retained possession of his personal property, Hawkins believed that the property should have been returned. Do you think the court agreed with him? Was the property abandoned? [*Hawkins v. Mahoney,* 990 P.2d 776 (1999).]

10. Thomas A. Carella filed for Chapter 7 bankruptcy. At the time, HSBC Bank USA held the sum of $16,540.94 on deposit in a joint bank account in the names of Carella and his father, Thomas J. Carella. The son sought to protect the money in the bank account, arguing that it was his father's account. The father had set up the joint account after finding out he needed to undergo heart bypass surgery. The father argues that he set up the joint account for convenience so that his son would have access to the money should the father pass away. The father survived the surgery and continued to manage the joint account. Only the father deposited or withdrew money from the account at any time. The son's bankruptcy trustee argued that the account was a gift *causa mortis* and thus is available as part of the bankruptcy. Did the joint account constitute a gift *causa mortis?* What are the necessary elements for establishing the joint account as a gift *causa mortis?* [*In re Thomas A. Carella,* 340 B.R. 710 (Bankr. W.D.N.Y. 2006).]

Looking for more review material?

The Online Learning Center at **www.mhhe.com/kubasek2e** contains this chapter's "Assignment on the Internet" and also a list of URLs for more information, entitled "On the Internet." Find both of them in the Student Center portion of the OLC, along with quizzes and other helpful materials.

CASE OPENER
Economic Redevelopment in Poletown

General Motors wanted to expand its facility, but when the company offered to purchase the property it needed, the owners would not accept the offers. The firm then approached the Detroit Economic Development Corporation with a request that the corporation use its power of eminent domain to acquire a large parcel of land on which members of the plaintiff organization, Poletown Neighborhood Council, resided and had small businesses. Once the corporation had acquired the land, it would be conveyed to General Motors for its plant expansion. The justification for the use of eminent domain was the creation of jobs for the economically depressed area.

The plaintiffs, who did not want their community destroyed, sued the city and the development corporation on the grounds that they were abusing their power of eminent domain to take private property for a private use.

1. Can business managers ask the city to buy real property for them when the owners do not wish to sell it?

2. What would determine whether the government can legally take the property for the corporation?

The Wrap-Up at the end of the chapter will answer these questions.

Ownership of real property seems to be one of the goals of most people in the United States. In this chapter we examine the nature of real property, the types of interests someone can own in real property, and how those interests can be transferred. As the opening scenario implies, transfers can be either voluntary or involuntary.

The Nature of Real Property

Real property, commonly referred to as *realty,* is land and everything permanently attached to it. The type of ownership interest a person has in a piece of property determines his or her rights to the property. In the next section, we describe these interests in detail. They may be conveyed or transferred under legal guidelines for property rights, most often voluntarily. However, for the benefit of the public, and to protect public health, safety, and welfare, the government may require involuntary transfers of property.

The definition of real property seems straightforward, but applying it is not always easy. Many disputes over whether an item is real or personal property have revolved around whether the item really is permanently attached. The courts have generally held that a given item is attached if its removal would hinder the functioning of the structure. Because removing built-in appliances would damage a building, these are held to be part of the real property; a freestanding appliance is personal property. Items not permanently attached but essential to the use of the building have been ruled part of the real property.

FIXTURES

A **fixture** is an item that was originally a piece of personal property but became part of the realty after it was permanently attached to the real property in question. For example, if a tenant installs a built-in dishwasher in the property he is renting, the dishwasher becomes part of the real property. When he leaves, the tenant may not take the dishwasher with him. However, there are two exceptions to this rule.

The first arises when there is a written agreement between the parties that specific features will be treated as personal property. The second exception applies to personal property attached to realty for the use of a business renting the property. Such items are known as *trade fixtures* and are treated as personal property on the basis of the presumption that neither party intends such fixtures to become a permanent part of the realty. For example, if a businessperson rents a storefront for a barbershop and installs barber chairs, these chairs are trade fixtures. If the businessperson relocates, he will need the chairs at a new location, and the next tenant will have her own needs.

This exception did not hold true, however, in a case in an Arizona state appellate court. Two air service businesses, Air Commerce Center, LLP, and Airport Properties, leased public land at Scottsdale Municipal Airport. Airport Properties had built air service–related improvements that it believed were trade fixtures. However, the court found that the improvements were the property of the city. Thus, if there is any concern on the part of the tenant about how improvements will be treated, it is best to get an agreement in writing if the tenant wants to retain possession of the material used in improving the property.

Legal Principle: A fixture is created when an item that was originally a piece of personal property is permanently attached to real property, thus becoming a part of the realty.

Exhibit 49-1
Extent of Real Property
Rights

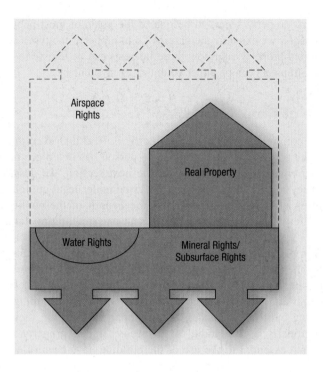

EXTENT OF OWNERSHIP

The landowner's rights to property go beyond simply the surface of the land. The airspace above the land, extending to the atmosphere, is also part of the legal concept of real property. Rights to airspace generally do not generate much controversy, but occasionally disputes arise over aircraft flying over individuals' property. A tree's branches may hang into the airspace of the property next door, and the owner of that airspace is entitled to cut them.

In dense, commercial urban areas, airspace may actually be an asset. Owners of two commercial buildings might want to build an overhead walkway adjoining their buildings across a parking lot you own. They will have to pay you handsomely for the right to build in your airspace.

The owner of real property also has *water rights,* the legal ability to use water flowing across or underneath the property. However, these rights are somewhat restricted; an owner cannot deprive landowners downstream of the use of the water by diverting it elsewhere.

Finally, ownership of real property extends to *mineral rights.* The landowner has the legal ability to dig or mine materials from the earth below the surface and may sell or give these rights to another. Ownership of these *subsurface rights* includes the right to enter onto the property to remove the underground materials.

The landowner's rights to property are illustrated in Exhibit 49-1.

Interests in Real Property

LO1

What are the interests in real property that someone can hold?

Interests in land range from temporary to permanent to future. The duration of a person's ownership interest and the power he or she has over use of the land depend on the type of *estate* the person holds. We discuss the various estates below and summarize them in Exhibit 49-2.

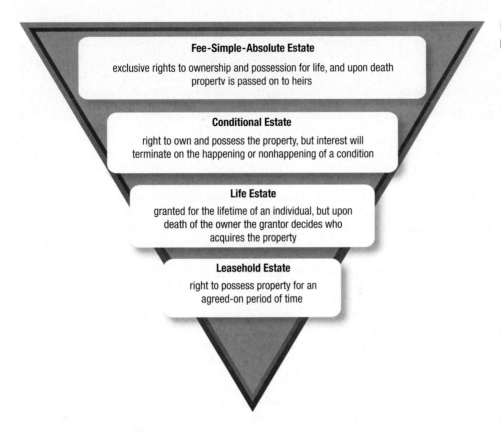

Exhibit 49-2
Hierarchy of Estates

FEE SIMPLE ABSOLUTE

A **fee simple absolute** is the most complete estate a person may have; it grants exclusive rights to ownership and possession of the land and is what most people refer to when they speak of "buying" a house or piece of land. This interest passes to the heirs when the owner dies.

CONDITIONAL ESTATE

The owner of a **conditional estate** possesses the same interest as the owner of a fee simple absolute, but it is subject to a condition. Should a prohibited event occur or a required event fail to occur, the interest will be terminated. Todd may be given property rights to a Victorian house on the condition that he preserve it in its original form. If he violates this condition by turning the house into a piano showroom or a beer hall, the house will either revert to the original owner or be transferred in accordance with the terms of the *deed,* the instrument used to convey real property.

LIFE ESTATE

A **life estate** is granted for the lifetime of an individual. On the death of this life holder, the property will go to another party designated by the original grantor. This future owner has an interest in seeing that the life tenant does not *waste* the property; if the life holder neglects or abuses the property, or fails to make necessary repairs such that its value diminishes, the future holder can bring legal action to recover damages for waste.

Case 49-1 illustrates what the courts have found as constituting waste.

SAULS v. CROSBY
DISTRICT COURT OF APPEALS OF FLORIDA
258 SO. 2D 326 (1972)

Annie Sauls, the defendant-appellant, conveyed a future interest in certain property to plaintiff-appellees Dan and Bertha Crosby and reserved a life estate in it. She attempted to cut timber on the property to sell, and the holders of the future interest sought to enjoin her from doing so. The district court held that Sauls was not entitled to cut timber and keep the proceeds for herself. She appealed the lower court's ruling.

JUDGE RAWLS: On the 9th day of October 1968, appellant conveyed to appellees certain lands situated in Hamilton County, Florida, with the following reservation set forth in said conveyance: "The Grantor herein, reserves a life estate in said property." By this appeal appellant now contends that the trial court erred in denying her, as a life tenant, the right to cut merchantable timber and enjoy the proceeds.

The English common law, which was transplanted on this continent, holds that it is waste for an ordinary life tenant to cut timber upon his estate when the sole purpose is to clear the woodlands. American courts today as a general rule recognize that an ordinary life tenant may cut timber and not be liable for waste if he uses the timber for fuel; for repairing fences and buildings on the estate; for fitting the land for cultivation; or for use as pasture if the inheritance is not damaged and the acts are conformable to good husbandry; and for thinning or other purposes which are necessary for the enjoyment of the estate and are in conformity with good husbandry.

In this jurisdiction a tenant for life or a person vested with an ordinary life estate is entitled to the use and enjoyment of his estate during its existence. The only restriction on the life tenant's use and enjoyment is that he not permanently diminish or change the value of the future estate of the remainderman. This limitation places on the "ordinary life tenant" the responsibility for all waste of whatever character.

An instrument creating a life tenancy may absolve the tenant of responsibility for waste by stating that the life tenant has the power to consume or that the life tenant is without impeachment for waste. Thus, there is a sharp distinction in the rights of an ordinary life tenant or life tenant without impeachment for waste or life tenant who has the power to consume. An ordinary life tenant has no right to cut the timber from an estate for purely commercial reasons and so to do is tortious conduct for which the remainderman may sue immediately.

In the case before us, the trial court was concerned with the rights of an ordinary life tenant and correctly concluded that appellant does not have the right to cut merchantable timber from the land involved in this suit unless the proceeds of such cutting and sale are held in trust for the use and benefit of the remaindermen. . . .

AFFIRMED in favor of plaintiff.

CRITICAL THINKING

What fact could you add to this case that would change the outcome?

ETHICAL DECISION MAKING

In rendering his decision, the judge gave primary weight to the interests of which stakeholders?

Legal Principle: **Waste occurs when the holder of a life estate uses the property in a way that reduces the value of the estate that the future holder will receive; it is unlawful.**

FUTURE INTEREST

The plaintiffs in Case 49-1 held a **future interest** in the estate, a present right to property ownership and possession in the future. Such an interest usually exists in conjunction

Property Interests in Vietnam

In the United States, we take for granted the right to purchase a piece of property if we have the money to do so. Property is not so freely available and transferable in all nations. Vietnam's new constitution, written in 1992, provides guidelines for the allocation, transfer, and sale of private property. However, it still asserts that the people, or the state, own all the land. Thus, if individuals or private enterprises want to use land, they must pay tax on it as a form of rent and are granted a "use of right" which entitles them to extended use and the freedom to transfer the property. Technically, they are transferring not the *property,* but rather the right to use it.

Transference of property can occur only with the approval of a state official. The official ensures the new owner intends to use the land for the original, state-approved purpose. Moreover, the new owner can never be given a longer term of right or more extensive rights over the land than the original owner had. Finally, the state official determines the price that the property will be transferred for. The government has specified certain prices depending on how the land is used.

with a life estate or a conditional estate. Suppose José owns a life estate in Oak Hills Apartments and on his death the property will pass to Sarah with fee-simple-absolute rights. Sarah holds a future interest in Oak Hills Apartments, and if José allows the buildings to deteriorate from neglect, she may sue to enjoin him from engaging in waste of the property.

LEASEHOLD ESTATE

The holder of a **leasehold** has a possessory but not an ownership interest. This interest is transferred by a contract known as a *lease.* Both the owner of the property (the lessor, or landlord) and the tenant (the lessee) sign the lease. The contract generally specifies the property to be leased, the amount of the rent payments and when they are due, the duration of the leasehold, and any special rights or duties of either party. A leasehold gives the lessee, or tenant, exclusive rights to the use and possession of the land, including the right to exclude the property owner under most circumstances, for the term specified by the lease.

The tenant's and landlord's rights and obligations may vary according to the lease, but some states require that landlords keep the property in good condition for the tenant's use, giving the tenant the right to withhold rent payments should the landlord fail to do so. Should the tenant fail to make the agreed-on payments *without* such grounds, the landlord may evict the tenant. The landlord is not allowed to enter the property, except in an emergency or when the tenant has given permission to make repairs. Near the end of the leasehold, the landlord may enter with notice to the tenant for the purpose of showing the property to a potential new tenant.

Subleasing of the property by the tenant to another party is permissible unless specifically prohibited by the lease. However, the initial tenant is liable throughout the entire term of the lease for payment of the rent to the landlord. We discuss leases in greater detail in Chapter 50, "Landlord-Tenant Law."

NONPOSSESSORY ESTATE

While most people think of interests in land as being possessory in nature, easements, profits, and licenses do not include the right to possess the property.

Easements and Profits. Easements and profits are similar in that they are neither ownership nor possessory interests. An **easement** is an irrevocable right to use some part of another's land for a specific purpose without taking anything from it. A **profit** is the right to go onto someone's land and take part of the land or a product of it away from the land. If Rashon has the right to drive his car across Jenny's property to get to his property, he has an easement, but if he has the right to go onto her property and remove the topsoil he needs from it for his landscaping business, he has a profit.

Owners of real property with a public easement have many rights regarding the land because they still own the fee. A construction manager, Albert Taub, believed that he could remove large quantities of dirt for his construction project from a public drainage easement because his actions improved the drainage. However, the court ruled that only the fee owner or the city could alter the property to improve the drainage and that Taub had no right to alter the easement.[1]

An easement or profit is *appurtenant* when it runs with land adjacent to the property on which it exists. If Rashon's property is adjacent to Jenny's, he has an easement (or profit) appurtenant, which only he can use and which can be transferred only in conjunction with the transfer of his property.

Easements or profits *in gross* are not dependent on owning property adjacent to the land on which the nonpossessory interest exists. The gas company may obtain an easement in gross to run gas lines across someone's property.

Easements and profits can be transferred by express agreement, inheritance, necessity, implication, or prescription. Transfer by *express agreement* occurs when the landowner expressly grants the agreed-on use of the land to the holder of the easement, such as allowing a farmer to run a ditch across part of his neighbor's property to drain a field. This easement should be recorded in the appropriate county office or described on the deed to protect the holder of the easement if the property is sold. If the transfer of the interest is to be by *inheritance,* its terms are simply incorporated into the property owner's will.

An **easement by prescription** is created by state law when certain conditions are met. In most states, if someone openly uses a portion of another's property for a statutory period (usually 25 years), an easement arises by law. If a piece of property is divided and one portion is landlocked as a result, an *easement by necessity* is created. For purposes of entrance to and exit from the land, the owner of the landlocked parcel has an easement to cross the other portion.

If the land that benefits from the easement or profit is sold, the nonpossessory interest goes with the property. Thus, if Rashon sold his land to Sonny, Sonny would also receive the easement across Jenny's property. If Jenny sold her property, the new owner would have the burden of Rashon's easement as long as it had been properly recorded. Of course, just as easements and profits can be created, they can also be terminated, most often by agreement. The easement holder may simply deed the easement back to the property owner. If the easement arose by necessity and the necessity no longer exists, the easement terminates.

An *easement by implication,* sometimes called *easement by necessity,* is said to exist when a piece of property is divided into two parcels in such a way that an already existing, obvious, and continuous use of the first parcel (such as for access) is necessary for the reasonable enjoyment of the second parcel. The owner of the second parcel has an easement by implication on the first parcel.

License.   A **license** is a temporary and revocable right to use another's property. Someone who purchases a theater ticket has the right to a specific use of the property for a limited time, subject to good behavior. No property interest goes to the license holder.

---

[1] *Gleason v. Taub,* 180 S.W.3d 711 (Tex. App. 2005).

Co-ownership

An interest in real property may be owned by a single individual, two or more persons, or a corporation. When more than one person possesses the same property rights, **co-ownership** exists. The type of co-ownership determines the ownership rights.

TENANCY IN COMMON

Tenancy in common is the most common type of co-ownership. It gives each co-owner the right to sell his or her interest without the consent of the others, to own an unequal share of the property, and to have a creditor attach his or her interest. The heirs of a tenancy in common receive the property interest on the tenant's death.

JOINT TENANCY

Joint tenants, like tenants in common, may sell their shares without the consent of the other owners, as well as have their interest attached by creditors. However, joint tenants all own *equal* shares of the property, and on the death of one the property is divided equally among the surviving joint owners.

TENANCY BY THE ENTIRETY

Tenancy by the entirety describes co-ownership by married couples: One owner cannot sell his or her interest without the other's consent, and creditors of one owner cannot attach the property. If one owner dies, the surviving spouse assumes full ownership. If the owners divorce, the interest becomes a tenancy in common.

In each of the three types of co-ownership, all tenants have the equal right to occupy all the property. This characteristic and others are listed in Exhibit 49-3.

CONDOMINIUMS AND COOPERATIVES

Two types of joint ownership are popular in this country, especially in cities. One is the *condominium* interest. It gives the holder exclusive ownership rights of a unit within the condominium and tenancy in common with the other condominium owners over the land, buildings, and improvements of the common areas of the development. The architecture

Exhibit 49-3
Joint Ownership

TYPE OF OWNERSHIP	POSSIBLE DIVISION OF OWNERSHIP	RIGHTS OF OWNERS' CREDITORS	OWNERSHIP OF PROPERTY UPON DEATH OF AN OWNER
Tenancy in Common	Shares can be equal or unequal.	Creditors can attach any owner's interest.	Deceased owner's share is transferred to heirs.
Joint Tenancy	Shares are equal.	Creditors can attach any owner's interest.	Deceased owner's share is divided among other joint tenants.
Tenancy by the Entirety	Shares are equal.	Owner's creditors cannot attach interest.	Deceased owner's share goes to surviving spouse.

and use of common areas are regulated by a condominium association, which has the power to levy assessments against the unit owners for maintenance of these areas. This association is directed by a *Declaration of Covenants, Conditions and Restrictions (CC&Rs)*, filed when the condominium is formed.

The second type of joint ownership is a *cooperative.* Here, the investor resident is a shareholder in the corporation owning (usually) an apartment building and receives a permanent lease on one unit of the facility upon acquiring stock. All the unit owners are governed by a board of directors, usually elected from among the unit owners to manage the property and establish rules for the owners. If a member violates these rules, the cooperative may evict the member and repurchase the evicted member's unit. In many cooperatives, before an apartment can be sold, the board must approve the buyer.

Voluntary Transfer of Real Property

LEGAL REQUIREMENTS

LO2

How is real property voluntarily transferred?

An owner may generally transfer any or all of his or her property to anyone for any price or no price, as the owner desires. This ability to transfer real property is part of the value of property.

The legal procedures that must be followed to effectuate such a transfer are *execution, delivery, acceptance,* and *recording,* with the last one being required to protect the recipient of the property. These procedures are outlined in Exhibit 49-4. The conveyance that results from following these procedural steps is presumed to be the conveyance of a fee simple absolute, unless the contrary is stated.

Execution.   Transfer of property is initiated by the *execution* (or preparation and signing) of the deed, which is the instrument of conveyance. There are different types of deeds, but any properly drafted deed must contain the following:

1. Identification of the *grantor,* the person conveying the property, and the *grantee,* the person receiving the property.
2. An expression of the grantor's intent to convey the property.

Exhibit 49-4   Steps in Voluntary Transfer of Property

Execution	Delivery	Acceptance	Recording
The deed must be properly drafted and signed by the granter and grantee	The deed must be given to the grantee with the intent of transferring ownership to the grantee	The grantee must express intent to possess property by accepting the deed	The deed should be properly filed

3. A legally sufficient description of the property, including its physical boundaries and any easements.

4. Any warranties or promises made by the grantor in conjunction with the conveyance.

The most commonly used deed, the **general warranty deed,** contains certain warranties or promises by the grantor. Such covenants may vary slightly by state but generally promise that:

1. The grantor owns the interest he or she is conveying.

2. The grantor has the right to convey the property.

3. There are no mortgages or liens against the property unless stated in the deed.

4. The grantee will not be disturbed by anyone who has a better claim to title of the property, and the grantor will defend the grantee's title against such claims or reimburse any money spent in their defense and/or settlement.

5. The grantor will provide any additional documents the grantee needs to perfect his or her title to the property.

A grantor may not necessarily feel comfortable making all those warranties and may instead execute a **special warranty deed,** which promises only that he or she has not done anything to lessen the value of the estate.

From the grantee's perspective, the least desirable type of deed is the **quitclaim deed.** It carries no warranties; the grantor simply conveys whatever interests he or she holds. Thus, if the grantor had a defective title, the grantee receives a defective title. Because of the insecurity of such a deed, very few grantees accept it.

Once a deed of any type has been properly drafted and signed by the grantor and grantee, it has been *executed.* In many states, it must also be witnessed or notarized. *Notarization* is certification by an official of the state that she or he saw the signing of the deed and was provided evidence that the signatories were who they claimed to be.

Delivery.   The next step in legal transfer of property is the *delivery* of the deed to the grantee, directly or through a third party, with the intent of transferring ownership.

Acceptance.   *Acceptance* is the grantee's expression of intent to possess the property, and it is assumed if the grantee retains possession of the deed.

Recording.   Recording is achieved by filing the deed, including any related documents such as mortgages, with the appropriate county office, thus giving the world official notice of the transfer. Although it is not a required step, recording is so important a protection of the grantee's rights that it should be part of every transfer. In fact, if two deeds allegedly convey the same piece of realty, many states give ownership to the person whose deed was recorded first.

Legal Principle: **To ensure that ownership of the property is transferred, the parties must follow the requisite steps of execution, delivery, acceptance, and recording of the deed.**

SALES TRANSACTIONS

Above we discussed the legal steps necessary for transfer of property. Now let's take a closer look at the actual sales process that generally leads to such a transfer.

Negotiation of a sales contract.   Generally, a person seeking to sell real property will contact a real estate agent, or broker. A broker is licensed by the state in which he or she operates and is familiar with real estate law, as well as available properties.

In exchange for a commission on the sale, the broker advertises the property, shows it to potential buyers, and guides the seller through the formalities of the transfer.

In most states, a broker cannot act for both buyer and seller (given their different interests) unless both parties consent. In some states, when the buyer does not have a broker or lawyer as a representative in the transaction, the seller's broker may handle all the necessary paperwork, but the buyer must sign a statement that acknowledges that he or she knows that the broker is working exclusively for the seller.

Once the buyer finds a desired property, she makes a written offer to purchase under specified conditions and puts up *earnest money* designed to establish the seriousness of her offer. If the seller accepts the offer, the earnest money will apply toward the purchase price. If the buyer changes her mind before the seller accepts, she forfeits the earnest money. If the seller does not accept the offer, the money is returned. Because the residents of Poletown did not accept General Motors' offer, they would have had to return any earnest money the company might have put up.

Failure to accept within the time limit in the offer is considered a rejection. As with any contract, the seller may make a counteroffer at a different price or under different conditions.

Once the offer has been accepted, a sales contract is drawn up in accordance with the offer's terms. The contract will generally include a description of the property, the names and addresses of the parties, the purchase price, the type of deed, and who will bear the risk of loss if the property is destroyed before the sale has been completed.

The contract generally requires that the buyer put a deposit in an *escrow account* maintained by a neutral third party until all the preliminary steps to the transfer can be made. The deposit, which varies in size depending on the part of the country and local custom, but is often around 10 percent of the purchase price, will be turned over to the seller at the *closing,* when the transfer is completed.

Seller's Duty to Disclose.   To what extent does the seller have a duty to disclose known defects to the buyer? The traditional answer was *caveat emptor,* or "Let the buyer beware," meaning that the seller had no obligation to tell the buyer about any problems. Can you tell which value is being replaced in the current move to a standard based more on reasonableness?

Today, most states require that the seller warn the buyer about any known defects that (1) the reasonable buyer could not discover through a thorough examination of the property and (2) materially affect the property's value. If the seller fails to disclose and the buyer discovers the defect only after the sales transaction has been completed, the buyer can sue the seller for fraud or misrepresentation.

Most states assume an implied warranty of habitability in the sale of a new home. With this warranty, comparable to the implied warranty of merchantability, the seller guarantees that everything in the house is of sound construction and in reasonable working order. If you purchased a new home during the winter and in warmer weather discovered the air conditioning did not run, you could sue the seller for breach of the implied warranty of habitability if he refused to fix the defective air conditioner.

Title Examination.   While the buyer's deposit is in escrow, a title company or representative of the buyer or seller will search the county records to make sure the seller in fact has legal title to the property, there are no liens on it, and there are no restrictions of which the buyer is not aware. A title free of such defects is called a marketable title.

If a material defect is found in the search that has not been disclosed in the sales contract, the seller has breached the contract. The buyer can file an action to rescind the agreement, obtain damages, or get an order for specific performance with a price reduction. A dispute arose between Sun International and Greenlands Realty during a title examination. Sun was attempting to purchase property from Greenlands but sought to void the sale, claiming that Greenlands did not possess marketable title to the property because a different, and then-defunct, realty company held part of the title. The court granted a motion for summary judgment in Greenlands' favor, determining that the defunct company had conveyed all its title in the property and therefore Greenlands did possess marketable title.

A title search may not reveal every single defect in the title, however, so most buyers purchase title insurance or have the seller purchase it for them. Title insurance protects the buyer from losses resulting from a defect in the title.

Financing.   Most buyers do not have the cash to purchase property, so most sales contracts are conditional on the buyer's being able to obtain financing within a certain period of time. In exchange for such a loan, the lender receives a security interest in the property, called a *mortgage.* While the buyer makes payments to the mortgagor or lender, the mortgagor or a third party holds title to the property and can sell it if the payments are not made.

Closing.   The closing is the meeting at which the transfer of title actually takes place and delivery and acceptance occur. The seller signs over the deed, and the buyer gives the seller a check for the amount due. If a mortgage was necessary, it is executed at this time. Following the closing, the deed and mortgage are recorded.

Involuntary Transfer of Real Property

The transfer of the owner's interest in real property is not always voluntary. It can occur without the owner's knowledge and even, in some cases, against his or her will, by either adverse possession or condemnation.

LO3

How is real property involuntarily transferred?

ADVERSE POSSESSION

In adverse possession, a person takes ownership of real property by treating it as his or her own, without protest or permission from the owner. Most states have established a length of time after which such a possessor receives ownership interest in the property. The adverse possession must be *actual* (the person lives on or uses the land as an owner would), *open* (not secretive), and *notorious* (without the owner's permission). In some states, the adverse possessor must have performed certain acts such as paying real estate taxes. In other states, the adverse possessor must operate "under color of title," or the assumption that he or she actually held title to the land.

The law is similar in Japan, where adverse possession for 20 years leads to a transfer of ownership as long as the possessor began with a nonnegligent good-faith belief that he or she had legal title to the property.

Legal Principle: **Transfer by adverse possession occurs when the adverse possession is actual, open (not secretive), and notorious for the amount of time specified by the state.**

CONDEMNATION

Condemnation is the legal process by which a transfer of property is made against the protest of the property owner. As you will remember from Chapter 5's discussion of the takings clause of the Fifth Amendment, the government has a constitutional right to take private property for the use of the public, upon providing the owner fair compensation.

This right is sometimes exercised on behalf of a private company operating to benefit the public. In the Poletown case, a private business argued that the creation of new jobs was essential to the economic future of the area, and reducing unemployment through job creation took precedence over the residents' individual property rights.

When the government decides to exercise its power of eminent domain, it will first offer to purchase the property for what it believes is the fair market value. If the owner does not want to sell or feels the price is too low, the government will initiate a condemnation proceeding and the court will determine whether it has a valid claim of legitimate public purpose. If it does, the court will determine, and the government will pay the owner, the fair market value of the property, and the property will be transferred to the government.

It is sometimes difficult to determine whether the exercise of eminent domain is actually for the public's benefit when the property will be conveyed to another private individual. In the Poletown case, a private corporation will clearly benefit from the government's taking of the residents' property. Could this benefit be for a public use? Since the 1980s, businesses have increasingly appealed to cities to exercise eminent domain to acquire land the owners did not want to sell, and state supreme courts have begun to address whether economic development is a public use under the constraints of the Fifth Amendment. Some courts found that job creation and expansion of the tax base did constitute public use. The U.S. Supreme Court finally settled the issue—at least for the present—in the 5–4 decision in Case 49-2. As you read it, ask yourself whether there are any significant differences between the facts in *Poletown* and those in Case 49-2.

CASE 49-2   KELO v. CITY OF NEW LONDON
UNITED STATES SUPREME COURT
126 S. CT. 326 (2005)

The city of New London approved an integrated development plan designed "to create in excess of 1,000 jobs, to increase tax and other revenues, and to revitalize an economically distressed city, including its downtown and waterfront areas." Using its development agent, the city purchased most of the property it needed for the project from willing sellers. A few property owners refused to sell, so the city initiated condemnation proceedings to take their property. The owners argued that this step would violate the "public use" restriction in the Fifth Amendment's Takings Clause. The trial court granted a permanent restraining order prohibiting the taking of some properties but allowing the taking of others. The Connecticut Supreme Court affirmed in part and reversed in part, upholding all the proposed takings. The United States Supreme Court agreed to hear the property owners' appeal.

JUSTICE STEVENS: . . . On the one hand, it has long been accepted that the sovereign may not take the property of A for the sole purpose of transferring it to another private

party B, even though A is paid just compensation. On the other hand, it is equally clear that a State may transfer property from one private party to another if future "use by the public" is the purpose of the taking. . . . Neither of these propositions, however, determines the disposition of this case.

As for the first proposition, the City would no doubt be forbidden from taking petitioners' land for the purpose of conferring a private benefit on a particular private party. . . . Nor would the City be allowed to take property under the mere pretext of a public purpose, when its actual purpose was to bestow a private benefit. The takings before us, however, would be executed pursuant to a "carefully considered" development plan. The trial judge and all the members of the Supreme Court of Connecticut agreed that there was no evidence of an illegitimate purpose in this case. Therefore, the City's development plan was not adopted "to benefit a particular class of identifiable individuals."

. . . On the other hand, this is not a case in which the City is planning to open the condemned land . . . to use by the general public. Nor will the private lessees of the land in any sense be required to operate like common carriers, making their services available to all comers. But . . . this "Court long ago rejected any literal requirement that condemned property be put into use for the general public."

The disposition of this case therefore turns on the question whether the City's development plan serves a "public purpose." . . . [O]ur cases have defined that concept broadly, reflecting our longstanding policy of deference to legislative judgments in this field. In *Berman v. Parker* (1954), this Court upheld a redevelopment plan targeting a blighted area of Washington, D.C., in which most of the housing for the area's 5,000 inhabitants was beyond repair. Under the plan, the area would be condemned and part of it utilized for the construction of streets, schools, and other public facilities. The remainder of the land would be leased or sold to private parties for the purpose of redevelopment, including the construction of low-cost housing. The owner of a department store located in the area challenged the condemnation, pointing out that his store was not itself blighted and arguing that the creation of a "better balanced, more attractive community" was not a valid public use. Justice Douglas refused to evaluate this claim in isolation, deferring instead to the legislative and agency judgment that the area "must be planned as a whole" for the plan to be successful. The Court explained that "community redevelopment programs need not, by force of the Constitution, be on a piecemeal basis—lot by lot, building by building." The public use underlying the taking was unequivocally affirmed. . . .

In *Hawaii Housing Authority v. Midkiff,* the Court considered a Hawaii statute whereby fee title was taken from lessors and transferred to lessees in order to reduce the concentration of land ownership. We unanimously upheld the statute and rejected the Ninth Circuit's view that it was "a naked attempt on the part of the state of Hawaii to take the property of A and transfer it to B solely for B's private use and benefit." Reaffirming *Berman's* deferential approach to legislative judgments in this field, we concluded that the State's purpose of eliminating the "social and economic evils of a land oligopoly" qualified as a valid public use. . . . "[I]t is only the taking's purpose, and not its mechanics," that matters in determining public use.

. . . For more than a century, our public use jurisprudence has wisely eschewed rigid formulas and intrusive scrutiny in favor of affording legislatures broad latitude in determining what public needs justify the use of the takings power.

Those who govern the City were not confronted with the need to remove blight in the Fort Trumbull area, but their determination that the area was sufficiently distressed to justify a program of economic rejuvenation is entitled to our deference. The City has carefully formulated an economic development plan that it believes will provide appreciable benefits to the community, including—but by no means

limited to—new jobs and increased tax revenue. . . . [T]he City is endeavoring to coordinate a variety of commercial, residential, and recreational uses of land, with the hope that they will form a whole greater than the sum of its parts. To effectuate this plan, the City has invoked a state statute that specifically authorizes the use of eminent domain to promote economic development. Given the comprehensive character of the plan, the thorough deliberation that preceded its adoption, and the limited scope of our review, it is appropriate for us, as it was in *Berman,* to resolve the challenges of the individual owners, not on a piecemeal basis, but rather in light of the entire plan. Because that plan unquestionably serves a public purpose, the takings challenged here satisfy the public use requirement of the Fifth Amendment.

To avoid this result, petitioners urge us to adopt a new bright-line rule that economic development does not qualify as a public use. . . . There is . . . no principled way of distinguishing economic development from the other public purposes that we have recognized.

Petitioners contend that using eminent domain for economic development impermissibly blurs the boundary between public and private takings. Again, our cases foreclose this objection. [T]he government's pursuit of a public purpose will often benefit individual private parties. . . . We cannot say that public ownership is the sole method of promoting the public purposes of community redevelopment projects.

It is further argued that without a bright-line rule nothing would stop a city from transferring citizen *A*'s property to citizen *B* for the sole reason that citizen *B* will put the property to a more productive use and thus pay more taxes. Such a one-to-one transfer of property, executed outside the confines of an integrated development plan, is not presented in this case. While such an unusual exercise of government power would certainly raise a suspicion that a private purpose was afoot, the hypothetical cases posited by petitioners can be confronted if and when they arise.

Alternatively, petitioners maintain that for takings of this kind we should require a "reasonable certainty" that the expected public benefits will actually accrue. Such a rule, however, would represent an even greater departure from our precedent. "When the legislature's purpose is legitimate and its means are not irrational, our cases make clear that empirical debates over the wisdom of takings—no less than debates over the wisdom of other kinds of socioeconomic legislation—are not to be carried out in the federal courts.". . . A constitutional rule that required postponement of the judicial approval of every condemnation until the likelihood of success of the plan had been assured would unquestionably impose a significant impediment to the successful consummation of many such plans.

Just as we decline to second-guess the City's considered judgments about the efficacy of its development plan, we also decline to second-guess the City's determinations as to what lands it needs to acquire in order to effectuate the project. . . . Once the question of the public purpose has been decided, the amount and character of land to be taken for the project and the need for a particular tract to complete the integrated plan rests in the discretion of the legislative branch.

. . . [N]othing in our opinion precludes any State from placing further restrictions on its exercise of the takings power. Indeed, many States already impose "public use" requirements that are stricter than the federal baseline. . . . This Court's authority, however, extends only to determining whether the City's proposed condemnations are for a "public use" within the meaning of the Fifth Amendment to the Federal Constitution.

AFFIRMED in favor of respondent City of New London.

JUSTICE O'CONNOR, WITH WHOM THE CHIEF JUSTICE, JUSTICE SCALIA, AND JUSTICE THOMAS JOIN, DISSENTING: Over two centuries ago, just after the Bill of Rights was ratified, Justice Chase wrote: ". . . [A] law that takes property from A. and gives it to B: It is against all reason and justice, for a people to entrust a Legislature with SUCH powers; and, therefore, it cannot be presumed that they have done it." . . .

Today the Court abandons this long-held, basic limitation on government power. Under the banner of economic development, all private property is now vulnerable to being taken and transferred to another private owner, so long as it might be upgraded—*i.e.,* given to an owner who will use it in a way that the legislature deems more beneficial to the public—in the process. To reason, as the Court does, that the incidental public benefits resulting from the subsequent ordinary use of private property render economic development takings "for public use" is to wash out any distinction between private and public use of property—and thereby effectively to delete the words "for public use" from the Takings Clause of the Fifth Amendment. Accordingly I respectfully dissent.

. . . [W]e have read the Fifth Amendment's language to impose two distinct conditions on the exercise of eminent domain: "the taking must be for a 'public use' and 'just compensation' must be paid to the owner." . . . These two limitations serve to protect "the security of Property." . . . Together they ensure stable property ownership by providing safeguards against excessive, unpredictable, or unfair use of the government's eminent domain power—particularly against those owners who, for whatever reasons, may be unable to protect themselves in the political process against the majority's will.

While the Takings Clause presupposes that government can take private property without the owner's consent, the just compensation requirement spreads the cost of condemnations and thus "prevents the public from loading upon one individual more than his just share of the burdens of government." . . . The public use requirement, in turn, imposes a more basic limitation, circumscribing the very scope of the eminent domain power: Government may compel an individual to forfeit her property for the *public's* use, but not for the benefit of another private person. This requirement promotes fairness as well as security. . . .

Where is the line between "public" and "private" property use? We give considerable deference to legislatures' determinations about what governmental activities will advantage the public. But were the political branches the sole arbiters of the public-private distinction, the Public Use Clause would amount to little more than hortatory fluff. An external, judicial check on how the public use requirement is interpreted, however limited, is necessary if this constraint on government power is to retain any meaning. . . . But "public ownership" and "use-by-the-public" are sometimes too constricting and impractical ways to define the scope of the Public Use Clause. Thus, we have allowed that, in certain circumstances and to meet certain exigencies, takings that serve a public purpose also satisfy the Constitution even if the property is destined for subsequent private use. . . .

The Court's holdings in *Berman* and *Midkiff* were true to the principle underlying the Public Use Clause. In both those cases, the extraordinary, precondemnation use of the targeted property inflicted affirmative harm on society—in *Berman* through blight resulting from extreme poverty and in *Midkiff* through oligopoly resulting from extreme wealth. And in both cases, the relevant legislative body had found that eliminating the existing property use was necessary to remedy the harm. Thus, a public purpose was realized when the harmful use was eliminated. Because each taking *directly* achieved a public benefit, it did not matter that the property was turned over to private use. Here, in contrast, New London does not claim that Susette Kelo's and Wilhelmina Dery's well-maintained homes are the source of any social harm. . . .

In moving away from our decisions sanctioning the condemnation of harmful property use, the Court today significantly expands the meaning of public use. It holds that the sovereign may take private property currently put to ordinary private use, and give it over for new, ordinary private use, so long as the new use is predicted to generate some secondary benefit for the public—such as increased tax revenue, more jobs, maybe even aesthetic pleasure. But nearly any lawful use of real private property can be said to generate some incidental benefit to the public. Thus, if predicted (or even guaranteed) positive side-effects are enough to render transfer from one private party to another constitutional, then the words "for public use" do not realistically exclude *any* takings, and thus do not exert any constraint on the eminent domain power.

CRITICAL THINKING

When you examine the reasoning in the majority and dissenting opinions, you can see a significant conflict because of the ambiguity of a key term. Identify this term, and explain how its interpretation affects the reasoning. How do you think the courts should define the term?

ETHICAL DECISION MAKING

Who are the primary stakeholders in this case? How are they affected by the ruling? What are the implications of this ruling in terms of the distinction between public and private property? Further, this case highlights an important value conflict. Can you explain how certain values would lead someone to support the majority opinion, whereas different values support the dissenting opinion? How might your values determine how you predict the implications of this ruling?

In *Kelo* and *Poletown,* government wants to take property from individuals to sell to companies, but sometimes the government seeks to take property from one company for use by another. In June 2000, Costco, a large retail chain, wanted to expand its warehouse in Lancaster, California. Afraid of losing the large store, which threatened to move if it could not expand, the city considered using eminent domain to acquire an adjacent 99 Cents Only store so that Costco could obtain the property. Even businesses may be at risk of losing their property to larger, more powerful firms.

State courts had been split fairly evenly over public use, so many people were surprised that the *Kelo* ruling generated a rare congressional outcry. Within a week, some members of Congress were drafting a bill attempting to limit the use of eminent domain for economic development purposes, while others were criticizing the proposed legislation as an unconstitutional attempt to interfere with the Supreme Court's exercise of its proper role.

The response to *Kelo* was dramatic and widespread. President George W. Bush issued an executive order limiting government's taking of private property to "situations in which the taking is for public use, with just compensation, and for the purpose of benefiting the general public, and not merely for the purpose of advancing the economic interest of private parties to be given ownership or use of the property taken." During the year and a half after *Kelo,* 30 state legislatures enacted statutes limiting the use of eminent domain. By some estimates, by 2009, 43 states had enacted new laws or adopted constitutional amendments aimed at preventing Kelo-type takings, typically by restricting the definition of public use to exclude economic development.[2]

Sadly, as of 2010, the land taken in the Kelo case was a vacant field because before the development was begun, Pfizer Corporation, whose research facility was to be the centerpiece of this new development, announced that it was pulling out of New London, so plans for the development were tabled.

To see how the use of eminent domain may distort market forces, please see the **Connecting to the Core** activity on the text Web site at www.mhhe.com/kubasek2e.

Restrictions on Land Use

No one is allowed to use land in a *completely* unrestricted manner; the doctrine of waste prohibits some uses and abuses of land. Other restrictions also exist, both voluntary and involuntary.

L04

How is the use of property restricted?

---

[2] James Ely, "A Report Card on Post-Kelo Eminent Domain Reforms," *OUPblog,* http://blog.oup.com/2009/03/eminent-domain/ (accessed October 10, 2010).

Restrictive Covenants

**Country Club Dist. Homes Assn. v.
Country Club Christian Church
Missouri Court of Appeals
118 S.W.3d 185 (Mo. Ct. App. 2003)**

All the property in the Hampstead Gardens Subdivision was covered by a restrictive covenant providing that "none of said lots shall be improved, used nor occupied for other than private residence purposes." The Country Club Christian Church owned three lots adjacent to the lot on which its church was located. It decided to turn these lots into parking lots, but the Country Club District Homeowners Association sued to enforce the restrictive covenant and obtain a permanent injunction. The trial court upheld the agreement and granted the injunction. The appellate court affirmed the lower court's ruling, stating that the terms of a restrictive covenant will not be enforced only where a defendant can prove that (1) there has been a radical change in conditions since the covenant was entered into, (2) as a result of the change, enforcement of the restriction will work an undue hardship on the defendant, and (3) continuing enforcement of the restriction provides no substantial benefit to the plaintiff. Given this standard, it is fairly easy to see why most restrictive covenants are upheld.

RESTRICTIVE COVENANTS

Property owners may voluntarily enter into **restrictive covenants,** that is, promises to use or not use their land in particular ways. These covenants, generally included in the deeds, are binding for lawful acts related to the land. A restrictive covenant not to construct only single-story dwelling houses on property is lawful and enforceable, whereas a covenant never to convey property to a woman is unlawful and unenforceable. A restriction that the land never be used for hog farming is related to the land and therefore valid, whereas a restriction that the owner always ride a bicycle to work is not. Finally, successors to the original makers of the covenant must have notice of it.

The most common use of restrictive covenants today is in urban developments sometimes called *planned communities.* Each deed binds the grantee to abide by community rules established by the developer and a homeowners' association. Such restrictions can be substantial, although some owners enjoy the assurance that their property will maintain its value. Courts will generally uphold these restrictive covenants. The Case Nugget above illustrates a typical court's treatment of a restrictive covenant.

Restrictive covenants are sometimes used in conjunction with the sale of a business, and sometimes they contain a provision for their termination. Such a situation appears in Case 49-3.

CASE 49-3

DOUBLE DIAMOND PROPERTIES v. BP PRODUCTS
U.S. COURT OF APPEALS FOR THE FOURTH CIRCUIT
277 FED. APPX. 312 (2008)

Double Diamond Properties purchased real property from BP Products on which to operate a gas station. The purchase agreement contained a restrictive covenant prohibiting Double Diamond from selling gasoline purchased from any source other than BP. When BP assigned to Miller Oil Company its right to supply gasoline, Double Diamond sought a declaratory judgment that the restrictive covenant was no longer enforceable, as well as damages based upon the difference in cost between obtaining BP fuel from the assignee and a cheaper distributor. The defendant received a declaratory judgment that the supplier still benefitted from the covenant despite its assignment, and that the covenant specified that it terminated only if the supplier stopped selling gasoline on a direct or indirect basis, which had not occurred. Double Diamond appealed.

PER CURIUM OPINION: . . . [C]ovenants restricting the free use of land are disfavored and must be strictly construed. . . . [T]he person claiming the benefit of the restrictions must prove that the covenants are applicable to the acts of which he complains. . . .

We will also apply Virginia principles of contract interpretation and "seek to determine the intent of the parties from the language expressed in the contract". . . . Contract terms that are clear and unambiguous will be afforded their plain and ordinary meaning, but extrinsic evidence may be used to interpret vague or ambiguous terms, and substantial doubts or ambiguity about the meaning of a restrictive covenant will be resolved in favor of the unrestricted use of land. . . .

Double Diamond argues that the restrictive covenant has expired according to its terms because BP no longer benefits from the covenant as a direct supplier of fuel to the Haygood station. Double Diamond contends that the language in the covenant concerning direct or indirect supply of fuel relates only to the scope of the restriction, meaning that Double Diamond may comply with the restriction by purchasing BP fuel either directly or indirectly. Double Diamond likewise contends that BP must benefit as a direct supplier of fuel if it does not benefit as an owner or lessee of land or as a fuel retailer, because the language describing the benefit to BP from the restriction does not include the description "indirect supplier."

We find, however, that BP still benefits from the restriction as an indirect supplier of fuel to the Haygood station. Arguably, BP would still benefit as a direct supplier of retail operations even if a particular retail operator chose to obtain its BP fuel indirectly, thereby maintaining the validity of the covenant while still giving meaning to the restriction. However, the restriction could be rendered meaningless under this construction if all retail operators in the area chose to obtain BP fuel indirectly, robbing BP of its status as a direct supplier through no action of its own. We conclude that the term "supplier" in the beneficiary sentence was intended to encompass acting as either an indirect supplier or a direct supplier, because both manners of supplying are contemplated by the description of the restriction. The circumstances surrounding the covenant also indicate that BP was clearly contemplating that it would no longer own land or operate retail facilities in the area, and strongly indicate that BP contemplated phasing out its role as a direct supplier of fuel to retail operations, at the time the covenant was made. Accordingly, because BP clearly benefits from the covenant as an indirect supplier of fuel, the covenant is still enforceable according to its terms.

A restraint on alienation of property is valid if it is reasonable. . . . A court must "consider (1) whether or not the agreement in question is reasonable as between the parties; and (2) if so, whether or not the agreement is injurious to the public interest by reason of its effect upon trade and, therefore, void." . . .

Double Diamond argues that the restrictive covenant is unreasonable because the requirement that only BP fuel be sold at the Haygood station is unreasonable when applied in conjunction with Miller Oil's exclusive right to distribute BP fuel to the Haygood station, because Miller Oil competes in the retail fuel market and because BP earns the same profit on fuel it supplies regardless of whether it uses Miller or another supplier. . . .

If Double Diamond were allowed to comply with the restrictive covenant by purchasing BP fuel for the Haygood station through the supplier of its choice, the burden of the restrictive covenant on the Haygood station and its owner, Double Diamond, would be reduced, because Double Diamond could negotiate a lower price for its fuel supply. The burden is arguably no greater than it would be if BP were the sole direct supplier of its fuel, however, because Double Diamond would have no choice as to the terms of its fuel supply agreement with BP. Although Miller Oil is a potential competitor with Double Diamond in the retail market, there is evidence in the record that Miller Oil does not operate any retail gas stations within two miles of the Haygood station, and is therefore not currently in direct competition. Although this is a close issue, the standard for reasonableness established by Virginia courts does not clearly compel the invalidation of the restrictive covenant as applied to Double Diamond.

(III) Validity of the Restrictive Covenant in Changed Circumstances

A change in circumstances that is "so radical as practically to destroy the essential objects and purposes of the [covenant]" will render a restrictive covenant null and void. . . . In order to determine the extent of the restriction imposed by a covenant, a court should "look to the substance—not the label—of the activity sought to be restricted."

Double Diamond argues that the restrictive covenant has expired due to changed circumstances because BP has radically altered its business practices by discontinuing its operations as a direct supplier of fuel to retail operations, instead supplying fuel for retail operations only indirectly. We hold that the circumstances surrounding the covenant have not changed so radically as to destroy the primary purpose of the covenant for its beneficiary, BP, namely to ensure a continuing retail market for its fuel in the Virginia Beach area. Although BP now benefits from the covenant as an indirect supplier of fuel, rather than a direct supplier, the essential purpose, to ensure an ultimate retail market for BP fuel, is still being met. . . . BP's ultimate purpose in enforcing the covenant is still served.

AFFIRMED in favor of BP Products.

CRITICAL THINKING

The facts of a case move it toward the court's conclusion. What facts, had they been true, would have caused this decision to have gone against BP Products?

ETHICAL DECISION MAKING

The court explains that the law frowns on restrictions against the free use of land. Whose interests are being protected by this legal principle?

Legal Principle: **Restrictive covenants are promises to use or not use land in particular ways, and they will be enforced as long as they are reasonable.**

ZONING

Zoning allows for the orderly growth and development of a community and protects the health, safety, and welfare of its citizens. It commonly restricts the type of use to which land may be put, such as residential, commercial, industrial, or agricultural. Zoning laws may also regulate land use on the basis of the intensity (single or multifamily dwellings), size, or placement of buildings.

There is generally a public hearing on proposed changes in zoning ordinances. Often the community allows an exception for a particular property, called a *nonconforming use*, if the zoning changes. An owner who wishes to use land in a manner prohibited by zoning laws may seek permission, called a *variance*, from the zoning board or planning commission. Variances are generally granted to prevent undue hardship.

Zoning is an exercise of police power, the power of the state to regulate to protect the health, safety, and welfare of the public. To be a valid exercise of such power, a zoning ordinance must not be arbitrary or unreasonable. It is unreasonable if (1) it encroaches on the private property rights of landowners without a substantial relationship to a legitimate government purpose such as public health, safety, or welfare or (2) there is no reasonable relationship between the ends to be obtained and the means used to attain them.

Although zoning laws typically restrict how owners of real property may use their property, they can also help protect the rights of landowners. A company, Vineyard Investments, wanted to open a wine and spirits store in Madison, Mississippi. Vineyard was in compliance with all zoning laws, but the City of Madison denied the building permit because the shopping center already had one liquor store and the city thought that having two would not convey the family-friendly atmosphere it wanted. The City of Madison told Vineyard that because it did not yet have a state permit to sell alcohol, the city could not approve the building permit. However, no zoning regulations required that Vineyard have the state permit before receiving the building permit, and Vineyard had a hearing already scheduled with the state board to receive the permit. The court ruled that because Vineyard was compliant with all the zoning regulations, the city must also abide by its zoning regulations and approve the building permit.[3]

[3] *Vineyard Investments v. City of Madison,* 999 So. 2d 438 (Miss. App. 2009).

Because zoning is intended to regulate property, not take it, it is unreasonable for a zoning ordinance to destroy the economic value of a piece of property. If it does, the zoning is considered a constructive taking of the property, and the owner is entitled to fair compensation. Frequently, but usually unsuccessfully, an owner will challenge zoning regulations on such grounds.

Legal Principle: **Zoning restricts the type of use to which land may be put, such as residential, commercial, industrial, or agricultural, or regulates land use on the basis of the intensity, size, or placement of buildings.**

OTHER STATUTORY RESTRICTIONS ON LAND USE

Another government restriction of property is the passing, in some states, of historic preservation statutes: Owners of buildings with historical importance are usually required to keep the building in good repair and obtain prior approval for any alterations to the façade.

As we are becoming more aware of environmental consequences with certain uses of land, governments are increasingly imposing restrictions on use of environmentally sensitive lands. These restrictions are often challenged in court as violating the private property owner's rights.

CASE OPENER WRAP-UP

Poletown

In the end, Detroit's Economic Redevelopment Corporation exercised its right of eminent domain and acquired the property in Poletown for General Motors. The plaintiffs argued that whatever incidental benefit may accrue to the public, assembling land to General Motors' specifications for its uncontrolled use in profit making is really a taking for *private* use because General Motors is the primary beneficiary, but the Michigan State Supreme Court disagreed. The court stated, "The determination of what constitutes a public purpose is primarily a legislative function, subject to review by the courts when abused, and the determination of the legislative body of that matter should not be reversed except in instances where such determination is palpable and manifestly arbitrary and incorrect."

The court found valid the legislature's determination that the proposed industrial site would alleviate and prevent unemployment and fiscal distress, meeting a public need and serving an essential public purpose. Thus, the taking was constitutional.

Interestingly, during spring 2005, just a few months before the *Kelo* decision, the Michigan Supreme Court had a chance to reconsider its reasoning in Poletown and, in the case of *Wayne v. Hathcock*, overruled it. The court stated that "Poletown's conception of a public use—that of 'alleviating unemployment and revitalizing the economic base of the community'—has no support in the Court's eminent domain jurisprudence." The persuasiveness of *Hathcock*, however, was rapidly overshadowed by the U.S. Supreme Court's decision in *Kelo*, because the reasoning in *Poletown* was consistent with that in *Kelo*.

Clearly, the question of what constitutes public use is not easily answered. While it appears from the high court's most recent pronouncement that public use is going to be interpreted broadly enough to include takings for economic redevelopment, even when they include some private benefit from the transfer of property from one private entity to another, such a transfer is much more likely to be upheld when it is part of a well-conceived plan for development and not just an individual transfer, as was the case in *Poletown*. And, as we noted earlier in this chapter, in response to this decision, many states are now passing statutes to tighten the circumstances under which state governments may use their power of eminent domain.

Key Terms

adverse possession   1089

closing   1089

condemnation   1089

conditional estate   1081

co-ownership   1085

easement   1083

easement by
    prescription   1084

fee simple absolute   1081

fixture   1079

future interest   1082

general warranty
    deed   1087

joint tenants   1085

leasehold   1083

license   1084

life estate   1081

marketable title   1088

profit   1083

quitclaim deed   1087

real property   1079

recording   1087

restrictive
    covenants   1094

special warranty deed   1087

tenancy by
    the entirety   1085

tenancy in common   1085

zoning   1096

Summary of Key Topics

The Nature of Real Property

Property is land and anything permanently affixed to the land.

Interests in Real Property

A *fee simple absolute* is the right to possess property for life and devise it to heirs on death; it is the most all-encompassing interest.

A *conditional estate* is an interest comparable to a fee simple absolute, except that the interest will terminate on the happening or nonhappening of a specified condition.

A *leasehold estate* is the right to possess property for an agreed-on period of time.

An *easement* is an irrevocable right to use a portion of someone else's land for a specified purpose.

A *license* is a right to temporarily use another's property.

Co-ownership

The traditional forms of co-ownership are:

Tenancy in common: Owners hold equal or unequal shares that can be attached by creditors and that pass on to heirs at death.

Joint tenancy: Equal shares are held by all owners, and on death the shares are divided among other owners.

Tenancy by the entirety: This form is available to married couples only, with equal shares that pass to the spouse on death.

Two newer forms of co-ownership are:

Condominium ownership: The owner acquires title to a "unit" within a condominium, along with an undivided interest in the land, buildings, and improvements of the common areas of the development.

Cooperative ownership: An investor resident acquires stock in the corporation owning the facility and receives a permanent lease on one unit of the facility.

Voluntary Transfer of Real Property

For a transfer to be legal, the transferor must follow the steps of *execution, delivery, acceptance,* and, to protect the recipient of the property, *recording.*

Involuntary Transfer of Real Property

There are two forms of involuntary transfers:

Adverse possession: When a person openly treats realty as his or her own, without protest or permission from the real owner, for a statutorily established period of time, ownership is automatically vested in that person.

Condemnation: The government acquires the ownership of private property for a public use for just compensation over the protest of the owner of the property.

Restrictions on Land Use

Restrictive covenants are agreements to use or not to use land in particular ways.

Zoning is the restriction of the use of property to allow for the orderly growth and development of a community and to protect the health, safety, and welfare of its citizens.

Point / Counterpoint

Should Legislatures Be Able to Use Eminent Domain to Give Private Property to Another Private Entity in the Name of "Public Use"?

NO	YES
The Fifth Amendment reads: "nor shall private property be taken for public use, without just compensation." This text suggests that government cannot use eminent domain unless the condemned property is available for use by the public. If, as in *Poletown,* the condemned property is transferred to a private corporation, the public cannot use it. Hence, this use of eminent domain does not comport with the plain meaning of the constitutional text.	Arguments emanating from constitutional text do not clearly support the position that eminent domain must yield property for use by the public. The text prohibits taking of private property for public use "without just compensation," but it says nothing about the taking of private property for *private* use. Thus, a literal reading of the constitutional text does not prohibit the use of eminent domain in question.
Even if the constitutional text allows this use of eminent domain, the Constitution does not hold corporations accountable for their promises to create jobs and generate tax revenues. If a corporation promises 6,500 jobs and $10 million in tax revenue to a local municipality in exchange for an advantageous piece of property, and only 3,000 jobs and $800,000 in tax revenue materialize, the corporation suffers no consequences. Thus, corporations have a perverse incentive to overstate the number of jobs and amount of tax revenue they are likely to create, and legislatures might use eminent domain when, had they known the actual state of affairs, they would not.	Moreover, even if the use of eminent domain creates perverse incentives for corporations to make unrealistic promises, the best solution is not a blanket ban on the practice. Rather, citizens can oppose the use of eminent domain at the ballot box: They can vote for local candidates who share their views. Many economic policies are unwise but not unconstitutional. As Justice Oliver Wendell Holmes wrote, the Constitution "does not enact Mr. Herbert Spencer's Social Statics." (Spencer's Social Statics was a popular economic theory during Holmes's time.) Justice Antonin Scalia once remarked that "[a] law can be both economic folly and constitutional."
A third strong argument against this use of eminent domain focuses on the alternative. If the private property in question is so desirable, the corporation can purchase it directly from the private owner. If the private owner is unwilling to give up her property for the price offered, the outcome is not necessarily bad. Indeed, economists would say the result is efficient because the property ends up where it is most highly valued: in the private owner's hands.	Finally, the argument that society ought to use markets instead of eminent domain ignores the possibility of *positive externalities*—benefits that accrue to third parties when two individuals engage in a market transaction. If the sale of private property to corporations is likely to produce positive externalities in the form of additional jobs and increased tax revenue, legislatures may want to compel more of these sales through the use of eminent domain.

Questions & Problems

1. Explain what a fixture is and when it is not treated as a part of the real property to which it is attached.

2. Explain the five possessory interests in land.

3. List the primary characteristics of three forms of joint ownership.

4. List the steps of the voluntary transfer of ownership of real property.

5. Explain how a piece of property could be involuntarily transferred.

6. Travis Scheible was riding his bicycle and started to cross the street from behind a mature tree that overhung the sidewalk and obscured his view of oncoming traffic. As he rode into the street, Travis was struck by an oncoming car and was killed. The tree was located on residential property that Jackson had sold to Smith about six months before the accident under a contract to be paid over the course of two years. Smith began residing on the property. Travis's mother, Christine Scheible, brought a wrongful-death action against Jackson and Smith. Jackson moved for summary judgment, arguing that he had no duty to Travis because he did not own, possess, or control the property at the time of the accident. Scheible argues that Jackson controlled the property, as proved by the facts that (1) Smith needed Jackson's permission before changing the property; (2) Smith paid Jackson to continue the liability coverage for the property in Jackson's name (Smith's name was never added to the policy); and (3) Smith eventually renounced his rights and returned the property to Jackson. What type of estate did Smith have when he purchased the property from Jackson, and how does this affect who is liable for the tree on the property and thus liable for Travis's death? What evidence leads to your conclusion? [*Jackson v. Scheible*, 902 N.E.2d 807 (Ind. 2009).]

7. Outdoor Systems Advertising (OSA), Inc., previously occupied a building owned by Jefferson Properties. When OSA vacated the building, it left behind two billboards located on the roof and east wall of the building. OSA notified Jefferson Properties of its ownership of the billboards and requested that the advertisements attached to the billboard structures be removed. The trial court held that the panel boards, the exterior portion of the billboards, belonged to OSA and that the billboard structures, which were attached to the building, were part of Jefferson Properties' realty. On appeal, OSA argued that both the panel boards and the billboard structures were trade fixtures. Jefferson Properties maintained that the billboard structures were fixtures and should remain affixed to the property. How do you think the court resolved this conflict? Were the billboard structures trade fixtures? [*Outdoor Systems Advertising, Inc. v. John J. Korth*, 1999 Mich. App. LEXIS 316.]

8. Carol Matoush owns property that grants her an easement dating back to 1901. The easement at issue here creates a right-of-way across David and Debra Lovingood's property for access between Matoush's property and an alley adjacent to the Lovingoods' property. The easement has not been used as a surface right-of-way across the Lovingoods' property since at least 1969. At some point before 1969, fences were built to enclose most of the easement area within the Lovingoods' backyard. Matoush attempted to sell her property to a buyer who inquired about using the easement as a driveway for vehicle access between Matoush's property and the alley. There is a driveway on Matoush's property that provides vehicle access to a garage located on Matoush's property. The buyer has proposed removing the driveway, relocating the garage, paving the easement area, and using the easement as a driveway for vehicle access between the alley and the new garage. Matoush brought an action against the Lovingoods to enforce her right to use the easement as a right-of-way for vehicle access between her property and the alley. The Lovingoods counterclaimed that use of the easement as a right-of-way was terminated by either abandonment, due to the lack of use, or adverse possession, due to the construction of fences obstructing the easement in 1969. Does Matoush still possess the easement across the Lovingoods' land? Why? [*Matoush v. Lovingood*, 177 P.3d 1262 (Colo. 2008).]

9. After they were married, Helen and Burr Dietz purchased real property as tenants by the entirety. Helen subsequently moved out, and the parties

agreed that if they were to become divorced, they would share the proceeds of the sale of their property. Helen and Burr divorced, and their tenancy by the entirety was converted into a tenancy in common. Burr continued to live in the residence, and Helen brought an action for the partition or sale of the property. She sought to receive half of the proceeds of the sale and rent for the period that she did not live on the property. The trial court determined that the property could not be partitioned, and therefore it directed the parties to sell the property and divide the proceeds accordingly. Burr did not want to sell the property and appealed the court's decision. How do you think the case was decided on appeal? [*Deitz v. Deitz,* 664 N.Y.S.2d 868 (1997).]

10. Denese Welch purchased property in 1980. The adjacent property was vacant. In 1985, Welch planted a tree on what she thought was her property. As it turned out, she planted the tree across the property line, on the vacant lot. Around 1994,

Welch built a woodshed behind the tree she had planted in 1985. Welch also landscaped around the shed. Before installing these improvements in 1994, Welch made some effort to locate the boundary between her lot and the vacant lot but failed to ascertain the true boundary. As a result, unbeknownst to Welch, the woodshed and the landscaping partially encroached on the vacant lot. The Harrisons purchased the vacant lot in March 2001. In June 2001, the Harrisons had the property surveyed. The survey revealed that the woodshed encroached up to 7.25 feet onto their lot and the landscaping encroached up to 9.8 feet. The total area of the encroachment amounted to 8 percent of the lot. The Harrisons sued Welch to remove the encroachment. Welch argued that she had right to the encroached land through, among other things, adverse possession. What does Welch need to prove to establish ownership through adverse possession? Was she successful? Why? [*Harrison v. Welch,* 11 Cal. Rptr. 3d 92 (Cal. Ct. App. 3d 2004).]

Looking for more review material?

The Online Learning Center at **www.mhhe.com/kubasek2e** contains this chapter's "Assignment on the Internet" and also a list of URLs for more information, entitled "On the Internet." Find both of them in the Student Center portion of the OLC, along with quizzes and other helpful materials.

50 Landlord-Tenant Law

LEARNING OBJECTIVES

After reading this chapter, you will be able to answer the following questions:

1   How is the landlord-tenant relationship created?

2   What are the rights and duties of the landlord and tenant?

3   What are landlords' liabilities for injuries on the premises?

4   How are interests in leased property transferred?

5   How are leases terminated?

CASE OPENER

Free to Choose?

Roommates.com operates a Web site that helps individuals find roommates. Individuals searching for roommates create profiles using questionnaires provided by the Web site. The questionnaires ask for information about age, sex, and sexual orientation, as well as whether the person lives with children. Roommates.com encourages users to supply additional information via profiles. Roommates.com then distributes e-mails to users after matching members on the basis of preferences. For example, if a person does not want to live with children, Roommates.com does not send that person information from potential roommates who live with children. The Fair Housing Councils of San Fernando Valley and San Diego have sued Roommates.com, alleging its business practices violate the federal Fair Housing Act and some California statutes. Roommates.com believes it enjoys immunity under the Communications Decency Act (CDA), which provides immunity from liability for providers of interactive computer services that publish information provided by others.

1. In this chapter, you will learn about how the landlord-tenant relationship is created. What is "fair housing," and how does the concept of fair housing affect landlord-tenant relationships?
2. Are tenants allowed to discriminate against potential roommates?

The Wrap-Up at the end of the chapter will answer these questions.

Suppose you are a manager for a new business. One of your responsibilities is to secure office space for the business. You meet with the business owner to talk about whether you should rent or purchase the office space. If you rent the office space, you will enter into a contractual agreement with the owner such that you will be responsible for paying a specific amount of money for a specific period of time to have temporary possession of a certain space. While this agreement will name a specific piece of property (i.e., provide the street address of the property), the lease is typically an agreement for use of some structure on the property. If you will potentially be renting housing or office space for your business, you should be aware of the laws that govern the landlord-tenant relationship.

A clear understanding of the language used in the landlord-tenant relationship is essential. The owner of the property is called the **landlord** or the **lessor.** In contrast, the **lessee,** or the **tenant,** is the party who assumes temporary ownership of the property. The property in question is called the **leasehold estate.** The actual agreement between the landlord and the tenant is called the **lease.**

In the landlord-tenant relationship, the landlord grants the tenant the temporary, exclusive right to occupy and use a specific space for a specific amount of time. In turn, the tenant is obligated to pay rent to the landlord, who retains the title to the land. This entire relationship is usually established in a contractual agreement. Usually, we think of landlord-tenant relationships as private. However, sometimes landlord-tenant relationships are public-private relationships. For example, the City of Orlando is in a relationship with RP Realty Partners, a landlord to tenant Orlando Movie Co., which operates Plaza Cinema Café. The development project is a public-private one, created when the city wanted a downtown movie theater to bring people into the city.

The landlord-tenant relationship has become more complex in recent years. In 1972, the National Conference of Commissioners on Uniform State Laws created the Uniform Residential Landlord and Tenant Act (URLTA), an act that created more uniformity among the state laws governing the landlord-tenant relationship.

The first part of this chapter explains how the landlord-tenant relationship is created. The next section explains the rights and responsibilities associated with the landlord-tenant relationship. The third section focuses on liability associated with injuries that occur on rental premises. The fourth section considers how landlords and tenants can transfer their interests in the rental property. The final section explains the ways a lease can be terminated.

Creation of the Landlord-Tenant Relationship

L01

How is the landlord-tenant relationship established? It is usually established by an oral or written contract. Generally, if the lease exceeds one year, it must be in writing. A landlord-tenant relationship requires the following elements: (1) the names of the tenant(s) and

How is the landlord-tenant relationship created?

landlord, (2) an express or implied intent to create a landlord-tenant relationship, (3) a description of the property, (4) the specific length of the lease, and (5) the amount of rent to be paid to the landlord.

The most distinguishing factor of the landlord-tenant relationship is the tenant's right to exclusive possession of the property named in the lease. If the landlord retains control of and access to the property, the relationship is likely not a landlord-tenant relationship because the tenant does not have an exclusive right to possession of the property.

Legal Principle: Exclusive right to possession of the property is a key characteristic of the landlord-tenant relationship.

TYPES OF LEASES

There are four categories of leases that can be created: definite term, period tenancy, tenancy at will, and tenancy at sufferance. Why should you understand the differences between these categories of leases? These categories are distinguishable by the duration of the agreement specified or unspecified in the lease. Some of these categories allow the landlord or tenant to terminate a lease at specific times, while other categories consider termination before the end of the term as a breach. As a future business manager, you need to be aware of the distinctions in the types of leases so that you know what kind of lease will and will not permit you to terminate the agreement.

First, a definite-term lease, also known as a *term for years,* automatically expires at the end of the specified term. The landlord is not required to give any notification of termination. Thus, a lease that states that the tenant has temporary possession of the property from August 1, 2000, to July 31, 2001, is an example of a definite-term lease. Second, a periodic-tenancy lease is created for a recurring term, such as month to month. The periodic-tenancy lease is distinct from the definite-term lease because the periodic-tenancy lease is for an indefinite time period. While either the landlord or the tenant can terminate during the recurring period, each party is required to give the other party sufficient notice. Third, parties to a tenancy-at-will lease may terminate the lease at any time. Fourth, if a tenant fails to leave the property after the termination of the lease, a tenancy-at-sufferance lease is created. The landlord may choose either to permit the tenant to remain on the property or to demand repossession of the property.

FAIR HOUSING ACT

When deciding to create a landlord-tenant relationship, the landlord has much freedom in deciding whether to accept someone as a tenant. If the individual has a history of not paying rent or severely damaging premises, the landlord does not have to enter into an agreement with this person. However, under the Fair Housing Act, the landlord may not discriminate against a prospective tenant with regard to race, color, sex, religion, national origin, or familial status. Thus, if a landlord denies a rental application because of the tenant's religion (or another protected class), the prospective tenant can bring a suit against the landlord. Case 50-1 considers the intersection between two federal laws, the Fair Housing Act (FHA) and the Communications Decency Act (CDA), which provides immunity from liability for providers of interactive computer services that publish information provided by others.

Plaintiff Chicago Lawyers' Committee for Civil Rights Under Law, Inc. (CLC) is a public interest consortium of forty-five law firms that promote and protect civil rights. CLC strives to eliminate discriminatory housing practices. It filed a lawsuit against Craigslist, a Delaware corporation located in San Francisco that operates a website that posts user-supplied information. One kind of information Craigslist posts is housing advertisements. CLC monitors Craigslist's website. CLC has found numerous allegedly objectionable statements within rental postings on Craigslist's website, e.g., "African Americans and Arabians tend to clash with me so that won't work out." "This is not in a trendy neighborhood-very Latino." "Owner lives on the first floor, so tenant must be respectful of the situation, preferably not 2 guys in their mid twenties, who throw parties all the time." "Christian single straight female needed." "Walk to shopping, restaurants, coffee shops, synagogue." CLC sued, alleging that Craigslist has violated the Fair Housing Act (FHA). Craigslist replied, asserting immunity under the Communications Decency Act (CDA).

ST. EVE, DISTRICT JUDGE: CLC alleges that . . . Craigslist publishes housing advertisements on its website that indicate a preference, limitation, or discrimination, or an intention to make a preference, limitation, or discrimination, on the basis of race, color, national origin, sex, religion, and familial status. . . . CLC alleges that [statements on Craigslist] discourage or prohibit home-seekers from pursuing housing and thus decrease the number of units available to them. . . .

Congress' purpose in providing the § 230 immunity [under the CDA] was thus evident. Interactive computer services have millions of users. The amount of information communicated via interactive computer services is therefore staggering. . . . It would be impossible for service providers to screen each of their millions of postings for possible problems. Faced with potential liability for each message republished by their services, interactive computer service providers might choose to severely restrict the number and type of messages posted. Congress considered the weight of the speech interests implicated and chose to immunize service providers to avoid any such restrictive effort. . . .

Applying Section 230 (c)(1) here, CLC's claim fails on the pleadings. First, Craigslist is a "provider of an interactive service" because . . . Craigslist operates a website that multiple users have accessed to create allegedly discriminatory housing notices. . . . These notices, in turn, are "information" that originates, not from Craigslist, but from "another important content provider," namely the users of Craigslist's website. As a "provider . . . of an interactive computer service" that serves as a conduit for "information provided by another information content provider," Craigslist "shall not be treated as a publisher." Because to hold Craigslist liable under [the FHA] would be to treat Craigslist as if it were the publisher of third-party content, the plain language of [the CDA] forecloses CLC's cause of action. . . .

[T]he Court grants Craigslist's Rule 12(c) motion for judgment on the pleadings.

MOTION GRANTED in favor of the defendant.

CRITICAL THINKING

Can you think of a situation in which a court might decide it *cannot* grant immunity to an interactive computer service provider? Use the court's rationale to generate ideas.

Could the court have granted Craigslist's motion for judgment on the pleadings and still encouraged Craigslist to take steps to prevent discrimination? How so? Be specific.

ETHICAL DECISION MAKING

If you were an employee of Craigslist, and you were a member of a protected group (e.g., gay, Muslim), what argument might you make to your employer that it should take some action to prevent discriminatory posts? Be specific.

Leases in French Law

Leases in France are governed by the Civil Code. Leases are under the code's jurisdiction because they engender personal contractual rights rather than property rights. The Civil Code places the rights of the tenant above the rights of the renter. Tenants are also given considerable freedom to engage in various agreements without the landlord's involvement or consent. If the lease is not renewed, the tenant has the right to collect compensation. The tenants' sovereignty, however, is a personal right. The landlord still maintains the property rights. The tenant is merely acting as his or her agent.

There are two special leases that transfer property rights to the tenant. The first is an *emphyteusis,* in which the tenant is going to be involved in extensive work on the property for anywhere between 18 and 99 years. During this period, the property rights of the land are given to the tenant, who pays a small rent fee in return. The second type of lease is a *construction lease.* It is similar to an *emphyteusis* in the sense that the tenant receives property rights for working on the land. Specifically, the tenant in a construction lease will be building and maintaining structures. If either of these leases is entered into, the property rights are ceded to the tenant for the period specified in the agreement.

CASE NUGGET

What Test Applies under the Fair Housing Act When a Mentally Impaired Tenant Seeks a Reasonable Accommodation?

Douglas v. Kriegsfeld Corporation
884 A.2d 1109 (2005)

In *Douglas v. Kriegsfeld,* a tenant (Douglas) with a mood disorder asked for "reasonable accommodation" under the Fair Housing Act. In particular, she wanted time and assistance in cleaning her apartment before the landlord could succeed in an action for possession. The landlord wanted to consider the impact Douglas's unclean apartment had on other tenants. Although the trial court was willing to consider this factor, the appellate court clarified that the test for establishing a reasonable-accommodation defense focuses on the landlord–tenant relationship, not on the impact one tenant has on other tenants. In particular, the court said:

> To establish a reasonable accommodation defense under the Fair Housing Act, the tenant must demonstrate that (1) she suffered from a "handicap" (or "disability"), (2) the landlord knew or should have known of the disability, (3) an accommodation of the disability may be necessary to afford the tenant an equal opportunity to use and enjoy her apartment, (4) the tenant has requested a reasonable accommodation, and (5) the landlord refused to grant a reasonable accommodation.

The court emphasized that each case should be judged on its unique facts, and it remanded the case to the lower court for consideration according to the test it had outlined.

Rights and Duties of the Landlord and the Tenant

LO2

What are the rights and duties of the landlord and tenant?

Both the landlord and the tenant gain certain rights and responsibilities when creating a lease. Each duty corresponds with a right: If the landlord has a duty to perform *X,* the tenant has the right to *X.* (See the examples in Exhibit 50-1.) As a future business manager, you could be either a landlord or a tenant; thus, it is important to understand what your responsibilities and rights would be as each party to the lease. These duties and rights can be classified under four main areas: possession, use, maintenance, and rent.

Exhibit 50-1

Examples of Duties and
Corresponding Rights
of Landlord and Tenant

DUTY
1. Landlord duty to put tenant in possession
2. Landlord duty of covenant of quiet enjoyment
3. Tenant duty not to commit waste

CORRESPONDING RIGHT
1. Tenant's right to retain possession
2. Tenant's right to quiet enjoyment of the property
3. Landlord right to reimbursement for tenant's waste

POSSESSION OF THE PREMISES

One of the few obligations that the landlord has to the tenant is to give the tenant possession of the premises. What exactly does *possession* mean? In the majority of states, the landlord is required to give the tenant physical possession of the premises. Suppose that you are supposed to move into your new office space tomorrow. Unfortunately, the previous tenant has refused to leave the premises. In the majority of states, the landlord is required to remove the previous tenant or break the agreement with the new tenant.

In contrast, in a minority of states, the landlord is required to simply provide legal possession of the premises. In other words, in the example above, you would be responsible for asserting your legal right to the premises and thus removing the previous tenant.

If, however, the tenant does not receive possession of the premises because of an act of the landlord, the landlord will be held liable. The tenant can bring an action for possession against the landlord.

Because the landlord has the duty to provide the tenant with possession of the premises, the tenant has the right to possession of the premises according to the terms of the lease. An element of the tenant's right to possess the premises is the right to quietly enjoy the premises. One of the most important promises that a landlord makes in a lease is the covenant of quiet enjoyment, a promise that the tenant has the right to quietly enjoy the land. What exactly does this mean? The landlord promises that he or she will not interfere with the tenant's use and enjoyment of the property. If the landlord does interfere, the tenant can sue the landlord for breach of this covenant. In Case 50-2, a New York city court explores the covenant of quiet enjoyment.

JANET I. BENITEZ v. SEBASTIANO RESTIFO
CITY COURT OF NEW YORK, YONKERS
167 MISC. 2D 967; 641 N.Y.S.2D 523; 1996 N.Y. MISC. LEXIS 106 (1996)

Janet I. Benitez was a tenant in a basement apartment in New York, and Sebastiano Restifo was her landlord. On August 10, 1995, a large amount of water fell through the ceiling in Benitez's apartment, causing severe damage to much of Benitez's property (e.g., carpet, a bed, clothing, etc.). Benitez replaced the carpet, mattress, bureau, and some clothing. The source of the water was from a third floor apartment rented by Mrs. Alamar, who had previously caused flooding in Benitez's apartment. According to Restifo, Mrs. Alamar was a "problem tenant" who would intentionally fill up her kitchen sink so that the water would overflow onto the kitchen floor and eventually flood Benitez's apartment. Restifo was aware that Alamar was responsible for the floods in Benitez's apartment but did not take steps to have Alamar evicted. Benitez brought suit to recover money based on a breach of covenant of quiet enjoyment.

JUDGE DICKERSON: In this case the plaintiff seeks to recover monies expended in replacing her personal property (carpet, furniture, bedding and clothing), all of which suffered water damage. In this case the water came from a third floor apartment in which a tenant intentionally allowed water to overflow onto her kitchen floor.

Based upon a review of the facts the court finds that plaintiff has asserted the following causes of action: (1) breach of the covenant of quiet enjoyment and (2) breach of the warranty of habitability as set forth in Real Property Law §235-b.

Breach of Covenant of Quiet Enjoyment

Implicit in the lease agreement between the landlord and tenant was a covenant of quiet enjoyment which "is an agreement on the part of the landlord that for the period of the term of the lease the tenant shall not be disturbed in his quiet enjoyment of the leased premises" (2 Rasch, New York Landlord and Tenant—Summary Proceedings 27.1 [3d ed]).

The breach of a covenant of quiet enjoyment requires actual or constructive eviction (2 Rasch, *op. cit.,* §28.1, 28.21). Constructive eviction arises when the landlord interferes with the tenant's possession of the premises to such an extent that the tenant is deprived of its beneficial enjoyment.

In this case it was the landlord's inaction and unwillingness to evict the third floor tenant, Mrs. Alamar, which directly led to the most recent flooding of the plaintiff's apartment. By failing to act, the defendant condoned and impliedly authorized Mrs. Alamar to leave the water running in her apartment, causing damage to plaintiff's apartment below (74 NY Jur 2d, Landlord and Tenant, §259-260, 265; *Brauer v Kaufman,* 72 Misc 2d 718, 721 [1972] ["It may well be that if a landlord by deliberate and affirmative action invites, encourages or permits lessees to engage in illegal and immoral conduct on the premises . . . result(s) in an endangerment to the life, health or safety of the other (tenants) . . . It should be on knowledge or upon a reckless disregard of the facts"]).

The defendant breached the covenant of quiet enjoyment in the lease agreement and is liable for all appropriate damages flowing therefrom.

JUDGMENT in favor of plaintiff.

CRITICAL THINKING

What would be the ramifications of not having a covenant of quiet enjoyment?

ETHICAL DECISION MAKING

How could the landlord have used the WPH framework to avoid this lawsuit?

EVICTION

Generally, interference with a tenant's quiet enjoyment of property is usually in the form of an eviction. Suppose you find that your landlord has changed the lock on your apartment and refuses to give you a new key for the apartment. The landlord has evicted you from

Using the Internet to Lay the Foundation for Good Landlord-Tenant Relationships

Smart, tech-savvy landlords and tenants gather as much information as possible before entering into a landlord-tenant relationship. They can use the Internet to gather information. Landlords need to use a rental application to find out as much information as possible regarding the tenant, from phone numbers, to references, to emergency contacts. Landlords and tenants may want to use www.anywho.com to gather information. Landlords and tenants may also want to check out local court Web sites to see whether either has been sued and, if so, for what. Tenants may want to find out about pending foreclosures on property. Landlords may want to find out whether prospective tenants have ever been sued for failing to pay rent. For an example of a state Web site to use for this search, see Maryland's, at http://casesearch.courts.state.md.us/inquiry/inquiry-index.jsp.

the premises and has thus interfered with your use and possession of the property. When a landlord physically prevents you from entering the leased premises, this eviction is known as an **actual eviction.**

An actual eviction may be full or partial. If a landlord physically prevents you from entering any part of the premises, it is a **full eviction.** However, if the landlord prevents you from entering a part of the premises, it is a **partial eviction.** For example, if you are renting an office building and the landlord changes the locks on certain offices in the building, you have been partially evicted. In both partial and full evictions, the tenant is released from the obligation to pay rent. Furthermore, the tenant can sue for damages or bring a suit against the landlord for breach of contract.

Although a landlord might not actively prevent a tenant from using and enjoying the property, a landlord might wrongfully perform or fail to perform certain acts that cause a substantial injury to the tenant's use and enjoyment of the property. If, after a tenant notifies the landlord of a problem, the premises become unsuitable for use because of the landlord's wrongful or omitted act, a **constructive eviction** has occurred. For example, suppose your heater in your office space breaks. You notify your landlord, who then refuses to repair your heater. Clearly, in the winter, the premises are unsuitable for use without heat. Consequently, you would be permitted to abandon the premises and terminate the lease. However, you must abandon the premises within a reasonable amount of time. If a constructive eviction occurs, the tenant may bring a suit to recover damages or to attempt to move back onto the property.

Legal Principle: Tenants have a legal expectation of quiet enjoyment of property; that is, the landlord cannot interfere with the tenant's use and enjoyment of the property by refusing to fix a major problem with the property, such as a problem with heat or water.

USE OF THE PREMISES

Generally, the landlord is not responsible for ensuring that the leased premises are tenantable. Why? Historically, the land was the more important element being leased. Some states have modified this rule to make the landlord more responsible for the dwellings on the property.

This rule has particularly been modified in the creation of residential leases. Most states have imposed an **implied warranty of habitability** of the premises, a requirement that the premises be fit for ordinary residential purposes. These states have recognized that most people currently enter into lease agreements because they are looking for shelter. Consequently, the dwelling, not the land, is the more important element of the lease.

Tenant Use of the Premises.   How may the tenant use the premises? A landlord and tenant may make an agreement to limit the uses of the premises. Obviously, if they agree that the premises will be used for certain purposes only, the tenant has a duty to abide by that agreement. If there is no agreement that limits the tenant's use of the property, the tenant may use the premises in any manner as long as the use is legal and does not impose substantial injury to the premises. However, the tenant must not use the premises in a way that creates a nuisance for surrounding tenants.

During the tenant's use of the leased property, the tenant has a duty not to commit waste. Any tenant conduct that causes permanent and substantial injury to the landlord's property is considered waste. For example, if a tenant cuts down several trees in the yard of the rental property without the landlord's permission, the tenant has committed waste.

Who is responsible for damages associated with use of the apartment? It depends. The tenant is not responsible for the ordinary wear and tear on the apartment. Thus, if the carpet in the rental unit becomes worn, the tenant is not responsible for replacing the carpet. If the tenant intentionally or negligently damages the apartment, however, the tenant will be responsible for paying for the damage. Consequently, if you have a party in your apartment and the guests spill drinks all over the carpet such that the carpet is permanently stained, you will likely be responsible for replacing the carpet.

Case 50-3 considers whether tobacco residue left inside an apartment constitutes ordinary wear and tear.

CASE 50-3   NANCY MCCORMICK v. ROBERT MORAN, SMALL CLAIMS #5176
JEFFERSON COUNTY CITY COURT OF WATERTOWN
699 N.Y.S.2D 273 (1999)

Nancy McCormick entered into a written lease with Robert Moran for an apartment for the period 7/13/98 to 7/12/99. McCormick brought suit against Moran to get a refund of McCormick's $375.00 security deposit. Moran responded by arguing that McCormick should pay $455.64 for the costs of the general cleaning of the apartment done after McCormick moved out. McCormick argued that such cleaning was unnecessary because she left the apartment in a better condition than when she moved in on 7/13/98. Moran argues that the extensive cleaning was necessary to remove the smoke residue from McCormick's heavy smoking.

JUDGE HARBERSON: The defendant's request for the cost to clean the floors, walls, windows, woodwork and carpets must be based on a showing such a clean-up was for conditions beyond ordinary "wear and tear" during reasonable use of the premises by the tenant. The landlord has the burden to prove such clean-up was for conditions caused by other than ordinary wear and tear due to

reasonable use of the apartment by the tenant or a violation of the lease terms.

The landlord testified that the basic reason such an extensive cleaning was required was due to the excessive smoking by the tenants leaving a smelly residue of tobacco smoke throughout the leasehold on the walls, woodwork, carpets and other surfaces.

The lease provides at B (2) "Tenant shall use reasonable care to keep the premises in such condition as to prevent health and sanitation problems from arising." Paragraph 3 states "the $375.00 security deposit . . . may be used . . . at the time premises vacated by tenant toward reimbursement . . . for charges for cleaning not performed prior to vacating. . . ."

In PBN Associates v. Xerox Corp., the Court acknowledged a cause of action for breaking "provisions" of a lease. In this case the Court finds the plaintiff had agreed to "use reasonable care to keep the premises in such condition as to prevent health . . . problems from arising" (paragraph B [2]). The Court finds that the plaintiff's conduct of excessive smoking while in the house caused the tobacco smoke residue to collect on various surfaces of the house creating an offensive odor and a potential health risk that may arise to others who may use the premises.

There is no question that the dangers of such a situation to health due to particulate matter on surfaces left by smoke from tobacco has been recognized by the State. . . . The expression of the State's concern in this area of public health is found in Public Health Law section 1399 - P(2) which allows hotel or motel operators "to implement a smoking policy for rooms rented to guests" and, if such a policy is adopted "shall post a notice . . . as to the availability . . . of rooms in which no smoking is allowed." Section 1399 - q(1) provides that Article 13 -E does not apply, however, "to private residences."

The Court finds that while Article 13 -E does not apply to private residences, the landlord could have specifically prohibited smoking in the leased premises as part of the lease contract for the obvious health reasons outlined above. Notwithstanding the failure to specifically prohibit tobacco smoking by the plaintiff in the lease, this omission did not relieve the tenant from the obligation assumed under the lease to use reasonable care to keep the premises in such a condition as "to prevent health . . . problems from arising" (para. B[2]). The Court finds that the tenant failed to use such "reasonable care" while smoking tobacco to prevent such indoor air pollution from tobacco smoke to occur in violation of this lease term and must reimburse the plaintiff for the cost to remedy the problems since the tenant failed to do so before leaving.

The defendant is awarded as provided at paragraph 3 of the lease "reimbursement for the charges for cleaning not performed prior to vacating" the house in the amount of $455.64 to remove the tobacco smoke residue on the various surfaces of the house.

In addition the Court finds that ordinary wear and tear should not leave a leasehold in a condition that violates the warranty of habitability. When the use of tobacco by a tenant causes such a pervasive coating of tobacco smoke residue on a leasehold's surfaces, this condition results in more than ordinary wear and tear to the premises because the residue must be removed to make the rooms habitable for the protection of the health of the next tenants—a condition which if it were not corrected would be "detrimental to their life, health or safety" possibly subjecting the landlord to a violation of the warranty of habitability under Section 235 - b of the Real Property Law.

The plaintiff's petition for refund of the security deposit is denied because the defendant's counterclaim damages exceed the amount remaining. The defendant is awarded $455.64 for the cost to clean the house of tobacco smoke residue. The plaintiff is entitled to an off-set for the $375.00 security deposit.

JUDGMENT in favor of defendant.

CRITICAL THINKING

There are several ambiguous phrases in this case, including "reasonable care," "health and sanitation problems," and "ordinary wear and tear." What do you think the implied definitions of these phrases are, given the context that the court uses them in? Would you define these phrases differently? How would various definitions change the validity of the court's conclusion? No evidence was provided that previous tenants of the residence did not contribute to the tobacco residue. Could there be rival causes for the presence of the residue? Can you tell from the facts provided?

ETHICAL DECISION MAKING

Suppose McCormick held the ethical theory of consequentialism. Would her decision to smoke in the apartment have been the same? Why or why not?

Suppose that you, as a tenant, want to put wallpaper in three rooms in the office space you are renting. Are you permitted to paint or wallpaper rooms in rental property? Alternatively, perhaps you want to construct a wall to divide one large room into two offices. Is construction of this wall permitted? In most states, tenants cannot make **alterations,** changes that affect the condition of the premises, without the landlord's consent. In a minority of states, tenants can make alterations as long as the alterations are necessary for the use of the property and do not reduce the value of the property.

Perhaps you want to install shelves in the offices in your rental space. Depending on the courts, you may or may not be permitted to remove these shelves later without paying for damages. Once the shelves become attached to the property, they are considered fixtures. In some states, fixtures may not be removed because they are considered the landlord's property.

MAINTENANCE OF THE PREMISES

Landlords must ensure that the premises meet certain safety and health codes. Earlier in the chapter, we discussed the implied warranty of habitability. In most states, if a landlord leases residential property, the landlord is responsible for ensuring that the property is habitable. Part of this responsibility is making certain repairs to the premises. The implied warranty of habitability generally ensures that the landlord is responsible for repairs to major defects in the rental property. For example, if there is a hole in the wall that interferes with the electricity in the rental unit, the landlord would be responsible for repairing the hole.

Moreover, the landlord is generally responsible for ensuring that the premises meet certain statutory requirements. For example, the city ordinances might have specific standards for building structures or wiring and plumbing within the premises. Thus, the landlord would be responsible for making repairs to rental units that do not meet these standards (assuming that tenant damage did not lead to the need for those repairs). For instance, a city health and safety law might require the installation of a fire hose and sprinkler system in all office buildings. The landlord would be required to pay for this change.

If you are the landlord of an office building or apartment complex, you would be responsible for repairs to **common areas,** areas such as yards, lobbies, elevators, stairs, and hallways that are used by all tenants. Thus, if certain steps in a stairway are in need of repair, you are responsible for the repairs.

The responsibility for repairs to a property in a long-term lease is a little more complicated. Suppose that you plan to rent an office space to a tenant for 10 years. Generally, when creating the lease, the parties determine who will be responsible for repairs to the rental unit. Typically, in long-term leases, the tenant is responsible for more of the repairs to the rental property. However, the tenant will usually not be required to pay for major repairs.

Pretend that you are leasing an apartment. What can you do if your landlord fails to maintain the leased property by making certain repairs? If the repairs breach the warranty of habitability or constitute constructive eviction, you have the option of terminating the lease. If you want to retain possession of the apartment, you have several options available.

First, you can withhold a rent payment. This withholding is usually justified by the landlord's breach of the implied warranty of habitability. If the tenant wishes to withhold a rent payment, he or she must usually place a specific amount of the rent due in an escrow account, an account held by an escrow agent such as the court. The funds will remain in this account until the landlord makes the repairs. However, the tenant cannot withhold all the rent; instead, the tenant can withhold only an amount associated with the defect.

Second, you might be able to have the repairs made and deduct the costs of the repairs from the rent due to your landlord. Several states have created repair-and-deduct statutes. However, the repair-and-deduct option may not be the best choice because some statutes restrict the amount of deductible rent. Furthermore, repair-and-deduct options are often restricted to essential services, such as gas, water, and electric services. However, before you attempt to repair and deduct, you must have notified the landlord, who must then refuse to make the repairs.

CASE NUGGET

How Does the Theory of Negligence Per Se Apply to Landlords?

Gradjelick v. Hance
646 N.W.2d 225 (2002)

Plaintiff Gradjelick was injured during a fire in the dwelling he rented from the Hance family. The fire was caused in part by careless smoking in another apartment, but it was allegedly exacerbated by the landlord's failure to maintain the premises. In particular, the tenant alleged that the landlord had violated several sections of the Uniform Building Code (UBC).

The court articulated the test for how the theory of negligence per se applies to landlords who allegedly violate the UBC. The court said:

[A] landlord is not negligent per se for code violations unless the following four elements are present:

(1) the landlord or owner knew or should have known of the Code violation;

(2) the landlord or owner failed to take reasonable steps to remedy the violation;

(3) the injury suffered was the kind the Code was meant to prevent; and

(4) the violation was the proximate cause of the injury or damage.

Third, you can sue the landlord for damages. You can attempt to recover damages associated with the landlord's breach of the implied warranty of habitability. When deciding what to do, make sure you do not defame your landlord. Recently, a landlord sued a former tenant after the tenant created a Twitter post accusing Horizon Realty Group of Chicago of responding poorly to a complaint that there was mold in the tenant's apartment. The tweet said, "Who said sleeping in a moldy apartment was bad for you? Horizon Realty thinks it's okay."[1] Horizon sued the tenant, indicating that mold was not found in the tenant's apartment.

RENT

Rent can be defined as the compensation paid to the landlord for the tenant's right to possession and exclusive use of the premises. The tenant has a duty to pay rent to the landlord. Rent can be paid in various forms, such as money or services to the landlord. The lease usually specifies the form of the rent as well as the payment schedule.

How much rent should be paid to the landlord? In some cases, the landlord has much freedom in determining how much rent should be charged. However, in other cases, the government establishes rent ceilings.

When the lease is initially created, the landlord typically asks the tenant to pay a security deposit, usually in the amount of one month's rent. This security deposit ensures that the tenant will fulfill the duties of the lease agreement.

At the expiration of the lease, the landlord is required to return to the tenant the security deposit minus any costs for damages caused by the tenant. If the landlord retains any portion of the security deposit, the landlord must provide the tenant with a list of the damages. Each state usually determines the amount of time that the landlord has to return the security deposit to the tenant. If the landlord exceeds this deadline, the tenant can recover the deposit, plus attorney fees. Recently, a court ruled that a landlord would have to pay a tenant $7,000 (security deposit plus attorney fees) because the landlord exceeded the deposit return deadline.

---

[1] Lisa Donovan, "Landlord Suing Tenant over Tweet: She Sued Us First," *Chicago Sun-Times,* July 29, 2009.

If a tenant fails to pay rent when it is due, the landlord may charge a late fee. This fee may not be excessive and must be related to the amount of rent past due. Thus, if you are two days late in paying a rent amount of $550, the landlord could not charge you $550 as a late fee. If the landlord wishes to terminate the lease because of a late payment, the landlord is generally required to give the tenant notice of the termination proceedings.

Once a lease has been signed, the landlord cannot increase the price of the rent unless there is a **rent escalation clause** included in the lease. This clause permits the landlord to increase the rent in association with increases in costs of living, property taxes, or the tenant's commercial business. A rent escalation clause would typically be found in a long-term lease.

Suppose you are a landlord, and you discover that one of your tenants has refused to pay rent. What are your options? First, you may sue the tenant to collect the unpaid rent. Second, depending on what state you live in, you might have the option of a **landlord's lien,** the right to some or all of the tenant's personal property. You would be required to initiate court proceedings so that the sheriff would seize the tenant's property. This property is often considered as security for the unpaid rent.

What can a landlord do if the tenant has vacated the premises and fails to pay rent? The tenant is responsible for paying rent to the landlord until the expiration of the lease. The landlord could choose to simply let the premises stand vacant until the expiration of the lease. Thus, the tenant would be responsible for the entire amount of rent.

Some states are requiring that landlords make a reasonable attempt to lease the property to another party. The tenant is liable for the unpaid rent for the time that it would reasonably take the landlord to find a new tenant. If a reasonable attempt to find a new tenant is made but the attempt is unsuccessful, the tenant remains responsible for the entire amount of the unpaid rent.

Liability for Injuries on the Premises

LO3

What are landlords' liabilities for injuries on the premises?

Suppose you own a building and you rent the ground floor of the building to a tenant who uses the space as a restaurant. One night, while you are watching the news, you see a story that a woman was critically injured by a large piece of ice that fell off your building. The woman was leaving the restaurant on the ground floor of your building. Will you be held responsible for the woman's injuries? Will the tenant?

These questions are tricky. Liability for injuries generally depends on who is in control of the area in which the injury occurred. The courts use the standard of reasonable care in deciding these cases. The person who is in control of the area must take the same precautions for safety that the reasonable person would take.

LANDLORD'S LIABILITY

When will the landlord be liable for injuries on the premises? Generally, the landlord is responsible for injuries that occur in common areas, such as elevators, hallways, and stairwells. For example, if you are a landlord for an apartment complex and an injury occurs in the elevator, you can be held responsible for the injury. The landlord is expected to inspect and repair the common areas.

Moreover, the landlord can be held responsible for injuries when he or she has a responsibility to make repairs to the premises yet wrongfully or negligently makes those repairs. Generally, the landlord has a certain amount of time to make the repairs. Thus, if a visitor to the restaurant described in the example above was injured by falling plaster from the ceiling and the landlord had assumed the responsibility for repairs to the premises, the

Landlord Liability in England

Landlords in England are not significantly restrained by common law in terms of their liability to the tenant at the time of letting. Landlords can be held liable if they violate the lease or if they are responsible for negligence or nuisance. The 1906 case of *Cavalier v. Pope* is the current precedent for the principle that the landlord owes no duty outside the contract with the tenant. For a landlord to be held liable due to negligence, he or she must have created the disputed defect. For instance, if a tenant were to injure himself on a standard feature of the rented property, the landlord could not be found guilty of negligence for letting a dangerous apartment because she did not actually create the disputed defect. The builder created the defect. A landlord may be held liable if he or she lets property without disclosing an obvious nuisance. However, if the court feels that the nuisance was not apparent, the landlord is cleared of liability. Because the statutes favor protection of the landlords, tenants need to be especially wary of any defects or nuisances on the property before signing a lease

landlord could be responsible for the visitor's injuries. However, the landlord's liability depends on the tenant's notification of need for repair.

If an injury occurs on the premises because of a condition that the landlord knew or should have known about, the landlord can be held responsible for the injury. Furthermore, if the landlord is aware of a dangerous condition but does not make the tenant aware of the condition or hides the condition from the tenant, the landlord will be responsible for the injury. Thus, if a landlord is aware that several beams within an office space are in need of repair but does not disclose this information to the tenant when signing the lease, the landlord would likely be liable if the tenant was injured by a falling beam.

If premises are used for commercial purposes, the landlord has a responsibility to ensure that the premises are in reasonably good condition before the tenant takes control of the property. However, the tenant is responsible for maintaining the premises. If injuries occur because the tenant was negligent in keeping the premises in good condition, the landlord will not be held responsible.

Legal Principle: Tenants can expect landlords to keep common areas safe; if an injury occurs in an elevator, hallway, or stairwell, the landlord is likely to be responsible for the injury.

TENANT'S LIABILITY

The tenant has a responsibility to keep the premises in which he or she is in control in a reasonably safe condition. For example, the tenant who runs the restaurant would be responsible for the injuries of a customer who slipped and fell on a wet floor inside the restaurant. However, if the customer slipped and fell after entering a room that said "Employees Only," the tenant would not be responsible. The tenant is responsible only for those areas in which the customer is reasonably expected to go.

Transferring Interests of Leased Property

Unless transfers are prohibited by the lease agreement, both the landlord and the tenant may transfer their respective interests in the property. Depending on the housing market in a particular time period, landlords and tenants take turns having a superior bargaining position. In 2009, for example, retail landlords were looking for ways to attract and keep tenants.[2] In Colorado Springs, retail landlords have been supporting good tenants.

LO4

How are interests in leased property transferred?

[2] Becky Hurly, "Retail Landlords Getting Creative to Help, Keep, Attract Tenants," *Colorado Springs Business Journal,* July 24, 2009.

For example, Kratt Commercial Properties believes that it is important to maintain retail centers well, by adding towers to increase visibility of stores such as Panera Bread, painting exteriors and adding façades for stores such as Mattress King, making sure that parking lots are striped, and enhancing landscaping.

LANDLORD TRANSFER OF INTEREST

Because the landlord is the owner of the leasehold estate, he or she can transfer that property. While the landlord can transfer ownership of the property to someone else, the lease is still legally binding. In other words, if you are renting an office space and the landlord sells the title to the leased property, the new owner could not force you to move out of your office space. The new owner becomes your landlord until your lease agreement expires.

Once a landlord provides possession of a property to a tenant, the landlord has the right to receive rent and other benefits for the property. The landlord can transfer this right to receive rent.

TENANT TRANSFER OF INTEREST

A tenant can transfer his or her interest in the leased property in two ways: assignments and subleases. Suppose you decide that you want to rent an office space to open your own business and you sign a lease that will begin next month. Unfortunately, you later discover that you don't have enough money to start your business at this time. You are still a party to the lease agreement, but you now have no use for the office space. However, your friend is interested in renting office space. You could transfer your entire interest in the leased property to your friend. A transfer of a tenant's entire interest in a leased property is an **assignment.**

Usually, a lease requires that the landlord must consent to a tenant's assignment of her interest in the lease. Why would the lease contain such a requirement? The requirement for a landlord's consent to an assignment is protection for the landlord. Perhaps the assignee, the person to whom the lease interests have been transferred, has a history of severely damaging property that he has previously rented. Consequently, if the tenant tries to assign the lease without the landlord's consent, the landlord may terminate the lease agreement. However, if the landlord knowingly accepts rent from the assignee, the landlord essentially waives the consent requirement.

Let's return to the example described above. Suppose that you make an assignment of your interest in the office space to your friend. Your friend acquires all your rights under the lease. However, your friend fails to make the rent payment for the first month. Who can be held liable for that rent? You can be. The assignment requires that your friend pay the rent, but it does not relieve you of your responsibility to pay the rent. You will have to pay the rent, but you have a right to be reimbursed by your friend. Thus, both you and your friend, the assignee, are liable to the landlord for failure to pay rent.

How is a sublease different from an assignment? Suppose that you are currently renting an office space but you decide to take a job that is three states away. Your lease for the office space ends in six months. You can try to find someone to sublease the office space for the six months. A **sublease** is a transfer of less than all the interest in a leased property. In essence, a sublease creates a landlord-tenant relationship between the original tenant and the sublessee. If you decided to sublease the office space to someone (with the consent of the landlord), this person would not have any legal obligations to the landlord. Instead, the legal obligations are to you, the tenant to the lease. Thus, if your sublessee does not pay rent, the landlord can hold you responsible for the rent payment.

Legal Principle: **Tenants should sublease with care, as landlords can hold them responsible for rent if the sublessee does not pay.**

Termination of the Lease

Generally, at the end of the term of a lease, the lease is terminated. The tenant returns possession of the premises to the landlord unless there is an option for renewal in the lease. The tenant must leave the premises.

Other than expiration of the term of the lease, there are several other ways in which a lease can be terminated. Remember that in almost all these cases, the termination of the lease agreement relieves the tenant from the obligation of rent.

L05

How are leases terminated?

BREACH OF CONDITION BY LANDLORD

As we discussed earlier, when a landlord interferes with a tenant's use and enjoyment of the property, the landlord has breached the covenant of quiet enjoyment. This interference usually takes place in the form of an eviction. One possible reaction to the eviction is that the tenant can choose to terminate the lease agreement.

FORFEITURE

Similarly, suppose that either the tenant or the landlord fails to perform a condition stated in the lease. That party's breach is referred to as forfeiture because the party is forfeiting his or her interest in the premises. For instance, if a tenant fails to pay rent by the date specified in the lease agreement, the tenant could be considered as forfeiting her interest in the property. Because forfeiture is quite severe, the courts generally do not favor upholding forfeiture.

DESTRUCTION OF THE PREMISES

If a fire or some other disaster has destroyed the subject matter of the lease, most states allow termination of the lease. The tenant is released from paying rent. If the landlord had not been able to do something to prevent the disaster, the landlord is generally not expected to restore and repair the premises.

SURRENDER

Suppose that you get a job offer to manage a business in California. You have to move, but you have one month left on your lease agreement for your apartment in Ohio. You speak with your landlord, who agrees to end the lease agreement early. You are surrendering, or returning, your interest in the premises, and the landlord is agreeing to accept the return of the interest. Thus, surrender is a mutual agreement between a landlord and a tenant. The landlord accepts the tenant's offer to surrender the interest in the premises. Generally, a surrender of property must be in writing.

ABANDONMENT

If a tenant moves out of leased premises before the end of the term, has no intent to return, and has defaulted on rent payments, the tenant is essentially making an offer of surrender to the landlord. This tenant behavior is called abandonment. If the landlord accepts the property, the tenant is usually relieved of the rent obligation and the lease is terminated.

To see a discussion of Financial Accounting Standards Board (FASB) requirements regarding how companies report leases on their balance sheets, please see the **Connecting to the Core activity** on the text Web site at www.mhhe.com/kubasek2e.

CASE OPENER WRAP-UP

Free to Choose?

The federal Fair Housing Act prohibits housing discrimination based on race, color, religion, sex, handicap, familial status, or national origin. This law applies to landlords and also to tenants looking for roommates. In the Roommates.com case, the U.S. Court of Appeals for the Ninth Circuit ruled that the CDA did not immunize Roommates.com from potential liability for drafting and posting questionnaires that asked questions about sexual orientation of potential roommates, among other characteristics. The court held that Roommates.com was involved in categorizing, channeling, and limiting distribution of user profiles. Its involvement with the profiles made it ineligible for immunity under the CDA. The CDA protects Web sites that allow content created by third parties. Roommates.com was actually a content provider, creating content by creating and distributing questionnaires. The organization was enabling discrimination. How is Roommates.com different from Craigslist, Inc.? How can Roommates.com change its business practices so that it enjoys immunity under the CDA?

Key Terms

abandonment   1117

actual eviction   1109

alterations   1111

assignment   1116

common areas   1112

constructive eviction   1109

covenant of quiet
   enjoyment   1107

definite-term lease   1104

forfeiture   1117

full eviction   1109

implied warranty of
   habitability   1109

landlord   1103

landlord's lien   1114

lease   1103

leasehold estate   1103

lessee   1103

lessor   1103

partial eviction   1109

periodic-tenancy
   lease   1104

rent   1113

rent escalation clause   1114

sublease   1116

surrender   1117

tenancy-at-
   sufferance lease   1104

tenancy-at-will lease   1104

tenant   1103

waste   1110

Summary of Key Topics

Creation of the Landlord-Tenant Relationship

The *landlord,* also known as the *lessor,* is the owner of the property.

The *tenant,* also called the *lessee,* is the party who assumes temporary ownership of the property.

A *leasehold estate* is the property in question.

A *lease* is the actual agreement between the landlord and the tenant.

Types of leases:

1. *Definite term:* The lease automatically expires at the end of a given term.
2. *Periodic tenancy:* The lease is created for a recurring term.
3. *Tenancy at will:* The lease may terminate at any time.
4. *Tenancy at sufferance:* The tenant fails to leave the property after the termination of the lease.

The *Fair Housing Act* prohibits landlords from discriminating on the basis of race, color, sex, religion, national origin, or familial status.

Rights and Duties of the Landlord and the Tenant	*Possession and use of the premises:*

A *covenant of quiet enjoyment* is a promise that the tenant has the right to quietly enjoy the land.

Eviction:

1. *Actual eviction* occurs when a landlord physically prevents the tenant from entering the premises; it can be full (prohibited from all parts) or partial (prohibited from some parts).
2. *Constructive eviction* occurs when the premises become unsuitable for use due to the landlord.

Use of the premises:

An *implied warranty of habitability* is a requirement that the premises be fit for ordinary residential purposes.

Tenant use of the premises:

Waste is tenant conduct that causes permanent and substantial injury to the landlord's property. *Alterations* are changes that affect the condition of the premises; generally, they cannot be made without the landlord's consent.

Maintenance of the premises:

Common areas are areas that are used by all the tenants and for which the landlord is responsible.

Tenants' options when repairs are not done:

1. Terminate the lease.
2. Withhold rent payment.
3. Repair and deduct costs.
4. Sue the landlord.

Rent is compensation paid to the landlord for the tenant's exclusive use of and right to possess the premises. Landlords may charge a late fee, but it must be related to the amount of rent past due.

A *rent escalation clause* is a clause included in the lease that allows the landlord to increase the rent for increases in cost of living, property taxes, or the tenant's commercial business.

A landlord's lien is a landlord's right to some or all of the tenant's property when rent is unpaid.

Liability for Injuries on the Premises	*Landlord liability:* A landlord can be held liable for injuries sustained in common areas and for injuries that occurred outside common areas due to repairs the landlord should have made. The landlord has the responsibility to ensure that the premises are in reasonably good condition before the tenant takes control. The foreseeability of a crime is also a factor in liability.

Tenant's liability: A tenant must keep the premises in a reasonably safe condition but is responsible only for those areas where a customer can be reasonably expected to go.

Transferring Interests of Leased Property	*Landlord transfer of interest:* A landlord may transfer property and the new owner becomes the landlord until the tenant's lease expires.

Tenant transfer of interest:

An *assignment* transfers the tenant's entire interest in the leased property.

A *sublease* transfers less than all of the tenant's interest in a leased property.

Termination of the Lease

Termination may occur in the following instances:

1. When the landlord *breaches a condition;* for example, the landlord interferes with the tenant's use and enjoyment of the premises.

2. Through *forfeiture,* which occurs when the tenant or landlord fails to perform conditions specified in the lease.

3. When a fire or other disaster *destroys the premises.*

4. Through *surrender,* that is, mutual agreement between landlord and tenant.

5. Through *abandonment,* which occurs when the tenant moves out of the leased premises before the end of the term.

Point / Counterpoint

Should State Legislatures Be Sensitive to the Unique Needs of Mobile-Home Owner-Tenants Who Face the Possibility of Eviction?*

Yes	No
Individuals who own a mobile home but rent a lot from a park owner are called *mobile home owner-tenants.* Mobile-home owner-tenants are in a landlord-tenant relationship with the park owner because they rent a lot, or "pad." Such landlord-tenant relationships are hybrid relationships—somewhere between owning and renting.	Individuals are free to enter into contracts with owners to rent property. The right to rent comes with responsibilities, especially the responsibility of paying for rented space. When mobile-home owner-tenants fail to pay their rent, they become undesirable tenants, and landlords have every right to evict them. Landlords who evict tenants are preserving their investment.

Currently, state laws vary with regard to the extent to which mobile-home owner-tenants are treated more like apartment renters or more like traditional homeowners. The extent to which mobile-home owner-tenants are treated like traditional homeowners is especially important when the landlord wants to evict the tenant for nonpayment of rent.

In some states, legislation treats mobile-home owner-tenants more like renters than owners. This is important because, unlike the case with an apartment dweller, when a mobile-home owner-tenant is evicted, the mobile-home owner-tenant must move both herself and her home.

Many people assume that mobile homes are easy to move. In reality, mobile homes are not very mobile. It is often difficult and expensive to move these homes. It is not as if a mobile-home owner can hitch the home to a vehicle and drive off. Often, mobile homes are designed to stay put once they are set down on a pad.

When a traditional homeowner gets behind on payments, this owner typically stays in the home 12 to 18 months before the lender can remove the owner from the home. Not so with the mobile-home owner-tenant. Park owners in some states can use eviction procedures that lock mobile-home owners out of their homes in less than a month!

Sometimes, state legislatures get involved in matters related to landlord-tenant relationships. They should get involved to address chronic, rather than temporary, problems.

Problems related to mobile-home owner-tenants are typically temporary problems. It is not a public policy issue when tenants cannot pay their bills. Issues between landlords and mobile-home owner-tenants are best resolved on a case-by-case basis.

If state legislatures do respond to the unique needs created by hybrid relationships, they should respond with an eye toward protecting owners. Owners provide an important contribution to society. They make it possible for good tenants to create stable homes. If state legislatures take any action at all, it should be to create incentives for park owners to enter into long-term relationships with good tenants, not with tenants who violate the fundamental terms of their contracts.

State legislatures should protect the sanctity of the American home for mobile-home owner-tenants by changing laws to respond to the unique needs created by hybrid relationships.

* This Point/Counterpoint is based primarily on information from J. Royce Fichtner, "The Iowa Mobile Home Park Landlord-Tenant Relationship: Present Eviction Procedures and Needed Reforms," 53 *Drake Law Review* 181 (Fall 2004). The "no" argument also relies on information from Paul Sullivan, "Security of Tenure for the Residential Tenant: An Analysis and Recommendations," 21 *Vermont Law Review* 1015 (1997).

Questions & Problems

1. What is the most distinguishing element of a landlord-tenant relationship?

2. As a tenant, what are the remedies available to you if the landlord breaches the implied warranty of habitability?

3. Explain the distinction between assignment and sublease.

4. In February 1998, Sutton Moore fell through a deck when he was visiting Jonathan and Kelly Hambrick. Moore was a guest of the Hambricks, who rented a house owned and maintained by Dennis Huard and his spouse. The Huards indicated that they maintained the deck regularly, having replaced rotten posts in 1995 and a broken step in 1997. The Hambricks had not noticed or reported any problems with the deck. Moore sued the Huards for negligence. What duty do the Huards, as landlords, owe to Moore, guests of the tenants? Who won? [*Moore v. Huard,* No. 31907-1-II, Slip. Op. (Wash. App. Div. 2, 2006).]

5. Hermes Reyes was injured when he was visiting his daughter at a summer rental property in 2003. When opening a sliding door and moving onto a deck, Reyes lost his balance and fell, sustaining injury. He contended that he lost his balance because there was an unexpected six-and-a-half-inch drop to the deck. Reyes brought suit against both the landlord (Egner) and the company that managed the property for the landlord (Prudential Fox & Roach Realtors). What was the result? [*Reyes v. Egner,* 962 A.2d 542 (2009).]

6. Stanley Jancik owned and rented apartments in a large housing complex. Though the apartments contained only one bedroom, they were large enough to house more than one person, and people of all ages, including children, lived in the housing complex. Jancik placed an advertisement in the newspaper stating that a "mature person" was preferred. When Jancik was contacted by potential tenants, he explained that he did not want any teenagers and that he was looking only for middle-aged tenants without children. He also inquired about the race of the potential tenants. Jancik was sued for violating a provision of the Fair Housing Act that makes discrimination based on "race, color, religion, sex, handicap, familial status, or national origin" unlawful. Do you think that his actions were unlawful? Why or why not? [*Jancik v. Department of Housing & Urban Development,* 44 F.3d 553 (7th Cir. 1995).]

7. Although his lease expired on December 31, Kevin Schill continued to live in his rented apartment. He had previously written a letter to the apartment management stating that the apartment "has severe water leaks and severe water damage." A.G. Spanos Development, Inc., the owner of the apartments, brought an action against Schill for nonpayment of the rent. Schill filed a counterclaim against Spanos, alleging that his property was damaged by the water leaks. The damages had occurred after the December 31 expiration. Because Schill had previously complained about the problem, Spanos argued that Schill voluntarily remained in the apartment notwithstanding his knowledge of the water leaks and, therefore, was responsible for any property damages. Do you think the courts agreed with Spanos? Why or why not? [*Schill v. A.G. Spanos Development, Inc.,* 457 S.E.2d 204 (Ga. App. 1995).]

8. Defendants John and Terry Hoffius advertised for rent a piece of residential property. The ad was

answered by Kristal McCready and Keith Kerr. After learning that McCready and Kerr were unmarried, the defendants refused to rent the property to them. Another unmarried couple, Rose Baiz and Peter Perusse, were also prevented from renting the property. The couples argued that they were unfairly discriminated against because of their marital status. The defendants argued that they were motivated by a strong religious belief that unmarried couples should not live together. Do you think that this is a reasonable reason for refusing to rent the property? Why or why not? [*McCready v. Hoffius,* 586 N.W.2d 723 (Mich. 1998).]

9. John McNamara was interested in leasing space from the Wilmington Mall Realty Corp. for the development of a custom jewelry store. He signed a five-year lease for the store and renovated the space at his own expense. An aerobic studio was subsequently located in the space next to McNamara's store. McNamara was informed that the studio would be soundproofed, but immediately after the studio opened, McNamara began to complain that the music from the studio could be heard in his store. The studio installed insulation, but McNamara still argued that the noise was disrupting his business. McNamara informed Wilmington that he would withhold rent until the matter was resolved. More insulation was installed, but McNamara still did not pay rent and eventually abandoned the space. He sued Wilmington on the basis of theories of constructive eviction and breach of the covenant of quiet enjoyment. Wilmington countersued

for the unpaid rent. The trial court found in favor of McNamara and awarded him $110,000 in damages. Wilmington appealed the decision. How do you think this conflict was resolved? [*McNamara v. Wilmington Mall Realty Corp.,* 466 S.E.2d 324 (N.C. App. 1996).]

10. Escobar, a college student, sustained injuries when he fell from a fourth-story window of the Mark Tower residence hall at the University of Southern California (USC). Before he fell, he had been sleeping on a bed that was placed against a window in Mark Tower. Escobar's friends had taken him to this residence hall so that he could sleep off the effects of excessive alcohol consumption. Escobar sued USC, alleging that the residence hall was dangerous, and USC had a duty to make the facility safe. USC sought to have the lawsuit dismissed because the fall was caused by Escobar's gross consumption of alcohol. Escobar contested USC's claim, alleging that his fall was caused by a dangerous condition in the residence hall. Specifically, when the university redesigned rooms in 1996, it created a dangerous condition by removing permanently affixed desks, which had prevented beds from being placed against the window. The university should have considered what its redesign would do to furniture arrangement and how new arrangements might place students at risk. Will Escobar get to go forward with his claim? [*Escobar v. University of Southern California,* No. B166522, Los Angeles Sup. Ct., No. BC259972, available at 2004 WL 2094602.]

Looking for more review material?

The Online Learning Center at **www.mhhe.com/kubasek2e** contains this chapter's "Assignment on the Internet" and also a list of URLs for more information, entitled "On the Internet." Find both of them in the Student Center portion of the OLC, along with quizzes and other helpful materials.

THE CONSTITUTION OF THE UNITED STATES OF AMERICA

Preamble

We the People of the United States, in Order to form a more perfect Union, establish Justice, insure domestic Tranquility, provide for the common defense, promote the general Welfare, and secure the Blessings of Liberty to ourselves and our Posterity, do ordain and establish this Constitution for the United States of America.

Article I

Section 1. All legislative Powers herein granted shall be vested in a Congress of the United States, which shall consist of a Senate and House of Representatives.

Section 2. The House of Representatives shall be composed of Members chosen every second Year by the People of the several States, and the Electors in each State shall have the Qualifications requisite for Electors of the most numerous Branch of the State Legislature.

No Person shall be a Representative who shall not have attained to the age of twenty five Years, and been seven Years a Citizen of the United States, and who shall not, when elected, be an Inhabitant of that State in which he shall be chosen.

Representatives and direct Taxes shall be apportioned among the several States which may be included within this Union, according to their respective Numbers, which shall be determined by adding to the whole Number of free Persons, including those bound to Service for a Term of Years, and excluding Indians not taxed, three fifths of all other Persons.[1] The actual Enumeration shall be made within three Years after the first Meeting of the Congress of the United States, and within every subsequent Term of ten Years, in such Manner as they shall by Law direct. The Number of Representatives shall not exceed one for every thirty Thousand, but each State shall have at Least one Representative, and until such enumeration shall be made, the State of New Hampshire shall be entitled to choose three, Massachusetts eight, Rhode-Island and Providence Plantations one, Connecticut five, New York six, New Jersey four, Pennsylvania eight, Delaware one, Maryland six, Virginia ten, North Carolina five, South Carolina five, and Georgia three.

When vacancies happen in the Representation from any State, the Executive Authority thereof shall issue Writs of Election to fill such Vacancies.

The House of Representatives shall chuse their Speaker and other Officers; and shall have the sole Power of Impeachment.

Section 3. The Senate of the United States shall be composed of two Senators from each State, chosen by the Legislature thereof,[2] for six Years; and each Senator shall have one Vote.

Immediately after they shall be assembled in Consequence of the first Election, they shall be divided as equally as may be into three Classes. The Seats of the Senators of the first Class shall be vacated at the Expiration of the second Year, of the second Class at the Expiration of the fourth Year, and of the third Class at the Expiration of the sixth Year, so that one third may

---

[1] Changed by the Fourteenth Amendment.

[2] Changed by the Seventeenth Amendment.

be chosen every second Year; and if Vacancies happen by Resignation, or otherwise, during the Recess of the Legislature of any State, the Executive thereof may make temporary Appointments until the next Meeting of the Legislature, which shall then fill such Vacancies.[3]

No Person shall be a Senator who shall not have attained to the Age of thirty Years, and been nine Years a Citizen of the United States, and who shall not, when elected, be an Inhabitant of that State for which he shall be chosen.

The Vice President of the United States shall be President of the Senate, but shall have no Vote, unless they be equally divided.

The Senate shall chuse their other Officers, and also a President pro tempore, in the Absence of the Vice President, or when he shall exercise the Office of President of the United States.

The Senate shall have the sole Power to try all Impeachments. When sitting for that Purpose, they shall be on Oath or Affirmation. When the President of the United States is tried, the Chief Justice shall preside: And no Person shall be convicted without the Concurrence of two thirds of the Members present.

Judgment in Cases of Impeachment shall not extend further than to removal from Office, and disqualification to hold and enjoy any Office of honor, Trust or Profit under the United States: but the Party convicted shall nevertheless be liable and subject to Indictment, Trial, Judgment and Punishment, according to Law.

Section 4. The Times, Places and Manner of holding Elections for Senators and Representatives, shall be prescribed in each State by the Legislature thereof; but the Congress may at any time by Law make or alter such Regulations, except as to the Places of chusing Senators.

The Congress shall assemble at least once in every Year, and such Meeting shall be on the first Monday in December, unless they shall by Law appoint a different Day.[4]

Section 5. Each House shall be the Judge of the Elections, Returns and Qualifications of its own Members, and a Majority of each shall constitute a Quorum to do Business; but a smaller Number may adjourn from day to day, and may be authorized to compel the Attendance of absent Members, in such Manner, and under such Penalties as each House may provide.

Each House may determine the Rules of its Proceedings, punish its Members for disorderly Behaviour, and with the Concurrence of two thirds, expel a Member.

Each House shall keep a Journal of its Proceedings, and from time to time publish the same, excepting such Parts as may in their Judgment require Secrecy; and the Yeas and Nays of the Members of either House on any question shall, at the Desire of one fifth of those Present, be entered on the Journal.

Neither House, during the Session of Congress, shall, without the Consent of the other, adjourn for more than three days, nor to any other Place than that in which the two Houses shall be sitting.

Section 6. The Senators and Representatives shall receive a Compensation for their Services, to be ascertained by Law, and paid out of the Treasury of the United States. They shall in all Cases, except Treason, Felony and Breach of the Peace, be privileged from Arrest during their Attendance at the Session of their respective Houses, and in going to and returning from the same; and for any Speech or Debate in either House, they shall not be questioned in any other Place.

No Senator or Representative shall, during the Time for which he was elected, be appointed to any civil Office under the Authority of the United States, which shall have been created, or the Emoluments whereof shall have been encreased during such time; and no Person holding any Office under the United States, shall be a Member of either House during his Continuance in Office.

---

[3] Changed by the Seventeenth Amendment.

[4] Changed by the Twentieth Amendment.

Section 7. All Bills for raising Revenue shall originate in the House of Representatives; but the Senate may propose or concur with Amendments as on other Bills.

Every Bill which shall have passed the House of Representatives and the Senate, shall, before it becomes a Law, be presented to the President of the United States; If he approves he shall sign it, but if not he shall return it, with his Objections to that House in which it shall have originated, who shall enter the Objections at large on their Journal, and proceed to reconsider it. If after such Reconsideration two thirds of that House shall agree to pass the Bill, it shall be sent, together with the Objections, to the other House, by which it shall likewise be reconsidered, and if approved by two thirds of that House, it shall become a Law. But in all such Cases the Votes of both Houses shall be determined by Yeas and Nays, and the Names of the Persons voting for and against the Bill shall be entered on the Journal of each House respectively. If any Bill shall not be returned by the President within ten Days (Sundays excepted) after it shall have been presented to him, the Same shall be a Law, in like Manner as if he had signed it, unless the Congress by their Adjournment prevent its Return, in which Case it shall not be a Law.

Every Order, Resolution, or Vote to which the Concurrence of the Senate and House of Representatives may be necessary (except on a question of Adjournment) shall be presented to the President of the United States; and before the Same shall take Effect, shall be approved by him, or being disapproved by him, shall be repassed by two thirds of the Senate and House of Representatives, according to the Rules and Limitations prescribed in the Case of a Bill.

Section 8. The Congress shall have Power To lay and collect Taxes, Duties, Imposts and Excises, to pay the Debts and provide for the common Defence and general Welfare of the United States; but all Duties, Imposts and Excises shall be uniform throughout the United States.

To borrow Money on the credit of the United States;

To regulate Commerce with foreign Nations, and among the several States, and with the Indian Tribes;

To establish an uniform Rule of Naturalization, and uniform Laws on the subject of Bankruptcies throughout the United States;

To coin Money, regulate the Value thereof, and of foreign Coin, and fix the Standard of Weights and Measures;

To provide for the Punishment of counterfeiting the Securities and current Coin of the United States;

To establish Post Offices and post Roads;

To promote the Progress of Science and useful Arts, by securing for limited Times to Authors and Inventors the exclusive Right to their respective Writings and Discoveries;

To constitute Tribunals inferior to the supreme Court;

To define and punish Piracies and Felonies committed on the high Seas, and Offences against the Law of Nations;

To declare War, grant Letters of Marque and Reprisal, and make Rules concerning Captures on Land and Water;

To raise and support Armies, but no Appropriation of Money to that Use shall be for a longer Term than two Years;

To provide and maintain a Navy;

To make Rules for the Government and Regulation of the land and naval Forces;

To provide for calling forth the Militia to execute the Laws of the Union, suppress Insurrections and repel Invasions;

To provide for organizing, arming, and disciplining, the Militia, and for governing such Part of them as may be employed in the Service of the United States, reserving to the States respectively, the Appointment of the Officers, and the Authority of training the Militia according to the discipline prescribed by Congress;

To exercise exclusive Legislation in all Cases whatsoever, over such District (not exceeding ten Miles square) as may, by Cession of particular States, and the Acceptance of Congress, become the Seat of the Government of the United States, and to exercise like Authority over all Places purchased by the Consent of the Legislature of the State in which the Same shall be, for the Erection of Forts, Magazines, Arsenals, dock-Yards, and other needful Buildings;—And

To make all Laws which shall be necessary and proper for carrying into Execution the foregoing Powers, and all other Powers vested by this Constitution in the Government of the United States, or in any Department or Officer thereof.

Section 9. The Migration or Importation of such Persons as any of the States now existing shall think proper to admit, shall not be prohibited by the Congress prior to the Year one thousand eight hundred and eight, but a Tax or duty may be imposed on such Importation, not exceeding ten dollars for each Person.

The Privilege of the Writ of Habeas Corpus shall not be suspended, unless when in Cases of Rebellion or Invasion the public Safety may require it.

No Bill of Attainder or ex post facto Law shall be passed.

No Capitation, or other direct, Tax shall be laid, unless in Proportion to the Census of Enumeration herein before directed to be taken.[5]

No Tax or Duty shall be laid on Articles exported from any State.

No Preference shall be given by any Regulation of Commerce or Revenue to the Ports of one State over those of another: nor shall Vessels bound to, or from, one State, be obliged to enter, clear, or pay Duties in another.

No Money shall be drawn from the Treasury, but in Consequence of Appropriations made by Law; and a regular Statement and Account of the Receipts and Expenditures of all public Money shall be published from time to time.

No Title of Nobility shall be granted by the United States: And no Person holding any Office of Profit or Trust under them, shall, without the Consent of the Congress, accept of any present, Emolument, Office, or Title, of any kind whatever, from any King, Prince, or foreign State.

Section 10. No State shall enter into any Treaty, Alliance, or Confederation; grant Letters of Marque and Reprisal; coin Money; emit Bills of Credit; make any Thing but gold and silver coin a Tender in Payment of Debts; pass any Bill of Attainder, ex post facto Law, or Law impairing the Obligation of Contracts, or grant any Title of Nobility.

No State shall, without the Consent of the Congress, lay any Imposts or Duties on Imports or Exports, except what may be absolutely necessary for executing its inspection Laws: and the net Produce of all Duties and Imposts, laid by any State on Imports or Exports, shall be for the Use of the Treasury of the United States; and all such Laws shall be subject to the Revision and Control of the Congress.

No State shall, without the consent of Congress, lay any Duty of Tonnage, keep Troops, or Ships of War in time of Peace, enter into any Agreement or Compact with another State, or with a foreign Power, or engage in War, unless actually invaded, or in such imminent Danger as will not admit of delay.

Article II

Section 1. The executive Power shall be vested in a President of the United States of America. He shall hold his Office during the Term of four Years, and, together with the Vice President, chosen for the same Term, be elected, as follows

Each state shall appoint, in such Manner as the Legislature thereof may direct, a Number of Electors, equal to the whole Number of Senators and Representatives to which the State may be entitled in Congress: but no Senator or Representative, or Person holding an Office of Trust or Profit under the United States, shall be appointed an Elector.

---

[5] Changed by the Sixteenth Amendment.

The Electors shall meet in their respective States, and vote by Ballot for two Persons, of whom one at least shall not be an inhabitant of the same State with themselves. And they shall make a List of all the Persons voted for, and of the Number of Votes for each; which List they shall sign and certify, and transmit sealed to the Seat of the Government of the United States, directed to the President of the Senate. The President of the Senate shall, in the Presence of the Senate and House of Representatives, open all the Certificates, and the Votes shall then be counted. The Person having the greatest Number of Votes shall be the President, if such Number be a Majority of the whole Number of Electors appointed; and if there be more than one who have such Majority, and have an equal Number of Votes, then the House of Representatives shall immediately chuse by Ballot one of them for President; and if no Person have a Majority, then from the five highest on the List the said House shall in like Manner chuse the President. But in chusing the President, the Votes shall be taken by States, the Representation from each State having one Vote; A quorum for this purpose shall consist of a Member or Members from two thirds of the States, and a Majority of all the States shall be necessary to a Choice. In every Case, after the Choice of the President, the Person having the greatest Number of Votes of the Electors shall be the Vice President. But if there should remain two or more who have equal Votes, the Senate shall chuse from them by Ballot the Vice President.[6]

The Congress may determine the Time of chusing the Electors, and the Day on which they shall give their Votes; which Day shall be the same throughout the United States.

No Person except a natural born Citizen, or a Citizen of the United States, at the time of the Adoption of this Constitution, shall be eligible to the Office of President; neither shall any Person be eligible to that Office who shall not have attained to the Age of thirty five Years, and been fourteen Years a Resident within the United States.

In Case of the Removal of the President from Office, or of his Death, Resignation, or Inability to discharge the Powers and Duties of the said Office, the Same shall devolve on the Vice President, and the Congress may by Law provide for the Case of Removal, Death, Resignation or Inability, both of the President and Vice President, declaring what Officer shall then act as President, and such Officer shall act accordingly, until the Disability be removed, or a President shall be elected.[7]

The President shall, at stated Times, receive for his Services, a Compensation, which shall neither be encreased nor diminished during the Period for which he shall have been elected, and he shall not receive within that Period any other Emolument from the United States, or any of them.

Before he enter on the Execution of his Office, he shall take the following Oath or Affirmation:—"I do solemnly swear (or affirm) that I will faithfully execute the Office of President of the United States, and will to the best of my Ability, preserve, protect, and defend the Constitution of the United States."

Section 2. The President shall be Commander in Chief of the Army and Navy of the United States, and of the Militia of the several States, when called into the actual Service of the United States; he may require the Opinion, in writing, of the principal Officer in each of the executive Departments, upon any Subject relating to the Duties of their respective Offices, and he shall have Power to grant Reprieves and Pardons for Offences against the United States, except in Cases of Impeachment.

He shall have Power, by and with the Advice and Consent of the Senate, to make Treaties, provided two thirds of the Senators present concur; and he shall nominate, and by and with the Advice and Consent of the Senate, shall appoint Ambassadors, other public Ministers and Consuls, Judges of the supreme Court, and all other Officers of the United States, whose Appointments are not herein otherwise provided for, and which shall be established

[6] Changed by the Twelfth Amendment.
[7] Changed by the Twenty-Fifth Amendment.

by Law; but the Congress may by Law vest the Appointment of such inferior Officers, as they think proper, in the President alone, in the Courts of Law, or in the Heads of Departments.

The President shall have Power to fill up all Vacancies that may happen during the Recess of the Senate, by granting Commissions which shall expire at the End of their next Session.

Section 3. He shall from time to time give to the Congress Information of the State of the Union, and recommend to their Consideration such Measures as he shall judge necessary and expedient; he may, on extraordinary Occasions, convene both Houses, or either of them, and in Case of Disagreement between them, with Respect to the Time of Adjournment, he may adjourn them to such Time as he shall think proper; he shall receive Ambassadors and other public Ministers; he shall take Care that the Laws be faithfully executed, and shall Commission all the Officers of the United States.

Section 4. The President, Vice President and all civil Officers of the United States, shall be removed from Office on Impeachment for, and Conviction of, Treason, Bribery, or other high Crimes and Misdemeanors.

Article III

Section 1. The judicial Power of the United States, shall be vested in one supreme Court, and in such inferior Courts as the Congress may from time to time ordain and establish. The Judges, both of the supreme and inferior Courts, shall hold their Offices during good Behaviour, and shall, at stated Times, receive for their Services, a Compensation, which shall not be diminished during their Continuance in Office.

Section 2. The judicial Power shall extend to all Cases, in Law and Equity, arising under this Constitution, the Laws of the United States, and Treaties made, or which shall be made, under their Authority;—to all Cases affecting Ambassadors, other public Ministers and Consuls;—to all Cases of admiralty and maritime Jurisdiction;—to Controversies to which the United States shall be a party;—to Controversies between two or more States;—between a State and Citizens of another State;[8]—between Citizens of different States;—between Citizens of the same State claiming Lands under Grants of different States, and between a State, or the Citizens thereof, and foreign States, Citizens or Subjects.

In all Cases affecting Ambassadors, other public Ministers and Consuls, and those in which a State shall be Party, the supreme Court shall have original Jurisdiction. In all the other Cases before mentioned, the supreme Court shall have appellate Jurisdiction, both as to Law and Fact, with such Exceptions, and under such Regulations as the Congress shall make.

The Trial of all Crimes, except in Cases of Impeachment, shall be by Jury: and such Trial shall be held in the State where the said Crimes shall have been committed; but when not committed within any State, the Trial shall be at such Place or Places as the Congress may by Law have directed.

Section 3. Treason against the United States, shall consist only in levying War against them, or in adhering to their Enemies, giving them Aid and Comfort. No Person shall be convicted of Treason unless on the Testimony of two Witnesses to the same overt Act, or on Confession in open Court.

The Congress shall have Power to declare the Punishment of Treason, but no Attainder of Treason shall work Corruption of Blood, or Forfeiture except during the Life of the Person attainted.

---

[8] Changed by the Eleventh Amendment.

Article IV

Section 1. Full Faith and Credit shall be given in each State to the public Acts, Records, and judicial Proceedings of every other State. And the Congress may by general Laws prescribe the Manner in which such Acts, Records and Proceedings shall be proved, and the Effect thereof.

Section 2. The Citizens of each State shall be entitled to all Privileges and Immunities of Citizens in the several States.

A Person charged in any State with Treason, Felony, or other Crime, who shall flee from Justice, and be found in another State, shall on Demand of the executive Authority of the State from which he fled, be delivered up, to be removed to the State having Jurisdiction of the Crime.

No Person held to Service or Labour in one State, under the Laws thereof, escaping into another, shall, in Consequence of any Law or Regulation therein, be discharged from such Service or Labour, but shall be delivered up on Claim of the Party to whom such Service or Labour may be due.[9]

Section 3. New States may be admitted by the Congress into this Union; but no new State shall be formed or erected within the Jurisdiction of any other State; nor any State be formed by the Junction of two or more States, or Parts of States, without the Consent of the Legislatures of the States concerned as well as of the Congress.

The Congress shall have Power to dispose of and make all needful Rules and Regulations respecting the Territory or other Property belonging to the United States; and nothing in this Constitution shall be so construed as to Prejudice any Claims of the United States, or of any particular State.

Section 4. The United States shall guarantee to every State in this Union a Republican Form of Government, and shall protect each of them against Invasion; and on Application of the Legislature, or of the Executive (when the Legislature cannot be convened) against domestic Violence.

Article V

The Congress, whenever two thirds of both Houses shall deem it necessary, shall propose Amendments to this Constitution, or, on the Application of the Legislatures of two thirds of the several States, shall call a Convention for proposing Amendments, which, in either Case, shall be valid to all Intents and Purposes, as Part of this Constitution, when ratified by the legislatures of three fourths of the several States, or by Conventions in three fourths thereof, as the one or the other Mode of Ratification may be proposed by the Congress; Provided that no Amendment which may be made prior to the Year One thousand eight hundred and eight shall in any Manner affect the first and fourth Clauses in the Ninth Section of the first Article; and that no State, without its Consent, shall be deprived of its equal Suffrage in the Senate.

Article VI

All Debts contracted and Engagements entered into, before the Adoption of this Constitution, shall be as valid against the United States under this Constitution, as under the Confederation.

The Constitution, and the Laws of the United States which shall be made in Pursuance thereof; and all Treaties made, or which shall be made, under the Authority of the United States,

---

[9] Changed by the Thirteenth Amendment.

shall be the supreme Law of the Land; and the Judges in every State shall be bound thereby, any Thing in the Constitution or Laws of any State to the Contrary notwithstanding.

The Senators and Representatives before mentioned, and the Members of the several State Legislatures, and all executive and judicial Officers, both of the United States and of the several States, shall be bound by Oath or Affirmation, to support this Constitution; but no religious Test shall ever be required as a Qualification to any Office or public Trust under the United States.

Article VII

The Ratification of the Conventions of nine States, shall be sufficient for the Establishment of this Constitution between the States so ratifying the Same.

Done in Convention by the Unanimous Consent of the States present the Seventeenth Day of September in the Year of our Lord one thousand seven hundred and eighty seven and of the Independence of the United States of America the Twelfth. In witness whereof We have hereunto subscribed our Names.

Amendments

[The first 10 amendments are known as the "Bill of Rights."]

AMENDMENT I (RATIFIED 1791)

Congress shall make no law respecting an establishment of religion, or prohibiting the free exercise thereof; or abridging the freedom of speech, or of the press; or the right of the people peaceably to assemble, and to petition the Government for a redress of grievances.

AMENDMENT 2 (RATIFIED 1791)

A well regulated Militia, being necessary to the security of a free State, the right of the people to keep and bear Arms, shall not be infringed.

AMENDMENT 3 (RATIFIED 1791)

No Soldier shall, in time of peace be quartered in any house, without the consent of the Owner, nor in time of war, but in a manner to be prescribed by law.

AMENDMENT 4 (RATIFIED 1791)

The right of the people to be secure in their persons, houses, papers, and effects, against unreasonable searches and seizures, shall not be violated, and no Warrants shall issue, but upon probable cause, supported by Oath or affirmation, and particularly describing the place to be searched, and the persons or things to be seized.

AMENDMENT 5 (RATIFIED 1791)

No person shall be held to answer for a capital, or otherwise infamous crime, unless on a presentment or indictment of a Grand Jury, except in cases arising in the land or naval forces, or in the Militia, when in actual service in time of War or public danger; nor shall any person be subject for the same offence to be twice put in jeopardy of life or limb; nor shall be compelled in any criminal case to be a witness against himself, nor be deprived of life, liberty, or property, without due process of law; nor shall private property be taken for public use, without just compensation.

AMENDMENT 6 (RATIFIED 1791)

In all criminal prosecutions, the accused shall enjoy the right to a speedy and public trial, by an impartial jury of the State and district wherein the crime shall have been committed, which district shall have been previously ascertained by law, and to be informed of the nature and cause of the accusation; to be confronted with the witnesses against him; to have compulsory process for obtaining Witnesses in his favor, and to have assistance of counsel for his defence.

AMENDMENT 7 (RATIFIED 1791)

In Suits at common law, where the value in controversy shall exceed twenty dollars, the right of trial by jury shall be preserved, and no fact tried by a jury, shall be otherwise re-examined in any Court of the United States, than according to the rules of the common law.

AMENDMENT 8 (RATIFIED 1791)

Excessive bail shall not be required, nor excessive fines imposed, nor cruel and unusual punishments inflicted.

AMENDMENT 9 (RATIFIED 1791)

The enumeration in the Constitution, of certain rights, shall not be construed to deny or disparage others retained by the people.

AMENDMENT 10 (RATIFIED 1791)

The powers not delegated to the United States by the Constitution, nor prohibited by it to the States, are reserved to the States respectively, or to the people.

AMENDMENT 11 (RATIFIED 1795)

The Judicial power of the United States shall not be construed to extend to any suit in law or equity, commenced or prosecuted against one of the United States by Citizens of another State, or by Citizens or Subjects of any Foreign State.

AMENDMENT 12 (RATIFIED 1804)

The Electors shall meet in their respective states, and vote by ballot for President and Vice-President, one of whom, at least, shall not be an inhabitant of the same state with themselves; they shall name in their ballots the person voted for as President, and in distinct ballots the person voted for as Vice-President, and they shall make distinct lists of all persons voted for as President, and of all persons voted for as Vice-President, and of the number of votes for each, which lists they shall sign and certify, and transmit sealed to the seat of the government of the United States, directed to the President of the Senate;—The President of the Senate shall, in the presence of the Senate and House of Representatives, open all the certificates and the votes shall then be counted;—The person having the greatest number of votes for President, shall be the President, if such number be a majority of the whole number of Electors appointed; and if no person have such majority, then from the persons having the highest numbers not exceeding three on the list of those voted for as President, the House of Representatives shall choose immediately, by ballot, the President. But in choosing the President, the votes shall be taken by states, the representation from each state having one vote; a quorum for this purpose shall consist of a member or members from two-thirds of the states, and a majority of all the states shall be necessary to a choice. And if the House of Representatives shall not choose a President whenever the right of choice shall devolve upon them, before the fourth day of March next following, then the Vice-President shall act as president, as in the case of the death or other constitutional disability of the President.[10]—The person having the greatest number of votes as Vice-President, shall be the Vice-President, if such number be a majority of the whole number of Electors appointed, and if no person have a majority, then from the two highest numbers on the list, the Senate shall choose the Vice-President; a quorum for the purpose shall consist of two-thirds of the whole number of Senators, and a majority of the whole number shall be necessary to a choice. But no person constitutionally ineligible to the office of President shall be eligible to that of Vice-President of the United States.

AMENDMENT 13 (RATIFIED 1865)

Section 1. Neither slavery nor involuntary servitude, except as a punishment for crime whereof the party shall have been duly convicted, shall exist within the United States, or any place subject to their jurisdiction.

Section 2. Congress shall have power to enforce this article by appropriate legislation.

AMENDMENT 14 (RATIFIED 1868)

Section 1. All persons born or naturalized in the United States, and subject to the jurisdiction thereof, are citizens of the United States and of the State wherein they reside. No State shall make or enforce any law which shall abridge the privileges or immunities of citizens of the United States; nor shall any State deprive any person of life, liberty, or property, without due process of law; nor deny to any person within its jurisdiction the equal protection of the laws.

Section 2. Representatives shall be apportioned among the several States according to their respective numbers, counting the whole number of persons in each State, excluding Indians not taxed. But when the right to vote at any election for the choice of electors for President and Vice President of the United States, Representatives in Congress, the Executive and Judicial officers of a State, or the members of the Legislature thereof, is denied to any of the male inhabitants of such State, being twenty-one[11] years of age, and citizens of the United States, or in any way abridged except for participation in rebellion, or other crime, the basis of representation therein shall be reduced in the proportion which the number of such male citizens shall bear to the whole number of male citizens twenty-one years of age in such State.

Section 3. No person shall be a Senator or Representative in Congress, or elector of President and Vice President, or hold any office, civil or military, under the United States, or under any State, who, having previously taken an oath, as a member of Congress, or as an officer of the United States, or as a member of any State legislature, or as an executive or judicial officer of any State, to support the Constitution of the United States, shall have engaged in insurrection or rebellion against the same, or given aid or comfort to the enemies thereof. But Congress may by a vote of two-thirds of each House, remove such disability.

Section 4. The validity of the public debt of the United States, authorized by law, including debts incurred for payment of pensions and bounties for services in suppressing insurrection or rebellion, shall not be questioned. But neither the United States nor any State shall assume or pay any debt or obligation incurred in aid of insurrection or rebellion against the United States, or any claim for the loss or emancipation of any slave; but all such debts, obligations and claims shall be held illegal and void.

[10] Changed by the Twentieth Amendment.

[11] Changed by the Twenty-Sixth Amendment.

Section 5. The Congress shall have power to enforce, by appropriate legislation, the provisions of this article.

AMENDMENT 15 (RATIFIED 1870)

Section 1. The right of citizens of the United States to vote shall not be denied or abridged by the United States or by any State on account of race, color, or previous condition of servitude.

Section 2. The Congress shall have power to enforce this article by appropriate legislation.

AMENDMENT 16 (RATIFIED 1913)

The Congress shall have power to lay and collect taxes on incomes, from whatever source derived, without apportionment among the several States, and without regard to any census or enumeration.

AMENDMENT 17 (RATIFIED 1913)

The Senate of the United States shall be composed of two Senators from each State, elected by the people thereof, for six years; and each Senator shall have one vote. The electors in each State shall have the qualifications requisite for electors of the most numerous branch of the State legislatures.

When vacancies happen in the representation of any State in the Senate, the executive authority of such State shall issue writs of election to fill such vacancies: *Provided,* That the legislature of any State may empower the executive thereof to make temporary appointments until the people fill the vacancies by election as the legislature may direct.

This amendment shall not be so construed as to affect the election or term of any Senator chosen before it becomes valid as part of the Constitution.

AMENDMENT 18 (RATIFIED 1919; REPEALED 1933)

Section 1. After one year from the ratification of this article the manufacture, sale, or transportation of intoxicating liquors within, the importation thereof into, or the exportation thereof from the United States and all territory subject to the jurisdiction thereof for beverage purposes is hereby prohibited.

Section 2. The Congress and the several States shall have concurrent power to enforce this article by appropriate legislation.

Section 3. This article shall be inoperative unless it shall have been ratified as an amendment to the Constitution by the legislatures of the several States, as provided in the Constitution, within seven years from the date of the submission hereof to the States by the Congress.[12]

AMENDMENT 19 (RATIFIED 1920)

The right of citizens of the United States to vote shall not be denied or abridged by the United States or by any State on account of sex.

Congress shall have power to enforce this article by appropriate legislation.

AMENDMENT 20 (RATIFIED 1933)

Section 1. The terms of the President and Vice President shall end at noon on the 20th day of January, and the terms of Senators and Representatives at noon on the 3rd day of January,

---

[12] Repealed by the Twenty-First Amendment.

of the years in which such terms would have ended if this article had not been ratified; and the terms of their successors shall then begin.

Section 2. The Congress shall assemble at least once in every year, and such meeting shall begin at noon on the 3rd day of January, unless they shall by law appoint a different day.

Section 3. If, at the time fixed for the beginning of the term of the President, the President elect shall have died, the Vice President elect shall become President. If a President shall not have been chosen before the time fixed for the beginning of his term, or if the President elect shall have failed to qualify, then the Vice President elect shall act as President until a President shall have qualified; and the Congress may by law provide for the case wherein neither a President elect nor a Vice President elect shall have qualified, declaring who shall then act as President, or the manner in which one who is to act shall be selected, and such person shall act accordingly until a President or Vice President shall have qualified.

Section 4. The Congress may by law provide for the case of the death of any of the persons from whom the House of Representatives may choose a President whenever the right of choice shall have devolved upon them, and for the case of the death of any of the persons from whom the Senate may choose a Vice President whenever the right of choice shall have devolved upon them.

Section 5. Sections 1 and 2 shall take effect on the 15th day of October following the ratification of this article.

Section 6. This article shall be inoperative unless it shall have been ratified as an amendment to the Constitution by the legislatures of three-fourths of the several States within seven years from the date of its submission.

AMENDMENT 21 (RATIFIED 1933)

Section 1. The eighteenth article of amendment to the Constitution of the United States is hereby repealed.

Section 2. The transportation or importation into any State, Territory, or possession of the United States for delivery or use therein of intoxicating liquors, in violation of the laws thereof, is hereby prohibited.

Section 3. This article shall be inoperative unless it shall have been ratified as an amendment to the Constitution by conventions in the several States, as provided in the Constitution, within seven years from the date of the submission hereof to the States by the Congress.

AMENDMENT 22 (RATIFIED 1951)

Section 1. No person shall be elected to the office of the President more than twice, and no person who has held the office of President, or acted as President, for more than two years of a term to which some other person was elected President shall be elected to the office of the President more than once. But this Article shall not apply to any person holding the office of President when this Article was proposed by the Congress, and shall not prevent any person who may be holding the office of President, or acting as President, during the term within which this Article becomes operative from holding the office of President or acting as President during the remainder of such term.

Section 2. This Article shall be inoperative unless it shall have been ratified as an amendment to the Constitution by the legislatures of three-fourths of the several States within seven years from the date of its submission to the States by the Congress.

AMENDMENT 23 (RATIFIED 1961)

Section 1. The District constituting the seat of Government of the United States shall appoint in such manner as the Congress may direct:

A number of electors of President and Vice President equal to the whole number of Senators and Representatives in Congress to which the District would be entitled if it were a State, but in no event more than the least populous State; they shall be in addition to those appointed by the States, but they shall be considered, for the purposes of the election of President and Vice President, to be electors appointed by a State; and they shall meet in the District and perform such duties as provided by the twelfth article of amendment.

Section 2. The Congress shall have power to enforce this article by appropriate legislation.

AMENDMENT 24 (RATIFIED 1964)

Section 1. The right of citizens of the United States to vote in any primary or other election for President or Vice President, for electors for President or Vice President, or for Senator or Representative in Congress, shall not be denied or abridged by the United States or any State by reason of failure to pay any poll tax or other tax.

Section 2. The Congress shall have power to enforce this article by appropriate legislation.

AMENDMENT 25 (RATIFIED 1967)

Section 1. In case of the removal of the President from office or of his death or resignation, the Vice President shall become President.

Section 2. Whenever there is a vacancy in the office of the Vice President, the President shall nominate a Vice President who shall take office upon confirmation by a majority vote of both Houses of Congress.

Section 3. Whenever the President transmits to the President pro tempore of the Senate and the Speaker of the House of Representatives his written declaration that he is unable to discharge the powers and duties of his office, and until he transmits to them a written declaration to the contrary, such powers and duties shall be discharged by the Vice President as Acting President.

Section 4. Whenever the Vice President and a majority of either the principal officers of the executive departments or of such other body as Congress may by law provide, transmit to the President pro tempore of the Senate and the Speaker of the House of Representatives their written declaration that the President is unable to discharge the powers and duties of his office, the Vice President shall immediately assume the powers and duties of the office as Acting President.

Thereafter, when the President transmits to the President pro tempore of the Senate and the Speaker of the House of Representatives his written declaration that no inability exists, he shall resume the powers and duties of his office unless the Vice President and a majority of either the principal officers of the executive department or of such other body as Congress may by law provide, transmit within four days to the President pro tempore of the Senate and the Speaker of the House of Representatives their written declaration that the President is unable to discharge the powers and duties of his office. Thereupon Congress shall decide the issue, assembling within forty-eight hours for that purpose if not in session. If the Congress, within twenty-one days after receipt of the latter written declaration, or, if Congress is not in session, within twenty-one days after Congress is required to assemble, determines by two-thirds vote of both Houses that the President is unable to discharge the powers and duties of his office, the Vice President shall continue to discharge the same as Acting President; otherwise, the President shall resume the powers and duties of his office.

AMENDMENT 26 (RATIFIED 1971)

Section 1. The right of citizens of the United States, who are eighteen years of age or older, to vote shall not be denied or abridged by the United States or by any State on account of age.

Section 2. The Congress shall have power to enforce this article by appropriate legislation.

AMENDMENT 27 (RATIFIED 1992)

No law, varying the compensation for the services of the Senators and Representatives, shall take effect, until an election of Representatives shall have intervened.

Appendix B

Uniform Commercial Code

Article 2—Sales

PART 1: SHORT TITLE, GENERAL CONSTRUCTION AND SUBJECT MATTER

§ 2–101. Short Title. This Article shall be known and may be cited as Uniform Commercial Code—Sales.

§ 2–102. Scope; Certain Security and Other Transactions Excluded from This Article. Unless the context otherwise requires, this Article applies to transactions in goods; it does not apply to any transaction which although in the form of an unconditional contract to sell or present sale is intended to operate only as a security transaction nor does this Article impair or repeal any statute regulating sales to consumers, farmers or other specified classes of buyers.

§ 2–103. Definitions and Index of Definitions.

(1) In this Article unless the context otherwise requires
    (a) "Buyer" means a person who buys or contracts to buy goods.
    (b) "Good faith" in the case of a merchant means honesty in fact and the observance of reasonable commercial standards of fair dealing in the trade.
    (c) "Receipt" of goods means taking physical possession of them.
    (d) "Seller" means a person who sells or contracts to sell goods.
(2) Other definitions applying to this Article or to specified Parts thereof, and the sections in which they appear are:

"Acceptance"	Section 2–606.
"Banker's credit"	Section 2–325.
"Between merchants"	Section 2–104.
"Cancellation"	Section 2–106(4).
"Commercial unit"	Section 2–105.
"Confirmed credit"	Section 2–325.
"Conforming to contract"	Section 2–106.
"Contract for sale"	Section 2–106.
"Cover"	Section 2–712.
"Entrusting"	Section 2–403.
"Financing agency"	Section 2–104.
"Future goods"	Section 2–105.
"Goods"	Section 2–105.
"Identification"	Section 2–501.
"Installment contract"	Section 2–612.
"Letter of Credit"	Section 2–325.
"Lot"	Section 2–105.

"Merchant"	Section 2–104.
"Overseas"	Section 2–323.
"Person in position of seller"	Section 2–707.
"Present sale"	Section 2–106.
"Sale"	Section 2–106.
"Sale on approval"	Section 2–326.
"Sale or return"	Section 2–326.
"Termination"	Section 2–106.

(3) The following definitions in other Articles apply to this Article:

"Check"	Section 3–104.
"Consignee"	Section 7–102.
"Consignor"	Section 7–102.
"Consumer goods"	Section 9–109.
"Dishonor"	Section 3–502.
"Draft"	Section 3–104.

(4) In addition Article 1 contains general definitions and principles of construction and interpretation applicable throughout this Article.

As amended in 1994.

See Appendix XI for material relating to changes made in text in 1994.

§ 2–104. Definitions: "Merchant"; "Between Merchants"; "Financing Agency".

(1) "Merchant" means a person who deals in goods of the kind or otherwise by his occupation holds himself out as having knowledge or skill peculiar to the practices or goods involved in the transaction or to whom such knowledge or skill may be attributed by his employment of an agent or broker or other intermediary who by his occupation holds himself out as having such knowledge or skill.

(2) "Financing agency" means a bank, finance company or other person who in the ordinary course of business makes advances against goods or documents of title or who by arrangement with either the seller or the buyer intervenes in ordinary course to make or collect payment due or claimed under the contract for sale, as by purchasing or paying the seller's draft or making advances against it or by merely taking it for collection whether or not documents of title accompany the draft. "Financing agency" includes also a bank or other person who similarly intervenes between persons who are in the position of seller and buyer in respect to the goods (Section 2–707).

(3) "Between merchants" means in any transaction with respect to which both parties are chargeable with the knowledge or skill of merchants.

§ 2–105. Definitions: "Transferability"; "Goods"; "Future" Goods; "Lot"; "Commercial Unit".

(1) "Goods" means all things (including specially manufactured goods) which are movable at the time of identification to the contract for sale other than the money in which the price is to be paid, investment securities (Article 8) and things in action. "Goods" also includes the unborn young of animals and growing crops and other identified things attached to realty as described in the section on goods to be severed from realty (Section 2–107).

(2) Goods must be both existing and identified before any interest in them can pass. Goods which are not both existing and identified are "future" goods. A purported present sale of future goods or of any interest therein operates as a contract to sell.

(3) There may be a sale of a part interest in existing identified goods.

(4) An undivided share in an identified bulk of fungible goods is sufficiently identified to be sold although the quantity of the bulk is not determined. Any agreed proportion of such a bulk or any quantity thereof agreed upon by number, weight or other measure may to the extent of the seller's interest in the bulk be sold to the buyer who then becomes an owner in common.

(5) "Lot" means a parcel or a single article which is the subject matter of a separate sale or delivery, whether or not it is sufficient to perform the contract.

(6) "Commercial unit" means such a unit of goods as by commercial usage is a single whole for purposes of sale and division of which materially impairs its character or value on the market or in use. A commercial unit may be a single article (as a machine) or a set of articles (as a suite of furniture or an assortment of sizes) or a quantity (as a bale, gross, or carload) or any other unit treated in use or in the relevant market as a single whole.

§ 2–106. Definitions: "Contract"; "Agreement"; "Contract for Sales"; "Sale"; "Present Sale"; "Conforming" to Contract; "Termination"; "Cancellation".

(1) In this Article unless the context otherwise requires "contract" and "agreement" are limited to those relating to the present or future sale of goods. "Contract for sale" includes both a present sale of goods and a contract to sell goods at a future time. A "sale" consists in the passing of title from the seller to the buyer for a price (Section 2–401). A "present sale" means a sale which is accomplished by the making of the contract.

(2) Goods or conduct including any part of a performance are "conforming" or conform to the contract when they are in accordance with the obligations under the contract.

(3) "Termination" occurs when either party pursuant to a power created by agreement or law puts an end to the contract otherwise than for its breach. On "termination" all obligations which are still executory on both sides are discharged but any right based on prior breach or performance survives.

(4) "Cancellation" occurs when either party puts an end to the contract for breach by the other and its effect is the same as that of "termination" except that the cancelling party also retains any remedy for breach of the whole contract or any unperformed balance.

§ 2–107. Goods to Be Severed from Realty: Recording.

(1) A contract for the sale of minerals or the like (including oil and gas) or a structure or its materials to be removed from realty is a contract for the sale of goods within this Article if they are to be severed by the seller but until severance a purported present sale thereof which is not effective as a transfer of an interest in land is effective only as a contract to sell.

(2) A contract for the sale apart from the land of growing crops or other things attached to realty and capable of severance without material harm thereto but not described in subsection (1) or of timber to be cut is a contract for the sale of goods within this Article whether the subject matter is to be severed by the buyer or by the seller even though it forms part of the realty at the time of contracting, and the parties can by identification effect a present sale before severance.

(3) The provisions of this section are subject to any third party rights provided by the law relating to realty records, and the contract for sale may be executed and recorded as a document transferring an interest in land and shall then constitute notice to third parties of the buyer's rights under the contract for sale. As amended in 1972.

PART 2: FORM, FORMATION AND READJUSTMENT OF CONTRACT

§ 2–201. Formal Requirements; Statute of Frauds.

(1) Except as otherwise provided in this section a contract for the sale of goods for the price of $500 or more is not enforceable by way of action or defense unless there is some writing sufficient to indicate that a contract for sale has been made between the parties and signed

by the party against whom enforcement is sought or by his authorized agent or broker. A writing is not insufficient because it omits or incorrectly states a term agreed upon but the contract is not enforceable under this paragraph beyond the quantity of goods shown in such writing.

(2) Between merchants if within a reasonable time a writing in confirmation of the contract and sufficient against the sender is received and the party receiving it has reason to know its contents, it satisfies the requirements of subsection (1) against such party unless written notice of objection to its contents is given within 10 days after it is received.

(3) A contract which does not satisfy the requirements of subsection (1) but which is valid in other respects is enforceable

(a) if the goods are to be specially manufactured for the buyer and are not suitable for sale to others in the ordinary course of the seller's business and the seller, before notice of repudiation is received and under circumstances which reasonably indicate that the goods are for the buyer, has made either a substantial beginning of their manufacture or commitments for their procurement; or

(b) if the party against whom enforcement is sought admits in his pleading, testimony or otherwise in court that a contract for sale was made, but the contract is not enforceable under this provision beyond the quantity of goods admitted; or

(c) with respect to goods for which payment has been made and accepted or which have been received and accepted (Section 2–606).

§ 2–202. Final Written Expression: Parol or Extrinsic Evidence.

Terms with respect to which the confirmatory memoranda of the parties agree or which are otherwise set forth in a writing intended by the parties as a final expression of their agreement with respect to such terms as are included therein may not be contradicted by evidence of any prior agreement or of a contemporaneous oral agreement but may be explained or supplemented

(a) by course of dealing or usage of trade (Section 1–205) or by course of performance (Section 2–208); and

(b) by evidence of consistent additional terms unless the court finds the writing to have been intended also as a complete and exclusive statement of the terms of the agreement.

§ 2–203. Seals Inoperative.

The affixing of a seal to a writing evidencing a contract for sale or an offer to buy or sell goods does not constitute the writing a sealed instrument and the law with respect to sealed instruments does not apply to such a contract or offer.

§ 2–204. Formation in General.

(1) A contract for sale of goods may be made in any manner sufficient to show agreement, including conduct by both parties which recognizes the existence of such a contract.

(2) An agreement sufficient to constitute a contract for sale may be found even though the moment of its making is undetermined.

(3) Even though one or more terms are left open a contract for sale does not fail for indefiniteness if the parties have intended to make a contract and there is a reasonably certain basis for giving an appropriate remedy.

§ 2–205. Firm Offers.

An offer by a merchant to buy or sell goods in a signed writing which by its terms gives assurance that it will be held open is not revocable, for lack of consideration, during the time stated or if no time is stated for a reasonable time, but in no event may such period of irrevocability exceed three months; but any such term of assurance on a form supplied by the offeree must be separately signed by the offeror.

§ 2–206. Offer and Acceptance in Formation of Contract.

(1) Unless otherwise unambiguously indicated by the language or circumstances
    (a) an offer to make a contract shall be construed as inviting acceptance in any manner and by any medium reasonable in the circumstances;
    (b) an order or other offer to buy goods for prompt or current shipment shall be construed as inviting acceptance either by a prompt promise to ship or by the prompt or current shipment of conforming or non-conforming goods, but such a shipment of non-conforming goods does not constitute an acceptance if the seller seasonably notifies the buyer that the shipment is offered only as an accommodation to the buyer.
(2) Where the beginning of a requested performance is a reasonable mode of acceptance an offeror who is not notified of acceptance within a reasonable time may treat the offer as having lapsed before acceptance.

§ 2–207. Additional Terms in Acceptance or Confirmation.

(1) A definite and seasonable expression of acceptance or a written confirmation which is sent within a reasonable time operates as an acceptance even though it states terms additional to or different from those offered or agreed upon, unless acceptance is expressly made conditional on assent to the additional or different terms.
(2) The additional terms are to be construed as proposals for addition to the contract. Between merchants such terms become part of the contract unless:
    (a) the offer expressly limits acceptance to the terms of the offer;
    (b) they materially alter it; or
    (c) notification of objection to them has already been given or is given within a reasonable time after notice of them is received.
(3) Conduct by both parties which recognizes the existence of a contract is sufficient to establish a contract for sale although the writings of the parties do not otherwise establish a contract. In such case the terms of the particular contract consist of those terms on which the writings of the parties agree, together with any supplementary terms incorporated under any other provisions of this Act.

§ 2–208. Course of Performance or Practical Construction.

(1) Where the contract for sale involves repeated occasions for performance by either party with knowledge of the nature of the performance and opportunity for objection to it by the other, any course of performance accepted or acquiesced in without objection shall be relevant to determine the meaning of the agreement.
(2) The express terms of the agreement and any such course of performance, as well as any course of dealing and usage of trade, shall be construed whenever reasonable as consistent with each other; but when such construction is unreasonable, express terms shall control course of performance and course of performance shall control both course of dealing and usage of trade (Section 1–205).
(3) Subject to the provisions of the next section on modification and waiver, such course of performance shall be relevant to show a waiver or modification of any term inconsistent with such course of performance.

§ 2–209. Modification, Rescission and Waiver.

(1) An agreement modifying a contract within this Article needs no consideration to be binding.
(2) A signed agreement which excludes modification or rescission except by a signed writing cannot be otherwise modified or rescinded, but except as between merchants such a requirement on a form supplied by the merchant must be separately signed by the other party.

(3) The requirements of the statute of frauds section of this Article (Section 2–201) must be satisfied if the contract as modified is within its provisions.

(4) Although an attempt at modification or rescission does not satisfy the requirements of subsection (2) or (3) it can operate as a waiver.

(5) A party who has made a waiver affecting an executory portion of the contract may retract the waiver by reasonable notification received by the other party that strict performance will be required of any term waived, unless the retraction would be unjust in view of a material change of position in reliance on the waiver.

§ 2–210. Delegation of Performance; Assignment of Rights.

(1) A party may perform his duty through a delegate unless otherwise agreed or unless the other party has a substantial interest in having his original promisor perform or control the acts required by the contract. No delegation of performance relieves the party delegating of any duty to perform or any liability for breach.

(2) Unless otherwise agreed all rights of either seller or buyer can be assigned except where the assignment would materially change the duty of the other party, or increase materially the burden or risk imposed on him by his contract, or impair materially his chance of obtaining return performance. A right to damages for breach of the whole contract or a right arising out of the assignor's due performance of his entire obligation can be assigned despite agreement otherwise.

(3) Unless the circumstances indicate the contrary a prohibition of assignment of "the contract" is to be construed as barring only the delegation to the assignee of the assignor's performance.

(4) An assignment of "the contract" or of "all my rights under the contract" or an assignment in similar general terms is an assignment of rights and unless the language or the circumstances (as in an assignment for security) indicate the contrary, it is a delegation of performance of the duties of the assignor and its acceptance by the assignee constitutes a promise by him to perform those duties. This promise is enforceable by either the assignor or the other party to the original contract.

(5) The other party may treat any assignment which delegates performance as creating reasonable grounds for insecurity and may without prejudice to his rights against the assignor demand assurances from the assignee (Section 2–609).

PART 3: GENERAL OBLIGATION AND CONSTRUCTION OF CONTRACT

§ 2–301. General Obligations of Parties.
The obligation of the seller is to transfer and deliver and that of the buyer is to accept and pay in accordance with the contract.

§ 2–302. Unconscionable Contract or Clause.

(1) If the court as a matter of law finds the contract or any clause of the contract to have been unconscionable at the time it was made the court may refuse to enforce the contract, or it may enforce the remainder of the contract without the unconscionable clause, or it may so limit the application of any unconscionable clause as to avoid any unconscionable result.

(2) When it is claimed or appears to the court that the contract or any clause thereof may be unconscionable the parties shall be afforded a reasonable opportunity to present evidence as to its commercial setting, purpose and effect to aid the court in making the determination.

§ 2–303. Allocation or Division of Risks.
Where this Article allocates a risk or a burden as between the parties "unless otherwise agreed", the agreement may not only shift the allocation but may also divide the risk or burden.

§ 2–304. Price Payable in Money, Goods, Realty, or Otherwise.

(1) The price can be made payable in money or otherwise. If it is payable in whole or in part in goods each party is a seller of the goods which he is to transfer.

(2) Even though all or part of the price is payable in an interest in realty the transfer of the goods and the seller's obligations with reference to them are subject to this Article, but not the transfer of the interest in realty or the transferor's obligations in connection therewith.

§ 2–305. Open Price Term.

(1) The parties if they so intend can conclude a contract for sale even though the price is not settled. In such a case the price is a reasonable price at the time for delivery if
  (a) nothing is said as to price; or
  (b) the price is left to be agreed by the parties and they fail to agree; or
  (c) the price is to be fixed in terms of some agreed market or other standard as set or recorded by a third person or agency and it is not so set or recorded.

(2) A price to be fixed by the seller or by the buyer means a price for him to fix in good faith.

(3) When a price left to be fixed otherwise than by agreement of the parties fails to be fixed through fault of one party the other may at his option treat the contract as cancelled or himself fix a reasonable price.

(4) Where, however, the parties intend not to be bound unless the price be fixed or agreed and it is not fixed or agreed there is no contract. In such a case the buyer must return any goods already received or if unable so to do must pay their reasonable value at the time of delivery and the seller must return any portion of the price paid on account.

§ 2–306. Output, Requirements and Exclusive Dealings.

(1) A term which measures the quantity by the output of the seller or the requirements of the buyer means such actual output or requirements as may occur in good faith, except that no quantity unreasonably disproportionate to any stated estimate or in the absence of a stated estimate to any normal or otherwise comparable prior output or requirements may be tendered or demanded.

(2) A lawful agreement by either the seller or the buyer for exclusive dealing in the kind of goods concerned imposes unless otherwise agreed an obligation by the seller to use best efforts to supply the goods and by the buyer to use best efforts to promote their sale.

§ 2–307. Delivery in Single Lot or Several Lots. Unless otherwise agreed all goods called for by a contract for sale must be tendered in a single delivery and payment is due only on such tender but where the circumstances give either party the right to make or demand delivery in lots the price if it can be apportioned may be demanded for each lot.

§ 2–308. Absence of Specified Place for Delivery. Unless otherwise agreed

  (a) the place for delivery of goods is the seller's place of business or if he has none his residence; but
  (b) in a contract for sale of identified goods which to the knowledge of the parties at the time of contracting are in some other place, that place is the place for their delivery; and
  (c) documents of title may be delivered through customary banking channels.

§ 2–309. Absence of Specific Time Provisions; Notice of Termination.

(1) The time for shipment or delivery or any other action under a contract if not provided in this Article or agreed upon shall be a reasonable time.

(2) Where the contract provides for successive performances but is indefinite in duration it is valid for a reasonable time but unless otherwise agreed may be terminated at any time by either party.

(3) Termination of a contract by one party except on the happening of an agreed event requires that reasonable notification be received by the other party and an agreement dispensing with notification is invalid if its operation would be unconscionable.

§ 2–310. Open Time for Payment or Running of Credit; Authority to Ship Under Reservation. Unless otherwise agreed

 (a) payment is due at the time and place at which the buyer is to receive the goods even though the place of shipment is the place of delivery; and

 (b) if the seller is authorized to send the goods he may ship them under reservation, and may tender the documents of title, but the buyer may inspect the goods after their arrival before payment is due unless such inspection is inconsistent with the terms of the contract (Section 2–513); and

 (c) if delivery is authorized and made by way of documents of title otherwise than by subsection (b) then payment is due at the time and place at which the buyer is to receive the documents regardless of where the goods are to be received; and

 (d) where the seller is required or authorized to ship the goods on credit the credit period runs from the time of shipment but postdating the invoice or delaying its dispatch will correspondingly delay the starting of the credit period.

§ 2–311. Options and Cooperation Respecting Performance.

(1) An agreement for sale which is otherwise sufficiently definite (subsection (3) of Section 2–204) to be a contract is not made invalid by the fact that it leaves particulars of performance to be specified by one of the parties. Any such specification must be made in good faith and within limits set by commercial reasonableness.

(2) Unless otherwise agreed specifications relating to assortment of the goods are at the buyer's option and except as otherwise provided in subsections (1)(c) and (3) of Section 2–319 specifications or arrangements relating to shipment are at the seller's option.

(3) Where such specification would materially affect the other party's performance but is not seasonably made or where one party's cooperation is necessary to the agreed performance of the other but is not seasonably forthcoming, the other party in addition to all other remedies

 (a) is excused for any resulting delay in his own performance; and

 (b) may also either proceed to perform in any reasonable manner or after the time for a material part of his own performance treat the failure to specify or to cooperate as a breach by failure to deliver or accept the goods.

§ 2–312. Warranty of Title and Against Infringement; Buyer's Obligation Against Infringement.

(1) Subject to subsection (2) there is in a contract for sale a warranty by the seller that

 (a) the title conveyed shall be good, and its transfer rightful; and

 (b) the goods shall be delivered free from any security interest or other lien or encumbrance of which the buyer at the time of contracting has no knowledge.

(2) A warranty under subsection (1) will be excluded or modified only by specific language or by circumstances which give the buyer reason to know that the person selling does not claim title in himself or that he is purporting to sell only such right or title as he or a third person may have.

(3) Unless otherwise agreed a seller who is a merchant regularly dealing in goods of the kind warrants that the goods shall be delivered free of the rightful claim of any third person by way of infringement or the like but a buyer who furnishes specifications to the seller must hold the seller harmless against any such claim which arises out of compliance with the specifications.

§ 2–313. Express Warranties by Affirmation, Promise, Description, Sample.

(1) Express warranties by the seller are created as follows:
  (a) Any affirmation of fact or promise made by the seller to the buyer which relates to the goods and becomes part of the basis of the bargain creates an express warranty that the goods shall conform to the affirmation or promise.
  (b) Any description of the goods which is made part of the basis of the bargain creates an express warranty that the goods shall conform to the description.
  (c) Any sample or model which is made part of the basis of the bargain creates an express warranty that the whole of the goods shall conform to the sample or model.
(2) It is not necessary to the creation of an express warranty that the seller use formal words such as "warrant" or "guarantee" or that he have a specific intention to make a warranty, but an affirmation merely of the value of the goods or a statement purporting to be merely the seller's opinion or commendation of the goods does not create a warranty.

§ 2–314. Implied Warranty: Merchantability; Usage of Trade.

(1) Unless excluded or modified (Section 2–316), a warranty that the goods shall be merchantable is implied in a contract for their sale if the seller is a merchant with respect to goods of that kind. Under this section the serving for value of food or drink to be consumed either on the premises or elsewhere is a sale.
(2) Goods to be merchantable must be at least such as
  (a) pass without objection in the trade under the contract description; and
  (b) in the case of fungible goods, are of fair average quality within the description; and
  (c) are fit for the ordinary purposes for which such goods are used; and
  (d) run, within the variations permitted by the agreement, of even kind, quality and quantity within each unit and among all units involved; and
  (e) are adequately contained, packaged, and labeled as the agreement may require; and
  (f) conform to the promise or affirmations of fact made on the container or label if any.
(3) Unless excluded or modified (Section 2–316) other implied warranties may arise from course of dealing or usage of trade.

§ 2–315. Implied Warranty: Fitness for Particular Purpose.
Where the seller at the time of contracting has reason to know any particular purpose for which the goods are required and that the buyer is relying on the seller's skill or judgment to select or furnish suitable goods, there is unless excluded or modified under the next section an implied warranty that the goods shall be fit for such purpose.

§ 2–316. Exclusion or Modification of Warranties.

(1) Words or conduct relevant to the creation of an express warranty and words or conduct tending to negate or limit warranty shall be construed wherever reasonable as consistent with each other; but subject to the provisions of this Article on parol or extrinsic evidence (Section 2–202) negation or limitation is inoperative to the extent that such construction is unreasonable.
(2) Subject to subsection (3), to exclude or modify the implied warranty of merchantability or any part of it the language must mention merchantability and in case of a writing must be conspicuous, and to exclude or modify any implied warranty of fitness the exclusion must be by a writing and conspicuous. Language to exclude all implied warranties of fitness is sufficient if it states, for example, that "There are no warranties which extend beyond the description on the face hereof."
(3) Notwithstanding subsection (2)
  (a) unless the circumstances indicate otherwise, all implied warranties are excluded by expressions like "as is", "with all faults" or other language which in common

understanding calls the buyer's attention to the exclusion of warranties and makes plain that there is no implied warranty; and

(b) when the buyer before entering into the contract has examined the goods or the sample or model as fully as he desired or has refused to examine the goods there is no implied warranty with regard to defects which an examination ought in the circumstances to have revealed to him; and

(c) an implied warranty can also be excluded or modified by course of dealing or course of performance or usage of trade.

(4) Remedies for breach of warranty can be limited in accordance with the provisions of this Article on liquidation or limitation of damages and on contractual modification of remedy (Sections 2–718 and 2–719).

§ 2–317. Cumulation and Conflict of Warranties Express or Implied.

Warranties whether express or implied shall be construed as consistent with each other and as cumulative, but if such construction is unreasonable the intention of the parties shall determine which warranty is dominant. In ascertaining that intention the following rules apply:

(a) Exact or technical specifications displace an inconsistent sample or model or general language of description.

(b) A sample from an existing bulk displaces inconsistent general language of description.

(c) Express warranties displace inconsistent implied warranties other than an implied warranty of fitness for a particular purpose.

§ 2–318. Third Party Beneficiaries of Warranties Express or Implied.

Note: *If this Act is introduced in the Congress of the United States this section should be omitted. (States to select one alternative.)*

Alternative A

A seller's warranty whether express or implied extends to any natural person who is in the family or household of his buyer or who is a guest in his home if it is reasonable to expect that such person may use, consume or be affected by the goods and who is injured in person by breach of the warranty. A seller may not exclude or limit the operation of this section.

Alternative B

A seller's warranty whether express or implied extends to any natural person who may reasonably be expected to use, consume or be affected by the goods and who is injured in person by breach of the warranty. A seller may not exclude or limit the operation of this section.

Alternative C

A seller's warranty whether express or implied extends to any person who may reasonably be expected to use, consume or be affected by the goods and who is injured by breach of the warranty. A seller may not exclude or limit the operation of this section with respect to injury to the person of an individual to whom the warranty extends.

As amended in 1966.

§ 2–319. F.O.B. and F.A.S. Terms.

(1) Unless otherwise agreed the term F.O.B. (which means "free on board") at a named place, even though used only in connection with the stated price, is a delivery term under which

(a) when the term is F.O.B. the place of shipment, the seller must at that place ship the goods in the manner provided in this Article (Section 2–504) and bear the expense and risk of putting them into the possession of the carrier; or

(b) when the term is F.O.B. the place of destination, the seller must at his own expense and risk transport the goods to that place and there tender delivery of them in the manner provided in this Article (Section 2–503);

(c) when under either (a) or (b) the term is also F.O.B. vessel, car or other vehicle, the seller must in addition at his own expense and risk load the goods on board. If the term is F.O.B. vessel the buyer must name the vessel and in an appropriate case the seller must comply with the provisions of this Article on the form of bill of lading (Section 2–323).

(2) Unless otherwise agreed the term F.A.S. vessel (which means "free alongside") at a named port, even though used only in connection with the stated price, is a delivery term under which the seller must

    (a) at his own expense and risk deliver the goods alongside the vessel in the manner usual in that port or on a dock designated and provided by the buyer; and

    (b) obtain and tender a receipt for the goods in exchange for which the carrier is under a duty to issue a bill of lading.

(3) Unless otherwise agreed in any case falling within subsection (1)(a) or (c) or subsection (2) the buyer must seasonably give any needed instructions for making delivery, including when the term is F.A.S. or F.O.B. the loading berth of the vessel and in an appropriate case its name and sailing date. The seller may treat the failure of needed instructions as a failure of cooperation under this Article (Section 2–311). He may also at his option move the goods in any reasonable manner preparatory to delivery or shipment.

(4) Under the term F.O.B. vessel or F.A.S. unless otherwise agreed the buyer must make payment against tender of the required documents and the seller may not tender nor the buyer demand delivery of the goods in substitution for the documents.

§ 2–320. C.I.F. and C. & F. Terms.

(1) The term C.I.F. means that the price includes in a lump sum the cost of the goods and the insurance and freight to the named destination. The term C. & F. or C.F. means that the price so includes cost and freight to the named destination.

(2) Unless otherwise agreed and even though used only in connection with the stated price and destination, the term C.I.F. destination or its equivalent requires the seller at his own expense and risk to

    (a) put the goods into the possession of a carrier at the port for shipment and obtain a negotiable bill or bills of lading covering the entire transportation to the named destination; and

    (b) load the goods and obtain a receipt from the carrier (which may be contained in the bill of lading) showing that the freight has been paid or provided for; and

    (c) obtain a policy or certificate of insurance, including any war risk insurance, of a kind and on terms then current at the port of shipment in the usual amount, in the currency of the contract, shown to cover the same goods covered by the bill of lading and providing for payment of loss to the order of the buyer or for the account of whom it may concern; but the seller may add to the price the amount of the premium for any such war risk insurance; and

    (d) prepare an invoice of the goods and procure any other documents required to effect shipment or to comply with the contract; and

    (e) forward and tender with commercial promptness all the documents in due form and with any indorsement necessary to perfect the buyer's rights.

(3) Unless otherwise agreed the term C. & F. or its equivalent has the same effect and imposes upon the seller the same obligations and risks as a C.I.F. term except the obligation as to insurance.

(4) Under the term C.I.F. or C. & F. unless otherwise agreed the buyer must make payment against tender of the required documents and the seller may not tender nor the buyer demand delivery of the goods in substitution for the documents.

§ 2–321. C.I.F. or C. & F.: "Net Landed Weights"; "Payment on Arrival"; Warranty of Condition on Arrival. Under a contract containing a term C.I.F. or C. & F.

(1) Where the price is based on or is to be adjusted according to "net landed weights", "delivered weights", "out turn" quantity or quality or the like, unless otherwise agreed the seller must reasonably estimate the price. The payment due on tender of the documents called for by

the contract is the amount so estimated, but after final adjustment of the price a settlement must be made with commercial promptness.

(2) An agreement described in subsection (1) or any warranty of quality or condition of the goods on arrival places upon the seller the risk of ordinary deterioration, shrinkage and the like in transportation but has no effect on the place or time of identification to the contract for sale or delivery or on the passing of the risk of loss.

(3) Unless otherwise agreed where the contract provides for payment on or after arrival of the goods the seller must before payment allow such preliminary inspection as is feasible; but if the goods are lost delivery of the documents and payment are due when the goods should have arrived.

§ 2–322. Delivery "Ex-Ship".

(1) Unless otherwise agreed a term for delivery of goods "ex-ship" (which means from the carrying vessel) or in equivalent language is not restricted to a particular ship and requires delivery from a ship which has reached a place at the named port of destination where goods of the kind are usually discharged.

(2) Under such a term unless otherwise agreed
   (a) the seller must discharge all liens arising out of the carriage and furnish the buyer with a direction which puts the carrier under a duty to deliver the goods; and
   (b) the risk of loss does not pass to the buyer until the goods leave the ship's tackle or are otherwise properly unloaded.

§ 2–323. Form of Bill of Lading Required in Overseas Shipment; "Overseas".

(1) Where the contract contemplates overseas shipment and contains a term C.I.F. or C. & F. or F.O.B. vessel, the seller unless otherwise agreed must obtain a negotiable bill of lading stating that the goods have been loaded in board or, in the case of a term C.I.F. or C. & F., received for shipment.

(2) Where in a case within subsection (1) a bill of lading has been issued in a set of parts, unless otherwise agreed if the documents are not to be sent from abroad the buyer may demand tender of the full set; otherwise only one part of the bill of lading need be tendered. Even if the agreement expressly requires a full set
   (a) due tender of a single part is acceptable within the provisions of this Article on cure of improper delivery (subsection (1) of Section 2–508); and
   (b) even though the full set is demanded, if the documents are sent from abroad the person tendering an incomplete set may nevertheless require payment upon furnishing an indemnity which the buyer in good faith deems adequate.

(3) A shipment by water or by air or a contract contemplating such shipment is "overseas" insofar as by usage of trade or agreement it is subject to the commercial, financing or shipping practices characteristic of international deep water commerce.

§ 2–324. "No Arrival, No Sale" Term. Under a term "no arrival, no sale" or terms of like meaning, unless otherwise agreed,

   (a) the seller must properly ship conforming goods and if they arrive by any means he must tender them on arrival but he assumes no obligation that the goods will arrive unless he has caused the non-arrival; and
   (b) where without fault of the seller the goods are in part lost or have so deteriorated as no longer to conform to the contract or arrive after the contract time, the buyer may proceed as if there had been casualty to identified goods (Section 2–613).

§ 2–325. "Letter of Credit" Term; "Confirmed Credit".

(1) Failure of the buyer seasonably to furnish an agreed letter of credit is a breach of the contract for sale.

(2) The delivery to seller of a proper letter of credit suspends the buyer's obligation to pay. If the letter of credit is dishonored, the seller may on seasonable notification to the buyer require payment directly from him.

(3) Unless otherwise agreed the term "letter of credit" or "banker's credit" in a contract for sale means an irrevocable credit issued by a financing agency of good repute and, where the shipment is overseas, of good international repute. The term "confirmed credit" means that the credit must also carry the direct obligation of such an agency which does business in the seller's financial market.

§ 2–326. Sale on Approval and Sale or Return; Consignment Sales and Rights of Creditors.

(1) Unless otherwise agreed, if delivered goods may be returned by the buyer even though they conform to the contract, the transaction is
   (a) a "sale on approval" if the goods are delivered primarily for use, and
   (b) a "sale or return" if the goods are delivered primarily for resale.

(2) Except as provided in subsection (3), goods held on approval are not subject to the claims of the buyer's creditors until acceptance; goods held on sale or return are subject to such claims while in the buyer's possession.

(3) Where goods are delivered to a person for sale and such person maintains a place of business at which he deals in goods of the kind involved, under a name other than the name of the person making delivery, then with respect to claims of creditors of the person conducting the business the goods are deemed to be on sale or return. The provisions of this subsection are applicable even though an agreement purports to reserve title to the person making delivery until payment or resale or uses such words as "on consignment" or "on memorandum". However, this subsection is not applicable if the person making delivery
   (a) complies with an applicable law providing for a consignor's interest or the like to be evidenced by a sign, or
   (b) establishes that the person conducting the business is generally known by his creditors to be substantially engaged in selling the goods of others, or
   (c) complies with the filing provisions of the Article on Secured Transactions (Article 9).

(4) Any "or return" term of a contract for sale is to be treated as a separate contract for sale within the statute of frauds section of this Article (Section 2–201) and as contradicting the sale aspect of the contract within the provisions of this Article on parol or extrinsic evidence (Section 2–202).

§ 2–327. Special Incidents of Sale on Approval and Sale or Return.

(1) Under a sale on approval unless otherwise agreed
   (a) although the goods are identified to the contract the risk of loss and the title do not pass to the buyer until acceptance; and
   (b) use of the goods consistent with the purpose of trial is not acceptance but failure seasonably to notify the seller of election to return the goods is acceptance, and if the goods conform to the contract acceptance of any part is acceptance of the whole; and
   (c) after due notification of election to return, the return is at the seller's risk and expense but a merchant buyer must follow any reasonable instructions.

(2) Under a sale or return unless otherwise agreed
   (a) the option to return extends to the whole or any commercial unit of the goods while in substantially their original condition, but must be exercised seasonably; and
   (b) the return is at the buyer's risk and expense.

§ 2–328. Sale by Auction.

(1) In a sale by auction if goods are put up in lots each lot is the subject of a separate sale.

(2) A sale by auction is complete when the auctioneer so announces by the fall of the hammer or in other customary manner. Where a bid is made while the hammer is falling in acceptance

of a prior bid the auctioneer may in his discretion reopen the bidding or declare the goods sold under the bid on which the hammer was falling.

(3) Such a sale is with reserve unless the goods are in explicit terms put up without reserve. In an auction with reserve the auctioneer may withdraw the goods at any time until he announces completion of the sale. In an auction without reserve, after the auctioneer calls for bids on an article or lot, that article or lot cannot be withdrawn unless no bid is made within a reasonable time. In either case a bidder may retract his bid until the auctioneer's announcement of completion of the sale, but a bidder's retraction does not revive any previous bid.

(4) If the auctioneer knowingly receives a bid on the seller's behalf or the seller makes or procures such a bid, and notice has not been given that liberty for such bidding is reserved, the buyer may at his option avoid the sale or take the goods at the price of the last good faith bid prior to the completion of the sale. This subsection shall not apply to any bid at a forced sale.

PART 4: TITLE, CREDITORS AND GOOD FAITH PURCHASERS

§ 2–401. Passing of Title; Reservation for Security; Limited Application of This Section.
Each provision of this Article with regard to the rights, obligations and remedies of the seller, the buyer, purchasers or other third parties applies irrespective of title to the goods except where the provision refers to such title. Insofar as situations are not covered by the other provisions of this Article and matters concerning title become material the following rules apply:

(1) Title to goods cannot pass under a contract for sale prior to their identification to the contract (Section 2–501), and unless otherwise explicitly agreed the buyer acquires by their identification a special property as limited by this Act. Any retention or reservation by the seller of the title (property) in goods shipped or delivered to the buyer is limited in effect to a reservation of a security interest. Subject to these provisions and to the provisions of the Article on Secured Transactions (Article 9), title to goods passes from the seller to the buyer in any manner and on any conditions explicitly agreed on by the parties.

(2) Unless otherwise explicitly agreed title passes to the buyer at the time and place at which the seller completes his performance with reference to the physical delivery of the goods, despite any reservation of a security interest and even though a document of title is to be delivered at a different time or place; and in particular and despite any reservation of a security interest by the bill of lading
   (a) if the contract requires or authorizes the seller to send the goods to the buyer but does not require him to deliver them at destination, title passes to the buyer at the time and place of shipment; but
   (b) if the contract requires delivery at destination, title passes on tender there.

(3) Unless otherwise explicitly agreed where delivery is to be made without moving the goods,
   (a) if the seller is to deliver a document of title, title passes at the time when and the place where he delivers such documents; or
   (b) if the goods are at the time of contracting already identified and no documents are to be delivered, title passes at the time and place of contracting.

(4) A rejection or other refusal by the buyer to receive or retain the goods, whether or not justified, or a justified revocation of acceptance revests title to the goods in the seller. Such revesting occurs by operation of law and is not a "sale".

§ 2–402. Rights of Seller's Creditors Against Sold Goods.

(1) Except as provided in subsections (2) and (3), rights of unsecured creditors of the seller with respect to goods which have been identified to a contract for sale are subject to the buyer's rights to recover the goods under this Article (Sections 2–502 and 2–716).

(2) A creditor of the seller may treat a sale or an identification of goods to a contract for sale as void if as against him a retention of possession by the seller is fraudulent under any rule of law of the state where the goods are situated, except that retention of possession in good faith and current course of trade by a merchant-seller for a commercially reasonable time after a sale or identification is not fraudulent.

(3) Nothing in this Article shall be deemed to impair the rights of creditors of the seller
   (a) under the provisions of the Article on Secured Transactions (Article 9); or
   (b) where identification to the contract or delivery is made not in current course of trade but in satisfaction of or as security for a pre-existing claim for money, security or the like and is made under circumstances which under any rule of law of the state where the goods are situated would apart from this Article constitute the transaction a fraudulent transfer or voidable preference.

§ 2–403. Power to Transfer; Good Faith Purchase of Goods; "Entrusting".

(1) A purchaser of goods acquires all title which his transferor had or had power to transfer except that a purchaser of a limited interest acquires rights only to the extent of the interest purchased. A person with voidable title has power to transfer a good title to a good faith purchaser for value. When goods have been delivered under a transaction of purchase the purchaser has such power even though
   (a) the transferor was deceived as to the identity of the purchaser, or
   (b) the delivery was in exchange for a check which is later dishonored, or
   (c) it was agreed that the transaction was to be a "cash sale", or
   (d) the delivery was procured through fraud punishable as larcenous under the criminal law.

(2) Any entrusting of possession of goods to a merchant who deals in goods of that kind gives him power to transfer all rights of the entruster to a buyer in ordinary course of business.

(3) "Entrusting" includes any delivery and any acquiescence in retention of possession regardless of any condition expressed between the parties to the delivery or acquiescence and regardless of whether the procurement of the entrusting or the possessor's disposition of the goods have been such as to be larcenous under the criminal law.

[*Publisher's Editorial Note: If a state adopts the repealer of Article 6—Bulk Transfers (Alternative A), subsec. (4) should read as follows:*]

(4) The rights of other purchasers of goods and of lien creditors are governed by the Articles on Secured Transactions (Article 9) and Documents of Title (Article 7).

[*Publisher's Editorial Note: If a state adopts Revised Article 6—Bulk Sales (Alternative B), subsec. (4) should read as follows:*]

(4) The rights of other purchasers of goods and of lien creditors are governed by the Articles on Secured Transactions (Article 9), Bulk Sales (Article 6) and Documents of Title (Article 7).

As amended in 1988.

For material relating to the changes made in text in 1988, see section 3 of Alternative A (Repealer of Article 6—Bulk Transfers) and Conforming Amendment to Section 2–403 following end of Alternative B (Revised Article 6—Bulk Sales).

PART 5: PERFORMANCE

§ 2–501. Insurable Interest in Goods; Manner of Identification of Goods.

(1) The buyer obtains a special property and an insurable interest in goods by identification of existing goods as goods to which the contract refers even though the goods so identified are non-conforming and he has an option to return or reject them. Such identification can be made at any time and in any manner explicitly agreed to by the parties. In the absence of explicit agreement identification occurs

(a)   when the contract is made if it is for the sale of goods already existing and identified;

(b)   if the contract is for the sale of future goods other than those described in paragraph (c), when goods are shipped, marked or otherwise designated by the seller as goods to which the contract refers;

(c)   when the crops are planted or otherwise become growing crops or the young are conceived if the contract is for the sale of unborn young to be born within twelve months after contracting or for the sale of crops to be harvested within twelve months or the next normal harvest season after contracting whichever is longer.

(2) The seller retains an insurable interest in goods so long as title to or any security interest in the goods remains in him and where the identification is by the seller alone he may until default or insolvency or notification to the buyer that the identification is final substitute other goods for those identified.

(3) Nothing in this section impairs any insurable interest recognized under any other statute or rule of law.

§ 2–502. Buyer's Right to Goods on Seller's Insolvency.

(1) Subject to subsection (2) and even though the goods have not been shipped a buyer who has paid a part or all of the price of goods in which he has a special property under the provisions of the immediately preceding section may on making and keeping good a tender of any unpaid portion of their price recover them from the seller if the seller becomes insolvent within ten days after receipt of the first installment on their price.

(2) If the identification creating his special property has been made by the buyer he acquires the right to recover the goods only if they conform to the contract for sale.

§ 2–503. Manner of Seller's Tender of Delivery.

(1) Tender of delivery requires that the seller put and hold conforming goods at the buyer's disposition and give the buyer any notification reasonably necessary to enable him to take delivery. The manner, time and place for tender are determined by the agreement and this Article, and in particular

(a)   tender must be at a reasonable hour, and if it is of goods they must be kept available for the period reasonably necessary to enable the buyer to take possession; but

(b)   unless otherwise agreed the buyer must furnish facilities reasonably suited to the receipt of the goods.

(2) Where the case is within the next section respecting shipment tender requires that the seller comply with its provisions.

(3) Where the seller is required to deliver at a particular destination tender requires that he comply with subsection (1) and also in any appropriate case tender documents as described in subsections (4) and (5) of this section.

(4) Where goods are in the possession of a bailee and are to be delivered without being moved

(a)   tender requires that the seller either tender a negotiable document of title covering such goods or procure acknowledgment by the bailee of the buyer's right to possession of the goods; but

(b)   tender to the buyer of a non-negotiable document of title or of a written direction to the bailee to deliver is sufficient tender unless the buyer seasonably objects, and receipt by the bailee of notification of the buyer's rights fixes those rights as against the bailee and all third persons; but risk of loss of the goods and of any failure by the bailee to honor the non-negotiable document of title or to obey the direction remains on the seller until the buyer has had a reasonable time to present the document or direction, and a refusal by the bailee to honor the document or to obey the direction defeats the tender.

(5) Where the contract requires the seller to deliver documents

(a)   he must tender all such documents in correct form, except as provided in this Article with respect to bills of lading in a set (subsection (2) of Section 2–323); and

(b)   tender through customary banking channels is sufficient and dishonor of a draft accompanying the documents constitutes non-acceptance or rejection.

§ 2–504. Shipment by Seller. Where the seller is required or authorized to send the goods to the buyer and the contract does not require him to deliver them at a particular destination, then unless otherwise agreed he must

(a) put the goods in the possession of such a carrier and make such a contract for their transportation as may be reasonable having regard to the nature of the goods and other circumstances of the case; and

(b) obtain and promptly deliver or tender in due form any document necessary to enable the buyer to obtain possession of the goods or otherwise required by the agreement or by usage of trade; and

(c) promptly notify the buyer of the shipment.

Failure to notify the buyer under paragraph (c) or to make a proper contract under paragraph (a) is a ground for rejection only if material delay or loss ensues.

§ 2–505. Seller's Shipment Under Reservation.

(1) Where the seller has identified goods to the contract by or before shipment:

(a) his procurement of a negotiable bill of lading to his own order or otherwise reserves in him a security interest in the goods. His procurement of the bill to the order of a financing agency or of the buyer indicates in addition only the seller's expectation of transferring that interest to the person named.

(b) a non-negotiable bill of lading to himself or his nominee reserves possession of the goods as security but except in a case of conditional delivery (subsection (2) of Section 2–507) a non-negotiable bill of lading naming the buyer as consignee reserves no security interest even though the seller retains possession of the bill of lading.

(2) When shipment by the seller with reservation of a security interest is in violation of the contract for sale it constitutes an improper contract for transportation within the preceding section but impairs neither the rights given to the buyer by shipment and identification of the goods to the contract nor the seller's powers as a holder of a negotiable document.

§ 2–506. Rights of Financing Agency.

(1) A financing agency by paying or purchasing for value a draft which relates to a shipment of goods acquires to the extent of the payment or purchase and in addition to its own rights under the draft and any document of title securing it any rights of the shipper in the goods including the right to stop delivery and the shipper's right to have the draft honored by the buyer.

(2) The right to reimbursement of a financing agency which has in good faith honored or purchased the draft under commitment to or authority from the buyer is not impaired by subsequent discovery of defects with reference to any relevant document which was apparently regular on its face.

§ 2–507. Effect of Seller's Tender; Delivery on Condition.

(1) Tender of delivery is a condition to the buyer's duty to accept the goods and, unless otherwise agreed, to his duty to pay for them. Tender entitles the seller to acceptance of the goods and to payment according to the contract.

(2) Where payment is due and demanded on the delivery to the buyer of goods or documents of title, his right as against the seller to retain or dispose of them is conditional upon his making the payment due.

§ 2–508. Cure by Seller of Improper Tender or Delivery; Replacement.

(1) Where any tender or delivery by the seller is rejected because non-conforming and the time for performance has not yet expired, the seller may seasonably notify the buyer of his intention to cure and may then within the contract time make a conforming delivery.

(2) Where the buyer rejects a non-conforming tender which the seller had reasonable grounds to believe would be acceptable with or without money allowance the seller may if he seasonably notifies the buyer have a further reasonable time to substitute a conforming tender.

§ 2–509. Risk of Loss in the Absence of Breach.

(1) Where the contract requires or authorizes the seller to ship the goods by carrier
  (a) if it does not require him to deliver them at a particular destination, the risk of loss passes to the buyer when the goods are duly delivered to the carrier even though the shipment is under reservation (Section 2–505); but
  (b) if it does require him to deliver them at a particular destination and the goods are there duly tendered while in the possession of the carrier, the risk of loss passes to the buyer when the goods are there duly so tendered as to enable the buyer to take delivery.
(2) Where the goods are held by a bailee to be delivered without being moved, the risk of loss passes to the buyer
  (a) on his receipt of a negotiable document of title covering the goods; or
  (b) on acknowledgment by the bailee of the buyer's right to possession of the goods; or
  (c) after his receipt of a non-negotiable document of title or other written direction to deliver, as provided in subsection (4)(b) of Section 2–503.
(3) In any case not within subsection (1) or (2), the risk of loss passes to the buyer on his receipt of the goods if the seller is a merchant; otherwise the risk passes to the buyer on tender of delivery.
(4) The provisions of this section are subject to contrary agreement of the parties and to the provisions of this Article on sale on approval (Section 2–327) and on effect of breach on risk of loss (Section 2–510).

§ 2–510. Effect of Breach on Risk of Loss.

(1) Where a tender or delivery of goods so fails to conform to the contract as to give a right of rejection the risk of their loss remains on the seller until cure or acceptance.
(2) Where the buyer rightfully revokes acceptance he may to the extent of any deficiency in his effective insurance coverage treat the risk of loss as having rested on the seller from the beginning.
(3) Where the buyer as to conforming goods already identified to the contract for sale repudiates or is otherwise in breach before risk of their loss has passed to him, the seller may to the extent of any deficiency in his effective insurance coverage treat the risk of loss as resting on the buyer for a commercially reasonable time.

§ 2–511. Tender of Payment by Buyer; Payment by Check.

(1) Unless otherwise agreed tender of payment is a condition to the seller's duty to tender and complete any delivery.
(2) Tender of payment is sufficient when made by any means or in any manner current in the ordinary course of business unless the seller demands payment in legal tender and gives any extension of time reasonably necessary to procure it.
(3) Subject to the provisions of this Act on the effect of an instrument on an obligation (Section 3–310), payment by check is conditional and is defeated as between the parties by dishonor of the check on due presentment.

As amended in 1994.
  See Appendix XI for material relating to changes made in text in 1994.

§ 2–512. Payment by Buyer Before Inspection.

(1) Where the contract requires payment before inspection non-conformity of the goods does not excuse the buyer from so making payment unless

(a) the non-conformity appears without inspection; or

(b) despite tender of the required documents the circumstances would justify injunction against honor under this Act (Section 5–109(b)).

(2) Payment pursuant to subsection (1) does not constitute an acceptance of goods or impair the buyer's right to inspect or any of his remedies.

As amended in 1995.

See Appendix XIV for material relating to changes made in text in 1995.

§ 2–513. Buyer's Right to Inspection of Goods.

(1) Unless otherwise agreed and subject to subsection (3), where goods are tendered or delivered or identified to the contract for sale, the buyer has a right before payment or acceptance to inspect them at any reasonable place and time and in any reasonable manner. When the seller is required or authorized to send the goods to the buyer, the inspection may be after their arrival.

(2) Expenses of inspection must be borne by the buyer but may be recovered from the seller if the goods do not conform and are rejected.

(3) Unless otherwise agreed and subject to the provisions of this Article on C.I.F. contracts (subsection (3) of Section 2–321), the buyer is not entitled to inspect the goods before payment of the price when the contract provides

(a) for delivery "C.O.D." or on other like terms; or

(b) for payment against documents of title, except where such payment is due only after the goods are to become available for inspection.

(4) A place or method of inspection fixed by the parties is presumed to be exclusive but unless otherwise expressly agreed it does not postpone identification or shift the place for delivery or for passing the risk of loss. If compliance becomes impossible, inspection shall be as provided in this section unless the place or method fixed was clearly intended as an indispensable condition failure of which avoids the contract.

§ 2–514. When Documents Deliverable on Acceptance; When on Payment.
Unless otherwise agreed documents against which a draft is drawn are to be delivered to the drawee on acceptance of the draft if it is payable more than three days after presentment; otherwise, only on payment.

§ 2–515. Preserving Evidence of Goods in Dispute.
In furtherance of the adjustment of any claim or dispute

(a) either party on reasonable notification to the other and for the purpose of ascertaining the facts and preserving evidence has the right to inspect, test and sample the goods including such of them as may be in the possession or control of the other; and

(b) the parties may agree to a third party inspection or survey to determine the conformity or condition of the goods and may agree that the findings shall be binding upon them in any subsequent litigation or adjustment.

PART 6: BREACH, REPUDIATION AND EXCUSE

§ 2–601. Buyer's Rights on Improper Delivery.
Subject to the provisions of this Article on breach in installment contracts (Section 2–612) and unless otherwise agreed under the sections on contractual limitations of remedy (Sections 2–718 and 2–719), if the goods or the tender of delivery fail in any respect to conform to the contract, the buyer may

(a) reject the whole; or

(b) accept the whole; or

(c) accept any commercial unit or units and reject the rest.

§ 2–602. Manner and Effect of Rightful Rejection.

(1) Rejection of goods must be within a reasonable time after their delivery or tender. It is ineffective unless the buyer seasonably notifies the seller.

(2) Subject to the provisions of the two following sections on rejected goods (Sections 2–603 and 2–604),

    (a) after rejection any exercise of ownership by the buyer with respect to any commercial unit is wrongful as against the seller; and

    (b) if the buyer has before rejection taken physical possession of goods in which he does not have a security interest under the provisions of this Article (subsection (3) of Section 2–711), he is under a duty after rejection to hold them with reasonable care at the seller's disposition for a time sufficient to permit the seller to remove them; but

    (c) the buyer has no further obligations with regard to goods rightfully rejected.

(3) The seller's rights with respect to goods wrongfully rejected are governed by the provisions of this Article on Seller's remedies in general (Section 2–703).

§ 2–603. Merchant Buyer's Duties as to Rightfully Rejected Goods.

(1) Subject to any security interest in the buyer (subsection (3) of Section 2–711), when the seller has no agent or place of business at the market of rejection a merchant buyer is under a duty after rejection of goods in his possession or control to follow any reasonable instructions received from the seller with respect to the goods and in the absence of such instructions to make reasonable efforts to sell them for the seller's account if they are perishable or threaten to decline in value speedily. Instructions are not reasonable if on demand indemnity for expenses is not forthcoming.

(2) When the buyer sells goods under subsection (1), he is entitled to reimbursement from the seller or out of the proceeds for reasonable expenses of caring for and selling them, and if the expenses include no selling commission then to such commission as is usual in the trade or if there is none to a reasonable sum not exceeding ten per cent on the gross proceeds.

(3) In complying with this section the buyer is held only to good faith and good faith conduct hereunder is neither acceptance nor conversion nor the basis of an action for damages.

§ 2–604. Buyer's Options as to Salvage of Rightfully Rejected Goods.

Subject to the provisions of the immediately preceding section on perishables if the seller gives no instructions within a reasonable time after notification of rejection the buyer may store the rejected goods for the seller's account or reship them to him or resell them for the seller's account with reimbursement as provided in the preceding section. Such action is not acceptance or conversion.

§ 2–605. Waiver of Buyer's Objections by Failure to Particularize.

(1) The buyer's failure to state in connection with rejection a particular defect which is ascertainable by reasonable inspection precludes him from relying on the unstated defect to justify rejection or to establish breach

    (a) where the seller could have cured it if stated seasonably; or

    (b) between merchants when the seller has after rejection made a request in writing for a full and final written statement of all defects on which the buyer proposes to rely.

(2) Payment against documents made without reservation of rights precludes recovery of the payment for defects apparent on the face of the documents.

§ 2–606. What Constitutes Acceptance of Goods.

(1) Acceptance of goods occurs when the buyer

    (a) after a reasonable opportunity to inspect the goods signifies to the seller that the goods are conforming or that he will take or retain them in spite of their non-conformity; or

(b) fails to make an effective rejection (subsection (1) of Section 2–602), but such acceptance does not occur until the buyer has had a reasonable opportunity to inspect them; or

(c) does any act inconsistent with the seller's ownership; but if such act is wrongful as against the seller it is an acceptance only if ratified by him.

(2) Acceptance of a part of any commercial unit is acceptance of that entire unit.

§ 2–607. Effect of Acceptance; Notice of Breach; Burden of Establishing Breach After Acceptance; Notice of Claim or Litigation to Person Answerable Over.

(1) The buyer must pay at the contract rate for any goods accepted.

(2) Acceptance of goods by the buyer precludes rejection of the goods accepted and if made with knowledge of a non-conformity cannot be revoked because of it unless the acceptance was on the reasonable assumption that the non-conformity would be seasonably cured but acceptance does not of itself impair any other remedy provided by this Article for non-conformity.

(3) Where a tender has been accepted

(a) the buyer must within a reasonable time after he discovers or should have discovered any breach notify the seller of breach or be barred from any remedy; and

(b) if the claim is one for infringement or the like (subsection (3) of Section 2–312) and the buyer is sued as a result of such a breach he must so notify the seller within a reasonable time after he receives notice of the litigation or be barred from any remedy over for liability established by the litigation.

(4) The burden is on the buyer to establish any breach with respect to the goods accepted.

(5) Where the buyer is sued for breach of a warranty or other obligation for which his seller is answerable over

(a) he may give his seller written notice of the litigation. If the notice states that the seller may come in and defend and that if the seller does not do so he will be bound in any action against him by his buyer by any determination of fact common to the two litigations, then unless the seller after seasonable receipt of the notice does come in and defend he is so bound.

(b) if the claim is one for infringement or the like (subsection (3) of Section 2–312) the original seller may demand in writing that his buyer turn over to him control of the litigation including settlement or else be barred from any remedy over and if he also agrees to bear all expense and to satisfy any adverse judgment, then unless the buyer after seasonable receipt of the demand does turn over control the buyer is so barred.

(6) The provisions of subsections (3), (4) and (5) apply to any obligation of a buyer to hold the seller harmless against infringement or the like (subsection (3) of Section 2–312).

§ 2–608. Revocation of Acceptance in Whole or in Part.

(1) The buyer may revoke his acceptance of a lot or commercial unit whose non-conformity substantially impairs its value to him if he has accepted it

(a) on the reasonable assumption that its non-conformity would be cured and it has not been seasonably cured; or

(b) without discovery of such non-conformity if his acceptance was reasonably induced either by the difficulty of discovery before acceptance or by the seller's assurances.

(2) Revocation of acceptance must occur within a reasonable time after the buyer discovers or should have discovered the ground for it and before any substantial change in condition of the goods which is not caused by their own defects. It is not effective until the buyer notifies the seller of it.

(3) A buyer who so revokes has the same rights and duties with regard to the goods involved as if he had rejected them.

§ 2–609. Right to Adequate Assurance of Performance.

(1) A contract for sale imposes an obligation on each party that the other's expectation of receiving due performance will not be impaired. When reasonable grounds for insecurity arise with respect to the performance of either party the other may in writing demand adequate assurance of due performance and until he receives such assurance may if commercially reasonable suspend any performance for which he has not already received the agreed return.

(2) Between merchants the reasonableness of grounds for insecurity and the adequacy of any assurance offered shall be determined according to commercial standards.

(3) Acceptance of any improper delivery or payment does not prejudice the aggrieved party's right to demand adequate assurance of future performance.

(4) After receipt of a justified demand failure to provide within a reasonable time not exceeding thirty days such assurance of due performance as is adequate under the circumstances of the particular case is a repudiation of the contract.

§ 2–610. Anticipatory Repudiation.
When either party repudiates the contract with respect to a performance not yet due the loss of which will substantially impair the value of the contract to the other, the aggrieved party may

(a) for a commercially reasonable time await performance by the repudiating party; or

(b) resort to any remedy for breach (Section 2–703 or Section 2–711), even though he has notified the repudiating party that he would await the latter's performance and has urged retraction; and

(c) in either case suspend his own performance or proceed in accordance with the provisions of this Article on the seller's right to identify goods to the contract notwithstanding breach or to salvage unfinished goods (Section 2–704).

§ 2–611. Retraction of Anticipatory Repudiation.

(1) Until the repudiating party's next performance is due he can retract his repudiation unless the aggrieved party has since the repudiation cancelled or materially changed his position or otherwise indicated that he considers the repudiation final.

(2) Retraction may be by any method which clearly indicates to the aggrieved party that the repudiating party intends to perform, but must include any assurance justifiably demanded under the provisions of this Article (Section 2–609).

(3) Retraction reinstates the repudiating party's rights under the contract with due excuse and allowance to the aggrieved party for any delay occasioned by the repudiation.

§ 2–612. "Installment Contract"; Breach.

(1) An "installment contract" is one which requires or authorizes the delivery of goods in separate lots to be separately accepted, even though the contract contains a clause "each delivery is a separate contract" or its equivalent.

(2) The buyer may reject any installment which is non-conforming if the non-conformity substantially impairs the value of that installment and cannot be cured or if the non-conformity is a defect in the required documents; but if the non-conformity does not fall within subsection (3) and the seller gives adequate assurance of its cure the buyer must accept that installment.

(3) Whenever non-conformity or default with respect to one or more installments substantially impairs the value of the whole contract there is a breach of the whole. But the aggrieved party reinstates the contract if he accepts a non-conforming installment without seasonably notifying of cancellation or if he brings an action with respect only to past installments or demands performance as to future installments.

§ 2–613. Casualty to Identified Goods. Where the contract requires for its performance goods identified when the contract is made, and the goods suffer casualty without fault of either party before the risk of loss passes to the buyer, or in a proper case under a "no arrival, no sale" term (Section 2–324) then

    (a)   if the loss is total the contract is avoided; and

    (b)   if the loss is partial or the goods have so deteriorated as no longer to conform to the contract the buyer may nevertheless demand inspection and at his option either treat the contract as avoided or accept the goods with due allowance from the contract price for the deterioration or the deficiency in quantity but without further right against the seller.

§ 2–614. Substituted Performance.

(1)   Where without fault of either party the agreed berthing, loading, or unloading facilities fail or an agreed type of carrier becomes unavailable or the agreed manner of delivery otherwise becomes commercially impracticable but a commercially reasonable substitute is available, such substitute performance must be tendered and accepted.

(2)   If the agreed means or manner of payment fails because of domestic or foreign governmental regulation, the seller may withhold or stop delivery unless the buyer provides a means or manner of payment which is commercially a substantial equivalent. If delivery has already been taken, payment by the means or in the manner provided by the regulation discharges the buyer's obligation unless the regulation is discriminatory, oppressive or predatory.

§ 2–615. Excuse by Failure of Presupposed Conditions. Except so far as a seller may have assumed a greater obligation and subject to the preceding section on substituted performance:

    (a)   Delay in delivery or non-delivery in whole or in part by a seller who complies with paragraphs (b) and (c) is not a breach of his duty under a contract for sale if performance as agreed has been made impracticable by the occurrence of a contingency the non-occurrence of which was a basic assumption on which the contract was made or by compliance in good faith with any applicable foreign or domestic governmental regulation or order whether or not it later proves to be invalid.

    (b)   Where the causes mentioned in paragraph (a) affect only a part of the seller's capacity to perform, he must allocate production and deliveries among his customers but may at his option include regular customers not then under contract as well as his own requirements for further manufacture. He may so allocate in any manner which is fair and reasonable.

    (c)   The seller must notify the buyer seasonably that there will be delay or non-delivery and, when allocation is required under paragraph (b), of the estimated quota thus made available for the buyer.

§ 2–616. Procedure on Notice Claiming Excuse.

(1)   Where the buyer receives notification of a material or indefinite delay or an allocation justified under the preceding section he may by written notification to the seller as to any delivery concerned, and where the prospective deficiency substantially impairs the value of the whole contract under the provisions of this Article relating to breach of installment contracts (Section 2–612), then also as to the whole,

    (a)   terminate and thereby discharge any unexecuted portion of the contract; or

    (b)   modify the contract by agreeing to take his available quota in substitution.

(2)   If after receipt of such notification from the seller the buyer fails so to modify the contract within a reasonable time not exceeding thirty days the contract lapses with respect to any deliveries affected.

(3)   The provisions of this section may not be negated by agreement except in so far as the seller has assumed a greater obligation under the preceding section.

PART 7: REMEDIES

§ 2–701. Remedies for Breach of Collateral Contracts Not Impaired.

Remedies for breach of any obligation or promise collateral or ancillary to a contract for sale are not impaired by the provisions of this Article.

§ 2–702. Seller's Remedies on Discovery of Buyer's Insolvency.

(1) Where the seller discovers the buyer to be insolvent he may refuse delivery except for cash including payment for all goods theretofore delivered under the contract, and stop delivery under this Article (Section 2–705).

(2) Where the seller discovers that the buyer has received goods on credit while insolvent he may reclaim the goods upon demand made within ten days after the receipt, but if misrepresentation of solvency has been made to the particular seller in writing within three months before delivery the ten day limitation does not apply. Except as provided in this subsection the seller may not base a right to reclaim goods on the buyer's fraudulent or innocent misrepresentation of solvency or of intent to pay.

(3) The seller's right to reclaim under subsection (2) is subject to the rights of a buyer in ordinary course or other good faith purchaser under this Article (Section 2–403). Successful reclamation of goods excludes all other remedies with respect to them.

As amended in 1966.

§ 2–703. Seller's Remedies in General. Where the buyer wrongfully rejects or revokes acceptance of goods or fails to make a payment due on or before delivery or repudiates with respect to a part or the whole, then with respect to any goods directly affected and, if the breach is of the whole contract (Section 2–612), then also with respect to the whole undelivered balance, the aggrieved seller may

    (a) withhold delivery of such goods;

    (b) stop delivery by any bailee as hereafter provided (Section 2–705);

    (c) proceed under the next section respecting goods still unidentified to the contract;

    (d) resell and recover damages as hereafter provided (Section 2–706);

    (e) recover damages for non-acceptance (Section 2–708) or in a proper case the price (Section 2–709);

    (f) cancel.

§ 2–704. Seller's Right to Identify Goods to the Contract Notwithstanding Breach or to Salvage Unfinished Goods.

(1) An aggrieved seller under the preceding section may

    (a) identify to the contract conforming goods not already identified if at the time he learned of the breach they are in his possession or control;

    (b) treat as the subject of resale goods which have demonstrably been intended for the particular contract even though those goods are unfinished.

(2) Where the goods are unfinished an aggrieved seller may in the exercise of reasonable commercial judgment for the purposes of avoiding loss and of effective realization either complete the manufacture and wholly identify the goods to the contract or cease manufacture and resell for scrap or salvage value or proceed in any other reasonable manner.

§ 2–705. Seller's Stoppage of Delivery in Transit or Otherwise.

(1) The seller may stop delivery of goods in the possession of a carrier or other bailee when he discovers the buyer to be insolvent (Section 2–702) and may stop delivery of carload, truckload, planeload or larger shipments of express or freight when the buyer repudiates or fails to make a payment due before delivery or if for any other reason the seller has a right to withhold or reclaim the goods.

(2) As against such buyer the seller may stop delivery until
   (a) receipt of the goods by the buyer; or
   (b) acknowledgment to the buyer by any bailee of the goods except a carrier that the bailee holds the goods for the buyer; or
   (c) such acknowledgment to the buyer by a carrier by reshipment or as warehouseman; or
   (d) negotiation to the buyer of any negotiable document of title covering the goods.
(3) (a) To stop delivery the seller must so notify as to enable the bailee by reasonable diligence to prevent delivery of the goods.
   (b) After such notification the bailee must hold and deliver the goods according to the directions of the seller but the seller is liable to the bailee for any ensuing charges or damages.
   (c) If a negotiable document of title has been issued for goods the bailee is not obliged to obey a notification to stop until surrender of the document.
   (d) A carrier who has issued a non-negotiable bill of lading is not obliged to obey a notification to stop received from a person other than the consignor.

§ 2–706. Seller's Resale Including Contract for Resale.

(1) Under the conditions stated in Section 2–703 on seller's remedies, the seller may resell the goods concerned or the undelivered balance thereof. Where the resale is made in good faith and in a commercially reasonable manner the seller may recover the difference between the resale price and the contract price together with any incidental damages allowed under the provisions of this Article (Section 2–710), but less expenses saved in consequence of the buyer's breach.
(2) Except as otherwise provided in subsection (3) or unless otherwise agreed resale may be at public or private sale including sale by way of one or more contracts to sell or of identification to an existing contract of the seller. Sale may be as a unit or in parcels and at any time and place and on any terms but every aspect of the sale including the method, manner, time, place and terms must be commercially reasonable. The resale must be reasonably identified as referring to the broken contract, but it is not necessary that the goods be in existence or that any or all of them have been identified to the contract before the breach.
(3) Where the resale is at private sale the seller must give the buyer reasonable notification of his intention to resell.
(4) Where the resale is at public sale
   (a) only identified goods can be sold except where there is a recognized market for a public sale of futures in goods of the kind; and
   (b) it must be made at a usual place or market for public sale if one is reasonably available and except in the case of goods which are perishable or threaten to decline in value speedily the seller must give the buyer reasonable notice of the time and place of the resale; and
   (c) if the goods are not to be within the view of those attending the sale the notification of sale must state the place where the goods are located and provide for their reasonable inspection by prospective bidders; and
   (d) the seller may buy.
(5) A purchaser who buys in good faith at a resale takes the goods free of any rights of the original buyer even though the seller fails to comply with one or more of the requirements of this section.
(6) The seller is not accountable to the buyer for any profit made on any resale. A person in the position of a seller (Section 2–707) or a buyer who has rightfully rejected or justifiably revoked acceptance must account for any excess over the amount of his security interest, as hereinafter defined (subsection (3) of Section 2–711).

§ 2–707. "Person in the Position of a Seller".

(1) A "person in the position of a seller" includes as against a principal an agent who has paid or become responsible for the price of goods on behalf of his principal or anyone who otherwise holds a security interest or other right in goods similar to that of a seller.

(2) A person in the position of a seller may as provided in this Article withhold or stop delivery (Section 2–705) and resell (Section 2–706) and recover incidental damages (Section 2–710).

§ 2–708. Seller's Damages for Non-acceptance or Repudiation.

(1) Subject to subsection (2) and to the provisions of this Article with respect to proof of market price (Section 2–723), the measure of damages for non-acceptance or repudiation by the buyer is the difference between the market price at the time and place for tender and the unpaid contract price together with any incidental damages provided in this Article (Section 2–710), but less expenses saved in consequence of the buyer's breach.

(2) If the measure of damages provided in subsection (1) is inadequate to put the seller in as good a position as performance would have done then the measure of damages is the profit (including reasonable overhead) which the seller would have made from full performance by the buyer, together with any incidental damages provided in this Article (Section 2–710), due allowance for costs reasonably incurred and due credit for payments or proceeds of resale.

§ 2–709. Action for the Price.

(1) When the buyer fails to pay the price as it becomes due the seller may recover, together with any incidental damages under the next section, the price
  (a) of goods accepted or of conforming goods lost or damaged within a commercially reasonable time after risk of their loss has passed to the buyer; and
  (b) of goods identified to the contract if the seller is unable after reasonable effort to resell them at a reasonable price or the circumstances reasonably indicate that such effort will be unavailing.

(2) Where the seller sues for the price he must hold for the buyer any goods which have been identified to the contract and are still in his control except that if resale becomes possible he may resell them at any time prior to the collection of the judgment. The net proceeds of any such resale must be credited to the buyer and payment of the judgment entitles him to any goods not resold.

(3) After the buyer has wrongfully rejected or revoked acceptance of the goods or has failed to make a payment due or has repudiated (Section 2–610), a seller who is held not entitled to the price under this section shall nevertheless be awarded damages for non-acceptance under the preceding section.

§ 2–710. Seller's Incidental Damages.

Incidental damages to an aggrieved seller include any commercially reasonable charges, expenses or commissions incurred in stopping delivery, in the transportation, care and custody of goods after the buyer's breach, in connection with return or resale of the goods or otherwise resulting from the breach.

§ 2–711. Buyer's Remedies in General; Buyer's Security Interest in Rejected Goods.

(1) Where the seller fails to make delivery or repudiates or the buyer rightfully rejects or justifiably revokes acceptance then with respect to any goods involved, and with respect to the whole if the breach goes to the whole contract (Section 2–612), the buyer may cancel and whether or not he has done so may in addition to recovering so much of the price as has been paid
  (a) "cover" and have damages under the next section as to all the goods affected whether or not they have been identified to the contract; or
  (b) recover damages for non-delivery as provided in this Article (Section 2–713).

(2) Where the seller fails to deliver or repudiates the buyer may also
  (a) if the goods have been identified recover them as provided in this Article (Section 2–502); or
  (b) in a proper case obtain specific performance or replevy the goods as provided in this Article (Section 2–716).

(3) On rightful rejection or justifiable revocation of acceptance a buyer has a security interest in goods in his possession or control for any payments made on their price and any expenses reasonably incurred in their inspection, receipt, transportation, care and custody and may hold such goods and resell them in like manner as an aggrieved seller (Section 2–706).

§ 2–712. "Cover"; Buyer's Procurement of Substitute Goods.

(1) After a breach within the preceding section the buyer may "cover" by making in good faith and without unreasonable delay any reasonable purchase of or contract to purchase goods in substitution for those due from the seller.
(2) The buyer may recover from the seller as damages the difference between the cost of cover and the contract price together with any incidental or consequential damages as hereinafter defined (Section 2–715), but less expenses saved in consequence of the seller's breach.
(3) Failure of the buyer to effect cover within this section does not bar him from any other remedy.

§ 2–713. Buyer's Damages for Non-delivery or Repudiation.

(1) Subject to the provisions of this Article with respect to proof of market price (Section 2–723), the measure of damages for non-delivery or repudiation by the seller is the difference between the market price at the time when the buyer learned of the breach and the contract price together with any incidental and consequential damages provided in this Article (Section 2–715), but less expenses saved in consequence of the seller's breach.
(2) Market price is to be determined as of the place for tender or, in cases of rejection after arrival or revocation of acceptance, as of the place of arrival.

§ 2–714. Buyer's Damages for Breach in Regard to Accepted Goods.

(1) Where the buyer has accepted goods and given notification (subsection (3) of Section 2–607) he may recover as damages for any non-conformity of tender the loss resulting in the ordinary course of events from the seller's breach as determined in any manner which is reasonable.
(2) The measure of damages for breach of warranty is the difference at the time and place of acceptance between the value of the goods accepted and the value they would have had if they had been as warranted, unless special circumstances show proximate damages of a different amount.
(3) In a proper case any incidental and consequential damages under the next section may also be recovered.

§ 2–715. Buyer's Incidental and Consequential Damages.

(1) Incidental damages resulting from the seller's breach include expenses reasonably incurred in inspection, receipt, transportation and care and custody of goods rightfully rejected, any commercially reasonable charges, expenses or commissions in connection with effecting cover and any other reasonable expense incident to the delay or other breach.
(2) Consequential damages resulting from the seller's breach include
    (a) any loss resulting from general or particular requirements and needs of which the seller at the time of contracting had reason to know and which could not reasonably be prevented by cover or otherwise; and
    (b) injury to person or property proximately resulting from any breach of warranty.

§ 2–716. Buyer's Right to Specific Performance or Replevin.

(1) Specific performance may be decreed where the goods are unique or in other proper circumstances.

(2) The decree for specific performance may include such terms and conditions as to payment of the price, damages, or other relief as the court may deem just.

(3) The buyer has a right of replevin for goods identified to the contract if after reasonable effort he is unable to effect cover for such goods or the circumstances reasonably indicate that such effort will be unavailing or if the goods have been shipped under reservation and satisfaction of the security interest in them has been made or tendered.

§ 2–717. Deduction of Damages from the Price.
The buyer on notifying the seller of his intention to do so may deduct all or any part of the damages resulting from any breach of the contract from any part of the price still due under the same contract.

§ 2–718. Liquidation or Limitation of Damages; Deposits.

(1) Damages for breach by either party may be liquidated in the agreement but only at an amount which is reasonable in the light of the anticipated or actual harm caused by the breach, the difficulties of proof of loss, and the inconvenience or nonfeasibility of otherwise obtaining an adequate remedy. A term fixing unreasonably large liquidated damages is void as a penalty.

(2) Where the seller justifiably withholds delivery of goods because of the buyer's breach, the buyer is entitled to restitution of any amount by which the sum of his payments exceeds
   (a) the amount to which the seller is entitled by virtue of terms liquidating the seller's damages in accordance with subsection (1), or
   (b) in the absence of such terms, twenty per cent of the value of the total performance for which the buyer is obligated under the contract or $500, whichever is smaller.

(3) The buyer's right to restitution under subsection (2) is subject to offset to the extent that the seller establishes
   (a) a right to recover damages under the provisions of this Article other than subsection (1), and
   (b) the amount or value of any benefits received by the buyer directly or indirectly by reason of the contract.

(4) Where a seller has received payment in goods their reasonable value or the proceeds of their resale shall be treated as payments for the purposes of subsection (2); but if the seller has notice of the buyer's breach before reselling goods received in part performance, his resale is subject to the conditions laid down in this Article on resale by an aggrieved seller (Section 2–706).

§ 2–719. Contractual Modification or Limitation of Remedy.

(1) Subject to the provisions of subsections (2) and (3) of this section and of the preceding section on liquidation and limitation of damages,
   (a) the agreement may provide for remedies in addition to or in substitution for those provided in this Article and may limit or alter the measure of damages recoverable under this Article, as by limiting the buyer's remedies to return of the goods and repayment of the price or to repair and replacement of non-conforming goods or parts; and
   (b) resort to a remedy as provided is optional unless the remedy is expressly agreed to be exclusive, in which case it is the sole remedy.

(2) Where circumstances cause an exclusive or limited remedy to fail of its essential purpose, remedy may be had as provided in this Act.

(3) Consequential damages may be limited or excluded unless the limitation or exclusion is unconscionable. Limitation of consequential damages for injury to the person in the case of consumer goods is prima facie unconscionable but limitation of damages where the loss is commercial is not.

§ 2–720. Effect of "Cancellation" or "Rescission" on Claims for Antecedent Breach.
Unless the contrary intention clearly appears, expressions of "cancellation" or "rescission" of the contract or the like shall not be construed as a renunciation or discharge of any claim in damages for an antecedent breach.

§ 2–721. Remedies for Fraud.
Remedies for material misrepresentation or fraud include all remedies available under this Article for non-fraudulent breach. Neither rescission or a claim for rescission of the contract for sale nor rejection or return of the goods shall bar or be deemed inconsistent with a claim for damages or other remedy.

§ 2–722. Who Can Sue Third Parties for Injury to Goods.
Where a third party so deals with goods which have been identified to a contract for sale as to cause actionable injury to a party to that contract

(a) a right of action against the third party is in either party to the contract for sale who has title to or a security interest or a special property or an insurable interest in the goods; and if the goods have been destroyed or converted a right of action is also in the party who either bore the risk of loss under the contract for sale or has since the injury assumed that risk as against the other;

(b) if at the time of the injury the party plaintiff did not bear the risk of loss as against the other party to the contract for sale and there is no arrangement between them for disposition of the recovery, his suit or settlement is, subject to his own interest, as a fiduciary for the other party to the contract;

(c) either party may with the consent of the other sue for the benefit of whom it may concern.

§ 2–723. Proof of Market Price: Time and Place.

(1) If an action based on anticipatory repudiation comes to trial before the time for performance with respect to some or all of the goods, any damages based on market price (Section 2–708 or Section 2–713) shall be determined according to the price of such goods prevailing at the time when the aggrieved party learned of the repudiation.

(2) If evidence of a price prevailing at the times or places described in this Article is not readily available the price prevailing within any reasonable time before or after the time described or at any other place which in commercial judgment or under usage of trade would serve as a reasonable substitute for the one described may be used, making any proper allowance for the cost of transporting the goods to or from such other place.

(3) Evidence of a relevant price prevailing at a time or place other than the one described in this Article offered by one party is not admissible unless and until he has given the other party such notice as the court finds sufficient to prevent unfair surprise.

§ 2–724. Admissibility of Market Quotations.
Whenever the prevailing price or value of any goods regularly bought and sold in any established commodity market is in issue, reports in official publications or trade journals or in newspapers or periodicals of general circulation published as the reports of such market shall be admissible in evidence. The circumstances of the preparation of such a report may be shown to affect its weight but not its admissibility.

§ 2–725. Statute of Limitations in Contracts for Sale.

(1) An action for breach of any contract for sale must be commenced within four years after the cause of action has accrued. By the original agreement the parties may reduce the period of limitation to not less than one year but may not extend it.

(2) A cause of action accrues when the breach occurs, regardless of the aggrieved party's lack of knowledge of the breach. A breach of warranty occurs when tender of delivery is made, except that where a warranty explicitly extends to future performance of the goods and discovery of the breach must await the time of such performance the cause of action accrues when the breach is or should have been discovered.

(3) Where an action commenced within the time limited by subsection (1) is so terminated as to leave available a remedy by another action for the same breach such other action may be commenced after the expiration of the time limited and within six months after the termination of the first action unless the termination resulted from voluntary discontinuance or from dismissal for failure or neglect to prosecute.

(4) This section does not alter the law on tolling of the statute of limitations nor does it apply to causes of action which have accrued before this Act becomes effective.

Article 2A: Leases

PART 1: GENERAL PROVISIONS

§ 2A–101. Short Title. This Article shall be known and may be cited as the Uniform Commercial Code—Leases.

See Appendix VI [following Amendment 24 therein] for material relating to changes in the Official Comment to conform to the 1990 amendments to various sections of Article 2A.

§ 2A–102. Scope. This Article applies to any transaction, regardless of form, that creates a lease.

§ 2A–103. Definitions and Index of Definitions.

(1) In this Article unless the context otherwise requires:
  (a) "Buyer in ordinary course of business" means a person who in good faith and without knowledge that the sale to him [or her] is in violation of the ownership rights or security interest or leasehold interest of a third party in the goods buys in ordinary course from a person in the business of selling goods of that kind but does not include a pawnbroker. "Buying" may be for cash or by exchange of other property or on secured or unsecured credit and includes receiving goods or documents of title under a preexisting contract for sale but does not include a transfer in bulk or as security for or in total or partial satisfaction of a money debt.
  (b) "Cancellation" occurs when either party puts an end to the lease contract for default by the other party.
  (c) "Commercial unit" means such a unit of goods as by commercial usage is a single whole for purposes of lease and division of which materially impairs its character or value on the market or in use. A commercial unit may be a single article, as a machine, or a set of articles, as a suite of furniture or a line of machinery, or a quantity, as a gross or carload, or any other unit treated in use or in the relevant market as a single whole.
  (d) "Conforming" goods or performance under a lease contract means goods or performance that are in accordance with the obligations under the lease contract.
  (e) "Consumer lease" means a lease that a lessor regularly engaged in the business of leasing or selling makes to a lessee who is an individual and who takes under the lease primarily for a personal, family, or household purpose [, if the total payments to be made under the lease contract, excluding payments for options to renew or buy, do not exceed $_____].
  (f) "Fault" means wrongful act, omission, breach, or default.
  (g) "Finance lease" means a lease with respect to which:
    (i) the lessor does not select, manufacture, or supply the goods;
    (ii) the lessor acquires the goods or the right to possession and use of the goods in connection with the lease; and

(iii) one of the following occurs:
  (A) the lessee receives a copy of the contract by which the lessor acquired the goods or the right to possession and use of the goods before signing the lease contract;
  (B) the lessee's approval of the contract by which the lessor acquired the goods or the right to possession and use of the goods is a condition to effectiveness of the lease contract;
  (C) the lessee, before signing the lease contract, receives an accurate and complete statement designating the promises and warranties, and any disclaimers of warranties, limitations or modifications of remedies, or liquidated damages, including those of a third party, such as the manufacturer of the goods, provided to the lessor by the person supplying the goods in connection with or as part of the contract by which the lessor acquired the goods or the right to possession and use of the goods; or
  (D) if the lease is not a consumer lease, the lessor, before the lessee signs the lease contract, informs the lessee in writing (a) of the identity of the person supplying the goods to the lessor, unless the lessee has selected that person and directed the lessor to acquire the goods or the right to possession and use of the goods from that person, (b) that the lessee is entitled under this Article to the promises and warranties, including those of any third party, provided to the lessor by the person supplying the goods in connection with or as part of the contract by which the lessor acquired the goods or the right to possession and use of the goods, and (c) that the lessee may communicate with the person supplying the goods to the lessor and receive an accurate and complete statement of those promises and warranties, including any disclaimers and limitations of them or of remedies.

(h) "Goods" means all things that are movable at the time of identification to the lease contract, or are fixtures (Section 2A–309), but the term does not include money, documents, instruments, accounts, chattel paper, general intangibles, or minerals or the like, including oil and gas, before extraction. The term also includes the unborn young of animals.

(i) "Installment lease contract" means a lease contract that authorizes or requires the delivery of goods in separate lots to be separately accepted, even though the lease contract contains a clause "each delivery is a separate lease" or its equivalent.

(j) "Lease" means a transfer of the right to possession and use of goods for a term in return for consideration, but a sale, including a sale on approval or a sale or return, or retention or creation of a security interest is not a lease. Unless the context clearly indicates otherwise, the term includes a sublease.

(k) "Lease agreement" means the bargain, with respect to the lease, of the lessor and the lessee in fact as found in their language or by implication from other circumstances including course of dealing or usage of trade or course of performance as provided in this Article. Unless the context clearly indicates otherwise, the term includes a sublease agreement.

(l) "Lease contract" means the total legal obligation that results from the lease agreement as affected by this Article and any other applicable rules of law. Unless the context clearly indicates otherwise, the term includes a sublease contract.

(m) "Leasehold interest" means the interest of the lessor or the lessee under a lease contract.

(n) "Lessee" means a person who acquires the right to possession and use of goods under a lease. Unless the context clearly indicates otherwise, the term includes a sublessee.

(o) "Lessee in ordinary course of business" means a person who in good faith and without knowledge that the lease to him [or her] is in violation of the ownership rights or security interest or leasehold interest of a third party in the goods, leases in ordinary course from a person in the business of selling or leasing goods of that kind but does not include a pawnbroker. "Leasing" may be for cash or by exchange of other property or on secured or unsecured credit and includes receiving goods or documents of title under a preexisting lease contract but does not include a transfer in bulk or as security for or in total or partial satisfaction of a money debt.

(p) "Lessor" means a person who transfers the right to possession and use of goods under a lease. Unless the context clearly indicates otherwise, the term includes a sublessor.

(q) "Lessor's residual interest" means the lessor's interest in the goods after expiration, termination, or cancellation of the lease contract.

(r) "Lien" means a charge against or interest in goods to secure payment of a debt or performance of an obligation, but the term does not include a security interest.

(s) "Lot" means a parcel or a single article that is the subject matter of a separate lease or delivery, whether or not it is sufficient to perform the lease contract.

(t) "Merchant lessee" means a lessee that is a merchant with respect to goods of the kind subject to the lease.

(u) "Present value" means the amount as of a date certain of one or more sums payable in the future, discounted to the date certain. The discount is determined by the interest rate specified by the parties if the rate was not manifestly unreasonable at the time the transaction was entered into; otherwise, the discount is determined by a commercially reasonable rate that takes into account the facts and circumstances of each case at the time the transaction was entered into.

(v) "Purchase" includes taking by sale, lease, mortgage, security interest, pledge, gift, or any other voluntary transaction creating an interest in goods.

(w) "Sublease" means a lease of goods the right to possession and use of which was acquired by the lessor as a lessee under an existing lease.

(x) "Supplier" means a person from whom a lessor buys or leases goods to be leased under a finance lease.

(y) "Supply contract" means a contract under which a lessor buys or leases goods to be leased.

(z) "Termination" occurs when either party pursuant to a power created by agreement or law puts an end to the lease contract otherwise than for default.

(2) Other definitions applying to this Article and the sections in which they appear are:

"Accessions"	Section 2A–310(1).
"Construction mortgage"	Section 2A–309(1) (d).
"Encumbrance"	Section 2A–309(1) (e).
"Fixtures"	Section 2A–309(1) (a).
"Fixture filing"	Section 2A–309(1) (b).
"Purchase money lease"	Section 2A–309(1) (c).

(3) The following definitions in other Articles apply to this Article:

"Account"	Section 9–106.
"Between merchants"	Section 2–104(3).
"Buyer"	Section 2–103(1) (a).
"Chattel paper"	Section 9–105(1) (b).
"Consumer goods"	Section 9–109(1).
"Document"	Section 9–105(1) (f).
"Entrusting"	Section 2–403(3).
"General intangibles"	Section 9–106.
"Good faith"	Section 2–103(1) (b).
"Instrument"	Section 9–105(1) (i).
"Merchant"	Section 2–104(1).
"Mortgage"	Section 9–105(1) (j).

"Pursuant to commitment"	Section 9–105(1) (k).
"Receipt"	Section 2–103(1) (c).
"Sale"	Section 2–106(1).
"Sale on approval"	Section 2–326.
"Sale or return"	Section 2–326.
"Seller"	Section 2–103(1) (d).

(4) In addition Article 1 contains general definitions and principles of construction and interpretation applicable throughout this Article.

As amended in 1990.

§ 2A–104. Leases Subject to Other Law.

(1) A lease, although subject to this Article, is also subject to any applicable:
  (a) certificate of title statute of this State: (list any certificate of title statutes covering automobiles, trailers, mobile homes, boats, farm tractors, and the like);
  (b) certificate of title statute of another jurisdiction (Section 2A–105); or
  (c) consumer protection statute of this State, or final consumer protection decision of a court of this State existing on the effective date of this Article.
(2) In case of conflict between this Article, other than Sections 2A–105, 2A–304(3), and 2A–305(3), and a statute or decision referred to in subsection (1), the statute or decision controls.
(3) Failure to comply with an applicable law has only the effect specified therein.

As amended in 1990.

§ 2A–105. Territorial Application of Article to Goods Covered by Certificate of Title.
Subject to the provisions of Sections 2A–304(3) and 2A–305(3), with respect to goods covered by a certificate of title issued under a statute of this State or of another jurisdiction, compliance and the effect of compliance or noncompliance with a certificate of title statute are governed by the law (including the conflict of laws rules) of the jurisdiction issuing the certificate until the earlier of (a) surrender of the certificate, or (b) four months after the goods are removed from that jurisdiction and thereafter until a new certificate of title is issued by another jurisdiction.

§ 2A–106. Limitation on Power of Parties to Consumer Lease to Choose Applicable Law and Judicial Forum.

(1) If the law chosen by the parties to a consumer lease is that of a jurisdiction other than a jurisdiction in which the lessee resides at the time the lease agreement becomes enforceable or within 30 days thereafter or in which the goods are to be used, the choice is not enforceable.
(2) If the judicial forum chosen by the parties to a consumer lease is a forum that would not otherwise have jurisdiction over the lessee, the choice is not enforceable.

§ 2A–107. Waiver or Renunciation of Claim or Right After Default.
Any claim or right arising out of an alleged default or breach of warranty may be discharged in whole or in part without consideration by a written waiver or renunciation signed and delivered by the aggrieved party.

§ 2A–108. Unconscionability.

(1) If the court as a matter of law finds a lease contract or any clause of a lease contract to have been unconscionable at the time it was made the court may refuse to enforce the lease contract, or it may enforce the remainder of the lease contract without the unconscionable

clause, or it may so limit the application of any unconscionable clause as to avoid any unconscionable result.

(2) With respect to a consumer lease, if the court as a matter of law finds that a lease contract or any clause of a lease contract has been induced by unconscionable conduct or that unconscionable conduct has occurred in the collection of a claim arising from a lease contract, the court may grant appropriate relief.

(3) Before making a finding of unconscionability under subsection (1) or (2), the court, on its own motion or that of a party, shall afford the parties a reasonable opportunity to present evidence as to the setting, purpose, and effect of the lease contract or clause thereof, or of the conduct.

(4) In an action in which the lessee claims unconscionability with respect to a consumer lease:

    (a) If the court finds unconscionability under subsection (1) or (2), the court shall award reasonable attorney's fees to the lessee.

    (b) If the court does not find unconscionability and the lessee claiming unconscionability has brought or maintained an action he [or she] knew to be groundless, the court shall award reasonable attorney's fees to the party against whom the claim is made.

    (c) In determining attorney's fees, the amount of the recovery on behalf of the claimant under subsections (1) and (2) is not controlling.

§ 2A–109. Option to Accelerate at Will.

(1) A term providing that one party or his [or her] successor in interest may accelerate payment or performance or require collateral or additional collateral "at will" or "when he [or she] deems himself [or herself] insecure" or in words of similar import must be construed to mean that he [or she] has power to do so only if he [or she] in good faith believes that the prospect of payment or performance is impaired.

(2) With respect to a consumer lease, the burden of establishing good faith under subsection (1) is on the party who exercised the power; otherwise the burden of establishing lack of good faith is on the party against whom the power has been exercised.

PART 2: FORMATION AND CONSTRUCTION OF LEASE CONTRACT

§ 2A–201. Statute of Frauds.

(1) A lease contract is not enforceable by way of action or defense unless:

    (a) the total payments to be made under the lease contract, excluding payments for options to renew or buy, are less than $1,000; or

    (b) there is a writing, signed by the party against whom enforcement is sought or by that party's authorized agent, sufficient to indicate that a lease contract has been made between the parties and to describe the goods leased and the lease term.

(2) Any description of leased goods or of the lease term is sufficient and satisfies subsection (1)(b), whether or not it is specific, if it reasonably identifies what is described.

(3) A writing is not insufficient because it omits or incorrectly states a term agreed upon, but the lease contract is not enforceable under subsection (1)(b) beyond the lease term and the quantity of goods shown in the writing.

(4) A lease contract that does not satisfy the requirements of subsection (1), but which is valid in other respects, is enforceable:

    (a) if the goods are to be specially manufactured or obtained for the lessee and are not suitable for lease or sale to others in the ordinary course of the lessor's business, and the lessor, before notice of repudiation is received and under circumstances that reasonably indicate that the goods are for the lessee, has made either a substantial beginning of their manufacture or commitments for their procurement;

    (b) if the party against whom enforcement is sought admits in that party's pleading, testimony or otherwise in court that a lease contract was made, but the lease contract is not enforceable under this provision beyond the quantity of goods admitted; or

    (c) with respect to goods that have been received and accepted by the lessee.

(5) The lease term under a lease contract referred to in subsection (4) is:

    (a) if there is a writing signed by the party against whom enforcement is sought or by that party's authorized agent specifying the lease term, the term so specified;

    (b) if the party against whom enforcement is sought admits in that party's pleading, testimony, or otherwise in court a lease term, the term so admitted; or

    (c) a reasonable lease term.

§ 2A–202. Final Written Expression: Parol or Extrinsic Evidence.

Terms with respect to which the confirmatory memoranda of the parties agree or which are otherwise set forth in a writing intended by the parties as a final expression of their agreement with respect to such terms as are included therein may not be contradicted by evidence of any prior agreement or of a contemporaneous oral agreement but may be explained or supplemented:

    (a) by course of dealing or usage of trade or by course of performance; and

    (b) by evidence of consistent additional terms unless the court finds the writing to have been intended also as a complete and exclusive statement of the terms of the agreement.

§ 2A–203. Seals Inoperative.

The affixing of a seal to a writing evidencing a lease contract or an offer to enter into a lease contract does not render the writing a sealed instrument and the law with respect to sealed instruments does not apply to the lease contract or offer.

§ 2A–204. Formation in General.

(1) A lease contract may be made in any manner sufficient to show agreement, including conduct by both parties which recognizes the existence of a lease contract.

(2) An agreement sufficient to constitute a lease contract may be found although the moment of its making is undetermined.

(3) Although one or more terms are left open, a lease contract does not fail for indefiniteness if the parties have intended to make a lease contract and there is a reasonably certain basis for giving an appropriate remedy.

§ 2A–205. Firm Offers.

An offer by a merchant to lease goods to or from another person in a signed writing that by its terms gives assurance it will be held open is not revocable, for lack of consideration, during the time stated or, if no time is stated, for a reasonable time, but in no event may the period of irrevocability exceed 3 months. Any such term of assurance on a form supplied by the offeree must be separately signed by the offeror.

§ 2A–206. Offer and Acceptance in Formation of Lease Contract.

(1) Unless otherwise unambiguously indicated by the language or circumstances, an offer to make a lease contract must be construed as inviting acceptance in any manner and by any medium reasonable in the circumstances.

(2) If the beginning of a requested performance is a reasonable mode of acceptance, an offeror who is not notified of acceptance within a reasonable time may treat the offer as having lapsed before acceptance.

§ 2A–207. Course of Performance or Practical Construction.

(1) If a lease contract involves repeated occasions for performance by either party with knowledge of the nature of the performance and opportunity for objection to it by the other, any course of performance accepted or acquiesced in without objection is relevant to determine the meaning of the lease agreement.

(2) The express terms of a lease agreement and any course of performance, as well as any course of dealing and usage of trade, must be construed whenever reasonable as consistent with each other; but if that construction is unreasonable, express terms control course of performance, course of performance controls both course of dealing and usage of trade, and course of dealing controls usage of trade.

(3) Subject to the provisions of Section 2A–208 on modification and waiver, course of performance is relevant to show a waiver or modification of any term inconsistent with the course of performance.

§ 2A–208. Modification, Rescission and Waiver.

(1) An agreement modifying a lease contract needs no consideration to be binding.

(2) A signed lease agreement that excludes modification or rescission except by a signed writing may not be otherwise modified or rescinded, but, except as between merchants, such a requirement on a form supplied by a merchant must be separately signed by the other party.

(3) Although an attempt at modification or rescission does not satisfy the requirements of subsection (2), it may operate as a waiver.

(4) A party who has made a waiver affecting an executory portion of a lease contract may retract the waiver by reasonable notification received by the other party that strict performance will be required of any term waived, unless the retraction would be unjust in view of a material change of position in reliance on the waiver.

§ 2A–209. Lessee Under Finance Lease as Beneficiary of Supply Contract.

(1) The benefit of a supplier's promises to the lessor under the supply contract and of all warranties, whether express or implied, including those of any third party provided in connection with or as part of the supply contract, extends to the lessee to the extent of the lessee's leasehold interest under a finance lease related to the supply contract, but is subject to the terms of the warranty and of the supply contract and all defenses or claims arising therefrom.

(2) The extension of the benefit of a supplier's promises and of warranties to the lessee (Section 2A–209(1)) does not: (i) modify the rights and obligations of the parties to the supply contract, whether arising therefrom or otherwise, or (ii) impose any duty or liability under the supply contract on the lessee.

(3) Any modification or rescission of the supply contract by the supplier and the lessor is effective between the supplier and the lessee unless, before the modification or rescission, the supplier has received notice that the lessee has entered into a finance lease related to the supply contract. If the modification or rescission is effective between the supplier and the lessee, the lessor is deemed to have assumed, in addition to the obligations of the lessor to the lessee under the lease contract, promises of the supplier to the lessor and warranties that were so modified or rescinded as they existed and were available to the lessee before modification or rescission.

(4) In addition to the extension of the benefit of the supplier's promises and of warranties to the lessee under subsection (1), the lessee retains all rights that the lessee may have against the supplier which arise from an agreement between the lessee and the supplier or under other law.

As amended in 1990.

§ 2A–210. Express Warranties.

(1) Express warranties by the lessor are created as follows:

   (a) Any affirmation of fact or promise made by the lessor to the lessee which relates to the goods and becomes part of the basis of the bargain creates an express warranty that the goods will conform to the affirmation or promise.

   (b) Any description of the goods which is made part of the basis of the bargain creates an express warranty that the goods will conform to the description.

   (c) Any sample or model that is made part of the basis of the bargain creates an express warranty that the whole of the goods will conform to the sample or model.

(2) It is not necessary to the creation of an express warranty that the lessor use formal words, such as "warrant" or "guarantee," or that the lessor have a specific intention to make a warranty, but an affirmation merely of the value of the goods or a statement purporting to be merely the lessor's opinion or commendation of the goods does not create a warranty.

§ 2A–211. Warranties Against Interference and Against Infringement; Lessee's Obligation Against Infringement.

(1) There is in a lease contract a warranty that for the lease term no person holds a claim to or interest in the goods that arose from an act or omission of the lessor, other than a claim by way of infringement or the like, which will interfere with the lessee's enjoyment of its leasehold interest.

(2) Except in a finance lease there is in a lease contract by a lessor who is a merchant regularly dealing in goods of the kind a warranty that the goods are delivered free of the rightful claim of any person by way of infringement or the like.

(3) A lessee who furnishes specifications to a lessor or a supplier shall hold the lessor and the supplier harmless against any claim by way of infringement or the like that arises out of compliance with the specifications.

§ 2A–212. Implied Warranty of Merchantability.

(1) Except in a finance lease, a warranty that the goods will be merchantable is implied in a lease contract if the lessor is a merchant with respect to goods of that kind.

(2) Goods to be merchantable must be at least such as
    (a) pass without objection in the trade under the description in the lease agreement;
    (b) in the case of fungible goods, are of fair average quality within the description;
    (c) are fit for the ordinary purposes for which goods of that type are used;
    (d) run, within the variation permitted by the lease agreement, of even kind, quality, and quantity within each unit and among all units involved;
    (e) are adequately contained, packaged, and labeled as the lease agreement may require; and
    (f) conform to any promises or affirmations of fact made on the container or label.

(3) Other implied warranties may arise from course of dealing or usage of trade.

§ 2A–213. Implied Warranty of Fitness for Particular Purpose.
Except in a finance lease, if the lessor at the time the lease contract is made has reason to know of any particular purpose for which the goods are required and that the lessee is relying on the lessor's skill or judgment to select or furnish suitable goods, there is in the lease contract an implied warranty that the goods will be fit for that purpose.

§ 2A–214. Exclusion or Modification of Warranties.

(1) Words or conduct relevant to the creation of an express warranty and words or conduct tending to negate or limit a warranty must be construed wherever reasonable as consistent with each other; but, subject to the provisions of Section 2A–202 on parol or extrinsic evidence, negation or limitation is inoperative to the extent that the construction is unreasonable.

(2) Subject to subsection (3), to exclude or modify the implied warranty of merchantability or any part of it the language must mention "merchantability", be by a writing, and be conspicuous. Subject to sub-section (3), to exclude or modify any implied warranty of fitness the exclusion must be by a writing and be conspicuous. Language to exclude all implied warranties of fitness is sufficient if it is in writing, is conspicuous and states, for example, "There is no warranty that the goods will be fit for a particular purpose".

(3) Notwithstanding subsection (2), but subject to subsection (4),
    (a) unless the circumstances indicate otherwise, all implied warranties are excluded by expressions like "as is," or "with all faults," or by other language that in common

understanding calls the lessee's attention to the exclusion of warranties and makes plain that there is no implied warranty, if in writing and conspicuous;

   (b) if the lessee before entering into the lease contract has examined the goods or the sample or model as fully as desired or has refused to examine the goods, there is no implied warranty with regard to defects that an examination ought in the circumstances to have revealed; and

   (c) an implied warranty may also be excluded or modified by course of dealing, course of performance, or usage of trade.

(4) To exclude or modify a warranty against interference or against infringement (Section 2A–211) or any part of it, the language must be specific, be by a writing, and be conspicuous, unless the circumstances, including course of performance, course of dealing, or usage of trade, give the lessee reason to know that the goods are being leased subject to a claim or interest of any person.

§ 2A–215. Cumulation and Conflict of Warranties Express or Implied.

Warranties, whether express or implied, must be construed as consistent with each other and as cumulative, but if that construction is unreasonable, the intention of the parties determines which warranty is dominant. In ascertaining that intention the following rules apply:

   (a) Exact or technical specifications displace an inconsistent sample or model or general language of description.

   (b) A sample from an existing bulk displaces inconsistent general language of description.

   (c) Express warranties displace inconsistent implied warranties other than an implied warranty of fitness for a particular purpose.

§ 2A–216. Third Party Beneficiaries of Express and Implied Warranties.

Alternative A

A warranty to or for the benefit of a lessee under this Article, whether express or implied, extends to any natural person who is in the family or household of the lessee or who is a guest in the lessee's home if it is reasonable to expect that such person may use, consume, or be affected by the goods and who is injured in person by breach of the warranty. This section does not displace principles of law and equity that extend a warranty to or for the benefit of a lessee to other persons. The operation of this section may not be excluded, modified, or limited, but an exclusion, modification, or limitation of the warranty, including any with respect to rights and remedies, effective against the lessee is also effective against any beneficiary designated under this section.

Alternative B

A warranty to or for the benefit of a lessee under this Article, whether express or implied, extends to any natural person who may reasonably be expected to use, consume, or be affected by the goods and who is injured in person by breach of the warranty. This section does not displace principles of law and equity that extend a warranty to or for the benefit of a lessee to other persons. The operation of this section may not be excluded, modified, or limited, but an exclusion, modification, or limitation of the warranty, including any with respect to rights and remedies, effective against the lessee is also effective against the beneficiary designated under this section.

Alternative C

A warranty to or for the benefit of a lessee under this Article, whether express or implied, extends to any person who may reasonably be expected to use, consume, or be affected by the goods and who is injured by breach of the warranty. The operation of this section may not be excluded, modified, or limited with respect to injury to the person of an individual to whom the warranty extends, but an exclusion, modification, or limitation of the warranty, including any with respect to rights and remedies, effective against the lessee is also effective against the beneficiary designated under this section.

§ 2A–217. Identification. Identification of goods as goods to which a lease contract refers may be made at any time and in any manner explicitly agreed to by the parties. In the absence of explicit agreement, identification occurs:

 (a) when the lease contract is made if the lease contract is for a lease of goods that are existing and identified;

 (b) when the goods are shipped, marked, or otherwise designated by the lessor as goods to which the lease contract refers, if the lease contract is for a lease of goods that are not existing and identified; or

 (c) when the young are conceived, if the lease contract is for a lease of unborn young of animals.

§ 2A–218. Insurance and Proceeds.

(1) A lessee obtains an insurable interest when existing goods are identified to the lease contract even though the goods identified are nonconforming and the lessee has an option to reject them.

(2) If a lessee has an insurable interest only by reason of the lessor's identification of the goods, the lessor, until default or insolvency or notification to the lessee that identification is final, may substitute other goods for those identified.

(3) Notwithstanding a lessee's insurable interest under subsections (1) and (2) , the lessor retains an insurable interest until an option to buy has been exercised by the lessee and risk of loss has passed to the lessee.

(4) Nothing in this section impairs any insurable interest recognized under any other statute or rule of law.

(5) The parties by agreement may determine that one or more parties have an obligation to obtain and pay for insurance covering the goods and by agreement may determine the beneficiary of the proceeds of the insurance.

§ 2A–219. Risk of Loss.

(1) Except in the case of a finance lease, risk of loss is retained by the lessor and does not pass to the lessee. In the case of a finance lease, risk of loss passes to the lessee.

(2) Subject to the provisions of this Article on the effect of default on risk of loss (Section 2A–220), if risk of loss is to pass to the lessee and the time of passage is not stated, the following rules apply:

 (a) If the lease contract requires or authorizes the goods to be shipped by carrier

  (i) and it does not require delivery at a particular destination, the risk of loss passes to the lessee when the goods are duly delivered to the carrier; but

  (ii) if it does require delivery at a particular destination and the goods are there duly tendered while in the possession of the carrier, the risk of loss passes to the lessee when the goods are there duly so tendered as to enable the lessee to take delivery.

 (b) If the goods are held by a bailee to be delivered without being moved, the risk of loss passes to the lessee on acknowledgment by the bailee of the lessee's right to possession of the goods.

 (c) In any case not within subsection (a) or (b), the risk of loss passes to the lessee on the lessee's receipt of the goods if the lessor, or, in the case of a finance lease, the supplier, is a merchant; otherwise the risk passes to the lessee on tender of delivery.

§ 2A–220. Effect of Default on Risk of Loss.

(1) Where risk of loss is to pass to the lessee and the time of passage is not stated:

 (a) If a tender or delivery of goods so fails to conform to the lease contract as to give a right of rejection, the risk of their loss remains with the lessor, or, in the case of a finance lease, the supplier, until cure or acceptance.

(b)   If the lessee rightfully revokes acceptance, he [or she], to the extent of any deficiency in his [or her] effective insurance coverage, may treat the risk of loss as having remained with the lessor from the beginning.

(2)   Whether or not risk of loss is to pass to the lessee, if the lessee as to conforming goods already identified to a lease contract repudiates or is otherwise in default under the lease contract, the lessor, or, in the case of a finance lease, the supplier, to the extent of any deficiency in his [or her] effective insurance coverage may treat the risk of loss as resting on the lessee for a commercially reasonable time.

§ 2A–221. Casualty to Identified Goods. If a lease contract requires goods identified when the lease contract is made, and the goods suffer casualty without fault of the lessee, the lessor or the supplier before delivery, or the goods suffer casualty before risk of loss passes to the lessee pursuant to the lease agreement or Section 2A–219, then:

(a)   if the loss is total, the lease contract is avoided; and

(b)   if the loss is partial or the goods have so deteriorated as to no longer conform to the lease contract, the lessee may nevertheless demand inspection and at his [or her] option either treat the lease contract as avoided or, except in a finance lease that is not a consumer lease, accept the goods with due allowance from the rent payable for the balance of the lease term for the deterioration or the deficiency in quantity but without further right against the lessor.

PART 3: EFFECT OF LEASE CONTRACT

§ 2A–301. Enforceability of Lease Contract. Except as otherwise provided in this Article, a lease contract is effective and enforceable according to its terms between the parties, against purchasers of the goods and against creditors of the parties.

§ 2A–302. Title to and Possession of Goods. Except as otherwise provided in this Article, each provision of this Article applies whether the lessor or a third party has title to the goods, and whether the lessor, the lessee, or a third party has possession of the goods, notwithstanding any statute or rule of law that possession or the absence of possession is fraudulent.

§ 2A–303. Alienability of Party's Interest Under Lease Contract or of Lessor's Residual Interest in Goods; Delegation of Performance; Transfer of Rights.

(1)   As used in this section, "creation of a security interest" includes the sale of a lease contract that is subject to Article 9, Secured Transactions, by reason of Section 9–102(1) (b).

(2)   Except as provided in subsections (3) and (4), a provision in a lease agreement which (i) prohibits the voluntary or involuntary transfer, including a transfer by sale, sublease, creation or enforcement of a security interest, or attachment, levy, or other judicial process, of an interest of a party under the lease contract or of the lessor's residual interest in the goods, or (ii) makes such a transfer an event of default, gives rise to the rights and remedies provided in subsection (5), but a transfer that is prohibited or is an event of default under the lease agreement is otherwise effective.

(3)   A provision in a lease agreement which (i) prohibits the creation or enforcement of a security interest in an interest of a party under the lease contract or in the lessor's residual interest in the goods, or (ii) makes such a transfer an event of default, is not enforceable unless, and then only to the extent that, there is an actual transfer by the lessee of the lessee's right of possession or use of the goods in violation of the provision or an actual delegation of a material performance of either party to the lease contract in violation of the provision. Neither the granting nor the enforcement of a security interest in (i) the lessor's interest under the lease contract or (ii) the lessor's residual interest in the goods is a transfer that

materially impairs the prospect of obtaining return performance by, materially changes the duty of, or materially increases the burden or risk imposed on, the lessee within the purview of subsection (5) unless, and then only to the extent that, there is an actual delegation of a material performance of the lessor.

(4) A provision in a lease agreement which (i) prohibits a transfer of a right to damages for default with respect to the whole lease contract or of a right to payment arising out of the transferor's due performance of the transferor's entire obligation, or (ii) makes such a transfer an event of default, is not enforceable, and such a transfer is not a transfer that materially impairs the prospect of obtaining return performance by, materially changes the duty of, or materially increases the burden or risk imposed on, the other party to the lease contract within the purview of subsection (5).

(5) Subject to subsections (3) and (4):

    (a) if a transfer is made which is made an event of default under a lease agreement, the party to the lease contract not making the transfer, unless that party waives the default or otherwise agrees, has the rights and remedies described in Section 2A–501(2);

    (b) if paragraph (a) is not applicable and if a transfer is made that (i) is prohibited under a lease agreement or (ii) materially impairs the prospect of obtaining return performance by, materially changes the duty of, or materially increases the burden or risk imposed on, the other party to the lease contract, unless the party not making the transfer agrees at any time to the transfer in the lease contract or otherwise, then, except as limited by contract, (i) the transferor is liable to the party not making the transfer for damages caused by the transfer to the extent that the damages could not reasonably be prevented by the party not making the transfer and (ii) a court having jurisdiction may grant other appropriate relief, including cancellation of the lease contract or an injunction against the transfer.

(6) A transfer of "the lease" or of "all my rights under the lease", or a transfer in similar general terms, is a transfer of rights and, unless the language or the circumstances, as in a transfer for security, indicate the contrary, the transfer is a delegation of duties by the transferor to the transferee. Acceptance by the transferee constitutes a promise by the transferee to perform those duties. The promise is enforceable by either the transferor or the other party to the lease contract.

(7) Unless otherwise agreed by the lessor and the lessee, a delegation of performance does not relieve the transferor as against the other party of any duty to perform or of any liability for default.

(8) In a consumer lease, to prohibit the transfer of an interest of a party under the lease contract or to make a transfer an event of default, the language must be specific, by a writing, and conspicuous.

As amended in 1990.

§ 2A–304. Subsequent Lease of Goods by Lessor.

(1) Subject to Section 2A–303, a subsequent lessee from a lessor of goods under an existing lease contract obtains, to the extent of the leasehold interest transferred, the leasehold interest in the goods that the lessor had or had power to transfer, and except as provided in subsection (2) and Section 2A–527(4), takes subject to the existing lease contract. A lessor with voidable title has power to transfer a good leasehold interest to a good faith subsequent lessee for value, but only to the extent set forth in the preceding sentence. If goods have been delivered under a transaction of purchase, the lessor has that power even though:

    (a) the lessor's transferor was deceived as to the identity of the lessor;

    (b) the delivery was in exchange for a check which is later dishonored;

    (c) it was agreed that the transaction was to be a "cash sale"; or

    (d) the delivery was procured through fraud punishable as larcenous under the criminal law.

(2) A subsequent lessee in the ordinary course of business from a lessor who is a merchant dealing in goods of that kind to whom the goods were entrusted by the existing lessee of that lessor before the interest of the subsequent lessee became enforceable against that

lessor obtains, to the extent of the leasehold interest transferred, all of that lessor's and the existing lessee's rights to the goods, and takes free of the existing lease contract.

(3) A subsequent lessee from the lessor of goods that are subject to an existing lease contract and are covered by a certificate of title issued under a statute of this State or of another jurisdiction takes no greater rights than those provided both by this section and by the certificate of title statute.

As amended in 1990.

§ 2A–305. Sale or Sublease of Goods by Lessee.

(1) Subject to the provisions of Section 2A–303, a buyer or sublessee from the lessee of goods under an existing lease contract obtains, to the extent of the interest transferred, the leasehold interest in the goods that the lessee had or had power to transfer, and except as provided in subsection (2) and Section 2A–511(4), takes subject to the existing lease contract. A lessee with a voidable leasehold interest has power to transfer a good leasehold interest to a good faith buyer for value or a good faith sublessee for value, but only to the extent set forth in the preceding sentence. When goods have been delivered under a transaction of lease the lessee has that power even though:
  (a) the lessor was deceived as to the identity of the lessee;
  (b) the delivery was in exchange for a check which is later dishonored; or
  (c) the delivery was procured through fraud punishable as larcenous under the criminal law.

(2) A buyer in the ordinary course of business or a sublessee in the ordinary course of business from a lessee who is a merchant dealing in goods of that kind to whom the goods were entrusted by the lessor obtains, to the extent of the interest transferred, all of the lessor's and lessee's rights to the goods, and takes free of the existing lease contract.

(3) A buyer or sublessee from the lessee of goods that are subject to an existing lease contract and are covered by a certificate of title issued under a statute of this State or of another jurisdiction takes no greater rights than those provided both by this section and by the certificate of title statute.

§ 2A–306. Priority of Certain Liens Arising by Operation of Law. If a person in the ordinary course of his [or her] business furnishes services or materials with respect to goods subject to a lease contract, a lien upon those goods in the possession of that person given by statute or rule of law for those materials or services takes priority over any interest of the lessor or lessee under the lease contract or this Article unless the lien is created by statute and the statute provides otherwise or unless the lien is created by rule of law and the rule of law provides otherwise.

§ 2A–307. Priority of Liens Arising by Attachment or Levy on, Security Interests in, and Other Claims to Goods.

(1) Except as otherwise provided in Section 2A–306, a creditor of a lessee takes subject to the lease contract.

(2) Except as otherwise provided in subsections (3) and (4) and in Sections 2A–306 and 2A–308, a creditor of a lessor takes subject to the lease contract unless:
  (a) the creditor holds a lien that attached to the goods before the lease contract became enforceable;
  (b) the creditor holds a security interest in the goods and the lessee did not give value and receive delivery of the goods without knowledge of the security interest; or
  (c) the creditor holds a security interest in the goods which was perfected (Section 9–303) before the lease contract became enforceable.

(3) A lessee in the ordinary course of business takes the leasehold interest free of a security interest in the goods created by the lessor even though the security interest is perfected (Section 9–303) and the lessee knows of its existence.

(4) A lessee other than a lessee in the ordinary course of business takes the leasehold interest free of a security interest to the extent that it secures future advances made after the secured party acquires knowledge of the lease or more than 45 days after the lease contract becomes enforceable, whichever first occurs, unless the future advances are made pursuant to a commitment entered into without knowledge of the lease and before the expiration of the 45-day period.

As amended in 1990.

§ 2A–308. Special Rights of Creditors.

(1) A creditor of a lessor in possession of goods subject to a lease contract may treat the lease contract as void if as against the creditor retention of possession by the lessor is fraudulent under any statute or rule of law, but retention of possession in good faith and current course of trade by the lessor for a commercially reasonable time after the lease contract becomes enforceable is not fraudulent.
(2) Nothing in this Article impairs the rights of creditors of a lessor if the lease contract (a) becomes enforceable, not in current course of trade but in satisfaction of or as security for a preexisting claim for money, security, or the like, and (b) is made under circumstances which under any statute or rule of law apart from this Article would constitute the transaction a fraudulent transfer or voidable preference.
(3) A creditor of a seller may treat a sale or an identification of goods to a contract for sale as void if as against the creditor retention of possession by the seller is fraudulent under any statute or rule of law, but retention of possession of the goods pursuant to a lease contract entered into by the seller as lessee and the buyer as lessor in connection with the sale or identification of the goods is not fraudulent if the buyer bought for value and in good faith.

§ 2A–309. Lessor's and Lessee's Rights When Goods Become Fixtures.

(1) In this section:
    (a) goods are "fixtures" when they become so related to particular real estate that an interest in them arises under real estate law;
    (b) a "fixture filing" is the filing, in the office where a mortgage on the real estate would be filed or recorded, of a financing statement covering goods that are or are to become fixtures and conforming to the requirements of Section 9–402(5);
    (c) a lease is a "purchase money lease" unless the lessee has possession or use of the goods or the right to possession or use of the goods before the lease agreement is enforceable;
    (d) a mortgage is a "construction mortgage" to the extent it secures an obligation incurred for the construction of an improvement on land including the acquisition cost of the land, if the recorded writing so indicates; and
    (e) "encumbrance" includes real estate mortgages and other liens on real estate and all other rights in real estate that are not ownership interests.
(2) Under this Article a lease may be of goods that are fixtures or may continue in goods that become fixtures, but no lease exists under this Article of ordinary building materials incorporated into an improvement on land.
(3) This Article does not prevent creation of a lease of fixtures pursuant to real estate law.
(4) The perfected interest of a lessor of fixtures has priority over a conflicting interest of an encumbrancer or owner of the real estate if:
    (a) the lease is a purchase money lease, the conflicting interest of the encumbrancer or owner arises before the goods become fixtures, the interest of the lessor is perfected by a fixture filing before the goods become fixtures or within ten days thereafter, and the lessee has an interest of record in the real estate or is in possession of the real estate; or
    (b) the interest of the lessor is perfected by a fixture filing before the interest of the encumbrancer or owner is of record, the lessor's interest has priority over any conflicting interest of a predecessor in title of the encumbrancer or owner, and the lessee has an interest of record in the real estate or is in possession of the real estate.

(5) The interest of a lessor of fixtures, whether or not perfected, has priority over the conflicting interest of an encumbrancer or owner of the real estate if:

    (a) the fixtures are readily removable factory or office machines, readily removable equipment that is not primarily used or leased for use in the operation of the real estate, or readily removable replacements of domestic appliances that are goods subject to a consumer lease, and before the goods become fixtures the lease contract is enforceable; or

    (b) the conflicting interest is a lien on the real estate obtained by legal or equitable proceedings after the lease contract is enforceable; or

    (c) the encumbrancer or owner has consented in writing to the lease or has disclaimed an interest in the goods as fixtures; or

    (d) the lessee has a right to remove the goods as against the encumbrancer or owner. If the lessee's right to remove terminates, the priority of the interest of the lessor continues for a reasonable time.

(6) Notwithstanding subsection (4) (a) but otherwise subject to subsections (4) and (5), the interest of a lessor of fixtures, including the lessor's residual interest, is subordinate to the conflicting interest of an encumbrancer of the real estate under a construction mortgage recorded before the goods become fixtures if the goods become fixtures before the completion of the construction. To the extent given to refinance a construction mortgage, the conflicting interest of an encumbrancer of the real estate under a mortgage has this priority to the same extent as the encumbrancer of the real estate under the construction mortgage.

(7) In cases not within the preceding subsections, priority between the interest of a lessor of fixtures, including the lessor's residual interest, and the conflicting interest of an encumbrancer or owner of the real estate who is not the lessee is determined by the priority rules governing conflicting interests in real estate.

(8) If the interest of a lessor of fixtures, including the lessor's residual interest, has priority over all conflicting interests of all owners and encumbrancers of the real estate, the lessor or the lessee may (i) on default, expiration, termination, or cancellation of the lease agreement but subject to the agreement and this Article, or (ii) if necessary to enforce other rights and remedies of the lessor or lessee under this Article, remove the goods from the real estate, free and clear of all conflicting interests of all owners and encumbrancers of the real estate, but the lessor or lessee must reimburse any encumbrancer or owner of the real estate who is not the lessee and who has not otherwise agreed for the cost of repair of any physical injury, but not for any diminution in value of the real estate caused by the absence of the goods removed or by any necessity of replacing them. A person entitled to reimbursement may refuse permission to remove until the party seeking removal gives adequate security for the performance of this obligation.

(9) Even though the lease agreement does not create a security interest, the interest of a lessor of fixtures, including the lessor's residual interest, is perfected by filing a financing statement as a fixture filing for leased goods that are or are to become fixtures in accordance with the relevant provisions of the Article on Secured Transactions (Article 9).

As amended in 1990.

§ 2A–310. Lessor's and Lessee's Rights When Goods Become Accessions.

(1) Goods are "accessions" when they are installed in or affixed to other goods.

(2) The interest of a lessor or a lessee under a lease contract entered into before the goods became accessions is superior to all interests in the whole except as stated in subsection (4).

(3) The interest of a lessor or a lessee under a lease contract entered into at the time or after the goods became accessions is superior to all subsequently acquired interests in the whole except as stated in subsection (4) but is subordinate to interests in the whole existing at the time the lease contract was made unless the holders of such interests in the whole have in writing consented to the lease or disclaimed an interest in the goods as part of the whole.

(4) The interest of a lessor or a lessee under a lease contract described in subsection (2) or (3) is subordinate to the interest of
    (a) a buyer in the ordinary course of business or a lessee in the ordinary course of business of any interest in the whole acquired after the goods became accessions; or
    (b) a creditor with a security interest in the whole perfected before the lease contract was made to the extent that the creditor makes subsequent advances without knowledge of the lease contract.
(5) When under subsections (2) or (3) and (4) a lessor or a lessee of accessions holds an interest that is superior to all interests in the whole, the lessor or the lessee may (a) on default, expiration, termination, or cancellation of the lease contract by the other party but subject to the provisions of the lease contract and this Article, or (b) if necessary to enforce his [or her] other rights and remedies under this Article, remove the goods from the whole, free and clear of all interests in the whole, but he [or she] must reimburse any holder of an interest in the whole who is not the lessee and who has not otherwise agreed for the cost of repair of any physical injury but not for any diminution in value of the whole caused by the absence of the goods removed or by any necessity for replacing them. A person entitled to reimbursement may refuse permission to remove until the party seeking removal gives adequate security for the performance of this obligation.

§ 2A–311. Priority Subject to Subordination. Nothing in this Article prevents subordination by agreement by any person entitled to priority.

As added in 1990.

PART 4: PERFORMANCE OF LEASE CONTRACT: REPUDIATED, SUBSTITUTED AND EXCUSED

§ 2A–401. Insecurity: Adequate Assurance of Performance.

(1) A lease contract imposes an obligation on each party that the other's expectation of receiving due performance will not be impaired.
(2) If reasonable grounds for insecurity arise with respect to the performance of either party, the insecure party may demand in writing adequate assurance of due performance. Until the insecure party receives that assurance, if commercially reasonable the insecure party may suspend any performance for which he [or she] has not already received the agreed return.
(3) A repudiation of the lease contract occurs if assurance of due performance adequate under the circumstances of the particular case is not provided to the insecure party within a reasonable time, not to exceed 30 days after receipt of a demand by the other party.
(4) Between merchants, the reasonableness of grounds for insecurity and the adequacy of any assurance offered must be determined according to commercial standards.
(5) Acceptance of any nonconforming delivery or payment does not prejudice the aggrieved party's right to demand adequate assurance of future performance.

§ 2A–402. Anticipatory Repudiation. If either party repudiates a lease contract with respect to a performance not yet due under the lease contract, the loss of which performance will substantially impair the value of the lease contract to the other, the aggrieved party may:
    (a) for a commercially reasonable time, await retraction of repudiation and performance by the repudiating party;
    (b) make demand pursuant to Section 2A–401 and await assurance of future performance adequate under the circumstances of the particular case; or
    (c) resort to any right or remedy upon default under the lease contract or this Article, even though the aggrieved party has notified the repudiating party that the aggrieved

party would await the repudiating party's performance and assurance and has urged retraction. In addition, whether or not the aggrieved party is pursuing one of the foregoing remedies, the aggrieved party may suspend performance or, if the aggrieved party is the lessor, proceed in accordance with the provisions of this Article on the lessor's right to identify goods to the lease contract notwithstanding default or to salvage unfinished goods (Section 2A–524).

§ 2A–403. Retraction of Anticipatory Repudiation.

(1) Until the repudiating party's next performance is due, the repudiating party can retract the repudiation unless, since the repudiation, the aggrieved party has cancelled the lease contract or materially changed the aggrieved party's position or otherwise indicated that the aggrieved party considers the repudiation final.

(2) Retraction may be by any method that clearly indicates to the aggrieved party that the repudiating party intends to perform under the lease contract and includes any assurance demanded under Section 2A–401.

(3) Retraction reinstates a repudiating party's rights under a lease contract with due excuse and allowance to the aggrieved party for any delay occasioned by the repudiation.

§ 2A–404. Substituted Performance.

(1) If without fault of the lessee, the lessor and the supplier, the agreed berthing, loading, or unloading facilities fail or the agreed type of carrier becomes unavailable or the agreed manner of delivery otherwise becomes commercially impracticable, but a commercially reasonable substitute is available, the substitute performance must be tendered and accepted.

(2) If the agreed means or manner of payment fails because of domestic or foreign governmental regulation:

    (a) the lessor may withhold or stop delivery or cause the supplier to withhold or stop delivery unless the lessee provides a means or manner of payment that is commercially a substantial equivalent; and

    (b) if delivery has already been taken, payment by the means or in the manner provided by the regulation discharges the lessee's obligation unless the regulation is discriminatory, oppressive, or predatory.

§ 2A–405. Excused Performance. Subject to Section 2A–404 on substituted performance, the following rules apply:

    (a) Delay in delivery or nondelivery in whole or in part by a lessor or a supplier who complies with paragraphs (b) and (c) is not a default under the lease contract if performance as agreed has been made impracticable by the occurrence of a contingency the nonoccurrence of which was a basic assumption on which the lease contract was made or by compliance in good faith with any applicable foreign or domestic governmental regulation or order, whether or not the regulation or order later proves to be invalid.

    (b) If the causes mentioned in paragraph (a) affect only part of the lessor's or the supplier's capacity to perform, he [or she] shall allocate production and deliveries among his [or her] customers but at his [or her] option may include regular customers not then under contract for sale or lease as well as his [or her] own requirements for further manufacture. He [or she] may so allocate in any manner that is fair and reasonable.

    (c) The lessor seasonably shall notify the lessee and in the case of a finance lease the supplier seasonably shall notify the lessor and the lessee, if known, that there will be delay or nondelivery and, if allocation is required under paragraph (b), of the estimated quota thus made available for the lessee.

§ 2A–406. Procedure on Excused Performance.

(1) If the lessee receives notification of a material or indefinite delay or an allocation justified under Section 2A–405, the lessee may by written notification to the lessor as to any goods involved, and with respect to all of the goods if under an installment lease contract the value of the whole lease contract is substantially impaired (Section 2A–510):

    (a)   terminate the lease contract (Section 2A–505(2)); or

    (b)   except in a finance lease that is not a consumer lease, modify the lease contract by accepting the available quota in substitution, with due allowance from the rent payable for the balance of the lease term for the deficiency but without further right against the lessor.

(2) If, after receipt of a notification from the lessor under Section 2A–405, the lessee fails so to modify the lease agreement within a reasonable time not exceeding 30 days, the lease contract lapses with respect to any deliveries affected.

§ 2A–407. Irrevocable Promises: Finance Leases.

(1) In the case of a finance lease that is not a consumer lease the lessee's promises under the lease contract become irrevocable and independent upon the lessee's acceptance of the goods.

(2) A promise that has become irrevocable and independent under subsection (1):

    (a)   is effective and enforceable between the parties, and by or against third parties including assignees of the parties; and

    (b)   is not subject to cancellation, termination, modification, repudiation, excuse, or substitution without the consent of the party to whom the promise runs.

(3) This section does not affect the validity under any other law of a covenant in any lease contract making the lessee's promises irrevocable and independent upon the lessee's acceptance of the goods.

As amended in 1990.

PART 5: DEFAULT

§ 2A–501. Default: Procedure.

(1) Whether the lessor or the lessee is in default under a lease contract is determined by the lease agreement and this Article.

(2) If the lessor or the lessee is in default under the lease contract, the party seeking enforcement has rights and remedies as provided in this Article and, except as limited by this Article, as provided in the lease agreement.

(3) If the lessor or the lessee is in default under the lease contract, the party seeking enforcement may reduce the party's claim to judgment, or otherwise enforce the lease contract by self-help or any available judicial procedure or nonjudicial procedure, including administrative proceeding, arbitration, or the like, in accordance with this Article.

(4) Except as otherwise provided in Section 1–106(1) or this Article or the lease agreement, the rights and remedies referred to in subsections (2) and (3) are cumulative.

(5) If the lease agreement covers both real property and goods, the party seeking enforcement may proceed under this Part as to the goods, or under other applicable law as to both the real property and the goods in accordance with that party's rights and remedies in respect of the real property, in which case this Part does not apply.

As amended in 1990.

§ 2A–502. Notice After Default. Except as otherwise provided in this Article or the lease agreement, the lessor or lessee in default under the lease contract is not entitled to notice of default or notice of enforcement from the other party to the lease agreement.

§ 2A–503. Modification or Impairment of Rights and Remedies.

(1) Except as otherwise provided in this Article, the lease agreement may include rights and remedies for default in addition to or in substitution for those provided in this Article and may limit or alter the measure of damages recoverable under this Article.

(2) Resort to a remedy provided under this Article or in the lease agreement is optional unless the remedy is expressly agreed to be exclusive. If circumstances cause an exclusive or limited remedy to fail of its essential purpose, or provision for an exclusive remedy is unconscionable, remedy may be had as provided in this Article.

(3) Consequential damages may be liquidated under Section 2A–504, or may otherwise be limited, altered, or excluded unless the limitation, alteration, or exclusion is unconscionable. Limitation, alteration, or exclusion of consequential damages for injury to the person in the case of consumer goods is prima facie unconscionable but limitation, alteration, or exclusion of damages where the loss is commercial is not prima facie unconscionable.

(4) Rights and remedies on default by the lessor or the lessee with respect to any obligation or promise collateral or ancillary to the lease contract are not impaired by this Article.

As amended in 1990.

§ 2A–504. Liquidation of Damages.

(1) Damages payable by either party for default, or any other act or omission, including indemnity for loss or diminution of anticipated tax benefits or loss or damage to lessor's residual interest, may be liquidated in the lease agreement but only at an amount or by a formula that is reasonable in light of the then anticipated harm caused by the default or other act or omission.

(2) If the lease agreement provides for liquidation of damages, and such provision does not comply with subsection (1), or such provision is an exclusive or limited remedy that circumstances cause to fail of its essential purpose, remedy may be had as provided in this Article.

(3) If the lessor justifiably withholds or stops delivery of goods because of the lessee's default or insolvency (Section 2A–525 or 2A–526), the lessee is entitled to restitution of any amount by which the sum of his [or her] payments exceeds:
    (a) the amount to which the lessor is entitled by virtue of terms liquidating the lessor's damages in accordance with subsection (1); or
    (b) in the absence of those terms, 20 percent of the then present value of the total rent the lessee was obligated to pay for the balance of the lease term, or, in the case of a consumer lease, the lesser of such amount or $500.

(4) A lessee's right to restitution under subsection (3) is subject to offset to the extent the lessor establishes:
    (a) a right to recover damages under the provisions of this Article other than subsection (1); and
    (b) the amount or value of any benefits received by the lessee directly or indirectly by reason of the lease contract.

§ 2A–505. Cancellation and Termination and Effect of Cancellation, Termination, Rescission, or Fraud on Rights and Remedies.

(1) On cancellation of the lease contract, all obligations that are still executory on both sides are discharged, but any right based on prior default or performance survives, and the cancelling party also retains any remedy for default of the whole lease contract or any unperformed balance.

(2) On termination of the lease contract, all obligations that are still executory on both sides are discharged but any right based on prior default or performance survives.

(3) Unless the contrary intention clearly appears, expressions of "cancellation," "rescission," or the like of the lease contract may not be construed as a renunciation or discharge of any claim in damages for an antecedent default.

(4) Rights and remedies for material misrepresentation or fraud include all rights and remedies available under this Article for default.

(5) Neither rescission nor a claim for rescission of the lease contract nor rejection or return of the goods may bar or be deemed inconsistent with a claim for damages or other right or remedy.

§ 2A–506. Statute of Limitations.

(1) An action for default under a lease contract, including breach of warranty or indemnity, must be commenced within 4 years after the cause of action accrued. By the original lease contract the parties may reduce the period of limitation to not less than one year.

(2) A cause of action for default accrues when the act or omission on which the default or breach of warranty is based is or should have been discovered by the aggrieved party, or when the default occurs, whichever is later. A cause of action for indemnity accrues when the act or omission on which the claim for indemnity is based is or should have been discovered by the indemnified party, whichever is later.

(3) If an action commenced within the time limited by subsection (1) is so terminated as to leave available a remedy by another action for the same default or breach of warranty or indemnity, the other action may be commenced after the expiration of the time limited and within 6 months after the termination of the first action unless the termination resulted from voluntary discontinuance or from dismissal for failure or neglect to prosecute.

(4) This section does not alter the law on tolling of the statute of limitations nor does it apply to causes of action that have accrued before this Article becomes effective.

§ 2A–507. Proof of Market Rent: Time and Place.

(1) Damages based on market rent (Section 2A–519 or 2A–528) are determined according to the rent for the use of the goods concerned for a lease term identical to the remaining lease term of the original lease agreement and prevailing at the times specified in Sections 2A–519 and 2A–528.

(2) If evidence of rent for the use of the goods concerned for a lease term identical to the remaining lease term of the original lease agreement and prevailing at the times or places described in this Article is not readily available, the rent prevailing within any reasonable time before or after the time described or at any other place or for a different lease term which in commercial judgment or under usage of trade would serve as a reasonable substitute for the one described may be used, making any proper allowance for the difference, including the cost of transporting the goods to or from the other place.

(3) Evidence of a relevant rent prevailing at a time or place or for a lease term other than the one described in this Article offered by one party is not admissible unless and until he [or she] has given the other party notice the court finds sufficient to prevent unfair surprise.

(4) If the prevailing rent or value of any goods regularly leased in any established market is in issue, reports in official publications or trade journals or in newspapers or periodicals of general circulation published as the reports of that market are admissible in evidence. The circumstances of the preparation of the report may be shown to affect its weight but not its admissibility.

As amended in 1990.

§ 2A–508. Lessee's Remedies.

(1) If a lessor fails to deliver the goods in conformity to the lease contract (Section 2A–509) or repudiates the lease contract (Section 2A–402), or a lessee rightfully rejects the goods (Section 2A–509) or justifiably revokes acceptance of the goods (Section 2A–517),

then with respect to any goods involved, and with respect to all of the goods if under an installment lease contract the value of the whole lease contract is substantially impaired (Section 2A–510), the lessor is in default under the lease contract and the lessee may:

(a) cancel the lease contract (Section 2A–505(1));

(b) recover so much of the rent and security as has been paid and is just under the circumstances;

(c) cover and recover damages as to all goods affected whether or not they have been identified to the lease contract (Sections 2A–518 and 2A–520), or recover damages for nondelivery (Sections 2A–519 and 2A–520);

(d) exercise any other rights or pursue any other remedies provided in the lease contract.

(2) If a lessor fails to deliver the goods in conformity to the lease contract or repudiates the lease contract, the lessee may also:

(a) if the goods have been identified, recover them (Section 2A–522); or

(b) in a proper case, obtain specific performance or replevy the goods (Section 2A–521).

(3) If a lessor is otherwise in default under a lease contract, the lessee may exercise the rights and pursue the remedies provided in the lease contract, which may include a right to cancel the lease, and in Section 2A–519(3).

(4) If a lessor has breached a warranty, whether express or implied, the lessee may recover damages (Section 2A–519(4)).

(5) On rightful rejection or justifiable revocation of acceptance, a lessee has a security interest in goods in the lessee's possession or control for any rent and security that has been paid and any expenses reasonably incurred in their inspection, receipt, transportation, and care and custody and may hold those goods and dispose of them in good faith and in a commercially reasonable manner, subject to Section 2A–527(5).

(6) Subject to the provisions of Section 2A–407, a lessee, on notifying the lessor of the lessee's intention to do so, may deduct all or any part of the damages resulting from any default under the lease contract from any part of the rent still due under the same lease contract.

As amended in 1990.

§ 2A–509. Lessee's Rights on Improper Delivery; Rightful Rejection.

(1) Subject to the provisions of Section 2A–510 on default in installment lease contracts, if the goods or the tender or delivery fail in any respect to conform to the lease contract, the lessee may reject or accept the goods or accept any commercial unit or units and reject the rest of the goods.

(2) Rejection of goods is ineffective unless it is within a reasonable time after tender or delivery of the goods and the lessee seasonably notifies the lessor.

§ 2A–510. Installment Lease Contracts: Rejection and Default.

(1) Under an installment lease contract a lessee may reject any delivery that is nonconforming if the nonconformity substantially impairs the value of that delivery and cannot be cured or the nonconformity is a defect in the required documents; but if the nonconformity does not fall within subsection (2) and the lessor or the supplier gives adequate assurance of its cure, the lessee must accept that delivery.

(2) Whenever nonconformity or default with respect to one or more deliveries substantially impairs the value of the installment lease contract as a whole there is a default with respect to the whole. But, the aggrieved party reinstates the installment lease contract as a whole if the aggrieved party accepts a nonconforming delivery without seasonably notifying of cancellation or brings an action with respect only to past deliveries or demands performance as to future deliveries.

§ 2A–511. Merchant Lessee's Duties as to Rightfully Rejected Goods.

(1) Subject to any security interest of a lessee (Section 2A–508(5)), if a lessor or a supplier has no agent or place of business at the market of rejection, a merchant lessee, after rejection of goods in his [or her] possession or control, shall follow any reasonable instructions received from the lessor or the supplier with respect to the goods. In the absence of those instructions, a merchant lessee shall make reasonable efforts to sell, lease, or otherwise dispose of the goods for the lessor's account if they threaten to decline in value speedily. Instructions are not reasonable if on demand indemnity for expenses is not forthcoming.

(2) If a merchant lessee (subsection (1)) or any other lessee (Section 2A–512) disposes of goods, he [or she] is entitled to reimbursement either from the lessor or the supplier or out of the proceeds for reasonable expenses of caring for and disposing of the goods and, if the expenses include no disposition commission, to such commission as is usual in the trade, or if there is none, to a reasonable sum not exceeding 10 percent of the gross proceeds.

(3) In complying with this section or Section 2A–512, the lessee is held only to good faith. Good faith conduct hereunder is neither acceptance or conversion nor the basis of an action for damages.

(4) A purchaser who purchases in good faith from a lessee pursuant to this section or Section 2A–512 takes the goods free of any rights of the lessor and the supplier even though the lessee fails to comply with one or more of the requirements of this Article.

§ 2A–512. Lessee's Duties as to Rightfully Rejected Goods.

(1) Except as otherwise provided with respect to goods that threaten to decline in value speedily (Section 2A–511) and subject to any security interest of a lessee (Section 2A–508(5)):

    (a) the lessee, after rejection of goods in the lessee's possession, shall hold them with reasonable care at the lessor's or the supplier's disposition for a reasonable time after the lessee's seasonable notification of rejection;

    (b) if the lessor or the supplier gives no instructions within a reasonable time after notification of rejection, the lessee may store the rejected goods for the lessor's or the supplier's account or ship them to the lessor or the supplier or dispose of them for the lessor's or the supplier's account with reimbursement in the manner provided in Section 2A–511; but

    (c) the lessee has no further obligations with regard to goods rightfully rejected.

(2) Action by the lessee pursuant to subsection (1) is not acceptance or conversion.

§ 2A–513. Cure by Lessor of Improper Tender or Delivery; Replacement.

(1) If any tender or delivery by the lessor or the supplier is rejected because nonconforming and the time for performance has not yet expired, the lessor or the supplier may seasonably notify the lessee of the lessor's or the supplier's intention to cure and may then make a conforming delivery within the time provided in the lease contract.

(2) If the lessee rejects a nonconforming tender that the lessor or the supplier had reasonable grounds to believe would be acceptable with or without money allowance, the lessor or the supplier may have a further reasonable time to substitute a conforming tender if he [or she] seasonably notifies the lessee.

§ 2A–514. Waiver of Lessee's Objections.

(1) In rejecting goods, a lessee's failure to state a particular defect that is ascertainable by reasonable inspection precludes the lessee from relying on the defect to justify rejection or to establish default:

    (a) if, stated seasonably, the lessor or the supplier could have cured it (Section 2A–513); or

(b) between merchants if the lessor or the supplier after rejection has made a request in writing for a full and final written statement of all defects on which the lessee proposes to rely.

(2) A lessee's failure to reserve rights when paying rent or other consideration against documents precludes recovery of the payment for defects apparent on the face of the documents.

§ 2A–515. Acceptance of Goods.

(1) Acceptance of goods occurs after the lessee has had a reasonable opportunity to inspect the goods and

(a) the lessee signifies or acts with respect to the goods in a manner that signifies to the lessor or the supplier that the goods are conforming or that the lessee will take or retain them in spite of their nonconformity; or

(b) the lessee fails to make an effective rejection of the goods (Section 2A–509(2)).

(2) Acceptance of a part of any commercial unit is acceptance of that entire unit.

§ 2A–516. Effect of Acceptance of Goods; Notice of Default; Burden of Establishing Default After Acceptance; Notice of Claim or Litigation to Person Answerable Over.

(1) A lessee must pay rent for any goods accepted in accordance with the lease contract, with due allowance for goods rightfully rejected or not delivered.

(2) A lessee's acceptance of goods precludes rejection of the goods accepted. In the case of a finance lease, if made with knowledge of a nonconformity, acceptance cannot be revoked because of it. In any other case, if made with knowledge of a nonconformity, acceptance cannot be revoked because of it unless the acceptance was on the reasonable assumption that the nonconformity would be seasonably cured. Acceptance does not of itself impair any other remedy provided by this Article or the lease agreement for nonconformity.

(3) If a tender has been accepted:

(a) within a reasonable time after the lessee discovers or should have discovered any default, the lessee shall notify the lessor and the supplier, if any, or be barred from any remedy against the party not notified;

(b) except in the case of a consumer lease, within a reasonable time after the lessee receives notice of litigation for infringement or the like (Section 2A–211) the lessee shall notify the lessor or be barred from any remedy over for liability established by the litigation; and

(c) the burden is on the lessee to establish any default.

(4) If a lessee is sued for breach of a warranty or other obligation for which a lessor or a supplier is answerable over the following apply:

(a) The lessee may give the lessor or the supplier, or both, written notice of the litigation. If the notice states that the person notified may come in and defend and that if the person notified does not do so that person will be bound in any action against that person by the lessee by any determination of fact common to the two litigations, then unless the person notified after seasonable receipt of the notice does come in and defend that person is so bound.

(b) The lessor or the supplier may demand in writing that the lessee turn over control of the litigation including settlement if the claim is one for infringement or the like (Section 2A–211) or else be barred from any remedy over. If the demand states that the lessor or the supplier agrees to bear all expense and to satisfy any adverse judgment, then unless the lessee after seasonable receipt of the demand does turn over control the lessee is so barred.

(5) Subsections (3) and (4) apply to any obligation of a lessee to hold the lessor or the supplier harmless against infringement or the like (Section 2A–211).

As amended in 1990.

§ 2A–517. Revocation of Acceptance of Goods.

(1) A lessee may revoke acceptance of a lot or commercial unit whose nonconformity substantially impairs its value to the lessee if the lessee has accepted it:
    (a) except in the case of a finance lease, on the reasonable assumption that its nonconformity would be cured and it has not been seasonably cured; or
    (b) without discovery of the nonconformity if the lessee's acceptance was reasonably induced either by the lessor's assurances or, except in the case of a finance lease, by the difficulty of discovery before acceptance.

(2) Except in the case of a finance lease that is not a consumer lease, a lessee may revoke acceptance of a lot or commercial unit if the lessor defaults under the lease contract and the default substantially impairs the value of that lot or commercial unit to the lessee.

(3) If the lease agreement so provides, the lessee may revoke acceptance of a lot or commercial unit because of other defaults by the lessor.

(4) Revocation of acceptance must occur within a reasonable time after the lessee discovers or should have discovered the ground for it and before any substantial change in condition of the goods which is not caused by the nonconformity. Revocation is not effective until the lessee notifies the lessor.

(5) A lessee who so revokes has the same rights and duties with regard to the goods involved as if the lessee had rejected them.

As amended in 1990.

§ 2A–518. Cover; Substitute Goods.

(1) After a default by a lessor under the lease contract of the type described in Section 2A–508(1) , or, if agreed, after other default by the lessor, the lessee may cover by making any purchase or lease of or contract to purchase or lease goods in substitution for those due from the lessor.

(2) Except as otherwise provided with respect to damages liquidated in the lease agreement (Section 2A–504) or otherwise determined pursuant to agreement of the parties (Sections 1–102(3) and 2A–503), if a lessee's cover is by a lease agreement substantially similar to the original lease agreement and the new lease agreement is made in good faith and in a commercially reasonable manner, the lessee may recover from the lessor as damages (i) the present value, as of the date of the commencement of the term of the new lease agreement, of the rent under the new lease agreement applicable to that period of the new lease term which is comparable to the then remaining term of the original lease agreement minus the present value as of the same date of the total rent for the then remaining lease term of the original lease agreement, and (ii) any incidental or consequential damages, less expenses saved in consequence of the lessor's default.

(3) If a lessee's cover is by lease agreement that for any reason does not qualify for treatment under subsection (2), or is by purchase or otherwise, the lessee may recover from the lessor as if the lessee had elected not to cover and Section 2A–519 governs.

As amended in 1990.

§ 2A–519. Lessee's Damages for Nondelivery, Repudiation, Default, and Breach of Warranty in Regard to Accepted Goods.

(1) Except as otherwise provided with respect to damages liquidated in the lease agreement (Section 2A–504) or otherwise determined pursuant to agreement of the parties (Sections 1–102(3) and 2A–503), if a lessee elects not to cover or a lessee elects to cover and the cover is by lease agreement that for any reason does not qualify for treatment under Section 2A–518(2), or is by purchase or otherwise, the measure of damages for nondelivery or repudiation by the lessor or for rejection or revocation of acceptance by the lessee is the present value, as of the date of the default, of the then market rent minus the present value as

of the same date of the original rent, computed for the remaining lease term of the original lease agreement, together with incidental and consequential damages, less expenses saved in consequence of the lessor's default.

(2) Market rent is to be determined as of the place for tender or, in cases of rejection after arrival or revocation of acceptance, as of the place of arrival.

(3) Except as otherwise agreed, if the lessee has accepted goods and given notification (Section 2A–516(3)), the measure of damages for nonconforming tender or delivery or other default by a lessor is the loss resulting in the ordinary course of events from the lessor's default as determined in any manner that is reasonable together with incidental and consequential damages, less expenses saved in consequence of the lessor's default.

(4) Except as otherwise agreed, the measure of damages for breach of warranty is the present value at the time and place of acceptance of the difference between the value of the use of the goods accepted and the value if they had been as warranted for the lease term, unless special circumstances show proximate damages of a different amount, together with incidental and consequential damages, less expenses saved in consequence of the lessor's default or breach of warranty.

As amended in 1990.

§ 2A–520. Lessee's Incidental and Consequential Damages.

(1) Incidental damages resulting from a lessor's default include expenses reasonably incurred in inspection, receipt, transportation, and care and custody of goods rightfully rejected or goods the acceptance of which is justifiably revoked, any commercially reasonable charges, expenses or commissions in connection with effecting cover, and any other reasonable expense incident to the default.

(2) Consequential damages resulting from a lessor's default include:
   (a) any loss resulting from general or particular requirements and needs of which the lessor at the time of contracting had reason to know and which could not reasonably be prevented by cover or otherwise; and
   (b) injury to person or property proximately resulting from any breach of warranty.

§ 2A–521. Lessee's Right to Specific Performance or Replevin.

(1) Specific performance may be decreed if the goods are unique or in other proper circumstances.

(2) A decree for specific performance may include any terms and conditions as to payment of the rent, damages, or other relief that the court deems just.

(3) A lessee has a right of replevin, detinue, sequestration, claim and delivery, or the like for goods identified to the lease contract if after reasonable effort the lessee is unable to effect cover for those goods or the circumstances reasonably indicate that the effort will be unavailing.

§ 2A–522. Lessee's Right to Goods on Lessor's Insolvency.

(1) Subject to subsection (2) and even though the goods have not been shipped, a lessee who has paid a part or all of the rent and security for goods identified to a lease contract (Section 2A–217) on making and keeping good a tender of any unpaid portion of the rent and security due under the lease contract may recover the goods identified from the lessor if the lessor becomes insolvent within 10 days after receipt of the first installment of rent and security.

(2) A lessee acquires the right to recover goods identified to a lease contract only if they conform to the lease contract.

§ 2A–523. Lessor's Remedies.

(1) If a lessee wrongfully rejects or revokes acceptance of goods or fails to make a payment when due or repudiates with respect to a part or the whole, then, with respect to any goods involved, and with respect to all of the goods if under an installment lease contract the

value of the whole lease contract is substantially impaired (Section 2A–510), the lessee is in default under the lease contract and the lessor may:

(a) cancel the lease contract (Section 2A–505(1));

(b) proceed respecting goods not identified to the lease contract (Section 2A–524);

(c) withhold delivery of the goods and take possession of goods previously delivered (Section 2A–525);

(d) stop delivery of the goods by any bailee (Section 2A–526);

(e) dispose of the goods and recover damages (Section 2A–527), or retain the goods and recover damages (Section 2A–528), or in a proper case recover rent (Section 2A–529);

(f) exercise any other rights or pursue any other remedies provided in the lease contract.

(2) If a lessor does not fully exercise a right or obtain a remedy to which the lessor is entitled under subsection (1), the lessor may recover the loss resulting in the ordinary course of events from the lessee's default as determined in any reasonable manner, together with incidental damages, less expenses saved in consequence of the lessee's default.

(3) If a lessee is otherwise in default under a lease contract, the lessor may exercise the rights and pursue the remedies provided in the lease contract, which may include a right to cancel the lease. In addition, unless otherwise provided in the lease contract:

(a) if the default substantially impairs the value of the lease contract to the lessor, the lessor may exercise the rights and pursue the remedies provided in subsections (1) or (2); or

(b) if the default does not substantially impair the value of the lease contract to the lessor, the lessor may recover as provided in subsection (2).

As amended in 1990.

§ 2A–524. Lessor's Right to Identify Goods to Lease Contract.

(1) After default by the lessee under the lease contract of the type described in Section 2A–523(1) or 2A–523(3) (a) or, if agreed, after other default by the lessee, the lessor may:

(a) identify to the lease contract conforming goods not already identified if at the time the lessor learned of the default they were in the lessor's or the supplier's possession or control; and

(b) dispose of goods (Section 2A–527(1)) that demonstrably have been intended for the particular lease contract even though those goods are unfinished.

(2) If the goods are unfinished, in the exercise of reasonable commercial judgment for the purposes of avoiding loss and of effective realization, an aggrieved lessor or the supplier may either complete manufacture and wholly identify the goods to the lease contract or cease manufacture and lease, sell, or otherwise dispose of the goods for scrap or salvage value or proceed in any other reasonable manner.

As amended in 1990.

§ 2A–525. Lessor's Right to Possession of Goods.

(1) If a lessor discovers the lessee to be insolvent, the lessor may refuse to deliver the goods.

(2) After a default by the lessee under the lease contract of the type described in Section 2A–523(1) or 2A–523(3) (a) or, if agreed, after other default by the lessee, the lessor has the right to take possession of the goods. If the lease contract so provides, the lessor may require the lessee to assemble the goods and make them available to the lessor at a place to be designated by the lessor which is reasonably convenient to both parties. Without removal, the lessor may render unusable any goods employed in trade or business, and may dispose of goods on the lessee's premises (Section 2A–527).

(3) The lessor may proceed under subsection (2) without judicial process if it can be done without breach of the peace or the lessor may proceed by action.

As amended in 1990.

§ 2A–526. Lessor's Stoppage of Delivery in Transit or Otherwise.

(1) A lessor may stop delivery of goods in the possession of a carrier or other bailee if the lessor discovers the lessee to be insolvent and may stop delivery of carload, truckload, planeload, or larger shipments of express or freight if the lessee repudiates or fails to make a payment due before delivery, whether for rent, security or otherwise under the lease contract, or for any other reason the lessor has a right to withhold or take possession of the goods.

(2) In pursuing its remedies under subsection (1), the lessor may stop delivery until
    (a) receipt of the goods by the lessee;
    (b) acknowledgment to the lessee by any bailee of the goods, except a carrier, that the bailee holds the goods for the lessee; or
    (c) such an acknowledgment to the lessee by a carrier via reshipment or as warehouseman.

(3) (a) To stop delivery, a lessor shall so notify as to enable the bailee by reasonable diligence to prevent delivery of the goods.
    (b) After notification, the bailee shall hold and deliver the goods according to the directions of the lessor, but the lessor is liable to the bailee for any ensuing charges or damages.
    (c) A carrier who has issued a nonnegotiable bill of lading is not obliged to obey a notification to stop received from a person other than the consignor.

§ 2A–527. Lessor's Rights to Dispose of Goods.

(1) After a default by a lessee under the lease contract of the type described in Section 2A–523(1) or 2A–523(3) (a) or after the lessor refuses to deliver or takes possession of goods (Section 2A–525 or 2A–526), or, if agreed, after other default by a lessee, the lessor may dispose of the goods concerned or the undelivered balance thereof by lease, sale, or otherwise.

(2) Except as otherwise provided with respect to damages liquidated in the lease agreement (Section 2A–504) or otherwise determined pursuant to agreement of the parties (Sections 1–102(3) and 2A–503), if the disposition is by lease agreement substantially similar to the original lease agreement and the new lease agreement is made in good faith and in a commercially reasonable manner, the lessor may recover from the lessee as damages (i) accrued and unpaid rent as of the date of the commencement of the term of the new lease agreement, (ii) the present value, as of the same date, of the total rent for the then remaining lease term of the original lease agreement minus the present value, as of the same date, of the rent under the new lease agreement applicable to that period of the new lease term which is comparable to the then remaining term of the original lease agreement, and (iii) any incidental damages allowed under Section 2A–530, less expenses saved in consequence of the lessee's default.

(3) If the lessor's disposition is by lease agreement that for any reason does not qualify for treatment under subsection (2), or is by sale or otherwise, the lessor may recover from the lessee as if the lessor had elected not to dispose of the goods and Section 2A–528 governs.

(4) A subsequent buyer or lessee who buys or leases from the lessor in good faith for value as a result of a disposition under this section takes the goods free of the original lease contract and any rights of the original lessee even though the lessor fails to comply with one or more of the requirements of this Article.

(5) The lessor is not accountable to the lessee for any profit made on any disposition. A lessee who has rightfully rejected or justifiably revoked acceptance shall account to the lessor for any excess over the amount of the lessee's security interest (Section 2A–508(5)).

As amended in 1990.

§ 2A–528. Lessor's Damages for Nonacceptance, Failure to Pay, Repudiation, or Other Default.

(1) Except as otherwise provided with respect to damages liquidated in the lease agreement (Section 2A–504) or otherwise determined pursuant to agreement of the parties (Sections 1–102(3) and 2A–503), if a lessor elects to retain the goods or a lessor elects to dispose of the goods and the disposition is by lease agreement that for any reason does not qualify for treatment under Section 2A–527(2), or is by sale or otherwise, the lessor may recover from the lessee as damages for a default of the type described in Section 2A–523(1) or 2A–523(3) (a), or, if agreed, for other default of the lessee, (i) accrued and unpaid rent as of the date of default if the lessee has never taken possession of the goods, or, if the lessee has taken possession of the goods, as of the date the lessor repossesses the goods or an earlier date on which the lessee makes a tender of the goods to the lessor, (ii) the present value as of the date determined under clause (i) of the total rent for the then remaining lease term of the original lease agreement minus the present value as of the same date of the market rent at the place where the goods are located computed for the same lease term, and (iii) any incidental damages allowed under Section 2A–530, less expenses saved in consequence of the lessee's default.

(2) If the measure of damages provided in subsection (1) is inadequate to put a lessor in as good a position as performance would have, the measure of damages is the present value of the profit, including reasonable overhead, the lessor would have made from full performance by the lessee, together with any incidental damages allowed under Section 2A–530, due allowance for costs reasonably incurred and due credit for payments or proceeds of disposition.

As amended in 1990.

§ 2A–529. Lessor's Action for the Rent.

(1) After default by the lessee under the lease contract of the type described in Section 2A–523(1) or 2A–523(3) (a) or, if agreed, after other default by the lessee, if the lessor complies with subsection (2), the lessor may recover from the lessee as damages:

   (a) for goods accepted by the lessee and not repossessed by or tendered to the lessor, and for conforming goods lost or damaged within a commercially reasonable time after risk of loss passes to the lessee (Section 2A–219), (i) accrued and unpaid rent as of the date of entry of judgment in favor of the lessor, (ii) the present value as of the same date of the rent for the then remaining lease term of the lease agreement, and (iii) any incidental damages allowed under Section 2A–530, less expenses saved in consequence of the lessee's default; and

   (b) for goods identified to the lease contract if the lessor is unable after reasonable effort to dispose of them at a reasonable price or the circumstances reasonably indicate that effort will be unavailing, (i) accrued and unpaid rent as of the date of entry of judgment in favor of the lessor, (ii) the present value as of the same date of the rent for the then remaining lease term of the lease agreement, and (iii) any incidental damages allowed under Section 2A–530, less expenses saved in consequence of the lessee's default.

(2) Except as provided in subsection (3), the lessor shall hold for the lessee for the remaining lease term of the lease agreement any goods that have been identified to the lease contract and are in the lessor's control.

(3) The lessor may dispose of the goods at any time before collection of the judgment for damages obtained pursuant to subsection (1). If the disposition is before the end of the remaining lease term of the lease agreement, the lessor's recovery against the lessee for damages is governed by Section 2A–527 or Section 2A–528, and the lessor will cause an appropriate credit to be provided against a judgment for damages to the extent that the amount of the judgment exceeds the recovery available pursuant to Section 2A–527 or 2A–528.

(4) Payment of the judgment for damages obtained pursuant to subsection (1) entitles the lessee to the use and possession of the goods not then disposed of for the remaining lease term of and in accordance with the lease agreement.

(5) After default by the lessee under the lease contract of the type described in Section 2A–523(1) or Section 2A–523(3) (a) or, if agreed, after other default by the lessee, a lessor who is held not entitled to rent under this section must nevertheless be awarded damages for nonacceptance under Section 2A–527 or Section 2A–528.

As amended in 1990.

§ 2A–530. Lessor's Incidental Damages.
Incidental damages to an aggrieved lessor include any commercially reasonable charges, expenses, or commissions incurred in stopping delivery, in the transportation, care and custody of goods after the lessee's default, in connection with return or disposition of the goods, or otherwise resulting from the default.

§ 2A–531. Standing to Sue Third Parties for Injury to Goods.

(1) If a third party so deals with goods that have been identified to a lease contract as to cause actionable injury to a party to the lease contract (a) the lessor has a right of action against the third party, and (b) the lessee also has a right of action against the third party if the lessee:
  (i)   has a security interest in the goods;
  (ii) has an insurable interest in the goods; or
  (iii) bears the risk of loss under the lease contract or has since the injury assumed that risk as against the lessor and the goods have been converted or destroyed.

(2) If at the time of the injury the party plaintiff did not bear the risk of loss as against the other party to the lease contract and there is no arrangement between them for disposition of the recovery, his [or her] suit or settlement, subject to his [or her] own interest, is as a fiduciary for the other party to the lease contract.

(3) Either party with the consent of the other may sue for the benefit of whom it may concern.

§ 2A–532. Lessor's Rights to Residual Interest.
In addition to any other recovery permitted by this Article or other law, the lessor may recover from the lessee an amount that will fully compensate the lessor for any loss of or damage to the lessor's residual interest in the goods caused by the default of the lessee.

As added in 1990.

Article 3–Negotiable Instruments

PART 1: GENERAL PROVISIONS AND DEFINITIONS

§ 3–101. Short Title.
This Article may be cited as Uniform Commercial Code—Negotiable Instruments.

§ 3–102. Subject Matter.

(a) This Article applies to negotiable instruments. It does not apply to money, to payment orders governed by Article 4A, or to securities governed by Article 8.

(b) If there is conflict between this Article and Article 4 or 9, Articles 4 and 9 govern.

(c) Regulations of the Board of Governors of the Federal Reserve System and operating circulars of the Federal Reserve Banks supersede any inconsistent provision of this Article to the extent of the inconsistency.

§ 3–103. Definitions.

(a) In this Article:

    (1) "Acceptor" means a drawee who has accepted a draft.

    (2) "Consumer account" means an account established by an individual primarily for personal, family, or household purposes.

    (3) "Consumer transaction" means a transaction in which an individual incurs an obligation primarily for personal, family, or household purposes.

    (4) "Drawee" means a person ordered in a draft to make payment.

    (5) "Drawer" means a person who signs or is identified in a draft as a person ordering payment.

    (6) ["Good faith" means honesty in fact and the observance of reasonable commercial standards of fair dealing.]

    (7) "Maker" means a person who signs or is identified in a note as a person undertaking to pay.

    (8) "Order" means a written instruction to pay money signed by the person giving the instruction. The instruction may be addressed to any person, including the person giving the instruction, or to one or more persons jointly or in the alternative but not in succession. An authorization to pay is not an order unless the person authorized to pay is also instructed to pay.

    (9) "Ordinary care" in the case of a person engaged in business means observance of reasonable commercial standards, prevailing in the area in which the person is located, with respect to the business in which the person is engaged. In the case of a bank that takes an instrument for processing for collection or payment by automated means, reasonable commercial standards do not require the bank to examine the instrument if the failure to examine does not violate the bank's prescribed procedures and the bank's procedures do not vary unreasonably from general banking usage not disapproved by this Article or Article 4.

    (10) "Party" means a party to an instrument.

    (11) "Principal obligor," with respect to an instrument, means the accommodated party or any other party to the instrument against whom a secondary obligor has recourse under this article.

    (12) "Promise" means a written undertaking to pay money signed by the person undertaking to pay. An acknowledgment of an obligation by the obligor is not a promise unless the obligor also undertakes to pay the obligation.

    (13) "Prove" with respect to a fact means to meet the burden of establishing the fact (Section 1–201(8)).

    (14) ["Record" means information that is inscribed on a tangible medium or that is stored in electronic or other medium and is retrievable in perceivable form.]

    (15) "Remitter" means a person who purchases an instrument from its issuer if the instrument is payable to an identified person other than the purchaser.

    (16) "Remotely-created consumer item" means an item drawn on a consumer account, which is not created by the payor bank and does not bear a handwritten signature purporting to be the signature of the drawer.

    (17) "Secondary obligor," with respect to an instrument, means (a) an indorser or an accommodation party, (b) a drawer having the obligation described in Section 3–414(d), or (c) any other party to the instrument that has recourse against another party to the instrument pursuant to Section 3–116(b).

(b) Other definitions applying to this Article and the sections in which they appear are:

"Acceptance"	Section 3–409.
"Accommodated party"	Section 3–419.
"Accommodation party"	Section 3–419.

"Account"	Section 4–104.
"Alteration"	Section 3–407.
"Anomalous indorsement"	Section 3–205.
"Blank indorsement"	Section 3–205.
"Cashier's check"	Section 3–104.
"Certificate of deposit"	Section 3–104.
"Certified check"	Section 3–409.
"Check"	Section 3–104.
"Consideration"	Section 3–303.
"Draft"	Section 3–104.
"Holder in due course"	Section 3–302.
"Incomplete instrument"	Section 3–115.
"Indorsement"	Section 3–204.
"Indorser"	Section 3–204.
"Instrument"	Section 3–104.
"Issue"	Section 3–105.
"Issuer"	Section 3–105.
"Negotiable instrument"	Section 3–104.
"Negotiation"	Section 3–201.
"Note"	Section 3–104.
"Payable at a definite time"	Section 3–108.
"Payable on demand"	Section 3–108.
"Payable to bearer"	Section 3–109.
"Payable to order"	Section 3–109.
"Payment"	Section 3–602.
"Person entitled to enforce"	Section 3–301.
"Presentment"	Section 3–501.
"Reacquisition"	Section 3–207.
"Special indorsement"	Section 3–205.
"Teller's check"	Section 3–104.
"Transfer of instrument"	Section 3–203.
"Traveler's check"	Section 3–104.
"Value"	Section 3–303.

(c)   The following definitions in other Articles apply to this Article:

"Banking day"	Section 4–104.
"Clearing house"	Section 4–104.
"Collecting bank"	Section 4–105.
"Depositary bank"	Section 4–105.
"Documentary draft"	Section 4–104.
"Intermediary bank"	Section 4–105.
"Item"	Section 4–104.
"Payor bank"	Section 4–105.
"Suspends payments"	Section 4–104.

(d) In addition, Article 1 contains general definitions and principles of construction and interpretation applicable throughout this Article.

Legislative Note. A jurisdiction that enacts this statute that has not yet enacted the revised version of UCC Article 1 should add to Section 3–103 the definition of "good faith" that appears in the official version of Section 1–201(b)(20) and the definition of "record" that appears in the official version of Section 1–201(b)(31). Sections 3–103(a)(6) and (14) are reserved for that purpose. A jurisdiction that already has adopted or simultaneously adopts the revised Article 1 should not add those definitions, but should leave those numbers "reserved." If jurisdictions follow the numbering suggested here, the subsections will have the same numbering in all jurisdictions that have adopted these amendments (whether they have or have not adopted the revised version of UCC Article 1).

§ 3–104. Negotiable Instrument.

(a) Except as provided in subsections (c) and (d), "negotiable instrument" means an unconditional promise or order to pay a fixed amount of money, with or without interest or other charges described in the promise or order, if it:
 (1) is payable to bearer or to order at the time it is issued or first comes into possession of a holder;
 (2) is payable on demand or at a definite time; and
 (3) does not state any other undertaking or instruction by the person promising or ordering payment to do any act in addition to the payment of money, but the promise or order may contain (i) an undertaking or power to give, maintain, or protect collateral to secure payment, (ii) an authorization or power to the holder to confess judgment or realize on or dispose of collateral, or (iii) a waiver of the benefit of any law intended for the advantage or protection of an obligor.

(b) "Instrument" means a negotiable instrument.

(c) An order that meets all of the requirements of subsection (a), except paragraph (1), and otherwise falls within the definition of "check" in subsection (f) is a negotiable instrument and a check.

(d) A promise or order other than a check is not an instrument if, at the time it is issued or first comes into possession of a holder, it contains a conspicuous statement, however expressed, to the effect that the promise or order is not negotiable or is not an instrument governed by this Article.

(e) An instrument is a "note" if it is a promise and is a "draft" if it is an order. If an instrument falls within the definition of both "note" and "draft," a person entitled to enforce the instrument may treat it as either.

(f) "Check" means (i) a draft, other than a documentary draft, payable on demand and drawn on a bank or (ii) a cashier's check or teller's check. An instrument may be a check even though it is described on its face by another term, such as "money order."

(g) "Cashier's check" means a draft with respect to which the drawer and drawee are the same bank or branches of the same bank.

(h) "Teller's check" means a draft drawn by a bank (i) on another bank, or (ii) payable at or through a bank.

(i) "Traveler's check" means an instrument that (i) is payable on demand, (ii) is drawn on or payable at or through a bank, (iii) is designated by the term "traveler's check" or by a substantially similar term, and (iv) requires, as a condition to payment, a countersignature by a person whose specimen signature appears on the instrument.

(j) "Certificate of deposit" means an instrument containing an acknowledgment by a bank that a sum of money has been received by the bank and a promise by the bank to repay the sum of money. A certificate of deposit is a note of the bank.

§ 3–105. Issue of Instrument.

(a) "Issue" means the first delivery of an instrument by the maker or drawer, whether to a holder or nonholder, for the purpose of giving rights on the instrument to any person.

(b) An unissued instrument, or an unissued incomplete instrument that is completed, is binding on the maker or drawer, but nonissuance is a defense. An instrument that is conditionally issued or is issued for a special purpose is binding on the maker or drawer, but failure of the condition or special purpose to be fulfilled is a defense.

(c) "Issuer" applies to issued and unissued instruments and means a maker or drawer of an instrument.

§ 3–106. Unconditional Promise or Order.

(a) Except as provided in this section, for the purposes of Section 3–104(a), a promise or order is unconditional unless it states (i) an express condition to payment, (ii) that the promise or order is subject to or governed by another record, or (iii) that rights or obligations with respect to the promise or order are stated in another record. A reference to another record does not of itself make the promise or order conditional.

(b) A promise or order is not made conditional (i) by a reference to another record for a statement of rights with respect to collateral, prepayment, or acceleration, or (ii) because payment is limited to resort to a particular fund or source.

(c) If a promise or order requires, as a condition to payment, a countersignature by a person whose specimen signature appears on the promise or order, the condition does not make the promise or order conditional for the purposes of Section 3–104(a). If the person whose specimen signature appears on an instrument fails to countersign the instrument, the failure to countersign is a defense to the obligation of the issuer, but the failure does not prevent a transferee of the instrument from becoming a holder of the instrument.

(d) If a promise or order at the time it is issued or first comes into possession of a holder contains a statement, required by applicable statutory or administrative law, to the effect that the rights of a holder or transferee are subject to claims or defenses that the issuer could assert against the original payee, the promise or order is not thereby made conditional for the purposes of Section 3–104(a); but if the promise or order is an instrument, there cannot be a holder in due course of the instrument.

§ 3–107. Instrument Payable in Foreign Money. Unless the instrument otherwise provides, an instrument that states the amount payable in foreign money may be paid in the foreign money or in an equivalent amount in dollars calculated by using the current bank offered spot rate at the place of payment for the purchase of dollars on the day on which the instrument is paid.

§ 3–108. Payable on Demand or at Definite Time.

(a) A promise or order is "payable on demand" if it (i) states that it is payable on demand or at sight, or otherwise indicates that it is payable at the will of the holder, or (ii) does not state any time of payment.

(b) A promise or order is "payable at a definite time" if it is payable on elapse of a definite period of time after sight or acceptance or at a fixed date or dates or at a time or times readily ascertainable at the time the promise or order is issued, subject to rights of (i) prepayment, (ii) acceleration, (iii) extension at the option of the holder, or (iv) extension to a further definite time at the option of the maker or acceptor or automatically upon or after a specified act or event.

(c) If an instrument, payable at a fixed date, is also payable upon demand made before the fixed date, the instrument is payable on demand until the fixed date and, if demand for payment is not made before that date, becomes payable at a definite time on the fixed date.

§ 3–109. Payable to Bearer or to Order.

(a)   A promise or order is payable to bearer if it:
  (1)   states that it is payable to bearer or to the order of bearer or otherwise indicates that the person in possession of the promise or order is entitled to payment;
  (2)   does not state a payee; or
  (3)   states that it is payable to or to the order of cash or otherwise indicates that it is not payable to an identified person.
(b)   A promise or order that is not payable to bearer is payable to order if it is payable (i) to the order of an identified person or (ii) to an identified person or order. A promise or order that is payable to order is payable to the identified person.
(c)   An instrument payable to bearer may become payable to an identified person if it is specially indorsed pursuant to Section 3–205(a). An instrument payable to an identified person may become payable to bearer if it is indorsed in blank pursuant to Section 3–205(b).

§ 3–110. Identification of Person to Whom Instrument Is Payable.

(a)   The person to whom an instrument is initially payable is determined by the intent of the person, whether or not authorized, signing as, or in the name or behalf of, the issuer of the instrument. The instrument is payable to the person intended by the signer even if that person is identified in the instrument by a name or other identification that is not that of the intended person. If more than one person signs in the name or behalf of the issuer of an instrument and all the signers do not intend the same person as payee, the instrument is payable to any person intended by one or more of the signers.
(b)   If the signature of the issuer of an instrument is made by automated means, such as a check writing machine, the payee of the instrument is determined by the intent of the person who supplied the name or identification of the payee, whether or not authorized to do so.
(c)   A person to whom an instrument is payable may be identified in any way, including by name, identifying number, office, or account number. For the purpose of determining the holder of an instrument, the following rules apply:
  (1)   If an instrument is payable to an account and the account is identified only by number, the instrument is payable to the person to whom the account is payable. If an instrument is payable to an account identified by number and by the name of a person, the instrument is payable to the named person, whether or not that person is the owner of the account identified by number.
  (2)   If an instrument is payable to:
    (i)   a trust, an estate, or a person described as trustee or representative of a trust or estate, the instrument is payable to the trustee, the representative, or a successor of either, whether or not the beneficiary or estate is also named;
    (ii)   a person described as agent or similar representative of a named or identified person, the instrument is payable to the represented person, the representative, or a successor of the representative;
    (iii)   a fund or organization that is not a legal entity, the instrument is payable to a representative of the members of the fund or organization; or
    (iv)   an office or to a person described as holding an office, the instrument is payable to the named person, the incumbent of the office, or a successor to the incumbent.
(d)   If an instrument is payable to two or more persons alternatively, it is payable to any of them and may be negotiated, discharged, or enforced by any or all of them in possession of the instrument. If an instrument is payable to two or more persons not alternatively, it is payable to all of them and may be negotiated, discharged, or enforced only by all of them. If an instrument payable to two or more persons is ambiguous as to whether it is payable to the persons alternatively, the instrument is payable to the persons alternatively.

§ 3–111. Place of Payment.
Except as otherwise provided for items in Article 4, an instrument is payable at the place of payment stated in the instrument. If no place of payment is stated, an instrument is payable at the address of the drawee or maker stated in the instrument. If no address is stated, the place of payment is the place of business of the drawee or maker. If a drawee or maker has more than one place of business, the place of payment is any place of business of the drawee or maker chosen by the person entitled to enforce the instrument. If the drawee or maker has no place of business, the place of payment is the residence of the drawee or maker.

§ 3–112. Interest.

(a) Unless otherwise provided in the instrument, (i) an instrument is not payable with interest, and (ii) interest on an interest bearing instrument is payable from the date of the instrument.

(b) Interest may be stated in an instrument as a fixed or variable amount of money or it may be expressed as a fixed or variable rate or rates. The amount or rate of interest may be stated or described in the instrument in any manner and may require reference to information not contained in the instrument. If an instrument provides for interest, but the amount of interest payable cannot be ascertained from the description, interest is payable at the judgment rate in effect at the place of payment of the instrument and at the time interest first accrues.

§ 3–113. Date of Instrument.

(a) An instrument may be antedated or postdated. The date stated determines the time of payment if the instrument is payable at a fixed period after date. Except as provided in Section 4–401(c), an instrument payable on demand is not payable before the date of the instrument.

(b) If an instrument is undated, its date is the date of its issue or, in the case of an unissued instrument, the date it first comes into possession of a holder.

§ 3–114. Contradictory Terms of Instrument.
If an instrument contains contradictory terms, typewritten terms prevail over printed terms, handwritten terms prevail over both, and words prevail over numbers.

§ 3–115. Incomplete Instrument.

(a) "Incomplete instrument" means a signed writing, whether or not issued by the signer, the contents of which show at the time of signing that it is incomplete but that the signer intended it to be completed by the addition of words or numbers.

(b) Subject to subsection (c), if an incomplete instrument is an instrument under Section 3–104, it may be enforced according to its terms if it is not completed, or according to its terms as augmented by completion. If an incomplete instrument is not an instrument under Section 3–104, but, after completion, the requirements of Section 3–104 are met, the instrument may be enforced according to its terms as augmented by completion.

(c) If words or numbers are added to an incomplete instrument without authority of the signer, there is an alteration of the incomplete instrument under Section 3–407.

(d) The burden of establishing that words or numbers were added to an incomplete instrument without authority of the signer is on the person asserting the lack of authority.

§ 3–116. Joint and Several Liability; Contribution.

(a) Except as otherwise provided in the instrument, two or more persons who have the same liability on an instrument as makers, drawers, acceptors, indorsers who indorse as joint payees, or anomalous indorsers are jointly and severally liable in the capacity in which they sign.

(b) Except as provided in Section 3–419(f) or by agreement of the affected parties, a party having joint and several liability who pays the instrument is entitled to receive from any party having the same joint and several liability contribution in accordance with applicable law.

§ 3–117. Other Agreements Affecting Instrument.

Subject to applicable law regarding exclusion of proof of contemporaneous or previous agreements, the obligation of a party to an instrument to pay the instrument may be modified, supplemented, or nullified by a separate agreement of the obligor and a person entitled to enforce the instrument, if the instrument is issued or the obligation is incurred in reliance on the agreement or as part of the same transaction giving rise to the agreement. To the extent an obligation is modified, supplemented, or nullified by an agreement under this section, the agreement is a defense to the obligation.

§ 3–118. Statute of Limitations.

(a) Except as provided in subsection (e), an action to enforce the obligation of a party to pay a note payable at a definite time must be commenced within six years after the due date or dates stated in the note or, if a due date is accelerated, within six years after the accelerated due date.

(b) Except as provided in subsection (d) or (e), if demand for payment is made to the maker of a note payable on demand, an action to enforce the obligation of a party to pay the note must be commenced within six years after the demand. If no demand for payment is made to the maker, an action to enforce the note is barred if neither principal nor interest on the note has been paid for a continuous period of 10 years.

(c) Except as provided in subsection (d), an action to enforce the obligation of a party to an unaccepted draft to pay the draft must be commenced within three years after dishonor of the draft or 10 years after the date of the draft, whichever period expires first.

(d) An action to enforce the obligation of the acceptor of a certified check or the issuer of a teller's check, cashier's check, or traveler's check must be commenced within three years after demand for payment is made to the acceptor or issuer, as the case may be.

(e) An action to enforce the obligation of a party to a certificate of deposit to pay the instrument must be commenced within six years after demand for payment is made to the maker, but if the instrument states a due date and the maker is not required to pay before that date, the six-year period begins when a demand for payment is in effect and the due date has passed.

(f) An action to enforce the obligation of a party to pay an accepted draft, other than a certified check, must be commenced (i) within six years after the due date or dates stated in the draft or acceptance if the obligation of the acceptor is payable at a definite time, or (ii) within six years after the date of the acceptance if the obligation of the acceptor is payable on demand.

(g) Unless governed by other law regarding claims for indemnity or contribution, an action (i) for conversion of an instrument, for money had and received, or like action based on conversion, (ii) for breach of warranty, or (iii) to enforce an obligation, duty, or right arising under this Article and not governed by this section must be commenced within three years after the [cause of action] accrues.

§ 3–119. Notice of Right to Defend Action.

In an action for breach of an obligation for which a third person is answerable over pursuant to this Article or Article 4, the defendant may give the third person notice of the litigation in a record, and the person notified may then give similar notice to any other person who is answerable over. If the notice states (i) that the person notified may come in and defend and (ii) that failure to do so will bind the person notified in an action later brought by the person giving the notice as to any determination of fact common to the two litigations, the person notified is so bound unless after seasonable receipt of the notice the person notified does come in and defend.

PART 2: NEGOTIATION, TRANSFER, AND INDORSEMENT

§ 3–201. Negotiation.

(a) "Negotiation" means a transfer of possession, whether voluntary or involuntary, of an instrument by a person other than the issuer to a person who thereby becomes its holder.

(b) Except for negotiation by a remitter, if an instrument is payable to an identified person, negotiation requires transfer of possession of the instrument and its indorsement by the holder. If an instrument is payable to bearer, it may be negotiated by transfer of possession alone.

§ 3–202. Negotiation Subject to Rescission.

(a) Negotiation is effective even if obtained (i) from an infant, a corporation exceeding its powers, or a person without capacity, (ii) by fraud, duress, or mistake, or (iii) in breach of duty or as part of an illegal transaction.

(b) To the extent permitted by other law, negotiation may be rescinded or may be subject to other remedies, but those remedies may not be asserted against a subsequent holder in due course or a person paying the instrument in good faith and without knowledge of facts that are a basis for rescission or other remedy.

§ 3–203. Transfer of Instrument; Rights Acquired by Transfer.

(a) An instrument is transferred when it is delivered by a person other than its issuer for the purpose of giving to the person receiving delivery the right to enforce the instrument.

(b) Transfer of an instrument, whether or not the transfer is a negotiation, vests in the transferee any right of the transferor to enforce the instrument, including any right as a holder in due course, but the transferee cannot acquire rights of a holder in due course by a transfer, directly or indirectly, from a holder in due course if the transferee engaged in fraud or illegality affecting the instrument.

(c) Unless otherwise agreed, if an instrument is transferred for value and the transferee does not become a holder because of lack of indorsement by the transferor, the transferee has a specifically enforceable right to the unqualified indorsement of the transferor, but negotiation of the instrument does not occur until the indorsement is made.

(d) If a transferor purports to transfer less than the entire instrument, negotiation of the instrument does not occur. The transferee obtains no rights under this Article and has only the rights of a partial assignee.

§ 3–204. Indorsement.

(a) "Indorsement" means a signature, other than that of a signer as maker, drawer, or acceptor, that alone or accompanied by other words is made on an instrument for the purpose of (i) negotiating the instrument, (ii) restricting payment of the instrument, or (iii) incurring indorser's liability on the instrument, but regardless of the intent of the signer, a signature and its accompanying words is an indorsement unless the accompanying words, terms of the instrument, place of the signature, or other circumstances unambiguously indicate that the signature was made for a purpose other than indorsement. For the purpose of determining whether a signature is made on an instrument, a paper affixed to the instrument is a part of the instrument.

(b) "Indorser" means a person who makes an indorsement.

(c) For the purpose of determining whether the transferee of an instrument is a holder, an indorsement that transfers a security interest in the instrument is effective as an unqualified indorsement of the instrument.

(d) If an instrument is payable to a holder under a name that is not the name of the holder, indorsement may be made by the holder in the name stated in the instrument or in the holder's name or both, but signature in both names may be required by a person paying or taking the instrument for value or collection.

§ 3–205. Special Indorsement; Blank Indorsement; Anomalous Indorsement.

(a) If an indorsement is made by the holder of an instrument, whether payable to an identified person or payable to bearer, and the indorsement identifies a person to whom it makes the instrument payable, it is a "special indorsement." When specially indorsed, an instrument becomes payable to the identified person and may be negotiated only by the indorsement of that person. The principles stated in Section 3–110 apply to special indorsements.

(b) If an indorsement is made by the holder of an instrument and it is not a special indorsement, it is a "blank indorsement." When indorsed in blank, an instrument becomes payable to bearer and may be negotiated by transfer of possession alone until specially indorsed.

(c) The holder may convert a blank indorsement that consists only of a signature into a special indorsement by writing, above the signature of the indorser, words identifying the person to whom the instrument is made payable.

(d) "Anomalous indorsement" means an indorsement made by a person who is not the holder of the instrument. An anomalous indorsement does not affect the manner in which the instrument may be negotiated.

§ 3–206. Restrictive Indorsement.

(a) An indorsement limiting payment to a particular person or otherwise prohibiting further transfer or negotiation of the instrument is not effective to prevent further transfer or negotiation of the instrument.

(b) An indorsement stating a condition to the right of the indorsee to receive payment does not affect the right of the indorsee to enforce the instrument. A person paying the instrument or taking it for value or collection may disregard the condition, and the rights and liabilities of that person are not affected by whether the condition has been fulfilled.

(c) If an instrument bears an indorsement (i) described in Section 4–201(b), or (ii) in blank or to a particular bank using the words "for deposit," "for collection," or other words indicating a purpose of having the instrument collected by a bank for the indorser or for a particular account, the following rules apply:

   (1) A person, other than a bank, who purchases the instrument when so indorsed converts the instrument unless the amount paid for the instrument is received by the indorser or applied consistently with the indorsement.

   (2) A depositary bank that purchases the instrument or takes it for collection when so indorsed converts the instrument unless the amount paid by the bank with respect to the instrument is received by the indorser or applied consistently with the indorsement.

   (3) A payor bank that is also the depositary bank or that takes the instrument for immediate payment over the counter from a person other than a collecting bank converts the instrument unless the proceeds of the instrument are received by the indorser or applied consistently with the indorsement.

   (4) Except as otherwise provided in paragraph (3), a payor bank or intermediary bank may disregard the indorsement and is not liable if the proceeds of the instrument are not received by the indorser or applied consistently with the indorsement.

(d) Except for an indorsement covered by subsection (c), if an instrument bears an indorsement using words to the effect that payment is to be made to the indorsee as agent, trustee, or other fiduciary for the benefit of the indorser or another person, the following rules apply:

   (1) Unless there is notice of breach of fiduciary duty as provided in Section 3–307, a person who purchases the instrument from the indorsee or takes the instrument from the indorsee for collection or payment may pay the proceeds of payment or the value given for the instrument to the indorsee without regard to whether the indorsee violates a fiduciary duty to the indorser.

(2) A subsequent transferee of the instrument or person who pays the instrument is neither given notice nor otherwise affected by the restriction in the indorsement unless the transferee or payor knows that the fiduciary dealt with the instrument or its proceeds in breach of fiduciary duty.

(e) The presence on an instrument of an indorsement to which this section applies does not prevent a purchaser of the instrument from becoming a holder in due course of the instrument unless the purchaser is a converter under subsection (c) or has notice or knowledge of breach of fiduciary duty as stated in subsection (d).

(f) In an action to enforce the obligation of a party to pay the instrument, the obligor has a defense if payment would violate an indorsement to which this section applies and the payment is not permitted by this section.

§ 3–207. Reacquisition. Reacquisition of an instrument occurs if it is transferred to a former holder, by negotiation or otherwise. A former holder who reacquires the instrument may cancel indorsements made after the reacquirer first became a holder of the instrument. If the cancellation causes the instrument to be payable to the reacquirer or to bearer, the reacquirer may negotiate the instrument. An indorser whose indorsement is canceled is discharged, and the discharge is effective against any subsequent holder.

PART 3: ENFORCEMENT OF INSTRUMENTS

§ 3–301. Person Entitled to Enforce Instrument. "Person entitled to enforce" an instrument means (i) the holder of the instrument, (ii) a nonholder in possession of the instrument who has the rights of a holder, or (iii) a person not in possession of the instrument who is entitled to enforce the instrument pursuant to Section 3–309 or 3–418(d). A person may be a person entitled to enforce the instrument even though the person is not the owner of the instrument or is in wrongful possession of the instrument.

§ 3–302. Holder in Due Course.

(a) Subject to subsection (c) and Section 3–106(d), "holder in due course" means the holder of an instrument if:

(1) the instrument when issued or negotiated to the holder does not bear such apparent evidence of forgery or alteration or is not otherwise so irregular or incomplete as to call into question its authenticity; and

(2) the holder took the instrument (i) for value, (ii) in good faith, (iii) without notice that the instrument is overdue or has been dishonored or that there is an uncured default with respect to payment of another instrument issued as part of the same series, (iv) without notice that the instrument contains an unauthorized signature or has been altered, (v) without notice of any claim to the instrument described in Section 3–306, and (vi) without notice that any party has a defense or claim in recoupment described in Section 3–305(a).

(b) Notice of discharge of a party, other than discharge in an insolvency proceeding, is not notice of a defense under subsection (a), but discharge is effective against a person who became a holder in due course with notice of the discharge. Public filing or recording of a document does not of itself constitute notice of a defense, claim in recoupment, or claim to the instrument.

(c) Except to the extent a transferor or predecessor in interest has rights as a holder in due course, a person does not acquire rights of a holder in due course of an instrument taken (i) by legal process or by purchase in an execution, bankruptcy, or creditor's sale or similar proceeding, (ii) by purchase as part of a bulk transaction not in ordinary course of business of the transferor, or (iii) as the successor in interest to an estate or other organization.

(d) If, under Section 3–303(a)(1), the promise of performance that is the consideration for an instrument has been partially performed, the holder may assert rights as a holder in due course of the instrument only to the fraction of the amount payable under the instrument equal to the value of the partial performance divided by the value of the promised performance.

(e) If (i) the person entitled to enforce an instrument has only a security interest in the instrument and (ii) the person obliged to pay the instrument has a defense, claim in recoupment, or claim to the instrument that may be asserted against the person who granted the security interest, the person entitled to enforce the instrument may assert rights as a holder in due course only to an amount payable under the instrument which, at the time of enforcement of the instrument, does not exceed the amount of the unpaid obligation secured.

(f) To be effective, notice must be received at a time and in a manner that gives a reasonable opportunity to act on it.

(g) This section is subject to any law limiting status as a holder in due course in particular classes of transactions.

§ 3–303. Value and Consideration.

(a) An instrument is issued or transferred for value if:
   (1) the instrument is issued or transferred for a promise of performance, to the extent the promise has been performed;
   (2) the transferee acquires a security interest or other lien in the instrument other than a lien obtained by judicial proceeding;
   (3) the instrument is issued or transferred as payment of, or as security for, an antecedent claim against any person, whether or not the claim is due;
   (4) the instrument is issued or transferred in exchange for a negotiable instrument; or
   (5) the instrument is issued or transferred in exchange for the incurring of an irrevocable obligation to a third party by the person taking the instrument.

(b) "Consideration" means any consideration sufficient to support a simple contract. The drawer or maker of an instrument has a defense if the instrument is issued without consideration. If an instrument is issued for a promise of performance, the issuer has a defense to the extent performance of the promise is due and the promise has not been performed. If an instrument is issued for value as stated in subsection (a), the instrument is also issued for consideration.

§ 3–304. Overdue Instrument.

(a) An instrument payable on demand becomes overdue at the earliest of the following times:
   (1) on the day after the day demand for payment is duly made;
   (2) if the instrument is a check, 90 days after its date; or
   (3) if the instrument is not a check, when the instrument has been outstanding for a period of time after its date which is unreasonably long under the circumstances of the particular case in light of the nature of the instrument and usage of the trade.

(b) With respect to an instrument payable at a definite time the following rules apply:
   (1) If the principal is payable in installments and a due date has not been accelerated, the instrument becomes overdue upon default under the instrument for nonpayment of an installment, and the instrument remains overdue until the default is cured.
   (2) If the principal is not payable in installments and the due date has not been accelerated, the instrument becomes overdue on the day after the due date.
   (3) If a due date with respect to principal has been accelerated, the instrument becomes overdue on the day after the accelerated due date.

(c) Unless the due date of principal has been accelerated, an instrument does not become overdue if there is default in payment of interest but no default in payment of principal.

§ 3–305. Defenses and Claims in Recoupment; Claims in Consumer Transactions.

(a)   Except as otherwise provided in this section, the right to enforce the obligation of a party to pay an instrument is subject to the following:

    (1)   a defense of the obligor based on (i) infancy of the obligor to the extent it is a defense to a simple contract, (ii) duress, lack of legal capacity, or illegality of the transaction which, under other law, nullifies the obligation of the obligor, (iii) fraud that induced the obligor to sign the instrument with neither knowledge nor reasonable opportunity to learn of its character or its essential terms, or (iv) discharge of the obligor in insolvency proceedings;

    (2)   a defense of the obligor stated in another section of this Article or a defense of the obligor that would be available if the person entitled to enforce the instrument were enforcing a right to payment under a simple contract; and

    (3)   a claim in recoupment of the obligor against the original payee of the instrument if the claim arose from the transaction that gave rise to the instrument; but the claim of the obligor may be asserted against a transferee of the instrument only to reduce the amount owing on the instrument at the time the action is brought.

(b)   The right of a holder in due course to enforce the obligation of a party to pay the instrument is subject to defenses of the obligor stated in subsection (a)(1), but is not subject to defenses of the obligor stated in subsection (a)(2) or claims in recoupment stated in subsection (a)(3) against a person other than the holder.

(c)   Except as stated in subsection (d), in an action to enforce the obligation of a party to pay the instrument, the obligor may not assert against the person entitled to enforce the instrument a defense, claim in recoupment, or claim to the instrument (Section 3–306) of another person, but the other person's claim to the instrument may be asserted by the obligor if the other person is joined in the action and personally asserts the claim against the person entitled to enforce the instrument. An obligor is not obliged to pay the instrument if the person seeking enforcement of the instrument does not have rights of a holder in due course and the obligor proves that the instrument is a lost or stolen instrument.

(d)   In an action to enforce the obligation of an accommodation party to pay an instrument, the accommodation party may assert against the person entitled to enforce the instrument any defense or claim in recoupment under subsection (a) that the accommodated party could assert against the person entitled to enforce the instrument, except the defenses of discharge in insolvency proceedings, infancy, and lack of legal capacity.

(e)   In a consumer transaction, if law other than this article requires that an instrument include a statement to the effect that the rights of a holder or transferee are subject to a claim or defense that the issuer could assert against the original payee, and the instrument does not include such a statement:

    (1)   the instrument has the same effect as if the instrument included such a statement;

    (2)   the issuer may assert against the holder or transferee all claims and defenses that would have been available if the instrument included such a statement; and

    (3)   the extent to which claims may be asserted against the holder or transferee is determined as if the instrument included such a statement.

(f)   This section is subject to law other than this article that establishes a different rule for consumer transactions.

Legislative Note: If a consumer protection law in this state addresses the same issue as subsection (g), it should be examined for consistency with subsection (g) and, if inconsistent, should be amended.

§ 3–306. Claims to an Instrument.

A person taking an instrument, other than a person having rights of a holder in due course, is subject to a claim of a property or possessory right in the instrument or its proceeds, including a claim to rescind a negotiation and to recover the instrument or its proceeds. A person having rights of a holder in due course takes free of the claim to the instrument.

§ 3–307. Notice of Breach of Fiduciary Duty.

(a) In this section:

    (1) "Fiduciary" means an agent, trustee, partner, corporate officer or director, or other representative owing a fiduciary duty with respect to an instrument.

    (2) "Represented person" means the principal, beneficiary, partnership, corporation, or other person to whom the duty stated in paragraph (1) is owed.

(b) If (i) an instrument is taken from a fiduciary for payment or collection or for value, (ii) the taker has knowledge of the fiduciary status of the fiduciary, and (iii) the represented person makes a claim to the instrument or its proceeds on the basis that the transaction of the fiduciary is a breach of fiduciary duty, the following rules apply:

    (1) Notice of breach of fiduciary duty by the fiduciary is notice of the claim of the represented person.

    (2) In the case of an instrument payable to the represented person or the fiduciary as such, the taker has notice of the breach of fiduciary duty if the instrument is (i) taken in payment of or as security for a debt known by the taker to be the personal debt of the fiduciary, (ii) taken in a transaction known by the taker to be for the personal benefit of the fiduciary, or (iii) deposited to an account other than an account of the fiduciary, as such, or an account of the represented person.

    (3) If an instrument is issued by the represented person or the fiduciary as such, and made payable to the fiduciary personally, the taker does not have notice of the breach of fiduciary duty unless the taker knows of the breach of fiduciary duty.

    (4) If an instrument is issued by the represented person or the fiduciary as such, to the taker as payee, the taker has notice of the breach of fiduciary duty if the instrument is (i) taken in payment of or as security for a debt known by the taker to be the personal debt of the fiduciary, (ii) taken in a transaction known by the taker to be for the personal benefit of the fiduciary, or (iii) deposited to an account other than an account of the fiduciary, as such, or an account of the represented person.

§ 3–308. Proof of Signatures and Status as Holder in Due Course.

(a) In an action with respect to an instrument, the authenticity of, and authority to make, each signature on the instrument is admitted unless specifically denied in the pleadings. If the validity of a signature is denied in the pleadings, the burden of establishing validity is on the person claiming validity, but the signature is presumed to be authentic and authorized unless the action is to enforce the liability of the purported signer and the signer is dead or incompetent at the time of trial of the issue of validity of the signature. If an action to enforce the instrument is brought against a person as the undisclosed principal of a person who signed the instrument as a party to the instrument, the plaintiff has the burden of establishing that the defendant is liable on the instrument as a represented person under Section 3–402(a).

(b) If the validity of signatures is admitted or proved and there is compliance with subsection (a), a plaintiff producing the instrument is entitled to payment if the plaintiff proves entitlement to enforce the instrument under Section 3–301, unless the defendant proves a defense or claim in recoupment. If a defense or claim in recoupment is proved, the right to payment of the plaintiff is subject to the defense or claim, except to the extent the plaintiff proves that the plaintiff has rights of a holder in due course which are not subject to the defense or claim.

§ 3–309. Enforcement of Lost, Destroyed, or Stolen Instrument.

(a) A person not in possession of an instrument is entitled to enforce the instrument if:

    (1) the person seeking to enforce the instrument:

        (i) was entitled to enforce the instrument when loss of possession occurred; or

        (ii) has directly or indirectly acquired ownership of the instrument from a person who was entitled to enforce the instrument when loss of possession occurred;

(2) the loss of possession was not the result of a transfer by the person or a lawful seizure; and

(3) the person cannot reasonably obtain possession of the instrument because the instrument was destroyed, its whereabouts cannot be determined, or it is in the wrongful possession of an unknown person or a person that cannot be found or is not amenable to service of process.

(b) A person seeking enforcement of an instrument under subsection (a) must prove the terms of the instrument and the person's right to enforce the instrument. If that proof is made, Section 3–308 applies to the case as if the person seeking enforcement had produced the instrument. The court may not enter judgment in favor of the person seeking enforcement unless it finds that the person required to pay the instrument is adequately protected against loss that might occur by reason of a claim by another person to enforce the instrument. Adequate protection may be provided by any reasonable means.

§ 3–310. Effect of Instrument on Obligation for Which Taken.

(a) Unless otherwise agreed, if a certified check, cashier's check, or teller's check is taken for an obligation, the obligation is discharged to the same extent discharge would result if an amount of money equal to the amount of the instrument were taken in payment of the obligation. Discharge of the obligation does not affect any liability that the obligor may have as an indorser of the instrument.

(b) Unless otherwise agreed and except as provided in subsection (a), if a note or an uncertified check is taken for an obligation, the obligation is suspended to the same extent the obligation would be discharged if an amount of money equal to the amount of the instrument were taken, and the following rules apply:

(1) In the case of an uncertified check, suspension of the obligation continues until dishonor of the check or until it is paid or certified. Payment or certification of the check results in discharge of the obligation to the extent of the amount of the check.

(2) In the case of a note, suspension of the obligation continues until dishonor of the note or until it is paid. Payment of the note results in discharge of the obligation to the extent of the payment.

(3) Except as provided in paragraph (4), if the check or note is dishonored and the obligee of the obligation for which the instrument was taken is the person entitled to enforce the instrument, the obligee may enforce either the instrument or the obligation. In the case of an instrument of a third person which is negotiated to the obligee by the obligor, discharge of the obligor on the instrument also discharges the obligation.

(4) If the person entitled to enforce the instrument taken for an obligation is a person other than the obligee, the obligee may not enforce the obligation to the extent the obligation is suspended. If the obligee is the person entitled to enforce the instrument but no longer has possession of it because it was lost, stolen, or destroyed, the obligation may not be enforced to the extent of the amount payable on the instrument, and to that extent the obligee's rights against the obligor are limited to enforcement of the instrument.

(c) If an instrument other than one described in subsection (a) or (b) is taken for an obligation, the effect is (i) that stated in subsection (a) if the instrument is one on which a bank is liable as maker or acceptor, or (ii) that stated in subsection (b) in any other case.

§ 3–311. Accord and Satisfaction by Use of Instrument.

(a) If a person against whom a claim is asserted proves that (i) that person in good faith tendered an instrument to the claimant as full satisfaction of the claim, (ii) the amount of the claim was unliquidated or subject to a bona fide dispute, and (iii) the claimant obtained payment of the instrument, the following subsections apply.

(b) Unless subsection (c) applies, the claim is discharged if the person against whom the claim is asserted proves that the instrument or an accompanying written communication contained a conspicuous statement to the effect that the instrument was tendered as full satisfaction of the claim.

(c) Subject to subsection (d), a claim is not discharged under subsection (b) if either of the following applies:

    (1) The claimant, if an organization, proves that (i) within a reasonable time before the tender, the claimant sent a conspicuous statement to the person against whom the claim is asserted that communications concerning disputed debts, including an instrument tendered as full satisfaction of a debt, are to be sent to a designated person, office, or place, and (ii) the instrument or accompanying communication was not received by that designated person, office, or place.

    (2) The claimant, whether or not an organization, proves that within 90 days after payment of the instrument, the claimant tendered repayment of the amount of the instrument to the person against whom the claim is asserted. This paragraph does not apply if the claimant is an organization that sent a statement complying with paragraph (1)(i).

(d) A claim is discharged if the person against whom the claim is asserted proves that within a reasonable time before collection of the instrument was initiated, the claimant, or an agent of the claimant having direct responsibility with respect to the disputed obligation, knew that the instrument was tendered in full satisfaction of the claim.

§ 3–312. Lost, Destroyed, or Stolen Cashier's Check, Teller's Check, or Certified Check.

(a) In this section:

    (1) "Check" means a cashier's check, teller's check, or certified check.

    (2) "Claimant" means a person who claims the right to receive the amount of a cashier's check, teller's check, or certified check that was lost, destroyed, or stolen.

    (3) "Declaration of loss" means a statement, made in a record under penalty of perjury, to the effect that (i) the declarer lost possession of a check, (ii) the declarer is the drawer or payee of the check, in the case of a certified check, or the remitter or payee of the check, in the case of a cashier's check or teller's check, (iii) the loss of possession was not the result of a transfer by the declarer or a lawful seizure, and (iv) the declarer cannot reasonably obtain possession of the check because the check was destroyed, its whereabouts cannot be determined, or it is in the wrongful possession of an unknown person or a person that cannot be found or is not amenable to service of process.

    (4) "Obligated bank" means the issuer of a cashier's check or teller's check or the acceptor of a certified check.

(b) A claimant may assert a claim to the amount of a check by a communication to the obligated bank describing the check with reasonable certainty and requesting payment of the amount of the check, if (i) the claimant is the drawer or payee of a certified check or the remitter or payee of a cashier's check or teller's check, (ii) the communication contains or is accompanied by a declaration of loss of the claimant with respect to the check, (iii) the communication is received at a time and in a manner affording the bank a reasonable time to act on it before the check is paid, and (iv) the claimant provides reasonable identification if requested by the obligated bank. Delivery of a declaration of loss is a warranty of the truth of the statements made in the declaration. If a claim is asserted in compliance with this subsection, the following rules apply:

    (1) The claim becomes enforceable at the later of (i) the time the claim is asserted, or (ii) the 90th day following the date of the check, in the case of a cashier's check or teller's check, or the 90th day following the date of the acceptance, in the case of a certified check.

    (2) Until the claim becomes enforceable, it has no legal effect and the obligated bank may pay the check or, in the case of a teller's check, may permit the drawee to pay the check. Payment to a person entitled to enforce the check discharges all liability of the obligated bank with respect to the check.

(3) If the claim becomes enforceable before the check is presented for payment, the obligated bank is not obliged to pay the check.

(4) When the claim becomes enforceable, the obligated bank becomes obliged to pay the amount of the check to the claimant if payment of the check has not been made to a person entitled to enforce the check. Subject to Section 4–302(a)(1), payment to the claimant discharges all liability of the obligated bank with respect to the check.

(c) If the obligated bank pays the amount of a check to a claimant under subsection (b)(4) and the check is presented for payment by a person having rights of a holder in due course, the claimant is obliged to (i) refund the payment to the obligated bank if the check is paid, or (ii) pay the amount of the check to the person having rights of a holder in due course if the check is dishonored.

(d) If a claimant has the right to assert a claim under subsection (b) and is also a person entitled to enforce a cashier's check, teller's check, or certified check which is lost, destroyed, or stolen, the claimant may assert rights with respect to the check either under this section or Section 3–309.

PART 4: LIABILITY OF PARTIES

§ 3–401. Signature.

(a) A person is not liable on an instrument unless (i) the person signed the instrument, or (ii) the person is represented by an agent or representative who signed the instrument and the signature is binding on the represented person under Section 3–402.

(b) A signature may be made (i) manually or by means of a device or machine, and (ii) by the use of any name, including a trade or assumed name, or by a word, mark, or symbol executed or adopted by a person with present intention to authenticate a writing.

§ 3–402. Signature by Representative.

(a) If a person acting, or purporting to act, as a representative signs an instrument by signing either the name of the represented person or the name of the signer, the represented person is bound by the signature to the same extent the represented person would be bound if the signature were on a simple contract. If the represented person is bound, the signature of the representative is the "authorized signature of the represented person" and the represented person is liable on the instrument, whether or not identified in the instrument.

(b) If a representative signs the name of the representative to an instrument and the signature is an authorized signature of the represented person, the following rules apply:

(1) If the form of the signature shows unambiguously that the signature is made on behalf of the represented person who is identified in the instrument, the representative is not liable on the instrument.

(2) Subject to subsection (c), if (i) the form of the signature does not show unambiguously that the signature is made in a representative capacity or (ii) the represented person is not identified in the instrument, the representative is liable on the instrument to a holder in due course that took the instrument without notice that the representative was not intended to be liable on the instrument. With respect to any other person, the representative is liable on the instrument unless the representative proves that the original parties did not intend the representative to be liable on the instrument.

(c) If a representative signs the name of the representative as drawer of a check without indication of the representative status and the check is payable from an account of the represented person who is identified on the check, the signer is not liable on the check if the signature is an authorized signature of the represented person.

§ 3–403. Unauthorized Signature.

(a) Unless otherwise provided in this Article or Article 4, an unauthorized signature is ineffective except as the signature of the unauthorized signer in favor of a person who in good faith pays the instrument or takes it for value. An unauthorized signature may be ratified for all purposes of this Article.

(b) If the signature of more than one person is required to constitute the authorized signature of an organization, the signature of the organization is unauthorized if one of the required signatures is lacking.

(c) The civil or criminal liability of a person who makes an unauthorized signature is not affected by any provision of this Article which makes the unauthorized signature effective for the purposes of this Article.

§ 3–404. Impostors; Fictitious Payees.

(a) If an impostor, by use of the mails or otherwise, induces the issuer of an instrument to issue the instrument to the impostor, or to a person acting in concert with the impostor, by impersonating the payee of the instrument or a person authorized to act for the payee, an indorsement of the instrument by any person in the name of the payee is effective as the indorsement of the payee in favor of a person who, in good faith, pays the instrument or takes it for value or for collection.

(b) If (i) a person whose intent determines to whom an instrument is payable (Section 3–110(a) or (b)) does not intend the person identified as payee to have any interest in the instrument, or (ii) the person identified as payee of an instrument is a fictitious person, the following rules apply until the instrument is negotiated by special indorsement:

    (1) Any person in possession of the instrument is its holder.

    (2) An indorsement by any person in the name of the payee stated in the instrument is effective as the indorsement of the payee in favor of a person who, in good faith, pays the instrument or takes it for value or for collection.

(c) Under subsection (a) or (b), an indorsement is made in the name of a payee if (i) it is made in a name substantially similar to that of the payee or (ii) the instrument, whether or not indorsed, is deposited in a depositary bank to an account in a name substantially similar to that of the payee.

(d) With respect to an instrument to which subsection (a) or (b) applies, if a person paying the instrument or taking it for value or for collection fails to exercise ordinary care in paying or taking the instrument and that failure substantially contributes to loss resulting from payment of the instrument, the person bearing the loss may recover from the person failing to exercise ordinary care to the extent the failure to exercise ordinary care contributed to the loss.

§ 3–405. Employer's Responsibility for Fraudulent Indorsement by Employee.

(a) In this section:

    (1) "Employee" includes an independent contractor and employee of an independent contractor retained by the employer.

    (2) "Fraudulent indorsement" means (i) in the case of an instrument payable to the employer, a forged indorsement purporting to be that of the employer, or (ii) in the case of an instrument with respect to which the employer is the issuer, a forged indorsement purporting to be that of the person identified as payee.

    (3) "Responsibility" with respect to instruments means authority (i) to sign or indorse instruments on behalf of the employer, (ii) to process instruments received by the employer for bookkeeping purposes, for deposit to an account, or for other disposition, (iii) to prepare or process instruments for issue in the name of the employer,

(iv) to supply information determining the names or addresses of payees of instruments to be issued in the name of the employer, (v) to control the disposition of instruments to be issued in the name of the employer, or (vi) to act otherwise with respect to instruments in a responsible capacity. "Responsibility" does not include authority that merely allows an employee to have access to instruments or blank or incomplete instrument forms that are being stored or transported or are part of incoming or outgoing mail, or similar access.

(b) For the purpose of determining the rights and liabilities of a person who, in good faith, pays an instrument or takes it for value or for collection, if an employer entrusted an employee with responsibility with respect to the instrument and the employee or a person acting in concert with the employee makes a fraudulent indorsement of the instrument, the indorsement is effective as the indorsement of the person to whom the instrument is payable if it is made in the name of that person. If the person paying the instrument or taking it for value or for collection fails to exercise ordinary care in paying or taking the instrument and that failure substantially contributes to loss resulting from the fraud, the person bearing the loss may recover from the person failing to exercise ordinary care to the extent the failure to exercise ordinary care contributed to the loss.

(c) Under subsection (b), an indorsement is made in the name of the person to whom an instrument is payable if (i) it is made in a name substantially similar to the name of that person or (ii) the instrument, whether or not indorsed, is deposited in a depositary bank to an account in a name substantially similar to the name of that person.

§ 3–406. Negligence Contributing to Forged Signature or Alteration of Instrument.

(a) A person whose failure to exercise ordinary care substantially contributes to an alteration of an instrument or to the making of a forged signature on an instrument is precluded from asserting the alteration or the forgery against a person who, in good faith, pays the instrument or takes it for value or for collection.

(b) Under subsection (a), if the person asserting the preclusion fails to exercise ordinary care in paying or taking the instrument and that failure substantially contributes to loss, the loss is allocated between the person precluded and the person asserting the preclusion according to the extent to which the failure of each to exercise ordinary care contributed to the loss.

(c) Under subsection (a), the burden of proving failure to exercise ordinary care is on the person asserting the preclusion. Under subsection (b), the burden of proving failure to exercise ordinary care is on the person precluded.

§ 3–407. Alteration.

(a) "Alteration" means (i) an unauthorized change in an instrument that purports to modify in any respect the obligation of a party, or (ii) an unauthorized addition of words or numbers or other change to an incomplete instrument relating to the obligation of a party.

(b) Except as provided in subsection (c), an alteration fraudulently made discharges a party whose obligation is affected by the alteration unless that party assents or is precluded from asserting the alteration. No other alteration discharges a party, and the instrument may be enforced according to its original terms.

(c) A payor bank or drawee paying a fraudulently altered instrument or a person taking it for value, in good faith and without notice of the alteration, may enforce rights with respect to the instrument (i) according to its original terms, or (ii) in the case of an incomplete instrument altered by unauthorized completion, according to its terms as completed.

§ 3–408. Drawee Not Liable on Unaccepted Draft.

A check or other draft does not of itself operate as an assignment of funds in the hands of the drawee available for its payment, and the drawee is not liable on the instrument until the drawee accepts it.

§ 3–409. Acceptance of Draft; Certified Check.

(a) "Acceptance" means the drawee's signed agreement to pay a draft as presented. It must be written on the draft and may consist of the drawee's signature alone. Acceptance may be made at any time and becomes effective when notification pursuant to instructions is given or the accepted draft is delivered for the purpose of giving rights on the acceptance to any person.

(b) A draft may be accepted although it has not been signed by the drawer, is otherwise incomplete, is overdue, or has been dishonored.

(c) If a draft is payable at a fixed period after sight and the acceptor fails to date the acceptance, the holder may complete the acceptance by supplying a date in good faith.

(d) "Certified check" means a check accepted by the bank on which it is drawn. Acceptance may be made as stated in subsection (a) or by a writing on the check which indicates that the check is certified. The drawee of a check has no obligation to certify the check, and refusal to certify is not dishonor of the check.

§ 3–410. Acceptance Varying Draft.

(a) If the terms of a drawee's acceptance vary from the terms of the draft as presented, the holder may refuse the acceptance and treat the draft as dishonored. In that case, the drawee may cancel the acceptance.

(b) The terms of a draft are not varied by an acceptance to pay at a particular bank or place in the United States, unless the acceptance states that the draft is to be paid only at that bank or place.

(c) If the holder assents to an acceptance varying the terms of a draft, the obligation of each drawer and indorser that does not expressly assent to the acceptance is discharged.

§ 3–411. Refusal to Pay Cashier's Checks, Teller's Checks, and Certified Checks.

(a) In this section, "obligated bank" means the acceptor of a certified check or the issuer of a cashier's check or teller's check bought from the issuer.

(b) If the obligated bank wrongfully (i) refuses to pay a cashier's check or certified check, (ii) stops payment of a teller's check, or (iii) refuses to pay a dishonored teller's check, the person asserting the right to enforce the check is entitled to compensation for expenses and loss of interest resulting from the nonpayment and may recover consequential damages if the obligated bank refuses to pay after receiving notice of particular circumstances giving rise to the damages.

(c) Expenses or consequential damages under subsection (b) are not recoverable if the refusal of the obligated bank to pay occurs because (i) the bank suspends payments, (ii) the obligated bank asserts a claim or defense of the bank that it has reasonable grounds to believe is available against the person entitled to enforce the instrument, (iii) the obligated bank has a reasonable doubt whether the person demanding payment is the person entitled to enforce the instrument, or (iv) payment is prohibited by law.

§ 3–412. Obligation of Issuer of Note or Cashier's Check.

The issuer of a note or cashier's check or other draft drawn on the drawer is obliged to pay the instrument (i) according to its terms at the time it was issued or, if not issued, at the time it first came into possession of a holder, or (ii) if the issuer signed an incomplete instrument, according to its terms when completed, to the extent stated in Sections 3–115 and 3–407. The obligation is owed to a person entitled to enforce the instrument or to an indorser who paid the instrument under Section 3–415.

§ 3–413. Obligation of Acceptor.

(a) The acceptor of a draft is obliged to pay the draft (i) according to its terms at the time it was accepted, even though the acceptance states that the draft is payable "as originally drawn" or equivalent terms, (ii) if the acceptance varies the terms of the draft, according to the terms of the draft as varied, or (iii) if the acceptance is of a draft that is an incomplete instrument, according to its terms when completed, to the extent stated in Sections 3–115 and 3–407. The obligation is owed to a person entitled to enforce the draft or to the drawer or an indorser who paid the draft under Section 3–414 or 3–415.

(b) If the certification of a check or other acceptance of a draft states the amount certified or accepted, the obligation of the acceptor is that amount. If (i) the certification or acceptance does not state an amount, (ii) the amount of the instrument is subsequently raised, and (iii) the instrument is then negotiated to a holder in due course, the obligation of the acceptor is the amount of the instrument at the time it was taken by the holder in due course.

§ 3–414. Obligation of Drawer.

(a) This section does not apply to cashier's checks or other drafts drawn on the drawer.

(b) If an unaccepted draft is dishonored, the drawer is obliged to pay the draft (i) according to its terms at the time it was issued or, if not issued, at the time it first came into possession of a holder, or (ii) if the drawer signed an incomplete instrument, according to its terms when completed, to the extent stated in Sections 3–115 and 3–407. The obligation is owed to a person entitled to enforce the draft or to an indorser who paid the draft under Section 3–415.

(c) If a draft is accepted by a bank, the drawer is discharged, regardless of when or by whom acceptance was obtained.

(d) If a draft is accepted and the acceptor is not a bank, the obligation of the drawer to pay the draft if the draft is dishonored by the acceptor is the same as the obligation of an indorser under Section 3–415(a) and (c).

(e) If a draft states that it is drawn "without recourse" or otherwise disclaims liability of the drawer to pay the draft, the drawer is not liable under subsection (b) to pay the draft if the draft is not a check. A disclaimer of the liability stated in subsection (b) is not effective if the draft is a check.

(f) If (i) a check is not presented for payment or given to a depositary bank for collection within 30 days after its date, (ii) the drawee suspends payments after expiration of the 30–day period without paying the check, and (iii) because of the suspension of payments, the drawer is deprived of funds maintained with the drawee to cover payment of the check, the drawer to the extent deprived of funds may discharge its obligation to pay the check by assigning to the person entitled to enforce the check the rights of the drawer against the drawee with respect to the funds.

§ 3–415. Obligation of Indorser.

(a) Subject to subsections (b), (c), (d), (e) and to Section 3–419(d), if an instrument is dishonored, an indorser is obliged to pay the amount due on the instrument (i) according to the terms of the instrument at the time it was indorsed, or (ii) if the indorser indorsed an incomplete instrument, according to its terms when completed, to the extent stated in Sections 3–115 and 3–407. The obligation of the indorser is owed to a person entitled to enforce the instrument or to a subsequent indorser who paid the instrument under this section.

(b) If an indorsement states that it is made "without recourse" or otherwise disclaims liability of the indorser, the indorser is not liable under subsection (a) to pay the instrument.

(c) If notice of dishonor of an instrument is required by Section 3–503 and notice of dishonor complying with that section is not given to an indorser, the liability of the indorser under subsection (a) is discharged.

(d) If a draft is accepted by a bank after an indorsement is made, the liability of the indorser under subsection (a) is discharged.

(e) If an indorser of a check is liable under subsection (a) and the check is not presented for payment, or given to a depositary bank for collection, within 30 days after the day the indorsement was made, the liability of the indorser under subsection (a) is discharged.

§ 3–416. Transfer Warranties.

(a) A person who transfers an instrument for consideration warrants to the transferee and, if the transfer is by indorsement, to any subsequent transferee that:
   (1) the warrantor is a person entitled to enforce the instrument;
   (2) all signatures on the instrument are authentic and authorized;
   (3) the instrument has not been altered;
   (4) the instrument is not subject to a defense or claim in recoupment of any party which can be asserted against the warrantor;
   (5) the warrantor has no knowledge of any insolvency proceeding commenced with respect to the maker or acceptor or, in the case of an unaccepted draft, the drawer; and
   (6) with respect to a remotely-created consumer item, that the person on whose account the item is drawn authorized the issuance of the item in the amount for which the item is drawn.

(b) A person to whom the warranties under subsection (a) are made and who took the instrument in good faith may recover from the warrantor as damages for breach of warranty an amount equal to the loss suffered as a result of the breach, but not more than the amount of the instrument plus expenses and loss of interest incurred as a result of the breach.

(c) The warranties stated in subsection (a) cannot be disclaimed with respect to checks. Unless notice of a claim for breach of warranty is given to the warrantor within 30 days after the claimant has reason to know of the breach and the identity of the warrantor, the liability of the warrantor under subsection (b) is discharged to the extent of any loss caused by the delay in giving notice of the claim.

(d) A [cause of action] for breach of warranty under this section accrues when the claimant has reason to know of the breach.

§ 3–417. Presentment Warranties.

(a) If an unaccepted draft is presented to the drawee for payment or acceptance and the drawee pays or accepts the draft, (i) the person obtaining payment or acceptance, at the time of presentment, and (ii) a previous transferor of the draft, at the time of transfer, warrant to the drawee making payment or accepting the draft in good faith that:
   (1) the warrantor is, or was, at the time the warrantor transferred the draft, a person entitled to enforce the draft or authorized to obtain payment or acceptance of the draft on behalf of a person entitled to enforce the draft;
   (2) the draft has not been altered;
   (3) the warrantor has no knowledge that the signature of the drawer of the draft is unauthorized; and
   (4) with respect to any remotely-created consumer item, that the person on whose account the item is drawn authorized the issuance of the item in the amount for which the item is drawn.

(b) A drawee making payment may recover from any warrantor damages for breach of warranty equal to the amount paid by the drawee less the amount the drawee received or is entitled to receive from the drawer because of the payment. In addition, the drawee is entitled to compensation for expenses and loss of interest resulting from the breach. The right of the drawee to recover damages under this subsection is not affected by any failure of the drawee to exercise ordinary care in making payment. If the drawee accepts the draft, breach of warranty is a defense to the obligation of the acceptor. If the acceptor makes payment with respect to the draft, the acceptor is entitled to recover from any warrantor for breach of warranty the amounts stated in this subsection.

(c)   If a drawee asserts a claim for breach of warranty under subsection (a) based on an unauthorized indorsement of the draft or an alteration of the draft, the warrantor may defend by proving that the indorsement is effective under Section 3–404 or 3–405 or the drawer is precluded under Section 3–406 or 4–406 from asserting against the drawee the unauthorized indorsement or alteration.

(d)   If (i) a dishonored draft is presented for payment to the drawer or an indorser or (ii) any other instrument is presented for payment to a party obliged to pay the instrument, and (iii) payment is received, the following rules apply:

    (1)   The person obtaining payment and a prior transferor of the instrument warrant to the person making payment in good faith that the warrantor is, or was, at the time the warrantor transferred the instrument, a person entitled to enforce the instrument or authorized to obtain payment on behalf of a person entitled to enforce the instrument.

    (2)   The person making payment may recover from any warrantor for breach of warranty an amount equal to the amount paid plus expenses and loss of interest resulting from the breach.

(e)   The warranties stated in subsections (a) and (d) cannot be disclaimed with respect to checks. Unless notice of a claim for breach of warranty is given to the warrantor within 30 days after the claimant has reason to know of the breach and the identity of the warrantor, the liability of the warrantor under subsection (b) or (d) is discharged to the extent of any loss caused by the delay in giving notice of the claim.

(f)   A [cause of action] for breach of warranty under this section accrues when the claimant has reason to know of the breach.

§ 3–418. Payment or Acceptance by Mistake.

(a)   Except as provided in subsection (c), if the drawee of a draft pays or accepts the draft and the drawee acted on the mistaken belief that (i) payment of the draft had not been stopped pursuant to Section 4–403 or (ii) the signature of the drawer of the draft was authorized, the drawee may recover the amount of the draft from the person to whom or for whose benefit payment was made or, in the case of acceptance, may revoke the acceptance. Rights of the drawee under this subsection are not affected by failure of the drawee to exercise ordinary care in paying or accepting the draft.

(b)   Except as provided in subsection (c), if an instrument has been paid or accepted by mistake and the case is not covered by subsection (a), the person paying or accepting may, to the extent permitted by the law governing mistake and restitution, (i) recover the payment from the person to whom or for whose benefit payment was made or (ii) in the case of acceptance, may revoke the acceptance.

(c)   The remedies provided by subsection (a) or (b) may not be asserted against a person who took the instrument in good faith and for value or who in good faith changed position in reliance on the payment or acceptance. This subsection does not limit remedies provided by Section 3–417 or 4–407.

(d)   Notwithstanding Section 4–215, if an instrument is paid or accepted by mistake and the payor or acceptor recovers payment or revokes acceptance under subsection (a) or (b), the instrument is deemed not to have been paid or accepted and is treated as dishonored, and the person from whom payment is recovered has rights as a person entitled to enforce the dishonored instrument.

§ 3–419. Instruments Signed for Accommodation.

(a)   If an instrument is issued for value given for the benefit of a party to the instrument ("accommodated party") and another party to the instrument ("accommodation party") signs the instrument for the purpose of incurring liability on the instrument without being a direct beneficiary of the value given for the instrument, the instrument is signed by the accommodation party "for accommodation."

(b) An accommodation party may sign the instrument as maker, drawer, acceptor, or indorser and, subject to subsection (d), is obliged to pay the instrument in the capacity in which the accommodation party signs. The obligation of an accommodation party may be enforced notwithstanding any statute of frauds and whether or not the accommodation party receives consideration for the accommodation.

(c) A person signing an instrument is presumed to be an accommodation party and there is notice that the instrument is signed for accommodation if the signature is an anomalous indorsement or is accompanied by words indicating that the signer is acting as surety or guarantor with respect to the obligation of another party to the instrument. Except as provided in Section 3–605, the obligation of an accommodation party to pay the instrument is not affected by the fact that the person enforcing the obligation had notice when the instrument was taken by that person that the accommodation party signed the instrument for accommodation.

(d) If the signature of a party to an instrument is accompanied by words indicating unambiguously that the party is guaranteeing collection rather than payment of the obligation of another party to the instrument, the signer is obliged to pay the amount due on the instrument to a person entitled to enforce the instrument only if (i) execution of judgment against the other party has been returned unsatisfied, (ii) the other party is insolvent or in an insolvency proceeding, (iii) the other party cannot be served with process, or (iv) it is otherwise apparent that payment cannot be obtained from the other party.

(e) If the signature of a party to an instrument is accompanied by words indicating that the party guarantees payment or the signer signs the instrument as an accommodation party in some other manner that does not unambiguously indicate an intention to guarantee collection rather than payment, the signer is obliged to pay the amount due on the instrument to a person entitled to enforce the instrument in the same circumstances as the accommodated party would be obliged, without prior resort to the accommodated party by the person entitled to enforce the instrument.

(f) An accommodation party who pays the instrument is entitled to reimbursement from the accommodated party and is entitled to enforce the instrument against the accommodated party. In proper circumstances, an accommodation party may obtain relief that requires the accommodated party to perform its obligations on the instrument. An accommodated party that pays the instrument has no right of recourse against, and is not entitled to contribution from, an accommodation party.

§ 3–420. Conversion of Instrument.

(a) The law applicable to conversion of personal property applies to instruments. An instrument is also converted if it is taken by transfer, other than a negotiation, from a person not entitled to enforce the instrument or a bank makes or obtains payment with respect to the instrument for a person not entitled to enforce the instrument or receive payment. An action for conversion of an instrument may not be brought by (i) the issuer or acceptor of the instrument or (ii) a payee or indorsee who did not receive delivery of the instrument either directly or through delivery to an agent or a co-payee.

(b) In an action under subsection (a), the measure of liability is presumed to be the amount payable on the instrument, but recovery may not exceed the amount of the plaintiff's interest in the instrument.

(c) A representative, other than a depositary bank, who has in good faith dealt with an instrument or its proceeds on behalf of one who was not the person entitled to enforce the instrument is not liable in conversion to that person beyond the amount of any proceeds that it has not paid out.

PART 5: DISHONOR

§ 3–501. Presentment.

(a) "Presentment" means a demand made by or on behalf of a person entitled to enforce an instrument (i) to pay the instrument made to the drawee or a party obliged to pay the instrument or, in the case of a note or accepted draft payable at a bank, to the bank, or (ii) to accept a draft made to the drawee.

(b) The following rules are subject to Article 4, agreement of the parties, and clearing-house rules and the like:

(1) Presentment may be made at the place of payment of the instrument and must be made at the place of payment if the instrument is payable at a bank in the United States; may be made by any commercially reasonable means, including an oral, written, or electronic communication; is effective when the demand for payment or acceptance is received by the person to whom presentment is made; and is effective if made to any one of two or more makers, acceptors, drawees, or other payors.

(2) Upon demand of the person to whom presentment is made, the person making presentment must (i) exhibit the instrument, (ii) give reasonable identification and, if presentment is made on behalf of another person, reasonable evidence of authority to do so, and (iii) sign a receipt on the instrument for any payment made or surrender the instrument if full payment is made.

(3) Without dishonoring the instrument, the party to whom presentment is made may (i) return the instrument for lack of a necessary indorsement, or (ii) refuse payment or acceptance for failure of the presentment to comply with the terms of the instrument, an agreement of the parties, or other applicable law or rule.

(4) The party to whom presentment is made may treat presentment as occurring on the next business day after the day of presentment if the party to whom presentment is made has established a cut-off hour not earlier than 2 p.m. for the receipt and processing of instruments presented for payment or acceptance and presentment is made after the cut-off hour.

§ 3–502. Dishonor.

(a) Dishonor of a note is governed by the following rules:

(1) If the note is payable on demand, the note is dishonored if presentment is duly made to the maker and the note is not paid on the day of presentment.

(2) If the note is not payable on demand and is payable at or through a bank or the terms of the note require presentment, the note is dishonored if presentment is duly made and the note is not paid on the day it becomes payable or the day of presentment, whichever is later.

(3) If the note is not payable on demand and paragraph (2) does not apply, the note is dishonored if it is not paid on the day it becomes payable.

(b) Dishonor of an unaccepted draft other than a documentary draft is governed by the following rules:

(1) If a check is duly presented for payment to the payor bank otherwise than for immediate payment over the counter, the check is dishonored if the payor bank makes timely return of the check or sends timely notice of dishonor or nonpayment under Section 4–301 or 4–302, or becomes accountable for the amount of the check under Section 4–302.

(2) If a draft is payable on demand and paragraph (1) does not apply, the draft is dishonored if presentment for payment is duly made to the drawee and the draft is not paid on the day of presentment.

(3) If a draft is payable on a date stated in the draft, the draft is dishonored if (i) presentment for payment is duly made to the drawee and payment is not made on the day the draft becomes payable or the day of presentment, whichever is later, or (ii) presentment for acceptance is duly made before the day the draft becomes payable and the draft is not accepted on the day of presentment.

(4) If a draft is payable on elapse of a period of time after sight or acceptance, the draft is dishonored if presentment for acceptance is duly made and the draft is not accepted on the day of presentment.

(c) Dishonor of an unaccepted documentary draft occurs according to the rules stated in subsection (b)(2), (3), and (4), except that payment or acceptance may be delayed without dishonor until no later than the close of the third business day of the drawee following the day on which payment or acceptance is required by those paragraphs.

(d) Dishonor of an accepted draft is governed by the following rules:

(1) If the draft is payable on demand, the draft is dishonored if presentment for payment is duly made to the acceptor and the draft is not paid on the day of presentment.

(2) If the draft is not payable on demand, the draft is dishonored if presentment for payment is duly made to the acceptor and payment is not made on the day it becomes payable or the day of presentment, whichever is later.

(e) In any case in which presentment is otherwise required for dishonor under this section and presentment is excused under Section 3–504, dishonor occurs without presentment if the instrument is not duly accepted or paid.

(f) If a draft is dishonored because timely acceptance of the draft was not made and the person entitled to demand acceptance consents to a late acceptance, from the time of acceptance the draft is treated as never having been dishonored.

§ 3–503. Notice of Dishonor.

(a) The obligation of an indorser stated in Section 3–415(a) and the obligation of a drawer stated in Section 3–414(d) may not be enforced unless (i) the indorser or drawer is given notice of dishonor of the instrument complying with this section or (ii) notice of dishonor is excused under Section 3–504(b).

(b) Notice of dishonor may be given by any person; may be given by any commercially reasonable means, including an oral, written, or electronic communication; and is sufficient if it reasonably identifies the instrument and indicates that the instrument has been dishonored or has not been paid or accepted. Return of an instrument given to a bank for collection is sufficient notice of dishonor.

(c) Subject to Section 3–504(c), with respect to an instrument taken for collection by a collecting bank, notice of dishonor must be given (i) by the bank before midnight of the next banking day following the banking day on which the bank receives notice of dishonor of the instrument, or (ii) by any other person within 30 days following the day on which the person receives notice of dishonor. With respect to any other instrument, notice of dishonor must be given within 30 days following the day on which dishonor occurs.

§ 3–504. Excused Presentment and Notice of Dishonor.

(a) Presentment for payment or acceptance of an instrument is excused if (i) the person entitled to present the instrument cannot with reasonable diligence make presentment, (ii) the maker or acceptor has repudiated an obligation to pay the instrument or is dead or in insolvency proceedings, (iii) by the terms of the instrument presentment is not necessary to enforce the obligation of indorsers or the drawer, (iv) the drawer or indorser whose obligation is being enforced has waived presentment or otherwise has no reason to expect or right to require that the instrument be paid or accepted, or (v) the drawer instructed the drawee not to pay or accept the draft or the drawee was not obligated to the drawer to pay the draft.

(b) Notice of dishonor is excused if (i) by the terms of the instrument notice of dishonor is not necessary to enforce the obligation of a party to pay the instrument, or (ii) the party whose obligation is being enforced waived notice of dishonor. A waiver of presentment is also a waiver of notice of dishonor.

(c) Delay in giving notice of dishonor is excused if the delay was caused by circumstances beyond the control of the person giving the notice and the person giving the notice exercised reasonable diligence after the cause of the delay ceased to operate.

§ 3–505. Evidence of Dishonor.

(a)   The following are admissible as evidence and create a presumption of dishonor and of any notice of dishonor stated:

    (1)   a document regular in form as provided in subsection (b) which purports to be a protest;

    (2)   a purported stamp or writing of the drawee, payor bank, or presenting bank on or accompanying the instrument stating that acceptance or payment has been refused unless reasons for the refusal are stated and the reasons are not consistent with dishonor;

    (3)   a book or record of the drawee, payor bank, or collecting bank, kept in the usual course of business which shows dishonor, even if there is no evidence of who made the entry.

(b)   A protest is a certificate of dishonor made by a United States consul or vice consul, or a notary public or other person authorized to administer oaths by the law of the place where dishonor occurs. It may be made upon information satisfactory to that person. The protest must identify the instrument and certify either that presentment has been made or, if not made, the reason why it was not made, and that the instrument has been dishonored by nonacceptance or nonpayment. The protest may also certify that notice of dishonor has been given to some or all parties.

PART 6: DISCHARGE AND PAYMENT

§ 3–601. Discharge and Effect of Discharge.

(a)   The obligation of a party to pay the instrument is discharged as stated in this Article or by an act or agreement with the party which would discharge an obligation to pay money under a simple contract.

(b)   Discharge of the obligation of a party is not effective against a person acquiring rights of a holder in due course of the instrument without notice of the discharge.

§ 3–602. Payment.

(a)   Subject to subsection (e), an instrument is paid to the extent payment is made by or on behalf of a party obliged to pay the instrument, and to a person entitled to enforce the instrument.

(b)   Subject to subsection (e), a note is paid to the extent payment is made by or on behalf of a party obliged to pay the note to a person that formerly was entitled to enforce the note only if at the time of the payment the party obliged to pay has not received adequate notification that the note has been transferred and that payment is to be made to the transferee. A notification is adequate only if it is signed by the transferor or the transferee; reasonably identifies the transferred note; and provides an address at which payments subsequently are to be made. Upon request, a transferee shall seasonably furnish reasonable proof that the note has been transferred. Unless the transferee complies with the request, a payment to the person that formerly was entitled to enforce the note is effective for purposes of subsection (c) even if the party obliged to pay the note has received a notification under this paragraph.

(c)   Subject to subsection (e), to the extent of a payment under subsections (a) and (b), the obligation of the party obliged to pay the instrument is discharged even though payment is made with knowledge of a claim to the instrument under Section 3–306 by another person.

(d)   Subject to subsection (e), a transferee, or any party that has acquired rights in the instrument directly or indirectly from a transferee, including any such party that has rights as a holder in due course, is deemed to have notice of any payment that is made under subsection (b) after the date that the note is transferred to the transferee but before the party obliged to pay the note receives adequate notification of the transfer.

(e) The obligation of a party to pay the instrument is not discharged under subsections (a) through (d) if:

    (1) a claim to the instrument under Section 3–306 is enforceable against the party receiving payment and (i) payment is made with knowledge by the payor that payment is prohibited by injunction or similar process of a court of competent jurisdiction, or (ii) in the case of an instrument other than a cashier's check, teller's check, or certified check, the party making payment accepted, from the person having a claim to the instrument, indemnity against loss resulting from refusal to pay the person entitled to enforce the instrument; or

    (2) the person making payment knows that the instrument is a stolen instrument and pays a person it knows is in wrongful possession of the instrument.

(f) As used in this section, "signed," with respect to a record that is not a writing, includes the attachment to or logical association with the record of an electronic symbol, sound, or process with the present intent to adopt or accept the record.

§ 3–603. Tender of Payment.

(a) If tender of payment of an obligation to pay an instrument is made to a person entitled to enforce the instrument, the effect of tender is governed by principles of law applicable to tender of payment under a simple contract.

(b) If tender of payment of an obligation to pay an instrument is made to a person entitled to enforce the instrument and the tender is refused, there is discharge, to the extent of the amount of the tender, of the obligation of an indorser or accommodation party having a right of recourse with respect to the obligation to which the tender relates.

(c) If tender of payment of an amount due on an instrument is made to a person entitled to enforce the instrument, the obligation of the obligor to pay interest after the due date on the amount tendered is discharged. If presentment is required with respect to an instrument and the obligor is able and ready to pay on the due date at every place of payment stated in the instrument, the obligor is deemed to have made tender of payment on the due date to the person entitled to enforce the instrument.

§ 3–604. Discharge by Cancellation or Renunciation.

(a) A person entitled to enforce an instrument, with or without consideration, may discharge the obligation of a party to pay the instrument (i) by an intentional voluntary act, such as surrender of the instrument to the party, destruction, mutilation, or cancellation of the instrument, cancellation or striking out of the party's signature, or the addition of words to the instrument indicating discharge, or (ii) by agreeing not to sue or otherwise renouncing rights against the party by a signed record.

(b) Cancellation or striking out of an indorsement pursuant to subsection (a) does not affect the status and rights of a party derived from the indorsement.

(c) In this section, "signed," with respect to a record that is not a writing, includes the attachment to or logical association with the record of an electronic symbol, sound, or process with the present intent to adopt or accept the record.

§ 3–605. Discharge of Secondary Obligors.

(a) If a person entitled to enforce an instrument releases the obligation of a principal obligor in whole or in part, and another party to the instrument is a secondary obligor with respect to the obligation of that principal obligor, the following rules apply:

    (1) Any obligations of the principal obligor to the secondary obligor with respect to any previous payment by the secondary obligor are not affected. Unless the terms of the release preserve the secondary obligor's recourse, the principal obligor is discharged, to the extent of the release, from any other duties to the secondary obligor under this article.

(2) Unless the terms of the release provide that the person entitled to enforce the instrument retains the right to enforce the instrument against the secondary obligor, the secondary obligor is discharged to the same extent as the principal obligor from any unperformed portion of its obligation on the instrument. If the instrument is a check and the obligation of the secondary obligor is based on an indorsement of the check, the secondary obligor is discharged without regard to the language or circumstances of the discharge or other release.

(3) If the secondary obligor is not discharged under paragraph (2), the secondary obligor is discharged to the extent of the value of the consideration for the release, and to the extent that the release would otherwise cause the secondary obligor a loss.

(b) If a person entitled to enforce an instrument grants a principal obligor an extension of the time at which one or more payments are due on the instrument and another party to the instrument is a secondary obligor with respect to the obligation of that principal obligor, the following rules apply:

(1) Any obligations of the principal obligor to the secondary obligor with respect to any previous payment by the secondary obligor are not affected. Unless the terms of the extension preserve the secondary obligor's recourse, the extension correspondingly extends the time for performance of any other duties owed to the secondary obligor by the principal obligor under this article.

(2) The secondary obligor is discharged to the extent that the extension would otherwise cause the secondary obligor a loss.

(3) To the extent that the secondary obligor is not discharged under paragraph (2), the secondary obligor may perform its obligations to a person entitled to enforce the instrument as if the time for payment had not been extended or, unless the terms of the extension provide that the person entitled to enforce the instrument retains the right to enforce the instrument against the secondary obligor as if the time for payment had not been extended, treat the time for performance of its obligations as having been extended correspondingly.

(c) If a person entitled to enforce an instrument agrees, with or without consideration, to a modification of the obligation of a principal obligor other than a complete or partial release or an extension of the due date and another party to the instrument is a secondary obligor with respect to the obligation of that principal obligor, the following rules apply:

(1) Any obligations of the principal obligor to the secondary obligor with respect to any previous payment by the secondary obligor are not affected. The modification correspondingly modifies any other duties owed to the secondary obligor by the principal obligor under this article.

(2) The secondary obligor is discharged from any unperformed portion of its obligation to the extent that the modification would otherwise cause the secondary obligor a loss.

(3) To the extent that the secondary obligor is not discharged under paragraph (2), the secondary obligor may satisfy its obligation on the instrument as if the modification had not occurred, or treat its obligation on the instrument as having been modified correspondingly.

(d) If the obligation of a principal obligor is secured by an interest in collateral, another party to the instrument is a secondary obligor with respect to that obligation, and a person entitled to enforce the instrument impairs the value of the interest in collateral, the obligation of the secondary obligor is discharged to the extent of the impairment. The value of an interest in collateral is impaired to the extent the value of the interest is reduced to an amount less than the amount of the recourse of the secondary obligor, or the reduction in value of the interest causes an increase in the amount by which the amount of the recourse exceeds the value of the interest. For purposes of this subsection, impairing the value of an interest in collateral includes failure to obtain or maintain perfection or recordation of the interest in collateral, release of collateral without substitution of collateral of equal value or equivalent reduction of the underlying obligation, failure to perform a duty to preserve the value of collateral owed, under Article 9 or other law, to a debtor or other person secondarily liable, and failure to comply with applicable law in disposing of or otherwise enforcing the interest in collateral.

(e) A secondary obligor is not discharged under subsections (a)(3), (b), (c), or (d) unless the person entitled to enforce the instrument knows that the person is a secondary obligor or has notice under Section 3–419(c) that the instrument was signed for accommodation.

(f) A secondary obligor is not discharged under this section if the secondary obligor consents to the event or conduct that is the basis of the discharge, or the instrument or a separate agreement of the party provides for waiver of discharge under this section specifically or by general language indicating that parties waive defenses based on suretyship or impairment of collateral. Unless the circumstances indicate otherwise, consent by the principal obligor to an act that would lead to a discharge under this section constitutes consent to that act by the secondary obligor if the secondary obligor controls the principal obligor or deals with the person entitled to enforce the instrument on behalf of the principal obligor.

(g) A release or extension preserves a secondary obligorís recourse if the terms of the release or extension provide that:

(1) the person entitled to enforce the instrument retains the right to enforce the instrument against the secondary obligor; and

(2) the recourse of the secondary obligor continues as if the release or extension had not been granted.

(h) Except as otherwise provided in subsection (i), a secondary obligor asserting discharge under this section has the burden of persuasion both with respect to the occurrence of the acts alleged to harm the secondary obligor and loss or prejudice caused by those acts.

(i) If the secondary obligor demonstrates prejudice caused by an impairment of its recourse, and the circumstances of the case indicate that the amount of loss is not reasonably susceptible of calculation or requires proof of facts that are not ascertainable, it is presumed that the act impairing recourse caused a loss or impairment equal to the liability of the secondary obligor on the instrument. In that event, the burden of persuasion as to any lesser amount of the loss is on the person entitled to enforce the instrument.

Appendix C

TITLE VII OF THE CIVIL RIGHTS ACT OF 1964

The U.S. Equal Employment Opportunity Commission

An Act

To enforce the constitutional right to vote, to confer jurisdiction upon the district courts of the United States to provide injunctive relief against discrimination in public accommodations, to authorize the attorney General to institute suits to protect constitutional rights in public facilities and public education, to extend the Commission on Civil Rights, to prevent discrimination in federally assisted programs, to establish a Commission on Equal Employment Opportunity, and for other purposes.

Be it enacted by the Senate and House of Representatives of the United States of America in Congress assembled, That this Act may be cited as the "Civil Rights Act of 1964."

***

DEFINITIONS

SEC. 2000e. *[Section 701].* For the purposes of this subchapter-

(a) The term "person" includes one or more individuals, governments, governmental agencies, political subdivisions, labor unions, partnerships, associations, corporations, legal representatives, mutual companies, joint stock companies, trusts, unincorporated organizations, trustees, trustees in cases under title 11 *[bankruptcy],* or receivers.

(b) The term "employer" means a person engaged in an industry affecting commerce who has fifteen or more employees for each working day in each of twenty or more calendar weeks in the current or preceding calendar year, and any agent of such a person, but such term does not include (1) the United States, a corporation wholly owned by the Government of the United States, an Indian tribe, or any department or agency of the District of Columbia subject by statute to procedures of the competitive service (as defined in section 2102 of title 5 *[of the United States Code]*), or (2) a bona fide private membership club (other than a labor organization) which is exempt from taxation under section 501(c) of title 26 *[the Internal Revenue Code of 1954],* except that during the first year after March 24, 1972 *[the date of enactment of the Equal Employment Opportunity Act of 1972],* persons having fewer than twenty five employees (and their agents) shall not be considered employers.

(c) The term "employment agency" means any person regularly undertaking with or without compensation to procure employees for an employer or to procure for employees opportunities to work for an employer and includes an agent of such a person.

(d) The term "labor organization" means a labor organization engaged in an industry affecting commerce, and any agent of such an organization, and includes any organization of any kind, any agency, or employee representation committee, group, association, or plan so engaged in which employees participate and which exists for the purpose, in whole or in part, of dealing with employers concerning grievances, labor disputes, wages, rates of pay, hours, or other terms or conditions of employment, and any conference, general committee, joint or system board, or joint council so engaged which is subordinate to a national or international labor organization.

(e) A labor organization shall be deemed to be engaged in an industry affecting commerce if (1) it maintains or operates a hiring hall or hiring office which procures employees for an employer or procures for employees opportunities to work for an employer, or (2) the number of its members (or, where it is a labor organization composed of other labor organizations or their representatives, if the aggregate number of the members of such other labor organization) is (A) twenty five or more during the first year after March 24, 1972 *[the date of enactment of the Equal Employment Opportunity Act of 1972]*, or (B) fifteen or more thereafter, and such labor organization-

(1) is the certified representative of employees under the provisions of the National Labor Relations Act, as amended *[29 U.S.C. 151 et seq.]*, or the Railway Labor Act, as amended *[45 U.S.C. 151 et seq.]*;

(2) although not certified, is a national or international labor organization or a local labor organization recognized or acting as the representative of employees of an employer or employers engaged in an industry affecting commerce; or

(3) has chartered a local labor organization or subsidiary body which is representing or actively seeking to represent employees of employers within the meaning of paragraph (1) or (2); or

(4) has been chartered by a labor organization representing or actively seeking to represent employees within the meaning of paragraph (1) or (2) as the local or subordinate body through which such employees may enjoy membership or become affiliated with such labor organization; or

(5) is a conference, general committee, joint or system board, or joint council subordinate to a national or international labor organization, which includes a labor organization engaged in an industry affecting commerce within the meaning of any of the preceding paragraphs of this subsection.

(f) The term "employee" means an individual employed by an employer, except that the term "employee" shall not include any person elected to public office in any State or political subdivision of any State by the qualified voters thereof, or any person chosen by such officer to be on such officer's personal staff, or an appointee on the policy making level or an immediate adviser with respect to the exercise of the constitutional or legal powers of the office. The exemption set forth in the preceding sentence shall not include employees subject to the civil service laws of a State government, governmental agency or political subdivision. **With respect to employment in a foreign country, such term includes an individual who is a citizen of the United States.**

(g) The term "commerce" means trade, traffic, commerce, transportation, transmission, or communication among the several States; or between a State and any place outside thereof; or within the District of Columbia, or a possession of the United States; or between points in the same State but through a point outside thereof.

(h) The term "industry affecting commerce" means any activity, business, or industry in commerce or in which a labor dispute would hinder or obstruct commerce or the free flow of commerce and includes any activity or industry "affecting commerce" within the meaning of the Labor Management Reporting and Disclosure Act of 1959 *[29 U.S.C. 401 et seq.]*, and further includes any governmental industry, business, or activity.

(i) The term "State" includes a State of the United States, the District of Columbia, Puerto Rico, the Virgin Islands, American Samoa, Guam, Wake Island, the Canal Zone, and Outer Continental Shelf lands defined in the Outer Continental Shelf Lands Act *[43 U.S.C. 1331 et seq.]*.

(j) The term "religion" includes all aspects of religious observance and practice, as well as belief, unless an employer demonstrates that he is unable to reasonably accommodate to an employee's or prospective employee's religious observance or practice without undue hardship on the conduct of the employer's business.

(k) The terms "because of sex" or "on the basis of sex" include, but are not limited to, because of or on the basis of pregnancy, childbirth, or related medical conditions; and women affected by pregnancy, childbirth, or related medical conditions shall be treated the same for all employment related purposes, including receipt of benefits under fringe benefit programs, as other persons not so affected but similar in their ability or inability to work, and nothing in section 2000e-2(h) of this title *[section 703(h)]* shall be interpreted to permit otherwise. This subsection shall not require an employer to pay for health insurance benefits for abortion, except where the life of the mother would be endangered if the fetus were carried to term, or except where medical complications have arisen from an abortion: Provided, That nothing herein shall preclude an employer from providing abortion benefits or otherwise affect bargaining agreements in regard to abortion.

(l) The term "complaining party" means the Commission, the Attorney General, or a person who may bring an action or proceeding under this subchapter.

(m) The term "demonstrates" means meets the burdens of production and persuasion.

(n) The term "respondent" means an employer, employment agency, labor organization, joint labor management committee controlling apprenticeship or other training or retraining program, including an on the job training program, or Federal entity subject to section 2000e-16 of this title.

EXEMPTION

SEC. 2000e-1. *[Section 702].*

(a) This subchapter shall not apply to an employer with respect to the employment of aliens outside any State, or to a religious corporation, association, educational institution, or society with respect to the employment of individuals of a particular religion to perform work connected with the carrying on by such corporation, association, educational institution, or society of its activities.

(b) It shall not be unlawful under section 2000e-2 or 2000e-3 of this title *[section 703 or 704]* for an employer (or a corporation controlled by an employer), labor organization, employment agency, or joint labor management committee controlling apprenticeship or other training or retraining (including on the job training programs) to take any action otherwise prohibited by such section, with respect to an employee in a workplace in a foreign country if compliance with such section would cause such employer (or such corporation), such organization, such agency, or such committee to violate the law of the foreign country in which such workplace is located.

(c) (1) If an employer controls a corporation whose place of incorporation is a foreign country, any practice prohibited by section 2000e-2 or 2000e-3 of this title *[section 703 or 704]* engaged in by such corporation shall be presumed to be engaged in by such employer.

(2) Sections 2000e-2 and 2000e-3 of this title *[sections 703 and 704]* shall not apply with respect to the foreign operations of an employer that is a foreign person not controlled by an American employer.

(3) For purposes of this subsection, the determination of whether an employer controls a corporation shall be based on-

(A) the interrelation of operations;

(B) the common management;

(C) the centralized control of labor relations; and

(D) the common ownership or financial control, of the employer and the corporation.

UNLAWFUL EMPLOYMENT PRACTICES

SEC. 2000e-2. *[Section 703].*

(a) It shall be an unlawful employment practice for an employer-

(1) to fail or refuse to hire or to discharge any individual, or otherwise to discriminate against any individual with respect to his compensation, terms, conditions, or privileges of employment, because of such individual's race, color, religion, sex, or national origin; or

(2) to limit, segregate, or classify his employees or applicants for employment in any way which would deprive or tend to deprive any individual of employment opportunities or otherwise adversely affect his status as an employee, because of such individual's race, color, religion, sex, or national origin.

(b) It shall be an unlawful employment practice for an employment agency to fail or refuse to refer for employment, or otherwise to discriminate against, any individual because of his race, color, religion, sex, or national origin, or to classify or refer for employment any individual on the basis of his race, color, religion, sex, or national origin.

(c) It shall be an unlawful employment practice for a labor organization-

(1) to exclude or to expel from its membership, or otherwise to discriminate against, any individual because of his race, color, religion, sex, or national origin;

(2) to limit, segregate, or classify its membership or applicants for membership, or to classify or fail or refuse to refer for employment any individual, in any way which would deprive or tend to deprive any individual of employment opportunities, or would limit such employment opportunities or otherwise adversely affect his status as an employee or as an applicant for employment, because of such individual's race, color, religion, sex, or national origin; or

(3) to cause or attempt to cause an employer to discriminate against an individual in violation of this section.

(d) It shall be an unlawful employment practice for any employer, labor organization, or joint labor management committee controlling apprenticeship or other training or retraining, including on the job training programs to discriminate against any individual because of his race, color, religion, sex, or national origin in admission to, or employment in, any program established to provide apprenticeship or other training.

(e) Notwithstanding any other provision of this subchapter, (1) it shall not be an unlawful employment practice for an employer to hire and employ employees, for an employment agency to classify, or refer for employment any individual, for a labor organization to classify its membership or to classify or refer for employment any individual, or for an employer, labor organization, or joint labor management committee controlling apprenticeship or other training or retraining programs to admit or employ any individual in any such program, on the basis of his religion, sex, or national origin in those certain instances where religion, sex, or national origin is a bona fide occupational qualification reasonably necessary to the normal operation of that particular business or enterprise, and (2) it shall not be an unlawful employment practice for a school, college, university, or other educational institution or institution of learning to hire and employ employees of a particular religion if such school, college, university, or other educational institution or institution of learning is, in whole or in substantial part, owned, supported, controlled, or managed by a particular religion or by a particular religious corporation, association, or society, or if the curriculum of such school, college, university, or other educational institution or institution of learning is directed toward the propagation of a particular religion.

(f) As used in this subchapter, the phrase "unlawful employment practice" shall not be deemed to include any action or measure taken by an employer, labor organization, joint labor management committee, or employment agency with respect to an individual who is a member of the Communist Party of the United States or of any other organization required to register as a Communist action or Communist front organization by final order of the Subversive Activities Control Board pursuant to the Subversive Activities Control Act of 1950 *[50 U.S.C. 781 et seq.]*.

(g) Notwithstanding any other provision of this subchapter, it shall not be an unlawful employment practice for an employer to fail or refuse to hire and employ any individual for any position, for an employer to discharge any individual from any position, or for an employment agency to fail or refuse to refer any individual for employment in any position, or for a labor organization to fail or refuse to refer any individual for employment in any position, if-

(1) the occupancy of such position, or access to the premises in or upon which any part of the duties of such position is performed or is to be performed, is subject to any requirement imposed in the interest of the national security of the United States under any security program in effect pursuant to or administered under any statute of the United States or any Executive order of the President; and

(2) such individual has not fulfilled or has ceased to fulfill that requirement.

(h) Notwithstanding any other provision of this subchapter, it shall not be an unlawful employment practice for an employer to apply different standards of compensation, or different terms, conditions, or privileges of employment pursuant to a bona fide seniority or merit system, or a system which measures earnings by quantity or quality of production or to employees who work in different locations, provided that such differences are not the result of an intention to discriminate because of race, color, religion, sex, or national origin, nor shall it be an unlawful employment practice for an employer to give and to act upon the results of any professionally developed ability test provided that such test, its administration or action upon the results is not designed, intended or used to discriminate because of race, color, religion, sex or national origin. It shall not be an unlawful employment practice under this subchapter for any employer to differentiate upon the basis of sex in determining the amount of the wages or compensation paid or to be paid to employees of such employer if such differentiation is authorized by the provisions of section 206(d) of title 29 *[section 6(d) of the Fair Labor Standards Act of 1938, as amended]*.

(i) Nothing contained in this subchapter shall apply to any business or enterprise on or near an Indian reservation with respect to any publicly announced employment practice of such business or enterprise under which a preferential treatment is given to any individual because he is an Indian living on or near a reservation.

(j) Nothing contained in this subchapter shall be interpreted to require any employer, employment agency, labor organization, or joint labor management committee subject to this subchapter to grant preferential treatment to any individual or to any group because of the race, color, religion, sex, or national origin of such individual or group on account of an imbalance which may exist with respect to the total number or percentage of persons of any race, color, religion, sex, or national origin employed by any employer, referred or classified for employment by any employment agency or labor organization, admitted to membership or classified by any labor organization, or admitted to, or employed in, any apprenticeship or other training program, in comparison with the total number or percentage of persons of such race, color, religion, sex, or national origin in any community, State, section, or other area, or in the available work force in any community, State, section, or other area.

(k) (1) (A) An unlawful employment practice based on disparate impact is established under this title only if-

(i) a complaining party demonstrates that a respondent uses a particular employment practice that causes a disparate impact on the basis of race, color, religion, sex, or national origin and the respondent fails to demonstrate that the challenged practice is job related for the position in question and consistent with business necessity; or

(ii) the complaining party makes the demonstration described in subparagraph (C) with respect to an alternative employment practice and the respondent refuses to adopt such alternative employment practice.

(B) (i) With respect to demonstrating that a particular employment practice causes a disparate impact as described in subparagraph (A)(i), the complaining party shall demonstrate that each particular challenged employment practice causes a disparate impact, except that if the complaining party can demonstrate to the court that the elements of a respondent's decision making process are not capable of separation for analysis, the decision making process may be analyzed as one employment practice.

(ii) If the respondent demonstrates that a specific employment practice does not cause the disparate impact, the respondent shall not be required to demonstrate that such practice is required by business necessity.

(C) The demonstration referred to by subparagraph (A)(ii) shall be in accordance with the law as it existed on June 4, 1989, with respect to the concept of "alternative employment practice".

(2) A demonstration that an employment practice is required by business necessity may not be used as a defense against a claim of intentional discrimination under this title.

(3) Notwithstanding any other provision of this title, a rule barring the employment of an individual who currently and knowingly uses or possesses a controlled substance, as defined in schedules I and II of section 102(6) of the Controlled Substances Act (21 U.S.C. 802(6)), other than the use or possession of a drug taken under the supervision of a licensed health care professional, or any other use or possession authorized by the Controlled Substances Act *[21 U.S.C. 801 et seq.]* or any other provision of Federal law, shall be considered an unlawful employment practice under this title only if such rule is

adopted or applied with an intent to discriminate because of race, color, religion, sex, or national origin.

(l) It shall be an unlawful employment practice for a respondent, in connection with the selection or referral of applicants or candidates for employment or promotion, to adjust the scores of, use different cutoff scores for, or otherwise alter the results of, employment related tests on the basis of race, color, religion, sex, or national origin.

(m) Except as otherwise provided in this title, an unlawful employment practice is established when the complaining party demonstrates that race, color, religion, sex, or national origin was a motivating factor for any employment practice, even though other factors also motivated the practice.

(n) (1) (A) Notwithstanding any other provision of law, and except as provided in paragraph (2), an employment practice that implements and is within the scope of a litigated or consent judgment or order that resolves a claim of employment discrimination under the Constitution or Federal civil rights laws may not be challenged under the circumstances described in subparagraph (B).

(B) A practice described in subparagraph (A) may not be challenged in a claim under the Constitution or Federal civil rights laws-

(i) by a person who, prior to the entry of the judgment or order described in subparagraph (A), had-

(I) actual notice of the proposed judgment or order sufficient to apprise such person that such judgment or order might adversely affect the interests and legal rights of such person and that an opportunity was available to present objections to such judgment or order by a future date certain; and

(II) a reasonable opportunity to present objections to such judgment or order; or

(ii) by a person whose interests were adequately represented by another person who had previously challenged the judgment or order on the same legal grounds and with a similar factual situation, unless there has been an intervening change in law or fact.

(2) Nothing in this subsection shall be construed to-

(A) alter the standards for intervention under rule 24 of the Federal Rules of Civil Procedure or apply to the rights of parties who have successfully intervened pursuant to such rule in the proceeding in which the parties intervened;

(B) apply to the rights of parties to the action in which a litigated or consent judgment or order was entered, or of members of a class represented or sought to be represented in such action, or of members of a group on whose behalf relief was sought in such action by the Federal Government;

(C) prevent challenges to a litigated or consent judgment or order on the ground that such judgment or order was obtained through collusion or fraud, or is transparently invalid or was entered by a court lacking subject matter jurisdiction; or

(D) authorize or permit the denial to any person of the due process of law required by the Constitution.

(3) Any action not precluded under this subsection that challenges an employment consent judgment or order described in paragraph (1) shall be brought in the court, and if possible before the judge, that entered such judgment or order. Nothing in this subsection shall preclude a transfer of such action pursuant to section 1404 of title 28, United States Code.

OTHER UNLAWFUL EMPLOYMENT PRACTICES

SEC. 2000e-3. *[Section 704].*

(a) It shall be an unlawful employment practice for an employer to discriminate against any of his employees or applicants for employment, for an employment agency, or joint labor management committee controlling apprenticeship or other training or retraining, including on the job training programs, to discriminate against any individual, or for a labor organization to discriminate against any member thereof or applicant for membership, because he has opposed

any practice made an unlawful employment practice by this subchapter, or because he has made a charge, testified, assisted, or participated in any manner in an investigation, proceeding, or hearing under this subchapter.

(b) It shall be an unlawful employment practice for an employer, labor organization, employment agency, or joint labor management committee controlling apprenticeship or other training or retraining, including on the job training programs, to print or publish or cause to be printed or published any notice or advertisement relating to employment by such an employer or membership in or any classification or referral for employment by such a labor organization, or relating to any classification or referral for employment by such an employment agency, or relating to admission to, or employment in, any program established to provide apprenticeship or other training by such a joint labor management committee, indicating any preference, limitation, specification, or discrimination, based on race, color, religion, sex, or national origin, except that such a notice or advertisement may indicate a preference, limitation, specification, or discrimination based on religion, sex, or national origin when religion, sex, or national origin is a bona fide occupational qualification for employment.

EQUAL EMPLOYMENT OPPORTUNITY COMMISSION

SEC. 2000e-4. *[Section 705].*

(a) There is hereby created a Commission to be known as the Equal Employment Opportunity Commission, which shall be composed of five members, not more than three of whom shall be members of the same political party. Members of the Commission shall be appointed by the President by and with the advice and consent of the Senate for a term of five years. Any individual chosen to fill a vacancy shall be appointed only for the unexpired term of the member whom he shall succeed, and all members of the Commission shall continue to serve until their successors are appointed and qualified, except that no such member of the Commission shall continue to serve (1) for more than sixty days when the Congress is in session unless a nomination to fill such vacancy shall have been submitted to the Senate, or (2) after the adjournment sine die of the session of the Senate in which such nomination was submitted. The President shall designate one member to serve as Chairman of the Commission, and one member to serve as Vice Chairman. The Chairman shall be responsible on behalf of the Commission for the administrative operations of the Commission, and, except as provided in subsection (b) of this section, shall appoint, in accordance with the provisions of title 5 *[United States Code]* governing appointments in the competitive service, such officers, agents, attorneys, administrative law judges *[hearing examiners],* and employees as he deems necessary to assist it in the performance of its functions and to fix their compensation in accordance with the provisions of chapter 51 and subchapter III of chapter 53 of title 5 *[United States Code],* relating to classification and General Schedule pay rates: Provided, That assignment, removal, and compensation of administrative law judges *[hearing examiners]* shall be in accordance with sections 3105, 3344, 5372, and 7521 of title 5 *[United States Code].*

(b) (1) There shall be a General Counsel of the Commission appointed by the President, by and with the advice and consent of the Senate, for a term of four years. The General Counsel shall have responsibility for the conduct of litigation as provided in sections 2000e-5 and 2000e-6 of this title *[sections 706 and 707].* The General Counsel shall have such other duties as the Commission may prescribe or as may be provided by law and shall concur with the Chairman of the Commission on the appointment and supervision of regional attorneys. The General Counsel of the Commission on the effective date of this Act shall continue in such position and perform the functions specified in this subsection until a successor is appointed and qualified.

　(2) Attorneys appointed under this section may, at the direction of the Commission, appear for and represent the Commission in any case in court, provided that the Attorney General shall conduct all litigation to which the Commission is a party in the Supreme Court pursuant to this subchapter.

(c) A vacancy in the Commission shall not impair the right of the remaining members to exercise all the powers of the Commission and three members thereof shall constitute a quorum.

(d) The Commission shall have an official seal which shall be judicially noticed.

(e) The Commission shall at the close of each fiscal year report to the Congress and to the President concerning the action it has taken *[the names, salaries, and duties of all individuals in its employ]* and the moneys it has disbursed. It shall make such further reports on the cause of and means of eliminating discrimination and such recommendations for further legislation as may appear desirable.

(f) The principal office of the Commission shall be in or near the District of Columbia, but it may meet or exercise any or all its powers at any other place. The Commission may establish such regional or State offices as it deems necessary to accomplish the purpose of this subchapter.

(g) The Commission shall have power-

(1) to cooperate with and, with their consent, utilize regional, State, local, and other agencies, both public and private, and individuals;

(2) to pay to witnesses whose depositions are taken or who are summoned before the Commission or any of its agents the same witness and mileage fees as are paid to witnesses in the courts of the United States;

(3) to furnish to persons subject to this subchapter such technical assistance as they may request to further their compliance with this subchapter or an order issued thereunder;

(4) upon the request of (i) any employer, whose employees or some of them, or (ii) any labor organization, whose members or some of them, refuse or threaten to refuse to cooperate in effectuating the provisions of this subchapter, to assist in such effectuation by conciliation or such other remedial action as is provided by this subchapter;

(5) to make such technical studies as are appropriate to effectuate the purposes and policies of this subchapter and to make the results of such studies available to the public;

(6) to intervene in a civil action brought under section 2000e-5 of this title *[section 706]* by an aggrieved party against a respondent other than a government, governmental agency or political subdivision.

(h) **(1)** The Commission shall, in any of its educational or promotional activities, cooperate with other departments and agencies in the performance of such educational and promotional activities.

(2) In exercising its powers under this title, the Commission shall carry out educational and outreach activities (including dissemination of information in languages other than English) targeted to-

(A) individuals who historically have been victims of employment discrimination and have not been equitably served by the Commission; and

(B) individuals on whose behalf the Commission has authority to enforce any other law prohibiting employment discrimination, concerning rights and obligations under this title or such law, as the case may be.

(i) All officers, agents, attorneys, and employees of the Commission shall be subject to the provisions of section 7324 of title 5 *[section 9 of the Act of August 2, 1939, as amended (the Hatch Act)]*, notwithstanding any exemption contained in such section.

(j) (1) The Commission shall establish a Technical Assistance Training Institute, through which the Commission shall provide technical assistance and training regarding the laws and regulations enforced by the Commission.

(2) An employer or other entity covered under this title shall not be excused from compliance with the requirements of this title because of any failure to receive technical assistance under this subsection.

(3) There are authorized to be appropriated to carry out this subsection such sums as may be necessary for fiscal year 1992.

ENFORCEMENT PROVISIONS

SEC. 2000e-5. *[Section 706]*.

(a) The Commission is empowered, as hereinafter provided, to prevent any person from engaging in any unlawful employment practice as set forth in section 2000e-2 or 2000e-3 of this title *[section 703 or 704]*.

(b) Whenever a charge is filed by or on behalf of a person claiming to be aggrieved, or by a member of the Commission, alleging that an employer, employment agency, labor organization, or joint labor management committee controlling apprenticeship or other training or retraining, including on the job training programs, has engaged in an unlawful employment practice, the Commission shall serve a notice of the charge (including the date, place and circumstances of the alleged unlawful employment practice) on such employer, employment agency, labor organization, or joint labor management committee (hereinafter referred to as the "respondent") within ten days, and shall make an investigation thereof. Charges shall be in writing under oath or affirmation and shall contain such information and be in such form as the Commission requires. Charges shall not be made public by the Commission. If the Commission determines after such investigation that there is not reasonable cause to believe that the charge is true, it shall dismiss the charge and promptly notify the person claiming to be aggrieved and the respondent of its action. In determining whether reasonable cause exists, the Commission shall accord substantial weight to final findings and orders made by State or local authorities in proceedings commenced under State or local law pursuant to the requirements of subsections (c) and (d) of this section. If the Commission determines after such investigation that there is reasonable cause to believe that the charge is true, the Commission shall endeavor to eliminate any such alleged unlawful employment practice by informal methods of conference, conciliation, and persuasion. Nothing said or done during and as a part of such informal endeavors may be made public by the Commission, its officers or employees, or used as evidence in a subsequent proceeding without the written consent of the persons concerned. Any person who makes public information in violation of this subsection shall be fined not more than $1,000 or imprisoned for not more than one year, or both. The Commission shall make its determination on reasonable cause as promptly as possible and, so far as practicable, not later than one hundred and twenty days from the filing of the charge or, where applicable under subsection (c) or (d) of this section, from the date upon which the Commission is authorized to take action with respect to the charge.

(c) In the case of an alleged unlawful employment practice occurring in a State, or political subdivision of a State, which has a State or local law prohibiting the unlawful employment practice alleged and establishing or authorizing a State or local authority to grant or seek relief from such practice or to institute criminal proceedings with respect thereto upon receiving notice thereof, no charge may be filed under subsection (a) of this section by the person aggrieved before the expiration of sixty days after proceedings have been commenced under the State or local law, unless such proceedings have been earlier terminated, provided that such sixty day period shall be extended to one hundred and twenty days during the first year after the effective date of such State or local law. If any requirement for the commencement of such proceedings is imposed by a State or local authority other than a requirement of the filing of a written and signed statement of the facts upon which the proceeding is based, the proceeding shall be deemed to have been commenced for the purposes of this subsection at the time such statement is sent by registered mail to the appropriate State or local authority.

(d) In the case of any charge filed by a member of the Commission alleging an unlawful employment practice occurring in a State or political subdivision of a State which has a State or local law prohibiting the practice alleged and establishing or authorizing a State or local authority to grant or seek relief from such practice or to institute criminal proceedings with respect thereto upon receiving notice thereof, the Commission shall, before taking any action with respect to such charge, notify the appropriate State or local officials and, upon request, afford them a reasonable time, but not less than sixty days (provided that such sixty day period shall be extended to one hundred and twenty days during the first year after the effective day of such State or local law), unless a shorter period is requested, to act under such State or local law to remedy the practice alleged.

(e) **(1)** A charge under this section shall be filed within one hundred and eighty days after the alleged unlawful employment practice occurred and notice of the charge (including the date, place and circumstances of the alleged unlawful employment practice) shall be served upon the person against whom such charge is made within ten days thereafter, except that in a case

of an unlawful employment practice with respect to which the person aggrieved has initially instituted proceedings with a State or local agency with authority to grant or seek relief from such practice or to institute criminal proceedings with respect thereto upon receiving notice thereof, such charge shall be filed by or on behalf of the person aggrieved within three hundred days after the alleged unlawful employment practice occurred, or within thirty days after receiving notice that the State or local agency has terminated the proceedings under the State or local law, whichever is earlier, and a copy of such charge shall be filed by the Commission with the State or local agency.

(2) For purposes of this section, an unlawful employment practice occurs, with respect to a seniority system that has been adopted for an intentionally discriminatory purpose in violation of this title (whether or not that discriminatory purpose is apparent on the face of the seniority provision), when the seniority system is adopted, when an individual becomes subject to the seniority system, or when a person aggrieved is injured by the application of the seniority system or provision of the system.

(f) (1) If within thirty days after a charge is filed with the Commission or within thirty days after expiration of any period of reference under subsection (c) or (d) of this section, the Commission has been unable to secure from the respondent a conciliation agreement acceptable to the Commission, the Commission may bring a civil action against any respondent not a government, governmental agency, or political subdivision named in the charge. In the case of a respondent which is a government, governmental agency, or political subdivision, if the Commission has been unable to secure from the respondent a conciliation agreement acceptable to the Commission, the Commission shall take no further action and shall refer the case to the Attorney General who may bring a civil action against such respondent in the appropriate United States district court. The person or persons aggrieved shall have the right to intervene in a civil action brought by the Commission or the Attorney General in a case involving a government, governmental agency, or political subdivision. If a charge filed with the Commission pursuant to subsection (b) of this section, is dismissed by the Commission, or if within one hundred and eighty days from the filing of such charge or the expiration of any period of reference under subsection (c) or (d) of this section, whichever is later, the Commission has not filed a civil action under this section or the Attorney General has not filed a civil action in a case involving a government, governmental agency, or political subdivision, or the Commission has not entered into a conciliation agreement to which the person aggrieved is a party, the Commission, or the Attorney General in a case involving a government, governmental agency, or political subdivision, shall so notify the person aggrieved and within ninety days after the giving of such notice a civil action may be brought against the respondent named in the charge (A) by the person claiming to be aggrieved or (B) if such charge was filed by a member of the Commission, by any person whom the charge alleges was aggrieved by the alleged unlawful employment practice. Upon application by the complainant and in such circumstances as the court may deem just, the court may appoint an attorney for such complainant and may authorize the commencement of the action without the payment of fees, costs, or security. Upon timely application, the court may, in its discretion, permit the Commission, or the Attorney General in a case involving a government, governmental agency, or political subdivision, to intervene in such civil action upon certification that the case is of general public importance. Upon request, the court may, in its discretion, stay further proceedings for not more than sixty days pending the termination of State or local proceedings described in subsection (c) or (d) of this section or further efforts of the Commission to obtain voluntary compliance.

(2) Whenever a charge is filed with the Commission and the Commission concludes on the basis of a preliminary investigation that prompt judicial action is necessary to carry out the purposes of this Act, the Commission, or the Attorney General in a case involving a government, governmental agency, or political subdivision, may bring an action for appropriate temporary or preliminary relief pending final disposition of such charge. Any temporary restraining order or other order granting preliminary or temporary relief shall be issued in accordance with rule 65 of the Federal Rules of Civil Procedure. It shall be the duty of a court having jurisdiction over

proceedings under this section to assign cases for hearing at the earliest practicable date and to cause such cases to be in every way expedited.

(3) Each United States district court and each United States court of a place subject to the jurisdiction of the United States shall have jurisdiction of actions brought under this subchapter. Such an action may be brought in any judicial district in the State in which the unlawful employment practice is alleged to have been committed, in the judicial district in which the employment records relevant to such practice are maintained and administered, or in the judicial district in which the aggrieved person would have worked but for the alleged unlawful employment practice, but if the respondent is not found within any such district, such an action may be brought within the judicial district in which the respondent has his principal office. For purposes of sections 1404 and 1406 of title 28 *[of the United States Code]*, the judicial district in which the respondent has his principal office shall in all cases be considered a district in which the action might have been brought.

(4) It shall be the duty of the chief judge of the district (or in his absence, the acting chief judge) in which the case is pending immediately to designate a judge in such district to hear and determine the case. In the event that no judge in the district is available to hear and determine the case, the chief judge of the district, or the acting chief judge, as the case may be, shall certify this fact to the chief judge of the circuit (or in his absence, the acting chief judge) who shall then designate a district or circuit judge of the circuit to hear and determine the case.

(5) It shall be the duty of the judge designated pursuant to this subsection to assign the case for hearing at the earliest practicable date and to cause the case to be in every way expedited. If such judge has not scheduled the case for trial within one hundred and twenty days after issue has been joined, that judge may appoint a master pursuant to rule 53 of the Federal Rules of Civil Procedure.

(g) **(1)** If the court finds that the respondent has intentionally engaged in or is intentionally engaging in an unlawful employment practice charged in the complaint, the court may enjoin the respondent from engaging in such unlawful employment practice, and order such affirmative action as may be appropriate, which may include, but is not limited to, reinstatement or hiring of employees, with or without back pay (payable by the employer, employment agency, or labor organization, as the case may be, responsible for the unlawful employment practice), or any other equitable relief as the court deems appropriate. Back pay liability shall not accrue from a date more than two years prior to the filing of a charge with the Commission. Interim earnings or amounts earnable with reasonable diligence by the person or persons discriminated against shall operate to reduce the back pay otherwise allowable.

(2) (A) No order of the court shall require the admission or reinstatement of an individual as a member of a union, or the hiring, reinstatement, or promotion of an individual as an employee, or the payment to him of any back pay, if such individual was refused admission, suspended, or expelled, or was refused employment or advancement or was suspended or discharged for any reason other than discrimination on account of race, color, religion, sex, or national origin or in violation of section 2000e-3(a) of this title *[section 704(a)]*.

(B) On a claim in which an individual proves a violation under section 2000e-2(m) of this title *[section 703(m)]* and a respondent demonstrates that the respondent would have taken the same action in the absence of the impermissible motivating factor, the court-

(i) may grant declaratory relief, injunctive relief (except as provided in clause (ii)), and attorney's fees and costs demonstrated to be directly attributable only to the pursuit of a claim under section 2000e-2(m) of this title *[section 703(m)]*; and

(ii) shall not award damages or issue an order requiring any admission, reinstatement, hiring, promotion, or payment, described in subparagraph (A).

(h) The provisions of chapter 6 of title 29 *[the Act entitled "An Act to amend the Judicial Code and to define and limit the jurisdiction of courts sitting in equity, and for other purposes," approved March 23, 1932 (29 U.S.C. 105-115)]* shall not apply with respect to civil actions brought under this section.

(i) In any case in which an employer, employment agency, or labor organization fails to comply with an order of a court issued in a civil action brought under this section, the Commission may commence proceedings to compel compliance with such order.

(j) Any civil action brought under this section and any proceedings brought under subsection (i) of this section shall be subject to appeal as provided in sections 1291 and 1292, title 28 *[United States Code].*

(k) In any action or proceeding under this subchapter the court, in its discretion, may allow the prevailing party, other than the Commission or the United States, a reasonable attorney's fee **(including expert fees)** as part of the costs, and the Commission and the United States shall be liable for costs the same as a private person.

CIVIL ACTIONS BY THE ATTORNEY GENERAL
SEC. 2000e-6. *[Section 707].*

(a) Whenever the Attorney General has reasonable cause to believe that any person or group of persons is engaged in a pattern or practice of resistance to the full enjoyment of any of the rights secured by this subchapter, and that the pattern or practice is of such a nature and is intended to deny the full exercise of the rights herein described, the Attorney General may bring a civil action in the appropriate district court of the United States by filing with it a complaint (1) signed by him (or in his absence the Acting Attorney General), (2) setting forth facts pertaining to such pattern or practice, and (3) requesting such relief, including an application for a permanent or temporary injunction, restraining order or other order against the person or persons responsible for such pattern or practice, as he deems necessary to insure the full enjoyment of the rights herein described.

(b) The district courts of the United States shall have and shall exercise jurisdiction of proceedings instituted pursuant to this section, and in any such proceeding the Attorney General may file with the clerk of such court a request that a court of three judges be convened to hear and determine the case. Such request by the Attorney General shall be accompanied by a certificate that, in his opinion, the case is of general public importance. A copy of the certificate and request for a three judge court shall be immediately furnished by such clerk to the chief judge of the circuit (or in his absence, the presiding circuit judge of the circuit) in which the case is pending. Upon receipt of such request it shall be the duty of the chief judge of the circuit or the presiding circuit judge, as the case may be, to designate immediately three judges in such circuit, of whom at least one shall be a circuit judge and another of whom shall be a district judge of the court in which the proceeding was instituted, to hear and determine such case, and it shall be the duty of the judges so designated to assign the case for hearing at the earliest practicable date, to participate in the hearing and determination thereof, and to cause the case to be in every way expedited. An appeal from the final judgment of such court will lie to the Supreme Court.

In the event the Attorney General fails to file such a request in any such proceeding, it shall be the duty of the chief judge of the district (or in his absence, the acting chief judge) in which the case is pending immediately to designate a judge in such district to hear and determine the case. In the event that no judge in the district is available to hear and determine the case, the chief judge of the district, or the acting chief judge, as the case may be, shall certify this fact to the chief judge of the circuit (or in his absence, the acting chief judge) who shall then designate a district or circuit judge of the circuit to hear and determine the case.

It shall be the duty of the judge designated pursuant to this section to assign the case for hearing at the earliest practicable date and to cause the case to be in every way expedited.

(c) Effective two years after March 24, 1972 *[the date of enactment of the Equal Employment Opportunity Act of 1972],* the functions of the Attorney General under this section shall be transferred to the Commission, together with such personnel, property, records, and unexpended balances of appropriations, allocations, and other funds employed, used, held, available, or to be made available in connection with such functions unless the President submits, and neither House of Congress vetoes, a reorganization plan pursuant to chapter 9 of title 5 *[United States Code],* inconsistent with the provisions of this subsection. The Commission shall carry out such functions in accordance with subsections (d) and (e) of this section.

(d) Upon the transfer of functions provided for in subsection (c) of this section, in all suits commenced pursuant to this section prior to the date of such transfer, proceedings shall continue without abatement, all court orders and decrees shall remain in effect, and the Commission shall be substituted as a party for the United States of America, the Attorney General, or the Acting Attorney General, as appropriate.

(e) Subsequent to March 24, 1972 *[the date of enactment of the Equal Employment Opportunity Act of 1972]*, the Commission shall have authority to investigate and act on a charge of a pattern or practice of discrimination, whether filed by or on behalf of a person claiming to be aggrieved or by a member of the Commission. All such actions shall be conducted in accordance with the procedures set forth in section 2000e-5 of this title *[section 706]*.

EFFECT ON STATE LAWS

SEC. 2000e-7. *[Section 708]*. Nothing in this subchapter shall be deemed to exempt or relieve any person from any liability, duty, penalty, or punishment provided by any present or future law of any State or political subdivision of a State, other than any such law which purports to require or permit the doing of any act which would be an unlawful employment practice under this subchapter.

INVESTIGATIONS, INSPECTIONS, RECORDS, STATE AGENCIES

SEC. 2000e-8. *[Section 709]*.

(a) In connection with any investigation of a charge filed under section 2000e-5 of this title *[section 706]*, the Commission or its designated representative shall at all reasonable times have access to, for the purposes of examination, and the right to copy any evidence of any person being investigated or proceeded against that relates to unlawful employment practices covered by this subchapter and is relevant to the charge under investigation.

(b) The Commission may cooperate with State and local agencies charged with the administration of State fair employment practices laws and, with the consent of such agencies, may, for the purpose of carrying out its functions and duties under this subchapter and within the limitation of funds appropriated specifically for such purpose, engage in and contribute to the cost of research and other projects of mutual interest undertaken by such agencies, and utilize the services of such agencies and their employees, and, notwithstanding any other provision of law, pay by advance or reimbursement such agencies and their employees for services rendered to assist the Commission in carrying out this subchapter. In furtherance of such cooperative efforts, the Commission may enter into written agreements with such State or local agencies and such agreements may include provisions under which the Commission shall refrain from processing a charge in any cases or class of cases specified in such agreements or under which the Commission shall relieve any person or class of persons in such State or locality from requirements imposed under this section. The Commission shall rescind any such agreement whenever it determines that the agreement no longer serves the interest of effective enforcement of this subchapter.

(c) Every employer, employment agency, and labor organization subject to this subchapter shall (1) make and keep such records relevant to the determinations of whether unlawful employment practices have been or are being committed, (2) preserve such records for such periods, and (3) make such reports therefrom as the Commission shall prescribe by regulation or order, after public hearing, as reasonable, necessary, or appropriate for the enforcement of this subchapter or the regulations or orders thereunder. The Commission shall, by regulation, require each employer, labor organization, and joint labor management committee subject to this subchapter which controls an apprenticeship or other training program to maintain such records as are reasonably necessary to carry out the purposes of this subchapter, including, but not limited to, a list of applicants who wish to participate in such program, including the chronological order in which applications were received, and to furnish to the Commission upon request, a detailed description of the manner in which persons are selected to participate in the apprenticeship or other training program. Any employer, employment agency, labor organization, or joint labor management committee which believes that the application to it of any regulation or order issued under this section would result in undue hardship may apply to the Commission for an exemption from the application of such regulation or order, and, if such application for an exemption is denied, bring a civil action in the United States district court for the district where such records are kept. If the Commission or the court, as the case may be, finds that the application of the regulation or order to the employer, employment agency, or labor organization in question would impose an undue hardship, the Commission or the court, as the case may be, may grant appropriate relief. If any person required to comply with the provisions of this subsection fails or refuses to do so, the United States district court for the district in which such person is found, resides, or transacts business, shall, upon application of the Commission, or the Attorney General in a case involving a government, governmental agency or political subdivision, have jurisdiction to issue to such person an order requiring him to comply.

(d) In prescribing requirements pursuant to subsection (c) of this section, the Commission shall consult with other interested State and Federal agencies and shall endeavor to coordinate its requirements with those adopted by such agencies. The Commission shall furnish upon request and without cost to any State or local agency charged with the administration of a fair employment practice law information obtained pursuant to subsection (c) of this section from any employer, employment agency, labor organization, or joint labor management committee subject to the jurisdiction of such agency. Such information shall be furnished on condition that it not be made public by the recipient agency prior to the institution of a proceeding under State or local law involving such information. If this condition is violated by a recipient agency, the Commission may decline to honor subsequent requests pursuant to this subsection.

(e) It shall be unlawful for any officer or employee of the Commission to make public in any manner whatever any information obtained by the Commission pursuant to its authority under this section prior to the institution of any proceeding under this subchapter involving such information. Any officer or employee of the Commission who shall make public in any manner whatever any information in violation of this subsection shall be guilty, of a misdemeanor and upon conviction thereof, shall be fined not more than $1,000, or imprisoned not more than one year.

INVESTIGATORY POWERS

SEC. 2000e-9. *[Section 710].* For the purpose of all hearings and investigations conducted by the Commission or its duly authorized agents or agencies, section 161 of title 29 *[section 11 of the National Labor Relations Act]* shall apply.

POSTING OF NOTICES; PENALTIES

SEC. 2000e-10. *[Section 711].*

(a) Every employer, employment agency, and labor organization, as the case may be, shall post and keep posted in conspicuous places upon its premises where notices to employees, applicants for employment, and members are customarily posted a notice to be prepared or approved by the Commission setting forth excerpts, from or, summaries of, the pertinent provisions of this subchapter and information pertinent to the filing of a complaint.

(b) A willful violation of this section shall be punishable by a fine of not more than $100 for each separate offense.

VETERANS' SPECIAL RIGHTS OR PREFERENCE

SEC. 2000e-11. *[Section 712].* Nothing contained in this subchapter shall be construed to repeal or modify any Federal, State, territorial, or local law creating special rights or preference for veterans.

RULES AND REGULATIONS

SEC. 2000e-12. *[Section 713].*

(a) The Commission shall have authority from time to time to issue, amend, or rescind suitable procedural regulations to carry out the provisions of this subchapter. Regulations issued under this section shall be in conformity with the standards and limitations of subchapter II of chapter 5 of title 5 *[the Administrative Procedure Act].*

(b) In any action or proceeding based on any alleged unlawful employment practice, no person shall be subject to any liability or punishment for or on account of (1) the commission by such person of an unlawful employment practice if he pleads and proves that the act or omission complained of was in good faith, in conformity with, and in reliance on any written interpretation or opinion of the Commission, or (2) the failure of such person to publish and file any information required by any provision of this subchapter if he pleads and proves that he failed to publish and file such information in good faith, in conformity with the instructions of the Commission issued under this subchapter regarding the filing of such information. Such a defense, if established, shall be a bar to the action or proceeding, notwithstanding that (A) after such act or omission, such interpretation or opinion is modified or rescinded or is determined by judicial authority to be invalid or of no legal effect, or (B) after publishing or filing the description and annual reports, such publication or filing is determined by judicial authority not to be in conformity with the requirements of this subchapter.

FORCIBLY RESISTING THE COMMISSION OR ITS REPRESENTATIVES

SEC. 2000e-13. *[Section 714].* The provisions of sections 111 and 1114, title 18 *[United States Code],* shall apply to officers, agents, and employees of the Commission in the performance of their official duties. Notwithstanding the provisions of sections 111 and 1114 of title 18 *[United States Code],* whoever in violation of the provisions of section 1114 of such title kills a person while engaged in or on account of the performance of his official functions under this Act shall be punished by imprisonment for any term of years or for life.

TRANSFER OF AUTHORITY

[Administration of the duties of the Equal Employment Opportunity Coordinating Council was transferred to the Equal Employment Opportunity Commission effective July 1, 1978, under the President's Reorganization Plan of 1978.]

EQUAL EMPLOYMENT OPPORTUNITY COORDINATING COUNCIL

SEC. 2000e-14. *[Section 715].* *[There shall be established an Equal Employment Opportunity Coordinating Council (hereinafter referred to in this section as the Council) composed of the Secretary of Labor, the Chairman of the Equal Employment Opportunity Commission, the Attorney General, the Chairman of the United States Civil Service Commission, and the Chairman of the United States Civil Rights Commission, or their respective delegates.]*

The Equal Employment Opportunity Commission *[Council]* shall have the responsibility for developing and implementing agreements, policies and practices designed to maximize effort, promote efficiency, and eliminate conflict, competition, duplication and inconsistency among the operations, functions and jurisdictions of the various departments, agencies and branches of the Federal Government responsible for the implementation and enforcement of equal employment opportunity legislation, orders, and policies. On or before October 1 *[July 1]* of each year, the Equal Employment Opportunity Commission *[Council]* shall transmit to the President and to the Congress a report of its activities, together with such recommendations for legislative or administrative changes as it concludes are desirable to further promote the purposes of this section.

EFFECTIVE DATE

SEC. 2000e-15. *[Section 716]*.

[(a) This title shall become effective one year after the date of its enactment.
(b) Notwithstanding subsection (a), sections of this title other than sections 703, 704, 706, and 707 shall become effective immediately.
(c)] The President shall, as soon as feasible after July 2, 1964 *[the enactment of this title]*, convene one or more conferences for the purpose of enabling the leaders of groups whose members will be affected by this subchapter to become familiar with the rights afforded and obligations imposed by its provisions, and for the purpose of making plans which will result in the fair and effective administration of this subchapter when all of its provisions become effective. The President shall invite the participation in such conference or conferences of (1) the members of the President's Committee on Equal Employment Opportunity, (2) the members of the Commission on Civil Rights, (3) representatives of State and local agencies engaged in furthering equal employment opportunity, (4) representatives of private agencies engaged in furthering equal employment opportunity, and (5) representatives of employers, labor organizations, and employment agencies who will be subject to this subchapter.

TRANSFER OF AUTHORITY

[Enforcement of Section 717 was transferred to the Equal Employment Opportunity Commission from the Civil Service Commission (Office of Personnel Management) effective January 1, 1979 under the President's Reorganization Plan No. 1 of 1978.]

EMPLOYMENT BY FEDERAL GOVERNMENT

SEC. 2000e-16. *[Section 717]*.

(a) All personnel actions affecting employees or applicants for employment (except with regard to aliens employed outside the limits of the United States) in military departments as defined in section 102 of title 5 *[United States Code]*, in executive agencies *[other than the General Accounting Office]* as defined in section 105 of title 5 *[United States Code]* (including employees and applicants for employment who are paid from nonappropriated funds), in the United States Postal Service and the Postal Rate Commission, in those units of the Government of the District of Columbia having positions in the competitive service, and in those units of the legislative and judicial branches of the Federal Government having positions in the competitive service, and in the Library of Congress shall be made free from any discrimination based on race, color, religion, sex, or national origin.

(b) Except as otherwise provided in this subsection, the Equal Employment Opportunity Commission *[Civil Service Commission]* shall have authority to enforce the provisions of subsection (a) of this section through appropriate remedies, including reinstatement or hiring of employees with or without back pay, as will effectuate the policies of this section, and shall issue such rules, regulations, orders and instructions as it deems necessary and appropriate to carry out its responsibilities under this section. The Equal Employment Opportunity Commission *[Civil Service Commission]* shall-

(1) be responsible for the annual review and approval of a national and regional equal employment opportunity plan which each department and agency and each appropriate unit referred to in subsection (a) of this section shall submit in order to maintain an affirmative program of equal employment opportunity for all such employees and applicants for employment;

(2) be responsible for the review and evaluation of the operation of all agency equal employment opportunity programs, periodically obtaining and publishing (on at least a semiannual basis) progress reports from each such department, agency, or unit; and

(3) consult with and solicit the recommendations of interested individuals, groups, and organizations relating to equal employment opportunity.

The head of each such department, agency, or unit shall comply with such rules, regulations, orders, and instructions which shall include a provision that an employee or applicant for employment shall be notified of any final action taken on any complaint of discrimination filed by him thereunder. The plan submitted by each department, agency, and unit shall include, but not be limited to-

(1) provision for the establishment of training and education programs designed to provide a maximum opportunity for employees to advance so as to perform at their highest potential; and

(2) a description of the qualifications in terms of training and experience relating to equal employment opportunity for the principal and operating officials of each such department, agency, or unit responsible for carrying out the equal employment opportunity program and of the allocation of personnel and resources proposed by such department, agency, or unit to carry out its equal employment opportunity program.

With respect to employment in the Library of Congress, authorities granted in this subsection to the Equal Employment Opportunity Commission *[Civil Service Commission]* shall be exercised by the Librarian of Congress.

(c) Within **90 days** of receipt of notice of final action taken by a department, agency, or unit referred to in subsection (a) of this section, or by the Equal Employment Opportunity Commission *[Civil Service Commission]* upon an appeal from a decision or order of such department, agency, or unit on a complaint of discrimination based on race, color, religion, sex or national origin, brought pursuant to subsection (a) of this section, Executive Order 11478 or any succeeding Executive orders, or after one hundred and eighty days from the filing of the initial charge with the department, agency, or unit or with the Equal Employment Opportunity Commission *[Civil Service Commission]* on appeal from a decision or order of such department, agency, or unit until such time as final action may be taken by a department, agency, or unit, an employee or applicant for employment, if aggrieved by the final disposition of his complaint, or by the failure to take final action on his complaint, may file a civil action as provided in section 2000e-5 of this title *[section 706],* in which civil action the head of the department, agency, or unit, as appropriate, shall be the defendant.

(d) The provisions of section 2000e-5(f) through (k) of this title *[section 706(f) through (k)],* as applicable, shall govern civil actions brought hereunder, **and the same interest to compensate for delay in payment shall be available as in cases involving nonpublic parties.**

(e) Nothing contained in this Act shall relieve any Government agency or official of its or his primary responsibility to assure nondiscrimination in employment as required by the Constitution and statutes or of its or his responsibilities under Executive Order 11478 relating to equal employment opportunity in the Federal Government.

SPECIAL PROVISIONS WITH RESPECT TO DENIAL, TERMINATION, AND SUSPENSION OF GOVERNMENT CONTRACTS

SEC. 2000e-17. *[Section 718].* No Government contract, or portion thereof, with any employer, shall be denied, withheld, terminated, or suspended, by any agency or officer of the United States under any equal employment opportunity law or order, where such employer has an affirmative action plan which has previously been accepted by the Government for the same facility within the past twelve months without first according such employer full hearing and adjudication under the provisions of section 554 of title 5 *[United States Code],* and the following pertinent sections: Provided, That if such employer has deviated substantially from such previously agreed to affirmative action plan, this section shall not apply: Provided further, That for the purposes of this section an affirmative action plan shall be deemed to have been accepted by the Government at the time the appropriate compliance agency has accepted such plan unless within forty five days thereafter the Office of Federal Contract Compliance has disapproved such plan.

Appendix D

THE CIVIL RIGHTS ACT OF 1991

The U.S. Equal Employment Opportunity Commission.

Title I—Federal Civil Rights Remedies

PROHIBITION AGAINST ALL RACIAL DISCRIMINATION IN THE MAKING AND ENFORCEMENT OF CONTRACTS

SEC. 101. Section 1977 of the Revised Statutes (42 U.S.C. 1981) is amended-

(1) by inserting "(a)" before "All persons within"; and

(2) by adding at the end the following new subsections:

"(b) For purposes of this section, the term 'make and enforce contracts' includes the making, performance, modification, and termination of contracts, and the enjoyment of all benefits, privileges, terms, and conditions of the contractual relationship.

"(c) The rights protected by this section are protected against impairment by nongovernmental discrimination and impairment under color of State law."

DAMAGES IN CASES OF INTENTIONAL DISCRIMINATION

SEC. 102. The Revised Statutes are amended by inserting after section 1977 (42 U.S.C. 1981) the following new section:

"SEC. 1977A. DAMAGES IN CASES OF INTENTIONAL DISCRIMINATION IN EMPLOYMENT. *[42 U.S.C. 1981a]*

"(a) Right of Recovery. -

"(1) Civil Rights. - In an action brought by a complaining party under section 706 or 717 of the Civil Rights Act of 1964 (42 U.S.C. 2000e-5) against a respondent who engaged in unlawful intentional discrimination (not an employment practice that is unlawful because of its disparate impact) prohibited under section 703, 704, or 717 of the Act (42 U.S.C. 2000e-2 or 2000e-3), and provided that the complaining party cannot recover under section 1977 of the Revised Statutes (42 U.S.C. 1981), the complaining party may recover compensatory and punitive damages as allowed in subsection (b), in addition to any relief authorized by section 706(g) of the Civil Rights Act of 1964, from the respondent.

"(2) Disability. - In an action brought by a complaining party under the powers, remedies, and procedures set forth in section 706 or 717 of the Civil Rights Act of 1964 (as provided in section 107(a) of the Americans with Disabilities Act of 1990 (42 U.S.C. 12117 (a)), and section 505(a)(1) of the Rehabilitation Act of 1973 (29 U.S.C. 794a(a)(1)), respectively) against a respondent who engaged in unlawful intentional discrimination (not an employment practice that is unlawful because of its disparate impact) under section 501 of the Rehabilitation Act of 1973 (29 U.S.C. 791) and the regulations implementing section 501, or who violated the requirements of section 501 of the Act or the regulations implementing section 501 concerning the provision of a reasonable accommodation, or section 102 of the Americans with Disabilities Act of 1990 (42 U.S.C. 12112), or committed a violation of section 102(b)(5) of the Act, against an individual, the complaining party may recover compensatory and punitive damages as allowed in subsection (b), in addition to any relief authorized by section 706(g) of the Civil Rights Act of 1964, from the respondent.

"(3) Reasonable Accommodation and Good Faith Effort. - In cases where a discriminatory practice involves the provision of a reasonable accommodation pursuant to section 102(b)(5) of the Americans with Disabilities Act of 1990 or regulations implementing section 501 of the

Rehabilitation Act of 1973, damages may not be awarded under this section where the covered entity demonstrates good faith efforts, in consultation with the person with the disability who has informed the covered entity that accommodation is needed, to identify and make a reasonable accommodation that would provide such individual with an equally effective opportunity and would not cause an undue hardship on the operation of the business.

"(b) Compensatory and Punitive Damages. -

"(1) Determination of punitive damages. - A complaining party may recover punitive damages under this section against a respondent (other than a government, government agency or political subdivision) if the complaining party demonstrates that the respondent engaged in a discriminatory practice or discriminatory practices with malice or with reckless indifference to the federally protected rights of an aggrieved individual.

"(2) Exclusions from compensatory damages. - Compensatory damages awarded under this section shall not include back pay, interest on back pay, or any other type of relief authorized under section 706(g) of the Civil Rights Act of 1964.

"(3) Limitations. - The sum of the amount of compensatory damages awarded under this section for future pecuniary losses, emotional pain, suffering, inconvenience, mental anguish, loss of enjoyment of life, and other nonpecuniary losses, and the amount of punitive damages awarded under this section, shall not exceed, for each complaining party -

"(A) in the case of a respondent who has more than 14 and fewer than 101 employees in each of 20 or more calendar weeks in the current or preceding calendar year, $50,000;

"(B) in the case of a respondent who has more than 100 and fewer than 201 employees in each of 20 or more calendar weeks in the current or preceding calendar year, $100,000; and

"(C) in the case of a respondent who has more than 200 and fewer than 501 employees in each of 20 or more calendar weeks in the current or preceding calendar year, $200,000; and

"(D) in the case of a respondent who has more than 500 employees in each of 20 or more calendar weeks in the current or preceding calendar year, $300,000.

"(4) Construction. - Nothing in this section shall be construed to limit the scope of, or the relief available under, section 1977 of the Revised Statutes (42 U.S.C. 1981).

"(c) Jury Trial. - If a complaining party seeks compensatory or punitive damages under this section -

"(1) any party may demand a trial by jury; and

"(2) the court shall not inform the jury of the limitations described in subsection (b)(3).

"(d) Definitions. - As used in this section:

"(1) Complaining party. - The term 'complaining party' means -

"(A) in the case of a person seeking to bring an action under subsection (a)(1), the Equal Employment Opportunity Commission, the Attorney General, or a person who may bring an action or proceeding under title VII of the Civil Rights Act of 1964 (42 U.S.C. 2000e et seq.); or

"(B) in the case of a person seeking to bring an action under subsection (a)(2), the Equal Employment Opportunity Commission, the Attorney General, a person who may bring an action or proceeding under section 505(a)(1) of the Rehabilitation Act of 1973 (29 U.S.C. 794a(a)(1)), or a person who may bring an action or proceeding under title I of the Americans with Disabilities Act of 1990 (42 U.S.C. 12101 et seq.).

"(2) Discriminatory practice. - The term 'discriminatory practice' means the discrimination described in paragraph (1), or the discrimination or the violation described in paragraph (2), of subsection (a).

ATTORNEY'S FEES

[This section amends section 722 of the Revised Statutes (42 U.S.C. 1988) by adding a reference to section 102 of the Civil Rights Act of 1991 to the list of civil rights actions in which reasonable attorney's fees may be awarded to the prevailing party, other than the United States.]

SEC. 103. The last sentence of section 722 of the Revised Statutes (42 U.S.C. 1988) is amended by inserting ",1977A" after "1977".

DEFINITIONS

SEC. 104. *[This section amends section 701 of the Civil Rights Act of 1964 (42 U.S.C. 2000e) by adding the following new subsections: (l) "complaining party," (m) "demonstrates," and (n) "respondent".]*

BURDEN OF PROOF IN DISPARATE IMPACT CASES

SEC. 105.

(a) *[This subsection amends section 703 of the Civil Rights Act of 1964 (42 U.S.C. 2000e-2) by adding a new subsection (k), on the burden of proof in disparate impact cases.]*

(b) No statements other than the interpretive memorandum appearing at Vol. 137 Congressional Record S 15276 (daily ed. Oct. 25, 1991) shall be considered legislative history of, or relied upon in any way as legislative history in construing or applying, any provision of this Act that relates to Wards Cove - Business necessity/cumulation/alternative business practice. *[42 U.S.C. 1981 note]*

PROHIBITION AGAINST DISCRIMINATORY USE OF TEST SCORES

SEC. 106. *[This section amends section 703 of the Civil Rights Act of 1964 (42 U.S.C. 2000e-2) by adding a new subsection (l), on the prohibition against discriminatory use of test scores.]*

CLARIFYING PROHIBITION AGAINST IMPERMISSIBLE CONSIDERATION OF RACE, COLOR, RELIGION, SEX, OR NATIONAL ORIGIN IN EMPLOYMENT PRACTICES

SEC. 107.

(a) In general. *[This subsection amends section 703 of the Civil Rights Act of 1964 (42 U.S.C. 2000e-2) by adding a new subsection (m), clarifying the prohibition against consideration of race, color, religion, sex, or national origin in employment practices.]*

(b) Enforcement provisions. *[This subsection amends section 706(g) of the Civil Rights Act of 1964 (42 U.S.C. 2000e-5(g)) by renumbering existing subsection (g), and adding at the end a new subparagraph (B) to provide a limitation on available relief in "mixed motive" cases (where the employer demonstrates it would have made the same decision in the absence of discrimination).]*

FACILITATING PROMPT AND ORDERLY RESOLUTION OF CHALLENGES TO EMPLOYMENT PRACTICES IMPLEMENTING LITIGATED OR CONSENT JUDGMENTS OR ORDERS

SEC. 108. *[This section amends section 703 of the Civil Rights Act of 1964 (42 U.S.C. 2000e-2) by adding a new subsection (n), on the resolution of challenges to employment practices implementing litigated or consent judgments or orders.]*

PROTECTION OF EXTRATERRITORIAL EMPLOYMENT

SEC. 109.

(a) Definition of Employee. *[This subsection amends the definition of "employee" in section 701(f) of the Civil Rights Act of 1964 (42 U.S.C. 2000e(f)) and section 101(4) of the Americans with Disabilities Act of 1990 (42 U.S.C. 12111(4)) by adding a sentence to the end of each definition to include U.S. citizens employed abroad within the laws' protections.]*

(b) Exemption. *[This subsection amends section 702 of the Civil Rights Act of 1964 (42 U.S.C. 2000e-1) by adding new subsections (b) (on compliance with the statute if violative of foreign law) and (c) (on the control of a corporation incorporated in a foreign country). This subsection similarly amends section 102 of the Americans with Disabilities Act of 1990 (42 U.S.C. 12112) by relettering the existing subsections and adding a new subsection (c) "Covered Entities in Foreign Countries."]*

(c) Application of Amendments. - The amendments made by this section shall not apply with respect to conduct occurring before the date of the enactment of this Act. *[42 U.S.C. 2000e note]*

TECHNICAL ASSISTANCE TRAINING INSTITUTE

SEC. 110.

(a) Technical Assistance. *[This subsection amends section 705 of the Civil Rights Act of 1964 (42 U.S.C. 2000e-4) by adding a new subsection (j), establishing the Technical Assistance Training Institute.]*

(b) Effective Date. - The amendment made by this section shall take effect on the date of enactment of this Act. *[42 U.S.C. 2000e-4 note]*

EDUCATION AND OUTREACH

SEC. 111. *[This section amends section 705(h) of the Civil Rights Act of 1964 (42 U.S.C. 2000e-4(h)) by renumbering the existing subsection and adding at the end a paragraph requiring the EEOC to engage in certain educational and outreach activities.]*

EXPANSION OF RIGHT TO CHALLENGE DISCRIMINATORY SENIORITY SYSTEMS

SEC. 112. *[This section amends section 706(e) of the Civil Rights Act of 1964 (42 U.S.C. 2000e-5(e)) by renumbering the subsection and adding at the end a paragraph to expand the right of claimants to challenge discriminatory seniority systems.]*

AUTHORIZING AWARD OF EXPERT FEES

SEC. 113.

(a) Revised Statutes. - Section 722 of the Revised Statutes is amended-

　(1) by designating the first and second sentences as subsections (a) and (b), respectively, and indenting accordingly; and

　(2) by adding at the end the following new subsection:

　"(c) In awarding an attorney's fee under subsection (b) in any action or proceeding to enforce a provision of section 1977 or 1977A of the Revised Statutes, the court, in its discretion, may include expert fees as part of the attorney's fee." *[42 U.S.C. 1988]*

(b) Civil Rights Act of 1964. *[This section amends section 706(k) of the Civil Rights Act of 1964 (42 U.S.C. 2000e-5(k)) to provide for recovery of expert fees as part of an attorney's fees award.]*

PROVIDING FOR INTEREST AND EXTENDING THE STATUTE OF LIMITATIONS IN ACTIONS AGAINST THE FEDERAL GOVERNMENT

SEC. 114. *[This section amends section 717 of the Civil Rights Act of 1964 (42 U.S.C. 2000e-16) by extending the time for federal employees or applicants to file a civil action from 30 to 90 days (from receipt of notice of final action taken by a department, agency or unit), and allowing federal employees or applicants the same interest to compensate for delay in payments as is available in cases involving nonpublic parties.]*

NOTICE OF LIMITATIONS PERIOD UNDER THE AGE DISCRIMINATION IN EMPLOYMENT ACT OF 1967

SEC. 115. *[This section amends section 7(e) of the Age Discrimination in Employment Act of 1967 (ADEA) (29 U.S.C. 626(e)) by eliminating the two- and three-year statute of limitations and making ADEA suit-filing requirements the same as those under Title VII, and requiring the EEOC to provide notice to charging parties upon termination of the proceedings.]*

LAWFUL, COURT-ORDERED REMEDIES, AFFIRMATIVE ACTION, AND CONCILIATION AGREEMENTS NOT AFFECTED

SEC. 116 *[42 U.S.C. 1981 note].* Nothing in the amendments made by this title shall be construed to affect court-ordered remedies, affirmative action, or conciliation agreements, that are in accordance with the law.

COVERAGE OF HOUSE OF REPRESENTATIVES AND THE AGENCIES OF THE LEGISLATIVE BRANCH

SEC. 117.

(a) Coverage of the House of Representatives. *[This subsection extends the rights and protections of Title VII of the Civil Rights Act of 1964, as amended, to employees of the U.S. House of Representatives. Procedures for processing discrimination complaints are handled internally by the House, not by the EEOC.] [2 U.S.C. 60l]*

(b) Instrumentalities of Congress. *[This subsection extends the rights and protections of the Civil Rights Act of 1991 and Title VII of the Civil Rights Act of 1964, as amended, to "Instrumentalities of Congress," which are defined to include: the Architect of the Capitol, the Congressional Budget Office, the General Accounting Office, the Government Printing Office, the Office of Technology Assessment, and the United States Botanic Garden. Each agency is to establish its own remedies and procedures for enforcement.]*

ALTERNATIVE MEANS OF DISPUTE RESOLUTION

SEC. 118 *[42 U.S.C. 1981 note].* Where appropriate and to the extent authorized by law, the use of alternative means of dispute resolution, including settlement negotiations, conciliation, facilitation, mediation, fact finding, minitrials, and arbitration, is encouraged to resolve disputes arising under the Acts or provisions of Federal law amended by this title.

Title II—Glass Ceiling

[This title sets up a "Glass Ceiling Commission" to focus attention on, and complete a study relating to, the existence of artificial barriers to the advancement of women and minorities in the workplace, and to make recommendations for overcoming such barriers. The Commission is to be composed of 21 members, with the Secretary of Labor serving as the Chairperson of the Commission. This title does not directly impose any responsibilities or obligations on the EEOC except to provide information and technical assistance as requested by the new Commission.] [42 U.S.C. 2000e note]

Title III—Government Employee Rights

GOVERNMENT EMPLOYEE RIGHTS ACT OF 1991

SEC. 301 *[2 U.S.C. 1201].*

(a) Short title. - This title may be cited as the "Government Employee Rights Act of 1991".

(b) Purpose. - The purpose of this title is to provide procedures to protect the right of Senate and other government employees, with respect to their public employment, to be free of discrimination on the basis of race, color, religion, sex, national origin, age, or disability.

(c) Definitions. - For purposes of this title:

(1) Senate employee. - The term "Senate employee" or "employee" means -

(A) any employee whose pay is disbursed by the Secretary of the Senate;

(B) any employee of the Architect of the Capitol who is assigned to the Senate Restaurants or to the Superintendent of the Senate Office Buildings;

(C) any applicant for a position that will last 90 days or more and that is to be occupied by an individual described in subparagraph (A) or (B); or

(D) any individual who was formerly an employee described in subparagraph (A) or (B) and whose claim of a violation arises out of the individual's Senate employment.

(2) Head of employing office. - The term "head of employing office" means the individual who has final authority to appoint, hire, discharge, and set the terms, conditions or privileges of the Senate employment of an employee.

(3) Violation. - The term "violation" means a practice that violates section 302 of this title.

DISCRIMINATORY PRACTICES PROHIBITED

SEC. 302 [2 U.S.C. 1202]. *[Sections 320 and 321 (which protect Presidential appointees and previously exempt state employees who may file complaints of discrimination with EEOC under this title) refer to the rights, protections and remedies of this section and section 307(h).]*

All personnel actions affecting employees of the Senate shall be made free from any discrimination based on -

(1) race, color, religion, sex, or national origin, within the meaning of section 717 of the Civil Rights Act of 1964 (42 U.S.C. 2000e-16);

(2) age, within the meaning of section 15 of the Age Discrimination in Employment Act of 1967 (29 U.S.C. 633a); or

(3) handicap or disability, within the meaning of section 501 of the Rehabilitation Act of 1973 (29 U.S.C. 791) and sections 102–104 of the Americans with Disabilities Act of 1990 (42 U.S.C. 12112-14).

[SECTIONS 303 THROUGH 306: Section 303 (2 U.S.C. 1203) establishes the Office of Senate Fair Employment Practices, which will administer the procedures set forth in sections 304 through 307. Section 304 (2 U.S.C. 1204) outlines the four-step procedure described in Sections 305 through 309 for consideration of alleged violations. Section 305 (2 U.S.C. 1205) describes the Step I counseling procedures. Section 306 (2 U.S.C. 1206) describes the Step II mediation process. Section 307 (2 U.S.C. 1207), described fully below, sets forth the formal complaint and hearing procedures.]

STEP III: FORMAL COMPLAINT AND HEARING

SEC. 307 [2 U.S.C. 1207]. *[SECTION 307, SUBSECTIONS (a) THROUGH (g), AND (i): Subsections (a) through (g), and (i) of Section 307 describe the process from the formal complaint through the hearing stage.]*

[Sections 320 and 321 (which protect Presidential appointees and previously exempt state employees who may file complaints of discrimination with EEOC under this title) refer to the rights, protections and remedies of section 302 and the following subsection.]

(h) Remedies. - If the hearing board determines that a violation has occurred, it shall order such remedies as would be appropriate if awarded under section 706 (g) and (k) of the Civil Rights Act of 1964 (42 U.S.C. 2000e-5 (g) and (k)), and may also order the award of such compensatory damages as would be appropriate if awarded under section 1977 and section 1977A (a) and (b)(2) of the Revised Statutes (42 U.S.C. 1981 and 1981A (a) and (b)(2)). In the case of a determination that a violation based on age has occurred, the hearing board shall order such remedies as would be appropriate if awarded under section 15(c) of the Age Discrimination in Employment Act of 1967 (29 U.S.C. 633a(c)). Any order requiring the payment of money must be approved by a Senate resolution reported by the Committee on Rules and Administration. The hearing board shall have no authority to award punitive damages.

[SECTIONS 308 THROUGH 313: Section 308 (2 U.S.C. 1208) describes the procedures by which a Senate employee or head of an employing office may request a review by the Select Committee on Ethics of a decision issued under Section 307. Section 309 (2 U.S.C. 1209) describes the circumstances under which a Senate employee or Member of the Senate may petition for a review by the United States Court of Appeals for the Federal Circuit. Section 310 (2 U.S.C. 1210) describes the procedures by which a complaint may be resolved. Section 311 (2 U.S.C. 1211) enumerates reimbursable costs of attending hearings. Section 312 (2 U.S.C. 1212) prohibits intimidation or reprisal against any employee because of the exercise of a right under this title. Section 313 (2 U.S.C. 1213) outlines confidentiality requirements for counseling, mediation, hearings, final decisions, and records.]

EXERCISE OF RULEMAKING POWER

SEC. 314 *[2 U.S.C. 1214]*. The provisions of this title, except for sections 309, 320, 321, and 322, are enacted by the Senate as an exercise of the rulemaking power of the Senate, with full recognition of the right of the Senate to change its rules, in the same manner, and to the same extent, as in the case of any other rule of the Senate. Notwithstanding any other provision of law, except as provided in section 309, enforcement and adjudication with respect to the discriminatory practices prohibited by section 302, and arising out of Senate employment, shall be within the exclusive jurisdiction of the United States Senate.

TECHNICAL AND CONFORMING AMENDMENTS

SEC. 315. *[This section makes technical and conforming amendments to section 509 of the Americans with Disabilities Act of 1990 (ADA) (42 U.S.C. 12209) with respect to Senate employees.]*

[SECTIONS 316 THROUGH 319: Section 316 (2 U.S.C. 1215) states that the consideration of political affiliation, domicile, and political compatibility with the employing office in an employment decision shall not be considered a violation of this title. Section 317 (2 U.S.C. 1216) states that a Senate employee may not commence a judicial proceeding to redress a prohibited discriminatory practice, except as provided in this title. Sec. 318 (2 U.S.C. 1217) expresses the Senate's view that legislation should be enacted to provide the same or comparable rights and remedies as are provided under this title to Congressional employees lacking such rights and remedies. Section 319 (2 U.S.C. 1218) reaffirms the Senate's commitment to Rule XLII of the Standing Rules of the Senate.]

COVERAGE OF PRESIDENTIAL APPOINTEES

SEC. 320 *[2 U.S.C. 1219]*.

(a) In General. -

(1) Application. - The rights, protections, and remedies provided pursuant to section 302 and 307(h) of this title shall apply with respect to employment of Presidential appointees.

(2) Enforcement by administrative action. - Any Presidential appointee may file a complaint alleging a violation, not later than 180 days after the occurrence of the alleged violation, with the Equal Employment Opportunity Commission, or such other entity as is designated by the President by Executive Order, which, in accordance with the principles and procedures set forth in sections 554 through 557 of title 5, United States Code, shall determine whether a violation has occurred and shall set forth its determination in a final order. If the Equal Employment Opportunity Commission, or such other entity as is designated by the President pursuant to this section, determines that a violation has occurred, the final order shall also provide for appropriate relief.

(3) Judicial review. -

(A) In general. - Any party aggrieved by a final order under paragraph (2) may petition for review by the United States Court of Appeals for the Federal Circuit.

(B) Law applicable. - Chapter 158 of title 28, United States Code, shall apply to a review under this section except that the Equal Employment Opportunity Commission or such other entity as the President may designate under paragraph (2) shall be an "agency" as that term is used in chapter 158 of title 28, United States Code.

(C) Standard of review. - To the extent necessary to decision and when presented, the reviewing court shall decide all relevant questions of law and interpret constitutional and statutory provisions. The court shall set aside a final order under paragraph (2) if it is determined that the order was -

(i) arbitrary, capricious, an abuse of discretion, or otherwise not consistent with law;

(ii) not made consistent with required procedures; or

(iii) unsupported by substantial evidence.

In making the foregoing determinations, the court shall review the whole record or those parts of it cited by a party, and due account shall be taken of the rule of prejudicial error.

(D) Attorney's fees. - If the presidential appointee is the prevailing party in a proceeding under this section, attorney's fees may be allowed by the court in accordance with the standards prescribed under section 706(k) of the Civil Rights Act of 1964 (42 U.S.C. 2000e-5(k)).

(b) Presidential appointee. - For purposes of this section, the term "Presidential appointee" means any officer or employee, or an applicant seeking to become an officer or employee, in any unit of the Executive Branch, including the Executive Office of the President, whether appointed by the President or by any other appointing authority in the Executive Branch, who is not already entitled to bring an action under any of the statutes referred to in section 302 but does not include any individual -

(1) whose appointment is made by and with the advice and consent of the Senate;

(2) who is appointed to an advisory committee, as defined in section 3(2) of the Federal Advisory Committee Act (5 U.S.C. App.); or

(3) who is a member of the uniformed services.

COVERAGE OF PREVIOUSLY EXEMPT STATE EMPLOYEES
SEC. 321 [2 U.S.C. 1220].

(a) Application. - The rights, protections, and remedies provided pursuant to section 302 and 307(h) of this title shall apply with respect to employment of any individual chosen or appointed, by a person elected to public office in any State or political subdivision of any State by the qualified voters thereof -

(1) to be a member of the elected official's personal staff;

(2) to serve the elected official on the policymaking level; or

(3) to serve the elected official as an immediate advisor with respect to the exercise of the constitutional or legal powers of the office.

(b) Enforcement by administrative action. -

(1) In general. - Any individual referred to in subsection (a) may file a complaint alleging a violation, not later than 180 days after the occurrence of the alleged violation, with the Equal Employment Opportunity Commission, which, in accordance with the principles and procedures set forth in sections 554 through 557 of title 5, United States Code, shall determine whether a violation has occurred and shall set forth its determination in a final order. If the Equal Employment Opportunity Commission determines that a violation has occurred, the final order shall also provide for appropriate relief.

(2) Referral to state and local authorities. -

(A) Application. - Section 706(d) of the Civil Rights Act of 1964 (42 U.S.C. 2000e-5(d)) shall apply with respect to any proceeding under this section.

(B) Definition. - For purposes of the application described in subparagraph (A), the term "any charge filed by a member of the Commission alleging an unlawful employment practice" means a complaint filed under this section.

(c) Judicial review. - Any party aggrieved by a final order under subsection (b) may obtain a review of such order under chapter 158 of title 28, United States Code. For the purpose of this review, the Equal Employment Opportunity Commission shall be an "agency" as that term is used in chapter 158 of title 28, United States Code.

(d) Standard of review. - To the extent necessary to decision and when presented, the reviewing court shall decide all relevant questions of law and interpret constitutional and statutory provisions. The court shall set aside a final order under subsection (b) if it is determined that the order was -

(1) arbitrary, capricious, an abuse of discretion, or otherwise not consistent with law;

(2) not made consistent with required procedures; or

(3) unsupported by substantial evidence.

In making the foregoing determinations, the court shall review the whole record or those parts of it cited by a party, and due account shall be taken of the rule of prejudicial error.

(e) Attorney's fees. - If the individual referred to in subsection (a) is the prevailing party in a proceeding under this subsection, attorney's fees may be allowed by the court in accordance with the standards prescribed under section 706(k) of the Civil Rights Act of 1964 (42 U.S.C. 2000e-5(k)).

SEVERABILITY

SEC. 322 [2 U.S.C. 1221]. Notwithstanding section 401 of this Act, if any provision of section 309 or 320(a)(3) is invalidated, both sections 309 and 320(a)(3) shall have no force and effect.

PAYMENTS BY THE PRESIDENT OR A MEMBER OF THE SENATE

SEC. 323 [2 U.S.C. 1222]. The President or a Member of the Senate shall reimburse the appropriate Federal account for any payment made on his or her behalf out of such account for a violation committed under the provisions of this title by the President or Member of the Senate not later than 60 days after the payment is made.

REPORTS OF SENATE COMMITTEES

SEC. 324 [2 U.S.C. 1223].

(a) Each report accompanying a bill or joint resolution of a public character reported by any committee of the Senate (except the Committee on Appropriations and the Committee on the Budget) shall contain a listing of the provisions of the bill or joint resolution that apply to Congress and an evaluation of the impact of such provisions on Congress.

(b) The provisions of this section are enacted by the Senate as an exercise of the rulemaking power of the Senate, with full recognition of the right of the Senate to change its rules, in the same manner, and to the same extent, as in the case of any other rule of the Senate.

INTERVENTION AND EXPEDITED REVIEW OF CERTAIN APPEALS

SEC. 325 [2 U.S.C. 1224].

(a) Intervention. - Because of the constitutional issues that may be raised by section 309 and section 320, any Member of the Senate may intervene as a matter of right in any proceeding under section 309 for the sole purpose of determining the constitutionality of such section.

(b) Threshold Matter. - In any proceeding under section 309 or section 320, the United States Court of Appeals for the Federal Circuit shall determine any issue presented concerning the constitutionality of such section as a threshold matter.

(c) Appeal. -

(1) In general. - An appeal may be taken directly to the Supreme Court of the United States from any interlocutory or final judgment, decree, or order issued by the United States Court of Appeals for the Federal Circuit ruling upon the constitutionality of section 309 or 320.

(2) Jurisdiction. - The Supreme Court shall, if it has not previously ruled on the question, accept jurisdiction over the appeal referred to in paragraph (1), advance the appeal on the docket and expedite the appeal to the greatest extent possible.

Title IV—General Provisions

SEVERABILITY

SEC. 401 *[42 U.S.C. 1981 NOTE].* If any provision of this Act, or an amendment made by this Act, or the application of such provision to any person or circumstances is held to be invalid, the remainder of this Act and the amendments made by this Act, and the application of such provision to other persons and circumstances, shall not be affected.

EFFECTIVE DATE

SEC. 402 *[42 U.S.C. 1981 NOTE].*

(a) In General. - Except as otherwise specifically provided, this Act and the amendments made by this Act shall take effect upon enactment.

(b) Certain Disparate Impact Cases. Notwithstanding any other provision of this Act, nothing in this Act shall apply to any disparate impact case for which a complaint was filed before March 1, 1975, and for which an initial decision was rendered after October 30, 1983.

Approved November 21, 1991.

Glossary

A

abandonment Behavior in which a tenant moves out of a leased premises before the end of the term and discontinues making rent payments.

absolute privilege A special right, immunity, permission, or benefit given to certain individuals that allows them to make any statements about someone without being held liable for defamation for any false statement made, regardless of intent or knowledge of the falsity of the claim.

absolutism A theory of ethics which requires that individuals defer to a set of rules to guide them in the ethical decision-making process. Whether an action is moral depends on whether it conforms to the given set of ethical rules.

abuse of process The malicious and deliberate misuse or perversion of a legal procedure.

acceptance A key factor in the agreement element of a contract; consists of the agreement of one party, the offeree, to the terms of the offer in the contract made by the other party, the offeror.

acceptor A person (drawee) who accepts and signs a draft to agree to pay the draft when it is presented.

accommodation party A party who signs an instrument to provide credit for another party who has also signed the instrument.

accord and satisfaction An arrangement between contracting parties whereby one of the parties substitutes a different performance for his or her original duty under the contract. The promise to perform the new duty is the *accord,* and the actual performance of that new duty is the *satisfaction.*

accountant-client privilege The right of an accountant to not reveal any information given in confidence by a client. The privilege is not granted by every state or by the federal government.

accounting A review and listing of all partnership assets and/or profit.

accredited investor A private investor who is allowed to accept private securities offerings under certain specific guidelines set by the SEC.

act utilitarianism A theory of ethics which requires that individuals examine all the potential actions in each situation and choose the action that yields the greatest amount of pleasure over pain for all involved.

actual cause The determination that the defendant's breach of duty resulted directly in the plaintiff's injury.

actual eviction An eviction in which a landlord physically prevents the lessee from entering the leased premises.

actual malice In defamation, either a person's knowledge that his or her statement or published material is false or the person's reckless disregard for whether it was false.

actual notice Notice of agency termination that is given by directly informing third parties, either orally or in writing.

actus reus Latin for "guilty act"; a wrongful behavior that is associated with the physical act of a declared crime.

ad substantiation An FTC standard requiring that advertisers have a reasonable basis for the claims made in their ads.

adhesion contract A contract created by a party to an agreement that is presented to the other party on a take-it-or-leave-it basis. Such contracts are legal but are sometimes rescinded on the grounds of unconscionability and the absence of one party's free will to enter a contract.

administrative agency Any government body created by the legislative branch (e.g., Congress, a state legislature, or a city council) to carry out specific duties.

administrative law The collection of rules and decisions made by administrative agencies to fill in particular details missing from constitutions and statutes.

administrative law judge (ALJ) A judge who presides over an administrative hearing; may attempt to get the parties to settle but has the power to issue a binding decision.

Administrative Procedures Act (APA) Federal legislation that places limitations on how agencies are run and contains very specific guidelines on rule making by agencies.

admission A statement made in court, under oath, or at some stage during a legal proceeding, in which a party against whom charges have been brought admits that an oral contract existed, even though the contract was required to be in writing.

advance directive A legal instrument in which a person expresses his wishes about efforts to prolong his life.

adversarial negotiation Negotiation in which each party seeks to maximize its own gain.

adverse possession An involuntary property transfer in which a person acquires ownership of property by treating a piece of real property as his or her own, without protest or permission from the owner.

affiliate A business enterprise located in one state that is directly or indirectly owned and controlled by a company located in another state. Also called *foreign subsidiary.*

affirm An appellate court decision that accepts a lower court's judgment in a case that has been appealed.

affirmative defense A defendant's response to a plaintiff's claim in which the defendant attacks the plaintiff's legal right to bring the action rather than attacking the fact of the claim or making excuses for unlawful behavior. Common affirmative defenses are expiration of the statute of limitations, mistake of fact, intoxication, insanity, duress, and entrapment.

after-acquired property   Property acquired by a debtor after the security arrangement is made.

Age Discrimination in Employment Act (ADEA) of 1967   Federal law that prohibits employers from refusing to hire, discharging, or discriminating in terms and conditions of employment on the basis of an employee's or applicant's being age 40 or older.

agency   The fiduciary relationship that arises when one person consents to have another act on his behalf and subject to his control and the other consents to do so.

agency by estoppel   See **apparent agency.**

agency coupled with an interest   An agency relationship that is created for the benefit of the agent, not the principal.

agency relationship   The association between one party and an agent who acts on behalf of that party.

agent   A party who has the authority to act on behalf of and bind another party.

agreement   One of the four elements necessary for a contract; consists of an offer made by one party, the offeror, and the acceptance of the offer by another party, the offeree.

alien corporation   A business that is incorporated in a foreign country.

allonge   Accompanying a negotiable instrument, a piece of paper that provides room for an endorsement if no room is available on the negotiable instrument itself.

alteration   (1) An unauthorized change to an instrument that modifies the obligation of a party to the instrument. (2) A change that affects the condition of the premises.

alternative dispute resolution (ADR)   The resolution of legal problems through methods other than litigation.

ambulatory   A term pertaining to the ability of a will to be changed by a testator.

Americans with Disabilities Act (ADA)   Federal law that prohibits discrimination against employees and job applicants with disabilities.

anatomical gift   All or part of an individual's body that the individual wishes to donate to a hospital, university, organ bank, etc.

answer   The response of the defendant to the plaintiff's complaint.

antidumping duties   Special tariffs that are imposed on imported goods in order to offset illegal dumping.

antilapse clause   In an insurance policy, a clause which states that the insured has a grace period in which to make an overdue payment.

apparent agency   An agency relationship created by operation of law when one party, by her actions, causes a third party to believe someone is her agent even though that person

actually has no authority to act as her agent. Also called *agency by estoppel.*

appeal   The act or fact of challenging the decision of a trial court after final judgment or some other legal ruling by taking the matter to the appropriate appellate court, and in some cases to the U.S. Supreme Court, in an attempt to reverse the decision.

appellate court   A higher court, usually consisting of more than one judge, that reviews the decision and results of a lower court (either a trial court or a lower-level appellate court) when a losing party files for an appeal. Appellate courts do not hold trials but may request additional oral and written arguments from each party; they issue written decisions, which collectively constitute case law or the common law. Also called *court of appellate jurisdiction.*

appraisal clause   A part of an insurance contract that calls for an assessment when parties disagree about the value and loss of a specific item.

appraisal right   A dissenting shareholder's right to have his or her shares appraised and to receive monetary compensation from the corporation for their value.

appropriation for commercial gain   A privacy tort that occurs when someone uses a person's name, likeness, voice, identity, or other identifying characteristics for commercial gain without that person's permission.

arbitration   A type of alternative dispute resolution wherein disputes are submitted for resolution to private nonofficial persons selected in a manner provided by law or the agreement of the parties.

arbitration clause   A part of an insurance contract that calls for a dispute to be settled by an arbitrator, a neutral third party.

arraignment   The first appearance in court by the defendant, at which the defendant is advised of the pending charges, the right to counsel, and the right to trial by jury and he or she enters a plea to the charge.

arrest   The action in which the police, or a person acting under the law, seize, hold, or take an individual into custody.

arson   The crime of intentionally setting fire to another's property.

articles of incorporation   A document that contains basic information about a corporation and is filed with the state.

articles of partnership   The written agreement that creates a partnership.

artisan's lien   A claim placed on personal property to satisfy a person's debt related to the property.

assault   A civil wrong that occurs when one person intentionally and voluntarily places another in fear or apprehension of an immediate, offensive physical harm. Assault does not require actual contact.

assignee   In a contract, the party who receives the rights of another party (an assignor) to collect what was contractually agreed on in the original contract.

assignment (1) A contracting party's (an assignor's) transfer of his or her rights to the contract to a third party (an assignee). (2) A transfer of a tenant's entire interest in a leased property.

assignor In a contract, the party who transfers his or her rights to a contract to a third party (an assignee), giving the assignee the right to collect what was contractually agreed on in the original contract.

assumption of the risk A defense whereby the defendant must prove that the plaintiff voluntarily assumed the risk that the defendant caused.

attachment (1) The point at which a creditor becomes the secured party who has a security interest in the collateral. (2) A court order permitting a local court officer to seize a debtor's property.

attempt to monopolize The use of certain business practices with the intent to gain market share by excluding competitors and thereby gain monopoly power.

automated teller machine (ATM) A machine connected to banking computers that enables customers to conduct transactions without having to enter their bank.

automatic stay After bankruptcy has been filed, a moratorium during which creditors cannot bring or continue action against the debtor or his or her property.

B

bail A thing of value, such as a money bail bond or any other form of property, that is given to the court to temporarily allow a person's release from jail and to ensure his or her appearance in court.

bailment (of personal property) A relationship that arises when one party (the bailer) gives possession of personal property to another (the bailee) with an advance agreement on the time period, the compensation, if any, and the bailee's treatment of the property.

bait-and-switch advertising A deceptive practice in which a seller advertises a low-priced item, generally unavailable to the consumer, and then pushes the consumer to buy a more expensive item.

Bankruptcy Abuse Prevention and Consumer Protection Act (BAPCPA) of 2005 Federal law that renovated the bankruptcy system by addressing the increased number of bankruptcy filings, significant losses associated with bankruptcy filings, loopholes and incentives that allowed for abuse, and the financial ability of debtors.

bankruptcy estate The assets that are collected from a debtor who files for bankruptcy.

battery A civil wrong that occurs when one person intentionally and voluntarily brings about a nonconsented harmful or offensive contact with a person or something closely associated with him or her. Battery requires an actual contact.

beachhead acquisition A takeover in which an aggressor gradually accumulates the target company's shares.

bearer instrument An instrument payable to cash or to whoever is in possession of the instrument.

bench trial A trial before a judge, with the judgment decided by the judge rather than a jury; occurs when the defendant has waived his or her right to a jury trial.

beneficiary (1) A person who can expect to benefit from a relationship. (2) A person who receives, or will receive, the proceeds from an insurance policy or a will.

bid rigging An agreement among firms to not bid against one another or to submit a certain level of bid.

bilateral contract A promise exchanged for a promise.

bilateral trade agreement An international agreement between two nations that relates to trade between them.

bill of lading A document issued by a person engaged in the business of transporting goods that verifies receipt of the goods for shipment.

binder An agreement that gives temporary insurance until the company decides to accept or reject the insurance application.

binding arbitration clause A contract provision mandating that all disputes arising under the contract must be settled by arbitration.

blank endorsement A payee's or last endorsee's signature on a negotiable instrument.

blank qualified endorsement A blank endorsement containing words that limit the enforceability of the check, such as the term *without recourse* (which means the endorser will not be liable).

blue-sky law A law that regulates the offering and sale of purely intrastate securities.

bond See **debt security.**

booking After an individual is arrested, the procedure of recording the name of the defendant and the alleged crime in the investigating agency's or police department's records.

bounty payment A government reward for an act that is beneficial to the public.

boycott A refusal to deal with, purchase goods from, or work for a business.

bribery A corrupt and illegal activity in which a person offers, gives, solicits, or receives money, services, or anything of value in order to gain an illicit advantage.

brief A written legal argument, which a party presents to a court, that explains why that party to the case should prevail. Also called *factum.*

burden of proof To convict a defendant, the duty of the plaintiff or prosecution to establish a claim or allegation by admissible evidence and to prove to the jury or court, beyond any reasonable doubt, that the defendant committed all the essential elements of the crime.

burglary   A crime in which someone unlawfully enters a building with intent to commit a felony or theft.

business ethics   The use of ethics and ethical principles to solve business dilemmas.

business law   The enforceable rules of conduct that govern the actions of buyers and sellers in market exchanges.

business trust   A business organization governed by a group of trustees who operate the trust for beneficiaries.

buyer in the ordinary course of business   A person who routinely buys goods in good faith from a person who routinely sells those goods.

bylaws   Rules and regulations that govern a corporation's internal management.

C

capacity   The legal ability to enter into a binding contract.

case law   The collection of legal interpretations made by judges. They are considered to be law unless otherwise revoked by a statutory law. Also known as *common law.*

case or controversy   A term used in the U.S. Constitution to describe the structure and requirements of conflicting claims of individuals that can be brought before a federal court for resolution. A case or controversy requires an actual dispute between parties over their legal rights that remains in conflict at the time the case is presented and that is a proper matter for judicial determination. Also referred to as *justifiable controversy.*

cash tender offer   A type of takeover in which the aggressor corporation offers to pay the target shareholders cash for their stock.

cashier's check   A check for which both drawer and drawee are the same bank.

casualty insurance   Insurance that protects a party from accidental injury.

categorical imperative   The principle that an act is ethical if we want all people to act according to its dictates.

cease-and-desist order   An FTC order requiring that a company stop its illegal behavior.

certificate of deposit (CD)   A document whereby a bank promises to pay a payee a certain amount of money at a future time.

certificate of incorporation   A document certifying that a corporation is incorporated in the state and is authorized to conduct business.

certificate of limited partnership   A document signed on the formation of a limited partnership and filed with the secretary of state.

certified check   Any check that is accepted by the bank from which the funds are drawn.

chain-style business operation   A type of franchise in which the franchise operates under the franchisor's business name and is required to follow the franchisor's standards and methods of business operation.

charging order   An order that entitles a creditor to collect a partner's profits.

chattel paper   A writing that indicates both a monetary obligation and a security interest in specific goods.

check   A special draft that orders a bank (the drawee) to pay a specified sum of money to the payee from the drawer's account.

choice-of-law clause   A contractual clause in which the parties specify which state's law will apply to the interpretation of the contract in the event of a dispute.

chose in action   After an acquisition, the surviving corporation's right to sue for debt and damages on behalf of the absorbed corporation.

circuit court of appeal   A court that hears appeals from the district courts located within its circuit, as well as appeals from decisions of federal administrative agencies. Also called *federal district court of appeal.*

civil law   The body of laws that govern the rights and responsibilities either between persons or between persons and their government.

Civil Rights Act (CRA) of 1964—Title VII   Federal law (as amended by the Civil Rights Act of 1991) that protects employees against discrimination based on race, color, religion, national origin, and sex; also prohibits harassment based on the same protected categories.

closely held corporation   A corporation that does not sell stock to the general public.

closing   The meeting at which a transfer of title takes place: The seller signs over the deed, and the buyer gives the seller a check for the amount due.

codicil   The document by which a testator changes his or her will.

collateral   The property that is subject to a secured interest.

collecting bank   Any bank, with the exception of the payor bank, that handles a check during the check collection process.

collective bargaining   The process whereby workers organize collectively and bargain with employers regarding the conditions of employment.

commerce clause   Clause 3 of Article I, Section 8, of the U.S. Constitution, which authorizes and empowers Congress "[t]o regulate Commerce with foreign Nations, and among the several States, and with the Indian Tribes."

commercial general liability policy   A policy that generally provides protection for the insured for bodily injury, as well as for third parties for property injury.

commercial insurance   Insurance that covers some type of business risk.

commercial reasonableness   Reasonable commercial standards of fair dealing, required of merchants in addition to honesty in fact.

commercial speech   Speech made by businesses about commercial matters, such as the sale of goods and services. It is protected by the First Amendment.

common areas   Areas that are used by all tenants.

common carrier   A carrier that is licensed to provide transportation services to the public.

common-carrier delivery contract   A type of contract in which purchased goods are delivered to the buyer via an independent contractor, such as a trucking line.

common law   See **case law.**

common stock   Corporate stock that does not convey any preference to its holders.

communication   In a contract, an offer made to the offeree or the offeree's agent.

comparative law   The study of the legal systems of different states.

compensatory damages   Money awarded to a plaintiff as reimbursement for her or his losses; based on the amount of actual damage or harm to property, lost wages or profits, pain and suffering, medical expenses, disability, etc.

complaint   A formal written document that begins a civil lawsuit; contains the plaintiff's list of allegations against the defendant, along with the damages the plaintiff seeks.

complete performance   Contract performance that occurs when all aspects of the parties' duties under the contract are carried out perfectly.

computer crime   Crime that is committed using a computer.

concealment   The active hiding of the truth about a material fact.

concurrent authority   Both the state and federal court systems have the power to render a binding verdict for this type of case.

concurrent conditions   In a contract, terms under which each party's performance is conditioned on the performance of the other; occur only when the parties are required to perform for each other simultaneously.

condemnation   The legal process by which a transfer of property is made against the protest of the property owner.

condition precedent   In a contract, an event that must occur in order for a party's duty to arise.

condition subsequent   In a contract, a future event that terminates the obligations of the parties when it occurs.

conditional contract   A contract that becomes enforceable only on the happening or termination of a specified condition.

conditional endorsement   An endorsement whereby payment can be made only on the fulfillment of a predecided condition, such as painting one's house.

conditional estate   An ownership interest in which the holder has the same interest as that in a fee simple absolute except that this interest is subject to a condition.

conditional privilege   A special right, immunity, permission, or benefit given to certain individuals that allows them to make any statements about someone without being held liable for defamation for any false statements made without actual malice.

conditional sales contract   A type of contract in which the sale itself is contingent on approval; can be either a sale-on-approval contract or a sale-or-return contract.

conforming goods   Goods that conform to contract specifications.

conglomerate merger   A merger in which a company merges with another company that is not a competitor or a buyer or seller to the company.

consent decree   An agreement that binds the violating party to cease his or her illegal behavior.

consent order   A statement in which a company agrees to stop disputed behavior but does not admit that it broke the law.

consequential damages   In a contract, foreseeable damages that result from special facts and circumstances arising outside the contract itself. The damages must be within the contemplation of the parties at the time the breach occurs. Also called *special damages.*

consequentialism   A general approach to ethical dilemmas which requires that we consider the consequences our actions will have on relevant people.

consideration   The bargained-for exchange; what each party gets in exchange for his or her promise under a contract.

Consolidated Omnibus Budget Reconciliation Act (COBRA)   Federal law which ensures that when employees lose their jobs or have their hours reduced to a level at which they would not be eligible to receive medical, dental, or optical benefits from their employer, the employees will be able to continue receiving benefits under the employer's policy for up to 18 months by paying the premiums for the policy.

consolidations   Combinations of two or more corporations where none of the original corporations continue to exist as a legal entity.

constitutional law   The general limits and powers of a government as interpreted from its written constitution.

constructive eviction   An eviction that occurs when a property has become unsuitable for use due to the unlivable quality of the property.

constructive notice   Notice of agency termination that is usually given by publishing an announcement in a newspaper.

constructive trust   (1) An implied trust in which a party is named to hold the trust for its rightful owner. (2) An equitable trust imposed on someone who wrongfully obtains or holds legal right to property he or she should not possess.

consumer good   A good used or bought for use primarily for personal, family, or household purposes.

consumer lease   A lease that has a value of $25,000 or less and exists between a lessor who is regularly engaged in the business of leasing or selling and a lessee who leases the goods primarily for a personal, family, or household purpose.

contract   A promise or set of promises for the breach of which the law gives a remedy or the performance of which the law in some way recognizes a duty.

contract clause   The clause in the U.S. Constitution that prohibits the government from unreasonably interfering with an existing contract.

contract under seal   Contracts simply identified with the word *seal* or the letters *L.S.* (an abbreviation for *locus sigilli*, which means "the place for the seal") at the end.

contractual capacity   The legal ability to enter into a binding agreement.

contributory negligence   A defense to negligence whereby the defendant can escape all liability by proving that the plaintiff failed to act in a way that would have protected him or her from an unreasonable risk of harm and that the plaintiff's negligent behavior contributed in some way to the plaintiff's accident.

Convention on the International Sale of Goods (CISG)   An international agreement applicable to transactions involving the commercial sale of goods.

conversion   Permanent interference with another's use and enjoyment of his or her personal property.

cooperative   An organization formed by individuals to market new products. Individuals in a cooperative pool their resources together to gain an advantage in the market.

co-ownership   A type of ownership in which multiple individuals possess ownership interests in a property.

copyright   The protection of the expression of a creative work; i.e., protection of the fixed form that expresses the ideas.

corporation   A legal entity formed by issuing stock to investors, who are the owners of the corporation.

corporation by estoppel   A defective corporation that has conducted business with a third party and therefore cannot deny its status as a corporation to escape liability.

corrective advertising   Advertising in which a company explicitly states that formerly advertised claims were untrue. Also called *counteradvertising*.

cost-benefit analysis   An economic school of jurisprudence in which all costs and benefits of a law are given monetary values. Those laws with the highest ratios of benefits to costs are then preferable to those with lower ratios.

counterclaim   A claim made by the defendant against the plaintiff that is filed along with the defendant's answer.

counteroffer   An offer made by an offeree to the offeror that relates to the same matter as the original offer but proposes a substituted bargain that differs from the one proposed in the original offer.

countervailing duties   Special tariffs imposed on subsidized goods to offset the beneficial effect of an illegal subsidy.

course of dealing   A history of previous commercial transactions between the same parties.

course of performance   The history of dealings between the parties in the particular contract at issue.

court of appellate jurisdiction   See **appellate court.**

court of original jurisdiction   See **trial court.**

covenant not to compete   An agreement not to compete against a party for a set period of time within a designated geographic area.

covenant of quiet enjoyment   A promise that a tenant has the right to quietly enjoy the land.

cover   A buyer's right to substitute goods for those due under a sales or lease agreement when the seller provides nonconforming goods.

creditor   An entity to which a debtor owes money.

creditor beneficiary   A third party who benefits from a contract in which the promisor agrees to pay the promisee's debt.

creditors' meeting   A meeting of all the creditors listed in the Chapter 7 required schedule for liquidation.

criminal fraud   A crime or an offense encompassing a variety of means by which an individual intentionally uses some sort of misrepresentation to gain an advantage over another person.

criminal law   A classification of law involving the rights and responsibilities an individual has with respect to the public as a whole.

criteria pollutant   Any of the six air pollutants that are subject to the National Ambient Air Quality Standards under the Clean Air Act.

critical-thinking skills   The ability to understand the structure and worth of an argument by evaluating the facts, issue, reasons, and conclusion of the argument.

cross-licensing   An illegal contractual arrangement in which two or more parties license each other to use their specified intellectual property *only* on the condition that neither licenses anyone else to use the property without the other's consent.

cure   A breaching party's right to provide conforming goods when nonconforming goods were initially delivered; subject to a reasonable time test.

customary international law   A general and consistent practice by nations that is accepted as binding law.

customs union   A free trade area with the additional feature of a common external tariff on products originating outside the union.

cyber terrorist   A hacker whose intention is the exploitation of a target computer or network to create a serious impact, such as the crippling of a communications network or the sabotage of a business or organization, which may have an impact on millions of citizens if the terrorist's attack is successful.

cyberlaw   A classification of law regulating business activities that are conducted online.

D

de facto **corporation**   Latin for "corporation in fact"; a corporation that has not substantially met the requirements of the state incorporation statutes.

de jure **corporation**   Latin for "lawful corporation"; a corporation that has met the mandatory statutory provisions and thus received its certificate of incorporation.

debt security   A security that represents a loan to a corporation. Also called *bond.*

debtor   An party that owes money to another party.

deceptive advertising   The practice of advertising with claims that mislead or could mislead a reasonable consumer.

defamation   A false statement or an action that harms the reputation or character of an individual, business, product, group, government, or nation.

default   Failure to make payments on a loan.

default judgment   Judgment for the plaintiff that occurs when the defendant fails to respond to the complaint.

defective corporation   A corporation whose incorporation process included an error or omission.

defendant   The person, party, or entity against whom a civil or criminal lawsuit is filed in a court of law.

definite and certain (terms)   The requirement, under common law, that a contract must include and clearly define all material terms.

definite-term lease   A type of lease that expires at the end of a specified term.

delegatee   A third party who is not part of the original contract but to whom duties to perform are transferred by one of the contracting parties (a delegator).

delegation   A contracting party's (a delegator's) transfer of his or her duty to perform to a third party who is not part of the original contract (a delegatee).

delegator   A party in a contract who transfers his or her duties to perform to a third party who is not a part of the original contract (a delegatee).

demand instrument   A type of draft that allows the payee to demand payment at any time from a holder.

deontology   The ethical theory which states that an action can be determined as ethical on the basis of right and wrong, regardless of its consequences.

depositary bank   The first bank that receives a check for payment.

deposition   A pretrial sworn and recorded testimony of a witness that is acquired out of court with no judge present.

design defect   A defect that is found in all products of a particular design and renders them dangerous.

digital cash   Money stored electronically and used in place of physical currency.

direct deposit   An electronic process, preauthorized by a customer, that allows funds to be deposited directly into the customer's bank account.

directed verdict   A ruling by the judge, after the plaintiff has presented her case but before any evidence is put forward by the defendant, in favor of the defendant because the plaintiff has failed to present the minimum amount of evidence necessary to establish his claim.

discharge   A written federal court order signed by a bankruptcy judge which states that the debtor is immune from creditor actions to collect debt; i.e., a release from liability.

disclosed principal   A principal whose identity is known to a third party. The third party is aware that the agent is making an agreement on behalf of the principal.

discovery   The pretrial phase in a lawsuit during which each party requests relevant documents and other evidence from the other side in an attempt to "discover" pertinent facts and to avoid any surprises in the courtroom during the trial. Discovery tools include requests for admissions, interrogatories, depositions, requests for inspection, and document production requests.

dishonored   Refused; specifically, a payment that has been refused despite a holder's presenting an instrument in a timely and proper manner.

dishonored instrument   An instrument that a party has refused to pay.

disparagement   A business tort that occurs when a statement is intentionally used to defame a business product or service.

disparate impact   A form of discrimination that arises when an employer's policy or practice appears to apply to everyone equally but its actual effect is that it disproportionately limits employment opportunities for a protected class.

disparate treatment   A form of intentional discrimination in which an employee is hired, fired, denied a promotion, or the like, on the basis of membership in a protected class.

Dispute Settlement Understanding   An agreement that is part of the WTO system whereby recognized governments of WTO member states may bring an action alleging a violation of GATT by other member states.

dissolution   The change in the relation of partners caused by any partner's ceasing to be associated with the carrying on of the partnership's business.

distributor   A merchant who purchases goods from a seller for resale in a foreign market.

distributorship   A type of franchise in which the franchisor manufactures a product and licenses a dealer to sell the product in an exclusive territory.

district court   A trial court in the federal system.

dividend   A distribution of corporate profits or income that is ordered by the directors and paid to the shareholders.

document of title   A transport document that, when appropriately made out, entitles the bearer to claim the goods from the carrier.

domestic corporation   A corporation located in the state in which it is incorporated.

donee beneficiary   A third party who benefits from a contract in which a promisor agrees to give a gift to the third party.

dormant commerce clause   A restriction on states' authority that is implied in the commerce clause of the U.S. Constitution: The power given to Congress to enact legislation that affects interstate commerce in effect prohibits a state from passing legislation that improperly burdens interstate commerce.

draft   An instrument validating an order by a drawer to a drawee to pay a payee.

dram shop act   A regulation under which bartenders can be held liable for injuries caused by individuals who become intoxicated in their bars.

drawee   The party that must obey an order. In the context of banking, the drawee is the bank that must pay the funds ordered by a customer's check.

drawer   The party that writes an order, or the person who writes a check.

due diligence defense   A defense in which the defendant argues that he or she applied the appropriate degree of attention, care, and research expected of a party in a given situation and had reasonable grounds to believe that certain facts and statements were accurate and had no omission of material facts.

due process clause   A clause in the Fifth Amendment of the U.S. Constitution which provides that the government cannot deprive an individual of life, liberty, or property without a fair and just hearing.

dumping   The practice wherein an exporter sells products in a foreign state for less than the price charged for the same or comparable goods in the exporter's home market.

durable power of attorney   A document which specifies that an agent's authority is intended to continue beyond the principal's incapacitation.

duress   Any unlawful act or threat exercised on a person whereby the person is forced to enter into an agreement or to perform some other act against his or her will.

duty   The standard of care a defendant must meet in order to not subject a person in the position of the plaintiff to an unreasonable risk of harm.

duty of loyalty   An agent's obligation to act in the interest of the principal.

duty of notification   An agent's obligation to inform the principal of the agent's actions on the principal's behalf and of all relevant information.

duty to compensate   A principal's obligation to pay an agent for his or her services.

E

easement   An irrevocable right to use some part of another's land for a specific purpose, without taking anything from it.

easement by prescription   An easement created by state law when certain conditions are met, most frequently by openly using a portion of another's property for a statutory period of time (usually 25 years).

effective date   The date that insurance takes effect.

efficiency   The economic principle of getting the most output from the least input.

Electronic Communications Privacy Act (ECPA) of 1986   Federal law that extended employees' privacy rights to electronic forms of communication including e-mail and cell phones; outlaws the intentional interception of electronic communications and the intentional disclosure or use of the information obtained through such interception.

electronic fund transfer (EFT)   The transfer of funds by an electronic terminal, telephone, or computer.

embezzlement   A wrongful conversion of another's funds or property by one who is lawfully in possession of those funds or that property.

e-money   Any electronic, nonphysical form of currency.

Employee Retirement Income Security Act (ERISA)   Federal law that sets minimum standards for most voluntarily established pension and health plans in private industry to provide protection for individuals in these plans.

employment-at-will doctrine   The doctrine which provides that either the employer or the employee can terminate the employment relationship at any time.

enabling legislation   A statute that specifies the name, functions, and specific powers of an administrative agency and grants the agency broad powers for the purpose of serving the "public interest, convenience, and necessity."

endorsee   One who receives an endorsement.

endorsement for deposit or collection only   The most common type of endorsement, which provides that the instrument can only be deposited into an account.

endorsement to prohibit further endorsement   An endorsement that provides increased protection to the endorsee.

endorser   One who issues an endorsement.

English rule   A rule which states that the first assignee to give notice of assignment to the obligor is the party with rights to the contract.

entrapment   A relatively common defense under which the defendant claims that he would not have committed the crime or broken the law if he had not been induced or tricked into doing so by law enforcement officials.

entrustment   The transfer of goods to a merchant who ordinarily deals in that type of goods. If the merchant subsequently sells them to a good-faith third-party purchaser, the buyer acquires good title to the goods.

environmental impact statement (EIS)   A document that must be filed whenever there is a major federal activity that might have a significant impact on the environment. It details the environmental impact of the proposed action, any adverse environmental effects of implementing the action, and other environmental considerations.

equal dignity rule   A rule requiring that contracts that would normally fall under the statute of frauds and need a writing if negotiated by the principal must be in writing even if negotiated by an agent.

Equal Pay Act (EPA) of 1963   Federal law that prohibits an employer from paying workers of one gender less than the wages paid to employees of the opposite gender for work that requires equal skill, effort, and responsibility.

equal protection clause   A clause in the Fourteenth Amendment of the U.S. Constitution that prevents states from denying "the equal protection of the laws" to any citizen. This clause implies that all citizens are created equal.

equity security   A security that represents ownership in a corporation.

establishment clause   One of two provisions in the First Amendment of the U.S. Constitution that protect citizens' freedom of religion. It prohibits (1) the establishment of a national religion by Congress and (2) the preference of one religion over another or of religion over nonreligious philosophies in general.

estate planning   The process whereby an individual decides what to do with his or her real and personal property during and after life.

ethical dilemma   A question about how a person should behave that requires the person to reflect about the advantages and disadvantages of the optional choices for various stakeholders.

ethical guideline   A simple tool to help determine whether an action is moral.

ethical relativism   The ethical theory that denies the existence of an ultimate ethical system, holding instead that a decision must be determined as ethical on the basis of its own context.

ethics   The study and practice of decisions about what is good or right.

ethics of care   The ethical theory that emphasizes human interaction, holding that what makes a decision ethical is how well it builds and promotes human relationships.

European Union   A customs union that consists of an association of states, has a basis in international law, and was formed for the purpose of forging closer ties among the peoples of Europe.

exchange tender offer   A type of takeover in which the aggressor corporation offers to exchange the target shareholders' current stock for its own stock.

exclusive-dealing contract   An agreement in which a seller requires that a buyer buy products supplied only by that seller.

exculpatory clause   A clause in a contract that basically frees one party (usually the drafter of the agreement) from all liability arising out of performance of the contract; generally based on factors such as consumer ignorance or a great deal of unexplained fine print that serve to deprive the less powerful party of a meaningful choice.

executed   A term applied to a contract whose terms have all been fully performed.

executive agency   An agency that is typically located within the executive branch, under one of the cabinet-level departments. The agency head is appointed by the president with the advice and consent of the Senate and may be discharged by the president at any time, for any reason. Also called *cabinet-level agency.*

executive order   A directive that has the force of law but is issued by a governor or the president.

executory   A term applied to a contract whose terms have not all been fully performed.

exemplary damages   See **punitive damages.**

exempted rule making   An APA exemption from rule making that allows an agency to decide whether public participation will be allowed. Exemptions include rule-making proceedings with regard to military or foreign affairs, agency management or personnel, and public property, loans, grants, benefits or contracts of an agency.

express condition   A condition specifically and explicitly stated in a contract and usually preceded by words such as *conditioned on, if, provided that,* or *when.*

express contract   A contract in which all the terms are clearly set forth in either written or spoken words.

express trust   A trust created either while the settlor is alive or by will.

express warranty   Any description of a good's physical nature or its use, either in general or specific circumstances, that becomes part of a contract.

expressed agency   An agency created in a written or oral agreement. Also called *agency by agreement.*

extortion   A criminal offense in which a person obtains money, property, and/or services from another by wrongfully threatening or inflicting harm to his or her person, property, or reputation. Also called *blackmail.*

F

failure to provide adequate warnings   A defect in which the product is not labeled to indicate that it can be dangerous.

Fair Labor Standards Act (FLSA)   Federal law which requires that a minimum wage of a specified amount be paid to all employees in covered industries; also mandates that employees who work more than 40 hours in a week be paid no less than 1½ times their regular wage for all hours beyond 40 worked in a given week.

fair-use doctrine   The doctrine which provides for the lawful use of a limited portion of another's work for purposes of criticism, comment, news reporting, teaching, scholarship, or research.

False Claims Act   An act that allows employees to sue employers on behalf of the federal government for fraud against the government. The employee retains a share of the recovery as a reward for his or her efforts.

false imprisonment   The unlawful restraint of another against the person's will.

false light   A privacy tort that occurs when highly offensive information is published about an individual that is not valid or places the person in a false light.

false pretense   A materially false representation of an existing fact, with knowledge of the falsity of the representation and with the intent to defraud.

Family and Medical Leave Act (FMLA)   Federal act requiring that employers provide all eligible employees with up to 12 weeks of leave during any 12-month period for several family-related occurrences (e.g., birth of a child, care of a sick spouse).

family incentive trust   A trust designed to take effect on the completion of a specified behavior.

federal preemption   A principle asserting the supremacy of federal legislation over state legislation when both pertain to the same subject matter.

Federal Register   The government publication in which an agency publishes each proposed rule, along with an explanation of the legal authority for issuing the rule and a description of how the public can participate in the rule-making process, and later publishes the final rule.

Federal Unemployment Tax Act (FUTA)   Federal law passed in 1935 that created a state system to provide unemployment compensation to qualified employees who lose their jobs.

federalism   A system of government in which power is divided between a central authority and constituent political units.

fee simple absolute   An ownership interest in which the holder has exclusive rights to ownership and possession of the land to the holder; the most comprehensive type of estate.

fellow servant rule   An outdated defense that prohibited an employee from suing an employer for negligence if the employee's injury was caused by another employee.

felony   A serious crime, such as murder, rape, or robbery, that is punishable by imprisonment for more than one year or death.

fictitious payee   Someone having no right to payment. Under the UCC fictitious-payee rule, any check made out to a fictitious payee and endorsed must be honored and is not considered a forgery.

finance lease   A type of lease in which the lessor does not select, manufacture, or supply the goods but acquires title to the goods or the right to their possession and use in connection with the terms of the lease.

financing statement   A document that lists the names and addresses of all the parties involved in the transaction, a description of the collateral, and the signature of the debtor.

fire insurance   Insurance that protects against property losses incurred by damage from fire.

firm offer   An offer made in writing and containing assurances that it will be irrevocable for a period of time not longer than three months despite a lack of consideration for the irrevocability.

first appearance   The initial appearance of an arrested individual before a judge, who determines whether there was probable cause for the arrest. If the judge ascertains that probable cause did not exist, the individual is freed.

first-assignment-in-time rule   A rule which states that the first party granted an assignment is the party correctly entitled to the contractual right.

fixture   An item that was originally a piece of personal property but becomes part of realty after it is permanently attached to the real property in question.

food disparagement   A tort that provides ranchers and farmers with a cause of action when someone spreads false information about the safety of a food product.

for-profit corporation   A corporation whose objective is to make a profit.

foreign corporation   A corporation that conducts business in a state in which it is not incorporated.

Foreign Corrupt Practices Act (FCPA)   Federal law prohibiting U.S. companies from offering or paying bribes to foreign government officials, political parties, and candidates for office for the purpose of obtaining or retaining business.

foreign sales representative   An agent who distributes, represents, or sells goods on behalf of a foreign seller, usually in return for the payment of a commission.

foreign subsidiary   See **affiliate.**

forfeiture   A party's forfeiting of his or her interest in the premises.

forgery   The fraudulent making or altering of a writing in a way that changes the legal rights and liabilities of another and with the intent to deceive or defraud.

formal contract   A contract that must have a special form or must be created in a specific manner.

formal rule making   A type of rule making that is used when legislation requires a formal hearing process with a complete transcript; consists of publication of the proposed rule in the *Federal Register*, a public hearing, publication of formal findings, and publication of the final rule if adopted.

forum selection agreement   A contractual clause in which the parties choose the location where disputes between them will be resolved.

franchise   A business arrangement between an owner of a trade name or trademark and a person who sells goods or services under the trade name or trademark.

franchise agreement   A contract whereby a company (the franchisor) grants permission (a license) to another entity (the franchisee) to use the franchisor's name, trademark, or copyright in the operation of a business and associated sale of goods in return for payment.

franchisee   The seller of goods or services under a trade name or trademark in a franchise.

franchisor   The owner of the trade name or trademark in a franchise.

fraud   (1) An intentional deception that causes harm to another. (2) A basis for contesting a will if the testator relied on false statements when he or she made the will.

fraud in the factum   A liability defense available to a party who signs a negotiable instrument without knowing that it is a negotiable instrument.

fraudulent misrepresentation   (1) The tort that occurs when a misrepresentation is made with intent to facilitate personal gain and with the knowledge that it is false. (2) In contracts, a false representation of a material fact that is consciously false and is intended to mislead the other party. Also called *intentional misrepresentation*.

fraudulent transfer   A transfer of property that is made with intent to defraud creditors or for an amount significantly lower than the property's fair market value and that occurs within two years of filing for bankruptcy.

free-exercise clause   A clause in the First Amendment of the U.S. Constitution. which states that government (state and federal) cannot make a law "prohibiting the free exercise" of religion; has been interpreted as including absolute freedom to believe and freedom to act, which may face state restriction.

free trade agreement   An international agreement between two or more nations whereby tariffs and other trade barriers are reduced and gradually eliminated.

Freedom of Information Act (FOIA)   Federal law passed in 1966 that mandates and facilitates public access to government information and records, including records about oneself. Sensitive information (e.g., on national security) is excluded.

friendly fire   A fire contained in a place where it is intended to burn.

full eviction   An eviction in which a landlord physically prevents the lessee from entering the leased premises.

full faith and credit clause   A clause in the U.S. Constitution (Article IV, Section 1) mandating that each state must recognize, respect, and enforce the public records, legislative acts, and judicial decisions of the other states.

future interest   A person's present right to property ownership and possession in the future.

G

gambling   Agreements in which parties pay consideration (money placed during bets) for the chance, or opportunity, to obtain an amount of money or property.

garnishment   An order that satisfies a debt by seizing a debtor's property that is being held by a third party.

General Agreement on Tariffs and Trade (GATT)   A comprehensive multilateral trading system designed to achieve distortion-free international trade through the minimization of tariffs and removal of artificial barriers.

general partnership   A partnership in which the partners divide profits and management responsibility and share unlimited personal liability for the partnership's debts.

general personal jurisdiction   A doctrine permitting adjudication of any claims against a defendant regardless of whether the claim has anything to do with the forum.

general power of attorney   A type of express authority that allows an agent to conduct all business for the principal.

general warranty deed   A deed containing a covenant in which the seller agrees to protect the buyer against being dispossessed because of any adverse claim against the land.

geographic market   An area in which a company competes with others in the relevant product market.

gift *causa mortis*   A gift that is made in contemplation of one's immediate death.

Golden Rule   The idea that we should act in the way that we would like others to act toward us.

good faith   Honesty in fact.

Good Samaritan statute   A statute that exempts from liability a person, such as a physician passerby, who voluntarily renders aid to an injured person but negligently, but not unreasonably negligently, causes injury while rendering the aid.

good title   Title acquired from someone who already owns the goods free and clear.

goods   All physically existing things that are movable at the time of identification in the contract for sale.

goods in bailment   Purchased goods that are in some kind of storage under the control of a third party, such as a warehouseman.

Government in Sunshine Act   Federal law which requires that agency business meetings be open to the public if the agency is headed by a collegiate body (i.e., two or more persons, the majority of whom are appointed by the president with the advice and consent of the Senate); also requires that agencies keep records of closed meetings.

green taxes   Taxes imposed on environmentally harmful activities.

gross negligence   An act committed with extreme reckless disregard for the property or life of another person.

group boycott   A boycott in which two or more competitors agree to refuse to deal with a certain person or company. Also called *refusal to deal.*

group insurance   Insurance that is purchased by neither the insured party nor the insurer.

guaranty   A type of contract which ensures that a third party is secondarily liable for the debt to be paid; similar to a suretyship.

H

hacker   A person who illegally accesses, or enters, another person's or company's computer system to obtain information or steal money.

Hague Evidence Convention   A multilateral convention establishing procedures for transnational discovery between private persons in different states.

half-truth   Information that is true but is not complete.

health care proxy   A document that empowers an agent to make medical decisions for a principal who is unable to make those decisions for himself or herself.

historical school   A school of jurisprudence that uses traditions as the model for future laws and behavior. Also called *tradition* or *custom.*

holder   A party in possession of a negotiable instrument.

holder in due course (HDC)   An individual who acquires a negotiable instrument in good faith.

homestead exemption   An exemption that allows a debtor to retain all or a portion of the family home so that the family will retain some form of shelter.

horizontal division of market   An agreement between two or more competitors to divide markets among themselves by geography, customers, or products.

horizontal merger   A merger between two or more competitors producing the same or similar products.

horizontal restraint of trade   An agreement between two competitors in the same market to engage in a practice that restrains trade.

hostile fire   A fire that occurs in a place where it was not intended.

hostile takeover   A takeover to which the management of the target corporation objects.

hybrid agency   An agency that has characteristics of both executive and independent agencies.

hybrid rule making   A type of rule making that combines features of both formal and informal rule making; consists of publication in the *Federal Register,* a written-comment period, and an informal public hearing with restricted cross-examination.

I

identification with the vulnerable   The school of jurisprudence of pursuing change on the grounds that some higher law or body of moral principles connects all of us in the human community.

illusory promise   A situation in which a party appears to commit to something but really has not committed to anything. It is not a promise and thus not consideration.

implied authority   The authority of an agent that arises by inference from the words and actions of the principal.

implied condition   A condition that is not specifically and explicitly stated but is inferred from the nature and language of the contract.

implied contract   A contract that arises not from words of agreement but from the conduct of the parties.

implied-contract exception   An exception to the employment at-will doctrine which provides that an implied employment contract may arise from statements the employer makes in an employment handbook or materials advertising the position.

implied covenant of good faith and fair dealing exception   An exception to the employment at-will doctrine that imposes a duty on the employer to treat employees fairly with respect to termination.

implied trust   A trust created by a court when (1) an express trust fails and the court can imply the existence of a trust from certain behavior and (2) the law steps in to protect someone from fraud or other wrongdoing.

implied warranty of fitness for a particular purpose   An assurance, inferred in any UCC sale, that when a seller/lessor knows or has reason to know (1) why the buyer/lessee is purchasing/leasing the goods and (2) that the buyer/lessee is relying on him or her to make the selection, the buyer/lessee has an enforceable warranty if such assurance is false.

implied warranty of habitability   A requirement that the premises be fit for ordinary residential purposes.

implied warranty of merchantability   An assurance, inferred in every sale unless clearly disclaimed, that merchantable goods will conform to a reasonable performance expectation. The purchaser must have purchased or leased the good from a merchant.

implied warranty of trade usage   An assurance, inferred in the context of certain UCC sales, depending on the circumstances, that can be created through a well-accepted course of dealing or trade usage.

imposter rule   A rule which holds that if one party obtains a negotiable instrument by impersonating another party and endorses it with the impersonated party's signature, the loss falls on the drawer of the instrument.

in pari delicto   In equal fault.

in personam **jurisdiction (jurisdiction in personam)**   Also called **personal jurisdiction.** The power of a court to require that a party (usually the defendant) or a witness come before the court; extends to the state's borders in the state court system and across the court's geographic district in the federal system. Also called *personal jurisdiction* and *jurisdiction in personam.*

in rem **jurisdiction**   The power of a court over the property or status of an out-of-state defendant located within the court's jurisdiction area.

incidental beneficiary   One who unintentionally gains a benefit from a contract between other parties.

income beneficiary   The recipient of the interest or appreciation generated by a trust.

incontestability clause   A part of an insurance contract that precludes an insurance company from challenging statements in an insurance application after a certain period of time.

incorporator   An individual who applies for incorporation on behalf of a corporation.

independent agency   An agency that is typically not located within a government department. It is governed by a board of commissioners appointed by the president with the advice and consent of the Senate.

indictment   A finding by the grand jury that there is evidence to charge the defendant and bring him or her to trial.

individual insurance   Insurance in which the insured party is an individual.

indivisible contract   A contract that cannot be divided and must be performed in its entirety.

industry guides   Interpretations of consumer laws created by the FTC to encourage businesses to stop unlawful behavior.

infant   A person who is not legally an adult (in most U.S. localities, a person under 18) and thus is considered to lack the mental capabilities of an adult. Infancy can be used as a partial defense to defuse the guilty-mind requirement of a crime.

informal contract   A contract that requires no formalities. Also called *simple contract.*

informal rule making   A type of rule making in which an agency publishes a proposed rule in the *Federal Register,* considers public comments, and then publishes the final rule.

information   A finding by a magistrate that there is enough evidence to charge the defendant and bring her or him to trial.

informational picketing   Picketing designed to truthfully inform the public of a labor dispute between an employer and the employees.

injunction   A court order either forcing a party to do something or prohibiting a party from doing something.

inland marine policy   A policy that protects against loss of ship and cargo from "perils of the sea" when a ship is traveling on inland waterways.

innkeepers   Entities that are regularly in the business of making lodging available to the public.

innocent misrepresentation   A false statement made about a material fact by a person who believed the statement was true.

insanity   An affirmative defense which claims that the defendant had a severe mental illness when the crime was committed that substantially impaired his or her capacity to understand and appreciate the moral wrongfulness of the act.

insider trading   Illegal buying or selling of a corporation's securities by corporate insiders, such as officers and directors, on the basis of material, nonpublic information and in breach of a fiduciary duty or some other relationship of trust and confidence.

insolvent debtor   A debtor who cannot pay debts in a timely fashion.

instrument   Any writing that serves as evidence of the right to payment of money.

insurable interest   A party who has an interest in property or life.

insurance   A contract in which the insured party makes payments to the insurer in exchange for the insurer's promise to make payment or transfer goods to another party in the event of injury or destruction to the insured party's property or life.

insured party   The party who makes a payment in exchange for payment in the event of damage or injury to property or person.

insurer   The party who receives payments from the insured party and makes the payment to the beneficiary.

integrated contract   A written contract intended to be the complete and final representation of the parties' agreement.

intellectual property   Intangible property that is the product of one's mind and not one's hands.

intended beneficiary   A third party to a contract whom the contracting parties intended to benefit directly from their contact.

intent   The intended purpose or goal of an action, especially in a contract.

intentional infliction of emotional distress   The tort that occurs when someone intentionally engages in outrageous conduct that is likely to cause extreme emotional distress to another person.

intentional interference with contract   The tort that occurs when someone intentionally takes an action that will cause a person to breach a contract that he or she has with another.

intentional misrepresentation   See **fraudulent misrepresentation.**

intentional tort   A civil wrong resulting from an intentional act committed on the person, property, or economic interest of another. Intentional torts include assault, battery, conversion, false imprisonment, intentional infliction of emotional distress, trespass to land, and trespass to chattels.

***inter vivos* gift**   A gift that is made by a person during his or her lifetime.

intermediary bank   Any bank, other than a payor or depositary bank, that transfers a check during the check collection process.

intermediate scrutiny   A standard of review under which a law must be necessary to achieve a substantial, or important, government interest and must be narrowly tailored to that interest.

international agreement   A written agreement between two or more nations that is governed by international law and relates to international subject matter.

International Labor Organization   An international organization operating under the principle that "labor should not be regarded merely as a commodity or article of commerce"; develops labor rights norms that serve as the basis for many international standards.

international law   The body of law that governs the conduct of nations and international organizations and their relations with one another and with natural and juridical persons.

interpretive rule   A rule that does not create any new rights or duties but is merely a detailed statement of an agency's interpretation of an existing law, including the actions a party must take to be in compliance with the law.

interrogatory   A formal set of written questions that one party to a lawsuit asks the opposing party during the pretrial discovery process to clarify matters of evidence and help determine what facts will be presented at a trial in the case. The questions must be answered in writing under oath or under penalty of perjury within a specified time. Also called *request for further information.*

Interstate Commerce Commission (ICC)   The first federal administrative agency; created to regulate the anticompetitive conduct of railroads.

intestacy statute   A statute that outlines how a person's property will be handled if that person dies without a will.

intestate   The state of dying without a will.

intrusion on an individual's affairs or seclusion   A physical, electronic, or mechanical intrusion that invades someone's solitude, seclusion, or personal affairs when he or she has the right to expect privacy. The tort occurs at the time of the intrusion; no publication is necessary.

involuntary intoxication   An affirmative defense in which the defendant claims that she took the intoxicant without awareness of its likely effect, mistook its identity, or was forced to ingest it and that it left her unable to understand that the act committed was wrong.

Islamic law   A legal system based on the fundamental tenet that law is derived from and interpreted in harmony with Shari'a (God's law) and the Koran.

J

joint and several liability   A type of liability in which a third party can choose to sue the partners separately or to sue all partners jointly in one action.

joint stock company   A partnership agreement in which company members hold transferable shares while all the goods of the company are held in the names of the partners.

joint tenancy   A type of co-ownership in which the joint tenants own equal shares of the property and, upon the death of one tenant, the property is divided equally among the surviving joint owners. The tenants may sell their shares without the consent of the other owners, and their interest can be attached by creditors.

joint tenants   Parties who hold property in joint tenancy.

joint venture   An association between two or more parties wherein the parties share profits and management responsibilities with respect to a specific project.

jointly liable   A term applied to partners who share liability for the partnership's debts.

judicial lien   A court order that allows a creditor to satisfy a debt by seizing the property of the debtor.

judicial review   The power of a court to review legislative and executive actions, such as a law or an official act of a government employee or agent, to determine whether they are constitutional.

jurisdiction   The power of a court to hear cases and resolve disputes.

justifiable use of force   The use of force that is necessary to prevent imminent death or great bodily harm to oneself or another or to prevent the imminent commission of a forcible felony.

L

lack of genuine assent   A defense to the agreement of a contract in which the offeree claims that the offeror secured the agreement through improper means, such as duress, fraud, undue influence, or misrepresentation.

landlord   The owner of a property being leased.

landlord's lien   A court order that allows a landlord, through a sheriff, to seize a tenant's personal property as security for unpaid rent.

Landrum-Griffin Act   Federal law that primarily governs the internal operations of labor unions. It requires financial disclosures by unions, establishes penalties for financial abuses by union officials, and includes "Labor's Bill of Rights" to protect employees from their own unions.

larceny   The unlawful taking, attempting to take, carrying, leading, or riding away of another person's property with intent to permanently deprive the rightful owner of the property.

last-clear-chance doctrine   A doctrine used by a plaintiff when the defendant establishes contributory negligence. If the plaintiff can establish that the defendant had the last opportunity to avoid the accident, the plaintiff may still recover, despite being contributorily negligent.

lease   A transfer of the right to possess and use goods for a period of time in return for consideration.

leasehold   A possessory interest, but not an ownership interest, transferred by contract (lease).

leasehold estate   The leased property.

legal assent   A promise to buy or sell that the courts will require that the parties obey.

legal object   To be enforceable, a contract cannot be either illegal or against public policy.

legal positivism   The school of jurisprudence which holds that because society requires authority, a legal and authoritarian hierarchy should exist. When a law is made, therefore, obedience is expected because authority created it.

legal realism   The school of jurisprudence which dictates that context must be considered as well as law. Context includes factors such as economic conditions and social conditions.

lessee   A person who acquires the right to possession and use of goods under a lease.

lessor   A person who transfers the right to possession and use of goods under a lease.

letter of credit   A binding document that a buyer obtains from his or her bank to guarantee that payment for goods will be made to the seller.

leveraged buyout (LBO)   A takeover-resistance strategy in which a group within the target corporation buys all the corporate stock held by the public, thereby turning the company into a privately held corporation.

lex mercatoria   The "law of merchants" as defined by customs or trade usages developed by merchants to facilitate business transactions.

liability insurance   Insurance that protects a business from tort liability to third parties.

liability without fault   See **strict liability.**

license   A revocable right to temporarily use another's property.

licensing agreement   A contract in which one company (the licensor) grants permission to another company (the licensee) to use the licensor's intellectual property in return for payment.

lien   A claim to property.

life estate   An ownership interest in which the holder has the right to possess the property until his or her death.

life insurance   A contract between a policy owner and an insurance company that requires the insurance company to pay a designated beneficiary a sum of money upon the occurrence of the insured's death.

limited liability company (LLC)   An unincorporated business that is taxed like a partnership, with the members paying personal income taxes, but has the limited liability of a corporation.

limited liability partnership (LLP)   A partnership in which all the partners assume liability for any partner's professional malpractice to the extent of the partnership's assets.

limited partnership   A partnership consisting of at least one general partner and at least one limited partner in which the general partners assume all liability for the partnerships's debts and the limited partners assume no responsibility beyond their originally invested capital.

liquidated damages   Damages specified as a term of the contract before a breach of contract occurs.

liquidated debt   Debt for which there is no dispute between the parties about the fact that money is owed and the amount of money owed.

liquidation   The process in which a debtor turns over all assets to a trustee.

living trust   A trust created by a trustor and administered by another party while the trustor is still alive.

living will   A document in which a person expresses his or her advance directives.

long-arm statute   A statute that enables a court to obtain jurisdiction against an out-of-state defendant as long as the defendant has sufficient minimum contacts within the state, such as committing a tort or doing business in the state.

M

mailbox rule   A rule which holds that an acceptance is valid when it is placed in the mailbox, whereas a revocation is effective only when received by the offeree. In some jurisdictions the mailbox rule has been expanded to faxes.

maker   A person who promises to pay a set sum to the holder of a promissory note or certificate of deposit.

malicious prosecution   A tort in which one person wrongfully subjects another to criminal or civil litigation for the sole purpose of causing problems for that other person, often in retaliation for previous litigation between the two.

malpractice action   A legal action filed against a professional person for failure to act in accordance with prevailing professional standards.

manifest   A document that records possession of hazardous waste from inception to disposal.

manufacturing arrangement   A type of franchise in which the franchisor provides the franchisee with a formula or ingredient that is necessary to manufacture a product.

manufacturing defect   A defect in an individual product that makes the product more dangerous than other, identical products.

marine insurance   Insurance that protects against loss of ships and cargo from the "perils of the sea."

market power   See **monopoly power.**

market share   A firm's fractional share of the relevant market.

marketable title   Title for property to which the seller has legal title and against which there are no liens or restrictions of which the buyer is not aware.

material breach   A substantial breach of a significant term or terms of a contract that excuses the nonbreaching party from further performance under the contract and gives the nonbreaching party the right to recover damages.

material terms   In a contract, the terms that allow a court to determine what the damages are in the event that one of the parties breaches the contract; include the subject matter, quantity, price, quality, and parties.

mechanic's lien   A claim placed on real property to satisfy the debt a person incurred to have improvements made to that property.

med-arb   A type of dispute resolution process in which both parties agree to start out in mediation and, if unsuccessful, to move on to arbitration.

mediation   A type of intensive negotiation in which disputing parties select a neutral party to help facilitate communication and suggest ways for the parties to solve their dispute.

meeting-the-competition defense   A defense to the Clayton Act in which a firm engages in price discrimination to compete in good faith with another seller's low price.

members   Owners of a limited liability company.

mens rea   Latin for "guilty mind"; the mental state accompanying a wrongful behavior.

merchant   A person who deals in goods of the kind or by his occupation holds himself out as having knowledge or skill peculiar to the practices or goods involved in the transaction, or a person who employs an intermediary who, by her occupation, holds herself out as having such knowledge or skill.

merger   A combination of two or more corporations in which only one of the corporations continues to exist.

merger clause   A clause in a written agreement within the statute of frauds which states that the written agreement accurately reflects the final, complete version of the agreement.

minitrial   A type of conflict resolution in which lawyers for each side present their arguments to a neutral adviser, who then offers an opinion on what the verdict will be if the case goes to trial. This decision is not binding.

minor   A person who has not yet reached the age of 18.

Miranda rights   The rights that are read to an arrested individual by a law enforcement agent before the individual is questioned about the commission of the crime.

mirror-image rule   A principle which holds that the terms of an acceptance must mirror the terms of the offer. If the terms of the acceptance do not mirror the terms of the offer, no contract is formed and the attempted acceptance is a counteroffer.

misappropriation theory   A theory of insider trading which holds that if an individual wrongfully acquires (misappropriates) and uses inside information for trading for his or her personal gain, that person is liable for insider trading.

misdemeanor   A crime that is less serious than a felony and is punishable by a fine and/or imprisonment for less than one year.

misrepresentation   An untruthful assertion by one of the parties about a material fact.

mistake   An erroneous belief about the facts of a contract at the time the contract is concluded. When a mistake occurs, legal assent is absent.

mistake of fact   (1) A mistake that is not caused by the neglect of a legal duty by the person committing the mistake but, rather, consists of unconscious ignorance of a past or present material event or circumstance. (2) An affirmative defense in which the defendant tries to prove that she or he made an honest and reasonable mistake that negates the guilty-mind element of a crime.

mixed sale   A contract that combines one or more goods with one or more services.

mock trial   A contrived or imitation trial, recruited by a jury selection firm, that attorneys sometimes use in preparing for a real trial in order to test theories, experiment with arguments, and try to predict the outcome of the real trial.

model law   See **uniform law.**

modified comparative negligence   In some states, a defense whereby the defendant is not liable for the percentage of harm that he or she proves can be attributed to the plaintiff's own negligence if the plaintiff's negligence is responsible for less than 50 percent of the harm. If the defendant establishes that the plaintiff's negligence caused more than 50 percent of the harm, the defendant has no liability.

modify   An appellate court decision that grants an alternative remedy in a case; granted when the court finds that the decision of the lower court was correct but the remedy was not.

monetary damages   Money claimed by or ordered paid to a party to compensate for injury or loss caused by the wrong of the opposite party.

money order   A signed document indicating that funds are to be paid from the drawee to the drawer.

monopoly power   The ability to control price and drive competitors out of the market.

moral hazard   Suggests that individuals who are insulated from risk sometimes behave differently.

most-favored-nation relations   See **normal trade relations.**

motion   In a civil case, a request made by either party that asks a judge or a court to issue an order in that party's favor.

motion for judgment on the pleadings   In a civil case, a request made by either party, after pleadings have been entered, that asks a judge or a court, to issue a judgment.

motion for summary judgment   In a civil case, a request made by either party that asks a judge or a court to promptly and expeditiously dispose of the case without a trial. Any evidence or information that would be admissible at trial may be considered on a motion for summary judgment. The court may hold oral arguments or decide the motion on the basis of the parties' briefs and supporting documentation alone.

motion to dismiss   In a civil case, a request by the defendant that asks a judge or a court to dismiss the case because even if all the allegations are true, the plaintiff is not entitled to any legal relief. Also called *demurrer.*

movability   The quality of a negotiable instrument that ensures it is mobile and available.

multilateral trade agreement   An international agreement between three or more nations that relates to trade between them.

multiple-product order   A form of cease-and-desist order issued by the FTC that applies not only to a specified product but also to other products produced by the same firm.

mutual (mistake)   The result of an error by both parties about a material fact, i.e., one that is important in the context of a particular contract.

N

National Labor Relations Board (NLRB)   An administrative agency created by the Wagner Act to interpret and enforce the National Labor Relations Act (NLRA).

national treatment   A GATT principle of trade law that prohibits WTO member states from regulating, taxing, or otherwise treating imported products any differently from domestically produced products.

natural law   A school of jurisprudence that recognizes the existence of higher law, or law that is morally superior to human laws.

necessary   A basic necessity of life, generally including food, clothing, shelter, and basic medical services.

necessity   An affirmative defense in which the defendant tries to prove that he or she was acting to prevent imminent harm and that there was no legal alternative to the action the defendant took.

negligence   Behavior that creates an unreasonable risk of harm to others.

negligence per se   A doctrine that allows a judge or jury to infer duty and breach of duty from the fact that a defendant violated a statute that was designed to prevent the type of harm that the plaintiff incurred.

negligent misrepresentation   A false statement of material fact made by a person who thinks it is true but who would have known the truth about the fact had he or she used reasonable care to discover or reveal it.

negligent tort   A civil wrong that occurs when the defendant acts in a way that subjects other people to an unreasonable risk of harm (i.e., the defendant is careless, to someone else's detriment). Negligence claims are usually used to achieve compensation for accidents and injuries.

negotiable instrument   A written document signed by a person who makes an unconditional promise to pay a specific sum of money on demand or at a certain time to the holder of the instrument; an acceptable medium for exchanging value from one person to another.

negotiation   (1) A bargaining process in which disputing parties interact informally to attempt to resolve their dispute. (2) The transfer of the rights to a negotiable instrument from one party to another.

New York Convention   An international agreement governing the use of arbitration as a method of resolving private international disputes.

no-par share   A stock share that does not have a par value.

nolo contendere   A plea in which the defendant does not admit guilt but agrees not to contest the charges.

nominal damages   Monetary damages awarded to a plaintiff in a very small amount, typically $1 to $5, to signify that the plaintiff has been wronged by the defendant even though the plaintiff suffered no compensable harm.

nondisclosure   The failure to provide pertinent information about a projected contract.

nonprobate property   Property that is not part of a probate estate.

nonprofit corporation   A corporation that operates for educational, charitable, social, religious, civic, or humanitarian purposes, rather than to earn a profit.

nontariff barrier   Any impediment to international trade other than tariffs.

normal trade relations   A GATT principle of trade law which requires that WTO member states treat like goods coming from other member states on an equal basis.

North American Free Trade Agreement (NAFTA)   An international agreement between the United States, Canada, and Mexico whereby tariffs and other trade barriers will be reduced and gradually eliminated.

note   A promise by the maker of the note to pay the payee of the note.

notice-and-comment rule making   See **informal rule making.**

novation   In a contract, the substitution of a third party for one of the original parties. The duties remain the same under the contract, but one original party is discharged and the third party takes that original party's place.

nuisance   A person's use of her property in a manner that unreasonably interferes with another's use and enjoyment of his land.

O

objective impossibility (of performance)   In a contract, a situation in which it is in fact not possible to lawfully carry out one's contractual obligations.

obligee   A contractual party who agrees to receive something from the other party.

obligor   A contractual party who agrees to do something for the other party.

Occupational Safety and Health Act (OSHA) of 1970   Federal law that established the Occupational Safety and Health Administration, the agency responsible for setting safety standards under the act and for enforcing the act through inspections and the levying of fines against violators.

ocean marine policy   An insurance policy that protects against loss of ship and cargo from "perils of the sea" when a ship is traveling on the ocean.

offer   A key factor in the agreement element of a contract; consists of the terms and conditions set by one party, the offeror, and presented to another party, the offeree.

Omnibus Crime Control and Safe Streets Act of 1968   Federal statute that prohibits employers from listening to the private telephone conversations of employees or disclosing the contents of these conversations. Employers may ban personal calls and monitor calls for compliance as long as they discontinue listening to any conversation once they determine it is personal.

option contract   An agreement whereby the offeree gives the offeror a piece of consideration in exchange for the offeror's agreement to hold the offer open for a specified period of time.

order   (1) An order to appear and bring specified documents. (2) A binding decision issued by an ALJ after a hearing.

order instrument   An instrument payable to a specific, named payee.

order of relief   An order stating that bankruptcy proceedings can continue.

organ donor card   A document that expresses a person's desire to donate organs or tissue.

output contract   An agreement in which the seller guarantees to sell everything he or she produces to one buyer and no quantity is stated; valid under the UCC but not under common law.

overdraft   A bank's action to pay an amount specified on a check, without there being sufficient funds in its customer's account.

P

par-value share   A stock share that has a fixed face value noted on the stock certificate.

parent-subsidiary merger   See **short-form merger.**

parol evidence rule   A common law rule which states that oral evidence of an agreement made prior to or contemporaneously with a written agreement is inadmissible when the parties intend to have the written agreement be the complete and final version of their agreement.

partial eviction   An eviction in which a landlord prevents the tenant from entering part of the leased premises.

partial performance   An exception to the statute of frauds in which the performance of portions of an unwritten agreement by one or both parties can constitute proof that an oral contract exists between the parties.

partially disclosed principal   A principal whose identity is not known by a third party, although the third party is aware that the agent is making an agreement on behalf of a principal. Also called *unidentified principal.*

partnership   A voluntary association between two or more people who co-own a business for profit.

past consideration   Something given or done in the past by one party that later prompts a promise by another party. As such, nothing has been given in exchange, and the court will not enforce the promise.

patent   Protection that grants the holder the exclusive right to produce, sell, and use the patented object for 20 years; can be obtained for a product, process, invention, or machine or a plant produced by asexual reproduction.

payee   The party that receives the benefit of an order (check, etc.).

payor bank   The bank responsible for disbursing the funds indicated on a check.

per se violation   An action that by its very existence carries with it liability, as opposed to an action that violates a rule of reason.

peremptory challenge   In a jury trial, the right of the plaintiff and the defendant in jury selection to reject, without stating a reason, a certain number of potential jurors who appear to have an unfavorable bias.

perfect tender rule   The requirement that a seller deliver goods in conformity with the contract, down to the last detail.

perfection   The series of legal steps a secured party takes to protect its right in collateral from other creditors that want to have their debts returned through the same collateral.

periodic-tenancy lease   A lease created for a recurring term.

personal defense   A liability defense that is not applicable to holders in due course.

personal insurance   Insurance that covers an individual's health or life.

personal jurisdiction   See *in personam* **jurisdiction.**

personal property   Any property that is not land or permanently affixed to the land.

personal representative   The person designated by a testator to collect the testator's property after he or she dies, pay the debts and taxes, and make sure the remainder of the estate gets distributed.

personal service   The process in which an officer of the court hands legal documents, such as a summons or complaint, to the defendant.

petit jury   A group of 6 to 12 citizens who are summoned to court and sworn in by the court to hear evidence presented by both sides and render a verdict in a trial.

petty offense   A minor crime that is punishable by a small fine and/or imprisonment for less than six months in a jail.

picketing   A labor activity in which individuals place themselves outside an employer's place of business for the purpose of informing passersby of the facts of a labor dispute.

plain-meaning rule   A rule of interpretation which states that words in a contract should be given their ordinary meaning.

plaintiff   The person or party who initiates a lawsuit (an action) before a court by filing a complaint with the clerk of the court against the defendant(s). Also known as *claimant* or *complainant.*

plea bargain   An agreement in which the prosecutor agrees to reduce charges, drop charges, or recommend a certain sentence if the defendant pleads guilty.

pledge   The transfer of collateral to a secured party.

point-of-sale system   An EFT system that enables consumers to directly transfer funds from a bank account to a merchant.

police power   The power retained by each state to pass laws that protect the health, safety, and welfare of its citizens.

policy   The insurance document signed by the insured party and the insurer.

policy statement   A general statement about the directions in which any agency intends to proceed with respect to its rule-making or enforcement activities; has no binding impact on anyone.

political speech   Speech that is used to support political candidates or referenda. Compared to other types of speech, it is given a high level of protection by the First Amendment.

posteffective period   In securities registration, the period that begins when the SEC declares the registration statement effective and ends when the issuer sells all the securities offered or withdraws them from sale.

posttrial motion   A request filed after a trial is over, by either party, to the trial court. Types include a motion for a new trial, a motion for judgment notwithstanding the verdict (JNOV), and a motion to amend or nullify the judgment.

power of attorney   A specific type of express authority that grants an agent specific powers.

precedent   A tool used by judges to make rulings on cases on the basis of key similarities to previous cases.

predatory pricing   The practice in which a company prices one product below normal cost until competitors are eliminated and then it sharply increases the price.

preexisting duty   A promise to do something that one is already obligated to do. It is not considered valid consideration.

preferential payment   A payment made by an insolvent debtor that gives preferential treatment to one creditor over another.

preferred stock   Stock that conveys preferences to its holder with respect to assets and dividends.

prefiling period   In securities registration, the period that begins when an issuer starts to think about issuing securities and ends when the issuer files the registration statement and prospectus with the SEC.

Pregnancy Discrimination Act (PDA) of 1987   Federal law that amended Title VII of the Civil Rights Act of 1964 by expanding the definition of sex discrimination to include discrimination based on pregnancy.

prejudicial error of law   An error of law that is so significant that it affects the outcome of the case.

premium   An insurance payment.

prenuptial agreement   An agreement two parties enter into before marriage that clearly states the ownership rights each party enjoys in the other party's property. To be enforceable, it must be in writing.

presentment   The act of making a demand for the drawee to pay.

presentment warranty   A warranty covering the parties accepting an instrument for payment; created to ensure that the accepting or paying party is paying the proper party.

pretrial   An event that includes consultation with attorneys, pleadings, the discovery process, and the pretrial conference.

pretrial conference   A meeting of the judge and the attorneys for both sides to narrow the issues for trial and identify witnesses for trial.

price discrimination   The practice of selling the same goods to different buyers at different prices.

price fixing   A restraint of trade in which two or more competitors agree to set prices for a product or service.prima facie Latin for "at first view"; term applied to evidence that is sufficient to raise a presumption that a wrong occurred.

primarily liable   Liable for paying the amount designated on an instrument when it is presented for payment.

primary boycott   A boycott against an employer with whom the union is directly engaged in a labor dispute.

primary-line injury   Under the Robinson-Patman Act, an injury that occurs when preferential treatment is given to a competitor.

principal   The party that an agent's authority can bind or act on behalf of.

principle of rights   The principle that judges the morality of a decision on the basis of how it affects the rights of all those involved.

Privacy Act   Federal law that mandates that a federal agency may not disclose information about an individual to other agencies or organizations without that individual's written consent.

privacy tort   A wrongful act in which invasion of privacy causes damage to an individual and for which a civil action can be brought. The four privacy torts are false light, public disclosure of private facts, appropriation for commercial gain, and intrusion on an individual's affairs or seclusion.

private corporation   A corporation that is created by private persons and does not have government duties.

private law   Law that involves suits between private individuals or groups.

private nuisance   A nuisance that affects only a single individual or a very limited number of individuals.

private placement exemption   An exemption from the SEC's securities registration process because the offerings are being made to private accredited investors and will not be advertised to the general public.

private trial   An ADR method in which a referee is selected and paid by the disputing parties to offer a legally binding judgment in a dispute.

privileges and immunities clause   The clause in the U.S. Constitution which requires that each state grant citizens of other states the same legal benefits that it grants its own citizens.

privity of contract   The relationship that exists between parties to a contract.

probable cause   Any essential element and/or standard by which a lawful officer may make a valid arrest, conduct a personal or property search, or obtain a warrant.

probate   The process of settling an estate.

problem-solving negotiation   Negotiation in which the parties seek to achieve joint gain.

procedural due process   The requirement that a government must use fair procedures before depriving a person of his or her life, liberty, or property.

procedural unconscionability   Unconscionability that derives from the process of making a contract.

proceeds   Something that is exchanged for a debtor's sold collateral.

product liability insurance   Insurance that protects a company from liability in the event that its customers suffer injury.

product market   A market in which all products identical to or substitutes for a company's product are sold.

professional insurance   Insurance that protects professionals from suits by third parties who claim negligent job performance.

profit   The right to go onto someone's land and take part of the land or a product of it away from the land.

promisee   In a third-party beneficiary contract, the party to the contract who owes something to the promisor in exchange for the promise made to the third-party beneficiary.

promisor   In a third-party beneficiary contract, the party to the contract who made the promise that benefits the third party.

promissory estoppel   The legal enforcement of an otherwise unenforceable contract due to a party's detrimental reliance on the contract.

promoter   A person who begins the corporate creation and organization process.

property insurance   Insurance that protects property from loss or damages.

prospectus   A written document filed with the SEC that contains a description of a security and other financial information regarding the company offering the security; also distributed as an advertising tool to potential investors.

proximate cause   The extent to which, as a matter of policy, a defendant may be held liable for the consequences of his or her actions. In the majority of states, proximate cause requires that the plaintiff and the type of injury suffered by the plaintiff were foreseeable at the time of the accident. In the minority of states, proximate cause exists if the defendant's actions led to the plaintiff's harm.

proxy   A writing signed by a shareholder that authorizes the individual named in the writing to exercise the shareholder's votes (corresponding to his or her shares of stock) at a shareholders' meeting.

proxy solicitation   The process of obtaining authority to vote on behalf of shareholders.

public corporation   A corporation that is created by government to help administer law.

public disclosure of private facts   A privacy tort that occurs when a person publishes a highly offensive private fact, such as information about one's sex life or failure to pay debts, about someone who did not waive his or her right to privacy.

public disclosure test   The ethical guideline that urges us to consider how others may view our actions when making a decision.

public figure privilege   A special right, immunity, or permission that allows people to make any statement about public figures, typically politicians and entertainers, without being held liable for defamation as long as false statements were not made with malice.

public law   Law that involves suits between private individuals or groups and their governments.

public policy exception   An exception to the employment at-will doctrine that prohibits employers from firing employees for doing something that is consistent with furthering public policy.

publicly held corporation   A corporation whose stock is available to the public.

puffing   The use of generalities and clear exaggerations.

punitive damages   Compensation awarded to a plaintiff that goes beyond reimbursement for actual losses and is imposed to punish the defendant and deter such conduct in the future. Also called *exemplary damages*.

purchase-money security interest (PMSI)   A security interest formed when a debtor uses borrowed money from the secured party to buy the collateral.

pure comparative negligence   A defense accepted in some states whereby the defendant is not liable for the percentage of harm that he or she can prove can be attributed to the plaintiff's own negligence.

Q

qualified endorsement   An endorsement that does not bind the endorser to the negotiable instrument in the event that the creator does not honor that instrument.

quantitative restriction   A limits on the importation of certain goods that is imposed on the basis of number of units, weight, or value for national economic reasons, or for the protection of domestic industry; prohibited by GATT.

quasi-contract   A court-imposed contractual obligation to prevent unjust enrichment.

quasi *in rem* jurisdiction   A type of jurisdiction exercised by a court over an out-of-state defendant's property that is within the jurisdictional boundaries of the court; applies to personal suits against a defendant in which the property is not the source of the conflict but is sought as compensation by the plaintiff. Also called *attachment jurisdiction*.

quick-look standard   In a restraint of trade case, the standard that allows a defendant to offer justification for his or her per se violation.

quitclaim deed   A deed that carries no warranties. The grantor simply conveys whatever interests he or she holds.

R

Racketeer Influenced and Corrupt Organizations (RICO) Act   Federal law that provides extended penalties for criminal acts performed as part of an ongoing criminal organization.

ratify   To approve an unauthorized agent's signature on an instrument.

rational-basis test   The lowest standard of review; requires that a law be designed to protect a legitimate state interest and be rationally related to that interest.

reaffirmation agreement   An agreement in which a debtor agrees to pay a debt even though it could have been discharged in bankruptcy.

real defense   A liability defense that applies universally to all parties.

real property   Land and everything permanently attached to it.

reasonable person standard   A measurement of the way members of society expect an individual to act in a given situation.

recognizance   An obligation in which a party acknowledges in court that he or she will perform some specified act and/or pay a price on failure to do so.

recording   Filing a deed, with any other related documents such as mortgages, with the appropriate county office, thereby giving official notice of the transfer to all interested parties.

red-herring prospectus   A prospectus with a warning written in red print at the top of the page telling investors that the registration has been filed with the SEC but not yet approved.

refusal to deal   See **group boycott.**

reg-neg   A type of rule making in which representatives of concerned interest groups and of the involved government agency participate in mediated bargaining sessions to reach an agreement, which is forwarded to the agency.

registration statement   A description, filed with the SEC, of securities being offered for sale; includes an explanation of how proceeds from the sale will be used, information on the registrant's business and properties, and certified financial statements.

rejection   Termination of a contract that occurs when an offeree does not accept the offer or terms of the contract.

relative permanence   The quality of a negotiable instrument that ensures its longevity.

remainderman   The recipient of the trust corpus, the property held in trust, when the trust is terminated.

remand   An appellate court decision that returns a case to the trial court for a new trial or for a limited hearing on a specified subject matter; rendered when the court decides that an error was committed that may have affected the outcome of the case.

rent   The compensation paid to a landlord for the tenant's right to possession and exclusive use of the premises.

rent escalation clause   In a lease, a clause that permits the landlord to increase the rent in association with increases in costs of living, property taxes, or the tenant's commercial business.

reply   A response by the plaintiff to the defendant's counterclaim.

request to produce documents   In a lawsuit, a discovery tool that forces the opposing party to produce certain information unless it is privileged or irrelevant to the case.

requirement contract   A contract in which a buyer agrees to purchase all his or her goods from one seller and no quantity is stated; valid under the UCC but not under common law.

res ipsa loquitur   A doctrine that allows a judge or jury to infer that, more likely than not, the defendant's negligence was the cause of the plaintiff's harm even though there is no direct evidence of the defendant's lack of due care.

resale-price maintenance agreement   An agreement in which a manufacturer and a retailer set a specific price for the resale of products.

rescind   To cancel a contract.

rescission   The termination of a contract.

respondeat superior   Latin for "let the superior speak"; the principle by which liability for harm caused by an agent/employee is held by the principal/employer.

Restatements of the Law   Summaries of common law rules in a particular area of the law. Restatements do not carry the weight of law but can be used to guide interpretations of particular cases.

restitution   The return of any property given up under a contract.

restricted security   A security that has limited transferability and is usually issued in a private placement.

restrictive covenant   A promise to use or not to use one's land in particular ways.

restrictive endorsement   An endorsement that limits the transferability of an instrument or controls the manner of payment under an instrument.

retained earnings   Profits that a corporation keeps.

reverse   An appellate court decision that overturns the judgment of a lower court, concluding that the lower court was incorrect and its verdict cannot be allowed to stand.

revocation   Termination of a contract that occurs when an offeror takes back the initial offer and annuls the opportunity for the offeree to accept the offer.

RICO Act   See **Racketeer Influenced and Corrupt Organizations (RICO) Act.**

right of first refusal   A method of restricting stock transferability whereby a corporation or its shareholders have the right to purchase any shares of stock offered for resale by a shareholder within a specified time frame.

right of survivorship   The right that specific partnership property will pass on to the surviving partner(s).

right to die   A person's right to place limits on other people's efforts to prolong her or his life.

rightfully dissolved   A term applied to the dissolution of a partnership in a way that does not violate the partnership agreement.

ripeness   A measure of the readiness of a case for a decision to be made; designed to prevent premature litigation for a dispute that is insufficiently developed. A claim is not ripe for litigation if it rests on contingent future events that may not occur as anticipated or may not occur at all.

risk   A potential loss.

risk management   The transfer and distribution of risk.

robbery   The unlawful taking or attempted taking of personal property by force or threat of force and/or by putting the victim in fear.

rule-of-reason analysis   An inquiry into the competitive effects of a company's anticompetitive behavior to determine whether the benefits of the behavior outweigh the harm.

rule utilitarianism   A subset of utilitarianism which holds that general rules that *on balance* produce the greatest amount of pleasure for all involved should be established and followed in each situation.

S

S corporation   A corporation that enjoys the tax status of a partnership.

Sabbath law   A law that prohibits the performance of certain activities on Sundays.

sale   The passing of title from a seller to a buyer for a price.

sale-on-approval contract   A contract in which the seller allows the buyer to take possession of the goods before deciding whether to complete the contract by making the purchase.

sale-or-return contract   A contract in which the buyer and seller agree that the buyer may return the goods at a later time.

Sarbanes-Oxley Act   Federal law that criminalizes specific nonaudit services when they are provided by a registered accounting firm to an audit client; also increases the punishment for a number of white-collar offenses. Also known as the *Public Company Accounting Reform and Investor Protection Act of 2002*.

scienter　Deliberately or knowingly.

search warrant　A court order that authorizes law enforcement agents to search for or seize items specifically described in the warrant.

secondarily liable　Liable for paying the amount designated on an instrument should the primarily liable party default.

secondary boycott　An illegal labor action in which unionized employees who have a labor dispute with their employer boycott another company to force it to cease doing business with their employer.

secondary-line injuries　Under the Robinson-Patman Act, an injury that is created when preferential treatment is granted to specific buyers.

secured interest　An interest in personal property or fixtures that secures payment or performance to a creditor.

secured party　The party that holds an interest in a secured property.

secured transaction　A transaction in which the payment of a debt is guaranteed by personal property owned by the debtor.

security　A financial instrument designated as a note, stock, or bond or any other instrument named in the Securities Act of 1933.

security agreement　An agreement in which a debtor gives a secured interest to a secured party.

self-dealing　Any instance in which directors or officers make decisions that violate their corporate duty of loyalty.

self-tender offer　A takeover-resistance strategy in which a target corporation offers to buy its shareholders' stock.

service of process　The procedure by which a court delivers a copy of the statement of claim or other legal documents, such as a summons, complaint, or subpoena, to a defendant.

settlor　A person who creates a trust.

severable contract　A contract whose terms can be divided.

sexual harassment　Unwelcome sexual advances, requests for sexual favors, and other verbal or physical conduct of a sexual nature that makes submission a condition of employment or a factor in employment decisions or that creates an intimidating, hostile, or offensive work environment. The two types are hostile environment and *quid pro quo*.

shadow jury　An unofficial jury, hired by a party in a legal case, that watches the actual trial and deliberates at the end of each day to give the attorney an idea of how the real jurors are reacting to the case.

shareholder　An investor who holds stock in a corporation, and thus is an owner of the corporation.

shareholder's derivative suit　A lawsuit filed by a shareholder on behalf of the corporation.

shelter principle　The principle which holds that when an item is transferred, the transferee acquires all the rights the transferor had to the item.

short-form merger　A merger in which a parent corporation absorbs a subsidiary corporation. Also called *parent-subsidiary merger.*

short-swing profits　Profits made from the sale of company stock within any six-month period by a statutory insider.

signal picketing　An unprotected form of picketing in which services and/or deliveries to the employer are cut off.

signature liability　Liability that is attributed because of a party's signature on an instrument.

simple contract　contract that is not a formal contract. Also called an *informal contract.*

simple delivery contract　A type of contract in which purchased goods are transferred to a buyer from a seller either at the time of the sale or sometime later by the seller's delivery.

situational ethics　An ethical theory which holds that to evaluate the morality of an action, we must imagine ourselves in the position of the person facing the ethical dilemma and then, on that basis, determine whether that person's action was ethical.

slander of quality　A business tort that occurs when false spoken statements criticize a business product or service and result in a loss of sales.

slander of title　A business tort that occurs when false published statements are related to the ownership of the business property.

smart card　A plastic card, similar to an ATM card, that contains a microchip for storing data; used to electronically transfer funds.

social responsibility of business　The responsibility of firms doing business within a community to meet the expectations that the community imposes on them.

socialist law　A legal system based on the premise that the rights of society as a whole outweigh the rights of the individual.

sole proprietor　The single person at the head of a sole proprietorship.

sole proprietorship　A business in which one person (sole proprietor) controls the management and profits.

special damages　See **consequential damages.**

special endorsement　An endorser's signature accompanying the name of the endorsee.

special power of attorney　A type of express authority that allows an agent to act on behalf of the principal only in regard to specifically outlined acts.

special qualified endorsement　A special endorsement containing words that limit the enforceability of the check, such as the term *without recourse* (which means the endorser will not be liable).

special warranty deed   A deed which promises only that the seller has not done anything to lessen the value of the estate.

specific performance   An order of the court requiring that a nonbreaching party fulfill the terms of the contract.

specific personal jurisdiction   A doctrine permitting adjudication of a claim against a defendant only if the defendant purposefully availed himself or herself of the protections of the forum and if the selected forum is reasonable.

stakeholders   The groups of people affected by a firm's decisions.

stale check   A check that is not presented to a bank within six months of its date.

standing   The legal right of a party to bring a lawsuit by demonstrating to the court sufficient connection to and harm from the law or action challenged (i.e., the plaintiff must demonstrate that he or she is harmed or will be harmed). Otherwise, the court will dismiss the case, ruling that the plaintiff "lacks standing" to bring the suit.

stare decisis   Latin for "standing by the decision"; a principle stating that rulings made in higher courts are binding precedent for lower courts.

statute of frauds   State-level legislation that addresses the enforceability of contracts that fail to meet the requirements set forth in the statute; serves to protect promisors from poorly considered oral contracts by requiring that certain contracts be in writing.

statutory insiders   Certain large stockholders, executive officers, and directors who are deemed insiders by the Securities Exchange Act of 1934.

statutory law   The assortment of rules and regulations put forth by legislatures.

stock certificate   A document that serves as a stockholder's proof of ownership in a corporation.

stock warrant   A type of security issued by a corporation (usually together with a bond or preferred stock) that gives the holder the right to purchase a certain amount of common stock at a stated price.

stop-payment order   An order by a drawer that instructs the drawee bank not to pay an issued check.

stored-value card   A plastic card that contains data regarding the value of the card, thereby allowing EFTs to be made.

strict liability   Liability in which responsibility for damages is imposed regardless of the existence of negligence. Also called *liability without fault*.

strict-liability offense   An offense for which no *mens rea* is required.

strict-liability tort   A civil wrong that occurs when a defendant takes an action that is inherently dangerous and cannot ever be undertaken safely, no matter what precautions the defendant takes. The defendant is liable for the plaintiff's damages without any requirement that the plaintiff prove that the defendant was negligent.

strict product liability   Under this, courts may hold the manufacturer, distributor, or retailer liable for any reasonably foreseeable injured party.

strict scrutiny   The most exacting standard of review used by the courts in determining the constitutionality of a statute; requires a compelling government interest and the least restrictive means of attaining that objective.

strike   A temporary, concerted withdrawal of labor.

subject-matter jurisdiction   The power of a court over the type of case presented to it.

subjective impossibility (of performance)   In a contract, a situation in which it would be very difficult for a party to carry out his or her contractual obligations.

sublease   A transfer of less than all of a tenant's interest in a leased property.

submission agreement   A contract which provides that a specific dispute will be resolved in arbitration.

subpoena   An order to appear at a particular time and place and provide testimony.

subpoena *duces tecum*   An order to appear and bring specified documents.

subscriber   An investor who agrees to purchase stock in a new corporation.

subscription agreement   An agreement between promoters (persons raising capital for a new corporation) and subscribers (investors) in which the subscribers agree to purchase stock in the new corporation.

subsidy   A financial contribution by a government that confers a benefit on a specific industry or enterprise.

substantial impairment   A concept, used to modify the perfect tender rule, whereby a buyer can revoke acceptance of goods or a buyer/lessee can reject an installment of a particular item only if the defects substantially impair the value of the goods.

substantial performance   Contract performance that occurs when nearly all the terms of the agreement have been met, there has been an honest effort to complete all the terms, and there has been no willful departure from the terms of the agreement.

substantive due process   The requirement that laws depriving an individual of life, liberty, or property be fair and not arbitrary.

substantive unconscionability   Unconscionability that derives from contract terms that are so one-sided, unjust, or overly harsh that the contract should not be enforced.

summary jury trial   An abbreviated trial that leads to a nonbinding jury verdict.

summons   A legal document issued by a court and addressed to a defendant that notifies him or her of a lawsuit and specifies how and when to respond to the complaint. A summons may be used in both civil and criminal proceedings.

supremacy clause   Article VI, Paragraph 2, of the U.S. Constitution, which states that the Constitution and all laws and treaties of the United States constitute the supreme law of the land. Thus, any state or local law that directly conflicts with the U.S. Constitution or federal laws or treaties is void.

suretyship   A contract between a creditor and a third party who agrees to pay another person's debt.

surrender   A mutual agreement between a landlord and a tenant in which the lessee returns his or her interest in the premises to the landlord.

syndicate   An investment group that comes together for the explicit purpose of financing a specific large project.

T

Taft-Hartley Act   Federal legislation designed to curtail some of the powers that unions had acquired under the Wagner Act; designates certain union actions as unfair. Also called *Labor-Management Relations Act*.

takings clause   A clause in the Fifth Amendment of the U.S. Constitution requiring that when government uses its power to take private property for public use, it must pay the owner just compensation, or fair market value, for the property. Also called *just-compensation clause*.

tariff   A tax levied on imported goods.

teller's check   A check for which the drawer and drawee are separate banks.

tenancy-at-sufferance lease   A lease that is created when a tenant who was lawfully in possession of a leased property remains in possession of that property unlawfully after the lease ends because the person with the power to evict him failed to do so.

tenancy-at-will lease   A lease that may be terminated by the parties at any time.

tenancy by the entirety   A type of co-ownership that is available only to married couples. The spouses' shares are equal, and if one owner dies, the surviving spouse assumes full ownership.

tenancy in common   A type of co-ownership in which each owner has the right to sell his or her interest without the consent of the other owners, may own an unequal share of the property, and may have a creditor attach his or her interest.

tenant   A person who assumes the temporary legal right to possess property.

tender   An offer by a contracting party to perform, along with being ready, willing, and able to perform, a duty outlined in the contract.

tender of delivery   A requirement that a seller/lessor have and hold conforming goods at the disposal of the buyer/lessee and give the buyer/lessee reasonable notification to enable him or her to take delivery.

tender offer   A type of takeover in which an aggressor corporation offers the target shareholders a price above their stock's current market value.

term-life insurance   Life insurance that provides coverage for a specified term.

termination   In a contract, the point at which an offer can no longer be accepted as part of a binding agreement or an offeree no longer has the power to form a legally binding contract by accepting the offer; can occur through revocation by the offeror, rejection by the offeree, death or incapacity of the offeror, destruction or subsequent illegality of the subject matter of the offer, or lapse of time or failure of another condition stated in the offer.

termination statement   An amendment to a financing statement which states that the debtor has no obligation to the secured party.

tertiary-line injury   Under the Robinson-Patman Act, an injury that occurs when someone who is given an illegally low price passes his savings on to his customers.

testamentary capacity   The minimum age required to write a legal will and be of sound mind.

testamentary trust   An express trust created by a will.

testator   A person who writes a will.

third-party beneficiary   A recipient of contractual benefits who is not one of the contracting parties; created when two parties enter into a contract with the intended purpose of benefiting a third party.

time instrument   A type of draft that allows the payee to collect payment only at a specific time in the future.

tippee   An individual who receives confidential information from an insider.

tipper   An insider who gives inside information to someone.

tipper/tippee theory   A theory of insider trading which holds that any individual (tippee) who acquires material inside information as a result of an insider's (tipper's) breach of duty has engaged in insider trading.

Title VII   See **Civil Rights Act (CRA) of 1964—Title VII.**

tombstone advertisement   A print advertisement that announces a forthcoming sale of securities in a format similar to that of a tombstone.

tort   A violation of another person's rights or a civil wrongdoing that does not arise out of a contract or statute; primary types are intentional, negligent, and strict-liability torts.

tortfeasor   A person who commits an intentional or through-negligence tort that causes a harm or loss for which a civil remedy may be sought.

trade dress   The overall appearance and image of a product.

trade libel   A business tort that occurs when false printed statements criticize a business product or service and result in a loss of sales.

trade secret   A process, product, method of operation, or compilation of information that gives a businessperson an advantage over his or her competitors.

trademark   A distinctive mark, word, design, picture, or arrangement that is used by a producer in conjunction with a product and tends to cause consumers to identify the product with the producer.

trademark dilution   The use of a distinctive or famous trademark, such as "McDonald's," in a manner that diminishes the value of the mark.

transfer warranty   A warranty regarding a negotiable instrument and its transfer; created by the party who transfers the instrument.

traveler's check   An order that is payable on demand, is drawn on or through a bank, is designated by the phrase *traveler's check,* and requires a countersignature by the person whose signature appears on the check.

treaty   A binding agreement between two nations or international organizations.

trespass to personalty   The temporary interference with a person's use or enjoyment of his or her personal property.

trespass to realty   A tort that occurs when someone goes on another's property without permission or places something on another's property without permission.

trial   An event in which parties to a dispute present evidence in court, before a judge or a jury, in order to achieve a resolution to their dispute.

trial court   A court in which most civil or criminal cases start when they first enter the legal system. The parties present evidence and call witnesses to testify. Trial courts are referred to as *courts of common pleas* or *county courts* in state court systems and *district courts* in the federal system. Also called *court of original jurisdiction* and *court of first instance.*

trust   A business arrangement in which stock owners appoint beneficiaries and place their securities with a trustee, who manages the company and pays a share of the earnings to the stockholders.

trust endorsement   An endorsement that is used when the instrument is being transferred to an agent or trustee for the benefit of either the endorser or a third party; gives the endorser the rights of a holder.

trustee   (1) In bankruptcy proceeding, an individual who takes over administration of a debtor's estate. (2) A person who operates a business trust for beneficiaries.

tying arrangement   Illegal agreement in which the sale of one product is tied to the sale of another.

U

unconscionability   Grounds for rescinding an unconscionable contract.

unconscionable   A term applied to a contract in which one party has so much more bargaining power than the other party that the powerful party dictates the terms of the agreement and eliminates the other party's free will.

underwriter   A party who receives payments from an insured party and makes the payment to the beneficiary.

undisclosed principal   A principal whose existence is not known by a third party. That is, the third party does not know that an agent is acting on behalf of a principal.

undue influence   The situation in which one person takes advantage of his or her dominant position in a relationship to unfairly persuade the other person and interfere with that person's ability to make his or her own decision.

unemployment compensation   The state system, created by the Federal Unemployment Tax Act, that provides unemployment compensation to qualified employees who lose their jobs.

unenforceable   A term applied to a contract that, because of a law, cannot be enforced by the courts.

unfair competition   The act of competing with another not to make a profit but for the sole purpose of driving that other out of business.

unfortunate accident   An incident that simply could not be avoided, even with reasonable care.

unidentified principal   See **partially disclosed principal.**

Uniform Commercial Code (UCC)   A statutory source of contract law in the United States that is applicable to transactions involving the sale of goods. The UCC was created in 1952 and adopted by all 50 states, the District of Columbia, and the Virgin Islands; it may be modified by each state to reflect the wishes of the state legislature.

uniform law   A law created to account for the variability of laws among states; serves to standardize the otherwise different interstate laws. Also called *model law.*

Uniform Probate Code   A statute that clarifies laws that govern transfers accomplished through wills and trusts.

unilateral   A mistake that is the result of an error by one party about a material fact, that is, a fact that is important in the context of the particular contract.

unilateral contract   A promise exchanged for an act.

unilateral mistake   The result of an error by one party about a material fact, i.e., a fact that is important in the context of a particular contract.

United Nations Convention on Contracts for the International Sale of Goods (CISG)   The legal structure for international sales, including business-to-business sales contracts.

universalization test   The ethical guideline that urges us to consider, before we act, what the world would be like if everyone acted in that way.

unliquidated debt   A debt for which the parties either dispute the fact that any money is owed or agree that some money is owed but dispute the amount.

unprotected speech   Speech that is not protected by the First Amendment; includes hate speech, insulting or fighting words, obscenity, and defamation.

unqualified opinion letter   A letter issued by an auditor when the financial statements presented are free of material misstatements and are in accordance with GAAP.

usage of trade   Any practice that members of an industry expect to be part of their dealings.

usury   The lending of money at an exorbitant or unlawful rate of interest.

utilitarianism   The ethical principle that urges individuals to act in a way that creates the most happiness for the largest number of people.

V

valid   A term applied to a contract that includes all four elements of a contract—agreement (offer and acceptance), consideration, contractual capacity, and legal object—and thus is enforceable.

values   Positive abstractions that capture our sense of what is good and desirable.

venue   The court with subject-matter and personal jurisdiction that is the most appropriate geographic location for the resolution of a dispute.

vertical merger   A merger in which a company at one level of the manufacturing-distribution system acquires a company at another level of the system.

vertical restraint against trade   An agreement between two parties at different levels in the manufacturing-distribution system to engage in a practice that restrains trade.

vest   To mature, as in the maturing of rights such that a party can legally act on the rights.

vicarious liability   The liability or responsibility imposed on a person, a party, or an organization for damages caused by another; most commonly used in relation to employment, with the employer held vicariously liable for the damages caused by its employees.

virtue ethics   The ethical system which proposes that a decision is ethical when it promotes positive character traits such as honesty, courage, or fairness.

virus   A computer program that rearranges, damages, destroys, or replaces computer data.

void   A term applied to a contract that is not valid because its object is illegal or it has a defect that is so serious that it is not a contract.

void title   Not true title; e.g., the title held by someone who knowingly or unknowingly purchased stolen goods.

voidable   A term applied to a contract that one or both parties have the ability to either withdraw from or enforce.

voidable title   Title that occurs when a contract between the original parties would be void but the goods have already been sold to a third party.

voir dire   The process of questioning potential jurors to ensure that the jury will be made up of nonbiased individuals.

W

Wagner Act   The first major piece of federal legislation adopted explicitly to encourage the formation of labor unions and provide for collective bargaining between employers and unions as a means of obtaining the peaceful settlement of labor disputes.

waiting period   In securities registration, the period between the time an issuer files a registration statement and prospectus with the SEC requesting to offer a security and the time the offer is approved by the SEC, which is a minimum of 20 days.

warehouse receipt   A receipt issued by one who is engaged in the business of storing goods for compensation.

warranty   (1) An assurance, either express or implied, by one party that the other party can rely on its representations of fact. (2) In sales, a binding promise regarding a product in the event that the product does not meet the manufacturer's or seller's promises.

warranty liability   Liability that is attributed when the transfer of an instrument breaches a warranty associated with an instrument.

warranty of title   An assurance, inferred in every UCC sales transaction, that the seller has good and valid title to the goods and has the right to transfer the title free and clear of any liens, judgments, or infringements of intellectual property rights of which the buyer does not have knowledge.

waste   Permanent and substantial injury to a landlord's property.

watered stock   Stock that is issued to individuals below its fair market value.

white-collar crime   A variety of nonviolent illegal acts against society that occur most frequently in the business context.

whole-life insurance   Life insurance that provides protection for the entire life of the insured person.

will   A legal document in which a person outlines how she wants her property to be distributed after her death.

winding up   The process of completing unfinished partnership business.

workers' compensation law   A state law that provides for financial compensation to employees or their dependents when the covered employee is injured on the job.

working papers   The various documents used and developed during an audit, including notes, calculations, copies, memorandums, and other papers constituting the accountant's work product.

World Trade Organization (WTO)   An international organization that facilitates international cooperation in opening markets and provides a forum for future trade negotiations and the settlement of international trade disputes.

WPH approach (to ethical decision making)   A set of ethical guidelines that urges us to consider whom an action affects, the purpose of the action, and how we view its morality (whether by utilitarian ethics, deontology, etc.).

writ of certiorari   A Supreme Court order, issued after the Court decides to hear an appeal, mandating that the lower court send to the Supreme Court the record of the appealed case.

writ of execution   A court order that authorizes a local law officer to seize and sell a debtor's real or personal nonexempt property, within the court's geographic jurisdiction, to enforce a judgment awarded by the court.

writing   A type of documentation that shows contractual intent and satisfies the statute of frauds requirement.

wrongful civil proceeding   A tort in which one person wrongfully subjects another to criminal or civil litigation that has no justifiable basis.

wrongful dissolution   A partnership dissolution that violates the partnership agreement.

Z

zoning   The process in which government places restrictions on the use of property to allow for the orderly growth and development of a community and to protect the health, safety, and welfare of its citizens.

Credits

Name Index

Subject Index